The Gender and Consumer Culture Reader

The Gender and Consumer Culture Reader

EDITED BY

Jennifer Scanlon

New York University Press

NEW YORK AND LONDON

NEW YORK UNIVERSITY PRESS
New York and London

Library of Congress Cataloging-in-Publication Data
The gender and consumer culture reader / edited by Jennifer Scanlon.
p. cm.
Includes bibliographical references and index.
ISBN 0-8147-8132-2 (pbk. : alk. paper)—ISBN 0-8147-8131-4 (alk. paper)
1. Women consumers—United States—History.   2. Consumers—United States—
History.   3. Consumption (Economics)—United States—History.
I. Scanlon, Jennifer, 1958–

HC110.C6 G457 2000
339.4'7'0820973—dc21   00-039448

Contents

Acknowledgments

Several institutions and many people deserve my thanks. The New York Public Library, with its vast collections in several locations, provided an excellent starting point for my exploration of published materials currently available in gender and consumer culture studies. Plattsburgh State University of New York, through a campus grants program in the Office of Sponsored Research, provided funding for my research trip to New York City. The librarians at Plattsburgh State provided me with much subsequent assistance as I ordered materials and explored computer databases. The administration at Plattsburgh State also deserve my thanks, as they supported my application for sabbatical to pursue a Fulbright Fellowship. The J. William Fulbright Foundation provided me with a lecturing/research Fulbright award in Trinidad and Tobago for the 1998–99 academic year and the opportunity to complete this project and several others. Finally, the Centre for Gender and Development Studies at the University of the West Indies, St. Augustine, Trinidad, provided me with a welcoming and stimulating home base for the year.

This work emerged from postpublication discussions with the editor of my first book, *Inarticulate Longings*, about the emerging field of consumer culture studies. That editor, Cecelia Cancellaro, encouraged me to develop this reader and speak with acquisitions editors at New York University (NYU) Press. Niko Pfund and Eric Zinner expressed an interest in the project, and Eric eagerly took it on, respecting and encouraging my determination to create a student-oriented reader. It has been a pleasure to work with him on this shared vision.

I thank my colleagues in the Women's Studies Program at Plattsburgh State University, most notably Lynda Ames and Robin Prenoveau, for keeping the program running and strong in my absence. In addition to all of her other responsibilities, Robin assisted me across the miles by organizing interlibrary loan requests, facilitating photocopying, and following through on correspondence with some difficult-to-reach authors and publishers. Daisy Hernandez, editorial assistant at NYU Press, also facilitated my work by responding to my seemingly endless E-mail requests for assistance with swift and helpful responses. My colleagues and friends at the Centre for Gender and Development Studies at the University of the West Indies (UWI) have my endless appreciation. Rhoda Reddock, senior lecturer and head of the Centre, was a wonderful host and inspiring colleague. Thanks also to Glenda St. Louis-Ottley, Amar Wahab, Susan Jacelon, Vanesa Martina, and all my students at UWI, who made my stay there enormously rewarding on so many levels.

Finally, thanks to my family, Michael Walton Arthur and Fynn Ajani Arthur, who, accompanying me to Trinidad, made sure that I participated in consumer culture outside the gates of campus as much as I contemplated it in the confines of the library.

Introduction

A Note for Students

One of the most significant but overlooked aspects of contemporary culture is consumer culture. After centuries of what can be called mass consumer culture, we shape our identities, at least in part, through purchasing: adolescent white suburbanites wear baggy jeans as they purchase black urban identity; young families choose to drive either the minivan or the sports utility vehicle and view the other choice with some degree of disdain; everyday Americans spend vast amounts of money on bottled water, regardless of its source, so they can brandish a health-conscious identity. Many of us even pay corporations to allow us to advertise for them: we wear Nike caps, Tommy Hilfiger jackets, Gap T-shirts. Consumer culture is ubiquitous, but understanding it can add greatly to our ability to comprehend individual and societal aspirations, conflicts, insecurities, and agendas.

Constantly bombarded with images of goods and the supposed "good life" they offer, we absorb some messages and reject others, but relatively few of us act as truly critical consumers in our everyday lives. The purpose of this book is to assist you in becoming a more critical consumer of consumer culture. One of the images that works well with my students is that of the fish in water. The fish swims around in the water all day long, yet does it ever realize it is wet? Consumer culture is, in part, the water we swim around in. It "understands" us every day by offering us products and the messages that will convince us to consume; our job is to work at understanding those messages, their providers, and our own complex motivations. The readings here will help you in that process.

This text is called *The Gender and Consumer Culture Reader*. But what is it about consumer culture that is gendered? When we make jokes about women who "shop 'til they drop," purchase an electric carving knife for a man but a set of ordinary kitchen knives for a woman, or think of a "bachelor pad" as a domestic space designed for men who want to entertain but not necessarily to commit to relationships with women, we engage with the gendered nature of consumer culture. Gender refers to the culturally and socially prescribed roles we play as women and as men, and certainly, we play particular roles in relation to consumer culture. In the generally agreed-upon formula, women are nondescript housewives or man-dependent young women who either unwittingly or obsessively spend the money they or their men earn; men, conversely, are either reluctant consumers who must be offered women's bodies as product accessories or eager advertising agents or retailers targeting the purses of female shoppers. The picture that has emerged from more recent scholarship, however, is far more nuanced than that, and this collection of readings will introduce you to new questions and new understandings of the gendered nature of consumer culture.

Gender is not, of course, the only aspect of our lives that has a relationship to consumer culture. We respond to invitations to purchase on the basis of social class, race, ethnicity, age, and sexual orientation, among other things. To give an example related to social class and age: Does your living-room wall feature a velvet Elvis, an original piece of art, a poster of Bob Marley, or a reproduction of a famous work of art? When you read that list of possibilities, what judgments might you make about the kinds of people who would have those items hanging on their walls? We convey messages about social class or social aspirations through our home decorations; in fact, one could argue, we speak to each other through the language of things.[1] We often come to conclusions about people long before we engage in conversation with them, by reading the language of their dress. Do you feel that you share critical information about yourself by inviting someone into your living room or by the way you dress, say, on a Saturday night out?

Although receiving an identity from and communicating through purchasing are not the only issues the writers in this collection tackle, they do provide a useful place to begin the process of exploring consumer culture in more detail. Do you purchase a particular brand of sneakers, for example, because name brands provide you with some guarantee of a high-quality product, because you want to identify yourself with others who wear that brand, because it is a good buy for the price, or because it makes you feel American/sexy/feminine/masculine/hip/rebellious/ black/ white/Latino/young/unique? Most likely you purchase that pair of sneakers because of a complex combination of several of the reasons cited above. But whether we actively seek to or not, we provide others with messages about ourselves through the brands of cigarettes, clothing, moisturizer, jeans, in-line skates, or soft drinks we purchase.[2] We also prove ourselves in the world by the quantity as well as the quality of our acquisitions. In many cases, more is better, although the environmental movement has influenced some among us to feel that less has a great deal to offer.[3]

Consumer culture is not unique to the United States. It is true, however, that it is recognized throughout the world as something quite American. The "ugly American" tourist, clad in garish clothing and expecting everyone everywhere to speak English, shops his or her way around the world and symbolizes the most negative aspects of the consumer culture. Americans themselves have used the symbolism of the consumer culture to claim their superiority in the world. During the cold war, for example, the media juxtaposed images of American abundance with images of Soviet scarcity; for many years, consumer goods functioned as one of the most important means to distinguish the pampered U.S. citizen from his or her apparently deprived Soviet counterpart. Television footage offered dismal images of Soviet citizens donning steel-gray clothing and waiting in long lines to purchase drab, low-quality consumer goods. American consumers, by contrast, felt "American" when they could walk down supermarket aisles that offered them twenty varieties of dish detergent or distinct shampoos for normal, dry, oily, permed, limp, color-treated, dandruff-tainted, and split-end-infested hair.

This collection of essays focuses primarily on the United States as it explores why we consume, what we get out of it—aside from the goods we purchase—who encourages this behavior, and how people resist or negotiate imposed messages and "use" the consumer culture as it uses them. Two of the essays focus on the British experience, however, and two others focus on the Caribbean. These pieces provide an important means of comparison and reveal the ways in which American methods and ideals of consumption have been, for centuries, both imported and exported, never without contestation.

Are you, as the saying goes, a "slave to fashion," or do you see your own style of dress as a means of engaging with but also rejecting parts of the culture's dominant messages about youth, clothing, and cultural assimilation? Do you recognize what else you buy when you purchase a product? Do you feel that consumers have rights, power, or responsibilities? The essays and archival material in this text invite you to engage with those questions and others. Please be an active reader and a critical consumer of the readings as well as the arguments they pose. Continually ask yourself: Why do I buy this?

The Emergence of Consumer Culture Studies

College courses that pay particular attention to consumer culture are a relatively recent phenomenon. Although consumer culture is so much a part of American culture, the Puritan inheritance that values work above leisure and considers the spending of money somewhat suspect encourages what one historian of consumer culture has called a "censorious attitude" toward the study of consumer culture.[4] Another scholar identifies, in addition to that so-called Puritan critique, the "Quaker critique," which attacks the pursuit of goods and favors a life of simplicity, and the "Republican critique," which attacks the consequences of pursuing consumer goods, namely, complacency and a subsequent lack of civic engagement.[5] So-called high culture, including the literary canon, classical music, and the fine arts, finds its way into scholarly examinations of people's lives, but what ordinary people do with their leisure time—the so-called low culture of dance halls, shopping, and supermarket tabloids—has long been deemed unworthy of serious scholarly attention.

Part of the hesitation to engage with the realities of consumer culture is simple fear. For centuries, cultural critics have feared that ordinary people would lose their sense of values as they responded to the lures of consumer culture. Nineteenth-century observer of American culture Alexis de Tocqueville argued that Americans who could ill afford to were being seduced into joining the growing group of those "whose desires grow much faster than their futures."[6] However, de Tocqueville's and others' fears about people's indulgences in consumer goods may have been poorly disguised fears about money in the hands of the less privileged. As Daniel Horowitz argues, many of these critics did not harbor the same level of fear about the reckless abandon of those who had always had money; instead, their diatribes against consumption revealed their righteous belief in the superiority of bourgeois life and their fears of immigrants and workers.[7] Nevertheless, this suspicion of people buying beyond their means and losing themselves in consumer culture has lived on; in fact, the terms *conspicuous* and *consumption* have become inextricably linked in many people's minds.[8]

Over the past several years, however, a transition has occurred in many academic fields. Those who study the uses and abuses of capital have come to recognize the value in looking also at what people do with the money, however little or much it is, that they earn. As social history has moved, as Lisa Tiersten puts it, "from an exploration of masses to a reconsideration of elites, from the public to the private domain, from the sphere of work to that of leisure, and often, from men's culture to women's culture," the study of spending as well as getting money has risen in importance.[9] Historians now fruitfully explore the complex relationships between those who produce and those who consume. Contemporary sociologists explore the ways in which consumption meets individual needs for both social identity and personal distinction. Anthropologists see consumption not as social control but as a cultural and psychological construct, arrived at through the active engagement of everyday people with the goods they purchase and indicative of cultural values. They see consumer culture as quite revealing. "Consumerism," writes Colin Campbell, "probably reflects the moral nature of contemporary human existence as much as any other widespread modern practice."[10] The contemporary study of consumer culture now explores such activities as vacations, gift giving, and cosmetic surgery in addition to shopping.[11]

The international research beyond the scope of this collection includes studies of the cultural significance of soap in colonial and postcolonial Zimbabwe, carnival in contemporary Trinidad, images of Elvis Presley in Indian films, Hollywood films in postwar Germany, and beauty pageants worldwide.[12] The questions scholars raise go well beyond the "good" or the "bad" of consumer culture to explore the multiple realities of this vital part of our cultural lives. This collection, too, invites you to participate in an interdisciplinary and international exploration of the seductive, subversive, and certainly significant nature of consumer culture.

The Emergence of Consumer Culture

Like many other historical issues, the "birth" of consumer culture has been hotly debated. The first scholars to explore the phenomenon located its emergence in Europe and in the United States in the late nineteenth and early twentieth centuries.[13] More recent inquiries, however, have demonstrated clearly that mass consumer culture was in the making as early as the eighteenth century, if not earlier.[14] Sociologist Chandra Mukerji argues that a consumer culture was developing in Europe as early as the sixteenth century.[15] Historian Carole Shammas explores the mass production and mass consumption of sugar products, caffeine, and tobacco in Europe during the early modern period and argues persuasively that the development of consumer culture offered something for everyone: "[b]ig profits for planters and merchants, relatively light weight for shippers, and cheap energy and relaxation for consumers."[16] J. H. Plumb also finds evidence of the mass consumption of goods in late seventeenth- and in eighteenth-century Europe through his study of reading, tourism, and traveling fairs, all of which were eagerly engaged in by the growing middle class.[17] By the late eighteenth century, most scholars now agree, the makings of a modern consumer culture were in place, and it is possible to speak of a "consumer revolution." As Daniel Horowitz writes, "People bought commodities, material possessions became a way of dramatizing social status, and the vision of an increased standard of living spread through most ranks of society."[18]

The process continued and grew tremendously in the nineteenth and twentieth centuries. At the turn of the twenty-first century, new markets continue to be identified; existing markets are expanded; and consumer culture makes further inroads into individual consciousness, group identification, and global decision making. For example, while one can argue that people act largely as consumers in the economic north of the world and largely as producers in the economic south, the articles in this collection that focus on the Caribbean vividly illustrate some of the ways in which consumer culture, some of which is imported from the United States, is part and parcel of everyday life for people throughout the world. The essays in this collection focus on nineteenth- and twentieth-century patterns and issues of consumption and collectively raise questions about the directions of both the scholarship and consumer culture itself as we move into the next millennium.

The Meaning of Goods and Their Acquisition

When we explore consumer culture, we can focus on many things: the goods, their producers, their consumers, their marketers. But what of these goods? As Mary Douglas and Baron Isherwood write, "It is extraordinary to discover that no one knows why people want goods."[19] If shopping is a significant leisure activity, what meaning do we attribute to the goods we look at, the goods we try on, the goods we purchase? One anthropologist has coined the term *neophiliacs* to describe those persons on an endless quest for novelty; we also speak of *shopaholics*, those who cannot control their urge to spend.[20] Do we see our possessions as extensions of our selves, or do we simply enjoy the act of looking and occasionally purchasing? And when we do buy, what meaning accompanies our purchases home with us? Does the good hold the same significance if we buy it on sale or at full price; through a catalog, on the internet, or in person; at a fashionable boutique, in a bargain basement, or at a garage sale? Material goods, the things we consume, reveal a great deal about us, scholars agree, but just what do they reveal? Perhaps the analysis that has most influenced subsequent scholars is that of anthropologists Mary Douglas and Baron Isherwood, who see goods as "live information systems." Possessions can be considered extensions of self or ephemeral items that leave our lives as quickly as they enter them. Possessions can be a means of fitting in to a group or a way of distinguishing ourselves in a group. How else are we to relate to the Joneses, Douglas and Isherwood ask only somewhat facetiously, if not by keeping up with them?[21]

Certainly, we use goods to compare our own station in life with that of others. Karl Marx noted this process when he spoke about the worker who finds a small house quite adequate—that is, at least, until someone nearby builds a far grander house. At this point, Marx noted, the worker's own house "shrinks from a little house to a hut." As he explained, "[O]ur desires and pleasure spring from society; we measure them, therefore, by society . . . they are of a relative nature."[22] The advertiser who offers us a particular set of goods may ascribe to them a social meaning, one deemed appealing to us as we measure ourselves against others. We may accept that meaning just as it is offered. We may also, at times, contest imposed meanings and apply ones that work more effectively for us. The process of sifting, absorbing, accepting, rejecting, and making meaning, in addition to the act of consuming, can be stifling or liberating; in either case, it is not a one-way street.

Consumer Culture as a Collaborative Process

For too long, historians of consumer culture regarded the consumer process as one comprised of perpetrators and victims. Capitalists, in this version of history, seem to control not only the means of production but also the minds of consumers; we, the consumers, act unwittingly and well. This analysis appeals to many people but fails to attribute agency to the people who consume. The process of consumption is truly a process rather than simply an act, a process involving people who continually make choices. Americans encounter a barrage of invitations to consume, whether it be to stave off the Russians, as described earlier; to develop an identity as a middle-class person; or to keep one's family free from the ravages of bacteria or dreadfulness of soggy breakfast cereal. It is easy to see how we are all victims of advertisers. But Americans, particularly over the course of the twentieth century, have themselves increasingly come to identify comfort and well-being with material possessions. They actively rather than passively respond to advertisements and products. In fact, they sometimes vex the capitalists who feel they do exercise control. Henry Ford, for example, who wanted to sell cars to the masses, maintained that more people would purchase cars if they featured low prices and few options. The American people had by then, however, come to desire variety and choice in their automobiles as well as in other aspects of their lives. They rejected Ford's monotonous offerings in favor of those of another manufacturer, ultimately favoring variety over price.[23]

Of course, this desire for comfort and style most often coincides with the ambitions of the forces above, most of whom remain quite eager to participate in the style wars that render goods costly or obsolete well before their time. In a variety of ways, consumers and producers collaborate in a process of granting these goods meaning. Think on the ways in which, for example, young people in the United States have given meaning to a simple commodity: baseball caps. They buy them, yes, but they have at varying times worn them backward, with the tags still on, or with the visor curled or straight, and for a variety of reasons: to demonstrate membership in a group or loyalty to a sports team or simply to cover up evidence of a bad hair day. These young people attribute to the caps meanings of their own design. Cap manufacturers and advertisers, consequently, are eager to observe and respond to those initiatives on the part of consumers, and the interplay continues.

Empowering and Disempowering Elements of Consumer Culture

When we ask why people want goods, we are also asking what the goods do "to" or "for" the people who purchase them. A good deal of scholarship has focused on the disempowering elements of consumer culture: the ways in which people are encouraged to buy beyond their means, females are portrayed as either simple-minded consumers or the bodies that provide male consumers with attractive consumer accessories, and people choose consumer culture over community-based leisure activities. The articles in this collection explore the insidious victimization apparent in consumer culture. At the same time, however, some of the authors included here argue that consumer culture can be liberating. By exploring what might be called the "politics of pleasure," they focus on the ways in which consumer culture makes offers that the rest of the culture ignores: men can actively engage in their domestic space; black women's attractiveness emanates from rather than in spite of their blackness; gay and lesbian citizens have a rightful place in the world of consumer culture as well as in culture in general.

Feminists have been among those who have objected most strongly to women's participation in the culture of consumption, viewing women as victims of male capitalists and male family members. Yet recent feminist scholarship, particularly that of historians and cultural theorists, has looked at the ways in which women play with the images thrust at them and, by so doing, disrupt dominant notions of femininity.[24] Cosmetics, for example, can be seen as consumer items that reinforce the importance of women's bodies rather than their minds. They have become so accepted as part of female identity that many women "become women" as they apply their makeup. At the same, however, one can argue that cosmetics allow women to use the female body in ways that give them autonomy and allow them both to see and to express themselves as sensual human beings, something the culture at large still has difficulty with.

Material goods certainly can make life easier, and shopping for those goods remains a pleasurable experience for many people. Shopping is the second most popular leisure pursuit in the United States, just after television, and with the advent of home shopping networks, people can pursue their number-one and number-two favorite leisure activities simultaneously.[25] The question remains, however, as consumer culture becomes more and more integrated into our daily lives: At what cost do we consume? Do we ever regain the elements of community life we lose when our downtown areas succumb to the malling of America?[26] Do we ever engage in the same way with others when the television, or perhaps the computer, becomes the central communication agent in the household? Will the demands for goods that advertising encourages us to pursue lead to further environmental and social degradation or to demands for a more equitable sharing of the world's resources? How empowering can the process ultimately become—or how disempowering? As the culture of consumption offers us an intoxicatingly strong invitation to live "the good life" as defined by purchasing, it leaves little room for us to consider other definitions of the good life. Contemporary consumer culture addresses primarily not our needs but our seemingly endless wants; but what will happen when we truly recognize all our wants and the limited ability of the consumer culture to actually meet them? As these questions and others raised in this collection make clear, there are no few things that the consumer culture does either "to" us or "for" us.

Organization of Essays in This Collection

This collection of essays and archival materials is divided into four parts. The first, "The Home: Stretching the Boundaries of the Domestic Sphere," explores the relationship between consumer culture and the realm most commonly thought of in relation to consumer culture: the home. In most of the scholarship on the domestic realm and consumer culture, women are seen as the consumers. As they decorate and maintain their homes and provide food and clothing for their families, housewives carve out a space for themselves in the private sphere. As historian Roland Marchand notes, wealthy and working-class women have been seen to have as their common denominator their consumption of goods for the private sphere: the "Colonel's lady" and "Judy O'Grady" were sisters under the skin.[27] The gendered nature of consumer culture in this regard has seemed utterly apparent: women purchase and men provide the incentive, either as wage-earning husbands or as purveyors of goods or the advertising surrounding those goods. More recently, however, scholars have examined the ways in which women have located both power in that domestic space and pleasure in the consumption of goods. They have also identified the ways in which consumer culture, rather than the culture at large, offers men greater access to the private sphere. The essays in this section explore the gendered nature of domestic life and the ways in which women and men both respond to and modify notions of gender and "the home."

The second part, "You Are What You Buy: Individual and Group Identity through Proper Consumption," explores the ways in which consumers are invited to or choose to integrate identities as they engage with the consumer culture. As Yiannis Gabriel and Tim Lang put it, "[C]onsumers are, above all, frequently presented as thirsting for identity and using commodities to quench this thirst."[28] In the case of the articles included here, people identify themselves as white, American, British, black, female, lesbian, or male through their interaction with various elements of consumer culture. Consumers also identify through opposition to, rather than identification with: white consumers are as much not black as they are white; male consumers are as much not female as they are male. The ways in which identity is both offered and consumed reveals a great deal about cultural attitudes and aspirations. One could say that we all "purchase" identities, although, as the authors make clear here, the motivations of the audience and the motivations of those who offer the images are not always one and the same. Purchased identities can be oppressive or liberating, passively accepted or actively pursued.

Part Three, "Under Whose Direction? Consumer Culture's Message Makers," explores what has been considered the hegemonic dimension of consumer culture: those people and organizations that direct consumers to consume. Advertising today accounts for 75 percent of the revenue of newspapers, 50 percent of the revenue of general-circulation magazines, and almost 100 percent of the revenue of broadcasters; clearly, the medium and the message are cleverly and inextricably woven together.[29] Scholars in a variety of disciplines have debated the gendered nature of the seemingly one-directional messages that result from these relationships. Women have long been the primary consumers of many commodities, actively seeking out goods and services, yet their image as passive victim predominates in much of the literature. Men have been viewed as the scientific observers of female consumption, the salesmen who knock on doors or sift through statistics, anxious to understand the buying psychology of women. The essays in this section both give credence to and complicate that simple gendered formula about the creators of consumer culture.

The final part of the book, "Purchasing Possibilities: Sexuality, Pleasure, and Resistance in Consumer Culture," explores in a more explicit fashion what will become apparent to readers who read the book straight through and then arrive at these essays: consumer culture truly is a collaborative process. Since the publication of Vance Packard's *The Hidden Persuaders* in the 1950s, scholarly critics and the general public alike have been quick to see the victim consumer, the dupe whose capacity for the production of goods has been all but completely manipulated into a passion for consuming them.[30] From discussions of subliminal messages in advertising, to the cultural acceptance that women's place truly is at the mall, to analyses of the use of women's bodies to sell alcohol or automobiles, critics see consumers largely as passive recipients of the directive to spend. But more recent scholarship has begun to explore the liberatory potential of consumer culture, keeping in mind issues of power. Part Four explores the significant role consumers play in defining and redefining the meaning of the products they purchase and the act of purchasing. As with other aspects of life, involvement in the consumer culture is both a continuous and a problematic process for its participants, who seek to influence as well as be influenced and whose own personal, gender, race, and sexual politics inform their decisions, actions, and acceptance of consumer culture.

A Note on Archival Materials following Each Part

At the end of each part you will find archival materials related in some way to the preceding essays. The purpose of these sections is to engage you with original materials related to consumer culture. The materials here include magazine articles and advertisements, cartoons, music lyrics, and poetry. My suggestion is that you use them individually or in groups, in class or outside, to illustrate points from individual readings, to look for connections among the readings, and to raise new questions about gender and consumer culture. These are not meant as appendixes to be looked at briefly; instead, my hope is that you will engage with them and "consume" them both thoroughly and critically.

NOTES

1. Consider the words *Xerox, thermos, zipper, escalator*, and *yo-yo*, all of which began as brand names but have since become part of our language. See Michael Schudson, "Historical Roots of Consumer Culture," in Roxanne Hovland and Gary B. Wilcox, eds., *Advertising in Society: Classic and Contemporary Readings on Advertising's Role in Society* (Lincolnwood, IL: NTC Business Books, 1990), 42–72, esp. 69.

2. Historian Stephen Heinze, exploring Jewish immigrant relationships to the culture of consumption in the United States, argued: "Easier to comprehend than the English language or the vote, they [consumer goods] served as the most accessible tools with which Jewish newcomers could forge an American Jewish identity" (*Adapting to Abundance: Jewish Immigrants, Mass Consumption, and the Search for American Identity* [New York: Columbia University Press, 1990], 5).

3. On the relationship between consumer culture and environmental issues, see Paul L. Wachtel, "Alternatives to the Consumer Culture," in David A. Crocker and Toby Linden, eds., *Ethics of Consumption: The Good Life, Justice, and Global Stewardship* (Lanham, MD: Rowman & Littlefield, 1998), 198–217. The United Nations has recently begun to publish information about consumption patterns that has led to people's questioning of unbridled consumption. For example, Americans spend $8 billion a year on cosmetics, $2 billion more than the estimated annual total needed to provide basic education for everyone in the world. Europeans spend $11 billion a year on ice cream, $2 billion more than the estimated annual total needed to provide clean water and safe sewers for the world's population. See United Nations Development Program (UNDP), *UNDP Human Development Report 1998* (New York: Oxford University Press, 1998).

4. Daniel Horowitz, *The Morality of Spending: Attitudes toward the Consumer Society* (Baltimore: Johns Hopkins University Press, 1985), xviii.

5. Michael Schudson, "Delectable Materialism," in Crocker and Linden, eds., *Ethics of Consumption*, 249–268, esp. 253.

6. Alexis de Tocqueville, quoted in Stuart Ewen, *All Consuming Images: The Politics of Style in Contemporary Culture* (New York: Basic Books, 1988), 59.

7. Horowitz, *Morality of Spending*, xviii.

8. On conspicuous consumption, see Thorstein Veblen, *The Theory of the Leisure Class: An Economic Study of Institutions* (1889; reprint, New York: Dover Publications, 1994); Roger S. Mason *Conspicuous Consumption* (New York: St. Martin's Press, 1981); Colin Campbell, "Conspicuous Confusion? A Critique of Veblen's Theory of Conspicuous Consumption," *Sociological Theory* 12, no. 2 (March 1994): 34–47.

9. Lisa Tiersten, "Redefining Consumer Culture: Recent Literature on Consumption and the Bourgeoisie in Western Europe," *Radical History Review* 57 (1993): 118.

10. Colin Campbell, "Consuming Goods and the Good of Consuming," in Crocker and Linden, eds., *Ethics of Consumption*, 139–154, esp. 152.

11. On vacations, see Gary Cross, *Time and Money: The Making of Consumer Culture*

(London: Routledge, 1993); on gift giving, see Marshall Sahlins, *Stone Age Economics* (Chicago: Aldine, 1972); on cosmetic surgery, see Sharon Batt, "Women and the Knife: Cosmetic Surgery and the Colonization of Women's Bodies," in Rose Weitz, ed., *The Politics of Women's Bodies: Sexuality, Appearance, and Behavior* (New York: Oxford University Press, 1998); Kathryn Pauly Morgan, "Medicalization of Racial Features: Asian-American Women and Cosmetic Surgery," in Weitz, ed., *The Politics of Women's Bodies;* and Hilary Radner, "Producing the Body: Jane Fonda and the New Public Feminine," in Pekka Sulkunen, John Holmwood, and Hilary Radner, eds., *Constructing the New Consumer Society* (New York: St. Martin's Press, 1997).

12. On Zimbabwe, see Timothy Burke, *Lifebuoy Men, Lux Women: Commodification, Consumption, and Cleanliness in Modern Zimbabwe* (Durham, NC: Duke University Press, 1996); on carnival in Trinidad, see Daniel Miller, *Modernity, an Ethnographic Approach: Dualism and Mass Consumption in Trinidad* (Oxford: Berg Publishers, 1994); on Elvis in Indian films, see Amit Rai, "An American Raj in Filmistan: Images of Elvis in Indian Films," *Screen* 35, no. 1 (Spring 1994): 51–77; on German women and the consumption of Hollywood films, see Erica Carter, *How German Is She? Postwar West German Reconstruction and the Consuming Woman* (Ann Arbor: University of Michigan Press, 1997); on beauty pageants, see Colleen Ballinero Cohen, Richard Wilk, and Beverly Stoeltze, eds., *Beauty Queens on the Global Stage: Gender, Contests and Power* (London: Routledge, 1995).

13. See T. J. Jackson Lears, "Beyond Veblen: Rethinking Consumer Culture in America," in Simon Bronner, ed., *Consuming Visions: Accumulation and Display of Goods in America, 1880–1920* (New York: W. W. Norton, 1989), 73–97. The literature on consumer culture in the nineteenth and twentieth centuries in the United States is far too extensive to include here. The most recent collection of essays on the period is Susan Strasser, Charles McGovern, and Matthias Judt, eds., *Getting and Spending: European and American Consumer Societies in the Twentieth Century* (New York: Cambridge University Press, 1988). Bibliographies include David Blanke, "A Selected Bibliographic Essay: Consumer Culture during the Gilded Age and Progressive Era" (h-net Gilded Age and Progressive Era List), November 22, 1996; Lynn Spigel and Denise Mann, "Women and Consumer Culture: A Selective Bibliography," *Quarterly Review of Film and Video* 11 (1989): 85–105; Ellen Furlough, "Gender and Consumption in Historical Perspective: A Selected Bibliography," in Victoria de Grazia, with Ellen Furlough, eds., *The Sex of Things: Gender and Consumption in Historical Perspective* (Berkeley: University of California Press, 1996), 389–409. Stephen Heinze notes that patterns of consumption changed considerably from the mid– to late nineteenth century and then again after World War II. By the 1880s, Americans spent 11 percent of their budget on expensive durable items, up from 2 percent at mid-century. The level stayed roughly the same until after World War II (Heinze, *Adapting to Abundance*, 11).

14. On the eighteenth century and earlier in Europe, see Neil McKendrick, John Brewer, and J. H. Plumb, eds., *The Birth of a Consumer Society: The Commercialization of Eighteenth-Century Europe* (Bloomington: Indiana University Press, 1982); John Brewer and Roy Porter, eds., *Consumption and the World of Goods* (London: Routledge, 1993); de Grazia, with Ellen Furlough, eds., *Sex of Things*; Grant McCracken, *Culture and Consumption: New Approaches to the Symbolic Character of Consumer Goods and Activities* (Bloomington: Indiana University Press, 1988).

15. Chandra Mukerji, *From Graven Images: Patterns of Modern Materialism* (New York: Columbia University Press, 1983).

16. Carole Shammas, "Changes in English and Anglo-American Consumption from 1550 to 1800," in Brewer and Porter, eds., *Consumption and the World of Goods*, 177–205, esp.

185. Shammas uses as a definition of "mass" goods that were bought by people of varied income levels on a more or less regular basis.

17. J. H. Plumb, "The Commercialization of Leisure," in McKendrick, Brewer, and Plumb, eds., *Birth of a Consumer Society*, 265–286.

18. Horowitz, *Morality of Spending*, xxv.

19. Mary Douglas and Baron Isherwood, *The World of Goods* (New York: Basic Books, 1979), 15. Douglas and Ishwerwood see consumer culture as "beyond commerce." In acquiring, using, and exchanging things, they argue, individuals come to have social lives.

20. Colin Campbell coined the term *neophiliacs*; see his "Conspicuous Confusion?" 34–47.

21. Douglas and Isherwood, *World of Goods*, 125. On the meaning of things, see also Arjun Appadurai, ed., *The Social Life of Things: Commodities in Cultural Perspective* (Cambridge: Cambridge University Press, 1986).

22. Karl Marx, *Wage Labour and Capital*, quoted in Schudson, "Delectable Materialism," 252.

23. Schudson, "Delectable Materialism," 256.

24. See, for example, Jane Gaines and Charlotte Herzog, eds., *Fabrications: Costume and the Female Body* (London: Routledge, 1990); Sarah Franklin, Celia Lury, and Jackie Stacey, eds., *Off-Centre: Feminism and Cultural Studies* (New York: HarperCollins, 1991); Janet Lee, "Subversive Sitcoms: Roseanne as Inspiration for Feminist Resistance," in Gail Dines and Jean M. Humez, eds., *Gender, Race and Class in Media: A Text-Reader* (Thousand Oaks, CA: Sage, 1995), 469–475; Kathy Peiss, *Cheap Amusements: Working Women and Leisure in Turn-of-the-Century New York* (Philadelphia: Temple University Press, 1986); Jennifer Scanlon, *Inarticulate Longings: The* Ladies' Home Journal, *Gender, and the Promises of Consumer Culture* (New York: Routledge, 1995); Beverly Skeggs, ed., *Feminist Cultural Theory: Process and Production* (Manchester: Manchester University Press, 1995).

25. On shopping as leisure pursuit, see Celia Lury, *Consumer Culture* (New Brunswick, NJ: Rutgers University Press, 1996), 29. On home shopping, see Mimi White, "Watching the Girls Go Buy: Shop-at-Home Television," chap. 3 of her *Tele-Advising: Therapeutic Discourse in America* (Chapel Hill: University of North Carolina Press, 1992), reprinted in Dines and Humez, eds., *Gender, Race and Class in Media*. White makes an interesting argument about the appeal of home shopping: "The viewer-shopper is not isolated in the home. On the contrary, shopping from the house with the club may be more personal and community-oriented than an afternoon at the local shopping mall. For here the viewer shares the experience with a host, who may even remember the last time she called, and with other shoppers who are part of the common culture of shop-at-home consumption" (158, Dines and Humez reprint). Note that White refers to the home shopper as "she." We can expect to see similar scholarship on internet shopping in the near future.

26. Kenneth T. Jackson argues that shopping malls have become "the common denominator of our national life" ("All the World's a Mall: Reflections on the Social and Economic Consequences of the Shopping Center, *American Historical Review* 101 [October 1996], 1111–21, esp. 1111.

27. Roland Marchand, *Advertising the American Dream: Making Way for Modernity* (Berkeley: University of California Press, 1985), 7.

28. Yiannis Gabriel and Tim Lang, *The Unmanageable Consumer: Contemporary Consumption and Its Fragmentation* (Thousand Oaks, CA: Sage, 1995), 81.

29. Gail Dines, introduction to "Advertising," in Dines and Humez, eds., *Gender, Race, and Class in Media*.

30. Vance Packard, *The Hidden Persuaders* (New York: Pocket Books, 1958).

Part One

The Home

Stretching the Boundaries of the Domestic Sphere

As Christopher Reed notes, "[I]f we isolate the values that comprise the notion of domesticity—separation from the workplace, privacy, comfort, focus on the family—we find that each has been identified by historians as a defining feature of the modern age."[1]

Scholars of gender and gender relations have explored the dualities associated with this modern domesticity—home and work, consumer and producer, female and male—recognizing the ways in which those dualities often keep women "in their place," literally, within the confines of the household. Consumer culture reinforces domesticity, urging women to buy washing machines and to prepare meals, for example, rather than to use commercial laundries or collective kitchens. At the same time, it seems to discourage men's involvement in the domestic sphere, regardless of changing work and family patterns. Yet, as the following essays demonstrate, consumer culture challenges as well as promotes traditional domesticity, and individual women and men have used the connection or disjunction between the domestic sphere and their own roles as consumers to break down as well as further these culturally imposed dualistic relationships. This part of the book engages the reader with issues of ethnicity, sexuality, and class as well as gender, all the while exploring the development of culturally mandated and culturally mediated messages about consumption and its relationship to the domestic sphere.

Victoria de Grazia argues, "Nothing about modern family attitudes toward consumption seems to have come naturally, least of all the sex-based division of labor between Mr. Breadwinner and Mrs. Consumer."[2] The four essays in this part reveal just how contentious the relationship has been between gender, consumer culture, and the domestic sphere. Through consumption, as Douglas and Isherwood argue, we attempt to "construct an intelligible universe."[3] We do the same, many would argue, through gendered identities. How do they work together? There is an adage, "A man's home is his castle," but women sarcastically rejoin, "Then let him clean it." Jokes like this reveal the tensions inherent in the gendered household and its relationship to consumer culture. Advertisers continue to market floor-cleaning products to women, in commercials that project images of stay-at-home wives, regardless of the statistics which state that few contemporary women fit the full-time homemaker pattern. Are advertisers ignorant of people's realities? Of course not. Instead, they respond to and encourage gendered household relationships in which women, regardless of employment outside the home, retain primary responsibility for housework and the consumption of products related to that housework; and men, regardless of their employment or contributions to the household, regard themselves as the recipients of the fruits of women's household and consumer work. Advertisers have found it profitable, for the most part, to ignore the realities of the people whose life experiences fall outside those limited parameters. One could argue as well that they have found it profitable to ignore the realities even of those whose life experiences most resemble these women and men in the advertisements, since few if any of those stay-at-home mothers actually gloat over floors clean enough to eat from.

The relationship between gender, consumer culture, and the domestic sphere is far more complicated than television commercials suggest. These essays articulate the ways in which both public and private spaces are constructed and contested by individual women and men. They reveal the ways in which women have derived power from domestic, including consumer, responsibilities; department store entrepreneurs have invited women to define the domestic sphere more broadly to include some public space; gay men have carved out domestic space for themselves in a world largely oblivious if not hostile to their lives; and heterosexual men have looked for and located "masculine" space inside the modern "female" household. Joan Kron argues that "surely the language of the home and its décor is one of the most complex languages in the world."[4] Cultural and gender differences in that language provide fascinating evidence of the diverse relationships people themselves have developed with consumer culture.

The first essay, "Jewish Women and the Making of an American Home," by Andrew Heinze, explores the ways in which a particular immigrant and ethnic group entered American domestic and consumer spaces. Jewish immigrant women experienced new freedoms in the United States in the early twentieth century, says Heinze, but "most expressed their new freedom within the confines of domestic life."[5] As they learned consumer skills in the marketplace, which they used to make their families' home lives more livable, Jewish women helped smooth the transition from one cultural experience to another for themselves, their families, and the other immigrants they helped acculturate. As Heinze argues, these women engaged, "virtually from the moment they entered the streets of the city, in a new cycle of consumption that defined a uniquely American approach to life."[6]

As Heinze reveals, historical and cultural circumstances assured that Jewish women would receive respect rather than derision in the "family purchasing agent" role.[7] Relieved from some of the most backbreaking of household work through increases in technology, Jewish women addressed the "mental strain of intelligent consumption" by playing an active role as consumers. They developed bargain-hunting skills and promoted the development of bargain shopping more generally, and they assimilated their families and relatives into patterns that allowed both the saving of needed pennies and the purchasing of the goods that identified one as an American rather than an immigrant or "greenhorn."[8] Heinze explores the activities of the "housewife," but his work reveals the necessary connections between the private world of domesticity and the public marketplace on the one hand and the powers certain women pursued in a seemingly powerless role on the other.

The second essay, " 'A New Era of Shopping': The Promotion of Women's Pleasure in London's West End," by Erika Rappaport, describes the department store as a necessary corollary to women's continued domestic role. A "monument to mass consumption," the department store offered women consumers a counterpart to the tedious workday at home.[9] As Rappaport interprets the invitations department stores offered women: "Whether imagined as an absolute need, a luxurious treat, a housewife's duty, a social activity, or a feminist demand, shopping was always a pleasure."[10] Interestingly, in an era when women could have abandoned far more of their domestic responsibilities, the department stores, recognizing the mutually dependent relationship between women as consumers and women as homemakers, did not invite them to do so. Selfridge's, the London department store in this study, acknowledged that household work could be terribly monotonous and invited women to look for their excitement outside the home but refrained from advocating that women retire altogether from the domestic role. "This businessman wanted to profit from the limited changes in women's activities underway. He did not want to alter gender norms dramatically," writes Rappaport of American-born entrepreneur Harry Gordon Selfridge. What Selfridge did, as a result, was attempt to create for women a kind of home away from home, a domestic space in public space, a "safe" space for women in the urban environment.

Rappaport also introduces another element related to gender, domesticity, and consumer culture: sexuality. Selfridge's department store promised women access to public spaces that "they had rarely entered and which recently had been tinged with associations of the sexual marketplace."[11] At the same time that it "cleaned up" those sexual spaces, though, it granted women sensual experiences in shopping. In fact, as Rappaport puts it, "sensual pleasures were given moral validity when placed within the language of domesticity."[12] In this case, the domestic sphere is carried into the public sphere; in the process, neither women's domestic lives nor that public space remains unchanged.

The themes of sexual expression and the blurred relationship between private and public domesticity is carried over in the third essay, "Lots of Friends at the YMCA: Rooming Houses, Cafeterias, and Other Gay Social Centers," by George Chauncey. While heterosexual women shopped and undertook domestic chores at home, gay men looked for domestic space to call their own. In the late nineteenth and early twentieth centuries, Chauncey notes, gay men in New York City created domestic spaces that, like those of Jewish women, provided "zones of camaraderie and security"[13] and, like those of Rappaport's shoppers, extended domestic space to the public realm. Many young men gravitated to New York and the gay world it offered; once there, they needed housing. The kinds of housing available to them dictated to some degree both their domestic arrangements and their relationship to the consumer culture. For example, much of the housing available to single men was located in rooming houses, which offered privacy but no cooking facilities. The same was true of the many "apartment hotels" that made it possible for a middle-class gay male world to develop. As a result, gay men used public places, namely, restaurants, as extensions of their domestic space.

The ways in which they created this domestic space in public space reveals a great deal about both gay life and the dominant heterosexual culture in which gay men lived. Because most gay men needed to "manage multiple identities and present themselves as straight" in so many social and domestic settings, the restaurants and cafeterias and lunch counters became places were they could be less guarded.[14] They turned these public spaces into "places where it did not seem queer to talk about an art show or a favorite torch singer, to laugh collectively about the morning paper's picture of the sailor with his arm wrapped around the cannon he was cleaning."[15] Restaurant owners, too, exercised a variety of responses to their gay clientele; most welcomed them as long as they remained an unobtrusive presence, while some actively facilitated a "muted gay ambience" without attracting too much attention from the outside. Moral reformers and law enforcement posed more active threats, and gay men sought ways to maintain a public presence in the face of that resistance. As Chauncey demonstrates, the ways in which gay men used both their private and public "domestic" space was always mediated through the larger culture and through their own experiences as gay people and as men.

The fourth and final essay in this part, "Do-It-Yourself: Constructing, Repairing, and Maintaining Domestic Masculinity," by Steven Gelber, examines one way in which a group of men has attempted to carve out space for themselves in the culturally mandated female sphere of the suburban home. Through the use of hand and power tools, symbols of masculinity, and in the feminine space of the home, heterosexual men reasserted male control over their domestic environments. By the 1950s, in fact, it was a "requirement of masculinity" to engage in some kind of do-it-yourself project in the home.[16] Men gloated over the difficulties of the work, taking pride in their manly ability to persevere in the face of the injuries they experienced or the need to redo work they initially thought they had completed. Like Heinze's Jewish arbiters of consumption, Rappaport's pleasure-seeking female shoppers, and Chauncey's space-claiming gay men, Gelber's do-it-yourselfers found something of merit in engaging with domestic affairs. In this case, heterosexual men, through their hobbies, helped redefine modern domestic life and refine definitions of masculinity.

Do-it-yourself was one of several activities suburban men undertook in their efforts to reassert a presence in the feminized domestic home. One thinks of the electric carving knife and the barbecue grill as specifically masculine household appliances. One also thinks of the Little League coach, the driver of the family automobile, and the handyman as family-related roles undertaken by suburban men. In each of these stereotypical but very real examples, men are able, as Gelber puts it, "to be both a part of the house and apart from it, sharing the home with their families while retaining a distinct masculine style."[17] A great deal of culturally significant activity takes place within and in relationship to the home, and men have found ways of participating in that culture without compromising their male identity—and, it must be noted, without relinquishing the privilege of ignoring much of the more tedious everyday work that takes place in that realm.

The archival material included at the end of this part comes from two 1956 volumes of *Playboy* magazine. The photograph of the first page of the article

"Playboy's Penthouse Apartment" provides yet one more depiction of domestic space and its relationship to gender and consumer culture. In this case, heterosexual men, bachelors, receive an invitation to consume domesticity; that is, they are invited to purchase a bachelor flat and all the consumer goods that go with it. Readers of *Playboy* learn that they can participate in the consumer culture as consumers in their own right rather than as recipients, however privileged, of women's consumption. *Playboy* magazine occupies a unique place in the publishing world in that, in addition to sexual images of women, it always provides "service" features, including information about the latest in consumer goods.[18] The very definition of the playboy for this advertising-revenue-driven magazine has, from its founding in 1953, included active participation in the consumer culture.

In a sense, the bachelor in the *Playboy* piece engages by contrast with the subjects of the essays by Heinze, Rappaport, Chauncey, and Gelber. Situated in his domestic space, the bachelor evokes the others in opposition: he is not the female housewife, not the female shopper, not the gay male, and not the heterosexual husband. Instead, clearly located in his own domestic space and surrounded by the artifacts of his own engagement with consumer culture, the playboy appropriates all that is inviting about that culture for the others—power, pleasure, comfort, and sensuality—yet he clearly rejects the association of domestic consumer culture with the female, the homoerotic, the "domesticated," the mundane.

NOTES

1. Christopher Reed, ed., *Not at Home: The Suppression of Domesticity in Modern Art and Architecture* (London: Thames and Hudson, 1996), 7–17.

2. Victoria de Grazia, "Establishing the Modern Consumer Household," in Victoria de Grazia and Ellen Furlough, eds., *The Sex of Things: Gender and Consumption in Historical Perspective* (Berkeley: University of California Press, 1996), 152.

3. Mary Douglas and Baron Isherwood, *The World of Goods* (New York: Basic Books, 1979), 65.

4. Joan Kron, "The Semiotics of Home Décor," in Sonia Maasik and Jack Solomon, eds., *Signs of Life in the U.S.A.: Readings on Popular Culture for Writers* (Boston: Bedford Books, 1994), 66–77, esp. 74.

5. Andrew Heinze, "Jewish Women and the Making of an American Home," originally published as chapter 6 of his *Adapting to Abundance: Jewish Immigrants, Mass Consumption, and the Search for American Identity* (New York: Columbia University Press, 1990), 105.

6. Ibid., 10.

7. Ibid., 109.

8. Ibid., 109, 112.

9. Erika D. Rappaport, " 'A New Era of Shopping': The Promotion of Women's Pleasure in London's West End, 1909–1914," originally published in Leo Cherney and Vanessa R. Schwartz, eds., *Cinema and the Invention of Modern Life* (Berkeley: University of California Press, 1995), 137.

10. Ibid., 137.

11. Ibid., 142.

12. Ibid., 146.

13. George Chauncey, "Lots of Friends at the YMCA: Rooming Houses, Cafeterias, and Other Gay Social Centers," originally published as chapter 6 of his *Gay New York: Gender, Urban Culture, and the Making of the Gay Male World, 1890–1940* (New York: Basic Books, 1994), 150–177; 152.

14. Ibid., 163.

15. Ibid.

16. Steven M. Gelber, "Do-It-Yourself: Constructing, Repairing and Maintaining Domestic Masculinity," originally published in *American Quarterly* 49 (March 1997): 100.

17. Ibid., 69.

18. See Gail Dines, " 'I Buy It for the Articles': *Playboy* Magazine and the Sexualization of Consumerism," in Gail Dines and Jean M. Humez, eds., *Gender, Race and Class in Media* (Thousand Oaks, CA: Sage, 1995), 254–262. As Dines puts it, participation in the consumer culture was at the core of the magazine, and *Playboy* owner Hugh Hefner's strategy of "offering a lifestyle, rather than just an ejaculation, quickly paid off" (257).

Chapter One

Jewish Women and the Making of an American Home

Andrew Heinze

Jewish women served as a catalyst for the adaptation of newcomers to the American standard of living. The increased prospects for consumption in urban America enabled Jewish homemakers to magnify their already powerful influence over family life. Through an expanded role as consumers and as managers of household consumption, these women smoothed the transition to a new way of life and emphasized the importance of new products to the cultural adjustment of Jews.

"There is no greater change from Eastern Europe to America," observed David Blaustein, in an address to the New York State Conference of Charities delivered in 1903, "than the change in the life of the women."[1] The foremost change experienced by women who had come to the United States involved personal freedom, particularly in marriage and career. The possibilities of freedom in these areas were conveyed brilliantly in the life of Emma Goldman, the prominent Russian Jewish anarchist who advocated the complete equality of the sexes during the thirty-three years that she spent in America before her deportation in 1919. Yet, most women, who ultimately married and raised children, expressed their new freedom within the confines of domestic life. The most conspicuous difference between the domestic power of women in America and in Europe was the magnitude of decision and control over family consumption.

Jewish immigrant women have often been characterized as old-fashioned and anxious about protecting their families from the pace of change in urban America. One of the more memorable images of the Jewish mother was composed by Henry Roth, whose rich novel of a Jewish immigrant family in New York City in the first decade of the twentieth century, *Call It Sleep*, was published in 1934. In Roth's story, the young mother lived in awe of the American city, rarely venturing beyond a small radius from her apartment. Periodically, with intense nostalgia, she dwelled on the picture of a farm that hung on the living-room wall as a reminder of the world left behind. The woman's conservative role in the family was emphasized by her being the sole emotional sanctuary for her son, a sensitive child abused by the outer world of callous men and rough boys.[2] The nostalgic image of the old-fashioned woman has also entered the historical literature. Jewish women have been portrayed as the primary force shielding the immigrant family from the supposedly pernicious temptations of urban consumption.[3]

In fact, the positive attitude of Jews toward new products and habits of consumption hinged on the activity of Jewish homemakers. Being the arbiter and director of domestic consumption was not a new experience for Jewish women—this had been one of their major responsibilities in the more traditional culture of eastern Europe. As consumers within the limited material environment of the shtetls and cities of the Pale, they laid a foundation for the larger role acquired in the United States.

The dynamic role of women in Jewish domestic life was summed up in the concept of the *baleboste*. A term without equivalent in English, baleboste was a Yiddish adaptation of the Hebrew phrase *baal-ha-bayit* which literally means "owner of the home" and implies the control of a household. It exemplified the capacity of Yiddish, which was essentially a variant of German strongly influenced by Hebrew, to use Hebrew words in order to expand the meaning of common concepts. Although Yiddish borrowed many words from German, the German word for housewife—"hausfrau"—was replaced by the Hebrew term "baal-ha-bayit," a phrase that magnified the Jewish conception of the woman's role in the home. As the masculine ideal in the traditional Jewish culture of eastern Europe was that of the scholar whose total attention focused on the study of Torah and Talmud, the complete direction of domestic affairs was considered the prerogative of women. As the term baleboste implied, the role was not underestimated.

Jewish women had inherited the task of overseeing an elaborate system of consumption that originated in the scriptural identification of pure and impure things. Despite the incipient decline of traditional Judaism in the late nineteenth century, particularly among urban people who viewed themselves as progressive thinkers, the majority of eastern Europeans appear to have maintained the observance of Jewish law, a central part of which was kashruth, the concept of purity in the preparation and consumption of food. The Jewish dietary code required of women scrupulous attention to the quality and preparation of food eaten by their families. In addition, the custom of honoring the Sabbath and holidays with special foods, clothes, and tableware added to the task of the baleboste the need to acquire and maintain luxury items with which to relieve the ongoing pressure of material scarcity. With white tablecloth, brass candlesticks, silver wine goblets, loaves of challah—the long, braided white bread rich in eggs—and a crowning dish of chicken or fish, the baleboste performed the wonder of creating a Sabbath atmosphere that consistently evoked affection in Jewish memoirs of eastern European life.[4]

Enhancing the role of the baleboste as an arbiter of consumption, Jewish women frequently involved themselves in the domain of petty commerce, where they sharpened their familiarity with the quality of merchandise and the activity of bargaining. The ideal of freeing one's husband for the study of the Law had made an unofficial commercial career a logical pursuit for Jewish wives. Under the economic duress of the late 1800s, the presence of women as shopkeepers became conspicuous. In an investigation of economic conditions among the Russian Jews shortly after 1900,

Isaac Rubinow found that the income of many petty merchants, whose ranks had swollen since the 1880s, was so small "that the wives are forced to sell something so as to earn a few cents a day."[5] Although their inventory of goods was limited by the reign of scarcity in the Pale, women operated a substantial number of the small stores in the region. In some places, they established a rudimentary form of the catering business, selling expertise in cooking and baking to local families preparing a *simkhe*, or celebration.[6] Despite the lack of statistics about women in commercial occupations, the scope of their involvement was suggested by a journalist who in 1898 observed of Bialystock, the second largest city in Lithuania, "generally the women are very much engaged in trade."[7]

In the more sophisticated material setting of American cities, the continuing involvement of women in retail trade produced familiarity with a higher grade of merchandise. Venturing successfully into the marketing of foods, garments, artificial flowers, and specialty items for American consumers, Jewish women sometimes attained public recognition for the high quality of their products.[8] Though limited to a minority, these commercial ventures benefited the community of Jewish women, as the knowledge of the entrepreneurs circulated among the multitude of shoppers. The engagement of women in trade enhanced the skills of Jewish consumers, but it was secondary to the activities of shopping and home management with which the majority of women were concerned. Through these activities, Jewish homemakers in America realized their potential as accomplished consumers.

The culmination of the Jewish woman's skill as a consumer in the United States depended on the belief that Jewish wives should avoid wage labor when possible. Out of deference to the role of the baleboste, an extremely small proportion of wives sought official employment. In 1911, a government investigation of immigrants in cities reported that in only 4.4 percent of the 297 Russian Jewish families surveyed did the wives take on official employment. The average percentage for all groups was 30.7 percent. Furthermore, between 1910 and 1925, the percentage of Jewish wives working for wages declined, whereas it increased for other groups of immigrants. Yet the father's income was not the sole support of most Russian Jewish families. Nearly 60 percent of wives contributed to the family income, often by taking in boarders. Twice as common in Russian Jewish homes as in the homes of other groups, this practice was more suited than was industrial labor to the role of the baleboste.[9]

Unlike many other immigrants, not only did Jews arrive with the motivation and the family structure for resettlement, but they endowed women with great authority to run the household economy. The significance of this factor appeared in comparison to Irish immigration. Like the eastern European Jews, most Irish newcomers were drawn by persecution to view America as a final destination, and they also included a large number of women. Irish women similarly aimed to raise their households to "lace curtain" status, and they had some commercial experience. Though probably not as extensively as Jews in eastern Europe, they entered the marketplace in Ireland by peddling household wares at local fairs, and running small shops in the towns. Yet, the rigid segregation of the sexes among the Irish made it more difficult for these homemakers to control the income and the consumption habits of their husbands, who tended to spend their money on drink and frivolities.[10]

The circumstances of the Irish suggested that household consumption was affected by the nature of domestic relations, and not simply by the amount of time the woman spent at home. Like eastern European Jews, Germans and Italians also tried to keep women at home as much as possible. But the patriarchal nature of these families made it difficult for housewives to exert full power over the family's habits. Compared to other European newcomers, Italian women were sheltered from American ways—they generally saw their role as one of maintaining traditional ways in opposition to outside influences.[11] Many German women also stayed home, as was indicated by several government surveys of immigrant households, which showed that they had a relatively low rate of participation in the work force.[12] Yet, German men upheld the deeply rooted custom of spending money on drink and entertainment at beer gardens and saloons, a habit that impaired the homemaker's ability to direct domestic consumption.[13]

The position of the Jewish woman as the manager of domestic consumption was buttressed by the comparative advantage of Jewish men in the work force. Remarkably few Jews were unskilled workers, whereas the Italians, Poles, Irish, and to a lesser extent Germans included a considerable number of common laborers. The concentration of Jews in skilled and semi-skilled trades and in white-collar occupations constituted one of the group's outstanding features.[14] Thus, Jewish homemakers rested on a comparatively sound economic base. Unlike many Italian women, they were not generally forced by the low wages of husbands to spend a lot of their time at home making artificial flowers, sewing garments, and doing other low-paid task work for local contractors.[15] Along with their low rate of alcoholism and their respect for their wives' domestic authority, the higher occupational status of Jewish men may have added an element of refinement to the home. In organizing household expenses and furnishing her apartment, the baleboste faced fewer manmade obstacles than did other immigrant women.

Emphasizing the role of the baleboste in the American city, Jewish women were able to increase their control over domestic consumption. In this respect, they approximated the situation of many American housewives. H. L. Mencken's sardonic remark that America was "a land where women rule and men are slaves" reflected at least one aspect of the relation between the sexes.[16] Prominent social workers and home economists agreed that the American wife was the "general purchasing agent" and the "financier" of the family, in both blue-collar and white-collar homes.[17] In the age of mass consumption, this was no small task. As new technology increasingly relieved women from backbreaking housework, the sophistication of the urban marketplace introduced the mental strain of intelligent consumption. "Housekeeping," explained Ellen H. Richards, a leading author on American domestic economy at the turn of the century, "no longer means washing dishes, scrubbing floors, making soap and candles; it means spending a given amount of money for a great variety of ready-prepared articles and so using the commodities as to produce the greatest satisfaction and the best possible mental, moral, and physical results."[18]

The energy of many urban American women had come to be invested in the activity of shopping, which offered Jewish women from eastern Europe an entirely new arena in which to sharpen their powers of discrimination as they widened the horizon of their demands. "Any one who thinks that all the good food is consumed in the upper end of the city . . . can learn something these days by visiting the open-air markets in the East Side," exclaimed a reporter for the *New York Sun* in 1900, on describing the active demand "among the wives and daughters of the East Side tailors" for expensive fish and imported vegetables—including dried mushrooms at eighty cents per pound![19]

The distinctive street markets of New York City allowed the accumulated experience of Jewish shoppers to surface in public, where it drew the attention of observers. In the first major report of the federal government on street marketing in New York City, published in 1925, the skills of Jewish women as consumers were a source of comment. The report noted how, amid a crowd of ten or twelve others, they would judge the merchandise on a pushcart solely by eye and simply call out the desired quantity. "The women of the Jewish race," it was concluded, "are rarely deceived when trading with the vendor."[20]

Through bargain hunting, these homemakers could obtain good-quality products for their families without compromising their sense of fiscal responsibility. The practice of bargain hunting was widespread in the United States as a result of the nation's peculiar social structure. In Europe, consumption had been profoundly influenced by a customary class structure, in which the aristocracy enjoyed luxuries carelessly while the multitude of working people lived in stoic want. American society, however, seemed to develop within the extremes of wealth and poverty, revolving as it did around a large population of people with moderate incomes but great expectations of comfort. In the early 1830s, Alexis de Tocqueville astutely observed the prominent tendency of the society that encouraged all to imagine affluence and that enabled many to attain a position of sufficient comfort to keep such an imagination. Tocqueville saw a multitude of Americans "whose wants are above their means, and who are very willing to take up with imperfect satisfaction, rather than abandon the object of their desires altogether."[21]

As a result of this tendency in the American population, bargain hunting—the search for good products at low prices—emerged as the definitive feature of urban shoppers and urban shops. Reporting on the enthusiasm with which consumers of all social classes redeemed manufacturers' coupons for gifts available at bargain outlets, the *New York Times* asserted in 1899 that city shoppers were driven by "the bargain-counter spirit."[22] The development of American retailing was defined by the passion of the people for bargain hunting. The two most prominent merchants in the United States during the nineteenth century were Alexander Turney Stewart, the New York City retailer who introduced many methods of modern selling between the 1820s and 1860s, and John Wanamaker, the Philadelphia department store owner who succeeded Stewart as the model of retail technique from the 1870s to the early 1900s. Both of these men had a distinct ability to locate, remake, and market products of good quality that could be sold at unusually low prices, an ability well-suited to the temperament of shoppers with moderate incomes and elite aspirations.

By the 1880s, bargain counters were becoming a normal part of American department stores. Established in 1879, the bargain basement of Marshall Field's store in Chicago enjoyed a booming business, expanding within a decade to include thirty departments of specially made, less expensive items in addition to discounted merchandise from the main store. By 1906, it had become a complete store in itself, with a volume of sales that kept pace with that of the original department store above and thus sustained the reduced level of prices. The trend at Marshall Field's was duplicated elsewhere, as merchants recognized the desire of urban people for potentially expensive products that did not carry a high price.[23]

By virtue of the important position of Jewish women as consumers, Jews were able to excel at the American custom of bargain hunting. In contrast to haggling, which revolved around the ability of a consumer to negotiate a lower price through clever talking, bargain hunting depended upon the activity of shopping. Emphasizing the value of spending time to investigate the comparative prices of merchandise, the baleboste turned the Lower East Side into a haven for bargain hunters. The bustling activity of Jewish shoppers was well depicted in a report of a fire sale held at a large store on Avenue A between Fourth and Fifth Streets in March 1899. The bargains on salvaged household furnishings drew tremendous crowds, causing a "riot" that required the supervision of the police and fire departments.[24]

The demand of Jewish shoppers for fine merchandise at discounted prices guided the development of retailing on the Lower East Side. In the 1880s, there emerged outlet known as "cheap stores" that marketed good-quality groceries and foodstuffs at moderate prices.[25] The evolution of Grand Street into a retail center also reflected the character of the newcomers as consumers. According to the *Tageblatt*, several large department stores that occupied this thoroughfare in the 1880s gave way to Jewish businesses because of their failure to understand "the psychology of the Jewish consumer," who wanted "more 'money's worth' with less ta-ra-ras."[26]

By enabling newcomers to view the spending of money as a means of saving money, bargain hunting legitimized the purchase of luxuries. During Jewish holidays, "Now Is Your Time to Save Money" became a familiar slogan of merchants on the Lower East Side whose businesses thrived on the desire of consumers to economize through calculated consumption.[27] Endemic to the situation of urban Americans, the custom of bargain hunting appealed to Jews as a way to reconcile the persistent need to save money with the intense desire to participate in the American pursuit of luxuries.

Not only as an economic exchange, but also as a social focus for urban women, shopping attracted newcomers. Through the institution of the department store, American women established the social ritual of shopping, which included getting together over lunch, and making comparisons of purchases with an eye to the fashion cycle. Although shopping limited the scope of female behavior by keeping women safely within the orbit of domestic affairs, it also provided an exhilirating freedom from the monotonous confinement of the home.[28] Substituting the Lower East Side's emporium of street markets and small shops for the palatial surroundings of the department store, Jewish women found similar satisfaction in the ritual of shopping. Describing Jewish shoppers on Hester Street in the autumn of 1895, the *New York Tribune* noted that "the pleasure they take in the excitement of marketing" dispelled any signs of stress from the faces of these immigrants. Shopping casually amid the intense barter of the street, they were "out to see and be seen as much as to buy."[29]

As an outlet for the personal striving and social competition that men found in the occupational world, shopping permitted newcomers an individualism that barely existed in eastern Europe. In 1906, under the provocative title "They Make Visits to Display Their Hats and Dresses," the *Forward* gave an account of two immigrant women who had adopted the American form of competitive shopping. One, from Berdichev, a city in the Ukraine, was the wife of a superintendent of a fire insurance company, and the other, from a shtetl, was married to a wage earner. Before her husband became a superintendent, the Berdichev woman was poor. Unable to dress nicely, she withdrew as much as possible from her circle of *landslayt*—people from the same region in Europe. Once her husband attained his position and earned forty dollars a week, she made a habit of wearing expensive outfits and visiting her friends. The wife of the wage earner, tired of these obvious displays on the part of her acquaintance, invited the Berdichev woman for a visit in two weeks. By that time, she had bought an exceptionally fine outfit which outclassed that of the superintendent's wife.[30]

In the realm of consumption, the American woman was ideally to be as up-to-date and time-conscious as the American businessman. The ethic of progressive consumption gradually infiltrated the concept of the baleboste in America. Yiddish advertising gave the best reflection of the changing ideal. Playing on the rhyme of the Yiddish words for yarn and lose—*gorn/farlorn*—a 1902 advertisement for Fleisher's yarn, a major American brand that was steadily promoted in the Yiddish press, contended that "a smart baleboste has no time to lose. She knits only with Fleisher's yarn."[31] The domestic equivalent of the popular American axiom "Time Is Money" found its way into the world of the Jewish newcomer.

The value of being up-to-date, as well as time-conscious, was reinforced by Yiddish advertisements. Fels Naptha soap, the well-known brand of a Jewish soap manufacturer, was regularly advertised with the character of "Aunty Drudge," a matron who instructed readers in the progressive approach to cleaning. At times, a drawing of an attractive, fashionably dressed young woman helped to convey the message that Fels Naptha would help keep a woman up-to-date.[32] When the New York Telephone Company began advertising in the Yiddish press near the end of the prewar period, it too reflected the idea of the Jewish woman as a progressive consumer. The advertising addressed "The Woman Who Keeps Herself Up-to-Date" and emphasized "A Telephone Makes Every Home Up-to-Date."[33]

Incorporating traits of the American consumer, the role of the baleboste extended to include control over consumption by other members of the family. "That a wife should accompany her husband in the store when he wants to buy a suit or a hat is with the Gentiles an old custom," the *Forward* exclaimed in 1905, "but to we sons of Israel this is just now becoming the way."[34] The newspaper depicted a scene that typified the new division of labor in regard to domestic consumption. Having just bought a new suit, the husband returns home to the scrutiny of his wife. She does not like the color, the suit does not "lie" quite right, and other problems arise. Inevitably, they return to the store, where a dismayed clerk must then deal with the more discriminating consumer of the pair!

Through her command over the household's consumers, the baleboste initiated newcomers in the adoption of American ways. Unlike many other immigrant women, Jewish wives played an active part in receiving the newly arrived. American immigration officials took note of the efforts of the women to provide the "green-horn" with a transition to American society. In one recorded case, a Russian Jewish family with seven children was met by the father's two sisters, who had been living in the United States for several years and who displayed the trappings of "a state of opulence that appeared to stagger the recently arrived brother."[35] The transition provided by these and many other women was based not only on the offer of temporary lodging and help in finding a job. It focused as well on instruction in the way an American looked and lived, lessons that primarily involved habits of consumption.

The baleboste also monitored and incorporated the demands of children for an American lifestyle. In the era of immigration from eastern Europe, the desire to give children greater educational opportunities was one reason for coming to the United States, and Jewish newcomers clearly emphasized the value of their children's success in America. The more sympathetic approach to childraising that had gained popularity in urban America during the late nineteenth century promoted the idea that the desires and the position of the young should be respected. Attracted by this notion, the Yiddish press excerpted advice about childrearing from leading American magazines. Jewish parents were told that American daughters had the right, not the privilege, to receive an allowance, and that American sons would turn into American gentlemen if they were treated as such at home.[36]

Given this type of respect, Jewish youngsters were able to persuade their elders to adopt American ways that they considered indispensable. Once children had entered the public schools, the pressure of conforming to American customs came powerfully to bear on the family. Schools taught the young that Americans were "the best, the brightest, the most educated and the strongest people in the world."[37]

Although parents often had to bridle at the insistent and sometimes insolent demands of their Americanizing children, Jewish mothers displayed an astute flexibility to the desire for a different lifestyle. In a memoir of the relationship between an immigrant mother and an American daughter, Elizabeth Stern, whose family had come from Russian Poland in 1891 when she was two years old, recalled the positive response of her mother to the new desire she felt on befriending non-Jews in high school. Once Stern began to yearn for a "sitting-room," her mother made provisions for one as soon as space allowed, even though the idea was completely foreign to her. Moreover, Stern commented, her mother strove to beautify the room by buying furniture, rugs, cabinets, a carpet, and by crocheting doilies and embroidering covers for the backs of chairs. "To the standards of the people I was coming to know," the daughter wrote of her mother, "she altered her standards, her speech, her dress. She even altered the whole plan of her home for me."[38]

The ability of Jewish women to respond to youth's desire for American ways reflected the enlarged role of the baleboste in America. Drawn by the sophistication of the urban marketplace, Jewish women sharpened the sense of discrimination about the material world that they had acquired in the traditional culture of eastern Europe. Through their skill as consumers, they extended the control of the baleboste over domestic consumption and thus facilitated Jewish adoption of American habits. Without the activity of women as arbiters of consumption, the pace and the form of Jewish adaptation to urban America would have been different.

NOTES

1. New York *Jewish Daily News (Yiddishes Tageblatt)*, November 22, 1903. The (New York) *Jewish Daily News* was the English page of the Yiddishes Tageblatt.

2. Henry Roth, *Call It Sleep* (New York, 1964). The literary stature of this fascinating novel about the life of Jewish immigrants in urban America was overlooked when the book was first published in 1934.

3. Elizabeth Ewen, *Immigrant Women in the Land of Dollars: Life and Culture on the Lower East Side, 1890–1925* (New York, 1985), pp. 203, 264–269.

4. Some good examples are Leon Stein, Abraham P. Conan, and Lynn Davison, eds., *The Education of Abraham Cahan* (Philadelphia, 1969), p. 36; Morris Raphael Cohen, *A Dreamer's Journey* (Boston, 1949), pp. 18, 34; Miriam Blaustein, ed., *Memoirs of David Blaustein* (New York, 1913), pp. 6–8; Benjamin L. Gordon, *Between Two Worlds: The Memoirs of a Physician* (New York, 1952), pp. 31, 75; Miriam Zunser, *Yesterday* (New York, 1939), pp. 42–48; Samuel Chotzinoff, *A Lost Paradise* (New York, 1955), pp. 73–74.

5. Isaac M. Rubinow, *Economic Condition of the Jews in Russia* (New York, 1975), p. 560. Rubinow's fine report appeared in 1907.

6. Abraham Ain, "Swislocz: Portrait of a Shtetl," in Irving Howe and Eliezer Greenberg, *Voices from the Yiddish* (Ann Arbor, 1972), p. 102; Joachim Schoenfeld, *Shtetl Memoirs* (Hoboken, NJ, 1985), p. 25.

7. *New York Jewish Daily News*, May 23, 1898.

8. Marc Lee Raphael, *Jews and Judaism in a Mid-Western Community, Columbus, Ohio, 1840–1975* (Columbus, 1979), p. 166; *New York Jewish Daily News*, July 18, 1898.

9. United States Immigration Commission, *Reports*, 41 vols. (Washington, D.C., 1911), vol. 1, *Immigrants in Cities*, pp. 229–230, 232, 198; Paula E. Hyman, "Culture and Gender: Women in the Immigrant Jewish Community," in David Berger, ed., *The Legacy of Jewish Migration: 1881 and Its Impact* (New York, 1983), pp. 161–62.

10. Hasia R. Diner, *Erin's Daughters in America: Irish Immigrant Women in the Nineteenth Century* (Baltimore, 1983), pp. 26–27, 67–69.

11. Virginia Yans-McLaughlin, *Family and Community: Italian Immigrants in Buffalo, 1880–1930* (Ithaca, 1977), pp. 203–206.

12. Dorothee Schneider, " 'For Whom Are All the Good Things in Life?': German-American Housewives Discuss Their Budgets," in Harmut Keil and John B. Jentz, eds.,

German Workers in Industrial Chicago, 1850–1910 (DeKalb, Ill., 1983), pp. 148–149; also see the table of income of women from different ethnic groups in Elizabeth H. Pleck, "A Mother's Wages: Income-Earning among Married Italian and Black Women," in Michael Gordon, ed., *The American Family in Social-Historical Perspective* (New York, 1978), p. 496.

13. Charles S. Bernheimer, *Russian Jew in the United States* (Philadelphia, 1905), p. 35.

14. Thomas Kessner, *The Golden Door: Italian and Jewish Immigrant Mobility in New York City, 1880–1915* (New York, 1977), pp. 59–64, 109–110.

15. Robert K. Foerster, *The Italian Emigration of Our Times* (Cambridge, Mass., 1919), p. 381.

16. Mencken's views on the status of American women and men are elaborated in the ironically titled book *In Defense of Women* (New York, 1918).

17. Christine Frederick, "How Advertising Looks to a Consumer," *Advertising and Selling* (June 30, 1914), 24:15; Louise B. More, "The Cost of Living for a Wage-Earner's Family in New York City," *Annals of the American Academy of Political and Social Science* (July 1913), 48:104; Louise Bolard More, *Wage-Earners' Budgets: Studies of Standards and Cost of Living in New York* (New York, 1907), p. 3.

18. Ellen H. Richards, *The Cost of Living as Modified by Sanitary Science* (New York, 1900), p. 103.

19. Excerpted in the *New York Jewish Daily News*, February 11, 1900.

20. United States Agricultural Economics Bureau, *Push Cart Markets in New York City* (Washington, D.C., 1925), p. 30.

21. Alexis de Tocqueville, *Democracy in America*, Richard D. Heffner, ed., (New York, 1956), p. 170. Tocqueville's classic interpretation of American society, based on a visit from May 1831 to February 1832, was first published in two parts, in 1835 and 1840.

22. *New York Times*, May 14, 1899; a good illustration of the passion for bargain hunting is given in the story "Priscilla Goes Shopping," *Ladies' Home Journal* (August 1906), 23:7.

23. Robert W. Twyman, *History of Marshall Field and Company, 1852–1906* (Philadelphia, 1954), pp. 112–114; "Bargain-Counters," *Printer's Ink* (February 3, 1897), 18:43; Ralph Hower, *The History of Macy's of New York, 1853–1919* (Cambridge, Mass., 1943), p. 381.

24. New York *Jewish Daily News*, March 8, 1899.

25. New York *Jewish Daily News*, February 19, 1899.

26. New York *Jewish Daily News*, March 20, 1910.

27. Ibid., March 26, 1896, for advertisement of Geiger and Braverman, a major furniture company of the Lower East Side, and *New York Forward*, March 24, 1900, for advertisement of the New York Furniture and Carpet Store.

28. Gunther Barth, *City People: The Rise of Modern City Culture in Nineteenth-Century America* (New York, 1982), pp. 123–124, 129–130, 136–137, 140–147; the book appeared first in 1980. Sheila M. Rothman, *Woman's Proper Place: A History of Changing Ideals and Practices, 1870 to the Present* (New York, 1978), pp. 19–21.

29. *New York Tribune*, November 3, 1895.

30. *New York Forward*, March 15, 1906.

31. New York *Jewish Daily News*, October 27, 1902.

32. Ibid., April 8, 1910.

33. *New York Forward*, February 2, 1914.

34. Ibid., September 15, 1905.

35. Quoted from Rudolf Glanz, *The Jewish Woman in America: Two Female Immigrant Generations, 1820–1929*, 2 vols. (New York, 1976), 2:61.

36. *Jewish Daily News*, August 14, 1898, May 10, 1898.

37. *New York Forward*, February 21, 1903.

38. Elizabeth G. Stern, *My Mother and I* (New York, 1917), p. 98. This evocative account of growing up in the New York City home of Jewish immigrants first appeared one year earlier, in 1916.

Chapter Two

"A New Era of Shopping"

The Promotion of Women's Pleasure in London's West End, 1909–1914

Erika D. Rappaport

"Thousands of women besiege the West," announced a *Daily Express* headline on 15 March 1909. The *Standard* proclaimed this day in early spring the beginning of "Woman's Week in London."[1] What drew these women to the West End and into the astonished consciousness of dozens of journalists? This female siege was part of a grand celebration of commerce launched by the opening of Gordon Selfridge's new Oxford Street department store, the simultaneous commemoration of Harrods' sixty-year jubilee, and the annual spring sales held in nearly every West End shop. A "lady correspondent" interpreted this intense retail competition as a benefit for women since it transformed "shopping" into "a fine art." Advertising, special sales, and opening celebrations, she argued, expanded the very meaning of shopping: "From Times immemorial woman has shopped . . . [but] it is only since Monday that we have understood what the word really means."[2] Stimulating excitement for this commercial extravaganza, the *Daily Express* declared the week to be the dawn of a "new era of shopping."[3]

Despite these assertions, however, decades of economic and cultural transformation had produced this "new era."[4] The opening of Selfridge's department store and the competing celebrations in older English shops in early spring 1909 was a moment when Edwardians reflected upon the commercial, class, and gender changes that had shaped their capital city since at least the 1860s. The overwhelming competition among retailers in the years before the war produced a new way of thinking about consumption, the city, and female pleasure. In particular, Gordon Selfridge's architectural style, along with his display and marketing strategies, sparked a widespread discussion on the nature and meaning of an expanding English commercial culture. This fevered debate among journalists, retailers, advertisers, and consumers prompted a redefinition of shopping and of women's place in the urban environment.

As the "lady correspondent" had declared, shopping had long been associated with women, but the meaning of this activity was by no means stable. For much of the Victorian era, shopping had been often denigrated as a wasteful, indulgent, immoral, and possibly disorderly female pleasure.[5] Selfridge and other Edwardian entrepreneurs rewrote the meaning of this indulgence. They used publicity, particularly the print media, to turn disorder and immorality into legitimate pleasures, transforming anxieties into profits. Shopping was advanced as pleasurable and respectable precisely because of its public setting, which Edwardian business presented as a context for female self-fulfillment and independence. Selfridge addressed women not only as urban actors but also as bodies to be satisfied, indulged, excited, and repaired. Shopping, he repeatedly stated, promised women access to a sensual and social metropolitan culture.

Nothing Selfridge offered, however, was truly novel. Department stores were not the only place where women shopped, nor were they the only institution that encouraged women to participate in West End commercial culture. Since the 1860s, restaurants, hotels, the theater, museums, exhibitions, women's clubs, guidebooks, and magazines had fostered an image of the West End of London as a place of commercial enjoyment and female exploration. The expansion of public transport, the advent of the cheap press, increasing economic opportunities for middle-class and working-class women, and shifting notions about class, gender, and the economy had produced what appeared as a "new era of shopping." Nonetheless, Gordon Selfridge successfully constructed a compelling narrative about consumption, novelty and pleasure, women and the city.

In this story, Selfridge became more than the founder of a unique shop. He fashioned himself as a builder of a female, consumer-oriented public culture and placed the department store at its center. The department store came to be privileged as a generator of this urban culture, rather than the result of a slowly developing and complex phenomenon.[6] This article examines the creation of this story and explores how mass retailing and the mass media collectively used publicity to create a powerful cultural narrative.

An American in London

A middle-aged Wisconsin native, Harry Gordon Selfridge had actively fostered pleasurable purchasing for more than twenty-five years in the United States.[7] As the second-in-command of the Marshall Field's store in Chicago, Selfridge claimed responsibility for many of the emporium's innovations: He introduced the first restaurant and bargain basement, invited foreign royalty for personal visits, and hired a well-known window-display artist to design spectacular show windows. Selfridge also believed in advertising, writing a good deal of the early copy himself.[8] Like many of his contemporaries, Selfridge hoped that luxurious decor, architecture, amenities, and entertainments, as well as extensive publicity, would encourage patrons to reimagine the way they viewed shopping. In these commercial environments, customers were asked to see buying not as an economic act but as a social and cultural event. Admittedly, Selfridge hoped he would reap the profits from his customers' pleasure. In 1904 he left Marshall Field's to open his own store. He came to England because of a professed affinity for English culture, particularly its economic ideals, later confessing, "I can buy merchandise there and put it on my counters more cheaply than anywhere else." [9]

London presented Selfridge with both a challenge and an opportunity. By 1909 the West End was a center of commercial leisure and pleasurable consumption for middle-class and even working-class men and women. Like New York's Times Square and similar districts in European cities, the West End had become "an attraction" that was both "bounded and free . . . familiar yet exotic . . . [a] pleasure zone."[10] Even working women window-shopped and dined in the West End. They met friends and lovers at such restaurants as the Criterion and occasionally enjoyed a visit to the music hall or similar amusement.

As a component of this commercialization, London department stores typically had grown from drapers' and grocers' shops founded in the early and middle decades of the nineteenth century.[11] These stores were both a symbol of and active player in the creation of the new West End. By the 1870s and 1880s, they sold every conceivable sort of household item, clothing, materials, toys, presents, furniture, food, and drink. They also offered patrons, particularly women, comfort and entertainment in the heart of the city. By the early twentieth century, shopping was closely associated with the idea of a pleasurable and comfortable mass urban culture. The author of a 1906 shopping guide, for example, remarked that "for the woman who knows her London, there is not a more moderate and satisfactory shopping place in the world. And daily it becomes more comfortable."[12]

Despite these commercial, social, and cultural changes, a large portion of this fashionable shopping district remained dedicated to serving its traditional aristocratic and upper-middle-class market. The aristocratic image of the West End had been centuries in the making, but during the early years of the nineteenth century it became even more firmly fixed when the Prince Regent fashioned a wide avenue to accommodate a public aristocratic culture of display and consumption.[13] By the 1850s, Regent Street was well known as a fashionable promenade, the "only spot," according to the Frenchman Frances Wey, "outside the park, where Society people are certain to meet." Its shops, which displayed "all the tempting treasures of the luxury trades,"[14] provided a glittering backdrop for upper-class society to flirt, stroll, and gossip. This aristocratic image strongly influenced the nature and perception of West End commercial culture into the Edwardian era. Bond Street, the Burlington Arcade, and the surrounding streets and squares largely served a small, elite clientele, while larger thoroughfares, such as Oxford Street, had a reputation as a middle-class marketplace.[15]

As late as 1909, only a few London stores approximated the size, services, and sensationalism of Marshall Field's or the Bon Marché in Paris.[16] Social, cultural, economic, and political forces had preserved the small scale and aristocratic tone of many West End shops.[17] Architecture, interior design, salesmanship, and advertising reflected a notion of a fixed and class-specific rather than a mass market. In the eighteenth century, English retailers were known for indulging in extremely elaborate and sophisticated forms of display.[18] By the twentieth century, these same techniques were criticized for being "backward"[19] and making shopping sometimes more painful than pleasurable. Rather than present a "unified whole," wrote Selfridge, West End stores were really an "agglomeration of shops" that were "form-less and inefficient." He assumed that "subdued and disciplined" interiors and employees discouraged browsing and fantasizing about goods. Selfridge remembered that when he had attempted to just look around a London shop, the shop-walker abruptly told him to " 'op it."[20]

Gordon Selfridge may have quietly left this shop, but he very loudly joined the West End business community. In less than a year, he constructed what was to be the largest, most luxurious, and most publicized store in London. After winning a struggle with the local city authorities over the proposed building's size and design, Selfridge used an innovative steel-frame structure and elaborate stonework to create a monument to mass consumption.[21] The Oxford Street emporium towered over its neighbors with eight floors, six acres of floor space, nine passenger lifts, and one hundred departments.[22] Eighty feet high, with huge stone columns and twenty-one of the largest plate glass windows in the world, Selfridge's [23] struck even the most critical Londoner as an imposing visual spectacle.

The interior, like the exterior, was considered an architectural masterpiece. The selling space had wide aisles, electric lighting, crystal chandeliers, and a striking color scheme in which white walls contrasted with thick green carpets. Although not everyone agreed with the reporter who described the interior as a scene of "unexampled perfection,"[24] architectural circles generally bestowed high praise on this ambitious new venture. While doing so, they also salvaged English reputations by portraying the store as a merger of the best of old and new, as modern American construction covered with an "elegantly English" exterior.[25]

Selfridge's embellishment of the store's physical structure turned its opening into a media event. The store's show windows, covered with large silk curtains, created a theatrical atmosphere. "Most impressive of all," one reporter claimed, "were the lights and shadows behind the drawn curtains of the great range of windows suggesting that a wonderful play was being arranged."[26] The sound of bugles announced the store's opening at exactly 9:00 A.M. on 15 March 1909. Employees drew back the curtains and revealed a sight so entertaining that one reporter described the window-gazing crowd as spectators of "a tableau in some drama of fashion." Instead of the traditional display of goods, each window "had a painted background . . . depicting a scene such as Watteau would have loved, and where ladies of the old French court would have wandered."[27] Nearly all descriptions of the opening emphasized the "new sensation" created by such "lofty" windows with "delicately painted" backgrounds.[28] Selfridge's window dressers used theatrical techniques to create tableaux that invested ordinary goods with cultural and social meanings, meanings filtered through and interpreted by a sympathetic media.

While there were numerous well-known and well-trained English window dressers, the press credited the American store with the production of a new visual landscape in which the street had been turned into a theater and the crowd had become an audience of a dramatic fashion show. Indeed, while reporting on the opening, the press created many of the meanings associated with shop windows and shopping in general. Readers unable or unwilling to venture to the West End could vicariously participate in this commercial spectacle by reading about it in dozens of journals, magazines, and newspapers.

The reporting on Selfridge's opening further tightened the relationship between mass retailing and mass journalism. Although long in its development, this partnership sold Selfridge's store by promoting a new notion of women, their pleasures, and the city. In representing the store as visual spectacle, the press produced Edwardian commercial culture in partnership with men such as Gordon Selfridge. Even while criticizing the new "monster shops," the press repeatedly figured consumption as a female, public, and sensual entertainment. Countless English writers thus joined a maverick American entrepreneur to create an international culture of pleasure in London's West End.

"A Time of Profit, Recreation, and Enjoyment"

Gordon Selfridge marketed his new store by promoting shopping as a delightful and respectable middle-class female pastime. Journalists then transformed this advertising message into accepted fact by writing about both Selfridge's new store and West End commercial culture in general. Selfridge's message flawlessly spread from the advertising to the news sections of even such unlikely journals as the *Church Daily Newspaper*. In writing about the store's opening, this paper's reporter loudly proclaimed that, at Selfridge's, "Shopping" had become "an Amusement."[29] Whether imagined as an absolute need, a luxurious treat, a housewife's duty, a social activity, or a feminist demand, shopping was always a pleasure.

Selfridge's central strategy was to undermine the pleasures of preexisting urban commercial culture in order to heighten the excitement and enjoyment of his new enterprise. His first advertisements, therefore, asserted that Selfridge's had transformed shopping from labor into leisure. A typical advertisement loudly proclaimed that the emporium influenced the "shopping habit of the public." For "previous to its opening . . . shopping was merely part of the day's WORK . . . to-day, shopping— at Selfridge's . . . is an important part of the day's PLEASURE, a time to PROFIT, RECREATION, and ENJOYMENT, that no Lady who has once experienced it will willingly forgo."[30] Another emphasized that "not until Selfridge's opened had English ladies understood the full meaning of 'shopping made easy.' Never had it been quite such a delightful pastime."[31]

Other advertisements and articles emphasized this transformation of shopping from work into pleasure by endlessly defining and elaborating upon those pleasures. In addition to the visual enjoyment of the advertisements and the store's window and interior decoration, countless promotions presented shopping at the core of a new publicly oriented social life, which included men and women and people of diverse classes. Selfridge and his commentators collectively promoted shopping by legitimating and defining a consumer-based, heterosocial urban culture. The romantic possibilities of shopping, for example, were subtly encoded in the imagery of the opening day advertisement. In "Herald Announcing the Opening" (fig. 2.1), Bernard Partridge illustrated the department store as a medieval prince on a faithful

Fig. 2.1. Bernard Partridge, "Herald Announcing the Opening," 15 March 1909. By kind permission of Selfridge's Archive at the History of Advertising Trust Archive, U.K.

steed; the powerful muscles and overwhelming size of the animal underscore the appeal of the handsome herald, who looms large in the foreground as he rides into the countryside to summon ladies and their spending power to the urban center. Despite this romantic image, the underlying economy of the buyer-seller relationship is identified in the combination of a pound and dollar sign, the store's symbol, emblazoned on the herald's breastplate. Yet the illustration also obscures the "foreign" background of the owner and his methods by linking the new venture to a representation of ancient English "tradition" and currently popular images of empire.[32]

Novelty and tradition, sensuality and consumption were thus bound together in a pastiche of medieval and Edwardian romantic imagery.[33] A second cartoon, "Leisurely Shopping," emphasized modernity and the romance of consumption by representing a fashionably dressed couple enjoying tea together (fig. 2.2). The attractive couple seems interested less in each other than in the viewer, who is invited to enjoy looking at the couple. Man or woman, the reader becomes both object and subject of the couple's gaze. The pleasures of shopping are encoded in the sexual exchange of the couple and in the voyeuristic pleasures of the reader. In contrast to this somewhat provocative drawing, the written text only indirectly encourages a sexual interplay. "Shopping at Selfridge's," it claims, is "A Pleasure—A Pastime—A Recreation . . . something more than merely shopping."[34] The advertisement constructed heterosexual and consumer desire in relation to each other and linked both to a public culture of looking and display.[35]

T. Friedelson united consumption with heterosocial culture by promotion window-shopping as visual pleasure. In "Selfridge's by Night," Friedelson illustrated a fashionable crowd streaming out of motorcars and carriages to gaze at the store's brightly lit windows (fig 2.3). The illustration and accompanying text implied that window shopping was an exciting but respectable evening entertainment. "By Night as well as Day Selfridge's will be a center of attraction," the copy boasted. The "brilliantly lit" and "frequently re-dressed" windows promised "to give pleasure to the artistic sense of every passer-by, and to make the 'Window Shows at Selfridge's in Oxford Street' worth a considerable detour to see."[36] This picture of evening street life both promoted shopping and suppressed the better-known image of the West End after dark.[37]

Indeed, Edwardian business owners and advertisers actively assaulted the reigning portrayal of the urban center as host to prostitution, gambling, and other illicit activities. Like the managers of West End restaurants, hotels, and theaters, Selfridge rebuilt the city's image as a modern, heterosocial, and commercial pleasure center.[38] These advertisements were part of the process, identified by Peter Bailey, by which capitalist managers promoted a new form of open, licit sexuality.[39] A distinct form of modernity was constructed from this limited and controlled form of sexuality.

Store advertisements and feature articles situated the department store and shopping, then, in a larger context of commercialized leisure. Copywriters and journalists drew upon a metaphorical repertoire from both urban high and low culture.[40] They described the store and the West End as a carnival, a fair, a public festival, a tourist sight, a women's club, and a pantomime. In interviews Gordon Selfridge even claimed that his emporium recaptured the sociability of the early modern

Fig. 2.2. Stanley Davis, "Leisurely Shopping," 19 March 1909. By kind permission of Selfridge's Archive at the History of Advertising Trust Archive, U.K.

Fig. 2.3. T. Friedelson, "Selfridge's by Night," 20 March 1909. By kind permission of Selfridge's Archive at the History of Advertising Trust Archive, U.K.

marketplace with its mixed-class and mixed-sex culture.[41] In 1913, for example, Selfridge discussed his store as a modern reincarnation of "the great Fairs" which flourished before "small shops began to do business behind thick walls and closed doors." With his own romantic vision of the history of commerce, he continued:

> We have lately emerged from a period when merchandising and merrymaking were kept strictly separate . . . 'Business was Business.' . . . But to-day . . . Stores—the modern form of market—are gaining something of the atmosphere of the old-time fair at its best; that is, before it became boisterous and degenerate. The sociability of Selfridge's is the sociability of the fair. It draws its visitors from far and near . . . to sell to them or merely to amuse and interest them.[42]

Selfridge argued that mass retailing reunited elite and popular culture, which he saw as having been separated during the Victorian era. He further implied that this separation had limited the pleasures of English shopping and urban culture during the Victorian era.

Selfridge's advertising also compared modern shopping to foreign or previously unrespectable forms of urban leisure. A typical promotion stated that the store served the same social function as a Continental café. "Abroad, it is the cafés," the ad suggested, "which are the familiar, lovable places where the populace resort . . . to meet their friends, to watch the world and his wife, to take a cup of coffee, or drink a glass of lager or absinthe." However, "in London . . . it is the Big Stores which are beginning to play the part of the charming foreign café; and . . . it was Selfridge's who deliberately began to create the necessary atmosphere."[43] Department stores then offered middle-class women a simulacrum of social spaces they had rarely entered and which until recently had been tinged with associations of the sexual marketplace.

Gordon Selfridge went further, however, and encouraged bourgeois women to experience city life in the role of the traditionally, but no longer exclusively, masculine character of the flâneur.[44] Walking alone through the city, this figure has been assumed to represent a masculine perspective on the city and modernity. However, this urban explorer had actually been figured as a woman in novels, guidebooks, magazines, and newspapers since at least the mid-nineteenth century.[45] Like these other texts, Selfridge positioned the shopper as a flâneuse whose urban ramble ended at his door. "What a wonderful street is Oxford-street," claimed one ad, for "it compels the biggest crowds of any street in London." "When people come here," it announced, "they feel they are in the centre of things . . . : Oxford Street is the most important highway of commerce in the world."[46] "An Ode to London in the Spring, Or, The Gentle Art of Advertisement" took up this theme by privileging the pleasures of an urban walk over those of a country stroll:

> Although the country lanes are sweet
> And though the blossom bloss,
> Yet what are these to Regent Street
> Or even Charing Cross?
> So catch a train, and thank your stars
> That there are trains to catch

And make your way this very day
To London, with dispatch.[47]

The excitement of looking at and being with strangers became enjoyable and respectable because the commercial West End was peopled with elite society rather than a dangerous mob. The shopper could become a queen,[48] or at least a queen of this elite crowd. In Lewis Baumer's advertisement entitled "At Home," middle-class shoppers were invited to a Society gathering of fur-wrapped and elegantly coiffed ladies. However, the picture and caption played on the two meanings of being at home. The illustration represented the formal ritualized sense of the term as a Society event, while the caption reminded readers of the comfortable domestic connotation of feeling "at home."[49] Other ads portrayed Selfridge's as a formal "event" in the Season's calendar. "Shopping" at Selfridge's, the text read, "has all the appearance of a Society gathering. . . . It holds a recognised position on the programme of events, and is responsible sartorially for much of the success of each function that takes place."[50]

Gordon Selfridge designed and publicized the department store as a blend of elite and mass culture. Compared to the private world of Ascot, the store also mirrored the public culture of the amusement park. In July 1909, for example, Selfridge displayed the Bleriot airplane, the first to fly between France and England, on the roof of his store. Despite his competitor's accusation that he was engaging in a cheap American publicity stunt, huge crowds rushed to his rooftop.[51] The *Daily Telegraph* reported that "the public interest in the monoplane yesterday was immense. Throughout the entire day, without cessation or diminution, a constant stream of visitors passed into Selfridge's and circled round the historic implement."[52] The stunt proved so successful that Selfridge eventually opened a rifle range, putting green, and skating rink on the top of the store.

In addition to these sensational entertainments, Selfridge's offered a range of services and amenities to create the feeling of both a homey environment and an escape from dull household routine. Indeed, while dozens of ads and articles promoted a heterosocial urban culture, others portrayed shopping and the city as an exclusively female social experience. These ads tended to emphasize such bodily comforts as eating and lounging more than the visual pleasures of shopping. However, many intertwined a variety of sensual experiences into one desirable consumer experience.

Since the 1870s, tea shops, women's clubs, restaurants, and hotels, as well as confectioners and department stores, served as places for women who were alone in the city to refresh themselves.[53] However, Gordon Selfridge marketed his store as the first and only provider of such services. Indeed, in a quasi-feminist tone stripped of any overtly political message, he painted his shop as the ideal female "rendezvous" or public meeting place. In the Callisthenes column entitled "Where Shall We Meet," the store became a haven for shoppers stranded in an unfriendly and supposedly inhospitable city. Before Selfridge's, the ad claimed, women had to resort to "a cold and draughty waiting-room at a railway station" or perhaps "a bleak, dusty, congested traffic-centre, such as Oxford Street." This supposed lack of an "ideal rendez-vous in London" was "called another of women's wrongs."

While "the City man had a number of favoured resorts . . . the poor ladies 'out shopping' have been at a single disadvantage."[54] By building a "private" place in public, Selfridge later told one of his executives, "I helped to emancipate women. . . . I came along just at the time when they wanted to step out on their own."[55] This businessman wanted to profit from the limited changes in women's activities already underway. He did not want to alter gender norms dramatically.

Countless ads described Selfridge's as both a public and private place, as an institution that catered to individual and social needs and desires. The vast restaurant, which served between two and three thousand patrons a day, was advertised as the largest and best in London.[56] Ads cheered its "excellent" food at "popular prices"[57] and argued that few luncheon and tea rooms in London were thought to have finer decor.[58] After lunch, patrons were encouraged to rest in the library and reading and writing rooms. French, German, American, and colonial reception rooms welcomed foreigners and allowed English shoppers to travel to foreign lands. The German shopper, for example, could relax in a dark-oak reception room decorated with old tapestries and designed to be a replica of a "sitting room in the Fatherland."[59] A fatigued or ill shopper had the choice between a first aid room that "looked very dainty and inviting"[60] and a "rest cure" in the Silence Room. Here, talking was forbidden, allowing customers to "retire from the whirl of bargains and build up energy."[61] Double windows excluded "street noises," while soft lights and chairs with deep cushions enabled shoppers "to find peace and recuperation."[62]

While a shopper rested, "skilled needlewomen" and a maid were always available "in case of any little accident to a button or hook-and-eye which might have occurred during the rough and tumble of a day's shopping."[63] With such free services, shopping was likened to a "rest cure" that reduced rather than increased anxiety. Underlying this nurturing image, however lay the more traditional views of the city as dangerous and dirty and of the female body as weak and in need of comfort and protection. Although Selfridge encouraged women to enter the city, like a good Edwardian patriarch, he also claimed to protect them once they were there.

Selfridge promised these women more than comfort, however. He offered them a space for legitimate indulgence. Modern shopping was more than just buying, but it was also more than "just looking."[64] Shopping, as William Leach has put it, was a visual culture of "color, glass and light,"[65] but it was also a bodily culture stimulating all the senses. Its decor and displays allowed one to feast one's eye and enjoy the feel of fine fabric. Its restaurants and services told shoppers to "treat" themselves to "delicious" luxuries. Even a visit to the Selfridge Bargain Basement could become a sensual wonderland for the frugal shopper. "What a shining feast for the eyes are the ribbon tables; what filmy piles of blouses are here . . . what a forest of silken and velvet flowers; what delicious scents are wafted to us from that mound of tinted soaps."[66] Materials provided "feasts" for the eyes, and colors and scents were "delicious," as if oral, tactile, and visual pleasures defined and amplified one another. All appetites were united in a single desiring body.

Emphasizing the exciting indulgence of Selfridge shopping, a large proportion of early ads focused on individual, and immediately gratifying, forms of consumption. Shoppers were enticed with bonbons and sweet-meats packaged in replicas of famous Italian monuments, buildings, and statues.[67] Sweets became "wonderfully nourishing," a "benefit," even a "necessity" that "makes an appetising and delicious appeal to every visitor in the Store."[68] The American-style soda fountain, a unique temptation, proved a strong selling point and the center of Selfridge's oral appeal. Luxurious ingestion almost became the heart of the consumer experience. A typical ad showed how the soda fountain transformed women who "hated shopping" into avid practitioners of the art. Two "large iced strawberries" could thoroughly reform women who had found shopping "frightfully boring," "a most decadent development," and a "hotbed of frivolous, senseless adornment."[69]

In order to contain the potentially radical message of women indulging in public pleasures, Selfridge's sometimes was imagined as a glorified bourgeois household. The department store became a huge bourgeois home, sustaining family life in the heart of the city. After defining "afternoon tea" as "the chief ritual to the household gods," an "unrivalled and unassailable" custom that was "one of the mainstays of family life," an advertisement reminded shoppers that "even when away from home, the solace of afternoon tea cannot be dispensed with."[70] This ad both created new and used preexisting domestic associations of afternoon tea with family, stability, and tradition in order to connect a new American-owned store with notions of bourgeois Englishness, to make local customers feel at home and visiting tourists feel English. Sensual pleasures were given moral validity when placed within the language of domesticity.

Selfridge's thereby became a home away from home, offering its customers space for what had been considered private forms of socializing. One journalist reported that women were even inviting their friends to formal shopping parties. This reporter claimed that these "parties are a new thing, which have sprung into existence to meet a new need. . . . The parties are small, select, numerous, and earnest."[71] They included buying but emphasized dining and browsing with friends. A common activity for nearly forty years, public dining was marketed by Selfridge as new modern, and fun years, as an updated image of Victorian women's culture.[72] Here, female friendship, like "the family," became a vehicle for legitimizing consumption.

Both paid and unpaid media publicity walked a tightrope between praising and denigrating the home and often did both at once. Indeed, Gordon Selfridge believed that women were responsive to his store's "sensuous appeal of beauty" because they had "little opportunity of escaping the deadening routine of homelife."[73] "Women needed Selfridge's," according to one ad, "to break the monotony that had invaded and made dull a daily round." Selfridge's provided "the variety which is the spice of life."[74] "I was lonely," complained one housewife,

> So I went to Selfridge's . . . one of the biggest and brightest places I could think of. I wanted crowds . . . a happy place . . . "home" in the open . . . caught up in a whirl of these jolly human, little businesses; made part of the crowd; all sense of isolation swept away.[75]

The store could be both " 'home' in the open" and contrasted with bourgeois home life, which in these ads denied rather than gave women pleasure. "I have a friend, and I want to meet her. Where shall the meeting-place be?" asked one character.

"At my home? I don't think so: women spend so much time among their own all too familiar chintzes." This consumer "wanted a place with music, where there were plenty of things to see, and a companionable sense of crowds."[76]

Advertising, news reports, publicity stunts, and social commentary promoted Selfridge's and the West End as a public sphere of female pleasure. Despite a considerable masculine presence on the streets, London was imagined as completely given over to women and consumption; indeed, the city seemed to have become a female space. One paper suggested that "the West End was given over to women," whose "laughter and the rustle of silken skirts enlivened the sound of buses crawling through the slush of the streets."[77] The city seemed invaded by an "army in furs and feather."[78] Although retailers' reports no doubt exaggerated the numbers of shoppers, there were possibly several million women visiting London in the third week of March 1909. Selfridge estimated that his store accommodated over a million visitors during its opening week.[79] How many could afford or even wanted to buy anything cannot be known. Nonetheless, during this week the West End appeared to offer something for everyone.[80]

In 1910 a Mrs. Stafford of Museum Cottage, Oxford, received a postcard from "Nannie."[81] On the back of a picture of a London hotel, a short note read: "Shall leave London tomorrow at 1.45, arrive at Oxford at 3. Am just off to Selfridges to tea with Annie Coleman. Had a P.C. [postcard] from Aunty. Much Love, Nannie."[82] By 1910 to the store was already a household word for a network of women. This postcard advertises a whole matrix of urban, commercial activities, including a system of public transport, a hotel, and a department store. Along with expensive ad campaigns, postcard, letters, and gossip also contributed to the imaginary creation of the West End. "Nannie" both experienced and promoted women's pleasure in London's West End.[83]

Despite the fact that men often shopped, shopping was represented as a uniquely feminine and urban pleasure. In Edwardian England, middle-class and lower-class women were invited to enjoy themselves in the heart of the metropolis. This promotion of shopping as feminine pleasure also served to construct the very notion of the West End as a female arena. The pleasure of shopping in the West End remained limited to particular areas and circumscribed by political, economic, and social constraints on women's full participation in public life. However, new images of femininity which highlighted the centrality of women in urban life were integral to the development and success of mass consumer culture in early twentieth-century England. Definitions of public and private, male and female, were necessarily renegotiated as women literally and metaphorically besieged the West End, occupying a central position in the economic and cultural life of the city.

NOTES

An earlier version of this article was presented at the Rutgers Center for Historical Analysis in December 1991. I am grateful to all the participants for their suggestions and comments. I also owe special thanks to Victoria de Grazia, John Gillis, Bonnie Smith, Cora Kaplan, Judy Walkowitz, Leo Charney, Vanessa Schwartz, and Jordan Witt for all their criticism and support.

1. *Daily Express*, 15 March 1909; *Standard*, 16 March 1909. Many of the newspaper references in this article were collected in scrapbooks housed at the Selfridges Department Store Archive and do not have page numbers.

2. *Standard*, 18 March 1909.

3. *Daily Express*, 15 March 1909.

4. For a broader discussion of this development, see Erika Rappaport. "The West End and Women's Pleasure: Gender and Commercial Culture in London, 1860–1914" (Ph.D. diss., Rutgers University, 1993). See, for example, William Leach, "Transformations in a Culture of Consumption: Women and Department Stores, 1890–1925,"*Journal of American History* 71 (September 1984): 319–342: Elizabeth Wilson, *Adorned in Dreams: Fashion and Modernity* (London: Virago, 1985); idem, *The Sphinx in the City: Urban Life, the Control of Disorder and Women* (Berkeley, Los Angeles, London: University of California Press, 1991); Rachel Bowlby, *Just Looking: Consumer Culture in Dreiser, Gissing, and Zola* (New York and London: Methuen, 1985).

5. Erika Rappaport, " 'A Husband and His Wife's Dresses': Consumer Credit and the Debtor Family in England, 1864–1914," in *The Sex of Things: Gender and Consumption in Historical Perspective*, ed. Victoria de Grazia and Ellen Furlough (Berkeley, Los Angeles, London: University of California Press, 1996).

6. This is most pronounced in business histories, such as Gordon Honeycombe, *Selfridges: Seventy-Five Years: The Story of the Stone* (London: Park Lane Press, 1984); Reginald Pound, *Selfridge: A Biography* (London: Heinemann, 1960); Alfred H. Williams, *No Name on the Door: A Memoir of Gordon Selfridge* (London: W. H. Allen. 1956); Richard S. Lambert, *The Universal Provider: A Study of William Whiteley and the Rise of the London Department Store* (London: George G. Harrap, 1938); Michael Moss and Alison Turton, *A Legend of Retailing: The House of Fraser* (London: Weidenfeld and Nicholson, 1989).

7. Lloyd Wendt and Herman Kogan, *Give the Lady What She Wants! The Story of Marshall Field and Company* (Chicago: Rand McNally, 1952), pp. 201–215. For the most detailed analysis of the role of the department store as an American cultural institution, see William Leach, *Land of Desire: Merchants, Power, and the Rise of a New American Culture* (New York: Pantheon Books, 1993); Susan Porter Benson, *Counter Cultures: Saleswomen, Managers, and Customers in American Department Stores* (Urbana and New York: University of Illinois Press, 1986); Elaine S. Abelson, *When Ladies Go A-Thieving: Middle-Class Shoplifters and the Victorian Department Store* (Oxford and New York: Oxford University Press, 1989). For a broader discussion of the cultural history of promotion in America, see Neil Harris, *Cultural Excursions: Marketing Appetites and Cultural Tastes in Modern America* (Chicago and London: University of Chicago Press, 1990); Susan Strasser, *Satisfaction Guaranteed: The Making of the American Mass Market* (New York: Pantheon, 1989); Simon J. Bronner, ed., *Consuming Visions: Accumulation and Display of Goods in America, 1880–1920* (New York: W. W. Norton, 1989).

8. Robert Hendrickson, *The Grand Emporiums: The Illustrated History of America's Great Department Stores* (New York: Stein and Day, 1979), pp. 86–87.

9. Pound, *op. cit.*, p. 32.

10. Jean Christophe Agnew, "Times Square: Secularization and Sacralization," in *Inventing Times Square: Commerce and Culture at the Crossroads of the World*, ed. William Taylor (New York: Russell Sage Foundation, 1991), p. 2.

11. James B. Jefferys, *Retail Trading in Great Britain, 1850–1950* (Cambridge: Cambridge University Press, 1954), p. 326. H. Pasdermadjian, *The Department Store: Its Origins, Evolution, and Economics* (London: Newman Books, 1954); David Chaney, "The Department Store as a Cultural Form," *Theory, Culture, and Society* 1 (1983): 22–31; Michael

Winstanley, *The Shopkeeper's World, 1830–1914* (Manchester: Manchester University Press, 1983). For a more general history of English retailing, see Alison Adburgham, *Shops and Shopping, 1800–1914: Where and in What Manner the Well-Dressed Englishwoman Bought her Clothes*, 2d ed. (London: Barrie and Jenkins, 1989); Dorothy Davis, *Fairs, Shops, and Supermarkets: A History of English Shopping* (Toronto: University of Toronto Press, 1966); Molly Harrison, *People and Shopping: A Social Background* (London: Ernest Benn, 1975); David Alexander, *Retailing in England During the Industrial Revolution* (London: The Athlone Press, 1970).

12. *Olivia's Shopping and How She Does It: A Prejudiced Guide to the London Shops* (London: Gay and Bird, 1906), p. 9.

13. Hermione Hobhouse, *A History of Regent Street* (London: Macdonald and Jane's and Queen Ann Press, 1975).

14. Frances Wey, *A Frenchman Sees the English in the 'Fifties*, trans. Valerie Pirie (1856; reprint, London: Sidgewick & Jackson, 1935), p. 72.

15. F. J. Fisher, "The Development of London as a Centre of Conspicuous Consumption in the Sixteenth and Seventeenth Centuries," in *Essays in Economic History*, vol. 2, ed. E. M. Carus-Wilson (London: Edward Arnold, 1962), pp. 197–207; Peter Earle, *The Making of the English Middle Class: Business, Society and Family Life in London, 1660–1730* (Berkeley, Los Angeles, London: University of California Press, 1989); Gareth Shaw, "The Role of Retailing in the Urban Economy," in *The Structure of Nineteenth-Century Cities*, ed. James H. Jonnson and Colin G. Pooley (London: Croom Helm and St. Martin's Press, 1982), pp. 171–194; P. J. Atkins, "The Spatial Configuration of Class Solidarity in London's West End, 1792–1939," *Urban History Yearbook* (1990): 36–65.

16. Bowlby, *op. cit.*, p. 8. For an analysis of the culture of the French department store, see Michael Miller, *The Bon Marché: Bourgeois Culture and the Department Store, 1869–1920* (Princeton: Princeton University Press, 1981); Rosalind Williams, *Dream Worlds: Mass Consumption in Late Nineteenth-Century France* (Berkeley, Los Angeles, London: University of California Press, 1982).

17. Rappaport, "West End and Women's Pleasure," pp. 287–292.

18. Neil McKendrick, John Brewer, and J. H. Plumb, eds., *The Birth of a Consumer Society: The Commercialization of Eighteenth-Century England* (Bloomington: Indiana University Press, 1982); Colin Campbell, *The Romantic Ethic and the Spirit of Modern Consumerism* (Oxford: Basil Blackwell, 1987); Hoh-Cheung and Lorna Mui, *Shops and Shopkeeping in Eighteenth-Century England* (Kingston and Montreal: McGill–Queen's University Press and Routledge, 1989); Lorna Weatherill, *Consumer Behavior and Material Culture in Britain, 1660–1760* (London and New York: Routledge, 1988). See also the recent collection of essays *Consumption and the World of Goods*, ed. John Brewer and Roy Porter (London and New York: Routledge, 1993).

19. Quoted in Alfred H. Williams, *op. cit.*, p. 80. This was a particularly strong theme in business journals at the time. See, for example, *The Magazine of Commerce* 4 (February 1904): 120.

20. Pound, *op. cit.*, p. 29.

21. Jeanne Lawrence, "Steel Frame Architecture Versus the London Building Regulations: Selfridges, The Ritz, and American Technology," *Construction History* 6 (1990): 23–46.

22. Honeycombe, *op. cit.*, p. 9.

23. The store's name is now Selfridges, without an apostrophe. However, at the time it opened, the name included the apostrophe.

24. *Daily Express*, 16 March 1909. For criticism, see *The Builder*, 20 March 1909.

25. *Black and White*, 20 March 1909.

26. *Daily Chronicle*, 15 March 1909.

27. *Daily Chronicle*, 16 March 1909.

28. *Christian World*, 18 March 1909.

29. *Church Daily Newspaper*, 19 March 1909.

30. *Daily Telegraph*, 11 April 1910.

31. *Daily Chronicle*, 17 March 1909.

32. Mark Girouard, *The Return to Camelot: Chivalry and the English Gentleman* (New Haven and London: Yale University Press, 1981).

33. Foreshadowing the techniques described as capitalist realism in Michael Schudson, *Advertising, the Uneasy Persuasion: Its Dubious Impact on American Society* (New York: Basic Books, 1984), pp. 214–215.

34. *Daily News, Telegraph*, and *Westminster Gazette*, 19 March 1909.

35. Indeed, all of Selfridge's advertising assumes that any consumer has what Lawrence Birken has termed the "polymorphous potential to desire everything" (Lawrence Birken, *Consuming Desire:Sexual Science and the Emergence of a Culture of Abundance, 1871–1914* [Ithaca and London: Cornell University Press, 1988], p. 50).

36. *Daily Chronicle*, 20 March 1909.

37. Judith R. Walkowitz, *City of Dreadful Delight: Narratives of Sexual Danger in Late-Victorian London* (Chicago: University of Chicago Press, 1992); Wilson, *op. cit.*, pp. 3–46; Tracy C. Davis, *Actresses as Working Women: Their Social Identity in Victorian Culture* (London and New York: Routledge, 1991), pp. 137–150.

38. Rappaport, "West End and Women's Pleasure," pp. 197–210.

39. Peter Bailey, "Parasexuality and Glamour: The Victorian Barmaid as Cultural Prototype," *Gender and History* 2 (summer 1990): 148–172.

40. For parallel examples, see Lauren Rabinovitz, "Temptations of Pleasure: Nickelodeons, Amusement Parks, and the Sights of Female Sexuality," *Camera Obscura* 23 (May 1990): 72–89; Tony Bennett, "A Thousand and One Troubles: Blackpool Pleasure Beach," in *Formations and Pleasure*, ed. Frederic Jameson (London: Routledge and Kegan Paul, 1983), pp. 138–155.

41. On the interplay between the market and visual entertainment in the early modern period, see Jean-Christophe Agnew, *Worlds Apart: The Market and the Theater in Anglo-American Thought, 1550–1750* (Cambridge: Cambridge University Press, 1986).

42. *Hardware Trade Journal*, 3 March 1913.

43. *Evening Standard*, 22 January 1912.

44. Several cultural critics have suggested that, as the object of the flâneur's gaze, women cannot occupy the same role. See Janet Wolff, "The Invisible Flâneuse: Women and the Literature of Modernity," *Theory, Culture, and Society* 2, no. 3 (1985): 37–46; Griselda Pollock, *Vision and Difference: Femininity, Feminism and Histories of Art* (London and New York: Routledge, 1988), pp. 50–90; Andreas Huyssen, "Mass Culture as Woman, Modernism's Other," in *Studies in Entertainment: Critical Approaches to Mass Culture*, ed. Tania Modleski (Bloomington: Indiana University Press), pp. 188–205; Susan Buck-Morss, "The Flâneur, The Sandwichman, and the Whore: The Politics of Loitering," *New German Critique* 39 (fall 1986): 99–140.

45. See, for example, Charlotte Brontë, *Villette* (1853; reprint, London: Penguin Books, 1979), p. 109; Rappaport, "West End and Women's Pleasure," pp. 211–274; Walkowitz, *op. cit.*, pp. 46–48; Elizabeth Wilson, "The Invisible Flâneur," *New Left Review* 191 (January–February 1992): 90–110.

46. *Evening Standard*, 11 December 1915.

47. Ibid., May 1912 (specific date not available).

48. See Thomas Richards, *The Commodity Culture of Victorian England: Advertising and Spectacle, 1851–1914* (Stanford: Stanford University Press, 1990), pp. 73–118.

49. *Standard*, 20 March 1909.

50. *Evening Standard* and *Pall Mall Gazette*, 13 May 1912.

51. Honeycombe, *op. cit.*, p. 39.

52. *Daily Telegraph*, 27 July 1909.

53. Robert Thorne, "Places of Refreshment in the Nineteenth-Century City," in *Buildings and Society: Essays on the Social Development of the Built Environment*, ed. Anthony D. King (London: Routledge and Kegan Paul, 1980), pp. 228–253.

54. *Evening Standard*, 23 March 1911. (Although readers thought Callisthenes was a composite of many English authors, it was a pseudonym for Selfridge and the employees whose copy he revised.)

55. Alfred H. Williams, *op. cit.*, p. 55.

56. *Daily Chronicle*, 22 March 1909.

57. *Church Daily Newspaper*, 19 March 1909.

58. *Morning Leader*, 17 March 1909.

59. *Daily News*, 22 March 1909.

60. *British Journal of Nursing*, 20 March 1909.

61. *Evening Standard*, 11 March 1909.

62. *Daily Mail*, 12 March 1909.

63. Ibid.

64. On the relation between looking and shopping, see Bowlby, *op. cit.*, pp. 32–34.

65. Leach, *Land of Desire*, pp. 39–70.

66. *Evening Standard*, 11 November 1915.

67. *Morning Post*, 30 October 1915.

68. *Pall Mall Gazette*, 6 November 1916.

69. *Evening Standard* and *Pall Mall Gazette*, 20 June 1912.

70. *Standard*, 10 April 1911.

71. *Daily Mail*, 15 March 1909.

72. Susan Porter Benson has argued that "women shared both knowledge and the experience of consumption in their kin and friendship networks" (Benson, *op. cit.*, p. 5). Businessmen recognized and used this culture in a variety of different ways.

73. Alfred H. Williams, *op. cit.*, p. 96.

74. *Evening Standard*, 21 April 1911.

75. Ibid., 16 July 1912.

76. Ibid., 23 November 1915.

77. *Daily Express*, 16 March 1909.

78. *Daily Graphic*, 15 March 1909.

79. *Daily Chronicle*, 22 March 1909.

80. *Daily Express*, 15 March 1909.

81. It is unclear whether "Nannie" was the former nanny of Mrs. Stafford, given how she signs the postcard.

82. Noble Collection, Box C23.3, 1910, Print Room, Guildhall Library, London.

83. However, this should not be read as a story of manipulation or seduction of passive female consumers by big business. As the sociologist Colin Campbell has noted, "Advertisements (and other product-promoting material) only constitute one part of the total set of cultural influences at work upon consumers" (Campbell, *op. cit.*, p. 47).

NIGHT NO. 10
in FAIRY-LAND

**Our Tireless Picket Tracks the Restless Androgyne to
CHILDS on Fifth Avenue and to LOUIS' on
49th Street.**

Fig. 3.1. Gay men and lesbians made numerous cafeterias and restaurants their meeting places. This sketch of a supposed gay drinking party appeared in *Broadway Brevities* in 1924. (*Collection of Leonard Finger.*)

Chapter Three

Lots of Friends at the YMCA
Rooming Houses, Cafeterias, and Other Gay Social Centers

George Chauncey

When Willy W. arrived in New York City in the 1940s, he did what many newcomers did: he took a room at the Sixty-third Street YMCA. As was true for many other young men, the friends he made at the Y remained important to him for years and helped him find his way through the city. Most of those friends were gay, and the gay world was a significant part of what they showed him. He soon moved on, though, to the St. George Hotel in Brooklyn, which offered more substantial accommodations. The St. George, it seemed to him, was "almost entirely gay," and the friends he met there introduced him to yet other parts of the gay world. After living briefly in a rooming house on Fiftieth Street near Second Avenue, he finally took a small apartment of his own, a railroad flat on East Forty-ninth Street near First Avenue, where he stayed for years. He moved there at the invitation of a friend he had met at Red's, a popular bar on Third Avenue at Fiftieth Street that had attracted gay men since its days as a speakeasy in the 1920s. The friend had an apartment in the building and wanted Willy to take the apartment next to his. An elderly couple had occupied it for years, and, since the walls were rather thin, the friend had never stopped worrying that they heard him late at night with gay friends and had grown suspicious of the company he kept. When they moved out he wanted to make sure that someone more understanding would take their place. Willy was happy to do so, and as other apartments opened up in the building he invited other friends to move in. Several friends did, and some of the newcomers encouraged their own friends to join them. The building's narrow railroad flats, if not luxurious, were adequate and cheap; the location, near the gay bar circuit on Third Avenue in the East Fifties, was convenient; and, most important, the other inhabitants were friendly and supportive. Within a few years, Willy remembered, "we took over." Gay men occupied fourteen of the sixteen apartments in the building.* Willy not only lived in a gay house, but in a growing gay neighborhood enclave, whose streets

---

*This was not the only predominantly gay apartment building Willy remembered. In the 1950s a major apartment house at Number 405 in a street in the East Fifties was so heavily gay that gay men nicknamed it the "Four out of Five."[1]

provided him with regular contact with other gay men. Although Willy's success in creating an almost completely gay apartment building was unusual, his determination to find housing that maximized his autonomy and his access to the gay world was not. In his movement from one dwelling to the next, Willy traced a path followed by many gay men in the first half of the century as they built a gay world in the city's hotels, rooming houses, and apartment buildings, and in its cafeterias, restaurants, and speakeasies. Gay men took full advantage of the city's resources to create zones of gay camaraderie and security.

Bachelor Housing

Although living with one's family, even in a crowded tenement, did not prevent a man from participating in the gay world that was taking shape in the city's streets, many gay men, like Willy, sought to secure housing that would maximize their freedom from supervision. For many, this meant joining the large number of unmarried workers living in the furnished-room houses (also called lodging or rooming houses) clustered in certain neighborhoods of the city. No census data exist that could firmly establish the residential patterns of gay men, but two studies of gay men incarcerated in the New York City Jail, conducted in 1938 and 1940, are suggestive. Sixty-one percent of the men investigated in 1940 lived in rooming houses, three-quarters of them alone and another quarter with a lover or other roommates; only a third lived in tenement houses with their own families or boarded with others.[2] Court records from the first three decades of the century provide relatively few accounts of men apprehended for sexual encounters in rooming houses (itself indirect evidence of the relative security of such encounters), but they do abound in anecdotal evidence of men who lived together in rooming houses or took other men to their rooms, and whose relationships or rendezvous came to the attention of the police only because of a mishap.*

Usually situated in rowhouses previously occupied by single families, rooming houses provided tenants with a small room, a bed, minimal furniture, and no kitchen facilities; residents were expected to take their meals elsewhere. Such housing had qualities that made it particularly useful to gay men as well as to transient workers of various sorts. The rooms were cheap, they were minimally supervised, and the fact that they were usually furnished and were rented by the week made them easy to leave if a lodger got a job elsewhere—or needed to disappear because of legal troubles.[4] Rooming houses also offered tenants a remarkable amount of privacy. Not only could they easily move out if trouble developed, the tenants at most houses compensated for the lack of physical privacy by maintaining a degree of respectful social distance. (Inclined to dislike anything they saw in the rooming houses, housing reformers, somewhat contradictorily, were as distressed by the lack

---

*Such information most frequently came to the attention of the police when a man who had been brought home assaulted or tried to blackmail his host, when parents discovered that a man had invited their son home, when the police followed men to a furnished room from some other, more public locale, or when one of the tenants sharing a room with his lover was arrested on another charge.[3]

of interest roomers took in one another's affairs as by the lack of privacy the houses afforded.) One study conducted in Boston in 1906 reported that in addition to taking their meals outside their cramped quarters, most roomers also developed their primary social ties elsewhere, at cheap neighborhood restaurants, at their workplaces, and in saloons.[5] Moreover, the absence of a parlor (which usually had been converted into a bedroom) in most rooming houses, the respect many land-ladies had for their tenants' privacy, and, perhaps most important, the competition among rooming houses for lodgers led many landladies to tolerate men and women visiting each other's rooms and bringing in guests of the other sex. Numerous landladies in the 1920s, when queried by male investigators posing as potential tenants, said straightforwardly that they could have women in their rooms: "Why certainly, this is your home" was the reassuring reply of one.[6]

Some landladies doubtless tolerated known homosexual lodgers for the same economic reasons they tolerated lodgers who engaged in heterosexual affairs, and others simply did not care about their tenants' homosexual affairs. But most ex-pected their tenants at least to maintain a decorous fiction about their social lives. The boundaries of acceptable behavior were, as a result, often unclear, and in many houses men felt constrained to try to conceal the gay aspects of their lives. The story of one black gay man who lived in the basement of a rooming house on West Fiftieth Street, between Fifth and Sixth Avenues, in 1919 suggests the latitude— and limitations—of rooming-house life. The tenant felt free to invite men whom he met on the street into his room. One summer evening, for instance, he invited an undercover investigator he had met while sitting on the basement stairs. But, as he later explained to his guest, while three "young fellows" had been visiting him in his room on a regular basis, he had finally decided to stop seeing the youths because they made too much noise, and he did not want the landlady "to get wise." Not only might he lose his room, he feared, but also his job as the house's chamber-maid.[7] The consequences of discovery could be even more severe. In 1900 a suspi-cious boardinghouse keeper on East Thirteenth Street barged into the room taken only a few days earlier by two waiters, a twenty-year-old German and seventeen-year-old American. She caught them having sex, had them arrested, and eventually had the German sent to prison for a year.[8]

In general, though, the same lack of supervision in the rooming houses that so concerned moral reformers made the houses particularly attractive to gay men, who were able to use their landladies' and fellow tenants' presumption that they were straight in order to disguise their liaisons with men. A male lodger attracted less attention when a man, rather than a woman, visited his room, and a male couple could usually take a room together without generating suspicion.[9] Moreover, the privacy and flexibility such accommodations provided often helped men develop gay social networks. Young men new to New York or the gay life often met other gay men in their rooming houses, and these men sometimes served as their guides as they explored gay society. The ease with which men could move from one rooming house to another also allowed them to pursue and strengthen new social ties by moving in with new friends (or lovers) or moving closer to restaurants or bars where their friends gathered.[10]

Moral reformers expressed concern that the casual intermingling of strangers in furnished-room houses could "assume a dangerous aspect," especially when it introduced young men and women to people of ill repute. In response to this threat, some sought to offer more secure environments to young migrants to the city.[11] Various groups established special hotels at the turn of the century in order to provide men with moral alternatives to the city's flophouses, transient hotels, and rooming houses. Ironically, though, such hotels often became major centers for the gay world and served to introduce men to gay life. In an all-male living situation, in which numerous men already shared rooms, it was virtually impossible for management to detect gay couples. The Seamen's Church Institute, for instance, had been established as a residential and social facility by a consortium of churches in order to protect seamen from the moral dangers the churchmen believed threatened them in the lodging houses of the waterfront areas. But gay seamen and other gay men interested in seamen could usually be found in the Institute's lobby. Men involved in relationships also had no difficulty taking rooms together: one seaman told an investigator in 1931 that he had lived with a youth at the Institute "for quite some time," and he had apparently encountered no censure there.[12] Similarly, the two massive Mills Houses, built by the philanthropist Darius O. Mills, were intended to offer unmarried workingmen moral accommodation in thousands of small but sanitary rooms. (The first one was built in 1896 directly across Bleecker Street from the building that had housed the notorious fairy resort, the Slide, just a few years earlier, as if to symbolize the reestablishment of moral order on the block; the second was built on Rivington Street in 1897.) Its attractiveness as a residence for working-class gay men is suggested by the frequency with which its residents appeared in the magistrate's courts. In March 1920, for instance, at least three residents of the two Mills Houses were arrested on homosexual charges (not on the premises): a forty-three-year-old Irish laborer, a forty-two-year-old Italian barber, and a thirty-eight-year-old French cook.[13]

The residential hotels built by the Young Men's Christian Association provide the most striking example of housing designed to reform men's behavior that gay men managed to appropriate for their own purposes. The YMCA movement had begun in the 1840s and 1850s with the intention of supplying young, unmarried migrants to the city with an urban counterpart to the rural family they had left behind. Its founders had expressed special concern about the moral dangers facing such men in the isolation of rooming-house life. The Y organized libraries, reading groups, and gymnasiums for such men, and in some cities established residential facilities, despite some organizers' fear that they might become as depraved and degrading as the lodging houses.[14] The New York YMCA began building dormitories in 1896, and by the 1920s the seven YMCA residential hotels in New York housed more than a thousand young men, whose profiles resembled those of most rooming-house residents: primarily in their twenties and thirties, nearly half of them were clerks, office workers, and salesmen, while smaller numbers were "professional men," artisans, mechanics, skilled workers, and, especially in the Harlem branch, hotel, restaurant, and domestic-service employees.[15]

The fears of the early YMCA organizers were realized. By World War I, the

YMCAs in New York and elsewhere had developed a reputation among gay men as centers of sex and social life. Sailors at Newport, Rhode Island, reported that "everyone" knew the Y was "the headquarters" for gay men, and the sailor's line in Irving Berlin's World War I show, *Yip, Yip, Yaphank*, about having lots of friends at the YMCA is said to have drawn a knowing laugh.[16] The reputation only increased in the Depression with the construction, in 1930, of two huge new YMCA hotels, which soon became famous within the gay world as gay residential centers. The enormous Sloane House, on West Thirty-fourth Street at Ninth Avenue, offered short-term accommodations to "transient young men" in almost 1,500 rooms, and the West Side Y, on Sixty-third Street at Central Park West, offered longer-term residential facilities as well. A man interviewed in the mid-1930s recalled of his stay at Sloane House:

> One night when I was coming in at 11:30 P.M. a stranger asked me to go to his room. They just live in one another's rooms although it's strictly forbidden. . . . This Y.M.C.A. is for transients but one further uptown [the West Side Y] is a more elegant brothel, for those who like to live in their ivory towers with Greek gods. If you go to a shower there is always someone waiting to have an affair. It doesn't take long.[17]

Such observations became a part of gay folklore in the 1930s, 1940s, and 1950s, when the extent of sexual activity at the Ys—particularly the "never ending sex" in the showers—became legendary within the gay world. A man living in New Jersey remembered that he stayed at Sloane House "many times, every chance I got . . . [because] it was very gay"; another man called it a "gay colony." Indeed, the Y had such a reputation for sexual adventure that some New Yorkers took rooms at Sloane House for the weekend, giving fake out-of-town addresses. "It was just a free for all," one man who did so several times recalled, "more fun than the baths."[18]

While the sexual ambience of the Ys became a part of gay folklore, the role of the Ys as gay social centers was also celebrated. Many gay New Yorkers rented rooms in the hotels, used the gym and swimming pool (where men swam naked), took their meals there, or gathered there to meet their friends. Just as important—and more ironic, given reformers' intentions—was the crucial role the hotels often played in introducing young men to the gay world. It was at the Y that many newcomers to the city made their first contacts with other gay men. Grant McGree arrived in the city in 1941, not knowing anyone, intimidated by the size of the city, and full of questions about his sexuality. But on his first night at the Y as he gazed glumly from his room into the windows of other men's rooms he suddenly realized that many of the men he saw sharing rooms were couples; within a week he had met many of them and begun to build a network of gay friends. As gay men used to put it, the letters Y-M-C-A stood for "Why I'm So Gay."[19]

Donald Vining's diary of his move to New York in search of work in the fall of 1942 provides a particularly detailed account of how the Y and similar residential hotels could serve to introduce men to the gay world. Upon arriving in New York, Vining took a room at Sloane House, and within a week was startled to have someone approach him in the shower room. Nothing happened that time, but, intrigued and emboldened, he initiated contact with someone else in the shower room a few days later. Within a week he had moved to the Men's Residence Club (formerly a YMCA hotel), on West Fifty-sixth Street, which he later wryly described as "a combination old men's home and whorehouse," where he continued to meet men. He soon took a job back at Sloane House, where he worked with several other gay men at the front desk. Within weeks of his arrival in the city, his contacts at the Y and the Club had supplied him with a large circle of friends, with whom he took his meals, went to the theater, and explored the gay life of the city. Although he eschewed the dominant institutions of the gay world, particularly bars and private parties, he created an extensive gay social circle based on the contacts he made at work and at home.[20]

The response of the YMCA's managers to such activity was ambiguous. At some residences they took steps to restrict contact between certain groups of men (and thus, in effect, to restrict the possibilities for liaisons), such as assigning servicemen to certain floors, segregating the floors by age or by other criteria, and prohibiting residents from taking outsiders to their rooms. It is not clear why the management developed such regulations; many gay men believed they had been designed precisely in order to hamper their socializing, but this, of course, reveals more about the extent to which they viewed the Y as a gay arena than it does about the actual concerns of management. The upper echelon of the Y's management occasionally indicated its concern about the situation by ordering crackdowns on homosexual activity. In general, however, the fate of gay residents depended on the personal predilections of the lower-level security staff and desk clerks. Some of them were gay themselves; as one man recalled, "The job was considered a plum—[the] fox guarding the hen house!"[21] Many of them, whatever their own inclinations, appear to have had little interest in spending their time ferreting out homosexual activity or in punishing the occasional homosexual liaisons of which they became aware, so long as the participants observed certain rules of decorum.

While both the YMCA and rooming houses offered a modicum of privacy to men of moderate means, the development of apartment hotels and houses in the last quarter of the nineteenth century made it possible for men with greater financial resources to acquire accommodations with greater privacy and respectability. Apartment hotels, originally introduced in the 1870s and built primarily in the late 1890s and 1900s, created new possibilities for independent living among unmarried men. A number of the earliest apartment hotels, such as the Bachelor Apartments, built at 15 East Forty-eighth Street in 1900, and the Hermitage Hotel, built in 1907 on Seventh Avenue just south of Forty-second Street, were specifically designed for well-off bachelors: they offered small but comfortable living quarters (without cooking facilities), a public restaurant, and communal lounging and writing rooms designed to resemble those of a gentlemen's club.

Although the superior social status of apartment *hotels* over rooming houses quickly allowed them to become respectable accommodations for middle-class bachelors, apartment *houses*, whose kitchen facilities made them more suitable for families, were initially eschewed by middle-class families. For most of the nineteenth century, a private rowhouse had been the mark of a successful family in a city whose immigrant masses were herded together in tenements, and most bourgeois families initially regarded the apartment house as little more than a better sort of tenement. The respectability and popularity of apartments grew in the last decade of the century, however, as the skyrocketing cost of land in desirable neighborhoods made individual home ownership unobtainable for all but the wealthy and as apartments became known for their size, convenience, and elegance. Middle-class New Yorkers began to accept them as the only way to live in desirable neighborhoods, and at the end of the depression of the mid-1890s, apartment construction commenced in earnest. By the 1920s, New York was well on its way to becoming a city of apartment dwellers.[22]

The increasing number and respectability of apartment houses and hotels helped make it possible for a middle-class gay male world to develop. At a minimum, they offered gay men greater privacy, space, and prestige than rooming houses. An employee-doorman, rather than an owner-landlady, observed their comings and goings, and residents generally sought to reproduce the privacy of an individual home by remaining aloof from the activities of their neighbors.* Such privacy allowed men to bring gay friends home and allowed couples to live together. More important, the ample space of an apartment allowed gay men to entertain friends on a large scale, a resource of inestimable value at a time when police harassment restricted their ability to gather in more public spaces.[24] Finally, the apartment offered middle-class gay men the unquestioned aura of respectability that eluded residents of rooming houses and flophouses. The "bachelor flat" became an established form of accommodation, and this made it easier for men whose backgrounds and occupations would not have allowed them to live at the Y to live outside the family system.

As apartment living became more financially accessible and commonplace in New York in the early decades of the century, it became the accommodation of choice for gay men as for other New Yorkers. In the 1920s and 1930s, growing numbers of tenements and railroad flats, which previously had been occupied by entire families (or even several families), were turned into apartments occupied by a single resident or a couple. A middle-class gay residential enclave developed on the Upper East Side in the 1930s, 1940s, and 1950s. Many gay men moved into the railroad flats in the East Fifties and Sixties east of the Third Avenue elevated train, which allowed them to live close to the elegance of Park Avenue (as well as the gay bars of Third Avenue) at a fraction of the cost. At the same time, a less wealthy gay enclave developed in the Forties west of Eighth Avenue, as large groups of poorer gay men, often youths, crowded into flats in the old tenements of Hell's Kitchen.

---

*One account of urban life in 1932 pointed to the still notable anonymity of life in the big midtown apartment buildings, "where your neighbor is just a number on the door." It illustrated its point with a description of an expensive building on West Fifty-sixth Street, whose two hundred apartments included not only the homes of "quiet families [who] know little or nothing about the activities of their neighbors," but also, it claimed, three flats on the ninth floor where lesbians lived, and another on the tenth occupied by a gay man.[23]

Cafeteria Society

Like most young, single residents of rooming houses, gay men took most of their meals at the cheap restaurants, cafeterias, and lunch counters that dotted the city's commercial and furnished-room districts. But such facilities took on special significance for many gay men. Most such men needed to manage multiple public identities and to present themselves as straight—or, at least, not gay—at work, at home, and in other consequential social settings. Numerous restaurants and cafeterias became important to them because they could "let their hair down" there and meet other gay people who accepted them as gay, even if they needed to guard against drawing the potentially hostile attention of other diners. Gay men turned many restaurants into places where they could gather with gay friends, gossip, ridicule the dominant culture that ridiculed them, and construct an alternative culture. They turned them into places where it did not seem queer to discuss opera or the latest Broadway show, to talk about an art show or a favorite torch singer, to laugh collectively about the morning paper's picture of the sailor with his arms wrapped around the cannon he was cleaning.[25] Restaurants became places, in short, where men branded as outsiders turned themselves into insiders by creating and sharing a gay reading of the world, a distinctive ironic, camp perspective that affirmed them and challenged the normativity of the world that branded them abnormal.

Particular restaurants served as the locus of particular gay social networks; overlapping groups of friends would meet regularly for dinner and camaraderie. The role of restaurants as social centers meant they often functioned as a crucial point of entry into the gay world for men just beginning to identify themselves as gay; for men already deeply involved in the gay world, they were a vital source of information about the gay scene, police activity, cultural events, and the like. The determination of gay men to claim space for themselves in the city's eating places—which they did boldly enough at some cafeterias to give them citywide reputations as "fairy hangouts," and surreptitiously enough at other places that they remained known only to other gay men—occasionally provoked a sharp reaction from social-purity forces. But gay men developed elaborate stratagems to protect such places, precisely because they played such an important role in their lives.

The number of cheap dining facilities increased rapidly in the late nineteenth and early twentieth centuries, in response to the growing number of unmarried clerks and shop workers living in the city. As more and more boardinghouses, whose landladies had provided meals for roomers, were converted into rooming houses, which served no meals and had no kitchen facilities, residents were forced to take meals elsewhere. The number of restaurants surged even further in the 1920s as Prohibition devastated their major sources of competition, closing both the saloons that had offered workingmen a free lunch and the businessmen's clubs that had offered more elegant fare, and making numerous suitable commercial spaces available for conversion into restaurants.[26]

The growth of such facilities is exemplified by the history of two of New York's most famous cafeteria chains, Childs and Horn & Hardart, both of which came to play major roles in the gay world. William and Samuel Childs opened the first of their many restaurants in 1889. Enormous, relatively inexpensive, and sparkling clean, they quickly became popular spots for white-collar workers to take their lunches, dinners, and after-theater suppers, and by 1898 there were nine Childs restaurants serving fifteen thousand to twenty thousand people a day. Childs sought to broaden its appeal further that year by introducing cafeteria-style eating to New York in a restaurant situated to pick up the lunch-hour business of Wall Street clerks. Following its success, the chain opened additional cafeterias throughout the city. By 1939, there were forty-four Childs cafeterias and restaurants in Manhattan, and several other chains, such as Bickford's, Schrafft's, Longchamps, and Caruso, had joined them in appealing to the ever-growing number of unmarried office workers and young families in which the wife continued to work before having children.[27] Following Child's lead, Horn & Hardart opened its first Automat in New York in 1903. Quickly growing in number, the Automats reached the height of their popularity during the Depression, when more than forty of them could be found in Manhattan alone.[28]

The cafeterias and Automats were not just cheap places to take meals. Many people also used them as meeting places, where they gathered on an almost nightly basis. In the 1930s they were known as the salons of the poorer bohemians of the Village, who wryly called their social world "Cafeteria Society Downtown," in contrast to the wealthier "Café Society Uptown."[29] The Automats appealed primarily to working people and the unemployed, but a cafeteria's clientele could vary enormously. It "all depends on where the restaurant is located," observed one guide in 1925, and, it might have added, on the time of day. Most of the Childs cafeterias were "the feeding ground of obscure and lowly folk" during the day, as the guide put it, but some also attracted a more affluent trade late at night, after the theater and supper clubs had closed.[30] Similarly, restaurants that served lunch to businessmen and dinner to families or theater-goers could cater to a less respectable clientele later at night. Investigators repeatedly warned during World War I and the postwar years that prostitutes and their customers were gathering at two and three in the morning at the Childs restaurants near Union Square, Penn Station, Columbus Circle, and 125th Street.[31]

Some of these cafeterias, Automats, and lunchrooms catered to a gay clientele, while others were simply taken over by gay men, who were allowed to remain so long as they increased business without drawing the attention of the police. Many gay men also had jobs in the city's restaurants,* and some tested the limits of managerial tolerance in the boldness with which they welcomed gay customers. Parker Tyler described the scene in the fall of 1929 when he visited a Childs in Brooklyn with several friends: "Well my dear considering that I was in a huge fur

---

*Of the two hundred men arrested on homosexual charges by the police in cooperation with the Society for the Suppression of Vice in 1920–21, thirty-nine were restaurant employees, by far the largest single occupational category represented. Frederick Whitin, general secretary of the Committee of Fourteen, surmised in 1921 that this might be related to the apparent move by homosexuals, like prostitutes, to turn restaurants into their major "resorts" after the closing of the saloons.[32]

coat of Clairmont's [one of his women companions] and must have looked very gorgeous, it isn't a surprise but that waiter started right in camping just as though there were *no law*!! And everybody in our party started camping after the waiter asked me: 'What will you have, gorgeous?', and I replied bitterly: 'Nothing you've got, dearie,' which really did upset everyone. And you can imagine how things went from bad to worse. So I concluded Brooklyn is wide open and N.Y. should be notified of its existence."[33]

Automats were among the safest refuges available to poorer gay men. They became even more secure during the Depression, when their rock-bottom prices and lack of supervision gave them a reputation as a sanctuary for social outcasts and the unemployed. The Automat on Forty-second Street across from Bryant Park became particularly well known as the site of raucous gatherings.[34]

While the Automats' clientele were particularly famous for their lack of inhibition, the atmosphere at even the large cafeterias in the very well established Childs chain could become astonishingly freewheeling, as Tyler's vignette suggests, particularly late at night, after the dinner hour, when managers tolerated a wide spectrum of customers and behavior in order to generate trade. Gay men quickly spread the word about which restaurants and cafeterias would let them gather without guarding their behavior. Several Childs cafeterias and restaurants located in heavily gay neighborhoods became known among gay men as meeting places; indeed, the campy antics of the more flamboyant among them became part of the draw for other customers. One gay man who lived in the city in the late 1920s recalled that the Childs restaurant in the Paramount Theater Building on Broadway at Forty-third Street was regularly "taken over" by "hundreds" of gay men after midnight. Even if his recollection exaggerates the situation, it suggests his sense of the extent to which gay men felt comfortable there; in any case, *Vanity Fair*'s 1931 guide to New York informed its readers that the Paramount Childs was particularly interesting because it "features a dash of lavender."[35]

The Paramount Childs was not the only restaurant in the chain to earn such a reputation. Two Childs located in the blocks of Fifth Avenue south of Central Park, which served as a major gay cruising area in the 1920s—one in the Falkenhayn apartment building on Fifth Avenue between Fifty-eighth and Fifty-ninth Streets and another on the Avenue near Forty-ninth Street—were also patronized by so many gay men that they became known in the gay world as meeting places.[36] But perhaps the most famous such rendezvous, christened "Mother Childs" by some, was the one on Fifty-ninth Street at Columbus Circle, close to Central Park cruising areas as well as to Broadway theaters. Numerous investigators in the early 1920s reported seeing "prostitutes, charity girls . . . cabaret performers [and] fairies" carrying on there, telling stories, camping, and moving from table to table to greet old friends and meet new ones.[37] A man who had moved to New York from a small town in North Dakota in 1922 recalled:

> After hours—you might say after the theater, [which brought] hordes of people together—Childs was a meeting place for gays and they would congregate and sit and have coffee and yak-yak and talk til three and four and five o'clock in the morning. . . . I was always there with friends, that was the social thing to do.[38]

The history of two cafeterias in the Village in the 1920s and 1930s, Stewart's and the Life Cafeteria, both located on Christopher Street at Sheridan Square, demonstrates even more clearly the extent to which gay men could be made part of the spectacle of an establishment, even as they turned it into a haven. Both cafeterias, like the turn-of-the-century Bowery resorts before them, seem to have premised their late-night operations on the assumption that by allowing lesbians and gay men to gather there they would attract sight-seers out to gawk at a late-night "fairy hangout." The *1939 WPA Guide to New York City* almost surely described the Life when it delicately explained that "a cafeteria [at Sheridan Square], curiously enough, is one of the few obviously Bohemian spots [left] in the Village, and evenings the more conventional occupy tables in one section of the room and watch the 'show' of the eccentrics on the other side."[39]

Many gay men and lesbians, in fact, especially younger people who felt they had less social position to lose, regularly tested the limits on their openness at restaurants, speakeasies, and other establishments, by dancing together, speaking loudly about their affairs, and camping for others. While at the Round Table in Greenwich Village one night in 1929, Parker Tyler was invited to join a group of lesbians and gay men who were clearly unwilling to brook any restrictions on their evening's fun: "Someone—Lesbian—rushed up and asked me to join their drinking party," Tyler wrote a gay friend, "and I did and someone who said he had just been brought out began making drunken love to me but he wasn't much and then someone—officially male—asked me to dance." The management had tolerated the gay flirtation at Tyler's table, but drew the line at same-sex dancing and promptly "ordered [them] off the floor." The woman who had invited him to join them dismissed the management's action by commenting curtly that "THEY DON'T UNDERSTAND OUR TYPE," as Tyler recalled in full capitals. Although Tyler sometimes declined invitations to dance for fear of such reprimands, he often tested the limits in precisely this way—and was almost as often told to stop dancing with men.[40]

Even Tyler, hardly reticent, was occasionally taken aback by how relentlessly some of his friends challenged hetero-normativity in their Village haunts—and by how insistently they demanded that he not present himself as anything other than gay. At a neighborhood speakeasy one night he found himself, somewhat to his surprise, beginning to neck with a woman he had just met. After a brief flirtation and "some drinks," he reported to a gay friend (in a reversal of the usual attempt to blame *homosexual* escapades on drink), "I found myself . . . kissing her madly." The fact that he was "kissing her madly" suggests the casual atmosphere of the place, though casual heterosexual interactions were usually treated more casually than homosexual. But his friends would have nothing of it, and turned his brief heterosexual flirtation into an occasion for asserting a gay presence in the speakeasy. "Who should come in about then," Tyler continued, "but Paula who exclaimed, 'What! Parker kissing a female!' " Tyler quieted his friend, but when he returned to the first woman and "started to kiss her again," a second friend, a gay man, "exclaimed in a booming voice: 'Parker! Why don't you tell this girl you're homosexual?' " Before Tyler could recover from his embarrassment, "who should positively BLOW in at that moment but a bitch named—(artist) who shouted at the top of his voice O HELLO MISS TYLER!" "And this was in a speakeasy," Tyler added immediately, as if even he found it astonishing that someone should be so overtly—and loudly—gay in such a space.[41] He had a similar reaction to the waiter at the Brooklyn Childs who "started right in camping just as though there were *no law*!!" For all his boldness, Tyler never forgot there *was* a law—informal as well as formal—against public expressions of gay culture, and it is doubtful that any other gay man did either. Nonetheless, many of them regularly tested the boundaries that law established.

Most managers, like the ones who stopped Tyler from dancing, never let matters get "out of hand." But when the informal injunction against gay visibility was successfully challenged by gay men and lesbians or gave way to public fascination with gay visibility, the formal agencies of the law—the police and social-purity organizations—sometimes stepped in to reestablish (the social) order. They sometimes did this with the connivance of skittish managers, who realized they had let things go "too far" by letting their gay clientele become too "obvious," as difficult as it might be to judge when that line had been crossed. In February 1927, for instance, after gay men had been congregating at the Forty-second Street Liggett's drugstore for some time, the management, perhaps sensing a temporary hardening of police attitudes or simply fearing for its reputation, suddenly called on the police to drive the men from its premises. The police raided the store and arrested enough men to fill two police vans.[42]

The state and social-purity groups intervened most commonly, though, against the wishes of managers who saw no harm and much profit in tolerating a gay presence. Some of those managers devised elaborate schemes to protect their businesses. The background to a raid on a Lower East Side cabaret in 1920 illustrates the strategies such establishments used to protect themselves and highlights the complex relationship between the social-purity societies, the police, the courts, and the entrepreneurs they sought to control, as well as the constraints affecting gay men who wished to socialize in public.

The Hotel Koenig, a small hotel and cabaret run by the German-born George Koenig on East Fourth Street near First Avenue, had developed a citywide reputation among gay men. Police records show that few of the men arrested there in a raid one night in 1920 were from the immediate neighborhood; most lived more than twenty blocks away, near Madison Square, in the midtown theater district, or in even more distant parts of Manhattan and Brooklyn, and two were visiting from Philadelphia. All were white and, like most of the city's bachelors, young: three-quarters were in their twenties, only a few were even in their thirties, and none was older. They seem to have taken care in choosing their housing and meeting places to ensure they could be openly gay, for about a quarter of them had come with roommates or live-in lovers. And they were quite open at Koenig's. One Committee of Fourteen investigator, who learned that fairies had begun to gather at the Koenig in the spring of 1920, reported that "most of the patrons paid more attention to the action of the fairies than to the cabaret performance." Koenig's tolerance of the men's flagrant campiness was consistent with his decision to permit prostitutes and other women to drink with the male patrons, "using vile language," according to the investigator, "and [not] behav[ing]." Koenig had clearly decided to cater to a rough crowd.[43]

While the Hotel Koenig was well known as a "fairy resort" to the cabaret's gay and straight patrons alike, court officials expressed surprise after the raid that such a place existed in the neighborhood at all, especially "without the knowledge of it being more general." As the Committee of Fourteen discovered in the course of its investigation, George Koenig had made arrangements to ensure that "knowledge of it" would be kept from the court, primarily by making his facilities freely available to a social club whose members included numerous patrolmen from the local precinct. On one occasion, for instance, the members, after taking in a burlesque show on West 125th Street, brought several female prostitutes and some of the "burlesque girls" down to the cabaret, where they drank and partied all night.

Such arrangements might have protected Koenig's indefinitely, had the Committee of Fourteen, an investigative group formed by moral reformers and city businessmen, not become involved during its postwar anti-gay campaign. The precautions Koenig had taken certainly made the Committee's job more difficult, requiring it to bypass the local precinct and persuade the chief inspector of the First Inspection District, a division of the police department independent of the precincts, to send four plainclothesmen to investigate the cabaret. Once it had prevailed upon the inspector to raid the place, the Committee needed to investigate the court schedule to ensure that the raid would be conducted on a night when a sympathetic judge would hear the case; "by all means we want to stay away from [certain judges]," the committee cautioned the inspector. On the last Saturday night in July 1920, when the judge they wanted to hear the case was sitting, the inspector's officers raided the cabaret and arrested thirty patrons, the manager, and the waitress. Koenig was charged with "keeping a disorderly house," a "resort for degenerates," and all of the arrested patrons were charged with degenerate disorderly conduct. Gay men appear to have been the only customers arrested.

No law specifically prohibited gay men from assembling in a public place at the time of the raid in 1920, but the police charged the men at Koenig's with "degenerate disorderly conduct." Indeed, the sentences the men received suggest how dangerous it could be to assert a gay presence at any public establishment. Twenty-three of the men were sentenced to ten days in the workhouse, and the remaining seven were fined fifty dollars. These sentences were unusually severe for men charged with disorderly conduct; sixteen men with similar backgrounds who appeared in court just before the Koenig group on the same charge, but with no implication of "degeneracy," were fined only one or two dollars apiece. Both the judge and the Committee nonetheless lamented that the penalties were relatively light for men charged with "degenerate" disorderly conduct. They considered them the harshest they dare impose, however, since their case was so weak, dependent on a sympathetic judge for successful prosecution. "As individual complaints had not been drawn and the defendants were all tried together," the judge confided to the Committee, he "was afraid the record would not stand on an appeal." No one had been charged with engaging in sexual acts or with any other particular incidents of disorderly conduct, in other words; as the judge well knew, he had convicted them simply for being members of a group of gay men congregating in a public place. Both the judge and the Committee settled on relatively light sentences because they feared that, with so many men involved, at least some would be provoked by a heavier sentence to make a successful appeal. None of the men did file an appeal, though, either because they realized they had gotten off *relatively* lightly—"only" ten days in the workhouse, compared to the sixty days often served by men convicted of degeneracy—or because they were simply too intimidated.

"Degenerate disorderly conduct," the offense for which the men at Koenig's were convicted, was the charge usually brought against gay men or lesbians found gathering on the streets or in public accommodations, or gay men trying to pick up other men. The use of the disorderly-conduct law against gay people was consistent with the intent of the law, which effectively criminalized a wide range of non-normative behaviors in public spaces, as defined by the dominant culture, be it loitering, gambling, failure to hire oneself out to an employer, failure to remain sober, or behaving in a public space in any other manner perceived as threatening the social order. The disorderly-conduct law was one of the omnibus legal measures used by the state to try to impose a certain conception of public order on the city's streets, and, in particular, to control the large numbers of immigrants from Ireland and southern and eastern Europe, as well as African-American migrants from the South—the so-called "dangerous classes" many bourgeois Anglo-Americans found frightening. Its purview was so general and ill defined, especially before the statute's revision in 1923, that the interpretation of its scope was left largely in the hands of the police, and it gave them a rationale for arresting people for a wide range of behaviors, even though the charges ultimately might be (and regularly were) dismissed by the courts in any particular case.

In the course of its general revision of the statute in 1923, the New York state legislature, for the first time, specified homosexual solicitation (a person "frequent[ing] or loiter[ing] about any public place soliciting men for the purpose of committing a crime against nature or other lewdness") as a form of disorderly conduct. In specifying the solicitation of men and a wide but unspecified range of "lewd" behavior, the new disorderly-conduct statute became the first law in the state's history to verge on specifying male homosexual conduct as a criminal offense. Even the statutes against sodomy and the crime against nature, which dated from the colonial era, had criminalized a wide range of nonprocreative sexual behavior between people of the same or different genders, without specifying male homosexual conduct or even recognizing it as a discrete sexual category. The criminalization of male homosexual conduct implicit in the wording of the law was made explicit in its enforcement, for Penal Law 722, section 8, "degenerate disorderly conduct," was used exclusively against men the police regarded as "degenerates." Although little evidence remains concerning the history of the legislature's decision, its timing surely reflects the degree to which the social-purity societies and the police had identified homosexuality as a distinct social problem during World War I.[44] The statute became one of the underpinnings of new state regulations after the repeal of Prohibition in 1933 that, for the first time, specifically and formally banned the assembly of gay people in a public space.

As the 1920 Koenig case and numerous other cases demonstrate, however, New York City's police and courts construed the disorderly-conduct statute to mandate a much broader ban on gay cultural practices than a narrow reading of its wording might suggest, both before and after its revision in 1923. They regularly used the statute to criminalize the assembly of gay men in a public place or their adoption of distinctive cultural styles, from camp behavior to dancing with people of the same gender or wearing clothes assigned to the other gender. The police and local courts construed such forms of "degenerate" conduct as *disorderly* conduct posing so dangerous a challenge to the social order that they merited imprisonment and fines, and for more than a decade before the law's revision in 1923, the authorities specified in their own records which disorderly-conduct arrests were for "degeneracy." Gay men managed to claim considerable space for themselves in the city's streets, cafeterias, and restaurants despite this policy, and the number of men actually arrested remained relatively small before the 1940s. But they had always to contend with the possibility of such penalties.*

Given both the lack of a specific legal prohibition against gay assembly before 1933 and the tolerant attitude toward gay men in certain quarters of the city, the use of the disorderly-conduct statute to arrest men gathering in a restaurant was episodic and depended to a large degree on the location of the restaurant and the strength of its political connections. Some smaller speakeasies, restaurants, and clubs that tolerated the open presence of lesbians and gay men flourished, but they were subject to the constant threat of harassment. An insider's review of the history of gay and lesbian meeting places in the 1920s, published in 1931, concluded that "it was not long before all the places were either raided or given up."[45]

A cafeteria in a well-established chain with a citywide reputation, such as Childs, on the other hand, had greater political clout and was less susceptible to police interference and raids than a smaller establishment run by a solitary entrepreneur. Large cafeterias in certain neighborhoods could maintain gay reputations for years, as the extraordinary resilience of Stewart's and the Life Cafeteria—which together served as well-known gay meeting places in the Village for almost two decades—demonstrates. Nonetheless, the police did occasionally raid the large cafeterias and Automats where gay people gathered, when they or the anti-vice societies thought the places had become too uproarious or the management, perhaps fearing the authorities were about to reach that conclusion, decided it was time to use the police to eliminate their "fairy" trade.

Gay men pursued a variety of strategies as they negotiated their presence in the city's restaurants, cafeterias, and speakeasies. Some of them boldly claimed their

---

*Lesbians arrested for assembling in a public place, dancing together, and the like were also often charged with disorderly conduct (although not with degenerate disorderly conduct). The revised 1923 statute did not specify lesbian conduct (by criminalizing the solicitation of women, for instance), but, as in the case of gay men before 1923, the police and courts did not need such a specific ban to construe lesbian visibility as a kind of disorderliness.

right to gather in public, speaking loudly about gay matters, dancing with their friends, even putting on a "show" for the other customers. Most men did not make themselves so noticeable, but they nonetheless claimed space in a large number of restaurants on a regular basis, meeting friends, talking about whatever they wanted, and noticing—and sometimes trying to gain the notice of—the other gay men around them. The latter group of men could meet in small, intimate restaurants and huge, impersonal cafeterias alike. The former group of men were more likely to be branded as "fairies" and restricted to the cafeterias or to restaurants located in sections of town with large concentrations of gay residents, such as the Village, Times Square, and Harlem. Although such men made their presence known throughout the early decades of the century, their numbers and boldness grew in the 1920s during Prohibition.

Both groups were protected, in part, by the preoccupation of the social-purity forces with female prostitution, which usually kept them from paying as much attention to gay meeting places as the Committee of Fourteen did in the case of Koenig's. They were also protected by the absence of a formal ban on gay assembly, the laissez-faire attitude of many New Yorkers and, often enough, of the police, and the complex system of bribes and political connections in which most small businessmen, ward politicians, and policemen were enmeshed. Above all, they were protected by the dominant popular image of the fairy, which was more likely to provoke fascination than outrage on the part of many New Yorkers, and, in any case, rendered most other gay men invisible to outsiders. The very brilliance of the fairy left most men safely in the shadows, and made it easier for them to meet their friends in restaurants throughout the city without provoking the attention of outsiders. Gay men seized the opportunities this portended.

NOTES

1. Willy W., interviewed.

2. George W. Henry and Alfred A. Gross, "The Homosexual Delinquent," *Mental Hygiene* 25 (1941): 426; idem, "Social Factors in the Case Histories of One Hundred Underprivileged Homosexuals," *Mental Hygiene* 22 (1938); 597. Each study surveyed 100 homosexuals. The figures for 1938 were roughly the same as those for 1940, but they showed a smaller percentage (49 percent) living in rooming houses and a higher percentage (39 percent) in tenements; the authors, however, considered the 1938 figures less reliable. The subjects of the studies had either been arrested on homosexual charges or been identified as homosexual once in the prison system. The findings should not be taken as entirely representative, since their subjects, like most men in prison, were relatively poorer than the average population from which they were drawn. In fact, it is likely that an unrepresentatively high percentage of the prisoners were found to be living in tenement apartments with families precisely because these men, who had the least privacy at home, were most likely to try to have sexual encounters in places where they might be apprehended by the police. Since the census data that historians customarily use to map the distribution of ethnic groups and classes in cities are unavailable for a study of gay men, most of the following analysis is necessarily based on literary rather than quantitative sources.

3. For examples, see *People v. Davis*, Manhattan District Attorney's papers, New York Municipal Archives 23,087 (Court of General Sessions, New York City 1898), in which two men were charged with forcible sodomy by the man they had met in Madison Square Park and taken to the West Twenty-fifth Street room one of them had occupied for three days (the actual facts of the case are unclear, but the circumstances suggest that the complainant may have been carrying through with a blackmail threat against the men he had gone home with, and the judge, perhaps for this reason, dismissed the charge); *People v. Mylott*, DAP 100,270 (CGS 1914), in which a man was assaulted by the man he had picked up and taken to his West Fifty-second Street room.

4. In my discussion of lodging houses and the social organization and implications of the housing market in general, I draw especially on Paul Groth's splendid study *Living Downtown: The History of Residential Hotels in the United States* (Berkeley: University of California Press, 1994), which I read in manuscript. See also Albert Benedict Wolfe, *The Lodging House Problem in Boston* (Boston and New York: Houghton Mifflin, 1906); Harvey Warren Zorbaugh, *The Gold Coast and the Slum: A Sociological Study of Chicago's Near North Side* (Chicago: University of Chicago Press, 1929), 69–86; Joanne J. Meyerowitz, *Women Adrift: Independent Wage Earners in Chicago, 1880–1930* (Chicago: University of Chicago Press, 1988); idem, "Sexual Geography and Gender Economy: The Furnished Room Districts of Chicago, 1890–1930," in *Gender and American History Since 1890*, ed. Barbara Mclosh (New York: Routledge, 1993), 43–71; and Mark Peel, "In the Margins: Lodgers and Boarders in Boston, 1860–1900," *Journal of American History* 72 (1986): 813–34.

5. Wolfe, *The Lodging House Problem*, 109–12.

6. Report on 53 W. 16th St., Sept. 27, 1928, box 36, Committee of Fourteen papers, New York Public Library; for other examples, see reports on 138 W. 49th St., Dec. 4, 1930, box 35; 52 W. 111th St., Jan. 19, 1927, box 36. Some proprietors did object, and others drew the line at women working as prostitutes on their premises; see, for example, 2272 Broadway, Jan. 27, 1932, box 35. The *Home News* began an editorial campaign against furnished-room houses as centers of vice and degradation in 1919; see, for example, the Mar. 5, 1919, issue. In the 1920s, after the Committee of Fourteen and other groups had succeeded in closing most of New York's brothels and pushing prostitutes off the streets, they discovered that prostitution had moved into such houses. Some were run as brothels, but most as smaller operations. Indeed, many hotels closed as disorderly houses were converted into furnished-room houses, since it was more economical for proprietors to reopen them as such than to convert them into tenements or business offices. In 1922, for instance, a prostitute took a vice squad officer to a furnished room in a building near Union Square which years earlier had been closed as a disorderly house: bulletin 1505, "A Hotel Problem," Jan. 17, 1922, box 88, COF; Committee of Fourteen, *Annual Report for 1922* (New York: Committee of Fourteen, 1923), 9–10.

7. Report on colored fairy, 63 W. 50th St., Aug. 2, 1919, box 34, COF.

8. *People v. Jagley and Walters*, DAP 31,547 (CGS 1900).

9. One gay man recalled living in the early twenties in a Milwaukee rooming house in which one of the other rooms was occupied by two middle-aged men who worked at the Gimbels department store. The other roomers suspected the nature of their relationship and joked about them behind their backs, but no one tried to have them evicted from their room, and no one suspected the observer, who lived alone (Leo, interviewed).

10. Such experiences were related by several men, including Roger Emmet and Bruhs Mero, in interviews with author.

11. Wolfe, *The Lodging House Problem*, 111–12. The classic statement of the debilitating

effects on young migrants of exposure to life in the cheapest of the city's lodging houses was provided by Jacob Riis in his chapters on the "Stale-Beer Dives" and "Cheap Lodging Houses" in *How the Other Half Lives* (1890; New York: Hill and Wang, 1957), 52–67.

12. Report on the Seamen's Church Institute and vicinity, July 15 and 16, 1931, box 35, COF.

13. Record of the arrests of Mills House residents appears in the entries for Mar. 9, 11, and 23, 1920, in the Society for the Suppression of Vice record books, vol. 4, 396–98, SSV. Robert A. M. Stern, Gregory Gilmartin, and John Montague Massengale, *New York 1900: Metropolitan Architecture and Urbanism, 1890–1915* (New York: Rizzoli, 1983), 272–79, includes floor plans for the Mills House.

14. Paul S. Boyer, *Urban Masses and Moral Order in America, 1820–1920* (Cambridge, Mass.: Harvard University Press, 1978), 108–19; David I. Macleod, *Building Character in the American Boy: The Boy Scouts, YMCA, and Their Forerunners, 1870–1920* (Madison: University of Wisconsin Press, 1983), 72–74, 127–28. The early history of the Y deserves further study with these questions in mind: Boyer notes that many of the early organizers of the Y were young, unmarried small businessmen and clerks.

15. On the construction of the first YMCA residential facilities in New York and the demographics of their residents, see "The Survey of the Young Men's Christian Association of the City of New York: June, 1925–July, 1926," Arthur L. Swift, Jr., director (published in mimeograph form by the Association Press, 1927), 172–209, especially 172–73, 177–85; and C. Howard Hopkins, *History of the Y.M.C.A. in North America* (New York: Association Press, 1951), 577–79.

16. Ronald Roberts, interviewed. *Yip, Yip, Yaphank* also included female impersonators trained by the vaudevillians Savoy and Brennan; see Anthony Slide, *Great Pretenders* (Lombard, Ill.: Wallace-Homestead, 1986), 33. As noted, this development was hardly unique to New York. Many gay men rented rooms at the Newport Army & Navy YMCA, took their meals there, and spent the evenings in the lobby, where they were widely recognized as "fairies"; see George Chauncey, "Christian Brotherhood or Sexual Perversion? Homosexual Identities and the Construction of Sexual Boundaries in the World War One Era," *Journal of Social History* 19 (Winter 1985): 190.

17. Louis E., quoted in George W. Henry, *Sex Variants* (New York: Paul B. Hoeber, 1941), 199–200. For other examples of men experimenting sexually or meeting other gay men at a YMCA in the 1920s and 1930s, see ibid., 298 (Archibald T.), 410 (Max N.), 471 (Peter R., about a man picking him up at a YMCA in Miami). Also see Perry M. Lichtenstein, "The 'Fairy' and the Lady Lover," *Medical Review of Reviews* 27 (1921): 370–71. Examples for the 1940s, 1950s, and 1960s were provided in interviews with Nat Fowler; Joe O'Connor; Al K.; Willy W.; and Grant McGree. In 1969, a Mattachine Society correspondent recommended that a prospective visitor to New York stay at the West Side Y, "if you would like a real, groovy place (gay)": Dick Griffo to A. V., Atlanta, Ga., Sept. 8, 1969, Mattachine Society of New York.

18. David Hearst, interviewed.

19. Grant McGree, interviewed; Joel Honig, interviewed.

20. Donald Vining, *A Gay Diary* (4 vols.; New York: Pepys Press, 1979–83), 1:231–34 (entries for Sept. 13, 14, 18, 23, 1942); 1:390 (entry for June 19, 1945); and passim.

21. Joel Honig, interviewed.

22. Elizabeth C. Cromley, *Alone Together: A History of New York's Early Apartments* (Ithaca, N.Y.: Cornell University Press, 1990); Richard Plunz, *A History of Housing in New York City: Dwelling Type and Social Change in the American Metropolis* (New York:

Columbia University Press, 1990); Amy Kallman Epstein, "Multifamily Dwellings and the Search for Respectability: Origins of the New York Apartment House," *Urbanism Past and Present*, no. 10 (Summer 1980): 29–39; Gwendolyn Wright, *Building the Dream: A Social History of Housing in America* (New York: Pantheon, 1981), 135–51; and Stern, Gilmartin, and Massengale, *New York 1900*, 272–79. *New York 1900* includes photographs of the Hermitage Hotel and the Bachelor Apartments as well as floor plans for the latter.

23. *Broadway Brevities*, Apr. 25, 1932.

24. Donald Vining, for one, forced by poor finances and the wartime housing shortage to live in a single room, was acutely aware of the social advantages of an apartment. See, for instance, Vining, *Diary*, 1:337 (entry for Feb. 11, 1945), and 1:419 (Oct. 13, 1945).

25. For similar readings of the meaning of leisure time for black people in the United States and Britain, see Robin D. G. Kelley, " 'We Are Not What We Seem': Rethinking Black Working-Class Opposition in the Jim Crow South," *Journal of American History* 80 (June 1993): 84–86; Paul Gilroy, "One Nation Under a Groove: The Cultural Politics of 'Race' and Racism in Britain," in *Anatomy of Racism*, ed. David Theo Goldberg (Minneapolis: University of Minnesota Press, 1990), 274. The newspaper image is drawn from Carl Van Vechten's scrapbook (Van Vechten papers, Yale Collection of American Literature, Beinecke Rare Books and Manuscript Library, Yale University, New Haven, Connecticut).

26. Harvey A. Levenstein, *Revolution at the Table: The Transformation of the American Diet* (New York: Oxford University Press, 1988), 185–89.

27. Michael and Ariane Batterberry, *On the Town in New York: From 1776 to the Present* (New York: Scribner's, 1973), 187–89; Stern, Gilmartin, and Massengale, *New York 1900*, 225–26; George Chappell, *The Restaurants of New York* (New York: Greenberg, 1925), 125; Perry R. Duis, *The Saloon; Public Drinking in Chicago and Boston, 1880–1920* (Urbana: University of Illinois Press, 1983), 194–95; *The WPA Guide to New York City* (New York: Random House, 1939), 24.

28. Horn & Hardart, *Directory of Horn & Hardart Automats*, n.d. [1939?], New York Historical Society; Jack Alexander, "The Restaurants That Nickels Built," *Saturday Evening Post*, Dec. 11, 1954, 22–23, 98ff.; *Saturday Evening Post*, Dec. 18, 1954, 30, 55ff; Batterberry, *On the Town*, 189. Using the advertising slogan "Less Work for Mother," the Automats also appealed to young women who had continued to work after marriage by establishing retail stores, beginning in 1924, where women could pick up meals to serve at home.

29. Richard Miller, *Bohemia: The Protoculture Then and Now* (Chicago: Nelson-Hall, 1977), 181.

30. Chappell, *Restaurants of New York*, 125.

31. Report on Taxi and Street Conditions, Broadway and 34th St., Nov. 1, 1917, box 25, COF; H. Kahan report, Sept. 30, 1921, and reports on Childs Restaurant, Columbus Circle, Jan. 12 and 19, 1919, and Aberdeen Hotel, Apr. 30–May 2, 1919, all in box 34, COF; report for June 27, 1924, 1924 Democratic National Convention folder, box 35, COF.

32. F. H. Whitin, "Sexual Perversion Cases in New York City Courts, 1916–1921," bulletin 1480, Nov. 12, 1921, box 88, COF.

33. Parker Tyler to Charles Henri Ford, Oct. 15, 1929.

34. *Broadway Brevities*, Nov. 2, 1931, 2. Frank Thompson reported in an interview that this was still the case in the 1940s.

35. Dorr Legg, interviewed; Charles G. Shaw, *Nightlife*: Vanity Fair's *Intimate Guide to New York* (New York: John Day, 1931), 66.

36. Report by H. Kahan, Sept. 14, 1926, box 35, COF; Jeffrey Gottfried, interviewed;

Broadway Brevities, October 1924, 48–49; *Broadway Brevities*, Nov. 16, 1931, 10. Additionally, a twenty-year-old actor explained in 1922 that after work he "most always" had his dinner at a place on Forty-ninth Street between Sixth and Seventh Avenues, "where I ate because lots of fags hang out there" (Samuel Kahn, *Mentality and Homosexuality* [Boston: Meador, 1937], 183). *Brevities* (Dec. 28, 1931, 7) also referred to the more general phenomenon, in its usual tone, when a columnist reported that "THE GARDENIA BOYS [a relatively uncommon slang term for gay men] are in again. . . . Under the chaperonage of Frankie (Drag) Carroll, they hold 'Midnight Teas' at various and well-known eateries in this versatile city of New Yawp." In later years certain cafeterias in gay bar districts, such as a Bickford's on Lexington Avenue in the East Fifties, were whimsically nicknamed "The Last Chance" or "The Last Stand," a place for men to take a final stab at picking someone up after the bars had closed (David Hearst, interviewed; Willy W., interviewed; Jeffrey Gottfried, interviewed).

37. *Broadway Brevities*, January 1924, 16; investigators' reports dated Apr. 4, 1921; Dec. 13, 1920; June 4, 1921; and July 19, 1921, box 34, COF.

38. Mark Stanley, interviewed. His further comments provide additional evidence of how well known the Columbus Circle Childs must have been, for he added that it "was the only [gay meeting] place that I was aware of New York having at that time"; he rarely participated in the gay scene, went only occasionally to this Childs, and apparently remained ignorant of the other cafeterias and the tearooms on MacDougal Street.

39. *WPA Guide to New York City*, 140.

40. Parker Tyler to Charles Henri Ford, July 22, 1929; on other reprimands, Mar. 11 and Apr. 2, 1929.

41. Parker Tyler to Charles Henri Ford, May 6, 1929. It is unclear whether Tyler's friends reacted so strongly because they found his carrying himself as if he were "heterosexual" an affront (and were, in effect, trying to police his sexual behavior and prohibit any indication of bisexuality) or because they wanted to prevent the woman from being hurt by his deception. It is also unclear whether Tyler was embarrassed because his friends had discovered his masquerade as a heterosexual or because they had publicly identified him as a homosexual.

42. Report on Fairies' hangout in basement, Times Square Bldg., 42nd St. and Broadway, Mar. 2, 1927, box 36, COF.

43. This account of the Koenig raid is based on the following sources: F. H. Whitin to Insp. Thomas MacDonald, First I.D., June 2, 1920, box 5, COF; investigator's reports for Apr. 30, June 12, and June 21, 1920, box 34, COF; bulletin 1391, "Police Action, East Side," Aug. 3, 1920, box 88, COF; bulletin 1438, "Finger Print Report, 1920," Mar. 15, 1921, box 88, COF; and bulletin 1480, "Sexual Perversion Cases in New York City," Nov. 12, 1921, box 88, COF. The COF bulletins do not give the date of the raid, which I determined by searching the Essex Market police court's record book for a record of arrests matching the description provided by the bulletins, that is, an arraignment of thirty men charged with degenerate disorderly conduct on a Saturday night in July (actually Sunday morning, Aug. 1, as it turned out), and given the penalties reported by the Committee: City Magistrates' Courts Record Book, Third Police Court, vol. 47 (July 26, 1920–Jan. 10, 1921), docket numbers 9242–73, New York Municipal Archives, Department of Records and Information Services, New York City.

44. *Cahill's Consolidated Laws of New York, Being the Consolidated Laws of 1909, as amended to July 1, 1923*, ed. James C. Cahill (Chicago: Callaghan, 1923), 1416. The legislative history of the statute's revision is obscure, since few records remain of New York State legislative deliberations of any sort from this period. One very short newspaper account

of the legislation suggests that one of its prime advocates was the United Real Estate Owners' Association, which intended to use the law against tenants who damaged their property, were "noisy and boisterous, . . . and [made] insulting, quarrelsome, and threatening remarks and actions." The article made no reference to the law's provisions restricting other forms of public "disorder" (*New York Times*, June 10, 1923, sec. 9, p. 1). Nonetheless, it seems likely that the moral-reform societies played some part in the legislature's decision to include homosexual solicitation in the measure, given their role in the development of legislation concerning related matters. On the significance of the shift from legislation criminalizing sodomy to that criminalizing a more amorphous "lewdness" (as the New York statute put it) or "gross indecency" (as the British statute, the subject of his article, put it), see Ed Cohen's insightful essay "Legislating the Norm: From Sodomy to Gross Indecency," *South Atlantic Quarterly* 88 (1989): 181–217.

45. *Broadway Brevities*, Nov. 16, 1931, 10.

Chapter Four

Do-It-Yourself
Constructing, Repairing, and Maintaining Domestic Masculinity

Steven M. Gelber

In the 1860s when Harriet Robinson annually set aside a full month for the spring cleaning of her Malden, Massachusetts home, she had the occasional assistance of hired help, but none from her husband, William. Over the years, as the Robinsons improved their house by installing weather stripping, repapering rooms, refinishing furniture, and putting in a new mantel, Harriet's biographer Claudia Bushman notes that neither she nor William "lifted a finger toward household maintenance."[1] Some eighty years later, immediately after World War II, when Eve and Sam Goldenberg moved into a somewhat decrepit apartment in the Bronx, Sam patched the holes in the wall himself and they both worked to scrub away the residual odor "of people who don't care."[2] After a few years in the Bronx, the Goldenbergs (now the Gordons) moved out to a new subdivision on Long Island where Sam built a brick patio and the surrounding fence, installed a new front door, and drew up plans to build a dormer window on the front facade. Real estate agents for the development would drive prospective buyers to the Gordons' house so they could admire Sam's handiwork and, in the words of the family chronicler Donald Katz, "see what a homeowner could do with old-fashioned, all American know-how . . . through the agency of his own hands."[3]

Only there was nothing at all "old-fashioned" about Sam's work around his suburban homestead in Island Park. Real old-fashioned husbands in the 1860s, even those in modest middle-class circumstances like William Robinson, usually hired professionals to do the smallest home repair or improvement. Robinson and his socio-economic peers may have been the titular heads of their households, but they had very little to do there. Their wives raised the children and supervised the servants; they retired to the library to smoke their cigars—or left the house altogether to pass their leisure hours with their male friends. One would have to go back to an even earlier time, before there were suburbs, when most people lived on farms, in order to find husbands who had the knowledge and inclination to use tools on their own homes. When industrialization separated living and working spaces it also separated men and women into non-overlapping spheres of competence, and men like Robinson fulfilled their familial obligations by bringing home the money with which their wives ran the household.

The metamorphosis of the restrained and distant Victorian father into the engaged and present suburban dad was one of the more significant changes in the structure of the modern family, and the male use of tools around the house was a critical component of that change. Historians Mark Carnes and Clyde Griffen recently asked, "When did Mr. Fixit and the master of the barbecue appear and did these circumscribed modifications in role alter the older division of gender spheres significantly?"[4] This article answers part of that question; "Mr. Fixit" put in his first formal appearance just after the turn of the century, although there had been calls and precursors as early as the 1870s. Furthermore, his appearance did indeed indicate an important alteration of the male sphere. By taking over chores previously done by professionals, the do-it-yourselfer created a new place for himself inside the house. In theory it overlapped with a widening female household sphere, but in practice it was sufficiently distinct so that by end of the 1950s the very term "do-it-yourself" would become part of the definition of suburban husbanding.

In the process of reacquainting themselves with manual skills, male householders renegotiated the way they functioned with their wives and the way that each related to their residence. The increasingly equalitarian rhetoric of democratic households in the twentieth century acknowledged the right of women to use tools in the same way as men, and calls for female emancipation on the tool front appeared for the first time in the Progressive era. Clearly, there was a steady expansion throughout the twentieth century of the kinds of do-it-yourself tasks women were willing to take on. Nevertheless, in most cases, wives limited themselves to helping their handyman husbands and acting as an appreciative audience to their household triumphs.

Men were able to move easily into home-based do-it-yourself activity because household construction, repair, and maintenance were free from any hint of gender-role compromise. In fact, do-it-yourself can be thought of as a reassertion of traditional direct male control of the physical environment through the use of heavy tools in a way that evoked pre-industrial manual competence. If, as numerous historians have asserted, industrialism and the rise of white-collar employment in sexually integrated work places made the job a more ambiguous source of masculine identity, then do-it-yourself provided men with an opportunity to recapture the pride that went along with doing a task from start to finish with one's own hands.[5] In periods of economic stress like the Great Depression, their labor could contribute directly to the family's standard of living and thus be a logical extension of work. However, even in good times such as the 1950s, when they might otherwise have been able to hire professional help, what men made or fixed around the house had some theoretical market value that gave do-it-yourself an aura of masculine legitimacy.

There is no doubt that single home ownership was a *sine qua non* for do-it-yourself activity; apartment dwellers do not normally have the space, the incentive, or even the right to fix up someone else's property. For this reason, the growth of do-it-yourself closely paralleled the growth of suburbs. Not only did the absolute number of owner-occupied homes go up from fewer than three million in 1890 to more than thirty million in 1960, but the percentage of dwellings that were occupied by their owners increased from 37 percent to over 60 percent. Thus, by the end of the 1950s there were ten times as many homeowners as there had been in the Gilded Age and proportionately fewer people living in rented housing.[6] Nevertheless, there was nothing inevitable about the do-it-yourself movement. The shift from professional to personal home maintenance, the growth of home workshops, the emergence of do-it-yourself as a hobby, and the unequal distribution of authority between men and women, were all functions of cultural forces beyond the mere growth in the number of privately owned homes.

Do-it-yourself had a series of distinct elements that permitted it to become virtually a male necessity by the 1950s. First, it drew on a pre-industrial yeoman/ artisan tradition of mastery over heavy tools. Second, what men did around the house may or may not have been necessary, but it had economic value and thus partook in the masculine legitimacy of skilled labor. Third, although work-like, household projects were undertaken more or less voluntarily. As self-directed and even playful, do-it-yourself was leisure—something to be embraced rather than avoided. Finally, do-it-yourself was the justification for men to claim a portion of their homes as a workshop for themselves. This new masculine space permitted men to be both a part of the house and apart from it, sharing the home with their families while retaining spatial and functional autonomy. Do-it-yourself was one of a series of roles that suburban men created so that they could actively participate in family activities while retaining a distinct masculine style. Outdoor cook, little league coach, driver of the car (when the whole family was present), and household handyman were all ways men could be intimate in family affairs without sacrificing their sense of maleness and recreate places for themselves in the homes they had left for factory and office.

Negotiating Domestic Space

Prior to the Civil War only 12 percent of Americans worked for somebody else; by 1910 more than two-thirds of all Americans were employees.[7] On the one hand, work in larger firms was more dependable than self-employment, making postbellum men better able to fulfill what Ileen DeVault has called the "social definition of masculinity"—the imperative to support their families.[8] On the other hand, as the more traditional sense of "manly independence" that came with being one's own boss became increasingly a thing of the past, Victorian men, as Carnes and Griffen point out, were forced to "devise new conceptions of masculinity."[9] While the job remained a—perhaps *the*—major source of personal identity for men, it appears to have been a less complete, less satisfying basis for feeling manly than self-employment had been.[10] As women began to work in offices, albeit in small numbers and limited roles, the fundamental demography of the workplace shifted and presented white-collar men with additional complications in defining masculinity through their jobs. Angel Kwolek-Folland discovered, for example, that the introduction of women into the life insurance business after the 1890s disturbed the traditional air (and language) of male camaraderie among the old-time clerks who felt they were being "civilized" and losing their manhood as a result.[11]

Historians of the postbellum era have suggested that male gender anxieties induced by industrialization found most of their resolutions away from the female-dominated home. In separate studies, both Mary Ann Clawson and Mark Carnes report that Victorian men spent many of their evenings at fraternal meetings that, like their jobs, kept them away from the female world of the house. According to Carnes, these ritual-filled meetings may have provided men with the psychological permission to break from the inhibiting bonds that tied them to their mothers.[12] Clawson goes even further, claiming that fraternalism "was an alternative to domesticity, one that worked to preserve rather than deny the primacy of masculine social organization."[13] These conclusions about fraternalism and masculinity have been reinforced by E. Anthony Rotundo's findings that boys and adolescent males formed homosocial groups that allowed them to retreat from the female-dominated household and practice the non-feminine values of aggression and competition that they would need in the workplace.[14] This picture of the father-as-stranger under his own roof is consistent with the general reluctance of nineteenth-century men to undertake work around the house. Their worlds of both work and leisure lay beyond the white picket fence. The rise of muscular Christianity and organized athletics, the continuation of fraternal orders, and the emergence of the Boy Scouts after 1900 are all indications that male groups remained an important, but no longer the sole, source of masculine identity into the new century.[15]

Along with this continuation of homosocial bonding, a counter-trend emerged in which men found companionship and masculine identity within the home. Beginning very tentatively in the nineteenth century, it took on a recognizably modern form at the beginning of the twentieth, as part of the rise of "masculine domesticity." Moving from the position of a somewhat remote *paterfamilias*, the new suburban husband was, according to Margaret Marsh, willing "to take on increased responsibility for some of the day-to-day tasks of bringing up children," and make "his wife, rather than his male cronies, his regular companion on evenings out."[16] Marsh notes in passing that part of this new role was some increased male attention to home decoration.[17] That increased attention to decoration was more than a part of the broader pattern of masculine domesticity; it was also an expression of a new relationship that developed between men and their houses in the first decades of the twentieth century. This relationship extended the concept of masculine domesticity to the structure itself and served both to broaden the man's sphere within the home and to further cement the partnership aspect of suburban married life. While it is true that men and women worked together more frequently on their houses, it is also important to understand that men staked out areas of activity at home that became their particular domains. By doing so they created what I prefer to call spheres of "domestic masculinity." Unlike masculine domesticity, which had men doing jobs that had once belonged to women, domestic masculinity was practiced in areas that had been the purview of professional (male) craftsmen, and therefore retained the aura of pre-industrial vocational masculinity. The two concepts are complementary, but the introduction of the idea of domestic masculinity recognizes the creation of a male sphere *inside* the house.

Whereas male do-it-yourself activity in the nineteenth century had been limited to minor household repairs and light maintenance with almost no crafts at all, as a result of the arts and crafts movement building things for pleasure became part of the masculine repertoire in the twentieth century.[18] As a form of work at home that was a relief from work on the job, the arts and crafts movement generated a whole set of psychotherapeutic arguments to augment the heretofore practical ones for do-it-yourself activity.[19] Under this new rubric, work around the house was not work; it was recreation that soothed the troubled minds of men when they returned from the city by providing them with a masculine alternative to effete office work. Typically, a 1910 article entitled "Recreation with Tools" explained that every person needed some interest aside from daily work in order to "maintain that balance and poise—physical and mental—which is so essential to right living."[20] Historian T. J. Jackson Lears seems to regret this palliative aspect of do-it-yourself when he notes that by World War I the arts and crafts ideal had "been reduced to a revivifying hobby for the affluent" in which the "nervous businessman would return refreshed to the office after a weekend of puttering at his basement workbench."[21] It is true that craft work had been "reduced" in the sense that the movement did not revolutionize industrial capitalism as many of its most ardent supporters had hoped, but it would provide generations of men with a sense of satisfaction that may have disappeared from their jobs.

The impact of the arts and crafts movement was amplified by its convergence with the spread of manual training in the public schools. Manual training had been introduced into the United States from Russia in 1876 as a form of vocational education for working-class children, but it combined with drawing instruction around the turn of the century to bring both the philosophy and techniques of the arts and crafts movement into middle- as well as working-class school rooms.[22] Shop courses introduced boys to the use of tools at a time when simpler house and furnishing styles made it easier for them, and their fathers, to make fashionable household items.[23] Ira Griffith, a manual arts teacher and do-it-yourself writer for *Suburban Life*, promoted the "plain, square Mission type of furniture" as both suitable for woodworking beginners and as compatible with the aesthetic dictum that form should follow function.[24] Manual arts classes legitimated constructive work for the middle class and recreated a home environment where fathers could once again pass on specific manly skills to their sons, a form of masculine bonding that was virtually universal before the industrial revolution but rare after it.[25] Beginning in the arts and crafts era and continuing through the 1950s, workshop plans frequently contained references to bringing fathers and sons closer.[26]

The House Becomes a Hobby

Judging from the dramatic increase in do-it-yourself literature, the role for men in caring for their homes grew so palpably during the interwar years that the house was transformed from a place *in* which to do things to a place *on* which to do things. Continuing the pattern that had begun in the Progressive era, and paralleling the general loosening of gender constraints, women also increased their role in home maintenance and repair, thus maintaining a rough proportionality with men. However, this was no zero-sum situation because both husbands and wives expanded their spheres of household competence. The only losers were professionals, the need for whose services continued to decline steadily. Because do-it-yourself was carving out new territory for householder activity, and because most of that activity was performed by men, home maintenance and repair became a major source of domestic masculinity in the 1920s and 1930s, slowing down only temporarily when World War II forced homeowners to exchange their hammers and saws for the tools of war.

Between 1890 and 1930 the number of privately owned homes more than tripled, while mass distribution of automobiles in the 1920s encouraged the growth of new housing developments beyond the confines of streetcar and rail lines.[27] As had been the case in the nineteenth century, this private housing boom was not restricted to the white-collar middle class. Richard Harris has shown that at the end of the Depression, the percentage of skilled workers who owned their own homes was actually higher than that of professional workers (41.9 percent versus 40.3 percent).[28] Although he has no precise figures, Harris is confident "that the families of male blue-collar workers did more work within and upon the home than did those of other groups."[29] Blue-collar workers who knew how to use tools and who risked no loss in status by doing so had everything to gain by working on their own homes. Trumpeting the benefits of his forty-hour work week in 1926, Henry Ford explained that his men "have been building houses for themselves, and to meet their demand for good and cheap lumber we have established a lumber yard where they can buy wood from our own forests."[30] And in lovely symmetry, the working men who bought the inexpensive cars produced by Ford's workers spent their free time building shelters for this first generation of cheap automobiles. When social worker Rose Feld investigated the leisure activities of steel workers who had just gotten an eight-hour workday in 1924 she discovered that a high percentage of them were constructing their own garages—which incidentally is additional testimony to the widespread private homeownership among blue collar workers.[31]

Because do-it-yourself was an artifact of homeownership, and because homeownership was widespread among blue-collar workers, do-it-yourself was an activity that transcended class more readily than gender. While common sense suggests that poorer householders had a greater economic stake in doing their own building, repairing, and maintenance than did richer homeowners, men from all classes appear to have had an essentially similar set of attitudes toward do-it-yourself. They recognized it as not-quite-a-chore, that is, something useful undertaken voluntarily. As such, do-it-yourself activities were a jumble of contradictions; they were leisure that was work-like and chores that were leisurely; they produced outcomes with real economic value that might actually cost more in time and money than the product was worth; they were performed by middle-class men acting like blue-collar workers and blue-collar workers acting like middle-class homeowners. It is precisely

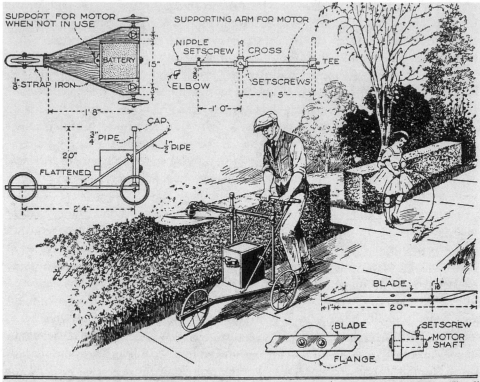

This Electrically Driven Hedge-Trimming Machine will Delight the Amateur Mechanic Who Prides Himself on the Appearance of His Grounds. It is Easily Made, and Quite Efficient

Fig. 4.1. Home-made, battery-powered hedge-trimmer was typical of make-it-yourself labor-saving devices in men's technology and do-it-yourself magazines in the 1920s. *Make It Yourself* (Chicago, 1927), 307.

this categorical fuzziness that allowed do-it-yourself to become so central to domestic masculinity. Its justifications and satisfactions were multiple, permitting men, depending on their circumstances, to rationalize it as money-saving, trouble-saving, useful, psychologically fulfilling, creative, or compensatory. It was, in other words, a hobby.

The large increase in the number of small-sized suburban houses after World War I made for a significant number of homeowners who could treat their homes playfully and act as an audience for increasing numbers of do-it-yourself articles. It was during the 1920s that the wonderful, if slightly nutty, tradition of home-made labor-savers got started.[32] Plans for devices like bicycle-driven lawn mowers, battery-run hedge trimmers, chicken-operated hen house doors, and remote electric ignition switches for water heaters, filled the pages of *Popular Mechanics* and other do-it-yourself magazines (fig. 4.1).[33] While these implements may in fact have saved some time and effort (if they ever worked), they contained an element of exuberance that made them as much playful as labor saving. The house itself was becoming a hobby, both the location and the object of leisure time activity.[34] To the extent that it was a hobby, the house was part of a pattern of "serious leisure," which, as sociologist Robert Stebbins has noted, is leisure pursued as though it were work.[35] Serious leisure is a strong source of personal identification, and a hobby that involved the use of traditional male skills contributed to a sense of domestic masculinity. By taking over work from professional craftsmen, this interwar generation of handymen expressed pride in their homes, much as they did in their cars, by tricking them out with gadgets and keeping them polished and purring.

With this new conception of the house as a pastime came the growing belief that do-it-yourself maintenance and repair work could be satisfying in the same way as more obviously creative constructive projects. The hobby label had been applied to furniture-building projects in the arts and crafts era; during the 1920s its application was broadened to include even routine work on the house itself. "Do It Yourself," urged the title of the first chapter in a 1924 home-repair book, because the best form of rest was taking up a "work hobby" that would provide a sense of accomplishment and ward off nervous collapse.[36] Saving money and avoiding inconvenience would remain the primary reasons for do-it-yourself household repair, but writers increasingly recognized the psychological satisfaction that could make household care as much a satisfying hobby as a chore.[37] The shifting balance between necessity and pleasure meant that, for the first time, how-to writers could begin to acknowledge what most homeowners had discovered for themselves; do-it-yourself did not necessarily save either money or aggravation, but could be pleasurable nevertheless. In a general how-to article on setting up a home workshop, James Tate advised "Mr. Amateur Mechanic" to be sure he had the tools necessary to fix a loose coffee pot handle, put up a few shelves, make the screen door fit, and repair the cord on the toaster. Tate was not advocating do-it-yourself repairs because they would save the homeowner money. On the contrary, he said he was addressing "the man who gets more fun out of twenty dollars' worth of time spent in tinkering with tools than in paying out five to have the job done."[38] In other words, Tate turned some of the traditional rationales for home repair upside-down. It was neither the cost saving, nor the convenience of bypassing professionals that mattered, it was the satisfaction of doing-it-yourself—even if you lost money in the process.

Following up on the inroads they had made during the 1910s, wives moved on to new challenges in do-it-yourself repair and maintenance in the 1920s, when, for the first time, detailed articles on such things as electrical appliance repair began appearing for women.[39] Although there is little hard data on female participation in do-it-yourself, the home-care literature indicates that the trend toward including wives in a house maintenance team continued and even expanded a bit during the Great Depression. With limited money to hire professionals or to buy new household items when the old ones wore out, the economic incentive to do-it-yourself became preeminent.[40] Indeed, the mid 1930s appear to have been something of a watershed for female incorporation in do-it-yourself. Women enjoyed the fact that they too could do-it-themselves, and did not have to depend on men. In 1936, when Martha Wirt Davis instructed women how to hammer in a nail—and how *not* to hammer in a screw, she did not cite financial savings as the reason women should gain competence with tools. What she did stress was the convenience and pride of being independent of men. She discovered that "there is quite a bit of satisfaction in being able to fix one's own cords, open stubborn windows, unstop stopped-up sinks, put new washers in leaky faucets or replace burned-out fuses without calling for male assistance."[41] Similarly, in 1938 when J. C. Woodin published what appears to be the first American textbook on home mechanics for girls, he explained that he hoped to "allow housewives to deal with minor, everyday problems without having to call professional repairmen or wait for their husbands to come home."[42] That women had to be encouraged to learn do-it-yourself tasks as elementary as hammering a nail or changing a fuse is testimony to both how andric household repair and maintenance remained and to a new rhetorical willingness to advocate female use of non-traditional tools.

Like hobbies in general, home workshops enjoyed a great boom during the depression. In a society where jobs were at a premium and the work ethic itself was under siege from unemployment, leisure time activities that replicated work activity and reinforced work values gave employed people a way to confirm the importance of productive labor as the core activity in modern society.[43] Advocates of do-it-yourself in the 1930s praised it both for its practicality in allowing homeowners to save money by doing their own work and for the sense of satisfaction it provided.[44] Workshop hobbyists consumed the fruits of their own production, and could argue they were saving money in the bargain. "I am sitting on a home-made chair," wrote one author, and "the greatest reward coming out of this piece of work was the fun of making it with my own hands." However, he went on point out that there was also "a dollar-and-cents moral to be drawn" because it cost him less than a commercially produced chair.[45]

Even while they were declaring the superiority of skill over wealth, do-it-yourselfers in the 1930s seemed to crave the affirmation that their mundane hobby was shared by those who were not economically constrained to work around the house. In good times craftsmanship was a sign of manly self-reliance, but in bad times it could be a sign of economic impotence. Thus, the knowledge that rich people were also do-it-yourselfers contributed to the sense, however illusory, that do-it-yourself was still more leisure than chore. In other words, gender transcended class. Home craftsmen could, and presumably rich ones did, look upon their efforts as an expression of masculinity rather than frugality, or even necessity. The *New York Times* made a point of describing doctors, lawyers and bankers who rolled up their sleeves in workshops that sometimes took up large portions of their homes.[46] Similarly, the Leisure League of America, a Depression-era organization that promoted the productive use of spare time, explained that "tucked away in a closet of one of the swankiest of New York's apartment hotels there happens to be a woodworker's bench, a power lathe and an amazing assortment of hand tools ready, at a moment's notice, to make the sawdust fly!"[47]

Just as the less affluent do-it-yourselfers might feel less self-conscious by knowing that the wealthy shared their hobby, home workshops allowed wealthier professionals and executives to establish their connection to the tradition of manly labor, which was experiencing a visual revival at the hands of New Deal artists. As Barbara Melosh points out, a disproportionately large number of broad-shouldered, barrel-chested workers peered down in mute disapproval of those who did not work with their hands, or did not work at all, from public buildings throughout the country.[48] In the Depression-era home workshop, however, the symbolic could still become real, and every office worker could imagine himself the heroic figure on the post office wall. Indeed, what little data we do have for the 1930s, confirms the classless nature of do-it-yourself. Approximately half of all home workshops were owned by middle-class college graduates and half by skilled blue-collar workers.[49]

The most dedicated and wealthy do-it-yourself hobbyists, like the one in the swanky New York apartment, equipped their shops with electrically driven tools. Some craft workers had motorized their foot-powered jigsaws and lathes as soon as small electric motors and electrically wired homes had appeared early in the century, but it was not until the end of the 1920s that craft writers could begin to assume that any significant number of their readers would have power tools at home.[50] The Delta corporation produced the first home power tool, a scroll saw, in 1923, and the new industry actually experienced a boomlet during the cash-starved years of the Great Depression.[51] It was a boomlet, not a boom, because of the price of the electrical tools. Walker-Turner, the leading manufacturer of home power tools in the 1930s, offered a motor-driven jigsaw, drill press, or lathe for about twenty dollars, and they were carried, at least for a while, by large department stores such as Macy's.[52] Other companies sold similar machines for thirty to forty dollars apiece, which did not include the cost of the motor used to run them. Because such prices amounted to 2–3 percent of the average worker's gross income, the market was limited to the wealthy or the highly motivated hobbyist.[53] A 1935 survey of home workshops in Lima, Ohio found that significantly fewer than half had any power equipment at all—and much of that was homemade.[54] On the other hand, a poll the same year of the more serious craftsmen who had joined the National Homeworkshop Guild determined that almost two-thirds of them had some sort of electrically driven tool, most commonly a lathe and circular saw.[55]

Expensive equipment distinguished wealthy from middle-class amateurs, but that difference was secondary to the sense of common masculine experience they shared. When one magazine printed an illustration of what it called a "typical" power-driven basement workshop in 1937, it belonged to the hardly typical Milwaukee industrialist Louis Allis. Yet the image is typical in a number of ways. Like the average Joe, Allis's workshop retreat was in his basement. It was, furthermore, a man's space, or at least a male's space, since Allis was pictured smoking a cigarette as he worked at his drill press while his son cut a pattern on an electric scroll saw. A second illustration depicts a similarly equipped basement shop with a large dog lying at the feet of his master. The article implies that while he might be a millionaire manufacturer of electric motors, Allis was also a craftsman participating in the democratic fraternity of home-based artisans, along with "bank and industrial executives, opera and movie stars, salesmen, professional men, mechanics and laborers," all of whom were numbered "among the ranks of the home shop operators."[56]

Rosie and Joe in War and Peace

During that brief period of prosperity between the outbreak of fighting in Europe and American entry into World War II, the pragmatic reasons for do-it-yourself shifted from lack of money to the shortage of qualified professional workers. American production for the European war absorbed skilled workers, which may be why there was a discernible change in attitudes toward women doing heavier work at home. As they had since the 1910s, most male do-it-yourselfers took it for granted that their wives would set the agenda, but that they would do the work.[57] Thus, the illustrator for a 1942 article in *Parents' Magazine* showed the wife directing her husband's use of heavy tools in four pictures, but doing light work herself in only one (fig. 4.2).[58] Yet three other articles from the same two-year period had women participating with their husbands in fairly heavy household projects, such as putting in a parking area and refinishing a basement.[59] There was a certain amount of ambivalence in the idea of women doing men's work. For example, when Rachel McKinley Bushong wrote an inspirational (as opposed to an instructional) article in *The American Home* that described how she painted walls and made furniture, the cartoon illustrations showed a woman hammering and sawing with much less competence than the determined self-taught do-it-yourselfer of the text (fig. 4.3).[60]

Official American entry into World War II at the end of 1941 erased that ambivalence. Women took over men's jobs in factories and at home. Sabina Ormsby Dean remembered being embarrassed as a girl by her mother who made her own window screens and installed her own plumbing. But when the war came and women everywhere were forced to learn the skills she had grown up with, she could boast in the title of a 1943 article, "It Didn't Take a War to Make a Carpenter Out of Mother."[61] A variety of organizations established adult education classes for women during the war so that they could nurse their ailing homes and appliances for the duration. The Young Women's Christian Association (YWCA), the U.S. Extension Service, and especially the American Women's Voluntary Services (a private war-time support organization) held classes to teach women to change fuses, splice wires, trouble-shoot appliances, paint, plumb, and do simple wood repairs.[62] War-time magazine articles on household repair routinely showed women using the heavy tools that had once been almost exclusively men's and proclaimed: "Every woman her own handy-man!"[63] Seldom did one find a traditional reference to the woman as instigator but not participant in household improvement—and even then she might be vulnerable to her husband's uniquely war-time response: "How can you say such things when you are a riveter?"[64]

From the perspective of household do-it-yourself, Rosie the Riveter and her GI Joe husband returned home after the war transformed by their experiences. Historians of the family often characterize gender roles in the 1950s as "neo-Victorian," and for good reason.[65] The crises of the 1930s and 1940s made the prospect of a husband at work and a wife at home with their children extremely attractive. The Victorian "cult of domesticity" returned with a vengeance in the late 1940s. Three million women left the labor force in the year after the war ended and gave birth at a rate 20 percent greater than during the war years.[66] Although by 1953 the number

Fig. 4.2. The son helps, the wife directs, the husband works. A typical division of responsibilities in home maintenance. Harold J. Hawkins, "Fixing Things Around the House," *Parents' Magazine* (Aug. 1942): 48.

Fig. 4.3. The article, written by a woman, described a highly competent female do-it-yourselfer. The illustrations showed a mechanical naïf who can't even keep her shoes on. Rachel McKinley Bushong, "Get Going! Not Brains, Not Talent, Not Skill—But Just Plain Work . . . Try It," *American Home* (Mar. 1941): 30.

of women in the labor force had actually regained its wartime peak, even women's return to work was domestically oriented; most of those who found jobs did so not to pursue careers but to support a material lifestyle, a major portion of which was a private home.[67]

The home of the 1950s, however, was not the home of the 1850s. Middle-class men and women did more with their own hands and did more together than their Victorian great-grandparents. Rather than neo-Victorian, a more apt, if excessively hyphenated, characterization of the 1950s family would be neo-pre-industrial. Like farm and artisan couples, husbands and wives in the 1950s had distinct jobs around the house, but ones that were done within sight of and in cooperation with each other.[68] Men were expected to be there for their wives, for their children, and for themselves. Being a father was no longer limited to bringing home the paycheck; men were also supposed to be warm and nurturing parents, but at the same time, popular images of emasculated suburban men seemed to warn of dangers in the role of suburban dad.[69] The increased calls for paternal presence clashed with the continuing assumptions of traditional gender models, catching men in a no-win position. Do-it-yourself provided at least a partial solution because household maintenance and repair permitted the suburban father to stay at home without feeling emasculated or being subsumed into an undifferentiated entity with his wife.[70]

The workshop, in particular, remained the man's realm. A 1954 advertisement for Corby's whiskey shows five men standing around in the garage workshop of what is clearly a very new house. The foreground is dominated by a large wood-lathe, with just enough wood shavings scattered about to make it clear this is a working shop. Hand tools and parts of power tools are hung neatly on the far wall. The casually dressed men have obviously stepped out of the house and away from their wives to admire a half-finished colonial-style Windsor rocking chair, while helping themselves to whiskey from a home-made serving cart.[71] Their collective retreat to the garage workshop to smoke, drink, and admire the artisanal prowess of the householder all bespeak male camaraderie built on a shared appreciation of the masculine role of suburban handyman.

These were just the men *Business Week* was referring to in its 2 June 1952 issue when it christened the new movement. Proclaiming the 1950s "the age of do-it-yourself," the magazine located the home improvement movement in the rapidly expanding postwar suburbs. Although the phrase "do-it-yourself" had been used from time to time at least as far back as 1912, this appears to be the earliest prominent use of the term in the 1950s and the one that gave it widespread currency.[72] Within the year, the phrase had become commonplace, spread in part by a series of "do-it-yourself" expositions, which themselves were additional evidence of the hands-on ownership trend.

Dad the Handyman

By mid-decade only reading and watching television were more popular forms of recreation than do-it-yourself among married men.[73] There were eleven million home workshops in the United States and do-it-yourselfers were, by some estimates, spending four to six billion dollars a year on newly developed materials and tools. Among the most popular innovations in materials were pre-trimmed wallpaper and washable, water-based latex paint applied with a roller, and floor covering tiles that did not require full-size layout and cutting. Painting and papering became the most common do-it-yourself projects, more than twice as popular as either electrical work or wood work, which followed in rank order.[74] The most significant of the new tools was the hand-held quarter inch drill.[75]

The Black & Decker Manufacturing Company had patented the first portable hand-held drill in 1914. The half-inch drill was large, expensive, and beyond the reach of most homeowners who, prior to World War II, jury-rigged portable drills by mounting drill bits on small jig saw motors, but the result was both awkward and weak.[76] In 1946 Black & Decker decided to try again. This time it produced a smaller, cheaper quarter-inch drill designed for home owners.[77] It was the right tool at the right time and became the symbol of the do-it-yourself movement. Suburban-ites bought an estimated fifteen million drills from Black & Decker and a variety of other manufacturers in the next eight years.[78] Originally priced at $16.95, the portable electric drill brought power equipment down to a price that fit the young family budget and to a size that fit in a toolbox as well as a workshop. Whereas in the 1930s, drills (in fact, drill presses) had lagged far behind lathes, saws, and grinders in popularity, in 1958 one survey found that almost three-quarters of handymen owned an electric hand-drill, twice as many as the next most popular power tool, a table saw.[79]

The postwar proliferation of power tools gave amateur craftsmen a sharply increased capacity to undertake larger and more complex projects. They could cut and drill quickly and accurately with much less training than required for the effective use of hand-tools. The widespread use of the new tools also confirmed a trend that had been apparent since the late 1920s; that is, home craftsmanship in the United States was as much product as process oriented. William Morris, the English founder of the arts and crafts movement, had envisioned a world where "all work which would be irksome to do by hand is done by immensely improved machinery; and in all work which it is a pleasure to do by hand, machinery is done without."[80] At the grass-roots level of the home workshop, that world had come to pass in the 1950s, a fact that Americans grasped more quickly than Morris's own countrymen. When a group of English experts toured American industrial education programs in 1950 they were disturbed by the large number of power tools they found in school shops. "What do your pupils do later if they wish to take up woodwork as a hobby, since they have been accustomed in school to do everything with power tools?" they asked. The answer was obvious: "they would, in taking up any hobby, first acquire the necessary machine tools."[81] For the English, hobbies were, almost by definition, activities that involved traditional methods of hand construction. For the Americans, hobbies were useful ways to occupy free time, and the instruments of that usefulness did not define the legitimacy of the enterprise.

For heavy tools, the new rule seemed to be, "men must, women may," but women were still ceded aesthetic preeminence with paint brush and needle.[82] For example, an exhaustively complete sixteen-hundred-page home repair handbook written by veteran do-it-yourself author Emanuele Stieri in 1950, pictured women on only two pages, those dealing with upholstery.[83] Victorian assumptions about inherent female superiority in aesthetic expression, especially with needle and brush, survived into the 1950s, but advice givers continued to add new possibilities for more substantial participation in household repair and improvement. Despite ongoing male domination of do-it-yourself, writers occasionally urged women to undertake heavy work on their own.[84] While a certain amount of this was journalistic hyperbole, it was also an indication that as men took on new household responsibilities, women were not going to surrender the right to participate. If power tools gave men additional opportunities, then do-it-yourself advocates could claim that using power tools to saw wood and drill holes was "simpler than threading, adjusting and running a sewing machine."[85] As they had periodically in the past, women pointed with pride to being able to do a "man's job"; the claim gained support from schools around the country as they began to open their shop classes to girls as well as boys.[86]

From a gender perspective the changes in do-it-yourself during the 1950s continued to enlarge the spheres of both men and women, but it was men who cemented their position as home handyman while at best, women expanded their role as assistant handyman. Women were now free to help with home improvements if they wanted to, but men were expected to. Most frequently women were depicted as helpers or partners for their husbands and, in fact, almost half of the men in one survey said they sometimes got help from their wives in performing do-it-yourself jobs. However, most of the time more than two-thirds of the men did these chores alone.[87] In an adult version of the tomboy pattern, the wife who did a man's work around the house was admired for her competence, but the husband who did not was less than a man. By the 1950s being handy had, like sobriety and fidelity, become an expected quality in a good husband. A sociological survey of Little Rock–area male homeowners near the end of the decade found that a significant number of them attributed their household activities to the "insistence of the wife," leading the interviewer to conclude that women were "the boss in the homes of Pulaski County, Arkansas."[88] This do-it-yourself environment gave rise to the ironic "honeydew" syndrome (honey do this, honey do that). Humorous complaints of henpecked husbands were a traditional form of male self-pity, but they had previously hinged on wives telling their spouses what they should not do (drink, gamble, ramble), not on what they should do (fix the faucet, put up a shelf, paint the kitchen).[89]

The henpecked do-it-yourselfer was not only being told do something he was expected to do, but also to do something his wife did not expect to do herself, even if she could. In other words, the image of the henpecked handyman was actually an image of continuing male dominance over the world of heavy tools. "He loves to putter around the house / To the great enjoyment of his spouse," ran the opening lines of an advertising ditty in 1945, and it ended by noting the admiration of the community: "Neighbors marvel; you'll hear them utter: / 'Wise little handyman, Peter Putter.' "[90] Such references imply that the male role of handyman was passing from voluntary to mandatory and confirm the social value placed on work around the house. The kinds of household repair, maintenance, and construction projects done by men did not change significantly during the 1950s, but the very doing of those projects became a requirement of masculinity.[91] Do-it-yourself was becoming for adult males what sports were for youths, a virtual badge of manhood. Just as boys took pride in their athletic ability, grown men boasted about their craft skills: "A man makes a chair, a desk, a house, puts a washer in a leaky faucet, builds a kayak, paints a crib, he spends the rest of his life and yours telling you about it."[92]

As they had as early as the 1920s, home handymen in the 1950s admitted that far from saving money, doing it yourself could actually be a distinct economic liability. A mordant commentator on the new do-it-yourself craze suggested that men who decided to build their own furniture usually ended up spending more just on the wood than a store-bought suite would have cost, and that they alienated their wives and children in the process.[93] Furthermore, frequent articles, and even a syndicated cartoon series of do-it-yourself disasters, made it clear that home-built was not necessarily better-built. In sharp contrast to earlier periods, in the 1950s almost nobody complained about poor professional work. It was, after all, unlikely that a professional would forget to install a staircase in the house he was building, wall up his wife in the attic bedroom he was constructing, or build a boat on the third floor of a New York City building so that it had to be lowered to sidewalk by piano movers.[94] "Make a professional feel better by viewing an amateur's botch," said one not-too-handy man, "and you've scattered a little sunshine."[95] To the extent that do-it-yourself had become part of the standard male repertoire, cost savings were secondary and even men who could afford to buy their work clothes at Abercrombie & Fitch, took their power tools to their country property to work on their second homes.[96]

Something more important than saving money was going on. The constant, often indulgently humorous, references to handyman disasters make it clear that for do-it-yourselfers there was pleasure in the pain. The quintessentially male pastime of reveling in self-inflicted discomfort had moved indoors. One no longer had to play football, climb mountains, or sail outside the harbor to experience the perverse joy of suffering. Now even the unathletic man could waste money, bruise his fingers, and make six return trips to the hardware store, thus participating in the community of manly perseverance. The ham-handed homeowner might make a mess, but at least it was his own mess, and he could take pride in confronting, if not always overcoming, obstacles.[97]

Conclusion

Just before World War II, a newspaper columnist and do-it-yourself author named Julian Starr praised leisure woodworking by describing the psychological benefits of creativity. The cure for the boredom of repetitive jobs, he said, was to find recreation "as far removed from daily occupation as a man can achieve." Starr claimed that sports could not fill that role because their competitiveness made them too work-like, but he then went on to promote shop work as a change of pace for white-collar workers precisely because it had the qualities of traditional artisan labor. For example, Starr celebrated the fact that "skill takes the place of thought, because 12 inches today is 12 inches tomorrow. A good joint, once learned is a good joint forever," and noted that "fixed values of this sort are a tremendous consolation in a world where the most fundamental concepts are subject to change without notice."[98] In other words, Starr's justification for do-it-yourself as leisure was an appeal to its intrinsically work-like qualities. Do-it-yourself might not be work, yet it had to be done, if not by the homeowner then by a paid professional; it might not be work, yet it was the exercise of creativity and productivity; it might not be work, yet it required planning, organization, knowledge and skill, the same values necessary for success on the job; it might not be work as it was—it was work as it might be.

Starr's contradictory assessment of the meaning of do-it-yourself derived from the culturally marginal location of the activity—it was leisure, yet it was work. By embracing two oppositional categories, do-it-yourself was able to become an instrument of domestic masculinity. As leisure, it could be done voluntarily, distinct from the arena of alienation that was the modern workplace. As manual work, it could confirm the homeowner's ties to his yeoman/artisan forefathers, thus creating and responding to a new cultural stereotype of masculinity. Over more than a century homeowner maintenance and amateur home production grew from somewhat suspect activities into a hobby that was a core component of suburban masculinity. The rise of do-it-yourself did not take place at the expense of women; they too expanded their role in the care and improvement of their suburban homes, albeit in a secondary capacity. Women, however, already had a place in the home (not in the workplace), which is why male do-it-yourself fits Margaret Marsh's definition of masculine domesticity. Do-it-yourself was an element in the more general pattern of increasing male involvement in the household. Unlike other aspects of masculine domesticity, however, do-it-yourself was always dominated by men and was therefore part of a process in which men reclaimed for themselves a legacy that had been lost when they swapped household for factory production.

Household maintenance, which started off as a money-saving convenience in the Victorian era, combined with amateur woodworking after the turn of the century to become a predominantly male domain defined by the use of heavy tools. There was a general acknowledgment of this activity as a hobby in the 1930s when its practicality complemented both the need to save money and the stress on traditional work values in an economically unstable world. The movement reached its culmination after World War II with the great suburban expansion and baby boom. Building on their war-time experiences, women joined men in improving their new tract homes, but female participation was optional. It seems likely that they did not challenge their husbands' dominance of do-it-yourself because it kept the men usefully occupied close to home. By ceding them space for a workshop and proprietary interest in the house, women helped perpetuate a male domestic sphere.

In 1959 *Popular Mechanics* reported that when a tourist asked actor Dick Powell's six-year-old daughter if a movie star lived in the house where she was playing, she answered no. She admitted, when pressed, that it was where Dick Powell lived, but assured the curious tourist that he was not a movie star. When asked what he did, she replied, "He fixes things." Headed by a picture of cowboy star Roy Rogers and his two young sons in his workshop, the article went on to list the do-it-yourself exploits of a dozen male actors, several of whom were described as building things with and for their children.[99] The article observed that these residents of a town known for "wild parties and wild spending" were now "climbing out of their glamorous occupational trappings into levis and becoming Mr. Fixits."[100] By the end of the 1950s, it would seem that actors, the most highly visible examples of idealized American manhood, could be held up as models of frugality, practicality, family orientation, and manual work through their participation in the do-it-yourself movement that had brought men back into the home by turning their houses into hobbies.

NOTES

1. Claudia L. Bushman, *A Good Poor Man's Wife* (Hanover, N.H., 1981), 116–17; see also, Faye E. Dudden, *Serving Women: Household Service in Nineteenth Century America* (Middletown, Conn., 1983), 158; Margaret Marsh, "Suburban Men and Masculine Domesticity, 1870–1915," *American Quarterly* 40 (June 1988): 172.

2. Donald Katz, *Home Fires: An Intimate Portrait of One Middle-Class Family in Postwar America* (New York, 1992), 29.

3. Ibid., 71.

4. Mark Carnes and Clyde Griffen, "Constructions of Masculinity in Friendship and Marriage," in *Meanings for Manhood: Constructions of Masculinity in Victorian America*, ed. Mark Carnes and Clyde Griffen (Chicago, 1990), 83. None of the historical data used in this article acknowledged race, and they are presumed to refer to whites. Whether African Americans, or any other ethnic group, behaved differently is a question that remains to be explored.

5. For discussions of masculinity and the work place see Peter G. Filene, *Him/Her/Self Gender Identities in Modern America* (New York, 1974), 73; Peter N. Stearns, *Be a Man! Males in Modern Society* (New York, 1979), 47–48, 109, 131; Michael S. Kimmel, "The Contemporary 'Crisis' of Masculinity in Historical Perspective," in *The Making of Masculinities: The New Men's Studies*, ed. Harry Brod (Boston, 1987), 138–39; Ava Baron, "Acquiring Manly Competence: The Demise of Apprenticeship and the Remasculinization of Printers' Work," in Carnes and Griffen *Meanings for Manhood*, 152–63; Ava Baron, ed., *Work Engendered: Toward a New History of American Labor* (Ithaca, N.Y., 1991); Joe L. Dubbert, *A Man's Place: Masculinity in Transition* (Englewood Cliffs, N.J., 1979), 15–28; Anthony E. Rotundo, *American Manhood: Transformations in Masculinity from the Revolution to the Modern Era* (New York, 1993), 167–68.

6. U.S. Bureau of the Census, *Historical Statistics of the United States, Colonial Times to 1970*, Part 2 (Washington, D.C., 1975), 646.

7. Kimmel, "The Contemporary 'Crisis,' " 138.

8. Ileen A. DeVault, " 'Give the Boys a Trade': Gender and Job Choice in the 1890s," in Baron, *Work Engendered*, 211; see also Baron, "Acquiring Manly Competence," 153.

9. Mark Carnes and Clyde Griffen, "Introduction," in Carnes and Griffen, *Meanings for Manhood*, 6

10. Stearns, *Be a Man!* 47–48; Dubbert, *A Man's Place*, 15, 18, 22, 28; Mary H. Blewett, "Manhood and the Market: The Politics of Gender and Class Among the Textile Workers of Fall River," in Baron, *Work Engendered*, 94–95; Rotundo, *American Manhood*, 167–68.

11. Angel Kwolek-Folland, "Gender, Self, and Work in the Life Insurance Industry, 1880–1930," in Baron, *Work Engendered*, 176–77.

12. Mark C. Carnes, "Middle-Class Men and the Solace of Fraternal Ritual," in Carnes and Griffen, *Meanings for Manhood*. 38–39, 46–48.

13. Mary Ann Clawson, *Constructing Brotherhood: Class, Gender, and Fraternalism* (Princeton, N.J., 1989), 174.

14. Rotundo, *American Manhood*, 31–74; see also Dubbert, *A Man's Place*, 99, 143.

15. Jeffrey P. Hantover, "The Boy Scouts and the Validation of Masculinity," in *The American Man*, ed. Elizabeth H. Pleck and Joseph H. Pleck (Englewood Cliffs, N.J., 1980), 285–301.

16. Marsh, "Suburban Men," 166.

17. Ibid., 181.

18. For some isolated examples of male hobby craftsmanship in the nineteenth century, see "Napkins and Handicrafts," *Godey's Magazine and Lady's Book* 42 (February 1851): 127; and "Hobbies," *Arthur's Home Magazine* 8 (Sept. 1856): 167–68.

19. T. J. Jackson Lears, *No Place of Grace: Antimodernism and the Transformation of American Culture* (New York, 1981), 47–58; Ruth Ellen Levine, "The Influence of the Arts and Crafts Movement on the Professional Status of Occupational Therapy," *American Journal of Occupational Therapy* 41 (Apr. 1987): 240.

20. Ira S. Griffith, "Recreation With Tools," *Suburban Life* 10 (June 1910): 22; see also, John R. Stilgoe, *Borderland: Origins of the American Suburb 1820–1939* (Cambridge, Mass., 1988), 262.

21. Lears, *No Place of Grace*, 65.

22. Eileen Boris, *Art and Labor: Ruskin, Morris, and the Craftsman Ideal in America* (Philadelphia, 1986), 82–98; Paul Hopkins Rule, "Industrial Arts in Education for Leisure" (master's thesis, University of Washington, 1940): 20–23; M. F. Johnston, "Arts and Crafts in Civic Improvements," *Chautauquan* 43 (June 1906): 382; Edgar Morton, "Home Work Shop," *American Homes and Gardens* 9 (Oct. 1912): sup. 18; Lewis Flint Anderson, *History of Manual and Industrial School Education* (New York, 1926), 188–90, 198.

23. Ira S. Griffith, "Three Things to Make in Your Own Workshop," *Suburban Life* 13 (Nov. 1911): 269.

24. Ira S. Griffith, "Cabinet Making as a Handicraft," *Suburban Life* 7 (Sept. 1910): 346; see also, D. H. Culyer, "Making a Magazine Stand," *The Circle* 2 (July 1907): 48; Griffith, "Three Things to Make," 269; A. Neely Hall, *Handicraft for Handy Boys* (Boston: Lathrop, Lee & Shepard, 1911), 111.

25. Robert L. Griswold, *Fatherhood in America: A History* (New York, 1993), 13–17, 26.

26. See for example, Arthur Wakeling, ed., *Things to Make in Your Home Workshop* (New York, 1930), v; Emanuele Stieri, *Home Craftsmanship* (New York, 1935), 277.

27. U.S. Bureau of the Census, *Historical Statistics*, 646; Kenneth T. Jackson, *Crabgrass Frontier: The Suburbanization of the United States* (New York, 1985), 116–37, 157–71.

28. Richard Harris, "Working-Class Home Ownership in the American Metropolis," *Journal of Urban History* 17 (Nov. 1990): 58.

29. Ibid., 54.

30. Samuel Crowther, "Henry Ford: Why I Favor Five Days' Work With Six Days' Pay," *The World's Work* 52 (Oct. 1926): 615.

31. Rose C. Feld, "Now That They Have It," *Century Magazine* 108 (Oct. 1924): 753, 756.

32. Mary Sies notes that architect-designed (rather than home-made) household gadgets got their start a generation earlier. Mary Corbin Sies, "American Country House Architecture in Context: The Suburban Ideal of Living in the East and Midwest" (Ph.D. diss., University of Michigan, 1987): 110.

33. *Make It Yourself* (Chicago: Popular Mechanics Press, 1927).

34. Note for example the title of Walter J. Coppock, *Make Your Home Your Hobby* (Yellow Springs, Ohio, 1945).

35. Robert A. Stebbins, *Amateurs, Professionals, and Serious Leisure* (Montreal, 1992).

36. Henry H. Saylor, *Tinkering With Tools* (New York, 1924), 3–11.

37. Arthur Wakeling, ed., *Fix It Yourself* (New York, 1929), 5; Arthur Wakeling, ed., *Home Workshop Manual* (New York, 1930), 1–2.

38. J. Tate, "Tools for the Home Mechanic," *Make It Yourself* (Chicago: Popular Mechanics Press, 1927), 2.

39. Stilgoe, *Borderland*, 266–67; for example, see James Tate, "Soldering for the Home Mechanic," in *Make It Yourself*, 158; Wakeling, *Fix It Yourself*, 149.

40. Marge E. Staunton, "Marge Does it Herself!" *American Home* 18 (Aug. 1937): 42.

41. Martha Wirt Davis, "Some Tips for Mrs. Fixit," *American Home* 15 (Apr. 1936): 44.

42. J. C. Woodin, *Home Mechanics for Girls* (Wichita, Kans., 1938), iii; for girls using woodworking machinery in a school in the 1930s, see W. Brewer, "Boys Not Allowed," *Texas Outlook* 33 (Dec. 1949): 16–18.

43. Steven M. Gelber, "A Job You Can't Lose: Work and Hobbies in the Great Depression," *Journal of Social History* 24 (summer 1991): 741–66.

44. Arthur W. Wilson, "Home Hobbyists Offer a Market," *Printers' Ink* 163 (4 May 1933): 69; H. J. Hobbs, "51 Hours a Week," *Better Homes and Gardens* 12 (Jan. 1934): 24.

45. Harry J. Hobbs, *Working With Tools* (New York, 1935), 63; see also, Clemens T. Schaefer, "Home Mechanics," in *Hobbies for Everybody*. ed. Ruth Lampland (New York: Harper, 1934), 216; Wakeling, *Things to Make*, v.

46. *New York Times*, 10 Jan. 1937, X112.

47. Ibid., 9.

48. Barbara Melosh, "Manly Work: Public Art and Masculinity in Depression America," in *Gender and American History Since 1890*, ed. Barbara Melosh (London, 1993), 182–206; see also, Steven M. Gelber, "Working to Prosperity: California's New Deal Murals," *California History* 61 (summer 1979): 98–127.

49. M. A. Powell, "A Survey of the National Home Workshop Guild" (master's thesis, Colorado State College of Education, Greeley, 1935), 5, 20–21, 26, 28–29, 37; U.S. Bureau of the Census, *Historical Statistics*, 380.

50. Wakeling, *Fix It Yourself*, 233; For illustrations of these tools, see Wakeling, *Home Workshop*, 51–65.

51. "History of the Delta Specialty Company, Delta Manufacturing Company, Rockwell Manufacturing Company, Rockwell International, Delta International Machinery Corp." [timeline], Delta International Machinery Corp., n.d. [c. 1993]; John Allen Murphy, "Sales Boom in Hobby Goods," *American Business* 6 (May 1936): 51.

52. Murphy, 51, 55; Robert K. Leavitt, "Mr. Macy, Meet the Guppy . . . and Mr. Advertiser, Meet the Hobby," *Advertising and Selling* 21 (22 June 1933): 17.

53. "Millions in Power Tools for Craftsmen Hobbies," *Steel* 100 (17 May 1937): 28–29.

54. Dean F. Kittle, "Activities and Equipment Found in the Home Workshops of Sixty Boys in Lima, Ohio" (master's thesis, Iowa State College, 1936): 26.

55. Powell, "Survey," 53; see also, Kittle, "Activities and Equipment," 26; C. L. Page, "A Survey of the Home Workshops in Ottumwa, Iowa" (master's thesis, Colorado State College of Education, Greeley, 1941): 32.

56. "Millions in Power Tools," 28–29.

57. Dick Rarnsell, "Diary of a Desperate Daddy," *Better Homes & Gardens* 20 (May 1942): 22–23.

58. Harold J. Hawkins, "Fixing Things Around the House," *Parents' Magazine* 17 (Aug. 1942): 48–49.

59. Esther Boulton Black, "Confessions of a Hostess," *American Home* 28 (June 1942): 77: "Family's Day for Repairs," *Parents' Magazine* 16 (Feb. 1941): 55; see also, William

Klenke, *Furniture a Girl Can Make* (Kansas City, Mo., 1940), 7; *Giant Home Workshop Manual* (New York, 1941), 67.

60. Rachel McKinley Bushong, "Get Going! Not Brains, Not Talent, Not Skill—But Just Plain Work . . . Try It," *American Home* 25 (Mar. 1941): 30–31; see also Klenke, *Furniture a Girl Can Make*, 2; Ruth Wyeth Spears, *Let's Make a Gift* (New York, 1941).

61. Sabina Ormsby Dean, "It Didn't Take a War to Make a Carpenter Out of Mother," *House Beautiful* 85 (Oct. 1943): 118–19; see also *New York Times*, 27 Dec. 1942, II2; F. C. Minaker, "Promotion to Hold Customer Interest," *American Business* 12 (Mar. 1942): 40.

62. For background on the AWVS see, Janet Flanner, "Ladies in Uniform," *New Yorker* 18 (4 July 1942): 21–29.

63. Mary Mardison, "Fixing It Yourself," *New York Times Magazine* (7 Mar. 1943): 24; see also, "How to Fix It: Home Owners All Over U.S. Learn to Make Own Repairs." *Life* 15 (26 July 1943): 87–95; Mrs. Robert C. Baker, "Everywoman's Primer of Home Repairs," *House and Garden* 83 (Mar. 1943): 35–42; Arthur Bohnen, "Be Your Own Handyman: Maintenance—Not Repair," *American Home* 29 (Jan. 1943): 36–38.

64. S. S. Pheiffer, "Never Tell Your Wife," *House Beautiful* 86 (Nov. 1944): 160.

65. See for example, Stephanie Coontz, *The Way We Never Were: American Families and the Nostalgia Trap* (New York, 1992), 27; Arlene Skolnick, *Embattled Paradise: The American Family in an Age of Uncertainty* (New York, 1991), 52.

66. U.S. Bureau of the Census, *Historical Statistics*, 49.

67. Filene, *Him/Her/Self*, 169: Skolnick *Embattled Paradise*, 53; U.S. Bureau of the Census, *Historical Statistics*, 131.

68. H. L. May and D. Petgen, *Leisure and Its Uses* (New York, 1928); Clifford Edward Clark, Jr., *The American Family Home, 1800–1960* (Chapel Hill, N.C., 1986); Jackson, *Crabgrass Frontier*, 231–45; Gwendolyn Wright, *Building the American Dream: A Social History of Housing in America* (New York, 1981), 248–55; Albert Roland, "Do-It-Yourself: A Walden for the Millions?" *American Quarterly* 10 (spring 1985): 161.

69. Griswold, *Fatherhood in America*, 207; Skolnick, *Embattled Paradise*, 71; Filene, *Him/Her/Self*, 173.

70. For an extended discussion of gender and lawn care see Virginia Scott Jenkins, *The Lawn: A History of an American Obsession* (Washington, D.C., 1994), 117–32.

71. Reproduced in Donna R. Braden, *Leisure and Entertainment in America* (Dearborn, Mich., 1988), 107.

72. "New Do-It-Yourself Market," *Business Week* (14 June 1952): 70.

73. William Astor and Charlotte Astor, "Private Associations and Commercial Activities," *The Annals of the American Academy of Political and Social Science* 313 (Sept. 1957): 96.

74. Yiron Nelson Hukill, "The Do-It-Yourself Movement in Pulaski County, Arkansas and Its Implications for Industrial Arts" (Ed. D. diss., University of Missouri–Columbia, (1958): 39; Phil Creden, "America Rediscovers Its Hands," *The American Magazine* 156 (Dec. 1953): 111; Nathan Kelne, "Is Your Product Ripe for the Four Billion Dollar Do-It-yourself Market?" *Printers' Ink* 245 (12 Nov. 1953): 46; "Do-It-yourself Gives America a New Look," *Senior Scholastic* 64 (7 Apr. 1954): 14.

75. Kelne, "Is Your Product Ripe," 46; "Do-It-yourself Gives America," 14; *New York Times*, 3 Jan. 1955, 91; see also, "The Shoulder Trade," *Time* 63 (2 Aug. 1954): 66; U.S. Bureau of the Census. Housing and Construction Reports, Series H101, No. 1, *Alterations and Repairs*, "Expenditures on Residential Owner-Occupied Properties January to May 1954,' (Washington, D.C., 1954), 3, 5; "Off the Editor's Chest," *Consumer's Research*

Bulletin 34 (Nov. 1954): 2; "For Handymen Only," *Newsweek* 43 (April 26, 1954): 77; *New York Times*, 19 Sept. 1954, III7.

76. Wakeling, *Home Workshop*, 65.

77. *Highlights of Progress* (Towson, Md., 1992).

78. Leonard A. Stevens, "America's Most Popular Gadget," *Collier's* 134 (9 July 1954): 80–81.

79. Hukill, "The Do-It-Yourself Movement," 30; see also, Stevens, "America's Most Popular Gadget," 83; *How to Use Power Tools* (Greenwich, Conn., 1953), 116; Kittle, "Activities and Equipment," 28; Powell, "Survey," 53.

80. Quoted in Robert W. Winter, "The Arroyo Culture," *California Design, 1910*, ed. Timothy J. Anderson, Eudorah M. Moore, Robert W. Winter (Santa Barbara, CA: Peregrine Smith, 1980) 20.

81. "Armory Show 1953," *Harper's Magazine* 206 (May 1953): 93.

82. For example, see Reed Millard, "Hobbies That Hold Your Family Together,"*Coronet* 31 (Jan. 1952): 136–38.

83. Emanuele Stieri, *Complete Home Repair Book* (New York, 1950), 354–55; see also, Kelne, "Is Your Product Ripe," 48; Roger W. Babson, "Do It Yourself—A New Industry," *Commercial and Financial Chronicle* 177 (5 Mar. 1953): 1012; Darrell Huff, "We've Found a Substitute for Income," *Harper's Magazine* 207 (Oct. 1953): 28, 29.

84. "Do-it-yourself Gives America a New Look," 15–16; Walt Durbhan, "Our House is Different—Yours Can Be Too," *American Magazine* 157 (Jan. 1954): 73.

85. *How To Use Power Tools*, 9; for examples of woodworking by women, see: H. Gunderson, "Hobby Crafts for Adults," *Industrial Arts and Vocational Education* 39 (Nov. 1950): 341–42; Dorothy Lambert Trumm, "Pleasure From Your Leisure, and Why Not?," *American Home* 54 (July 1955): 31–33; Rose McAfee, "A Lady and a Jig Saw," *Profitable Hobbies* 11 (Feb. 1955): 2–5; Elizabeth Krusell Hall, "My Wood Working Hobby Paid Off," *American Home* 57 (Mar. 1957): 109–10.

86. Mary N. Borton, "Hobbies Can Build Character," *Parents Magazine* 26 (May 1951): 44–46; William G. Poole, "Coeducation Wood Shop," *Industrial Arts and Vocational Education* 47 (Sept. 1958): 205–6.

87. Hukill, "The Do-It-Yourself Movement," 65.

88. Ibid., 85–86; see also, Sprague Holden, "Education of a House Husband," *House Beautiful* 89 (Sept. 1947): 128.

89. Edward C. Fisher, "You're Going to Make a Chair," *Profitable Hobbies* 7 (Jan. 1951): 44–47.

90. "The ABC of Home Repair" [advertisement] *American Home* 31 (0Sept. 1945): 43.

91. For examples see, John Webster, "Handsome Furniture You Can Build," *Better Homes and Gardens* 29 (Mar. 1951): 258–59; *Build It* (Greenwich, Conn., 1954), 2, 66, 104–5; Henry Humphrey, ed., *Woman's Home Companion Household Book* (New York, 1950), 501; Herbert J. Gans, *The Levittowners: Ways of Life and Politics in a New York Suburban Community* (New York, 1967), 270; *New York Times*, 24 Oct. 1955, 24; *New York Times*, 9 Feb. 1958, IIII; "Sap Is Running in Do-It-Yourself," *Business Week* (27 Mar. 1954): 122; "What's New in Do-It-Yourself," *Changing Times* 10 (Feb. 1956): 37; Babson, "Do It Yourself," 1012.

92. Eugene Rachlis, "How Not to Do-It-Yourself," *New York Times Magazine* (15 Aug. 1954): VI, 34; but see also, *New York Times*, 19 Sept. 1954, VI4.

93. Rachlis, "How Not to," 34.

94. "Shoulder Trade," 64, 66; David Dempsey, "Home Sweet (Homemade) Homes,"

New York Times Magazine (31 Mar. 1957): 26; Huff, "We've Found," see illustrations by Julius Kroll, 27, 29; *New York Times*, 10 Sept. 1955, 32.

95. Sprague Holden, "Education of a House Husband," *House Beautiful* 89 (Sept. 1947): 129; see also, V. C. Barnett, "Hints for the Gentleman Mechanic: or, How to Use a Tinker's Dam," *Better Homes and Gardens* 25 (May 1947): 190–93; "Off the Editor's Chest," 29; Margaret E. Mulac, *Hobbies: The Creative Use of Leisure* (New York, 1959).

96. Dempsey, "Home," 71.

97. See for examples, Huff, "We've Found," 28; Francis Coughlin, "Is There a Handyman Handy?" *Science Digest* 43 (Mar. 1958): 72.

98. Julian Starr, Jr., *Fifty Things to Make for the Home* (New York, 1941), 3–5.

99. Julian Tusher, "Do It Yourself . . . Hollywood Does," *Popular Mechanics* 112 (Aug. 1959): 125–29; for earlier and somewhat more modest versions of the star-as-craftsman, see: "Our Hobby Parade: 68 Unusual American Collections," *House and Garden* 82 (July 1942): 43; Kay Campbell, "And What's Your Hobby?" *American Home* 37 (Apr. 1947): 32–36. Some of these stories may have been the result of a deliberate campaign by the Screen Actors' Guild to promote family values, see Coontz, *The Way We Never Were*, 27–28.

100. Tusher, "Do It Yourself," 126.

Chapter Five

Archival Material
Playboy's Penthouse Apartment

A man yearns for quarters of his own. More than a place to hang his hat, a man dreams of his own domain, a place that is exclusively his. PLAYBOY has designed, planned and decorated, from the floor up, a penthouse apartment for the urban bachelor—a man who enjoys good living, a sophisticated connoisseur of the lively arts, of food and drink and congenial companions of both sexes. A man very much, perhaps, like you. In such a place, you might live in elegant comfort, in a man's world which fits your moods and desires, which is a tasteful, gracious setting for an urbane personality. Here is the key. Let's use it together and take a tour of discovery.

It is just after dark on an evening with a tang of autumn in the air. The front door (that's at the lower left) takes us into a hallway with a facing wall of primavera panels. One slides easily aside, a light goes on automatically within and we hang our topcoats in a dust-proof closet. To our right is an illuminated aquarium and a wall-and-ceiling skylight, lending a romantic atmosphere to the entrance-way, and to our left, at the end of the hall, the apartment beckons warmly.

Coming down the hallway, we are able to view the entire width of the apartment and through the open casements, see the terrace and the winking towers of the city beyond. Then, quite suddenly, we are in the apartment proper—a modern kitchen adjoins the dining room and before us is the main living area.

The fire in the raised and recessed Swedish grate casts a magnetic glow on the couch facing it, forming an intimately confined area, a romantic setting for a tête-à-tête. The floor beneath us is cork tile. The smooth plaster wall is in dramatic contrast to the stone hearth, which has a painting on its right and a raised planter with climbing vine on its left. The apartment's sense of masculine richness and excitement stems in part from such juxtapositions of textures—the smooth wall, the stone, the planter, the cork floor—and for visual impact the unadorned brick wall which closes off the bath and the kitchen area. Turn to the window wall. Here's drama and contrast again, a view of the city through casements richly hung with white dacron and slate gray silk shantung overdrapes. Below these are continuous hanging storage cabinets.

The rest of the living room is best seen by utilizing a unique feature of the couch. It flips, literally: at the touch of a knob on its end, the back becomes seat and vice versa—and now we're facing the other way. Immediately before us are four low square tables, placed together. Each has a foam rubber cushion. Right now, two of the tables are being used as such and two for seating; with all four cushions in place, it becomes a large area for very casual lounging; with all cushions removed, it serves as a low table for drinks for up to eight guests sozzled enough to be sitting on the floor. A Saarinen couch and the classic Saarinen armchair with Versen floor lamp complete a charmed circle, a conversational grouping held together texturally and visually by the deep-pile green nylon rug. And remember the foyer closet where we hung our things? We're now facing its living room side, a fourteen-foot wall faced with two-foot-square primavera panels, with flush-mounted color TV and built-in stereophonic speakers and hi-fi components behind them. This is our electronic entertainment installation. From it, lines go to individual speaker installations in every room, each with its own on-off and volume control. Here we can stack mood-music recordings on the automatic changer, or flood the apartment with music for dancing. Or, if the occasion calls for serious listening—to Bach or Baker— we switch to the manually-operated transcription turntable and pick up for the highest in fi. Here, too, are long-and short-wave radio tuners, FM tuner and tape recorder. Also, movie and stereo projectors that can throw pictures on a beaded screen which lines the back of the painting by the fireplace.

And speaking of entertainment one of the hanging Knoll cabinets beneath the windows holds a built-in bar. This permits the canny bachelor to remain in the room while mixing a cool one for his intended quarry. No chance of missing the proper psychological moment—no chance of leaving her cozily curled up on the couch with her shoes off and returning to find her mind changed, purse in hand, and the young lady ready to go home, damn it. Here, conveniently at hand, too, is a self-timing rheostat which will gradually and subtly dim the lights to fit the mood—as opposed to the harsh click of a light switch that plunges all into sudden darkness and may send the fair game fleeing.

The same advance thinking prompted the placing of an on-off widget for the phone within the cabinet, too, so that the jangling bell or, what's worse, a chatty call from the date of the night before, won't shatter the spell being woven. (Don't worry about missing out on any fun this way: there's a phone-message-taker hooked to the tape recorder.)

The PLAYBOY apartment brings back the dining room—done away with in many another modern apartment—but this is a dining room with multiple functions. For intimate dining *à deux* and in style, the four-leaf Mathesson gateleg table can have just one leaf raised. For less intimate occasions—say a midnight after-theater snack—the Shoji screens which close off the kitchen may be rolled back, and the kitchen's island counter becomes a cozy, handy spot to set up chafing dish and silver ice bucket in which nestles a bottle of Mumm's Gold Label.

For large formal dinners, the Mathesson table can be expanded to seat twelve, but for casual get-togethers or big informal parties it folds practically flat against a wall, where one leaf can be raised for cold or hot buffet.

It is when we wish to host a host of folks that the flexibility of the apartment's separate areas comes into full play. By moving aside the Saarinen chair, which acts as a psychological room divider between living and dining rooms, by rolling back the kitchen's Shoji screens and opening the terrace windows, all these areas become united and we can entertain half a hundred, if we've a mind. This is possible because the apartment is not divided into cell-like rooms, but into function areas well delineated for relaxation, dining, cooking, wooing and entertaining, all interacting and yet inviting individual as well as simultaneous use.

Consider again the dining room's multiple uses. Obviously, it's ideal for a full-production gala dinner, as no "dining alcove" is. Or, with its pull-down globe lighting, it's perfect for all-night poker games, stag or strip. Yet we've seen how simple it is to join it to the living room. Similarly, the kitchen may be closed off from the other rooms by pulling closed the sliding screens. But since the urban male prides himself on his culinary artistry it may, more often, be open onto the dining room, so the host can perform for an admiring audience while sharing in conversation.

And now let's enter the kitchen. Your first thought may be: where is everything? It's all there, as you shall see, but all is neatly stowed and designed for efficiency with the absolute minimum of fuss and hausfrau labor. For this is a bachelor kitchen, remember, and unless you're a very odd-ball bachelor indeed, you like to cook and whomp up short-order specialties to exactly the same degree that you actively dislike dishwashing, marketing and tidying up. All that's been taken care of here. Let's look it over.

Notice, first, that it's clean and functional, but doesn't have the antiseptic, medical look of so many modern kitchens. The walls are smooth gray, the floor of vinyl. Those hinged wood panels on the rear wall house a vertical freezer where you'll keep frozen fruits, vegetables, seafood, game, and plenty of meat. Even if your apartment's a haven for drop-in guests as well as planned pleasures, there's ample space here for weeks of good eating. Next to the freezer is a vertical wine bin, a honeycomb framework which holds the bottles horizontally. There's sufficient capacity here so you can exercise your canny skills in finding buys in, say, a special half case of rosé, a rich Burgundy that's on sale, or a few choice bottles of vintage Riesling—just right to go with your tossed-greens salad. Below the wine, which is stored hand height, are compartments for larger bottles, i.e., your stronger potations and *vin ordinaire,* which you order in bulk and pour as needed into decanters. Next come dry-storage shelves and a utility closet where your once-a-week servant stores brooms and vacuum.

And now we come to something you're going to like: that standing white cabinet in the center of the wall is an ultrasonic dishwasher. Stack its rack with greasy dishes, with glasses that bear the imprint of a lipsticky kiss, with eggy knives and forks. Shut the door and all is bathed in water and bombarded by ultrasonic sound waves which remove all dirt. Next in the automatic dish-doing cycle is warm-air drying and ultra-violet sterilization. And now we're ready to put the dishes away—but we don't have to. Relax. Light up. Talk to your girl. Play a Stan Kenton recording. The dishes stay right where they are, behind the panel, ready for their next use, since this machine also acts as a storage unit.

And now for the damndest island counter you've ever seen. At one end is a radiant broiler-roaster. Here, under the transparent dome, you can broil a four-inch sirloin or roast a pheasant—or a standing rib roast—to a turn, with all fumes drawn off and out of the house by a built-in blower which turns on when you turn on the heat. Lifting the hinged dome automatically brings the base of the unit to counter height. It's our bet that the manipulation of this broiler, and the sight through the dome of a sizzling steak, will prove for your guests a rival attraction to the best on TV. And you'll be the director of this show.

From the broiler on down the counter, for about half its length, is a smooth Carrara glass surface on which you can sit or lean—if you have no keys or coins in your pockets or ring on your finger. Because this, believe it or not, is your stove, although there's not a burner in sight and it's stone cold even when it's on. That's because it heats only metallic objects in its field, by induction; it's the pots and pans that do the cooking, not the stove top and you can be mixing a cool salad right beside a hot pot of potatoes. Pilot lights beneath the translucent glass top wink on or off to show what cooks when you twiddle the dials on the dashboard.

Beneath the stove and work counter is more storage space, hand-height utensil drawers and, down toward the vertical freezer, a refrigerator to hold a few days' food, chilled mixers, beer and soft drinks, your pre-chilled Martini beaker and vermouth atomizer, canapés and cheeses, and an ample supply of ice cubes.

Playboy's Penthouse Apartment

A MAN'S HOME is not only his castle, it is or should be, the outward reflection of his inner self—a comfortable, livable, and yet exciting expression of the person he is and the life he leads. But the overwhelming percentage of homes are furnished by women. What of the bachelor and his need for a place to call his own? Here's the answer, PLAYBOY's penthouse apartment, home for a sophisticated man of parts, a fit setting for his full life and a compliment to his guests of both sexes. Here a man, perhaps like you, can live in masculine elegance.

At first glance, it obviously looks like a hell of a fine place to live and love and be merry, a place to relax in alone or to share for intimate hours with some lucky lass, a wonderful setting for big or small parties—in short, a bachelor's dream place. It is all these, but it's more, too—thanks to the fact that it doesn't follow the conventional plan of separated rooms for various purposes. Instead, there are two basic areas, an active zone for fun and partying and a quiet zone for relaxation, sleep and such.

The living room, with its cozy shadow-box fireplace suggests a tête-à-tête on the couch—but it's just as inviting to a cordial crowd of fellow hi-fi enthusiasts. The electronic entertainment center, recessed in the giant storage wall that separates living room from foyer, contains binaural hi-fi, FM, TV, tape recorder, movie and slide projectors. And merely moving that blue Saarinen armchair makes living room and dining room one—for gala entertaining. Kitchen and dining room, too, many be used separately or together, thanks to the sliding Shoji screens which divide them. These areas comprise the apartment's active zone, which was described in detail last month.

A huge bed dominates the penthouse bedroom. This is a magnificent sleeping

Fig. 5.1. Playboy's Penthouse Apartment. Copyright © 1956 by Playboy.

platform of veneer plywood on steel legs, 8 feet long and 4½ feet wide. The 4" airfoam mattress stops short enough of the foot so that the platform's end serves as a bench on which to slouch while donning or doffing shoes and socks.

Casement windows stretch across one entire wall, framing an ever-changing, living mural of our man's city. In the corner nook formed by windows and the Modernfold door which closes off the study, is a charmed circle where a bachelor may have a romantic nightcap with a chosen guest. Grouped here are a Saarinen chair (the mate of the one in the living room), a walnut Eames chair and free-form Noguchi table. Across from you (but hidden in the illustration by the brick wall) is a hanging wall cabinet wherein is cannily concealed a built-in bar and small refrigerator, just large enough for ice cubes, mixers and midnight snacks—a boon to the barefoot bachelor in PJs who's reluctant to trek to the kitchen for his good-night potation, or perhaps unwilling to interrupt the dulcet dialogue he's been sharing.

Now, we've sipped the nocturnal dram and it is bed time; having said "nighty-night" (or "come along, now, dearest") to the last guest, it's time to sink into the arms of Morpheus (or a more comely substitute). Do we go through the house turning out the lights and locking up? No sir: flopping on the luxurious bed, we have within easy reach the multiple controls of its unique headboard. Here we have silent mercury switches and a rheostat that control every light in the place and can subtly dim the bedroom lighting to just the right romantic level. Here, too, are the switches which control the circuits for front door and terrace window locks. Beside them are push buttons to draw the continuous, heavy, pure-linen, lined draperies on sail track, which can insure darkness at morn—or noon. Above are built-in speakers fed by the remotely-controlled hi-fi and radio based in the electronic entertainment installation in the living room. On either side of the bed are storage cupboards with doors that hinge downward to create bedside tables. Within are telephone, with on-off switch for the bell, and miscellaneous bed-time items. Soft mood music flows through the room and the stars shine in the casements as you snuggle down.

At the start of a new day, the chime alarm sounds, morning music comes on and the headboard's automatic controls again prove their value: reaching lazily to the control panel, you press the buttons for the kitchen circuits and immediately the raw bacon, eggs, bread and ground coffee you did the right things with the night before (while the ultrasonic washer was doing the dishes) start their metamorphosis into crisp bacon, eggs fried just right, and steaming-hot fresh java. Now you flip the switch that draws the curtains and opens the terrace doors to let in the brisk morning air. Don't just lie there, man, rise and shine!

Even a bachelor in his own domain needs a place like our apartment's study, where he can get away from the rest of the house and be really alone, where if he wishes he can leave papers on the desk in seeming disarray (actually in that precious disorder in which he alone can lay hands on just what he wants). This is the sanctum sanctorum, where women are seldom invited, where we can work or read or just sit and think while gazing into the fireplace.

With a study like this, even the most dedicated pub crawler or theatre and nightclub buff will be tempted to stay at home of an evening, content within his own surroundings and savoring the city's glamour via the enchanted view from the window wall. But suppose the playboy master of the house decides that now, with the winter season starting, he wants to hold a real big shindig. By folding back that accordion door between study and bedroom the two are merged into one magnificent room, with the continuous carpeting from end to end and the matched draperies tying it all together. Now the whole apartment's a grownup's playground for rollicking, fancy-free fun 'til down lights the windows and it's time for prairie oysters and breakfast.

Throughout the apartment, its strikingly different atmosphere is achieved by the bold though harmonious use of solid color and interesting texture. Entering the bedroom from the living room we are immediately aware of the textural difference between the living room's cork floor and the luxurious wall-to-wall carpeting of the bedroom, which seems to invite a barefoot romp but which also bespeaks rich smartness. The dramatic brick wall between living room and bath projects into the quiet area, establishing visual continuity between the apartment's two zones and providing a sight barrier between the living room and the sleeping area of the bedroom, just as the headboard unit visually separates sleeping and dressing. Lighting—ample and glareless—is provided by those conical fixtures called "top hats," which are recessed into the ceiling at strategic locations. Lamps, which would impede the clean, open look of the place, are virtually dispensed with: there is a complete absence of bric-a-brac, patterned fabrics, pleats and ruffles.

This is the kind of pre-planning in design and furnishing which makes PLAYBOY's penthouse apartment a bachelor haven of virile good looks, a place styled for a man of taste and sophistication. This is *his* place, to fit his moods, suit his needs, reflect his personality. *ironic, Playboy's personality NOT the man's.*

Part Two

You Are What You Buy
Individual and Group Identity through Proper Consumption

This part explores perhaps the most puzzling issue related to gender and consumer culture: the ways in which consumers seek, and products and their marketers offer, identities through purchasing. As Yiannis Gabriel and Tim Lang put it, "[C]onsumers are, above all, frequently presented as thirsting for identity and using commodities to quench this thirst."[1] According to this view, consumers literally absorb images and goods in their own quests for individual and group identity in life. Steven Heinze's essay in Part One explores the ways in which Jewish immigrants found an American identity through purchasing. "For the context of immigration," Heinze writes, "the consumption of American products becomes a visible way to express a change in identity, as newcomers transfer themselves psychologically from the old world to the new."[2] Perhaps *psychologically* is the key word here, as the discussion of identity and consumer culture by necessity points to the psychological connections people make with themselves and each other through the culture of consumption.

Neither the purchasers nor the process, however, lend themselves to a simple explanation. A working-class woman does not once and for all acquire the identity of a wealthy sophisticate through her purchase of a particular perfume or handbag. An "average guy" does not once and for all acquire the identity of a debonair man-about-town through the purchase of a particular automobile or brand of whiskey. In fact, we put on and take off identities over the course of a day, at work, at play, at home, much as we put on and remove clothing. At times we may feel that we shed our identities at the same time that we shed our suits: the business woman at work in a suit becomes the athletic woman at the gym in spandex, the shopper at the mall in jeans and a sweater, and the relaxed person at home in sweatpants and sweatshirt.

The identities we purchase are fluid, as are our desires. Advertisers continue to offer us distinct identities through products, and we choose and discard those identities and those purchases as we ourselves grow and change, make new friends, or pass through new stages in life. Advertisers speak of "brand loyalty," the commitment on the part of consumers that draws them back over years to the same product. While they may count on that loyalty, advertisers do not take it for granted. Instead, they attempt to maintain brand loyalty by continually devising appeals to us based on what they know to be our changing realities and identities. The reasons one chooses a particular brand of cigarettes at age seventeen, for example, are not the same reasons one chooses that brand or another at age forty. As Gabriel and Lang assert, "Urban living, anonymous organizations, impersonal work, mass production, social and physical movement, the proliferation of choice, in short modernity itself conspires against fixed identities."[3] Identity comes from many aspects of our life experiences, including our engagement with consumer culture, and it is constructed continuously through those life experiences and that engagement. In fact, some scholars argue that today's postmodern consumers seek not one but multiple identities and feel quite comfortable putting them on and taking them off. "They are content with diverse personas, all products of artifice, all inauthentic, often at odds with each other. Schizophrenia becomes a perennial condition for the postmodern consumer."[4] Others see consumer goods as bridges individuals use between their real and their ideal selves.[5]

Consumers also mediate what it is to be female or male through consumption. Some women will not go out of the house without first putting on makeup. Clearly they feel that makeup makes them female—that their identity as female is dependent, at least in part, on cosmetics. What, then, does it really mean to be female? Is femaleness determined biologically, culturally, or in the marketplace? Does that consumer culture definition of female work in women's favor, allowing them the freedom to put on and take off identities at will, or does it work against them, furthering cultural insecurities in the groups of women who do wear makeup and the groups of women who do not?[6]

Inevitably offerings of identity such as these will leave out as many people as they invite in, collide with other identities, and effect alienation from as well as affinity with consumer culture and culture at large. Early Hollywood films and the cinemas they played in, for example, functioned in consumer culture by inviting certain people in as spectators and consumers. These audiences, working-class and middle-class white Americans (at least at first), responded positively to films that depicted people who looked and acted like them as morally and intellectually superior to those who did not look and act like them. One of the first groups to feel the "outsider status" of identity through consumption was Mexicans and Chicanos, who functioned in these films as a counterpoint to whites and as "the vilest of characters, who indulged in banditry, pillage, plundering, rape, and murder." The portrayals were so severe that the Mexican government banned many films in 1922 after filing a written protest in 1919 that went unheeded.[7]

As the essays that follow demonstrate, the acquisition of identity through purchasing is a complicated and contentious endeavor. In these discussions, white Americans purchase identity through the consumption of images of American Indians; white colonial subjects purchase identity through the consumption of images of black colonial subjects; white lesbians purchase identity through the consumption of black lesbian territory; and men seek identity through the conformity of khakis. Consumer culture offers "choice," but that choice is often predicated on difference, and the differences depicted fall into stereotypical divisions of race, gender, and class. The offer of one type of identity may well be accompanied by visions of an identity to be had by not engaging with the consumer culture at this moment: sophisticated versus unworldly, male versus female, white versus person of color, American versus foreign. Such dichotomous representations have worked well in consumer culture and continue both to defy and to misrepresent changing realities.[8]

The first essay in this part, "Reduced to Images: American Indians in Nineteenth-Century Advertising," by Jeffrey Steele, explores the ways in which images of American Indians were used both to marginalize the cultural position of Native Americans and to buttress the position of the white consumer.[9] As Steele explains it, for white people the process of gaining identity as citizens in the nineteenth century was also the process of gaining identity as consumers. As with the immigrants in Heinze's study, white Americans dealt with their own insecurities and with changing social realities by accepting the definition that consumer equals citizen. Advertising provided images to further that definition; in this case, images of American Indians proliferated and, in the contrast they provided to white consumers, offered clear pictures of who the consumer "naturally" was and was not.

Steele's study focuses on advertising trade cards, which, like Wild West shows and minstrel shows, turned groups of Americans into fetishized images that "satisfied the hunger for entertainment and disposable commodities."[10] The fact that American Indians had what was considered exotic appeal made them "a natural vehicle" for advertising, which sought to reach people's fantasies about themselves and about the marginalized "other."[11] These trade cards are particularly important in that, ephemeral as they were meant to be, they were unattached to newspapers or magazines and thus free of the editorial constraints that might have contained their use of stereotypes. In an era of tremendous social change and insecurity, when white Americans preferred to view Native Americans as savages in tribal costume rather than as their neighbors and fellow citizens, these trade cards provided them the images with which to maintain the most egregious stereotypes both of Native Americans and, by contrast, of themselves.

The second essay in this part, "Soft-Soaping Empire: Commodity Racism and Imperial Advertising," by Anne McClintock,[12] explores some similar themes to those explored in the Steele essay. In this case, McClintock's setting is early twentieth-century Britain, and the advertisements she explores offer, in a troubled empire, redemption through consumption. McClintock traces a shift from scientific racism, in which people are determined as different based on real or imaginary biological differences, to commodity racism, in which the market introduces and cements racial differences. In this case, the Victorian middle-class home is linked with and contrasted to the British colonies, Africa in particular, and the people who live there. McClintock's examination of soap advertising reveals the ways in which white identity is developed and furthered by contrast with black identity, in a colonial context, and through organized racism. Soap becomes the link, and advertising agents act as the "empire builders" who bring their products and their images of British superiority to the unwashed African masses and to the "clean" British consumer.[13]

McClintock's essay also explores the concept of the "fetish" in advertising. In this case, four fetishes—soap, a mirror, light, and white clothing—function to naturalize imperialism and to further British unity through consumer culture. Soap, the commodity, functions as the cleansing agent that keeps the white male colonizer clean and "white," and as the symbol of whiteness, supposedly eagerly embraced by blacks in the colonies. The mirror provides the white colonial agent with the reassurance of his own identity as he interacts with those people of color. The light signifies both rationality and spirituality as defined by the British. Finally, the white clothing provides further validation of whiteness in general. Pears' soap, in one ad, is literally introduced as "a potent factor in brightening the dark corners of the earth." Interestingly, as McClintock reveals, the images of domesticity offered in the service of commodity culture erase the female who, most likely, would actually use the product. Race and gender and nation work in fascinating ways in this exploration of identity through engagement with consumer culture.

The third essay, "Lesbian Chic: Experimentation and Repression in the 1920s," by Lillian Faderman,[14] explores the ways in which sexual expression was linked with consumer culture in the 1920s. Freudianism invaded U.S. culture in the 1910s and 1920s, and sexual experimentation accompanied the cultural discourse that viewed sexuality as natural for women as well as for men. Faderman describes as "lesbian chic" the bisexual experimentation that went on during the decade of the 1920s and the connection between white bisexual or lesbian women, black bisexual or lesbian women, and black culture in Harlem at the time. In this case, a disenfranchised group of white people saw in Harlem, a black location, some of the freedom to explore sexuality that they did not feel in their own neighborhoods. Since it already functioned as a "synonym for naughtiness" in the white imagination, Harlem had a particular appeal that few examined critically but many participated in eagerly. White women felt that Harlem gave them the permission to act on their desires; perhaps, instead, they took permission to act on their desires in that location. The ways in which these women purchased identities and purchased a location in which to act them out reveals a great deal about the relationship between Harlem and the larger city of New York, the relationship between white women and black culture, and the ways in which mutual "minority" status can provide opportunities for tolerance, if not acceptance.

Faderman's essay also explores the culture of black lesbians in Harlem, where the relative tolerance that formed one aspect of the culture's resistance to racism permitted black lesbians "to socialize openly in their own communities instead of seeking alien turf as white lesbians generally felt compelled to do."[15] Exploring the relationship between open discussions of sexuality and the blues tradition, the essay reveals the ways in which women used consumer culture to talk openly about sexual desires and sexual practices, including lesbianism. Interestingly, although many black women in Harlem were bisexual, they put into the public context lesbian identity, as that was considered more provocative and, perhaps, a "better sell." As Faderman explains, Harlem provided a location where black and white women alike could purchase an identity of sexual freedom and experimentation, where they "could pretend, at least, that the 1920s was a decade of true sexual rebellion and freedom."[16]

The fourth essay in this part, "Consumerism and the Construction of Black

Female Identity in Twentieth-Century America," by Robert Weems,[17] relates specifically to the Steele and McClintock articles that precede it. Whereas McClintock's examination of imperial advertising reveals the ways in which white consumers purchased white identity, Weems explores the different ways in which black women have responded to seemingly similar invitations. In a historical analysis of cosmetics and hair care products marketed to black women, Weems argues that although a cursory glance at cosmetics advertising might suggest that black women indeed sought whiteness through the use of these products, both the invitations they received and their own decisions to purchase provide a more complex picture. Steele's essay on Native Americans and advertising ends when Native Americans receive their first invitations to participate in the consumer culture; Weems's essay begins in a similar place, as advertisers responded to the buying power and promise of African American women with invitations to purchase cosmetics.

The use of personal care and beauty products by African American women has long been a contentious cultural issue. Advertisements for these products were the richest contracts for the Negro Press in the first decades of the twentieth century and remain an important source of advertising revenue today. At the same time, the equation of the use of hair straighteners and skin lighteners with a quest for whiteness has been debated in academic circles and in many people's everyday lives. What identity did and do black women purchase, for example, when they straighten their hair? And what of the businesses that seem to invite African American women to purchase whiteness? Weems explores the approaches to black women taken by both black- and white-owned businesses over the course of the twentieth century. He finds that black-owned businesses approached black women as beautiful whereas white-owned businesses approached black women as potentially beautiful. Because of this tremendous difference in approach, Weems argues, black women today would benefit from some economic nationalism as they participate in the consumer culture.

The fifth and final essay in Part Two, "Listening to Khakis: What America's Most Popular Pants Tell Us about the Way Guys Think," by Malcolm Gladwell,[18] explores the still-ambivalent relationship American men have with the culture of consumption. Gladwell analyzes the Dockers campaign, one of the most successful advertising campaigns in U.S. history. As he puts it, "This is a remarkable fact for a number of reasons, not the least of which is that the Dockers campaign was aimed at men, and no one had even thought you could hit a home run like that trying to sell fashion to the American male."[19] Male identity and consumer identity, in spite of the best efforts of *Esquire* and *Playboy* and contemporary advertisers, are still only loosely linked in today's culture of consumption.

Gladwell's essay reveals the distinct reasons for the success of the Dockers campaign. Since men are not eager to be seen as consumers, the ads sell sameness rather than the variety often promoted in consumer culture. As he argues, one cannot imagine a successful clothing line targeted at women where the uniformity of the product would be one of its most significant selling points. Men, however, do not want to be seen as too interested in their clothing, so Dockers, which do not vary from size to size or season to season, appeal to them. The advertising campaign succeeded so well because it sold men an identity that underemphasized rather than accentuated their individuality. It also sold men images of male friendship, something that baby boomer men seem to lack in their real lives. Gladwell's analysis provides an example of how one advertising campaign provides consumers with identity, part of which corresponds to their real lives and part of which corresponds to their imagined lives. In this case and several others mentioned by Gladwell, unlike the case of African American women described by Weems, the consumers apparently did respond to the invitations to consume on the terms offered them by advertisers.

The archival material in this section, two advertisements from the 1920s, provides visual representations of some of the issues raised in the essays. The Paramount Pictures ad provides consumer identities for several groups and individuals: the family, the married couple, the children, the wife, the husband. Each has a particular and well-defined relationship to the domestic sphere as it is mediated through consumer culture. In this case, the implication is that men and boys will, with invitations only consumer culture can provide, accept definitions of themselves that include domestic responsibility. It is the consumer culture, rather than women's complaints or their own realizations of privilege, that will draw men and boys into the kitchen. The Linit soap advertisement juxtaposes the white consuming woman with the black servant woman. Their relationships to each other are also mediated through consumer culture; in fact, the placement of the two white women and the one black woman makes clear that outside consumer culture they have little, if any, relationship at all. The white woman consumes the product and white identity through her ability to have the black woman both in and not in her domestic space. These two advertisements offer clear visual images of the problematic and complex ways in which identity is conceptualized, offered, and purchased in consumer culture.

NOTES

1. Yiannis Gabriel and Tim Lang, *The Unmanageable Consumer: Contemporary Consumption and Its Fragmentation* (Thousand Oaks, CA: Sage, 1995), 81.

2. Steven Heinze, *Adapting to Abundance: Jewish Immigrants, Mass Consumption, and the Search for American Identity* (New York: Columbia University Press, 1990), 8.

3. Gabriel and Lang, *Unmanageable Consumer*, 85.

4. Ibid., 91.

5. See Grant McCracken, *Culture and Consumption: New Approaches to the Symbolic Character of Consumer Goods and Activities* (Bloomington: Indiana University Press, 1988).

6. See Kathy Peiss, "Making Up, Making Over: Cosmetics, Consumer Culture, and Women's Identity," in *The Sex of Things: Gender and Consumption in Historical Perspective*, ed. Victoria de Grazia and Ellen Furlough (Berkeley: University of California Press, 1996), 311–336.

7. Clint C. Wilson and Felix Gutierrez, eds., *Race, Multiculturalism, and the Media* (Thousand Oaks, CA: Sage, 1995), 73, 75.

8. On the ways in which Japanese culture has functioned as either "aestheticized" or

"demonized" culture for consumption in American films, see Sumiko Higashi, "Touring the Orient with Lafcadio Hearn and Cecil B. DeMille: Highbrow Versus Lowbrow in a Consumer Culture," in Daniel Bernardi, ed., *The Birth of Whiteness: Race and the Emergence of U.S. Cinema* (New Brunswick, NJ: Rutgers University Press, 1996), 329–353.

9. Jeffrey Steele, "Reduced to Images: American Indians in Nineteenth-Century Advertising," originally published in S. Elizabeth Bird, ed., *Dressing in Feathers: The Construction of the Indian in American Popular Culture* (Boulder, CO: Westview Press, 1995), 45–64.

10. Ibid., 45–46.

11. Ibid., quoting Robert Jay, 48.

12. Anne McClintock, "Soft-Soaping Empire: Commodity Racism and Imperial Advertising," originally published as chapter 5 of her *Imperial Leather: Race, Gender, and Sexuality in the Colonial Contest* (NY: Routledge, 1994), 207–231.

13. Ibid., 214.

14. Lillian Faderman, "Lesbian Chic: Experimentation and Repression in the 1920s," originally published as chap. 3 of her *Odd Girls and Twilight Lovers: A History of Lesbian Life in Twentieth-Century America* (New York: Columbia University Press, 1991), 67–72.

15. Ibid., 73.

16. Ibid., 67.

17. Robert Weems, Jr., "Consumerism and the Construction of Black Female Identity in Twentieth-Century America," originally published in this book.

18. Malcolm Gladwell, "Listening to Khakis," originally published in the *New Yorker*, July 28, 1997, 54–65.

19. Ibid., 54.

Chapter Six

Reduced to Images
American Indians in Nineteenth-Century Advertising

Jeffrey Steele

Stereotypes sell. To this day, consumers recognize the stylized Indian chief on cans of Calumet baking powder and the kneeling Indian maiden on packages of Land O'Lakes butter. The athletic fortunes of the Braves, Indians, Chiefs, Redskins, and Black Hawks are followed by professional sports fans across the country. In the past, images of Indian warriors, chiefs, and maidens helped to market products as diverse as Bow-Spring dental rubber, Hiawatha canned corn, Cherokee coal, Red Warrior axes, and Savage rifles.[1] From the late nineteenth century to the present, numerous manufacturers, promoters, and advertisers have chosen the image of an American Indian to symbolize their products. Although some of these symbols and trademarks were designed as recently as the 1950s, the majority date from the period 1870–1910—the era of warfare and legislation that effectively contained American Indian cultures on the margins of U.S. society.

This containment of cultures is evident in the forms of racialized entertainment that arose in the closing decades of the century. Emerging at roughly the same time, the minstrel show and the Wild West show both reinforced racial stereotypes during an era when the roles of African-Americans and American Indians were rapidly changing. After the departure of federal troops from the South during the 1870s, the civil and voting rights of American blacks became the source of violent contention. With their images of happy slaves and benign songs and dances, minstrel shows helped to perpetuate the myth that the old days of plantation slavery represented the high point in black-white relations. In answer to the more disturbing racial anxieties of the time (such as those expressed in the growing epidemic of lynchings), the images of happy, banjo-playing plantation laborers reassured viewers that "blacks were under control."[2]

In many respects, Wild West shows, with their mock combats showing the defeat of Indian warriors, enacted a similar containment. Maintaining the illusion that American Indians dwelled in regions far removed from eastern urban centers, extravaganzas like "The Wild West: Buffalo Bill's and Doc Carver's Mountain and Prairie Exhibition" constructed "the image of the Plains Sioux as the quintessential American Indian."[3] From the safety of their seats in the grandstand, viewers were exposed to "Indians as savages from a wild land . . . inimical to civilization"; in one scene, for example, "Buffalo Bill and his cowboys would ride to the rescue of [stagecoach] passengers before Indians could commit their final treachery."[4] It is ironic that such racial myths came into conflict with the official policy of the Bureau of Indian Affairs, which attempted "to break up the reservations and accelerate the transformation of Indians into property owners and U.S. citizens" after the passage of the Dawes Act in 1887.[5] But not surprisingly, the image of assimilated Indians with 160-acre farms was much less appealing to the popular imagination than Buffalo Bill's horse-riding, stagecoach-attacking warriors.

Rather than acknowledging a continuity between their world and that of American Indians, such shows fixed the image of the Indian in time "as if the only true Indian were a past one."[6] In this format, the heroism of Indian braves could be appreciated as a remnant of vanquished and "vanishing" cultures that posed little threat to the hegemony of white civilization.[7] Forcibly removed from any contexts that would threaten the imaginative security of consumers, American Indians (like African-Americans) were being turned into fetishized images that satisfied the hunger for entertainment and disposable commodities.

Contemporaneously with the rise of the Wild West show, images appropriated from native cultures began to appear on advertisements for products found in numerous American households. As "the volume of American advertising increased by more than tenfold" from 1870 to 1900, advertising trade cards became the most important form of mass-market advertising.[8] Produced in the thousands, these postcard-size, lithographed images were widely distributed in stores and as premiums packaged with some products. The "narrative richness" of these cards, limited by little more than the imaginative energies of printers, artists, and manufacturers, is of great interest to the modern historian.[9] A form of what is now known as "printed ephemera," trade cards were given away by merchants, who quickly restocked new cards to feed the growing hunger for images and the commodities they represented.

In a few cases, manufacturers hit upon stable images that solidified into recognizable trademarks; but most often, designs proliferated, as one eye-catching image after another was used to lure potential customers. As chromolithography became the most effective technology for mass-producing images, there emerged a "swelling trade in images" that contributed to what Jackson Lears has characterized as the "rich and complex carnivalesque tradition" operating "in nineteenth-century American advertising."[10] Many products (especially patent medicines) seemed "to conjure up the magic of self-transformation through purchase"—a magical "aura" that was captured by the fantastic "floating signifiers" found on trade cards.[11]

This riot of images, churned out by numerous printers, facilitated the release of racial fantasies that might have been contained in more stable circumstances. Since "advertisers using trade cards were able to avoid the editorial constraints imposed by periodicals and even more public forms of advertising," nothing prevented their producers from digging deep into the mine of racial fantasy.[12] Focusing upon the characteristics of various racial and ethnic minorities, many advertisements created a sense of white, middle-class consumer solidarity at the expense of subordinate groups. Although they were not totally without buying power, Irish servants, African-Americans, Chinese Americans, and American Indians were often depicted in demeaning postures and caricatures that reveal the assumption that such individuals stood outside the mainstream of American consumerism. As a result, nineteenth-century trade cards remain to this day the most graphic examples of racial and ethnic stereotypes being used as marketing tools.

On some cards, eye-catching humor (often cartoons at the expense of blacks and the Irish) captured the attention of white consumers. On others, specific product characteristics were highlighted through association with racialized attributes of marginalized groups. Manufacturers of both thread and stove polish, for example, promoted the blackness of their products through images that exploited stereotypes of African-Americans. On one card, an African-American boy riding a spool of

Fig. 6.1. Trade card, J & P Coats "Fast Black" Thread. Bren-Dor Americana; photo, Jeffrey Steele.

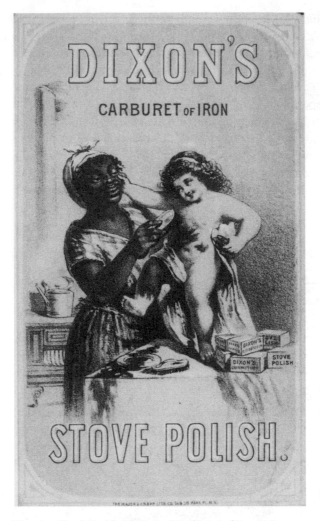

Fig. 6.2. Trade card, Dixon's "Carburet of Iron" Stove
Polish, Jos. Dixon Crucible Co., Jersey City, N.J.;
printed by Major & Knapp Lith. Co., N.Y. Bren-Dor
Americana; photo, Jeffrey Steele.

"fast black" thread points to a worried-looking sun and proclaims that "We never
fade!!" In similar fashion, an image promoting Dixon's black stove polish shows an
African-American mammy washing a young white girl who has gotten into the
stove polish—a whitening operation that the mammy cannot perform on herself
(figs. 6.1, 6.2).

Both images depend upon the exclusion of a racial other whose marginalized
presence buttresses the identity of white consumers. The dynamics of this process
are perhaps most apparent on a remarkable card produced to market Muzzy's
cornstarch: A Chinese laundry worker holds up before a white, middle-class family
a freshly starched and ironed shirt, which is so shiny the woman can see her own
reflection (fig. 6.3). In this image, we find depicted a mythologized image of identity

construction in which whiteness (we notice that the laundry worker holds up a *white* shirt) depends upon the presence of a subordinate, racialized other. Recently, Toni Morrison has argued that the white imagination depends upon the presence of a racial other in the form of an "Africanist presence"; in her eyes, the most fundamental white American ideals—"freedom . . . autonomy . . . authority"— were "made possible by, shaped by, activated by . . . Africanism, deployed as rawness and savagery."[13] Images of American Indian "savagery" served a similar function, validating the smug self-certainty of nineteenth-century proponents of what is now called "scientific racism": the belief that the different races of human beings exist on an evolutionary continuum ranging from "savagery" through "barbarism" to "civilization."[14]

To explore the role that racial ideologies played in the early stages of product identification and marketing psychology, it is useful to compare images of African-Americans and American Indians on trade cards. Not surprisingly, African-Americans are depicted in a wide variety of occupations, including sports, domestic roles, and public performances; American Indians, by contrast, are found in a narrower range of occupations and activities—imagery that suggests a more alien status in the white imagination. African-Americans, wearing familiar clothing, are often depicted indoors in domestic or vocational scenes, whereas American Indians are almost always shown outdoors in traditional, native attire (for example, moccasins, leggings, and headdresses). It is extremely rare to find black cards that refer to specific historical events; Indian cards, on the other hand, often refer to specific treaties and scenes of warfare, as if the image of the Indian were fixed at a specific time.

According to Robert Jay, in the late nineteenth century, "the Indian was little more than a romanticized abstraction for most white Americans, and was seen firsthand only in medicine and wild west shows, if at all"—a situation that gave

Fig. 6.3. Trade card, Muzzy's Corn Starch. Bren-Dor Americana; photo, Jeffrey Steele.

Fig. 6.4. Trade card, Dryeas Improved Corn Starch. Bren-Dor Americana; photo, Jeffrey Steele.

Fig. 6.5. Trade card, Abe Loebenberg's Arcade Clothing House, 10 West Washington Street, Indianapolis. Bren-Dor Americana; photo, Jeffrey Steele.

Indians an "exotic appeal" that made them "a natural vehicle for advertising."[15] More accurately, those American Indians still remaining east of the Mississippi, many of whom had adopted western dress and manners, had become largely invisible. The Indian maidens and warriors depicted on trade cards belonged to worlds that stood outside those of white, eastern consumers. Either they were located in historical scenes from the past or they were shown in picturesque locales far removed from the domain of middle-class, urban homes. As in the case of picture postcards mass-produced a generation later, such representations created a fictitious sense of "reality" in which contemporary American Indians found little reflection of their daily lives.[16]

For example, an advertisement for Duryeas Improved Corn Starch depicts a scene far removed from eastern cities (fig. 6.4). In the foreground, an Indian man attempts to quiet a bucking horse, which he holds by the bridle. In the background, Indian women near tepees cultivate corn, prepare food, and care for children. Other cards produced during this era illustrate plains Indians hunting buffalo on horseback or fighting with government troops. The clothing on many cards enforces a similar sense of distance. For example, the young man and woman on a card advertising Abe Loebenberg's Arcade Clothing House (fig. 6.5) wear traditional outfits that cut them off from the cosmopolitan world of Washington, D.C., portrayed in the background. On a card advertising Tippecanoe Spring Preparation (fig. 6.6), eight Indians in various types of tribal attire carefully conduct their birch bark canoe through rapids. Their canoe does not tip and presumably, these hardy warriors do not suffer from motion sickness and thus are immune from "dyspepsia," "stomach

Fig. 6.6. Trade card, "Tippecanoe" Spring Preparation. Bren-Dor Americana; photo, Jeffrey Steele.

Fig. 6.7. Advertising booklet, "The Golden Secret of the 'Oswego,' " Austen's Oswego Bitters, 1882. Bren-Dor Americana; photo, Jeffrey Steele.

disorders," "feeble appetite," or any of the other disorders of civilization that the Tippecanoe nostrum allegedly cures. In this instance, the advertiser exploits the perceived distance between Indian and white cultures (signified through setting and dress) by the suggestion that "the red man, in his unique communion with nature, possessed knowledge of its curative powers unrevealed to civilized man."[17]

The Kickapoo Indian Remedy was one of numerous patent medicines to exploit the myth that American Indians were more closely attuned to the rhythms of nature. One of the more elaborate variations of this theme is found in a sixteen-page advertising booklet produced to market Austen's Oswego Bitters in 1882 (fig. 6.7), which contains a short story entitled "The Witch-Woman's Revenge; or, the Golden Secret of the Oswego." In a familiar fairy-tale plot, Winona, a beautiful Indian girl, is forbidden by her mother (the "witch-woman") to marry the son of the man who killed her father. Illustrating the way that images of American Indians were fixed in the past, this tale is set in the distant era before the "foot of a white man had trod" the country now covered by the city of Oswego, New York.

In order to enforce the separation between Winona and her beloved Wanketo, the witch-woman has cast a curse that is rapidly killing all the members of his tribe. Miraculously, a lightning bolt kills the wicked mother, freeing Winona to use her family's herbal lore to save Wanketo's village. Gathering "simple herbs which none has ever thought to use as medicines," she administers the "health-giving" and "life-giving" remedy.

Through some miracle of transmission, the booklet concludes, this remedy has come into the possession of "the well-known firm, W. J. Austen & Co., Oswego, N.Y.": "Gradually its benefits were extended to the whites, and as the Indians faded away before the onward march of civilization the secret passed from their hands into those of the conquering race." "Almost as soon as they had taken the Indians' land," Jackson Lears comments, "white settlers began to claim access to their medical lore."[18] In striking support of such cultural imperialism, this booklet provides a compendium of nineteenth-century racial myths: The Indian characters, existing lower on the scale of civilization, live closer to nature and its secrets; as a 'vanishing' race, Indians yield effortlessly to the "onward march of civilization"; Winona is a "wonderfully beautiful" Indian maiden; her betrothed, "a perfect specimen of forest manhood," exhibits the characteristics of the "noble savage."

Superimposed on this racialized framework is a seductive narrative that exploits nineteenth-century stereotypes of age and gender. The attractive and healthy young couple prosper in their "free and simple lives," while the "withered crone" (Winona's interfering mother) dies. Youth (and, by implication, the sexual energies of youth) conquer in this simple tale that culminates with the marriage of Winona and Wanketo, who become the progenitors of "many generations." Similar associations are found in the trade cards produced to market Indian Queen Perfume. On one card (not pictured here), an attractive Indian woman, standing in the midst of luxuriant foliage, cradles a bow in her left arm as she gathers nectar dropping from a flower into a shell held in her right hand.[19] In an image that "represents the colonized world as the feminine," the exploitable bounties of nature are associated with the eroticized image of a native woman from a dominated race.[20]

Another card advertising Indian Queen Perfume makes even more explicit the conjunction of racialized myths of beauty, nature, and female fecundity (fig. 6.8). A demure-looking Indian woman, with limpid eyes and bowed head, cradles an infant in her left arm, while she holds a magical-looking feathered wand in her right hand. Wearing a cowrie-shell necklace, feathered headdress, and surrounded by luxuriant foliage, she seems the mythical embodiment of nature's maternal, soothing power. In the terms of Jackson Lears, she is a mythical representation of the female source of abundance—a symbol commonly found in nineteenth-century advertising.[21] To complete the picture, a butterfly (a sign of grace or immortality) hovers above her child's head in an apparent blessing.

In somewhat different fashion, male figures are used to symbolize nature's abundance. In an advertisement for a fertilizer called Bradley's Super-Phosphate of Lime (fig. 6.9), an Indian man in traditional dress stands in a field of corn; he holds a (phallic-looking) lance and stares into the distance. Behind him are two corn plants: a short plant with the legend "without phosphate" and a tall plant labeled "with

Fig. 6.8. Trade card, Indian Queen Perfume, Bean &
Brother, Philadelphia. Bren-Dor Americana; photo,
Jeffrey Steele.

phosphate." This figure's kingly potency (associated with the generative qualities of
Bradley's *fertilizer*) is reinforced by a verse from Ecclesiastes: "The profit of the
earth is for all; the king himself is served by the field." Significantly, the image on
this card is framed by a border that appropriates this regal and generative power
for the white-controlled arena of scientific agricultural management (an act that
narrows the definition of the earth's "profit" to an idea of commercial gain).
"Bradley's Phosphate furnishes the elements of plant-food in proper proportions,"
this border reads. "By using Bradley's Phosphate you return to the soil the plant-
food constituents your crops are constantly taking from it."

Nature's masculine abundance is even more apparent on an 1886 card used to
advertise Diamond lawnmowers (fig. 6.10). An example of the popular and Widely
used "vegetable people" series, this advertisement depicts a "corned Indian" whose
body is an ear of corn; hands and feet, corn husk. Melded with this agricultural
motif is the figure of an Indian whose posture, clothing, and staff resemble to a

close degree those found on the previous card. An even more primordial representation of natural bounty and potency, this image suggests the extent to which racial myth (based upon the deep-seated association of American Indians with their staple, corn) could be blended with fantasy and desire in the service of commerce. Merging deeply rooted images of oral gratification, masculine sexuality, and racialized iconography, this card represents the American Indian as a consumable product—as food. In the face of white imperialism, this card suggests, Indian cultures (like the products appropriated from them) could be absorbed at will.

Such disposition is even more apparent on trade cards that used images derived from history. William Penn's 1682 treaty with Delaware tribal leaders might seem like an odd choice for a nineteenth-century advertisement. But the use of this event on two different trade cards suggests some of the ways in which historical references served commercial ambitions. Although Penn's treaty was famous for "acknowledg-

Fig. 6.9. Trade card, Bradley's Super-Phosphate of Lime, Bradley Fertilizer Co., Boston. Bren-Dor Americana; photo, Jeffrey Steele.

Fig. 6.10. Trade card, "A Corned Indian," Diamond
Lawnmowers, C. W. Hackett Hardware Co., St. Paul,
Minn.; printed 1886 by L. P. Griffith & Co.,
Baltimore. Bren-Dor Americana; photo, Jeffrey Steele.

ing Indian title to land, and establishing strict and fair procedures for its purchase,"
white settlers "managed to evade regulations . . . through leases of Indian lands,"
"outright encroachment," and "official fraud."[22] Two hundred years later, in the
1880s, it was easy to use this historical event as a self-congratulatory symbol
substantiating whites' "enlightened" policy toward Indians (at least in the East).
Why go to the trouble of conquering Indian territories, these cards suggest, when
they can be easily appropriated through seemingly fair treaties? On both cards, the
"treaties" represented are actually advertisements: for Ayer's Cherry Pectoral and
for Enterprise Bone, Shell, and Corn Mills, respectively.

The Enterprise card (fig. 6.11) is especially interesting—both for its graphic
design and because of a verse embedded in the center of the card. The text reads:

In sixteen eighty two, you surely have heard
How William Penn an honest treaty made.

All good Indians mourn him still
And remember his proclamation of good will
To use the Enterprise Bone, Shell, and Corn Mill.

In this context, Penn's "honest treaty" commits unwitting Indians to the consumption of the product he is peddling—in an unequal relationship that cements the image of white paternalism. According to this card, "good Indians" know their place and their proper role—to be unquestioning consumers. But in reality this card advertises a form of agricultural technology of little use to the American Indians depicted, who seem to have stepped out of a cartoon world. Their function, it would seem, is to signify an act of consumption that they cannot fill, for more than anything, they seem to be playing with the Enterprise mill.

The visual categories pioneered by Erving Goffman can be applied to this card

Fig. 6.11. Trade card, Enterprise Bone, Shell, and Corn Mill, Enterprise Mfg. Co., Philadelphia; printed 1893 by Donaldson Brothers, N.Y. Bren-Dor Americana; photo, Jeffrey Steele.

to reveal a number of familiar signs of dominance and subordination. This power differential is reinforced by the placement and posture of the figures: a smug-looking William Penn stands in the background overlooking three Indian figures who seem totally absorbed with (if not amazed by) their new mill. The position of the figures provides an obvious "function ranking": Penn stands in a paternal position of control, "a little outside the physical circle," surveying the entire scene and holding pen and paper (the tools of literacy), while the Indian figures have their attention more narrowly focused on the mill.[23] The playful, even childish, expressions on the faces of the Indian figures express an emotionality and lack of restraint that diminishes their status in contrast to the more staid figure of Penn and suggests their distance from his mastery.[24]

In addition to the portrayal of human figures, this card conveys its message through the conjunction of "multiple planes of meaning" (to use Lears's phrase) that are conjoined but do not meet.[25] The Enterprise mill (a modern machine) belongs to a world distinct from that of William Penn and his seventeenth-century treaty with the Delawares. The effect of this disjunction is to underscore the distance between the world of native culture and the nineteenth-century realm of technological and mechanical power. In another way, the gap between white and Indian cultures is signified by the presence, at the bottom of the card, of an imposing edifice designated the "Electrical Building." As an aspect of the card's design, this building seems out of place. But as a signifier demonstrating the evident "superiority" of white civilization, it bespeaks a kind of economic manifest destiny. The three Indian figures depicted above the Electrical Building are provided with no valid place in a world where such structures exist.

In contrast to treaties, scenes of Indian warfare and violence were an even more popular subject on trade cards. As is to be expected, depictions of Custer's Last Stand made their way onto these advertisements. One unusual card, for example, depicts the "Death of Custer" as part of "Forepaugh's Equestrian Spectacular Tragedy"—evidently a Wild West show staging scenes from recent history.[26] Other cards, which had the merit of not raising unsettling questions about recent U.S. Indian policy, portrayed military scenes from the past. The 1811 Battle of Tippecanoe (fought in Indiana) was featured on an 1883 advertisement for Tippecanoe tonic—a graphic card that depicts a number of Indian warriors in the act of being slaughtered. A sensational scene from the Black Hawk War, identified on the back as "Defeat of Black Hawk and his Indians, 1832," was one of three vignettes of Wisconsin history depicted on an 1892 card for Arbuckle Brothers Coffee (fig. 6.12). Part of a series of fifty cards "giving a pictorial history of the United States and territories," the Arbuckle card is worth closer examination. Both the pictorial elements on the front of the card and the text on the back (a synopsis of Wisconsin history) contribute to a complicated act of racial mythmaking.

The battle scene, occupying the center of the card, is given visual emphasis by the diagonal lines at the left (the French explorers "Marquette and Joliet crossing the portage from the Fox to the Wisconsin River"), a visual element echoed in the position of muskets and arms in the center panel. The right-hand scene, which provides a sense of closure to the design, portrays a party of white tourists in

Fig. 6.12. Trade card, Arbuckle Brothers Coffee, Arbuckle Bros., N.Y.; printed 1892 by Donaldson Brothers, N.Y. Bren-Dor Americana; photo, Jeffrey Steele.

contemporary dress on top of "Stand Rock in the 'Dells.' " Both the left- and right-hand panels place human figures in recognizable natural landscapes, while presenting a visual narrative that stresses the progression from exploration to present-day tourism. In contrast, the center panel stands out from the card as an intrusion; it contains no natural features and seems to have been unscrolled, rolling across and disrupting the narrative of exploration, implied settlement, and tourism. The text on the back of the card reinforces this narrative of "manifest destiny" by asserting that "the Black Hawk War (1832) was an important factor in the opening of the region to public view."

Appealing to consumers' prurient interest, the central panel shows a scene of close combat in which a bare-breasted Indian woman, kneeling over a dead man, raises her arm in a futile effort to stop the killing. Significantly, this image depicts an Indian woman in a state of seminudity that no white woman could occupy.[27] In the visual economy of this advertisement, the American Indian is implicitly identified with this figure, whose state of vulnerable undress seems a sign of "savagery," at the same time that her resistance seems particularly pathetic and ineffectual. The viewer's sympathy is stirred but quickly overwhelmed by the implied message: Here is a powerful emblem of the "vanishing Indian," powerless to resist the white military pressure that was successful in "opening the region [like this female figure] to public view." Just as this eroticized image of an American Indian woman was made available for white-male erotic fantasy, Indians (in general) were reduced to images that could be made to play allotted roles in nineteenth-century fantasies of cultural imperialism.

In different ways, a number of trade cards (some of them illustrating historical subjects) contributed to the argument for "manifest destiny" by illustrating scenes of savagery and violence. As a group, these cards provide graphic images of "the Indian as . . . alien to the White."[28] A Kickapoo Indian Medicines booklet, for example, depicts a sleeping Indian who dreams of hunting, Custer's Last Stand, and a massacre.[29] In the massacre scene (placed directly beneath the word "Indian"), a number of warriors slaughter and scalp white men, women, and children. The motif of scalping was picked up in even more graphic fashion on a card advertising Taylor's Sure Cure.[30] A sleeping Indian, his gun leaning against him, dreams two scenes: embracing a large, life-size bottle labeled "Fire Water"; and killing a horrified missionary, his tracts scattered at his feet and eyes wide open, who prays for his life. Superimposed on this amazing image is the following verse:

> The Indian dreams of days gone by,
> When he raised hair, his knife for a lever;
> His country is gone, but then he has left
> Taylor's Sure Cure for chills and fever.

In this vision of commercial expansion, the lost lands and violent past of the Indian figure are compensated for by his new "role" as consumer. But in reality, the sleeping Indian is not being presented as a potential customer but rather as a source of entertainment for a white populace whose sense of identity is bolstered by its perceived distance from such "savagery."

Images on two Arbuckle Brothers coffee cards reinforce this stereotype of savagery. The first, part of the series illustrating scenes from state history, depicts as one of three historical tableaux a scene identified on the reverse as "Massacre by the Sioux" in Iowa (fig. 6.13). The explanatory text relates that "in 1830 the Sioux

Fig. 6.13. Trade card, Arbuckle Brothers Coffee, Arbuckle Bros., N.Y.; printed 1892 by Donaldson Brothers, N.Y. Bren-Dor Americana; photo, Jeffrey Steele.

Fig. 6.14. Trade card, Arbuckle Brothers Coffee, Arbuckle Bros., N.Y., printed 1893 by Kaufmann & Strauss. Bren-Dor Americana; photo, Jeffrey Steele.

annihilated a large party of the Sacs and Foxes (including ten chiefs) on the Mississippi River, near Dubuque." The only problem with this explanation is that the inflammatory image on the front portrays a white family being killed and scalped. Perhaps it was unthinkable for the anonymous artist who drew this scene to imagine anyone other than white settlers as the victims of American Indian violence! The lapse is revealing and eloquently illustrates the ways in which stereotyped images of American Indians took on a life of their own.

The second Arbuckle card (dated 1893), titled "American Indians," is particularly interesting because it is part of an ethnocentric series of fifty cards "giving a pictorial history of the Sports and Pastimes of all Nations" (fig. 6.14). In addition to hunting, spearfishing, and riding, one of these "pastimes" was the war dance. In this illustration, a ceremony related to the cultural survival of American Indian nations (who were subject to constant encroachment and attack from white troops and settlers) is turned into an amusement, as if it were no more serious than the waltz or polka. The text on the reverse continues this vein of cultural chauvinism: "The war-dance, principal of their terpsichorean exercises was more horrible than graceful, and suggested the sanguinary atrocities of bloodshed." The Latinate euphemisms ("terpsichorean," "sanguinary") make a show of disguising the bloody "reality" behind the war dance, as if more direct language would offend the reader's "civilized" sensibilities. But in actuality, these terms (as well as the text as a whole) reveal a colonizing mind-set that uses ornate language as a sign of cultural superiority and presumed distance from "sanguinary atrocities" (as if only American Indians were responsible for savage acts of violence).

Equally revealing is the writer's use of the past tense throughout the explanatory text (which provides a graphic example of the image of the "noble savage"): "No hardier or more rugged race than the Indians of North America *ever existed*. Their endurance and tenacity *were* more than human, their stoicism *was* remarkable, their courage *shrank* from nothing, and their skill and agility *were* the development of generations of outdoor life." In the scale of cultural evolution, this suggests, the American Indian represented an earlier, more primitive race that had long since been superseded by the "civilized" races of the world, who fit more clearly into the scale of humanity (not being "more than human").

Very few nineteenth-century trade cards escaped from the cultural imperialism of the cards described above. This should not be surprising, considering that most of these cards were produced in the late 1880s and early 1890s, at the end of two decades of active warfare between government troops and Indian nations in the West. After the completion of the transcontinental railroad in 1869, western settlement had rapidly accelerated. Armed conflicts became inevitable as struggles broke out over valuable lands. Between 1866 and 1886, wars were fought with the Teton Sioux, Cheyennes, and Arapahos in Wyoming and Montana; with the Paiutes in Oregon and Idaho; with the Cheyennes, Arapahos, Sioux, Comanches, and Kiowas in the Central Plains; with the Modocs in California; with the Lakota Sioux, Cheyennes, and Arapahos in Montana and Wyoming; with the Nez Percé in the Northwest; with the Bannocks, Paiutes, and Cayuses in Idaho and Oregon; with the Utes in Colorado; and with the Apaches in the Southwest.[31] By 1890, after the conclusion of these armed conflicts, millions of acres of ceded land were being opened up for white settlement throughout the West.

As these wars ended and especially after the passage of the Dawes Act in 1887, the roles of American Indians were rapidly changing. In the eyes of many whites, Indian cultures—vanquished by the U.S. military—had disappeared. Other more enlightened individuals realized that surviving members of tribes would need a new economic foundation for their cultures, since traditional patterns of hunting and food gathering had been destroyed by the numerous wars and the consequent relocation of Indians to reservations. The Dawes Act, with its system of land allotments, represented an attempt to transform American Indians into citizens and farmers. The Salishan author Mourning Dove captured the turmoil of this situation in her posthumously published autobiography:

> My birth happened in the year 1888. In that year the Indians of my tribe, the Colvile, were well into the cycle of history involving their readjustment in living conditions. They were in a pathetic state of turmoil caused by trying to learn to till the soil for a living, which was being done on a very small and crude scale. It was no easy matter for members of this aboriginal stock, accustomed to making a different livelihood (by the bow and arrow), to handle the plow and sow seed for food. Yet I was born long enough ago to have known people who lived in the ancient way before everything started to change.[32]

Not surprisingly, very few trade cards illustrated these changing circumstances. One card that did, however, was produced to advertise Keystone Agricultural Implements around 1890 (fig. 6.15). Uncle Sam stands in front of an illustration of

Fig. 6.15. Trade card, Keystone Line of Agricultural Implements, Keystone Manufacturing Co., Sterling, Ill.; printed ca. 1890 by G. H. Dunston, Buffalo, N.Y. Bren-Dor Americana; photo, Jeffrey Steele.

a new disc harrow, which he points out to sixteen male viewers. All of the members of his audience represent recognizable ethnic types, among them Scottish, Irish, German, Scandinavian, Turkish, Chinese, Arabian, and African. Significantly, this family of nations includes an American Indian, who looks on as attentively as the others. In this unusual advertisement, the American Indian is granted space, along with the others, to join in the cultivation of the nation. Although such space rarely appears in nineteenth-century trade cards, its presence in this instance suggests how varied and rich a medium they represent. Advertisers used whatever would help sell their products; and as the nation began to change at the turn of the century, even American Indians (long used as emblems of racial otherness) gained a foothold in the nation's commercial culture. No longer positioned solely as entertaining icons used to symbolize products, they began to gain a role as accepted consumers in their own right.

NOTES

1. Hal Morgan, *Symbols of America* (New York: Viking Press, 1986), pp. 57–59, 61–62.
2. Eric Sundquist, *To Wake the Nations: Race in the Making of American Literature* (Cambridge: Harvard University Press, 1993), p. 473.
3. L. G. Moses, "Wild West Shows, Reformers, and the Image of the American Indian, 1887–1914," *South Dakota History* 14 (fall 1984): 195.
4. Ibid., pp. 194, 197.
5. Ronald Takaki, *A Different Mirror: A History of Multicultural America* (Boston, Toronto, London: Little, Brown, 1993), p. 234. Moses (cited earlier) notes that "by the end of the 1880s, considerable sentiment against the use of Indians in shows rose among leaders in Indian policy reform" (p. 199).

6. Robert F. Berkhofer, Jr., *The White Man's Indian: Images of the American Indian from Columbus to the Present* (New York: Vintage Books, 1979), p. 67.

7. In a modern example of this viewpoint, Morgan in *Symbols of America* observes that "after the last Indian resistance in the West had been crushed," it "became safe to look back fondly on a great and noble culture that had been largely destroyed" (p. 57).

8. Robert Jay, *The Trade Card in Nineteenth-Century America* (Columbia: University of Missouri Press, 1987), pp. 34, 39.

9. Ibid., p. 60.

10. J. Lears, *Fables of Abundance: A Cultural History of Advertising in America* (New York: Basic Books, 1994), pp. 41, 54.

11. Ibid., pp. 42, 20, 55.

12. Jay, *The Trade Card*, p. 60.

13. Toni Morrison, *Playing in the Dark: Whiteness and the Literary Imagination* (New York: Vintage Books, 1993), pp. 38, 44.

14. For a discussion of these matters, see Berkhofer's *White Man's Indian*, chapter 2, under the section " 'Scientific' Racism and Human Diversity in Nineteenth-Century Social Sciences."

15. Jay, *The Trade Card*, pp. 70–71.

16. Patricia C. Albers and William R. James, "Utah's Indians and Popular Photography in the American West: A View from the Picture Post Card," *Utah Historical Quarterly* 52 (winter 1984): 91.

17. Jay, *The Trade Card*, p. 71.

18. Lears, *Fables*, p. 64.

19. Kit Barry, *Reflections: Ephemera from Trades, Products, and Events*, vol. 1 (Brattleboro, Vt.: Iris Publishing, 1993), p. 52.

20. David Spurr, *The Rhetoric of Empire: Colonial Discourse in Journalism, Travel Writing, and Imperial Administration* (Durham, N.C. and London: Duke University Press, 1993), p. 170.

21. Lears, *Fables*, pp. 107, 109.

22. Carl Waldman, *Atlas of the North American Indian* (New York and London: Facts on File, 1985), p. 171.

23. Erving Goffman, *Gender Advertisements* (New York: Harper and Row, 1979), pp. 32, 39.

24. Goffman discusses a similar dynamic in the advertisements he studies, in which "the female is likely to be exhibiting a more expansive expression than is the male" (p. 69).

25. Lears, *Fables*, p. 153.

26. Kit Barry, *Reflections: Ephemera from Trades, Products, and Events*, vol. 2 (Brattleboro, Vt.: Iris Publishing, 1994), p. 27.

27. One famous example of contemporary standards of erotic display involved a Merrick Thread card depicting a mother playing with two children at the ocean. In its original state, the woman, shown seated on a rock, was depicted with bare breasts, but because of public outcry, the printer was forced to alter the card by covering the offending flesh with extra hair.

28. Berkhofer, *White Man's Indian*, p. xv.

29. Barry, *Reflections*, vol. 1, p. 123.

30. Barry, *Reflections*, vol. 2, p. 173.

31. Waldman, *Atlas*, p. 129.

32. Mourning Dove, *A Salishan Autobiography*, ed. Jay Miller (Lincoln and London: University of Nebraska Press, 1990), p. 3.

Chapter Seven

Soft-Soaping Empire
Commodity Racism and Imperial Advertising

Anne McClintock

Soap is Civilization
> —Unilever Company Slogan

Doc: My, it's so clean.
Grumpy: There's dirty work afoot.
> —Snow White and the Seven Dwarfs

Soap and Civilization

At the beginning of the nineteenth century, soap was a scarce and humdrum item and washing a cursory activity at best. A few decades later, the manufacture of soap had burgeoned into an imperial commerce; Victorian cleaning rituals were peddled globally as the God-given sign of Britain's evolutionary superiority, and soap was invested with magical, fetish powers. The soap saga captured the hidden affinity between domesticity and empire and embodied a triangulated crisis in value: the *undervaluation* of women's work in the domestic realm, the *overvaluation* of the commodity in the industrial market and the *disavowal* of colonized economies in the arena of empire. Soap entered the realm of Victorian fetishism with spectacular effect, notwithstanding the fact that male Victorians promoted soap as the icon of nonfetishistic rationality.

Both the cult of domesticity and the new imperialism found in soap an exemplary mediating form. The emergent middle class values—monogamy ("clean" sex, which has value), industrial capital ("clean" money, which has value), Christianity ("being washed in the blood of the lamb"), class control ("cleansing the great unwashed") and the imperial civilizing mission ("washing and clothing the savage")—could all be marvelously embodied in a single household commodity. Soap advertising, in particular the Pears' soap campaign, took its place at the vanguard of Britain's new commodity culture and its civilizing mission.

In the eighteenth century, the commodity was little more than a mundane object to be bought and used—in Marx's words, "a trivial thing."[1] By the late nineteenth century, however, the commodity had taken its privileged place not only as the fundamental form of a new industrial economy but also as the fundamental form of a new cultural system for representing social value.[2] Banks and stock exchanges rose up to manage the bonanzas of imperial capital. Professions emerged to administer the goods tumbling hectically from the manufactures. Middle-class domestic space became crammed as never before with furniture, clocks, mirrors, paintings, stuffed animals, ornaments, guns and myriad gewgaws and knicknacks. Victorian novelists bore witness to the strange spawning of commodities that seemed to have lives of their own, and huge ships lumbered with trifles and trinkets plied their trade among the colonial markets of Africa, the East and the Americas.[3]

The new economy created an uproar not only of things but of signs. As Thomas Richards has argued, if all these new commodities were to be managed, a unified system of cultural representation had to be found. Richards shows how, in 1851, the Great Exhibition at the Crystal Palace served as a monument to a new form of consumption: "What the first Exhibition heralded so intimately was the complete transformation of collective and private life into a space for the spectacular exhibition of commodities."[4] As a "semiotic laboratory for the labor theory of value," the World Exhibition showed once and for all that the capitalist system had not only created a dominant form of exchange but was also in the process of creating a dominant form of representation to go with it: the voyeuristic panorama of surplus as spectacle. By exhibiting commodities not only as goods but as an organized system of images, the World Exhibition helped fashion "a new kind of being, the consumer and a new kind of ideology, consumerism."[5] The mass consumption of the commodity spectacle was born.

Victorian advertising reveals a paradox, however, for, as the cultural form that was entrusted with upholding and marketing abroad those founding middle-class distinctions—between private and public, paid work and unpaid work—advertising also from the outset began to confound those distinctions. Advertising took the intimate signs of domesticity (children bathing, men shaving, women laced into corsets, maids delivering nightcaps) into the public realm, plastering scenes of domesticity on walls, buses, shopfronts and billboards. At the same time, advertising took scenes of empire into every corner of the home, stamping images of colonial conquest on soap boxes, matchboxes, biscuit tins, whiskey bottles, tea tins and chocolate bars. By trafficking promiscuously across the threshold of private and public, advertising began to subvert one of the fundamental distinctions of commodity capital, even as it was coming into being.

From the outset, moreover, Victorian advertising took explicit shape around the reinvention of racial difference. Commodity kitsch made possible, as never before, the mass marketing of empire as an organized system of images and attitudes. Soap flourished not only because it created and filled a spectacular gap in the domestic market but also because, as a cheap and portable domestic commodity, it could persuasively mediate the Victorian poetics of racial hygiene and imperial progress.

Commodity racism became distinct from scientific racism in its capacity to expand beyond the literate, propertied elite through the marketing of commodity spectacle. If, after the 1850s, scientific racism saturated anthropological, scientific and medical journals, travel writing and novels, these cultural forms were still relatively class-bound and inaccessible to most Victorians, who had neither the means nor the education to read such material. Imperial kitsch as consumer spectacle, by contrast, could package, market and distribute evolutionary racism on a hitherto unimagined scale. No preexisting form of organized racism had ever before been able to reach so large and so differentiated a mass of the populace. Thus, as domestic commodities were mass marketed through their appeal to imperial jingoism, commodity jingoism itself helped reinvent and maintain British national unity in the face of deepening imperial competition and colonial resistance. The cult of domesticity became indispensable to the consolidation of British national identity, and at the center of the domestic cult stood the simple bar of soap.[6]

Yet soap has no social history. Since it purportedly belongs in the female realm of domesticity, soap is figured as beyond history and beyond politics proper.[7] To begin a social history of soap, then, is to refuse, in part, to accept the erasure of women's domestic value under imperial capitalism. It cannot be forgotten, moreover, that the history of European attempts to impose a commodity economy on African cultures was also the history of diverse African attempts either to refuse or to transform European commodity fetishism to suit their own needs. The story of soap reveals that fetishism, far from being a quintessentially African propensity, as nineteenth-century anthropology maintained, was central to industrial modernity, inhabiting and mediating the uncertain threshold zones between domesticity and industry, metropolis and empire.

Soap and Commodity Spectacle

Before the late nineteenth century, clothes and bedding washing was done in most households only once or twice a year in great, communal binges, usually in public at streams or rivers.[8] As for body washing, not much had changed since the days when Queen Elizabeth I was distinguished by the frequency with which she washed: "regularly every month whether she needed it or not."[9] By the 1890s, however, soap sales had soared, Victorians were consuming 260,000 tons of soap a year, and advertising had emerged as the central cultural form of commodity capitalism.[10]

Before 1851, advertising scarcely existed. As a commercial form, it was generally regarded as a confession of weakness, a rather shabby last resort. Most advertising was limited to small newspaper advertisements, cheap handbills and posters. After midcentury, however, soap manufacturers began to pioneer the use of pictorial advertising as a central part of business policy.

The initial impetus for soap advertising came from the realm of empire. With the burgeoning of imperial cotton on the slave plantations came the surplus of cheap cotton goods, alongside the growing buying power of a middle class that could afford for the first time to consume such goods in large quantities. Similarly, the sources for cheap palm oil, coconut oil and cottonseed oil flourished in the imperial plantations of West Africa, Malay, Ceylon, Fiji and New Guinea. As rapid changes in the technology of soapmaking took place in Britain after midcentury, the prospect dawned of a large domestic market for soft body soaps, which had previously been a luxury that only the upper class could afford.

Economic competition with the United States and Germany created the need for a more aggressive promotion of British products and led to the first real innovations in advertising. In 1884, the year of the Berlin Conference, the first wrapped soap was sold under a brand name. This small event signified a major transformation in capitalism, as imperial competition gave rise to the creation of monopolies. Henceforth, items formerly indistinguishable from each other (soap sold simply as soap) would be marketed by their corporate signature (Pears, Monkey Brand, etc). Soap became one of the first commodities to register the historic shift from myriad small businesses to the great imperial monopolies. In the 1870s, hundreds of small soap companies plied the new trade in hygiene, but by the end of the century, the trade was monopolized by ten large companies.

In order to manage the great soap show, an aggressively entrepreneurial breed of advertisers emerged, dedicated to gracing each homely product with a radiant halo of imperial glamour and racial potency. The advertising agent, like the bureaucrat, played a vital role in the imperial expansion of foreign trade. Advertisers billed themselves as "empire builders" and flattered themselves with "the responsibility of the historic imperial mission." Said one: "Commerce even more than sentiment binds the ocean sundered portions of empire together. Anyone who increases these commercial interests strengthens the whole fabric of the empire."[11] Soap was credited not only with bringing moral and economic salvation to Britain's "great unwashed" but also with magically embodying the spiritual ingredient of the imperial mission itself.

In an ad for Pears, for example, a black and implicitly racialized coalsweeper holds in his hands a glowing, occult object. Luminous with its own inner radiance, the simple soap bar glows like a fetish, pulsating magically with spiritual enlightenment and imperial grandeur, promising to warm the hands and hearts of working people across the globe.[12] Pears, in particular, became intimately associated with a purified nature magically cleansed of polluting industry (tumbling kittens, faithful dogs, children festooned with flowers) and a purified working class magically cleansed of polluting labor (smiling servants in crisp white aprons, rosy-cheeked match girls and scrubbed scullions).[13]

Nonetheless, the Victorian obsession with cotton and cleanliness was not simply a mechanical reflex of economic surplus. If imperialism garnered a bounty of cheap cotton and soap oils from coerced colonial labor, the middle class Victorian fascination with clean, white bodies and clean, white clothing stemmed not only from the rampant profiteering of the imperial economy but also from the realms of ritual and fetish.

Soap did not flourish when imperial ebullience was at its peak. It emerged commercially during an era of impending crisis and social calamity, serving to preserve, through fetish ritual, the uncertain boundaries of class, gender and race identity in a social order felt to be threatened by the fetid effluvia of the slums, the belching smoke of industry, social agitation, economic upheaval, imperial competition and anticolonial resistance. Soap offered the promise of spiritual salvation and regeneration through commodity consumption, a regime of domestic hygiene that could restore the threatened potency of the imperial body politic and the race.

The Pears' Campaign

In 1789 Andrew Pears, a farmer's son, left his Cornish village of Mevagissey to open a barbershop in London, following the trend of widespread demographic migration from country to city and the economic turn from land to commerce. In his shop, Pears made and sold the powders, creams and dentifrices used by the rich to ensure the fashionable alabaster purity of their complexions. For the elite, a sun-darkened skin stained by outdoor manual work was the visible stigma not only of a class obliged to work under the elements for a living but also of far-off, benighted races marked by God's disfavor. From the outset, soap took shape as a technology of social purification, inextricably entwined with the semiotics of imperial racism and class denigration.

In 1838 Andrew Pears retired and left his firm in the hands of his grandson, Francis. In due course, Francis' daughter, Mary, married Thomas J. Barratt, who became Francis' partner and took the gamble of fashioning a middle-class market for the transparent soap. Barratt revolutionized Pears by masterminding a series of dazzling advertising campaigns. Inaugurating a new era of advertising, he won himself lasting fame, in the familiar iconography of male birthing, as the "father of advertising." Soap thus found its industrial destiny through the mediation of domestic kinship and that peculiarly Victorian preoccupation with patrimony.

Through a series of gimmicks and innovations that placed Pears at the center of Britain's emerging commodity culture, Barratt showed a perfect understanding of the fetishism that structures all advertising. Importing a quarter of a million French centime pieces into Britain, Barratt had the name Pears stamped on them and put the coins into circulation—a gesture that marvelously linked exchange value with the corporate brand name. The ploy worked famously, arousing much publicity for Pears and such a public fuss that an Act of Parliament was rushed through to declare all foreign coins illegal tender. The boundaries of the national currency closed around the domestic bar of soap.

Georg Lukács points out that the commodity lies on the threshold of culture and commerce, confusing the supposedly sacrosanct boundaries between aesthetics and economy, money and art. In the mid-1880s, Barratt devised a piece of breathtaking cultural transgression that exemplified Lukács' insight and clinched Pears' fame. Barratt bought Sir John Everett Millais' painting "Bubbles" (originally entitled "A Child's World") and inserted into the painting a bar of soap stamped with the totemic word *Pears*. At a stroke, he transformed the artwork of the best-known painter in Britain into a mass produced commodity associated in the public mind with Pears.[14] At the same time, by mass reproducing the painting as a poster ad, Barratt took art from the elite realm of private property to the mass realm of commodity spectacle.[15]

In advertising, the axis of possession is shifted to the axis of spectacle. Advertising's chief contribution to the culture of modernity was the discovery that by manipulating the semiotic space around the commodity, the unconscious as a public space could also be manipulated. Barratt's great innovation was to invest huge sums of money in the creation of a visible aesthetic space around the commodity. The development of poster and print technology made possible the mass reproduction of such a space around the image of a commodity.[16]

In advertising, that which is disavowed by industrial rationality (ambivalence, sensuality, chance, unpredictable causality, multiple time) is projected onto image space as a repository of the forbidden. Advertising draws on subterranean flows of desire and taboo, manipulating the investment of surplus money. Pears' distinction, swiftly emulated by scores of soap companies including Monkey Brand and Sunlight, as well as countless other advertisers, was to invest the aesthetic space around the domestic commodity with the commercial cult of empire.

Empire of the Home: Racializing Domesticity

The Soap

Four fetishes recur ritualistically in soap advertising: soap itself, white clothing (especially aprons), mirrors and monkeys. A typical Pears' advertisement figures a black child and a white child together in a bathroom (fig. 7.1). The Victorian bathroom is the innermost sanctuary of domestic hygiene and by extension the private temple of public regeneration. The sacrament of soap offers a reformation allegory whereby the purification of the domestic body becomes a metaphor for the regeneration of the body politic. In this particular ad, a black boy sits in the bath, gazing wide-eyed into the water as if into a foreign element. A white boy, clothed in a white apron—the familiar fetish of domestic purity—bends benevolently over his "lesser" brother, bestowing upon him the precious talisman of racial progress. The magical fetish of soap promises that the commodity can regenerate the Family of Man by washing from the skin the very stigma of racial and class degeneration.

Soap advertising offers an allegory of imperial progress as spectacle. In this ad, the imperial topos that I call panoptical time (progress consumed as a spectacle from a point of privileged invisibility) enters the domain of the commodity. In the second frame of the ad, the black child is out of the bath and the white boy shows him his startled visage in the mirror. The black boy's body has become magically white, but his face—for Victorians the seat of rational individuality and self-consciousness—remains stubbornly black. The white child is thereby figured as the agent of history and the male heir to progress, reflecting his lesser brother in the European mirror of self-consciousness. In the Victorian mirror, the black child witnesses his predetermined destiny of imperial metamorphosis but remains a passive racial hybrid, part black, part white, brought to the brink of civilization by the twin commodity fetishes of soap and mirror. The advertisement discloses a crucial element of late Victorian commodity culture: the metaphoric transformation of

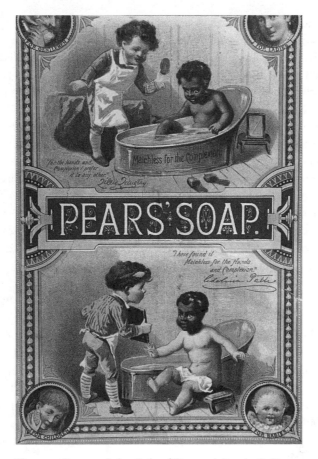

Fig. 7.1. Race and the Cult of Domesticity. A. & F. Pears, Ltd.

imperial *time* into consumer *space*—imperial progress consumed at a glance as domestic spectacle.

The Monkey

The metamorphosis of imperial time into domestic space is captured most vividly by the advertising campaign for Monkey Brand Soap. During the 1880s, the urban landscape of Victorian Britain teemed with the fetish monkeys of this soap. The monkey with its frying pan and bar of soap perched everywhere, on grimy hoardings and buses, on walls and shop fronts, promoting the soap that promised magically to do away with domestic labor: "No dust, no dirt, no labor." Monkey Brand Soap promised not only to regenerate the race but also to magically erase the unseemly spectacle of women's manual labor.

In an exemplary ad, the fetish soap-monkey sits cross-legged on a doorstep, the threshold boundary between private domesticity and public commerce—the embodiment of anachronistic space. Dressed like an organ grinder's minion in a gentleman's ragged suit, white shirt and tie, but with improbably human hands and feet, the monkey extends a frying pan to catch the surplus cash of passersby. On the doormat before him, a great bar of soap is displayed, accompanied by a placard that reads: "My Own Work." In every respect the soap-monkey is a hybrid: not entirely ape, not entirely human; part street beggar, part gentleman; part artist, part advertiser. The creature inhabits the ambivalent border of jungle and city, private and public, the domestic and the commercial, and offers as its handiwork a fetish that is both art and commodity.

Monkeys inhabit Western discourse on the borders of social limit, marking the place of a contradiction in social value. As Donna Haraway has argued: "the primate body, as part of the body of nature, may be read as a map of power."[17] Primatology, Haraway insists, "is a Western discourse . . . a political order that works by the negotiation of boundaries achieved through ordering differences."[18] In Victorian iconography, the ritual recurrence of the monkey figure is eloquent of a crisis in value and hence anxiety at possible boundary breakdown. The primate body became a symbolic space for reordering and policing boundaries between humans and nature, women and men, family and politics, empire and metropolis.

Simian imperialism is also centrally concerned with the problem of representing *social change*. By projecting history (rather than fate, or God's will) onto the theater of nature, primatology made nature the alibi of political violence and placed in the hands of "rational science" the authority to sanction and legitimize social change. Here, "the scene of origins," Haraway argues, "is not the cradle of civilization, but the cradle of culture . . . the origin of sociality itself, especially in the densely meaning-laden icon of the family."[19] Primatology emerges as a theater for negotiating the perilous boundaries between the family (as natural and female) and power (as political and male).

The appearance of monkeys in soap advertising signals a dilemma: *how to represent domesticity without representing women at work*. The Victorian middle-class house was structured around the fundamental contradiction between women's paid and unpaid domestic work. As women were driven from paid work in mines, factories, shops and trades to private, unpaid work in the home, domestic work became economically undervalued and the middle-class definition of femininity figured the "proper" woman as one who did not work for profit. At the same time, a *cordon sanitaire* of racial degeneration was thrown around those women who did work publicly and visibly for money. What could not be incorporated into the industrial formation (women's domestic economic value) was displaced onto the invented domain of the primitive, and thereby disciplined and contained.

Monkeys, in particular, were deployed to legitimize social boundaries as edicts of nature. Fetishes straddling nature and culture, monkeys were seen as allied with the dangerous classes: the "apelike" wandering poor, the hungry Irish, Jews, prostitutes, impoverished black people, the ragged working class, criminals, the insane and female miners and servants, who were collectively seen to inhabit the threshold of racial degeneration. When Charles Kingsley visited Ireland, for example, he lamented: "I am haunted by the human chimpanzees I saw along that hundred miles of horrible country. . . . But to see white chimpanzees is dreadful; if they were black, one would not feel it so much, but their skins, except where tanned by exposure, are as white as ours."[20]

In the Monkey Brand advertisement, the monkey's signature of labor ("My Own Work") signals a double disavowal. Soap is masculinized, figured as a male product, while the (mostly female) labor of the workers in the huge, unhealthy soap factories is disavowed. At the same time, the labor of social transformation in the daily scrubbing and scouring of the sinks, pans and dishes, labyrinthine floors and corridors of Victorian domestic space vanishes—refigured as anachronistic space, primitive and bestial. Female servants disappear and in their place crouches a phantasmic male hybrid. Thus, domesticity—seen as the sphere most separate from the marketplace and the masculine hurly-burly of empire—takes shape around the invented ideas of the primitive and the commodity fetish.

In Victorian culture, the monkey was an icon of metamorphosis, perfectly serving soap's liminal role in mediating the transformations of nature (dirt, waste and disorder) into culture (cleanliness, rationality and industry). Like all fetishes, the monkey is a contradictory image, embodying the hope of imperial progress through commerce while at the same time rendering visible deepening Victorian fears of urban militancy and colonial misrule. The soap-monkey became the emblem of industrial progress and imperial evolution, embodying the double promise that nature could be redeemed by consumer capital and that consumer capital could be guaranteed by natural law. At the same time, however, the soap-monkey was eloquent of the degree to which fetishism structures industrial rationality.

The Mirror

In most Monkey Brand advertisements, the monkey holds a frying pan, which is also a mirror. In a similar Brooke's Soap ad, a classical female beauty with bare white arms stands draped in white, her skin and clothes epitomizing the exhibition value of sexual purity and domestic leisure, while from the cornucopia she holds flows a grotesque effluvium of hobgoblin angels. Each hybrid fetish embodies the doubled Victorian image of woman as "angel in the drawing room, monkey in the bedroom," as well as the racial iconography of evolutionary progress from ape to angel. Historical time, again, is captured as domestic spectacle, eerily reflected in the frying pan/mirror fetish.

In this ad, the Brooke's Soap offers an alchemy of economic progress, promising to make "copper like gold." At the same time, the Enlightenment idea of linear, rational time leading to angelic perfection finds its antithesis in the other time of housework, ruled by the hobgoblins of dirt, disorder and fetishistic, nonprogressive time. Erupting on the margins of the rational frame, the ad displays the irrational consequences of the idea of progress. The mirror/frying pan, like all fetishes, visibly expresses a crisis in value but cannot resolve it. It can only embody the contradiction, frozen as commodity spectacle, luring the spectator deeper and deeper into consumerism.

Mirrors glint and gleam in soap advertising, as they do in the culture of imperial kitsch at large. In Victorian middle-class households, servants scoured and polished every metal and wooden surface until it shone like a mirror. Doorknobs, lamp stands and banisters, tables and chairs, mirrors and clocks, knives and forks, kettles and pans, shoes and boots were polished until they shimmered, reflecting in their gleaming surfaces other object-mirrors, an infinity of crystalline mirrors within mirrors, until the interior of the house was all shining surfaces, a labyrinth of reflection. The mirror became the epitome of commodity fetishism: erasing both the signs of domestic labor and the industrial origins of domestic commodities. In the domestic world of mirrors, objects multiply without apparent human intervention in a promiscuous economy of self-generation.

Why the attention to surface and reflection? The polishing was dedicated, in part, to policing the boundaries between private and public, removing every trace of labor, replacing the disorderly evidence of working women with the exhibition of domesticity as veneer, the commodity spectacle as surface, the house arranged as a theater of clean surfaces for commodity display. The mirror/commodity renders the value of the object as an exhibit, a spectacle to be consumed, admired and displayed for its capacity to embody a twofold value: the man's market worth and the wife's exhibition status. The house existed to display femininity as bearing exhibition value only, beyond the marketplace and therefore, by natural decree, beyond political power.

An ad for Stephenson's Furniture Cream figures a spotless maid on all fours, smiling up from a floor so clean that it mirrors her reflection. The cream is "warranted not to fingermark." A superior soap should leave no telltale smear, no fingerprint of female labor. As Victorian servants lost individuality in the generic names their employers imposed on them, so soaps erased the imprint of women's work on middle-class history.

Domesticating Empire

By the end of the century, a stream of imperial bric-a-brac had invaded Victorian homes. Colonial heroes and colonial scenes were emblazoned on a host of domestic commodities, from milk cartons to sauce bottles, tobacco tins to whiskey bottles, assorted biscuits to toothpaste, toffee boxes to baking powder.[21] Traditional national fetishes such as the Union Jack, Britannia, John Bull and the rampant lion were marshaled into a revamped celebration of imperial spectacle (fig.7.2 and 7.3). Empire was seen to be patriotically defended by Ironclad Porpoise Bootlaces and Sons of the Empire soap, while Henry Morton Stanley came to the rescue of the Emin of Pasha laden with outsize boxes of Huntley and Palmers Biscuits.

Late Victorian advertising presented a vista of Africa conquered by domestic commodities.[22] In the flickering magic lantern of imperial desire, teas, biscuits, tobaccos, Bovril, tins of cocoa and, above all, soaps beach themselves on far-flung shores, tramp through jungles, quell uprisings, restore order and write the inevitable legend of commercial progress across the colonial landscape. In a Huntley and Palmers' Biscuits ad, a group of male colonials sit in the middle of a jungle on biscuit crates, sipping tea (fig. 7.4). Moving toward them is a stately and seemingly endless procession

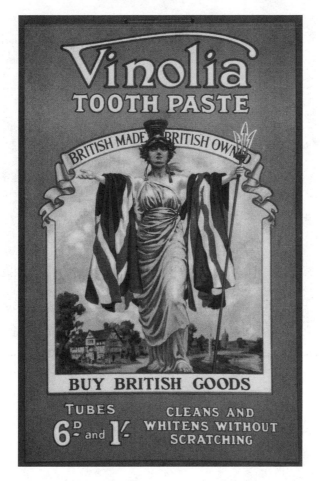

Fig. 7.2. Britannia and Domesticity. Robert Opie Collection.

of elephants, loaded with more biscuits and colonials, bringing tea time to the heart of the jungle. The serving attendant in this ad, as in most others, is male. Two things happen in such images: women vanish from the affair of empire, and colonized men are feminized by their association with domestic servitude.

Liminal images of oceans, beaches and shorelines recur in cleaning ads of the time. An exemplary ad for Chlorinol Soda Bleach shows three boys in a soda box sailing in a phantasmic ocean bathed by the radiance of the imperial dawn (fig. 7.5). In a scene washed in the red, white and blue of the Union Jack, two black boys proudly hold aloft their boxes of Chlorinol. A third boy, the familiar racial hybrid of cleaning ads, has presumably already applied his bleach, for his skin is blanched an eery white. On red sails that repeat the red of the bleach box, the legend of black people's purported commercial redemption in the arena of empire reads: "We are going to use 'Chlorinol' and be like de white nigger."

The ad vividly exemplifies Marx's lesson that the mystique of the commodity fetish lies not in its use value but in its exchange value and its potency as a sign:

Fig. 7.3. National Fetishism. Robert Opie Collection.

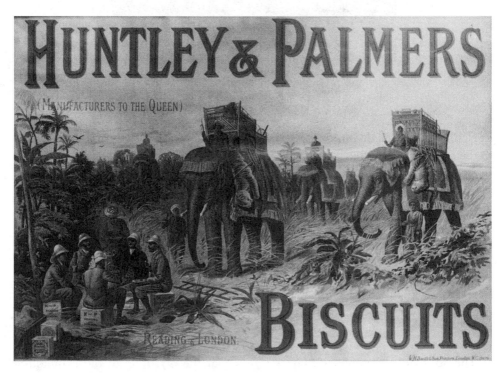

Fig. 7.4. Tea Time Comes to the Jungle. Robert Opie Collection.

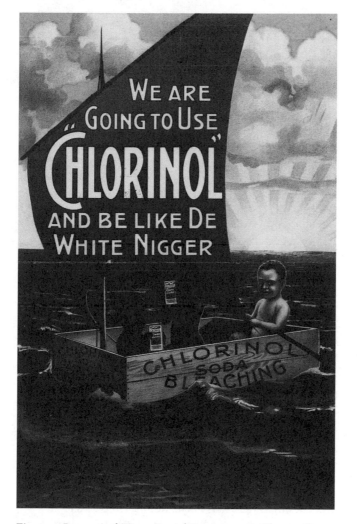

Fig. 7.5. Panoptical Time: Racial Progress at a Glance. Copy
1/264, Public Record Office, London.

"So far as [the commodity] is a value in use, there is nothing mysterious about it."
For three naked children, clothing bleach is less than useful. Instead, the whitening
agent of bleach promises an alchemy of racial upliftment through historical contact
with commodity culture. The transforming power of the civilizing mission is
stamped on the boat-box's sails as the objective character of the commodity itself.

More than merely a *symbol* of imperial progress, the domestic commodity becomes the *agent* of history itself. The commodity, abstracted from social context
and human labor, does the civilizing work of empire, while radical change is figured
as magical, without process or social agency. Hence the proliferation of ads featuring magic (fig. 7.6). In similar fashion, cleaning ads such as Chlorinol's foreshadow
the "before and after" beauty ads of the twentieth century, a crucial genre directed
largely at women, in which the conjuring power of the product to alchemize change

Fig. 7.6. Commodity Magic and the Vanishing of Women's Work. Copy 1/144 Pt. 1, Public Record Office, London.

is all that lies between the temporal "before and after" of women's bodily transformation.

The Chlorinol ad displays a racial and gendered division of labor. Imperial progress from black child to "white nigger" is consumed as commodity spectacle—as panoptical time. The self-satisfied, hybrid "white nigger" literally holds the rudder of history and directs social change, while the dawning of civilization bathes his enlightened brow with radiance. The black children simply have exhibition value as potential consumers of the commodity, there only to uphold the promise of capitalist commerce and to represent how far the white child has evolved—in the iconography of Victorian racism, the condition of "savagery" is identical to the condition of infancy. Like white women, Africans (both women and men) are figured not as historic agents but as frames for the commodity, valued for *exhibition* alone. The working women, both black and white, who spent vast amounts of energy bleaching the white sheets, shirts, frills, aprons, cuffs and collars of imperial clothes are nowhere to be seen. It is important to note that in Victorian advertising, black women are very seldom rendered as consumers of commodities, for, in imperial lore, they lag too far behind men to be agents of history. Imperial domesticity is therefore a domesticity without women.

In the Chlorinol ad, women's creation of social value through housework is displaced onto the commodity as its own power, fetishistically inscribed on the children's bodies as a magical metamorphosis of the flesh. At the same time, military subjugation, cultural coercion and economic thuggery are refigured as benign domestic processes as natural and healthy as washing. The stains of Africa's disobligingly complex and tenacious past and the inconvenience of alternative economic and cultural values are washed away like grime.

Incapable of themselves actually engendering change, African men are figured only as "mimic men," to borrow V. S. Naipaul's dyspeptic phrase, destined simply to ape the epic white march of progress to self-knowledge. Bereft of the white raimants of imperial godliness, the Chlorinol children appear to take the fetish literally, content to bleach their skins to white. Yet these ads reveal that, far from being a quintessentially African propensity, the faith in fetishism was a faith fundamental to imperial capitalism itself.

The Myth of First Contact

By the turn of the century, soap ads vividly embodied the hope that the commodity alone, independent of its use value, could convert other cultures to "civilization." Soap ads also embody what can be called *the myth of first contact*: the hope of capturing, as spectacle, the pristine moment of originary contact fixed forever in the timeless surface of the image. In another Pears ad, a black man stands alone on a beach, examining a bar of soap he has picked from a crate washed ashore from a shipwreck (fig. 7.7). The ad announces nothing less than the "The Birth Of Civilization." Civilization is born, the image implies, at the moment of first contact with the Western commodity. Simply by touching the magical object, African man is inspired into history. An epic metamorphosis takes place, as Man the Hunter-gatherer (anachronistic man) evolves instantly into Man the Consumer. At the same time, the magical object effects a gender transformation, for the consumption of the domestic soap is racialized as a male birthing ritual, with the egg-shaped commodity as the fertile talisman of change. Since women cannot be recognized as agents of history, it is necessary that a man, not a woman, be the historic beneficiary of the magical cargo and that the male birthing occur on the beach, not in the home.[23]

In keeping with the racist iconography of the gender degeneration of African men, the man is subtly feminized by his role as historic exhibit. His jaunty feather represents what Victorians liked to believe was African men's fetishistic, feminine and lower-class predilection for decorating their bodies. Thomas Carlyle, in his prolonged cogitation on clothes, *Sartor Resartus*, notes, for example: "The first spiritual want of a barbarous man is Decoration, as indeed we still see amongst the barbarous classes in civilized nations."[24] Feminists have explored how, in the icon-

Fig. 7.7. The Myth of First Contact. A. & F. Pears,
Ltd.

ography of modernity, women's bodies are exhibited for visual consumption, but
very little has been said about how, in imperial iconography, black men were figured
as spectacles for commodity exhibition. If, in scenes set in the Victorian home,
female servants are *racialized* and portrayed as frames for the exhibition of the
commodity, in advertising scenes set in the colonies, African men are *feminized* and
portrayed as exhibition frames for commodity display. Black women, by contrast,
are rendered virtually invisible. Essentialist assumptions about a universal "male
gaze" elide a great many important historical complexities.

Marx noted how under capitalism "the exchange value of a commodity assumes
an independent existence."[25] Toward the end of the nineteenth century, the commodity itself disappears from many ads, and the corporate signature, as the embodiment of pure exchange value in monopoly capital, finds an independent existence.
Another ad for Pears features a group of disheveled Sudanese "dervishes" awestruck

by a white legend carved on the mountain face: PEARS SOAP IS THE BEST. The significance of the ad, as Richards notes, is its representation of the commodity as a magical medium capable of enforcing and enlarging British power in the colonial world, even without the rational understanding of the mesmerized Sudanese.[26] What the ad more properly reveals is the colonials' own fetishistic faith in the magic of brand names to work the causal power of empire. In a similar ad, the letters BOVRIL march boldly over a colonial map of South Africa—imperial progress consumed as spectacle, as panoptical time. In an inspired promotional idea, the world had been recognized as tracing the military advance of Lord Roberts across the country, yoking together, as if writ by nature, the simultaneous lessons of colonial domination and commodity progress. In this ad, the colonial map explicitly enters the realm of commodity spectacle.

The poetics of cleanliness is a poetics of social discipline. Purification rituals prepare the body as a terrain of meaning, organizing flows of value across the self and the community and demarcating boundaries between one community and another. Purification rituals, however, can also be regimes of violence and constraint. People who have the power to invalidate the boundary rituals of another people thereby demonstrate their capacity to violently impose their culture on others. Colonial travel writers, traders, missionaries and bureaucrats carped constantly at the supposed absence in African culture of "proper domestic life," in particular Africans' purported lack of hygiene.[27] But the inscription of Africans as dirty and undomesticated, far from being an accurate depiction of African cultures, served to legitimize the imperialists' violent enforcement of their cultural and economic values, with the intent of purifying and thereby subjugating the unclean African body and imposing market and cultural values more useful to the mercantile and imperial economy. The myth of imperial commodities beaching on native shores, there to be welcomed by awestruck natives, wipes from memory the long and intricate history of European commercial trade with Africans and the long and intricate history of African resistance to Europe and colonization. Domestic ritual became a technology of discipline and dispossession.

The crucial point is not simply the formal contradictions that structure fetishes, but also the more demanding historical question of how certain groups succeed, through coercion or hegemony, in foreclosing the ambivalence that fetishism embodies by successfully imposing their economic and cultural system on others.[28] Cultural imperialism does not mean that the contradictions are permanently resolved, nor that they cannot be used against the colonials themselves. Nonetheless, it seems crucial to recognize that what has been vaunted by some as the permanent undecidability of cultural signs can also be violently and decisively foreclosed by superior military power or hegemonic dominion.

Fetishism in the Contest Zone

Enlightenment and Victorian writers frequently figured the colonial encounter as the journey of the rational European (male) mind across a liminal space (ocean, jungle or desert) populated by hybrids (mermaids and monsters) to a prehistoric zone of dervishes, cannibals and fetish-worshippers. Robinson Crusoe, in one of the first novelistic expressions of the idea, sets Christian lands apart from those whose people "prostrate themselves to Stocks and Stones, worshipping Monsters, Elephants, horrible shaped animals and Statues, or Images of Monsters."[29] The Enlightenment mind was felt to have transcended fetish worship and could look indulgently upon those still enchanted by the magical powers of "stocks and stones." But as Mitchell notes, "the deepest magic of the commodity fetish is its denial that there is anything magical about it."[30] Colonial protestations notwithstanding, a decidedly fetishistic faith in the magical powers of the commodity underpinned much of the colonial civilizing mission.

Contrary to the myth of first contact embodied in Victorian ads, Africans had been trading with Europeans for centuries by the time the British Victorians arrived. Intricate trading networks were spread over west and north Africa, with complex intercultural settlements and long histories of trade negotiations and exchanges, sporadically interrupted by violent conflicts and conquests. As John Barbot, the seventeenth-century trader and writer, remarked of the Gold Coast trade: "The Blacks of the Gold Coast, having traded with Europeans since the 14th century, are very well skilled in the nature and proper qualities of all European wares and merchandise vended there."[31] Eighteenth-century voyage accounts reveal, moreover, that European ships plying their trade with Africa were often loaded not with "useful" commodities but with baubles, trinkets, beads, mirrors and "medicinal" potions.[32] Appearing in seventeenth-century trade lists, among the salt, brandy, cloth and iron, are items such as brass rings, false pearls, bugles (small glass beads), looking glasses, little bells, false crystals, shells, bright rags, glass buttons, small brass trumpets, amulets and arm rings.[33] Colonials indulged heavily in the notion that, by ferrying these cargoes of geegaws and knick-knacks across the seas, they were merely pandering to naive and primitive African tastes. Merchant trade lists reveal, however, that when the European ships returned from West Africa, they were laden not only with gold dust and palm oil but also with elephant tusks, "teeth of sea-horses" (hippopotami), ostrich feathers, beeswax, animal hides and "cods of musk."[34] The absolute commodification of humanity and the colonial genuflection to the fetish of profit was most grotesquely revealed in the indiscriminate listing of slaves amongst the trifles and knick-knacks.

By defining the economic exchanges and ritual beliefs of other cultures as "irrational" and "fetishistic," the colonials tried to disavow them as legitimate systems. The huge labor that went into transporting cargoes of trifles to the colonies had less to do with the appropriateness of such fripperies to African cultural systems than with the systematic undervaluation of those systems with respect to merchant capitalism and market values in the European metropolis.

A good deal of evidence also suggests that the European traders, while vigorously denying their own fetishism and projecting such "primitive" proclivities onto white women, Africans and children, took their own "rational" fetishes with the utmost seriousness.[35] By many accounts, the empire seems to have been especially fortified by the marvelous fetish of Eno's Fruit Salt. If Pears could be entrusted with cleaning the outer body, Eno's was entrusted with "cleaning" the inner body. Most importantly, the internal purity guaranteed by Eno's could be relied upon to ensure male potency in the arena of war. As one colonial vouched: "During the Afghan war, I verily believe Kandahar was won by us all taking up large supplies of ENO's FRUIT SALT and so arrived fit to overthrow half-a-dozen Ayub Khans."[36] He was not alone in strongly recommending Eno's power to restore white supremacy. Commander A. J. Loftus, hydrographer to His Siamese Majesty, swore that he never ventured into the jungle without his tin of Eno's. There was only one instance, he vouched, during four years of imperial expeditions that any member of his party fell prey to fever: "and that happened after our supply of FRUIT SALT ran out."[37]

Fetishism became an intercultural space in that both sides of the encounter appear occasionally to have tried to manipulate the other by mimicking what they took to be the other's specific fetish. In Kenya, Joseph Thomson posed grandly as a white medicine man by conjuring an elaborate ruse with a tin of Eno's for the supposed edification of the Masai: "Taking out my sextant," he records with some glee:

> and putting on a pair of kid gloves—that accidentally I happened to have and that impressed the natives enormously, I intently examined the contents . . . getting ready some ENO'S FRUIT SALT, I sang an incantation—in general something about "Three Blue Bottles"—over it. My voice . . . did capitally for a wizard's. My preparations complete and Brahim [*sic*] being ready with a gun, I dropped the Salt into the mixture; simultaneously the gun was fired and, lo! up fizzed and sparkled the carbonic acid . . . the chiefs with fear and trembling taste as it fizzes away.[38]

While amusing himself grandly at the imagined expense of the Masai, Thomson reveals his own faith in the power of his fetishes (gloves as a fetish of class leisure, sextant and gun as a fetish of scientific technology and Eno's as a fetish of domestic purity) to hoodwink the Masai. "More amusing," however, as Hindley notes, is Thomson's own naivete, for the point of the story is that "to persuade the Masai to take his unfamiliar remedies, Thomson laid on a show in which the famous fruit salt provided only the 'magic' effects."[39] Eno's power as domestic fetish was eloquently summed up by a General Officer, who wrote and thanked Mr. Eno for his good powder: "Blessings on your Fruit Salt," he wrote, "I trust it is not profane to say so, but I swear by it. There stands the cherished bottle on the Chimney piece of my sanctum, my little idol—at home my household god, abroad my vade mecum."[40] The manufacturers of Eno's were so delighted by this fulsome dedication to their little fetish that they adopted it as regular promotional copy. Henceforth, Eno's was advertised by the slogan: "At home my household god, abroad my vade mecum."

In the colonial encounter, Africans adopted a variety of strategies for countering colonial attempts to undervalue their economies. Amongst these strategies, mimicry, appropriation, revaluation and violence figure the most frequently. Colonials carped rancorously at the African habit of making off with property that did not belong to them, a habit that was seen not as a form of protest, nor as a refusal of European notions of property ownership and exchange value, but as a primitive incapacity to understand the value of the "rational" market economy. Barbot, for example, describes the Eket as "the most trying of any of the Peoples we had to deal with . . . Poor Sawyer had a terrible time; the people had an idea they could do as they liked with the factory keeper and would often walk off with the goods without paying for them, that Mr Sawyer naturally objected to, usually ending in a free fight, sometimes my people coming off second best."[41] Richards notes how Henry Morton Stanley, likewise, could not make Africans (whom he saw primarily as carriers of western commodities) understand that he endowed the goods they carried with an abstract exchange value apart from their use value. Since these goods "lack any concrete social role for them in the customs, directives and taboos of their tribal lives, the carriers are forever dropping, discarding, misplacing, or walking away with them. Incensed, Stanley calls this theft."[42]

From the outset, the fetishism involved an intercultural contestation that was fraught with ambiguity, miscommunication and violence. Colonials were prone to fits of murderous temper when Africans refused to show due respect to their flags, crowns, maps, clocks, guns and soaps. Stanley, for one, records executing three African carriers for removing rifles, even though he admits that the condemned did not understand the value of the rifles or the principle for which they were being put to death.[43] Other carriers were executed for infringements such as dropping goods in rivers.

Anecdotes also reveal how quickly colonial tempers flared when Africans failed to be awestruck by the outlandish baubles the colonials offered them, for it wasn't long before the non-Europeans' curiosity and tolerance turned to derision and contempt. In Australia, Cook carped at the local inhabitants' ungrateful refusal to recognize the value of the baubles he brought them: "Some of the natives would not part with a hog, unless they received an axe in exchange; but nails and beads and other trinkets, that, during our former voyages, had so great a run at this island, were now so much despised, that few would deign so much to look at them."[44]

De Bougainville similarly recalls how a native from the Moluccas, when given "a handkerchief, a looking-glass and some other trifles . . . laughed when he received these presents and did not admire them. He seemed to know the Europeans."[45] As Simpson points out: "The handkerchief is an attribute of 'civilization,' the tool for making away with the unseemly sweat of the brow, the nasal discharge of cold climates and perhaps the tears of excessive emotion." The white handkerchief was also (like white gloves) the Victorian icon of domestic purity and the erasure of signs of labor. The Moluccan's refusal of handkerchief and mirror expressed a frank refusal of two of the central icons of Victorian middle-class consumerism.[46]

In some instances, elaborate forms of mimicry were created by Africans to maintain control of the mercantile trade. As the Comaroffs point out, the Tlhaping, the southernmost Tswana, having obtained beads for themselves, tried to deter Europeans from venturing further into the interior by mimicking European stereotypes of black savagery and portraying their neighbors as "men of ferocious habits" too barbaric to meddle with.[47]

In the imperial contest zone, fetishes embodied conflicts in the realm of value and were eloquent of a sustained African refusal to accept Europe's commodities and boundary rituals on the colonials' terms. The soap saga and the cult of domesticity vividly demonstrates that fetishism was original neither to industrial capitalism nor to precolonial economies, but was from the outset the embodiment and record of an incongruous and violent encounter.

NOTES

1. Karl Marx, "Commodity Fetishism," *Capital,* vol. 1 (New York: Vintage Books, 1977), p. 163.

2. See Thomas Richards's excellent analysis, *The Commodity Culture of Victorian Britain: Advertising and Spectacle, 1851–1914* (London: Verso, 1990), especially the introduction and ch. 1.

3. See David Simpson's analysis of novelistic fetishism in *Fetishism and Imagination: Dickens, Melville, Conrad* (Baltimore: Johns Hopkins University Press, 1982).

4. Richards, *The Commodity Culture,* p. 72.

5. Richards, *The Commodity Culture,* p. 5.

6. In 1889, an ad for Sunlight Soap featured the feminized figure of British nationalism, Britannia, standing on a hill and showing P. T. Barnum, the famous circus manager and impresario of the commodity spectacle, a huge Sunlight Soap factory stretched out below them. Britannia proudly proclaims the manufacture of Sunlight Soap to be: "The Greatest Show On Earth." See Jennifer Wicke's excellent analysis of P. T. Barnum in *Advertising Fiction: Literature, Advertisement and Social Reading* (New York: Columbia University Press, 1988).

7. See Timothy Burke, " 'Nyamarira That I Loved': Commoditization, Consumption and the Social History of Soap in Zimbabwe," *The Societies of Southern Africa in the 19th and 20th Centuries: Collected Seminar Papers,* vol. 17, no. 42 (London: University of London, Institute of Commonwealth Studies, 1992), pp. 195–216.

8. Leonore Davidoff and Catherine Hall, *Family Fortunes: Men and Women of the English Middle Class* (Routledge: London, 1992).

9. David T. A. Lindsey and Geoffrey C. Bamber, *Soap-Making. Past and Present, 1876–1976* (Nottingham: Gerard Brothers Ltd, 1965), p. 34.

10. Lindsey and Bamber, *Soap-Making,* p. 38. Just how deeply the relation between soap and advertising became embedded in popular memory is expressed in words such as "soft-soap" and "soap opera." For histories of advertising, see also Blanche B. Elliott, *A History of English Advertising* (London: Business Publications Ltd., 1962); and T. R. Nevett, *Advertising in Britain. A History* (London: Heinemann, 1982).

11. Quoted in Diana and Geoffrey Hindley, *Advertising in Victorian England, 1837–1901* (London: Wayland, 1972), p. 117.

12. Mike Dempsey, ed., *Bubbles: Early Advertising Art from A. & F. Pears Ltd.* (London: Fontana, 1978).

13. Laurel Bradley, "From Eden to Empire: John Everett Millais' Cherry Ripe," Victorian Studies, vol. 34, no. 2 (Winter 1991): 179–203. See also, Michael Dempsey, *Bubbles.*

14. Barratt spent £2200 on Millais' painting and £30,000 on the mass production of millions of individual reproductions of the painting. In the 1880s, Pears was spending between £300,000 nd £400,000 on advertising alone.

15. Furious at the pollution of the sacrosanct realm of art with economics, the art world lambasted Millais for trafficking (publicly instead of privately) in the sordid world of trade.

16. See Jennifer Wicke, *Advertising Fiction*, p. 70.

17. Donna Haraway, *Primate Visions: Gender; Race, and Nature in the World of Modern Science* (London: Routledge, 1989), p. 10.

18. Haraway, *Primate Visions*, p. 10.

19. Haraway, *Primate Visions*, pp. 10–11.

20. Charles Kingsley, Letter to his wife, 4 July 1860, in *Charles Kingsley: His Letters and Memories of His Life*, Francis E. Kingsley, ed. (London: Henry S. King and Co, 1877), p. 107. See also Richard Kearney, ed., *The Irish Mind* (Dublin: Wolfhound Press, 1985); L. P. Curtis Jr., *Anglo-Saxons and Celts: A Study of Anti-Irish Prejudice in Victorian England* (Bridgeport: Conference on British Studies of University of Bridgeport, 1968); and Seamus Deane, "Civilians and Barbarians," *Ireland's Field Day* (London: Hutchinson, 1985), pp. 33–42.

21. During the Anglo-Boer War, Britain's fighting forces were seen as valiantly fortified by Johnston's Corn Flour, Pattisons' Whiskey and Frye's Milk Chocolate. See Robert Opie, *Trading on the British Image* (Middlesex: Penguin, 1985), for an excellent collection of advertising images.

22. In a brilliant chapter, Richards explores how the imperial conviction of the explorer and travel writer Henry Morton Stanley that he had a mission to civilize Africans by teaching them the value of commodities "reveals the major role that imperialists ascribed to the commodity in propelling and justifying the scramble for Africa." Richards, *The Commodity Culture*, p. 123.

23. As Richards notes: "A hundred years earlier the ship offshore would have been preparing to enslave the African bodily as an object of exchange; here the object is rather to incorporate him into the orbit of exchange. In either case, this liminal moment posits that capitalism is dependent on a noncapitalist world, for only by sending commodities into liminal areas where, presumably, their value will not be appreciated at first can the endemic overproduction of the capitalist system continue." Richards, *The Commodity Culture*, p. 140.

24. Thomas Carlyle, *Sartor Resartus*, in *The Works of Thomas Carlyle*, vol. 1 (London: Chapman and Hall, 1896–1899), p. 30.

25. Karl Marx, "Theories of Surplus Value," quoted in G. A. Cohen, *Karl Marx's Theory of History: A Difference* (Princeton: Princeton University Press, 1978), pp. 124–25.

26. Richards, *The Commodity Culture*, pp. 122–23.

27. But palm-oil soaps had been made and used for centuries in west and equatorial Africa. In *Travels in West Africa* Mary Kingsley records the custom of digging deep baths in the earth, filling them with boiling water and fragrant herbs, and luxuriating under soothing packs of wet clay. In southern Africa, soap from oils was not much used, but clays, saps and barks were processed as cosmetics, and shrubs known as "soap bushes" were used for cleansing. Mary H. Kingsley, *Travels in West Africa* (London: Macmillan, 1899). Male Tswana activities like hunting and war were elaborately prepared for and governed by taboo. "In each case," as Jean and John Comaroff write, "the participants met beyond the boundaries of the village, dressed and armed for the fray, and were subjected to careful ritual washing (go foka marumo)." Jean and John Comaroff, *Of Revelation and Revolution: Christianity, Colonialism and Consciousness in South Africa*, vol. 1 (Chicago: University of Chicago Press, 1991), p. 164. In general, people creamed, glossed and sheened their bodies with a variety of oils, ruddy orchres, animal fats and fine colored clays.

28. For an excellent exploration of colonial hegemony in Southern Africa see Jean and

John Comaroff, "Home-Made Hegemony: Modernity, Domesticity and Colonialism in South Africa," in Karen Hansen, ed., *Encounters With Domesticity* (New Brunswick: Rutgers University Press, 1992), pp. 37–74.

29. Daniel Defoe, *The Farther Adventures of Robinson Crusoe*, in *The Shakespeare Head Edition of the Novels and Selected Writings of Daniel Defoe*, vol. 3 (Oxford: Basil Blackwell, 1927–1928), p. 177.

30. For an excellent analysis of commodity fetishism, see W. J. T. Mitchell, *Iconology: Image, Text, Ideology* (University of Chicago Press: Chicago, 1986), p. 193. See also Wolfgang Fritz Haug, *Critique of Commodity Aesthetics: Appearance, Sexuality and Advertising in Capitalist Society*, trans. Robert Bock (Minneapolis: University of Minnesota Press, 1986). See Catherine Gallagher's review essay in *Criticism*, vol. 29, no. 2 (1987): pp. 233–42. On the ritual character of commodities, see Arjun Appadurai, ed., *The Social Life of Things: Commodities in Cultural Perspective* (Cambridge: Cambridge University Press, 1986). See also Sut Jhally, *The Codes of Advertising: Fetishism and the Political Economy of Meaning in the Consumer Society* (London: Routledge, 1990); and, for the language of commodification, see Judith Williamson, *Decoding Advertisements: Ideology and Meaning in Advertising* (London: Marian Boyars, 1978).

31. Cited in Mary H. Kingsley, *Travels in West Africa*, p. 622.

32. Simpson, *Fetishism and Imagination*, p. 29.

33. "Trade Goods Used in the Early Trade with Africa as Given by Barbot and Other Writers of the Seventeenth Century," in Kingsley, *Travels in West Africa*, pp. 612–25.

34. Kingsley, *Travels in West Africa*, p. 614.

35. Fetishism was often defined as an infantile predilection. In Herman Melville's *Typee*, the hero describes the people's fetish-stones as "childish amusement . . . like those of a parcel of children playing with dolls and baby houses." *The Writings Of Herman Melville*, The Northwestern-Newberry Edition, Harrison Hayford, Hershel Parker and G. Thomas Tanselle, eds. (Evanston: Northwestern University Press; Chicago: The Newberry Library, 1968), pp. 174–77.

36. D. and G. Hindley, *Advertising in Victorian England*, p. 99.

37. D. and G. Hindley, *Advertising in Victorian England*, p. 98.

38. D. and G. Hindley, *Advertising in Victorian England*, p. 98.

39. D. and G. Hindley, *Advertising in Victorian England*, p. 98.

40. D. and G. Hindley, *Advertising in Victorian England*, p. 99.

41. Kingsley, *Travels in West Africa*, p. 594.

42. Richards, *The Commodity Culture*, p. 125.

43. Richards, *The Commodity Culture*, p. 125.

44. James Cook, *A Voyage to the Pacific Ocean, Undertaken by the Command of His Majesty, for Making Discoveries in the Northern Hemisphere* (vol. 2 (London: James Cook, 784), p. 10.

45. Lewis de Bougainville, *A Voyage Round the World, Performed by the Order of His Most Christian Majesty, in the Years 1766, 1767, 1768, and 1769*, trans. John Reinhold Forster (London: 1772), p. 360.

46. Barbot admits that the Africans on the west coast "have so often been imposed on by the Europeans, who in former ages made no scruple to cheat them in the quality, weight and measures of their goods which at first they received upon content, because they say it would never enter into their thoughts that white men . . . were so base as to abuse their credulity . . . examine and search very narrowly all our merchandize, piece by piece." It did not take

long, it seems, for Africans to invent their own subterfuges to hoodwink the Europeans and win the exchange. By Barbot's account, they would half-fill their oil casks with wood, add water to their oil, or herbs to the oil to make it ferment and thus fill up casks with half the oil. Kingsley, *Travels in West Africa*, pp. 582.

47. Jean and John L. Comaroff, *Of Revelation and Revolution*, p. 166.

Chapter Eight

Lesbian Chic
Experimentation and Repression in the 1920s

Lillian Faderman

The Roots of Bisexual Experimentation

By the 1920s in the United States, there were already a few established communities of women who identified themselves as lesbians, in some astonishing places such as Salt Lake City as well as in more likely areas such as San Francisco. But few women, regardless of their sexual experiences, became part of the fledgling lesbian community. Even if they did not marry and had affectional relationships only with other women, they lived usually without a lesbian subculture. In small towns where heterosexuals often "never even knew that homosexuals existed," according to oral histories of those who lived in such towns through the 1920s, they passed easily for heterosexual spinsters.[1]

But although there were no huge numbers of women who suddenly identified as lesbians, statistics gathered by a 1920s sociologist, Katharine Bement Davis, indicate that many women were giving themselves permission to explore sex between women. Davis' study of 2200 females (primarily of the middle class) shows that 50.4 percent admitted to intense emotional relations with other women and half of that number said that those experiences were either "accompanied by sex or recognized as sexual in character." They frequently saw the relationship as an isolated experience (or one of several isolated experiences), and they expected eventually to marry and live as heterosexuals, though the times seemed to some of them to permit experimentation.[2]

The etiology of "lesbian chic," the bisexual experimentation of the 1920s, has been traced by some social critics to World War I. But the war, in which the United States was engaged for only two years, did not have so significant an effect in establishing a lesbian subculture in America as it seems to have had in some areas of Europe, where it was fought for five years and with much more female participation than American women were permitted. According to Radclyffe Hall's 1920s works, "Miss Ogilvy Finds Herself" and *The Well of Loneliness*, for example, in World War I many English female "sexual inverts" took jobs such as ambulance driving and had the opportunity to meet others who were attracted to the active life that war service offered. It was not until the Second World War, in which American women participated on a much larger scale, that their war effort experiences actually did stimulate an unprecedented growth of an American lesbian subculture.

But while no large lesbian subculture was established in the United States as a result of World War I, the period seems to have marked the beginning of some self-conscious sexual experimentation between women. In the midst of women's Freudian enlightenment about the putative power of sexual drives, two million men were sent overseas and many more were called away from home for the war effort. It has been speculated that women, turning to each other *faute de mieux*, found they liked sex with other women just fine. As one blues composer wag of the era suggested in his song "Boy in the Boat," it was then that women learned about cunnilingus, manipulating "the boy in the boat" (the clitoris) with each other:

> Lot of these dames had nothing to do.
> Uncle Sam thought he'd give 'em a fightin' chance,
> Packed up all the men and sent 'em on to France,
> Sent 'em over there the Germans to hunt,
> Left the women at home to try out all their new stunts.[3]

Despite the composer's humorous intent, there is probably some element of truth in his explanation of the growth of sexual relations between women during those years when the relative paucity of men encouraged same-sex intimacy not only among middle-class college and professional women, who had had the freedom to enjoy each other's company for some time now, but also among a broader spectrum, of females who might have married (if not out of love, then out of ordinary social pressure) had it not been for the war.

In addition to the effects of Freud and the war, bisexual experimentation was also encouraged in some circles by a new value placed on the unconventional and daring. By the 1920s, young American intellectuals, bohemians, and generic nonconformists were determined to rout with a vengeance the last vestiges of Victorianism in the country. To many of them it was clear that their parents had known nothing anyway and it was that ignorance that had not only involved the world in a fruitless war but also caused untold personal suffering in the form of harmful repression and absurd legislation. In metropolitan areas these young people often determined the temper of the times through their preference for literature and art that challenged tradition, as well as through their resistance to laws such as Prohibition, their adoption of new fashions such as bobbed hair and short skirts for women, and their rejection of received notions regarding sexuality. Freud provided them with a license to explore sex openly, but there was a particular charm in explorations that would have previously been considered especially unorthodox, that would have shocked Lewis's Babbit, flown in the face of convention, shown an ability to live originally and dangerously. These became goals for the 1920s rebels— and in some circles, bisexuality seemed to address all those goals.

Unlike in earlier eras, love between women was now often assumed to be sexual (perhaps even in cases where it was not), and it was popularly described by the bald term "homo*sexuality*." With regard to sexual awareness, much of this generation had traveled a vast distance from their parent generation and the sophisticated would now have been incredulous over the concept of romantic friendship. But not only could they not believe in platonic love; they were also voyeuristically intrigued with lesbianism. The extent to which the subject fascinated the public is suggested by its popularity in American fiction of the era. Ernest Hemingway, for example, deals with the subject both briefly and extensively in his fiction of the '20s: in *The Sun Also Rises (1926)*, with the character of the "boyish" Brett Ashley; in *A Farewell to Arms* (1929), with Catherine Barkley's nurse friend, Fergy, who is in love with her; in the short story "The Sea Change," which is about a woman trying to explain to her male companion her erotic involvement with another woman; and in his posthumously published novel *The Garden of Eden*, set in the 1920s, whose major focus is a triangle that includes two women who are sexually enamoured with each other. Sherwood Anderson shows American women "experimenting" with lesbianism in two novels of the '20s, *Poor White (1920)* and *Dark Laughter (1925)*. A bisexual woman in *Dark Laughter* suggests that American wives played with lesbianism with great ease since American men "knew so little" about love and sex between women.[4] But the writers were working as hard as they could, along with the Freudians, to inform them. Minor novelists also, such as James Huneker (*Painted Veils, 1920*) and Wanda Fraiken Neff (*We Sing Diana, 1928*), and playwrights such as Henry Gribble (*March Hares, 1921)* and Thomas Dickinson (*Winter Bound, 1929)* all brought fascinated views of lesbians to literature and the American stage. The English novel *The Well of Loneliness*, published in the United States in 1928, became a huge *succès de scandale*.

It is difficult to assess just what that widespread interest in lesbianism meant, to American men in particular. Clearly there was ambivalence in their response. But perhaps the exoticism of the concept captured their curiosity and sexual imagination. Or perhaps the image of love between women aroused subconscious anxiety that was then cathartically soothed in these fictional works, since they almost invariably ended by confirming conventional sexuality: the girl seldom got the girl— most often a male came in and stole the booty. The old, reassuring sexual order was restored after experimentation with the new.

Although there was considerable interest in unconventional sexuality among sophisticates of the 1920s, the official voice was not remarkably different from that of the earlier eras and lesbianism, while discussed more openly than it had ever been before in America, was greeted with outrage by the guardians of morality who were nowhere near ready to accept such autonomous sexuality in women. In 1923 *Theatre Magazine*, an important voice of Broadway, said of Sholom Asch's *God of Vengeance*, one of the earliest plays with a lesbian theme to appear on Broadway: "A more foul and unpleasant spectacle has never been seen in New York." The producer, director, and cast of twelve were all hauled off to court on charges of obscenity. Edouard Bourdet's play *The Captive*, about a young woman who cannot be happy in her marriage because she is obsessed by another woman, met a similar fate in 1926 on Broadway, as well as in San Francisco, Los Angeles, and Detroit, when it appeared in those cities in 1927. Another play, *Sin of Sins*, opened in Chicago in 1926 and closed after a three-week run and a series of scandalized reviews such as that in *Variety*, which described the lesbian subject matter as being "not fit for public presentation."[5]

But despite such vestiges of suppression, public curiosity about the subject could not be stopped. In cosmopolitan areas like New York, the intrigue with homosexuality for the 1920s' "rebels" was manifested by drag balls where some men wore evening gowns and some women wore tuxedos and many came to be spectators. The balls were held in "respectable" ballrooms such as the ritzy Savoy and Hotel Astor and in the huge Madison Square Garden. Despite the voices of censorship such as those that occasionally emerged in response to Broadway plays, these events were officially sanctioned by police permits and attracted large numbers, as one Broadway gossip sheet of the 1920s announced in a headline: "6000 Crowd Huge Hall as Queer Men and Women Dance."[6]

Although the headline hints at a clear distinction between the "queers" and the spectators, the fiction of the period suggests that the lines sometimes blurred as the "heterosexual" tourists made contacts that were more than social among the avowedly homosexual participants. Such balls were for many sophisticates what the '20s was all about—the ultimate in rebellion and a good laugh at the naive world that took as self-evident matters such as sex and gender.

But although the "heterosexuals" in such places may have played for a while with homosexuality, they generally did not see themselves as homosexual. Since "homosexual" was in the process of becoming an identity, one now might feel forced to chose either to accept or reject that label. But an erotic interest in another female, and even sex with another female, was not necessarily sufficient to make a woman a lesbian. She might consider her experiences simply bisexual experimentation, which was even encouraged in certain milieus. One had to *see* oneself as a lesbian to be a lesbian. But despite the apparent sexual liberalism of many in the 1920s, the era was not far removed in time from the Victorian age, and to admit to an aberrant sexual identity must not yet have been easy for any but the most brave, unconventional, committed, or desperate.

White "Slumming" in Harlem

While a lesbian identity was impossible for many women to assume during the '20s, sex with other women was the great adventure, and literature and biography suggest that many women did not hesitate to partake of it. Of course some of the women who had sex with other women did indeed accept a lesbian identity and committed themselves to a new lesbian lifestyle. By 1922, as Gertrude Stein's "Miss Furr and Miss Skeene" indicates, such women were already calling themselves "gay," as homosexual men were.[7] But whether they identified as "gay" or were "just exploring," those who wanted to experience the public manifestations of lesbianism looked for recently emerged enclaves in America. The era saw the emergence of little areas of sophistication or places where a laissez-faire "morality" was encouraged, such as Harlem and Greenwich Village, which seemed to provide an arena in which like-minded cohorts could pretend, at least, that the 1920s was a decade of true sexual rebellion and freedom.

Harlem had a particular appeal for whites who wanted to indulge in rebel sexuality. Perhaps there was a certain racism in their willingness to think of Harlem as a free-for-all party or, as *Colliers Magazine* said in the 1920s, "a synonym for naughtiness." White fascination with Harlem seems to have smacked of a "sexual colonialism," in which many whites *used* Harlem as a commodity, a stimulant to sexuality. And as in many colonized countries, Harlem itself, needing to encourage tourism for economic reasons, seemed to welcome the party atmosphere. Whites went not only to cabarets such as the Cotton Club, which presented all-black entertainment to all-white audiences, but also to speakeasies—the Drool Inn, the Clam House, the Hot Feet—that were located in dark basements, behind locked doors with peepholes. Whites snickered and leered in places that specialized in double entendre songs. They peeked into or participated in sex circuses and marijuana parlors. And they went to Harlem to experience homosexuality as the epitome of the forbidden: they watched transvestite floorshows; they rubbed shoulders with homosexuals; they were gay themselves in mixed bars that catered to black and white, heterosexual and homosexual. Made braver by bootlegged liquor, jazz, and what they saw as the primitive excitement of Africa, they acted out their enchantment with the primal and the erotic. They were fascinated with putative black naturalness and exoticism, and they romantically felt that those they regarded as the "lower class" had something to teach them about sexual expression that their middle-class milieu had kept from them. They believed Harlem gave them permission—or they simply took permission there—to explore what was forbidden in the white world. They could do in Harlem what they dared not do anywhere else.[8]

But it was not simply that whites took callous advantage of Harlem. To those who already defined themselves as homosexual, Harlem seemed a refuge, for which they were grateful. With an emerging homosexual consciousness, they began, probably for the first time in America, to see themselves as a minority that was not unlike racial minorities. They compared their social discomfort as homosexuals in the world at large with the discomfort of black people in the white world. Some sensed, as one character says in a novel about the period, *Strange Brother*, a bond between themselves and blacks because both groups flourished under heavy odds, and they believed that blacks also acknowledged that bond: "In Harlem I found courage and joy and tolerance. I can be myself there. . . . They know all about me and I don't have to lie."[9]

In fact, however, blacks were generally as ambivalent about homosexuality as whites, but there were clubs in Harlem that did indeed welcome homosexuals, if only as one more exotic drawing card to lure tourists. Urban blacks in the 1920s did not all simply accept homosexuality as a "fact of life," as gay whites liked to think they did, but Harlem's reliance on tourism created at least the illusion of welcome.

Black novels of the 1920s show how thin that illusion really was. Claude McKay, a black writer who was himself bisexual, depicts Harlem's ambivalence about homosexuality in his novel *Home to Harlem (1928)*. Raymond, an intellectual black waiter, is eloquent in his romantic characterization of lesbianism. He tells Jake, a kitchen porter, that he is reading a book by Alphonse Daudet, *Sapho*:

> It's about a sporting woman who was beautiful like a rose. . . . Her lovers called her Sapho. . . . Sappho was a real person. A wonderful woman, a great Greek poet. . . . Her story gave two lovely words to modern language. . . . Sapphic and Lesbian— beautiful words.

But it is Jake who seems to speak for the Harlem masses when he realizes that "lesbian" is "what we calls bulldyker in Harlem," and he declares, "Them's all ugly womens." Raymond continues his liberal defense in correcting him, "Not *all*. And that's a damned ugly name." But he realistically recognizes "Harlem is too savage about some things." McKay illustrates more of Harlem's ridicule, good-natured as it may sometimes have been, when he presents in this novel a nightclub called The Congo that does cater to homosexuals along with heterosexuals, but the "wonderful drag blues" to which everyone dances suggests that the heterosexuals responded to the homosexuals around them with a gentle contempt: "And there is two things in Harlem I don't understan'/ It is a bulldyking woman and a faggoty man./ Oh, baby, how are you?/ Oh, baby, what are you?"[10]

Other novels by black writers also make it clear that while lesbians in Harlem of the 1920s went unmolested, they were seldom approved of. In Wallace Thurman's 1929 novel *The Blacker the Berry*, lesbian characters are a part of everyday Harlem, but there is always a hint of discomfort when they appear. Alva, a black bisexual who is a scoundrel, runs around with a creole lesbian, which emphasizes his unsavory character. Emma Lou, the heroine, goes hunting for a room to rent and encounters the absurd Miss Carrington, who places her hand on Emma Lou's knee, promising, "Don't worry anymore, dearie, I'll take care of you from now on," and tells her, "There are lots of nice girls living here. We call this the 'Old Maid's Home.' We have parties among ourselves and just have a grand time. Talk about fun! I know you'd be happy here." Emma Lou is frightened off by what seems to her a bizarre sexuality, although obviously there is a whole boarding house full of lesbians who are allowed to live in Harlem undisturbed.[11] But the tone in which this phenomenon is presented, by a black writer who was himself gay, makes it clear that Harlem sees these women as "queers."

Yet most white writers who dealt with gay Harlem of the 1920s preferred the illusion of an "anything goes" atmosphere in which no one blinks an eye or expresses disapproval. In Blair Niles' *Strange Brother* when a white woman begs "to see the other Harlem" she is taken to the Lobster Pot, which vibrates with variety, both in color and sexual orientation. At the Lobster Pot,

> three white women had just taken the table next to [several Negro] dandies. One of them was a girl, rather lovely, with delicately chiseled features and short dark hair brushed severely back from a smooth low forehead. From the waist up she was dressed like a man, in a loose shirt of soft white silk and a dark tailored coat. She sat with one arm around the woman beside her.

No one makes wisecracks or exhibits disdain at such a sight. The most prominent lesbian figure in *Strange Brother* is Sybil, the black piano player at the Lobster Pot, perhaps modeled on Gladys Bentley, a lesbian transvestite Harlem entertainer. Sybil is a totally happy soul. She "filled the room with her vast vitality" and performed "as though to live was so gorgeous an experience that one must dance and sing in thanksgiving." She lives with another woman, her "wife," whom she married in a lesbian wedding, Sybil in tuxedo, the other woman in bridal veil and orange blossoms. A white character says, "They're happy and nobody they know thinks any the less of them."[12] But as black novelists suggested, such uncomplicated acceptance was less than certain.

In reality as well as in fiction, whites were reluctant to see Harlem's ambivalence toward homosexuality. Instead, they saw that Harlem appeared "wide open" sexually and, typical of many who enjoy the fruits of colonialism, they did not analyze why or even question Harlem's limits. They "slummed" in Harlem as though they were taking a trip into their id. The white women who went to Harlem to "be lesbian" were sometimes only "trying it on," taking advantage of what they assumed was the free spirit of the 1920s in Harlem to explore a variety of sexual possibilities. Some of these women considered themselves bisexual. More often they simply considered themselves adventurous, since there was not yet a pressing need to declare, even to one's self, one's "sexual orientation." They were frequently married or looking for a husband but saw that as no obstacle to their right to explore, either with the black women or with other white women they might meet in Harlem. In John Dos Passos' *The Big Money*, a novel about America after World War I, Dick Savage is implored by Patricia Doolittle (puns intended), one of the Junior League women in his group of wealthy friends, "Do take me some place low. . . . I'm the new woman. . . . I want to see life." They end up in a black, homosexual basement bar in Harlem, where Patricia dances with "a pale pretty mulatto girl in a yellow dress," while Dick dances with a "brown boy" in a tight suit who calls himself "Gloria Swanson." When Dick insists on taking Patricia home so that he can carry on without her as a witness, she screams at him, "You spoil everything. . . . You'll never go through with anything," piqued because she too had intended something further with her female partner. He later returns to the bar alone and takes "Gloria" and another young man, "Florence," home with him.[13] It is night time Harlem that unleashes inhibitions in these repressed whites. They permit themselves to live out fantasy in a world that is not quite real to them. They no longer have to "behave" as they do in white society which "matters."

Such fiction appears to have accurately reflected real life, in which wealthy whites were fascinated with "seeing life" and playing at it in various Harlem night spots that were open to displays of unconventional sexuality. Libby Holman, the celebrated singer of the '20s, who was married to a man, nevertheless came to Harlem, where she could not only act as a lesbian but even be outrageously gay. With one of her lovers, Louisa Carpenter du Pont Jenney, heiress to a great number of the du Pont millions, she visited Harlem almost nightly during one period, both dressed in identical men's dark suits and bowler hats such as they probably could not have worn with impunity in most other areas of the United States. There they were joined by other women celebrities and high-livers, most of them also married to men but out for a good time with other bisexual females: Beatrice Lillie, Tallulah Bankhead, Jeanne Eagles (who was Sadie Thompson in the first version of *Rain*), Marilyn Miller (the quintessential Ziegfield girl), and Lucille Le Sueur (who later became Joan Crawford). Sometimes they went to the Lafayette to listen to another bisexual woman singer, Bessie Smith, or they visited Helen Valentine, the famous entrepeneur of 140th Street who staged sex circuses that featured homosexual as well as heterosexual acts.[14]

They encouraged some Harlem entertainers even to flaunt lesbianism, to make it a spectacle and an attraction to those who expected the *outre* from Harlem. Gladys Bentley, a three-hundred-pound "male impersonator" who sometimes played under the name Bobby Minton, appeared in men's suits not only onstage at the popular Clam House and the night spot she later opened, Barbara's Exclusive Club, but also on the streets of Harlem. It was said that her appearance "drew celebrities like flies." Dressed in a tuxedo, she announced her homosexuality by marrying a woman in a New Jersey civil ceremony, like her fictional counterpart Sybil in *Strange Brother*. Her blatant transvestism and homosexual behavior were part of her risqué appeal. She was the epitome of the stereotype of the lesbian that the public came to Harlem to gawk at. Gladys was in reality bisexual, but in her exceptional case it was more profitable to hide that aspect of her life from the public, which was fascinated with her outrageous image.[15]

That whites permitted themselves to act in Harlem as they probably would not elsewhere was obviously not without opportunism and a racist conviction that nothing really counted in the fantasy world of tourist Harlem. Perhaps their behavior can be attributed to a feeling that their skin color served as armor here, making them impervious to any manner of attack or insult. But what they saw as the greater vitality of black people, "their more basic and healthier eroticism," permitted these white women to reach into those areas of their psyches (whose existence the Freudians had recently charted like a newly discovered planet) in order to discover and express desires they might have suppressed elsewhere. Many of them must have been grateful for the permission Harlem appeared to give them.

Black Lesbians in Harlem

A black lesbian subculture could be established fairly early in Harlem for several reasons. One root of that subculture might have been the demiworld. Black women who had been to jail learned there not only about lesbian sexuality but also about "mama" and "papa" sexual roles that had developed in institutionalized situations in America by the beginning of this century.[16] They sometimes established similar "butch/femme" arrangements once they were released from the institution, and perhaps they helped to bring such patterns into the fledgling subculture and to give it a clear, identifiable image.

But it was also easy for black lesbians to form a subculture in Harlem relatively early because although many Harlemites treated homosexuality with some ridicule, there was nevertheless more tolerance there than elsewhere for what the world of Babbit would have seen as outcasts and oddities, since blacks in general felt themselves to be outside the pale in white America. While homosexual men were sometimes being run out of small white towns, as Sherwood Anderson suggests in his post–World War I collection of stories *Winesburg, Ohio* ("Hands"), in Harlem tolerance extended to such a degree that black lesbians in butch/femme couples married each other in large wedding ceremonies, replete with bridesmaids and attendants. Real marriage licenses were obtained by masculinizing a first name or having a gay male surrogate apply for a license for the lesbian couple. Those licenses were actually placed on file in the New York City Marriage Bureau. The marriages were often common knowledge among Harlem heterosexuals.[17]

Such relative tolerance permitted black lesbians to socialize openly in their own communities instead of seeking out alien turf as white lesbians generally felt compelled to do. While heterosexual Harlemites often made fun of lesbians, they were willing to share bars and dance floors with them. There were thus plenty of places where black lesbians could amuse themselves and meet other lesbians in Harlem. The nightclubs that catered to gays and straights together that were described in novels such as *Home to Harlem, Strange Brother, The Big Money*, and Carl Van Vechten's *Nigger Heaven* all had counterparts in reality. The Lobster Pot, where Sybil sings and dances in *Strange Brother*, for instance, was probably the Clam House, where Gladys Bentley entertained for many years. There were numerous other bars and dance places, such as Connie's Inn, the Yeahman, the Garden of Joy, and Rockland Palace, where homosexuals and heterosexuals rubbed shoulders, although, as Van Vechten shows in *Nigger Heaven*, heterosexuals sometimes quit a club when they perceived that "too many bulldikers" were taking over.[18]

Institutions that had no counterparts in the white world also flourished in gay Harlem of the 1920s. "Buffet flats," apartments where sex circuses were staged, cafeteria style, for a paying clientele, occasionally catered to homosexual audiences. Ruby Walker Smith recalls such establishments where there were "nothing but faggots and bulldaggers. . . . everybody that's in the life. . . . everything goes." According to Smith, people would pay as they came in and then be free to roam around: "They had shows in every room, two women goin' together, a man and a man goin' together. . . . and if you interested they do the same thing to you." While buffet flats appear to have begun as a heterosexual institution, there were enough individuals who were interested in homosexuality to make a gay buffet flat a profitable proposition. Equivalent buffet flats still catered to heterosexuals as well, not only in New York, but in the ghettos of Chicago, Detroit, Philadelphia, and Washington.[19]

While there were black lesbians in 1920s Harlem who committed themselves to "the life" and sometimes lived with other women in butch/femme couples, many who had affairs with other females were married to men, either because they were bisexual, they needed to marry for economic reasons, or front marriages permitted them to continue functioning with less stigma in the very sexually aware and ambivalent black community. Among Harlem women of wealth or fame, bisexuality was not uncommon, though few would have admitted to exclusive homosexuality. Perhaps to Harlem sophisticates, who in this respect do not appear to have been very different from white sophisticates of the 1920s, the former seemed like adventure while the latter seemed like disease. In any case, there is a good deal of evidence of bisexuality among Harlem entertainers in particular. For instance, blues singer Bessie Smith's lesbian interests were well known among her show business intimates, although she was a married woman and took pains to cultivate that image as well. Many of the women in Bessie's mid-1920s show, *Harlem Frolics*, were also known to have had relationships with each other.[20]

The complex attitudes with regard to female homosexual relations that were prevalent among sophisticated Harlemites in the 1920s are sometimes reflected in lyrics of the blues. Those songs, which are often satirical or funny, do not deal with bisexuality, perhaps because that affectional preference lent itself less readily to humorous caricature than did blatant lesbianism. Instead, they sometimes present extreme lesbian stereotypes (especially the mannish lesbian image that the term "bulldiker" connoted), which allowed the listener to recognize the situation without introducing subtle complications and to laugh at the in-joke. With the usual goal of titillation, the songs also satirically probed masculine uneasiness about the suspicion that women know how to "do it" better to each other than men do. And they frequently admitted to an ambivalent fascination.

In some of these songs the characterization of the lesbian combines images of freakishness with a bravado that is at once laughable and admirable. The lesbian is ridiculed for her illicit and unorthodox sexuality. But she is also an outlaw, which makes her a bit of a culture hero in an oppressed community. In Ma Rainey's "Prove It on Me Blues" the singer seems to invite jeers: she admits to wearing a collar and a tie, to being "crooked," to liking "to watch while the women pass by." But the black audience is forced to identify with her because she and they understand stigmatization. And she is also rescued from being ludicrous because she can toy with the audience. She is the jokester they must, at least grudgingly, admire. She teasingly admits that she means to follow another woman everywhere she goes and that she wants the whole world to know it. But she pretends to dangle ambiguity in front of her listeners:

> Went out last night with a crowd of my friends,
> They must've been women, 'cause I don't like no men. . . .
>
> They say I do it, ain't nobody caught me,
> They sure got to prove it on me. . . . [21]

Her message is finally that she doesn't give a damn what they think and until she is caught *in flagrante delicto* no one can prove anything about her anyway. But the audience is meant to understand that she does indeed "do it" and to simultaneously laugh at her and cheer her on for her boldness.

It is not surprising that sophisticated heterosexuals, both blacks and the tourists who were intrigued with black life and environs, were taken with such lyrics—they were characteristic of the era: They flaunt unorthodoxy with a vengeance, but at the same time they exhibit the vestiges of discomfort toward female nonconformity and sexual autonomy that individuals who scoffed at the conventional nevertheless maintained. That discomfort, as much as it is mitigated by laughter in these songs, suggests that even those who chose to reject the mainstream culture or who were cast outside it by virtue of their race could go no further in their own unconventionality than to be ambivalent about sexual love between women.

NOTES

1. Lesbian communities in Salt Lake City and San Francisco are discussed in Vern Bullough and Bonnie Bullough, "Lesbianism in the 1920s and 1930s: A New Found Study," *Signs* (Summer 1977), 2(4):895–904. Discussion of small town homosexuality in the 1920s is in Bob Skiba, "Pansies, Perverts, and Pegged Pants," *Gay and Lesbian Community Guide to New England*, 1982, p. 3, in New York Lesbian Herstory Archives, file: 1920s.

2. Katharine Bement Davis, *Factors in the Sex Life of Twenty-Two Hundred Women* (New York: Harper and Row, 1929), p. 247. See also my analysis of Davis' data in *Surpassing the Love of Men: Romantic Friendship and Love Between Women from the Renaissance to the Present* (New York: William Morrow, 1981), pp. 326–27.

3. George Hannah, "Boy in the Boat," *AC-DC Blues: Gay Jazz Reissues*, side B, Stash Records, ST-106.

4. Hemingway's most recent biographer, Kenneth Lynn, observes "a larger drama of sexual confusion" in Hemingway's life: a mother who was a lesbian, sisters who wished to be boys, obsession with women's short hair, cross dressing. He was intrigued by Gertrude Stein's lesbianism and was also close friends with other expatriate lesbians such as Djuna Barnes and Natalie Barney. Lynn suggests that Hemingway derived the name of his impotent hero in *The Sun Also Rises* from them: "Jacob" from Natalie's famous address, 20 rue Jacob, and "Barnes" from Djuna's last name. Jake is in love with Brett who is sexually aggressive and mannish, and Lynn states that his "dilemma is that, like a lesbian, he cannot penetrate his loved one's body"; Kenneth S. Lynn, *Hemingway* (New York: Simon and Schuster, 1987). But Hemingway's interest in lesbians may be explained as easily in the context of his times as in the context of his personal life. Sherwood Anderson, *Dark Laughter* (New York: Boni and Liveright, 1925), pp. 150–55.

5. Kaier Curtin discusses the flurry over *God of Vengeance, Sin of Sins*, and *The Captive* in *"We Can Always Call Them Bulgarians": Lesbians and Gay Men on the American Stage* (Boston: Alyson, 1987). When Thomas Dickinson's *Winter Bound*, a play that seems to be influenced by D. H. Lawrence's novella of lesbian defeat, *The Fox*, appeared on Broadway at the end of the decade it caused little stir, perhaps because by then the public had become more used to the subject of lesbianism, particularly through *The Well of Loneliness*, which was published in America shortly before the production of *Winter Bound* (1929) and quickly became a best-seller.

6. Quoted in "That Was New York," *New Yorker*, Feb. 1940, pp. 35–38.

7. Gertrude Stein, "Miss Furr and Miss Skeene" (1922; reprinted in *The Selected Writings of Gertrude Stein*, ed. Carl Van Vechten [New York: Random House, 1962], pp. 561–68).

8. "Synonym," quoted in John B. Kennedy, "So This Is Harlem," *Colliers*, October 28, 1933, p. 27+. Straight/gay Harlem in the '20s described in George Chauncey, Jr., "The Way

We Were," *Village Voice*, July 1, 1986, pp. 29–30+; Blair Niles, *Strange Brother* (1931; reprint, New York: Arno, 1975), p. 210; Milt Machlin, *Libby* (New York: Tower, 1980), p. 59.

9. Niles, pp. 151–52.

10. On Harlem Renaissance homosexuality see Eric Garber, " 'Tain't Nobody's Business: Homosexuality in Harlem in the 1920s," *Advocate*, May 13, 1982, pp. 39–43+. On Mc-Kay's homosexuality see Wayne F. Cooper, *Claude McKay: Rebel Sojourner in the Harlem Renaissance* (Baton Rouge: Louisiana State University Press, 1987), passim. Claude McKay, *Home to Harlem* (1928; reprint, Chatham, New Jersey: Chatham 1973), pp. 128–29, 91–92. Bessie Smith recorded a slightly different version of the song called "Foolish Man Blues":

> There's two things got me puzzled,
> There's two things I don't understand,
> That's a mannish-acting woman,
> And a skippin', twistin', woman-acting man.

In Chris Albertson, *Bessie* (New York: Stein and Day, 1972), p. 125. In Smith's version its razzing nature is mitigated through the title, which laughs at the speaker, and through the fact of the singer's own bisexuality.

11. Wallace Thurman, *The Blacker the Berry* (1929; reprint, New York: Arno, 1969), pp. 211, 135–36.

12. Niles, pp. 47, 56, 155–56.

13. John Dos Passos, *The Big Money* (New York: Harcourt Brace, 1936), pp. 514–17.

14. Machlin, pp. 69–71. See also Mercedes de Acosta, *Here Lies the Heart* (1960; reprint, New York: Arno Press, 1975), p. 128, and Lee Israel, *Miss Tallulah Bankhead* (New York: Dell, 1973), pp. 68–70.

15. Jervis Anderson, *This Was Harlem: A Cultural Portrait, 1900–1950* (New York: Farrar, Straus and Giroux, 1982), p. 169; Roi Ottley and William Weatherby, eds., *The Negro in New York: An Informal Social History* (Dobbs Ferry, N.Y.: Oceana, 1967), p. 249; Gladys Bentley, "I Am a Woman Again," *Ebony* (August 1952), pp. 92–98; personal interview with Mabel Hampton, cohort of Bentley, age 85, New York, October 4, 1987.

16. Margaret Otis discussed early twentieth-century black and white lesbian behavior in jails in "A Perversion Not Commonly Noted," *Journal of Abnormal Psychology* (June–July 1913), 8(2): 113–16.

17. Luvenia Pinson, "The Black Lesbian—Times Past, Times Present," *Womanews*, May 1980. See also Niles, for Harlemites' knowledge of black lesbian marriages.

18. Gloria Hull, in "Under the Days: The Buried Life and Poetry of Angelina Weld Grimke," *Conditions: Five, The Black Women's Issue* (Autumn 1979), 2(2):23, suggests that Grimke was not more prolific because she felt she had to hide her lesbianism. But it is actually unclear to what extent Grimke felt it necessary to be secretive about her affectional preference. Some ostensibly lesbian poems by Grimke did appear during her lifetime, such as "Mona Lisa," in Countee Cullen, ed., *Caroling Dusk: An Anthology of Verse by Negro Poets* (New York: Harper and Row, 1927), p. 42. See also the poems of May V. Cowdery, who published frequently in *Crisis* during the 1920s. Cowdery's book of collected verse, *We Lift Our Voices and Other Poems* (Philadelphia: Alpress, 1936), contains several poems that appear to be lesbian, such as "Insatiate," a sardonic poem about how only jealousy can keep the speaker faithful to her woman lover (pp. 57–58). Information about clubs from Bentley; Machlin, pp. 69–70; Garber, p. 41; and personal interview with Mabel Hampton. Carl Van Vechten, *Nigger Heaven* (rpt. New York: Harper and Row, 1971), pp. 12, 137.

19. Interview with Ruby Smith by Chris Albertson, 1971, *AC-DC Blues*, side A. See also Albertson, *Bessie*, p. 123. History of buffet flats in Garber, p. 41; McKay, p. 103; Machlin, p. 71.

20. Elaine Feinstein, *Bessie Smith* (New York: Viking, 1985), p. 38. Albertson, *Bessie*, chatper 5.

21. Ma Rainey, "Prove It on Me Blues," on *AC-DC Blues: Gay Jazz Reissues*, side A, Stash Records, ST-106.

Chapter Nine

Consumerism and the Construction of Black Female Identity in Twentieth-Century America

Robert E. Weems, Jr.

African Americans, of both genders, have historically viewed consumption as a means to construct an "identity." African Americans, in fact, have placed greater emphasis than other groups on "identity construction" through consumption. Because blacks possess the dubious distinction of being the only group in the United States to have once been designated as slaves, many African Americans continue to view consumerism, and in fact, conspicuous consumption, as a means to separate themselves from a "degraded past."

Although African American men and women share a mutual "need" to consume, this essay focuses on a gender-specific aspect of twentieth-century black female consumption. Perhaps the most controversial and complex aspect of African American female consumption during this century—especially in terms of using consumption to help construct an identity—has been black women's use of personal care items and beauty products.

There is a growing body of literature that clearly demonstrates that African American women, for much of the twentieth century, have been "culturally assaulted" by most purveyors of beauty care products. Advertisers, consciously or unconsciously, deemed the natural physical attributes of black women "ugly." Consequently, black women, especially before mid-century, were urged to buy a myriad of concoctions to straighten their hair, whiten their skin, and thin their lips.[1]

African American newspapers represented the most widely used medium to reach black female consumers during the first decades of the twentieth-century. In one of the chapters ("What Is in a Negro Paper") of his classic 1922 study *The Negro Press in the United States*, Frederick G. Detweiler noted the following:[2]

> There are certain sorts of advertising that strike the reader as unusually prominent. First among those come the cosmetics. The persons and firms who do hairdressing or sell skin bleaches and hair straighteners are legion . . . The most successful Chicago paper had twenty-five advertisements of this character in a random issue. A Memphis paper had twenty-two in one issue. Another city paper gives 40 percent of its advertising to this business, two others in large southern cities give just about half, and a religious paper more than half of all its advertising.

Three years later, sociologist Guy B. Johnson published a study titled "Newspaper Advertisements and Negro Culture" that examined advertising in six prominent African American newspapers: the Chicago *Defender*, the *Negro World* (published by Marcus Garvey's Universal Negro Improvement Association), the Norfolk *Journal and Guide*, the Atlanta *Independent*, and the Houston *Informer*. Similar to Detweiler, Johnson discovered an overwhelming predominance of ads marketing various beauty preparations. Moreover, he asserted that most of these ads "make their appeal to the desire for straight hair and light complexion."[3] To buttress his point, Johnson's article featured advertisements that appeared in the newspapers he surveyed. The following examples graphically illustrate this marketing genre.[4]

New 3-Way Skin Discovery Gives You WHITE SKIN BEAUTY OVERNIGHT—OR NO COST. Amazing Bleach works Under the Skin. Science has perfected a new 3-way treatment to harmlessly bleach, lighten and make any ugly blotchy skin beautiful—or the treatment costs nothing. . . . Used by stage stars and prominent people everywhere. You will love these creations—results often the first night. The treatment is complete. Skin beauty can be yours.

MAKE YOUR HAIR STRAIGHT AND BEAUTIFUL. Try this quick and simple method which thousands now use. Don't envy your friends who have gleaming masses of straight hair. Have it yourself. It is a simple matter to achieve that glossy black, wavy effect, which our entire Race admires. Convince yourself of this by using our patented Dixie Curve-Tooth Straightening Comb.

Succeeding decades would witness an increased diversity of products advertised in African American newspapers, as advertisers recognized and responded to blacks' buying power and promise. Nevertheless, Vishnu V. Oak's 1948 book *The Negro Newspaper* noted that advertisements of hair and skin lotions remained "the richest advertising contracts for the Negro Press."[5]

The proliferation of racially derogatory advertising aimed at black women in early twentieth-century African American newspapers raises several questions. First, since these ads offered blacks the "wonders of whiteness" (i.e., straight hair and lighter skin) in a jar or bottle, did some black readers indeed respond to these products on that basis? What about black companies that marketed personal care/beauty products to black women? Were they selling African American women "whiteness" or something else entirely?

The issue of blacks' use of certain personal care products to repudiate one identity (the "ugly" African) and aspire toward another identity (the "pretty" or "handsome" European) remains controversial and emotionally charged. One of the more blunt assessments of this phenomenon appeared in John Moffatt Mecklin's 1921 book *Democracy and Race Friction*. Mecklin, a white professor of philosophy at the University of Pittsburgh, included the following in his discussion of African Americans:[6]

The columns of Negro newspapers from Massachusetts to Texas are full of advertisements of "anti-kink" nostrums accompanied by illustrations of heads of long and flowing hair. . . . This slavish imitation of the white, even to the attempted obliteration of physical characteristics, such as woolly hair, is almost pathetic and exceedingly significant as indicating the absence of feelings of race pride or integrity. Any imitation of one race by another of such a wholesale and servile kind as to involve complete race self-abnegation, must be disastrous to all concerned.

But in a May 1925 article in the *Journal of Social Forces* titled "Conflicting Forces in Negro Progress," Francis Marion Dunford offered a somewhat different and intriguing assessment of African American usage of hair straighteners and skin whiteners. While Dunford, like most white scholars of the era, still conveyed a sense of condescension toward blacks,[7] his observations about black use of hair straighteners and skin whiteners challenge the notion that black consumers simply attempted to purchase whiteness.

Like Frederick Detweiler and Guy B. Johnson, Dunford included examples of the various types of the advertisements aimed at African American interested in straightening their hair or lightening their skin. The most outrageous went as follows:[8]

At last! The lighter complexion that increases beauty and is so popular among refined members of the Race. Makes Skin So Light Would Hardly Know She Is Colored. When Mrs. Gresham says Ko-Verra made her skin so white that folks would hardly know that she is colored, you can know what this amazing new preparation can do for any person who wants the beauty of lighter skin. Mrs. Gresham has just been appointed by the governor of Iowa to attend the Illiteracy Conference at Washington, you can be sure she won't travel without KO-VERRA . . . Ko-Verra makes the darkest skin look much lighter, and those with tan skin look several shades lighter.

After presenting several ads like the one quoted above, Dunford continued:[9]

To make a statement regarding the percentage of Negroes using such preparations would be to make a hazardous guess, but that the number is quite large is evident from the wide and persistent prevalence of advertisements concerning them in many of the leading Negro periodicals. Farmers are not the only producers who abandon and cease to cultivate unfertile fields.

Although most black newspapers accepted such advertisements because of the revenue they generated, Dunford discovered that some refused these ads out of principle. According to a representative example he presented, however—an editorial in the May 3, 1924, issue of the Chicago *Whip*—"principle" dealt with potentially harmful preparations rather than any real opposition to the practice of bleaching the skin or straightening the hair:[10]

Last week "a Kinkout" preparation burned all of the combined locks from the head of a foolish user. . . . There ought to be a limit somewhere upon these "Kinkout" chemists, who are for the most part white men who are seeking to filch the money out of the pockets of black people. Every man and woman should make himself or herself as attractive as possible, but a rule of reason should be used and that rule should not include the use of caustic potash to straighten hair nor the use of mercury and tannic acid whereby to lighten a dark skin. . . . Be beautiful if you can, but don't burn your brains out in the attempt.

Ironically, the proliferation of skin whitener and hair straightener ads in African American newspapers during the early to mid-1920s appeared at a time of increasing black pride and consciousness. Marcus Garvey's Universal Negro Improvement Association and the renowned Harlem Renaissance, along with the dramatic growth of black-owned businesses during this decade, signaled that African Americans were, indeed, capable of self-determining activity. Dunford's analysis of this contradictory situation of simultaneous black empowerment and the continued purchase of these products has enduring relevance:[11]

> Can the Negro continue to build up race pride and solidarity, however, and at the the same time persist in the hiding of those physical characteristics which are peculiarly his own? Are we to answer this question in the negative, or are we to conclude that "kinkouts" and skin whiteners are merely the creation of Dame Fashion and that while a few Negroes may use them to be more like the white race, the majority do so without forethought, merely because smooth hair and light skin are in vogue?

Kathy Peiss's 1995 essay "Making Up, Making Over: Cosmetics, Consumer Culture, and Women's Identity" provides important insights related to the questions raised by Dunford seventy years earlier. Peiss cogently suggests that, notwithstanding the claims of various products to straighten the hair and whiten the skin, only the most gullible blacks believed that the use of these concoctions would actually allow them subsequently to "pass" for white.[12] Yet she notes, "European aesthetic domination shaped status distinctions among African-Americans. Lighter skin, straight hair, and European features were believed advantageous for gaining job opportunities and good marriage partners."[13]

To many early-twentieth-century African Americans, decades before the late 1960s Black Power and Black Consciousness movements, dark skin, pronounced Negroid features, and kinky hair were not objects of pride. Considering the overt cultural assault experienced by African Americans up to this point, Kathy Peiss's observations do not come as a surprise. Nevertheless, as Noliwe M. Rooks's important 1996 book *Hair Raising: Beauty, Culture, and African American Women* confirms, many early-twentieth-century African American women experienced complex motivations in addressing these elements of their selves and identities with the use of purchased products. Principally, according to Rooks, those women who straightened their hair sought not to emulate whiteness but rather to enhance their natural beauty through the promotion of healthy hair and scalps.

Interestingly, most of the racially derogatory hair straightening ads chronicled by Detweiler, Johnson, and Dunford were produced by white-owned companies. Black entrepreneurs seeking the early-twentieth-century black female consumer market, such as Madame C. J. Walker and Annie Malone, did not disparage natural African American hair as "ugly," "kinky," or "unruly" in their ads.[14] They marketed healthy hair growth, rather than straight hair, to African American female consumers. In fact, Walker, who is credited with inventing the hair straightening comb in 1905, "consistently asked editors and writers to refrain from using the term 'hair straightener' when writing about her in their newspapers and magazines."[15]

Not only did black female consumers respond enthusiastically to Madame C. J.

Walker's and other black entrepreneurs' ads by purchasing their products, but thousands also became active agents for these black firms. Moreover, as *Hair Raising* indicates, these women were specifically trained to promote, rather than negate, their customers' sense of self-esteem in their pursuit of sales:[16]

> She [Walker] instructed her agents to create an atmosphere in which African American women would feel pampered and valued while giving the hair "proper attention." Indeed, agents interested in the Walker system of treatment learned a philosophy of inner as well as outer beauty. . . . Beauty, they were taught, referred to outer manifestations such as physical cleanliness and good health as well as inner things such as mental cleanliness. . . . Walker considered the ritual of her system to be as important as the actual hairstyle, thus shifting the terrain of the debate over hair straightening from dissatisfaction with African physical features to a focus on health as well as physical and mental well-being.

Significantly, the positive ambiance that Madame C. J. Walker sought to associate with her products continued after her death. Rooks notes this in her comparative analysis of mid-century marketing campaigns of the white-owned Lustrasilk Company and the Madame C. J. Walker Company.[17]

> A 1948 Lustrasilk advertisement shows us that the manufacturers wish African American women to believe that their lives need to be and will be substantially changed by the purchase of this product. . . . When we contrast this view with that of the Madame C. J. Walker Company during the same year, we find a great difference in the message. Walker's company says her products are "For Women of Beauty," whereas the white-owned company emphasizes a "lack."

Although this more recent research has successfully repudiated earlier notions that black women straightened their hair based *solely* on "servile imitativeness," the use of various apparatuses and formulas to alter the natural texture of African hair, for whatever reason, raises issues of identity construction. Among other things, it could represent yet another manifestation of the contradictory psychological state of African Americans that W. E. B. Du Bois so eloquently described: "One ever feels his twoness—an American, a Negro; two souls, two thoughts, two unreconciled strivings; two warring ideals in one dark body."[18]

Much of African American history has featured and continues to feature black individuals' internal conflict regarding their *basic* identity. Yet, for a tantalizingly brief period during the late 1960s and early 1970s, a significant number of African Americans solved this dilemma by choosing to accentuate the African within. Coinciding with what is generally referred to as the Black Power movement, African Americans, especially the young, viewed themselves as foot soldiers in a cultural revolution against historic white supremacy.

The Black Power movement's emphasis on cultural and psychological regeneration, while linked to such historic figures as Henry McNeal Turner and Marcus Garvey, appeared more closely connected to the teachings and speeches of the recently martyred Malcolm X. For example, when Malcolm organized the Organization of African American Unity in mid-1964, he told his followers that "we must recapture our heritage and our identity if we are to ever liberate ourselves from the bonds of white supremacy." Furthermore, he argued, "we must launch a cultural revolution to unbrainwash an entire people."[19]

One of the first areas Black Power advocates focused on to "unbrainwash" the African American masses was that of hair care. Specifically, African Americans were told that only "Negroes" would use hair straightening devices and formulas. Consequently, one of the first steps toward becoming a self-determining "black" was to wear one's hair in a natural, "Afro" style. In his 1992 book *New Day in Babylon: The Black Power Movement and American Culture, 1965–1975*, William L. Van Deburg elaborates on this phenomenon:[20]

> What was so "righteous" about the natural? While some variants of the new grooming technique may have been simpler to care for and cheaper to maintain, the fundamental attraction went beyond convenience and utility. A natural hair style served as a highly visible imprimatur of blackness, a tribute to group unity, a statement of self-love and personal significance. "We have to stop being ashamed of being black," asserted Stokely Carmichael in 1966. "A broad nose, a thick lip and nappy hair is us and we are going to call that beautiful whether they like it or not. We are not going to fry our hair anymore."

While some contemporary observers, both black and white, sought to portray Stokely Carmichael and other Black Power advocates as the "lunatic fringe" of the African American community, research indicates that their pronouncements related to hair reached a mainstream black audience. A 1977 content analysis of advertisements in *Ebony* magazine between January 1949 and December 1972 clearly indicated that "Black Is Beautiful" represented more than an empty slogan. This study, which sought to determine if the Black Power movement changed African American notions of "identity," examined the prevalence of advertisements for hair straightening and skin lightening products in *Ebony* during this period. The project's coordinators, who published their findings in the spring 1977 issue of *Phylon*, identified two major trends. First, while the number of *Ebony* ads promoting hair straightening and skin lightening products declined between 1949 and 1972, the most dramatic drop occurred between the years 1968 and 1972. Conversely, ads promoting the "Afro" hairstyle did not appear until *Ebony*'s December 1967 issue, yet by 1972, such ads predominated in the magazine.[21]

Although the widespread wearing of Afros, especially by African American women, gave way to the Jheri Curl phenomenon of the late 1970s, black female consumers had been changed forever by the cultural ramifications of the Black Power movement. Moreover, the white purveyors of personal care products aimed at black women, cognizant of this positive change in the psyche of African American women, dramatically changed their marketing strategy to reach this market.

Corporate marketers of women's beauty and personal care products subsequently sought to link African American women's enhanced sense of self-worth to increased spending on beauty and personal care products. This trend, while focused on black females, was not necessarily unique. As Kathy Peiss's 1990 article "Making Faces: The Cosmetics Industry and the Cultural Construction of Gender, 1890–1930" convincingly demonstrates, American women, regardless of race, had long been socialized to equate self-worth with personal appearance.[22] Since the 1970s, the purveyors of beauty and personal care products to African American women have sought to sell black women both beauty and status.

While the Black Power movement provided black women with a rejuvenated sense of "beauty," the Civil Rights movement provided them with a rejuvenated sense of "status." Enhanced African American socioeconomic mobility associated with the mid-century struggle for racial justice helped improve the economic position of many black women during this period. For instance, because 55 percent of black women in the labor force during the 1970s had at least a high school diploma, as compared to 45 percent of black men, African American females were especially well situated to take advantage of new employment opportunities. Moreover, commencing in the late 1960s, there existed an increased demand for clerical workers, teachers, and nurses—occupations that traditionally attracted women.[23] Among other things, this phenomenon allowed a significant number of African American women to express their enhanced sense of self by purchasing premium cosmetics.

The Flori Roberts Company, established in 1965, was one of the first companies to take advantage of black women's increased interest in higher-priced beauty products. Roberts, a white woman with an extensive background in the fashion industry, started this company because of her knowledge of the problems faced by black models seeking desirable facial makeup. With financial and technical assistance from her physician husband, Flori Roberts began her product line, which, from the beginning, was sold only in department stores. By the mid-1970s, Flori Roberts Products had satisfied customers throughout the United States and in Africa.[24]

Another important player in the premium 1970s black beauty products market was the Fashion Fair Cosmetics Company. This firm represented an outgrowth of *Ebony* magazine and its popular *Ebony* Fashion Fair Show. The models with this traveling fashion show, along with their fashion coordinators, regularly mixed and blended various cosmetics to devise a look they felt satisfied with. After each show, women in the audience participated by inquiring as to how they could duplicate the "look" of the models.[25] Because of this interest, the *Ebony* Fashion Fair Show, using *Ebony* magazine as a test marketing venue, offered black women a relatively high-priced kit containing samples of the cosmetics used by its models. Black women's overwhelmingly positive response to this campaign convinced the *Ebony* Fashion Fair Show to accentuate its new Fashion Fair Cosmetics division. By the mid-1970s, with the probable assistance of *Ebony*'s influential publisher, John H. Johnson, Fashion Fair Cosmetics were being marketed in such upscale department stores as Bloomingdale's in New York City, Marshall Field in Chicago, and Nieman Marcus in Dallas.[26]

Although there existed a sizable market for high-priced black cosmetics during the 1970s, the beauty and personal care products industry did not ignore the needs of less-affluent African American women. For example, the August 1977 issue of *American Druggist* featured an article titled "Selling Black Cosmetics Proves a Tricky Business," which provided advice to drugstores on how best to reach black women seeking more economical products.

First and foremost, *American Druggist* advised its readers that if African Americans comprised at least 30 percent of the population surrounding their place of business, this warranted carrying black cosmetics. The trade journal, however, appeared far less definite in advising how black cosmetics should be displayed. Some retailers believed that black cosmetics should be highlighted separately; others felt that black cosmetics should be included in the regular cosmetic department. Significantly, notions related to identity underscored this discrepancy. As one retailer explained:[27]

> There's a dichotomy here and I don't know how to solve it. Blacks have a definite desire for ethnic cosmetics. But psychologically, no one wants to be singled out by announcing, in effect, "I'm black and I have to buy black cosmetics." With Revlon's Polished Ambers, she feels more comfortable because everyone buys Revlon. But if she buys Ultra Sheen, she's saying she's different. And in America, everybody wants to be the same.

Along with the purveyors of beauty and personal care products, *Essence*, established as a magazine for black women in 1970, also profited from black women's growing sense of "beauty" and "status." The dramatic rise in the magazine's advertising revenues between 1970 and 1980 clearly suggests that corporate marketers came to view the magazine as an ideal mechanism to reach increasingly important African American female consumers.[28]

Ironically, while *Essence* publicly portrayed itself as the magazine of the "new," confident African American woman, comments attributed to the magazine's first publisher, Clarence Smith, suggest that his message to corporate marketers maintained that the best way to reach black female consumers was to exploit their racially based feminine insecurity. The December 1977 issue of *Product Marketing*, a national newsletter surveying the cosmetics, toiletries, and drug industries, quoted Smith:[29]

> In not studying the purchasing habits of Black women, marketers are overlooking an important aspect of the Black woman's psyche. They don't see how much Black women are competing with White women to prove they are as good or better. Since childhood they have been inundated with media images of beauty as the White woman. They want to be as attractive as possible and show the Black man that her beauty is fine. Marketers should see that she is overcompensating in buying products to dispel negative stereotypes.

Armed with such information about the alleged "psyche" of African American women and with evidence of the increasingly lucrative nature of the industry, white-owned companies in the personal care products industry stepped up their efforts to reach this market. One result of their increased interest was greater choice for African American female consumers. Another, however, was that black-owned producers of African American personal care products found themselves losing ground in an increasingly crowded and competitive marketplace.

The experiences of the Chicago-based Johnson Products Company epitomize the problems faced by black beauty entrepreneurs during this period. Ironically, before the late 1970s, Johnson Products Company represented one of the more spectacular instances of African American business success. In fact, the overwhelming success of the company's Afro-Sheen product line helped it become, in 1973, the first black firm to be listed on a major stock exchange.[30] Johnson Products' fortunes began to change for the worse in 1975, however, after the Federal Trade Commission (FTC) forced the company to sign a consent decree acknowledging safety problems with its Ultra Sheen Permanent Creme Relaxer. According to the FTC, this product contained sodium hydroxide, which could cause both hair loss and eye and skin damage. Consequently, the FTC mandated that Johnson Products place a special warning for consumers on all its hair straightening products that improper use could result in eye and skin damage.[31]

George Johnson, president of Johnson Products, agreed to the consent decree with the distinct impression that his competitors, including the white-owned Revlon Company, would quickly be forced to follow suit. To his surprise and disappointment, Revlon was not required to place a similar warning on its advertising and similar products until nearly two years later. In the meantime, black female consumers were given the impression that Revlon's French Perm and Realistic Protein Creme Relaxer, which also contained sodium hydroxide, were safer products than Johnson Products' Ultra Sheen Permanent Creme Relaxer.[32] An understandably bitter Johnson later asserted that the FTC's actions represented a conscious attempt to inhibit black business development. In fact, by the 1990s white-owned cosmetic and personal care products companies had dramatically expanded their control of this part of the overall African American consumer market.

The recent decline of black-owned personal care products companies such as Johnson Products represents more than a business phenomenon. It is also linked to contemporary African American females' changed notions of identity. Earlier in the century, African American women clearly felt a special affinity with black-owned enterprises. For instance, the Detroit Housewives' League, which grew from fifty to ten thousand members between 1930 and 1935 and spawned similar organizations in other cities, represented an important historical attempt to use black dollars to enhance African American community development. To join the league, African American women pledged to support black businesses, buy black-produced products, and patronize black professionals. Considering that African American women generally coordinated their families' spending patterns, the league sought to mobilize this power toward community development.[33] Darlene Clark Hine's 1994 essay "The Housewives' League of Detroit: Black Women and Economic Nationalism" aptly referred to this strategy as "economic housekeeping."[34]

Despite this legacy, today's black female consumers, largely unaware of this history and responding to a barrage of advertising aimed at them by white companies in the personal care products industry, appear far less committed to supporting entrepreneurs of their race. Many white-owned personal care products companies, with their history of denigrating African American women, have convinced a significant number of contemporary black female consumers that the best way to achieve "beauty" and "status" is through the use of their products.[35]

A watershed event in the recent wooing of African American female consumers was the Maybelline Company's 1991 introduction of Shades of You, a collection of face and lip makeup specifically for black women. This represented the first time a major cosmetic company had created a mass-market line for African American women.[36] Still, Maybelline's historic maneuver appeared to have been motivated primarily by its potential profitability rather than by a strong commitment to serving the needs of black females. As a December 17, 1991, article in *Advertising Age* that previewed Maybelline's campaign reported:[37]

> For Maybelline, its latest move may prove a way to regain lost ground. The company is now the No. 2 cosmetics marketer, with an estimated 17.5% share, trailing No. 1 Cover Girl's 23% but ahead of No. 3 Revlon's 13%.... "It's a smart move," said industry consultant Allan Motus of Maybelline's new line. "Instead of going eyeball to eyeball with Cover Girl, they can go for a specific segment for incremental market share. That's shrewd.

Other white-owned cosmetic companies caught onto Maybelline's strategy and launched their own campaigns to reach the black woman of the 1990s. The Estee Lauder Company's 1991 creation of Prescriptives All Skins appeared especially significant.

Estee Lauder had long been considered one of the premier cosmetic lines. In fact, before 1991, the company cultivated an image that linked its products with upper-class white women. Yet, as 1990 census data revealed an African American female population that was growing in both numbers and affluence, Estee Lauder decided to expand its clientele to include black women. Similar to Maybelline's profitable Shades of You line, Estee Lauder's Prescriptive All Skins, which offered over one hundred custom-blended makeup shades, attracted nearly fifty thousand new black customers during its first year.[38]

The increasing beauty options of contemporary black women have generated a mixed reaction in the African American community. A June 1993 *Black Enterprise* article titled "Redefining Beautiful" captured the essence of this debate when it asserted:[39]

> [M]ore than a dozen makeup lines and line extensions have been thrust at the black female consumer in the last two years. And there are more on the horizon. Without question, the onslaught of competition in the ethnic market is good news for black women, who for the first time have the dizzying array of cosmetic choices that white women have long enjoyed. But it could herald disaster for smaller and some black-owned companies, who lack the deep pockets needed for massive advertising campaigns as well as the financial clout to demand adequate shelf space.... There is no way for the beauty industry's major players to hit their sales targets without cutting deeply into consumer bases of smaller, more established ethnic cosmetic companies.

One black-owned cosmetics firm that reacted aggressively to increased white competition was Fashion Fair Cosmetics. Because Fashion Fair Cosmetics was a subsidiary of the Johnson Publishing Company and received extensive advertising space in *Ebony* and *Jet*, it had long been the number-one marketer of cosmetics to African American women. Increased competition however, forced Fashion Fair both to refine and to redefine its product line. In 1992, the company redesigned the packaging of its products to enhance their aura of elegance. During the same year, Fashion Fair and Johnson Publishing introduced the new Ebone' cosmetic line. Unlike Fashion Fair Cosmetics, which were aimed at an upscale black female clientele, Ebone' sought to attract younger and less affluent black women. In the short term, both of Fashion Fair Cosmetics' maneuvers proved profitable.[40]

As Fashion Fair Cosmetics and the remaining black-owned companies in the African American personal care/beauty products industry become further marginalized, their future appears increasingly tenuous. In fact, it seems that unless black women rediscover the nuances of economic nationalism, the business tradition linked with such historic figures as Madame C. J. Walker and Annie Turnbo Malone will be totally relegated to the footnotes of African American history. This would be especially paradoxical considering that, for much of the twentieth century, *only* the black-owned companies in this industry linked their products with positive notions of black female identity. Contrary to their white competitors, whose advertisements often denigrated the natural features of African people, historically black-owned personal care products companies pioneered the belief that the terms *black* and *beautiful* can be mutually inclusive characteristics.

NOTES

1. For example, see Noliwe M. Rooks, *Hair Raising: Beauty, Culture, and African American Women* (New Brunswick, NJ: Rutgers University Press, 1996); Natalie R. Weathers, "Braided Sculptures and Smokin' Combs: African-American Women's Hair-Culture," *SAGE: Journal of Women and Culture* 8 (Summer 1991), 58–61; Kobena Mercer, "Black Hair/Style Politics," in Russell Ferguson, Martha Gever, Trinh T. Minh-ha, and Cornel West, eds., *Marginalization and Contemporary Cultures* (Cambridge, MA: MIT Press, 1990), 247–264; and bell hooks, "Straightening Our Hair," *Z Magazine* (Summer 1998), 33–37. A recent useful master's thesis is De Anna J. Reese's "Intertwining Paths: Respectability, Character, Beauty, and the Making of Community among St. Louis Black Women 1900–1920" (University of Missouri–Columbia, 1996).

2. Frederick G. Detweiler, *The Negro Press in the United States* (Chicago: University of Chicago Press, 1922), 113–14.

3. Guy B. Johnson, "Newspaper Advertisements and Negro Culture," *Journal of Social Forces* 3 (May 1925): 707.

4. Ibid.

5. Vishnu V. Oak, *The Negro Newspaper* (Yellow Springs, OH: Antioch Press, 1948), 119.

6. John Moffatt Mecklin, *Democracy and Race Friction* (New York: Macmillan Co., 1921), 98–99.

7. Francis Marion Dunford, "Conflicting Forces in Negro Progress," *Journal of Social Forces* 3 (May 1925): 701. For example, he noted, "Coming from Africa some two hundred and fifty years ago, in a condition of almost stark nakedness—both from a physical and cultural standpoint—the Negro has achieved truly remarkable results in the assimilation of the white man's civilization."

8. Ibid., 702.

9. Ibid.

10. Ibid., 703.

11. Ibid., 705.

12. Kathy Peiss, "Making Up, Making Over: Cosmetics, Consumer Culture, and Women's Identity," in *The Sex of Things: Gender and Consumption in Historical Perspective*, ed. Victoria DeGrazia and Ellen Furlough (Berkeley: University of California Press, 1996), 327.

13. Ibid.

14. Noliwe M. Rooks, *Hair Raising: Beauty, Culture, and African American Women* (New Brunswick: Rutgers University Press, 1996), 48–49, 61.

15. Ibid., 63.

16. Ibid., 63–64.

17. Ibid., 128.

18. William Edward Burghardt DuBois, *The Souls of Black Folk* (1903; reprint, Greenwich, CT: Fawcett Publications, Inc., 1961), 17.

19. William L. Van Deburg, *New Day in Babylon: The Black Power Movement and American Culture, 1965–1975* (Chicago: University of Chicago Press, 1992), 5.

20. Ibid., 198, 201.

21. Ibid., 49–52.

22. Kathy Peiss, "Making Faces: The Cosmetics Industry and the Cultural Construction of Gender, 1890–1930," *Genders* 7 (Spring 1990): 143–69.

23. Robert E. Weems, Jr., *Desegregating the Dollar: African American Consumerism in the Twentieth Century* (New York: New York University Press, 1998), 90.

24. Catherine Ellis Hunter, "Flori Roberts: White Success in Black Cosmetics," *Drug and Cosmetic Industry* 122 (June 1978): 32–36.

25. Charles Marticorena, "Ethnic Market: Biggest Potential for Growth in Cosmetics Industry," *Chemical Marketing Reporter* 207 (June 23, 1975): 38.

26. Ibid.

27. "Selling Black Cosmetics Proves a Tricky Business," *American Druggist* 176 (August 1977): 60.

28. "Records of Essence Magazine," Publishers Information Bureau, Inc./Magazine Publishers of America, New York, New York. Essence's advertising revenue for the years 1970–1973 is unavailable. Between the years 1974 and 1980, however, the magazine's advertising revenue grew from $1,868,788 to $7,957,772.

29. "Essence Urges R & D for Blacks," *Product Marketing* 6 (December 1977): 31.

30. Grayson Mitchell, "Battle of the Rouge," *Black Enterprise* 9 (August 1978): 25.

31. Ibid.

32. Ibid.

33. Darlene Clark Hine, Elsa Barkley Brown, and Rosalyn Terborg-Penn, *Black Women in America: An Historical Encyclopedia* (Brooklyn: Carlson Publishing Company, 1993), 584–86.

34. Darlene Clark Hine, *Hine Sight: Black Women and the Re-Construction of American History* (Bloomington: Indiana University Press, 1994), 133.

35. Pat Sloan, "New Maybelline Line Targets Blacks," *Advertising Age* 61 (December 17, 1991): 1. Contemporary African American males, too, have exhibited a tendency not to support historic black-owned business enterprises. The worsening plight of African American insurance companies in recent decades is one clear manifestation of this trend. See my *Desegregating the Dollar*, chap. 5 and 7.

36. Sloan, "New Maybelline Line, 1."

37. Ibid.

38. Caroline V. Clarke, "Redefining Beautiful," *Black Enterprise* 23 (June 1993): 243, 246, 248.

39. Ibid., 244.

40. Ibid., 248.

Chapter Ten

Listening to Khakis

What America's Most Popular Pants Tell Us about the Way Guys Think

Malcolm Gladwell

In the fall of 1987, Levi Strauss & Co. began running a series of national television commercials to promote Dockers, its new brand of men's khakis. All the spots—and there were twenty-eight—had the same basic structure. A handheld camera would follow a group of men as they sat around a living room or office or bar. The men were in their late thirties, but it was hard to tell, because the camera caught faces only fleetingly. It was trained instead on the men from the waist down—on the seats of their pants, on the pleats of their khakis, on their hands going in and out of their pockets. As the camera jumped in quick cuts from Docker to Docker, the men chatted in loose, overlapping non sequiturs—guy-talk fragments that, when they are rendered on the page, achieve a certain Dadaist poetry. Here is the entire transcript of "Poolman," one of the first—and, perhaps, best—ads in the series:

> "She was a redhead about five foot six inches tall."
> "And all of a sudden this thing starts spinning, and it's going round and round."
> "Is that Nelson?"
> "And that makes me safe, because with my wife, I'll never be that way."
> "It's like your career, and you're frustrated. I mean that—that's—what you want."
> "Of course, that's just my opinion."
> "So money's no object."
> "Yeah, money's no object."
> "What are we going to do with our lives, now?"
> "Well . . ."
> "Best of all . . ."
> [Voice-over] *"Levi's one-hundred-percent-cotton Dockers. If you're not wearing Dockers, you're just wearing pants."*
> "And I'm still paying the loans off."
> "You've got all the money in the world."
> "I'd like to at least be your poolman."

By the time the campaign was over, at the beginning of the nineties, Dockers had grown into a six-hundred-million-dollar business—a brand that if it had spun off from Levi's would have been (and would still be) the fourth-largest clothing brand in the world. Today, seventy per cent of American men between the ages of twenty-five and forty-five own a pair of Dockers, and khakis are expected to be as popular as bluejeans by the beginning of the next century. It is no exaggeration to call the original Dockers ads one of the most successful fashion-advertising campaigns in history.

This is a remarkable fact for a number of reasons, not the least of which is that the Dockers campaign was aimed at men, and no one had ever thought you could hit a home run like that by trying to sell fashion to the American male. Not long ago, two psychologists at York University, in Toronto—Irwin Silverman and Marion Eals—conducted an experiment in which they had men and women sit in an office for two minutes, without any reading material or distraction, while they ostensibly waited to take part in some kind of academic study. Then they were taken from the office and given the real reason for the experiment: to find out how many of the objects in the office they could remember. This was not a test of memory so much as it was a test of awareness—of the kind and quality of unconscious attention that people pay to the particulars of their environment. If you think about it, it was really a test of fashion sense, because, at its root, this is what fashion sense really is—the ability to register and appreciate and *remember* the details of the way those around you look and dress, and then reinterpret those details and memories yourself.

When the results of the experiment were tabulated, it was found that the women were able to recall the name and the placement of seventy per cent more objects than the men, which makes perfect sense. Women's fashion, after all, consists of an endless number of subtle combinations and variations—of skirt, dress, pants, blouse, T-shirt, hose, pumps, flats, heels, necklace, bracelet, cleavage, collar, curl, and on and on—all driven by the fact that when a woman walks down the street she knows that other women, consciously or otherwise, will notice the name and the placement of what she is wearing. Fashion works for women because women can appreciate its complexity. But when it comes to men what's the point? How on earth do you sell fashion to someone who has no appreciation for detail whatsoever?

The Dockers campaign, however, proved that you could sell fashion to men. But that was only the first of its remarkable implications. The second—which remains as weird and mysterious and relevant to the fashion business today as it was ten years ago—was that you could do this by training a camera on a man's butt and having him talk in yuppie gibberish.

I watched "Poolman" with three members of the new team handling the Dockers account at Foote, Cone & Belding (F. C. B.), Levi's ad agency. We were in a conference room at Levi's Plaza, in downtown San Francisco, a redbrick building decorated (appropriately enough) in khakilike earth tones, with the team members— Chris Shipman, Iwan Thomis, and Tanyia Kandohla—forming an impromptu critical panel. Shipman, who had thick black glasses and spoke in an almost inaudible laid-back drawl, put a videocassette of the first campaign into a VCR—stopping, starting, and rewinding—as the group analyzed what made the spots so special.

"Remember, this is from 1987," he said, pointing to the screen, as the camera began its jerky dance. "Although this style of filmmaking looks everyday now, that kind of handheld stuff was very fresh when these were made."

"They taped real conversations," Kandohla chimed in. "Then the footage was cut together afterward. They were thrown areas to talk about. It was very natural, not at all scripted. People were encouraged to go off on tangents."

After "Poolman," we watched several of the other spots in the original group— "Scorekeeper" and "Dad's Chair," "Flag Football," and "The Meaning of Life"— and I asked about the headlessness of the commercials, because if you watch too many in a row all those anonymous body parts begin to get annoying. But Thomis maintained that the headlessness was crucial, because it was the absence of faces that gave the dialogue its freedom. "They didn't show anyone's head because if they did the message would have too much weight," he said. "It would be too pretentious. You know, people talking about their hopes and dreams. It seems more genuine, as opposed to something stylized."

The most striking aspect of the spots is how different they are from typical fashion advertising. If you look at men's fashion magazines, for example, at the advertisements for the suits of Ralph Lauren or Valentino or Hugo Boss, they almost always consist of a beautiful man, with something interesting done to his hair, wearing a gorgeous outfit. At the most, the man may be gesturing discreetly, or smiling in the demure way that a man like that might smile after, say, telling the supermodel at the next table no thanks he has to catch an early-morning flight to Milan. But that's all. The beautiful face and the clothes tell the whole story. The Dockers ads, though, are almost exactly the opposite. There's no face. The camera is jumping around so much that it's tough to concentrate on the clothes. And instead of stark simplicity, the fashion image is overlaid with a constant, confusing patter. It's almost as if the Dockers ads weren't primarily concerned with clothes at all—and in fact that's exactly what Levi's intended. What the company had discovered, in its research, was that baby-boomer men felt that the chief thing missing from their lives was male friendship. Caught between the demands of the families that many of them had started in the eighties and career considerations that had grown more onerous, they felt they had lost touch with other men. The purpose of the ads—the chatter, the lounging around, the quick cuts—was simply to conjure up a place where men could put on one-hundred-per-cent-cotton khakis and reconnect with one another. In the original advertising brief, that imaginary place was dubbed Dockers World.

This may seem like an awfully roundabout way to sell a man a pair of pants. But that was the genius of the campaign. One of the truisms of advertising is that it's always easier to sell at the extremes than in the middle, which is why the advertisements for Valentino and Hugo Boss are so simple. The man in the market for a thousand-dollar suit doesn't need to be convinced of the value of nice clothes. The man in the middle, though—the man in the market for a forty-dollar pair of khakis—does. In fact, he probably isn't comfortable buying clothes at all. To sell him a pair of pants you have to take him somewhere he *is* comfortable, and that was the point of Dockers World. Even the apparent gibberish of lines like " 'She was a redhead about five foot six inches tall.' / 'And all of a sudden this thing starts spinning, and it's going round and round.'/'Is that Nelson?' " have, if you listen closely enough, a certain quintessentially guy-friendly feel. It's the narrative equivalent of the sports-highlight reel—the sequence of five-second film clips of the best plays from the day's basketball or football or baseball games, which millions of American men watch every night on television. This nifty couplet from "Scorekeeper," for instance—" 'Who remembers their actual first girlfriend?' / 'I would have done better, but I was bald then, too' "—is not nonsense but a twenty-minute conversation edited down to two lines. A man schooled in the highlight reel no more needs the other nineteen minutes and fifty-eight seconds of that exchange than he needs to see the intervening catch and throw to make sense of a sinking liner to left and a close play at the plate.

"Men connected to the underpinnings of what was being said," Robert Hanson, the vice-president of marketing for Dockers, told me. "These guys were really being honest and genuine and real with each other, and talking about their lives. It may not have been the truth, but it was the fantasy of what a lot of customers wanted, which was not just to be work-focused but to have the opportunity to express how you feel about your family and friends and lives. The content was very important. The thing that built this brand was that we absolutely nailed the emotional underpinnings of what motivates baby boomers."

Hanson is a tall, striking man in his early thirties. He's what Jeff Bridges would look like if he had gone to finishing school. Hanson said that when he goes out on research trips to the focus groups that Dockers holds around the country he often deliberately stays in the background, because if the men in the group see him "they won't necessarily respond as positively or as openly." When he said this, he was wearing a pair of stone-white Dockers, a deep-blue shirt, a navy blazer, and a brilliant-orange patterned tie, and these worked so well together that it was obvious what he meant. When someone like Hanson dresses up that fabulously in Dockers, he makes it clear just how many variations and combinations are possible with a pair of khakis—but that, of course, defeats the purpose of the carefully crafted Dockers World message, which is to appeal to the man who wants nothing to do with fashion's variations and combinations. It's no coincidence that every man in every one of the group settings profiled in each commercial is wearing—albeit in different shades—*exactly the same kind of pants*. Most fashion advertising sells distinctiveness. (Can you imagine, say, an Ann Taylor commercial where a bunch of thirtyish girlfriends are lounging around chatting, all decked out in matching sweater sets?) Dockers was selling conformity.

"We would never do anything with our pants that would frighten anyone away," Gareth Morris, a senior designer for the brand, told me. "We'd never do too many belt loops, or an unusual base cloth. Our customers like one-hundred-per-cent-cotton fabrics. We would never do a synthetic. That's definitely in the market, but it's not where we need to be. Styling-wise, we would never do a wide, wide leg. We would never do a peg-legged style. Our customers seem to have a definite idea of what they want. They don't like tricky openings or zips or a lot of pocket flaps and details on the back. We've done button-through flaps, to push it a little bit. But we usually do a welt pocket—that's a pocket with a button-through. It's funny. We have focus groups in New York, Chicago, and San Francisco, and whenever we show them a pocket with a flap—it's a simple thing—they hate it. They won't buy the pants. They complain, 'How do I get my wallet?' So we compromise and do a welt. That's as far as they'll go. And there's another thing. They go, 'My butt's big enough. I don't want flaps hanging off of it, too.' They like inseam pockets. They like to know where they put their hands." He gestured to the pair of experimental prototype Dockers he was wearing, which had pockets that ran almost parallel to the waistband of the pants. "This is a stretch for us," he said. "If you start putting more stuff on than we have on our product, you're asking for trouble."

The apotheosis of the notion of khakis as nonfashion-guy fashion came several years after the original Dockers campaign, when Haggar Clothing Co. hired the Goodby, Silverstein & Partners ad agency, in San Francisco, to challenge Dockers' khaki dominance. In retrospect, it was an inspired choice, since Goodby, Silverstein is Guy Central. It does Porsche ("Kills Bugs Fast") and Isuzu and the recent "Got Milk?" campaign and a big chunk of the Nike business, and it operates out of a gutted turn-of-the-century building downtown, refurbished in what is best described as neo–Erector set. The campaign that it came up with featured voice-overs by Roseanne's television husband, John Goodman. In the best of the ads, entitled "I Am," a thirtyish man wakes up, his hair all mussed, pulls on a pair of white khakis, and half sleepwalks outside to get the paper. *"I am not what I wear. I'm not a pair of pants, or a shirt,"* Goodman intones. The man walks by his wife, handing her the front sections of the paper. *"I'm not in touch with my inner child. I don't read poetry, and I'm not politically correct."* He heads away from the kitchen, down a hallway, and his kid grabs the comics from him. *"I'm just a guy, and I don't have time to think about what I wear, because I've got a lot of important guy things to do."* All he has left now is the sports section and, gripping it purposefully, he heads for the bathroom. *"One-hundred-per-cent-cotton wrinkle-free khaki pants that don't require a lot of thought. Haggar. Stuff you can wear."*

"We softened it," Richard Silverstein told me as we chatted in his office, perched on chairs in the midst of—among other things—a lacrosse stick, a bike stand, a gym bag full of yesterday's clothing, three toy Porsches, and a giant model of a Second World War Spitfire hanging from the ceiling. "We didn't say 'Haggar Apparel' or 'Haggar Clothing.' We said, 'Hey, listen, guys, don't worry. It's just *stuff*. Don't worry about it.' The concept was 'Make it approachable.' " The difference between this and the Dockers ad is humor. F. C. B. assiduously documented men's inner lives. Goodby, Silverstein made fun of them. But it's essentially the same message. It's instructive, in this light, to think about the Casual Friday phenomenon of the past decade, the loosening of corporate dress codes that was spawned by the rise of khakis. Casual Fridays are commonly thought to be about men rejecting the uniform of the suit. But surely that's backward. Men started wearing khakis to work because Dockers and Haggar made it sound as if khakis were going to be even easier than a suit. The khaki-makers realized that men didn't want to get rid of uniforms; they just wanted a better uniform.

The irony, of course, is that this idea of nonfashion—of khakis as the choice that diminishes, rather than enhances, the demands of fashion—turned out to be a white lie. Once you buy even the plainest pair of khakis, you invariably also buy a sports jacket and a belt and a whole series of shirts to go with it—maybe a polo knit for the weekends, something in plaid for casual, and a button-down for a dressier look—and before long your closet is thick with just the kinds of details and options that you thought you were avoiding. You may not add these details as brilliantly or as consciously as say, Hanson does, but you end up doing it nonetheless. In the past seven years, sales of men's clothing in the United States have risen an astonishing twenty-one per cent, in large part because of this very fact—that khakis, even as they have simplified the bottom half of the male wardrobe, have forced a steady revision of the top. At the same time, even khakis themselves— within the narrow constraints of khakidom—have quietly expanded their range. When Dockers were launched, in the fall of 1986, there were just three basic styles: the double-pleated Docker in khaki, olive, navy, and black; the Steamer, in cotton canvas; and the more casual flat-fronted Docker. Now there are twenty-four. Dockers and Haggar and everyone else has been playing a game of bait and switch: lure men in with the promise of a uniform and then slip them, bit by bit, fashion. Put them in an empty room and then, ever so slowly, so as not to scare them, fill the room with objects.

There is a puzzle in psychology known as the canned-laughter problem, which has a deeper and more complex set of implications about men and women and fashion and why the Dockers ads were so successful. Over the years, several studies have been devoted to this problem, but perhaps the most instructive was done by two psychologists at the University of Wisconsin, Gerald Cupchik and Howard Leventhal. Cupchik and Leventhal took a stack of cartoons (including many from *The New Yorker*), half of which an independent panel had rated as very funny and half of which it had rated as mediocre. They put the cartoons on slides, had a voice-over read the captions, and presented the slide show to groups of men and women. As you might expect, both sexes reacted pretty much the same way. Then Cupchik and Leventhal added a laugh track to the voice-over—the subjects were told that it was actual laughter from people who were in the room during the taping—and repeated the experiment. This time, however, things got strange. The canned laughter made the women laugh a little harder and rate the cartoons as a little funnier than they had before. But not the men. They laughed a bit more at the good cartoons but much more at the bad cartoons. The canned laughter also made them rate the bad cartoons as much funnier than they had rated them before, but it had little or no effect on their ratings of the good cartoons. In fact, the men found a bad cartoon with a laugh track to be almost as funny as a good cartoon without one. What was going on?

The guru of male-female differences in the ad world is Joan Meyers-Levy, a professor at the University of Chicago business school. In a groundbreaking series of articles written over the past decade, Meyers-Levy has explained the canned-laughter problem and other gender anomalies by arguing that men and women use fundamentally different methods of processing information. Given two pieces of evidence about how funny something is—their own opinion and the opinion of others (the laugh track)—the women came up with a higher score than before because they added the two clues together: they integrated the information before them. The men, on the other hand, picked one piece of evidence and ignored the other. For the bad cartoons, they got carried away by the laugh track and gave out hugely generous scores for funniness. For the good cartoons, however, they were so wedded to their own opinion that suddenly the laugh track didn't matter at all.

This idea—that men eliminate and women integrate—is called by Meyers-Levy the "selectivity hypothesis." Men are looking for a way to simplify the route to a conclusion, so they seize on the most obvious evidence and ignore the rest, while women, by contrast, try to process information comprehensively. So-called bandwidth research, for example, has consistently shown that if you ask a group of people to sort a series of objects or ideas into categories, the men will create fewer and larger categories than the women will. They use bigger mental bandwidths. Why? Because the bigger the bandwidth the less time and attention you have to pay to each individual object. Or consider what is called the invisibility question. If a woman is being asked a series of personal questions by another woman, she'll say more if she's facing the woman she's talking to than she will if her listener is invisible. With men, it's the opposite. When they can't see the person who's asking them questions, they suddenly and substantially open up. This, of course, is a condition of male communication which has been remarked on by women for millennia. But the selectivity hypothesis suggests that the cause of it has been misdiagnosed. It's not that men necessarily have trouble expressing their feelings; it's that in a face-to-face conversation they experience emotional overload. A man can't process nonverbal information (the expression and body language of the person asking him questions) and verbal information (the personal question being asked) at the same time any better than he can process other people's laughter and his own laughter at the same time. He has to select, and it is Meyers-Levy's contention that this pattern of behavior suggests significant differences in the way men and women respond to advertising.

Joan Meyers-Levy is a petite woman in her late thirties, with a dark pageboy haircut and a soft voice. She met me in the downtown office of the University of Chicago with three large folders full of magazine advertisements under one arm, and after chatting about the origins and the implications of her research she handed me an ad from several years ago for Evian bottled water. It has a beautiful picture of the French Alps and, below that, in large type, "Our factory." The text ran for several paragraphs, beginning:

> You're not just looking at the French Alps. You're looking at one of the most pristine places on earth. And the origin of Evian Natural Spring Water.
>
> Here, it takes no less than 15 years for nature to purify every drop of Evian as it flows through mineral-rich glacial formations deep within the mountains. And it is here that Evian acquires its unique balance of minerals.

"Now, is that a male or a female ad?" She asked. I looked at it again. The picture baffled me. But the word "factory" seemed masculine, so I guessed male.

She shook her head. "It's female. Look at the picture. It's just the Alps, and then they label it 'Our factory.' They're using a metaphor. To understand this, you're going to have to engage in a fair amount of processing. And look at all the imagery they're encouraging you to build up. You're not just looking at the French Alps. It's 'one of the most pristine places on earth' and it will take nature 'no less than fifteen years' to purify." Her point was that this is an ad that works only if the viewer appreciates all its elements—if the viewer integrates, not selects. A man, for example, glancing at the ad for a fraction of a second, might focus only on the words "Our factory" and screen out the same picture of the Alps entirely, the same way he might have screened out the canned laughter. Then he wouldn't get the visual metaphor. In fact, he might end up equating Evian with a factory, and that would be a disaster. Anyway, why bother going into such detail about the glaciers if it's just going to get lost in the big male bandwidth?

Meyers-Levy handed me another Evian advertisement. It showed a man—the Olympic Gold Medal swimmer Matt Biondi—by a pool drinking Evian, with the caption "Revival of the fittest." The women's ad had a hundred and nineteen words of text. This ad had just twenty-nine words: "No other water has the unique, natural balance of minerals that Evian achieves during its 15-year journey deep within the French Alps. To be the best takes time." Needless to say, it came from a men's magazine. "With men, you don't want the fluff," she said. "Women, though, participate a lot more in whatever they are processing. By giving them more cues, you give them something to work with. You don't have to be so literal. With women you can be more allusive, so you can draw them in. They will engage in elaboration, and the more associations they make the easier it is to remember and retrieve later on."

Meyers-Levy took a third ad from her pile, this one for the 1997 Mercury Mountaineer four-wheel-drive sport-utility vehicle. It covers two pages, has the heading "Take the Rough with the Smooth," and shows four pictures—one of the vehicle itself, one of a mother and her child, one of a city skyline, and a large one of the interior of the car, over which the ad's text is superimposed. Around the border of the ad are forty-four separate, tiny photographs of roadways and buildings and construction sites and manhole covers. *Female.* Next to it on the table she put another ad—this one a single page, with a picture of the Mountaineer's interior, fifteen lines of text, a picture of the car's exterior, and, at the top, the heading: "When the Going Gets Tough, the Tough Get Comfortable." *Male.* "It's details, details. They're saying lots of different stuff," she said, pointing to the female version. "With men, instead of trying to cover everything in a single execution, you'd probably want to have a whole series of ads, each making a different point."

After a while, the game got very easy—if a bit humiliating: Meyers-Levy said that her observations were not antimale—that both the male and the female strategies have their strengths and their weaknesses—and, of course, she's right. On the other hand, reading the gender of ads makes it painfully obvious how much the advertising world—consciously or not—talks down to men. Before I met Meyers-

Levy, I thought that the genius of the famous first set of Dockers ads was their psychological complexity, their ability to capture the many layers of eighties guyness. But when I thought about them again after meeting Meyers-Levy, I began to think that their real genius lay in their heroic simplicity—in the fact that F. C. B. had the self-discipline to fill the allotted thirty seconds with as *little* as possible. Why no heads? The invisibility rule. Guys would never listen to that Dadaist extemporizing if they had to process nonverbal cues, too. Why were the ads set in people's living rooms *and* at the office? Bandwidth. The message was that khakis were wide-bandwidth pants. And why were all the ads shot in almost exactly the same way, and why did all the dialogue run together in one genial, faux-philosophical stretch of highlight reel? Because of canned laughter. Because if there were more than one message to be extracted men would get confused.

In the early nineties, Dockers began to falter. In 1992, the company sold sixty-six million pairs of khakis, but in 1993, as competition from Haggar and the Gap and other brands grew fiercer, that number slipped to fifty-nine million six hundred thousand, and by 1994 it had fallen to forty-seven million. In marketing-speak, user reality was encroaching on brand personality; that is, Dockers were being defined by the kind of middle-aged men who wore them, and not by the hipper, younger men in the original advertisements. The brand needed a fresh image, and the result was the "Nice Pants" campaign currently being shown on national television—a campaign widely credited with the resurgence of Dockers' fortunes.

In one of the spots, "Vive la France," a scruffy young man in his early twenties, wearing Dockers, is sitting in a café in Paris. He's obviously a tourist. He glances up and sees a beautiful woman (actually, the supermodel Tatjana Patitz) looking right at him. He's in heaven. She starts walking directly toward him, and as she passes by she says, *"Beau pantalon."* As he looks frantically through his French phrase book for a translation, the waiter comes by and cuffs him on the head: "Hey, she says, 'Nice pants.' " Another spot in the series, "Subway Love," takes place on a subway car in Chicago. He (a nice young man wearing Dockers) spots her (a total babe), and their eyes lock. Romantic music swells. He moves toward her, but somehow, in a sudden burst of pushing and shoving, they get separated. Last shot: she's inside the car, her face pushed up against the glass. He's outside the car, his face pushed up against the glass. As the train slowly pulls away, she mouths two words: "Nice pants."

It may not seem like it, but "Nice Pants" is as radical a campaign as the original Dockers series. If you look back at the way that Sansabelt pants, say, were sold in the sixties, each ad was what advertisers would call a pure "head" message: the pants were comfortable, durable, good value. The genius of the first Dockers campaign was the way it combined head and heart: these were all purpose, no-nonsense pants that connected to the emotional needs of baby boomers. What happened to Dockers in the nineties, though, was that everyone started to do head and heart for khakis. Haggar pants were wrinkle-free (head) and John Goodman-guy (heart). The Gap, with its brilliant billboard campaign of the early nineties—"James Dean wore khakis," "Frank Lloyd Wright wore khakis"—perfected the heart message by forgoing an emotional connection between khakis and a particular nostalgic, glamorous all-Americanness. To reassert itself, Dockers needed to go an extra step. Hence "Nice Pants," a campaign that for the first time in Dockers history raises the subject of sex.

"It's always been acceptable for a man to be a success in business," Hanson said, explaining the rationale behind "Nice Pants." "It's always been expected of a man to be a good provider. The new thing that men are dealing with is that it's O.K. for men to have a sense of personal style, and that it's O.K. to be seen as sexy. It's less about the head than about the combination of the head, the heart, and the groin. It's those three things. That's the complete man."

The radical part about this, about adding the groin to the list, is that almost no other subject for men is as perilous as the issue of sexuality and fashion. What "Nice Pants" had to do was talk about sex the same way that "Poolman" talked about fashion, which was to talk about it by not talking about it—or, at least to talk about it in such a coded, cautious way that no man would ever think Dockers was suggesting that he wear khakis in order to look *pretty*. When I took a videotape of the "Nice Pants" campaign to several of the top agencies in New York and Los Angeles, virtually everyone agreed that the spots were superb, meaning that somehow F. C. B. had managed to pull off this balancing act.

What David Altschiller, at Hill, Holliday/Altschiller, in Manhattan, liked about the spots, for example, was that the hero was naïve: in neither case did he know that he had on nice pants until a gorgeous woman told him so. Naïveté, Altschiller stressed, is critical. Several years ago, he did a spot for Claiborne for Men cologne in which a great-looking guy in a bar, wearing a gorgeous suit, was obsessing neurotically about a beautiful woman at the other end of the room: *"I see this woman. She's perfect. She's looking at me. She's smiling. But wait. Is she smiling at me? Or laughing at me? . . . Or looking at someone else?"* You'd never do this in an ad for women's cologne. Can you imagine? "I see this guy. He's perfect. Ohmigod. Is he looking at me?" In women's advertising, self-confidence is sexy. But if a man is self-confident—if he knows he is attractive and is beautifully dressed—then he's not a man anymore. He's a fop. He's effeminate. The cologne guy had to be neurotic or the ad wouldn't work. "Men are still abashed about acknowledging that clothing is important," Altschiller said. "Fashion can't be important to me as a man. Even when, in the first commercial, the waiter says 'Nice pants,' it doesn't compute to the guy wearing the nice pants. He's thinking, What do you mean, 'Nice pants?'" Altschiller was looking at a videotape of the Dockers ad as he talked—standing at a forty-five-degree angle to the screen, with one hand on the top of the monitor, one hand on his hip, and a small, bemused smile on his lips. "The world may think they are nice, but so long as he doesn't think so he doesn't have to be self-conscious about it, and the lack of self-consciousness is very important to men. Because '*I don't care.*' Or 'Maybe I care, but I can't be *seen* to care.' " For the same reason, Altschiller liked the relative understatement of the phrase "nice pants," as opposed to something like "great pants," since somewhere between "nice" and "great" a guy goes from just happening to look good to the unacceptable position of actually trying to look good. "In focus groups, men said that to be told you had 'nice pants' was one of the highest compliments a man could wish for," Tanyia Kandohla told me later, when I asked about the slogan. "They wouldn't want more attention drawn to them than that."

In many ways, the "Nice Pants" campaign is a direct descendant of the hugely successful campaign that Rubin-Postaer & Associates, in Santa Monica, did for Bugle Boy Jeans in the early nineties. In the most famous of those spots, the camera opens on an attractive but slightly goofy-looking man in a pair of jeans who is hitchhiking by the side of a desert highway. Then a black Ferrari with a fabulous babe at the wheel drives by, stops, and backs up. The babe rolls down the window and says, "Excuse me. Are those Bugle Boy Jeans that you're wearing?" The goofy guy leans over and pokes his head in the window, a surprised half smile on his face: "Why, yes, they *are* Bugle Boy Jeans."

"Thank you," the babe says, and she rolls up the window and drives away.

This is really the same ad as "Nice Pants"—the babe, the naïve hero, the punch line. The two ads have something else in common. In the Bugle Boy spot, the hero wasn't some stunning male model. "I think he was actually a boxboy at Vons in Huntington Beach," Larry Postaer, the creative director of Rubin-Postaer & Associates, told me. "I guess someone"—at Bugle Boy—"liked him." He's O.K.-looking, but not nearly in the same class as the babe in the Ferrari. "In Subway Love," by the same token, the Dockers man is medium-sized, almost small, and gets pushed around by much tougher people in the tussle on the train. He's cute, but he's a little bit of a wimp. Kandohla says that F. C. B. tried very hard to find someone with that look—someone who was, in her words, "aspirational real," not some "buff, muscle-bound jock." In a fashion ad for women, you can use Claudia Schiffer to sell a cheap pair of pants. But not in a fashion ad for men. The guy has to be *believable*. "A woman cannot be too gorgeous," Postaer explained. "A man, however, can be too gorgeous, because then he's not a man anymore. It's pretty rudimentary. Yet there are people who don't buy that, and have gorgeous men in their ads. I don't get it. Talk to Barneys about how well that's working. It couldn't stay in business trying to sell that high-end swagger to a mass market. The general public wouldn't accept it. Look at beer commercials. They always have these gorgeous girls—even now, after all the heat—and the guys are always just guys. That's the way it is. We only reflect what's happening out there, we're not creating it. Those guys who run the real high-end fashion ads—they don't understand that. They're trying to remold how people think about gender. I can't explain it, though I have my theories. It's like a Grecian ideal. But you can't be successful at advertising by trying to re-create the human condition. You can't alter men's minds, particularly on subjects like sexuality. It'll never happen."

Postaer is a gruff, rangy guy, with a Midwestern accent and a gravelly voice, who did Budweiser commercials in Chicago before moving West fifteen years ago. When he wasn't making fun of the pretentious style of East Coast fashion advertising, he was making fun of the pretentious questions of East Coast writers. When, for example, I earnestly asked him to explain the logic behind having the goofy guy screw up his face in such a—well, goofy—way when he says, "Why, yes, they *are* Bugle Boy Jeans," Postaer took his tennis shoes off his desk, leaned forward bemusedly in his chair, and looked at me as if my head came to a small point. "Because that's the only way he could say it," he said. "I suppose we might have had him say it a little differently if he could actually *act*."

Incredibly, Postaer said, the people at Bugle Boy wanted the babe to invite the goofy guy into the car, despite the fact that this would have violated the most important rule that governs this new style of groin messages in men's-fashion advertising, which is that the guy absolutely cannot *ever* get the girl. It's not just that if he got the girl the joke wouldn't work anymore; it's that if he got the girl it might look as if he had deliberately dressed to get the girl, and although at the back of every man's mind as he's dressing in the morning there is the thought of getting the girl, any open admission that that's what he's actually trying to do would undermine the whole unself-conscious, antifashion statement that men's advertising is about. If Tatjana Patitz were to say *"Beau garçon"* to the guy in "Vive la France," or the babe on the subway were to give the wimp her number, Dockers would suddenly become terrifyingly conspicuous—the long-pants equivalent of wearing a tight little Speedo to the beach. And if the Vons boxboy should actually get a ride from the Ferrari babe, the ad would suddenly become believable only to that thin stratum of manhood which thinks that women in Ferraris find twenty-four-dollar jeans irresistible. "We fought that tooth and nail," Postaer said. "And it more or less cost us the account, even though the ad was wildly successful." He put his tennis shoes back up on the desk. "But that's what makes this business fun—trying to prove to clients how wrong they are."

The one ad in the "Nice Pants" campaign which isn't like the Bugle Boy spots is called "Motorcycle." In it a nice young man happens upon a gleaming Harley on a dark back street of what looks like downtown Manhattan. He strokes the seat and then, unable to contain himself, climbs aboard the bike and bounces up and down, showing off his Dockers (the "product shot") but accidentally breaking a mirror on the handlebar. He looks up. The Harley's owner—a huge, leather-clad biker—is looking down at him. The biker glowers, looking him up and down, and says, "Nice pants." Last shot: the biker rides away, leaving the guy standing on the sidewalk in just his underwear.

What's surprising about this ad is that, unlike "Vive la France" and "Subway Love," it *does* seem to cross the boundaries of acceptable sex talk. The rules of guy advertising so carefully observed in those spots—the fact that the hero has to be naïve, that he can't be too good-looking, that he can't get the girl, and that he can't be told anything stronger than "Nice pants"—are all, in some sense, reactions to the male fear of appearing too concerned with fashion, of being too pretty, of not being masculine. But what is "Motorcycle"? It's an ad about a sweet-looking guy down in the Village somewhere who loses his pants to a butch-looking biker in leather. "I got so much feedback at the time of 'Well, God, that's kind of *gay*, don't you think?' " Robert Hanson said. "People were saying, 'This buff guy comes along and he rides off with the guy's pants. I mean, what the hell were they doing?' It came from so many different people within the industry. It came from some of our most conservative retailers. But do you know what? If you put these three spots up—

'Vive la France,' 'Subway Love,' and 'Motorcycle'—which one do you think men will talk about ad nauseam? 'Motorcycle.' It's No. 1. It's because he's really cool. He's in a really cool environment, and it's every guy's fantasy to have a really cool, tricked-out fancy motorcycle."

Hanson paused, as if he recognized that what he was saying was quite sensitive. He didn't want to say that men failed to pick up the gay implications of the ad because they're stupid, because they aren't stupid. And he didn't want to sound condescending, because Dockers didn't build a six-hundred-million-dollar business in five years by sounding condescending. All he was trying to do was point out the fundamental exegetical error in calling this a gay ad, because the only way for a Dockers man to be offended by "Motorcycle" would be if he thought about it with a little imagination, if he picked up on some fairly subtle cues, if he integrated an awful lot of detail. In other words, a Dockers man could only be offended if he did precisely what, according to Meyers-Levy, men don't do. It's not a gay ad because it's a guy ad. "The fact is," Hanson said, "that most men's interpretation of that spot is: You know what? Those pants must be really cool, because they prevented him from getting the shit kicked out of him."

Chapter Eleven

Archival Material
Paramount Pictures and Linit Advertisements

Everybody steps lively on Paramount night

GOOD motion pictures knit a family closer together. Mother might be willing to let the others go to the ball game without her, but watch her step lively when Dad, Son and Daughter declare that tonight's a Paramount night!

Immediately there's a new spirit of lend-Mother-and-Sis-a-hand, and the evening takes on a swift and lively air that soon merges into the silence of expectation as they all take their seats at the theatre that has announced a Paramount Picture.

Nothing but a great record of great entertainment regularly delivered could have put the reputation of Paramount Pictures where it is today in the minds of thousands of families in every State in the Union.

Nothing but the work of the greatest directors, the brightest stars, the most eminent dramatists, would have stood up and stood out and achieved and kept supremacy in the face of the steady inspection of the whole nation over a period of years.

And nothing but an astounding *uniformity* of such clean and thrilling quality of entertainment could have kept that public opinion unanimous.

Little wonder then that more than 10,000 theatres in every important town and state of the U. S. make Paramount Pictures the backbone of their program of entertainment for you.

Little wonder that you and the other millions of theatre patrons are steadily supporting their policy with enthusiasm.

And mark well this fact wherever you go, that the theatre that shows Paramount Pictures and makes it well known that it shows them always plays to crowded houses.

When you have learned to look in the theatre's advertisements, and in their lobbies and on the placards, for the phrase *"It's a Paramount Picture"* you have learned it all.

Because *there's* the best show in town!

Paramount Pictures

Fig. 11.1. Paramount Pictures ad. Paramount Pictures promised female consumers that male identity in the household would change, not because of changes in consciousness but, instead, through their engagement with consumer culture. *Ladies' Home Journal*, May 1921, p. 30.

HOW TO MAKE EVEN ORDINARY COTTON GOODS
LOOK AND FEEL LIKE LINEN

THE new and easy method of making all wash garments and household fabrics look and feel like linen is simply to starch with Linit, the remarkable new starch.

Linit is entirely different from any starch you have ever used. When ready for use, your Linit mixture is thin and free running like water. When you dip your fabrics into this Linit mixture, Linit instantly penetrates every thread. This fastens back into place all loosening bits of thread fibre and lint. Each thread strengthened by Linit and the life of your garment thereby prolonged. You'll notice too that your ironing is much easier.

Linit restores to all fabrics that soft, cool, pliable finish you admire in new goods at the store.

Once you starch with Linit, you will never go back to old-fashioned starches.

IMPORTANT NOTICE

Every effort is being made to supply grocers, our only distributors, throughout the country. If your grocer cannot supply you with LINIT, send in this coupon and we will send you by return mail prepaid, the amount of LINIT you desire.

CORN PRODUCTS REFINING CO.
DEP'T 12, ARGO, ILLINOIS

Enclosed is _____ ¢ for which please send me _____ full size 10¢ packages of Linit. [Enclose 10¢ for each package Linit desired]

NAME_____

ADDRESS_____

TOWN_____

GROCER'S NAME_____

Fig. 11.2. Linit ad. Advertisers have often offered white women a consumer identity that relies on race as a counterpoint. In this case, the white women not only define themselves as consumers of a particular household product; they purchase whiteness as well. *Ladies' Home Journal*, September 1924, p. 107.

Part Three

Under Whose Direction?
Consumer Culture's Message Makers

Critics of consumer culture have mined numerous and rich examples of the ways in which the purveyors of consumer culture exploit, deceive, and victimize the public. They grant those individuals and groups varied degrees of power over us but agree that manipulation is the aim, if not always the result; that manufacturers and advertisers have on the whole been enormously successful in their endeavors; and that it is imperative that consumers engage actively in the critical consumption of messages and of products. One vivid contemporary illustration of consumer manipulation is that of the Phillip Morris Corporation, which, anticipating resistance to cigarette advertising and in particular to the ethnicity-based advertising campaigns currently underway, trains its staff to deal with potentially disruptive participants at promotional events. "You're killing my people," screams an actress, while Phillip Morris employees determine how they could most effectively respond to such a situation in real life.[1] Manufacturers and advertisers clearly have a great deal to gain from "understanding" us: what lures us in, what pushes us away—why we eagerly embrace or vigorously reject their appeals. They hope, of course, that in the end their messages will be the loudest, the most seductive, the most effective ones we hear, more appealing even than the countermessages in our own heads or hearts. The essays in this part of the book explore the supply side of consumer culture: the exhortations to consume and the individuals and groups that design those messages. As the title of this part asks, under whose direction do we participate in this culture of consumption?[2]

Spending money as a leisure-time activity appeals to many people, regardless of the positive or negative messages we receive about it. Daniel Horowitz raises the example of Henry Ward Beecher, who wrote in an 1853 publication, *Lectures to Young Men*, that "satisfaction is not the product of excess, or of indolence, or of riches; but of industry, temperance, and usefulness."[3] Regardless of his best advice to others, however, Beecher himself was a consummate shopper, spending more than he could afford to on books and semiprecious stones, then going out on the lecture circuit to pay his bills. Nearly a century and a half later, we receive far more invitations to consume than did Beecher in his day. The ever-more-present nature of consumer culture raises questions: To what degree would we embrace the culture of consumption if we did not receive continuous invitations to do so? Why is it that the messages to participate are often more seductive than those that urge us to abstain? Where does the control sit: with us, with the purveyors of the messages, or in a mediated relationship between "us" and "them"?

The notion of control raises many additional questions. Do we participate in consumer culture because people tell us to? because their messages are the most numerous of the many messages about social life we encounter each day? because we receive pleasure from consuming? or because we hope to alleviate some of our own cultural anxieties through active engagement with this part of our culture? All of these explanations apply to all of us at one point of that engagement or another. From early childhood on, we receive training in the culture of consumption. Children learn to recognize name brands long before they learn to read. One could argue, in fact, that the language of advertising or consumer culture is one of the first languages we master.[4] Given all that, one might attribute to the purveyors of consumer culture a seemingly omnipotent hold on consumers. Do they know and understand our every move? Are they not also implicated in various ways as consumers as well as carriers of these messages? How do they see themselves? What makes them tick? And what should we think of them? The essays that follow explore these questions and others as they reveal the diverse experiences, aims, and successes of the purveyors of consumer culture.

The first essay in this part, "Advertising Women: The J. Walter Thompson Company Women's Editorial Department," by Jennifer Scanlon, challenges the formula of the exploitative male and the victimized female popular in studies of consumer culture. This analysis explores the lives and work of one of the first groups of women to work in the advertising field in the United States. In the early decades of the twentieth century, as greater numbers of women earned college degrees and subsequently sought employment, the world of business in general and advertising in particular held a special appeal. Unlike teaching, nursing, or social work, women's traditional occupations, the business world offered respectable wages and, equally important, social respect. Advertising was a good match for women interested in "exploring their creativity, maintaining their autonomy, and achieving job or career advancements."[5] Scanlon's women, who sought to create in the J. Walter Thompson Company an "alternative institution," wrote advertisements that urged other women to consume and to identify themselves primarily as housewives and agents of consumption. Significantly, the advertising women did so in their own quests to remain largely outside that limited and limiting cultural definition of womanhood. This essay explores the disparities often evident between the lives of the people who produce the messages and the people who consume them. How well did the upper-middle-class female producers understand their working-class and middle-class contemporaries? Were they simply exploiting the women they "served," or was their experience more complex?

Scanlon's essay raises the contested issue of sex appeal as an advertising tool. Contemporary observers of advertising are quick to see the ways in which women are exploited in formulas that dictate their use as sexual accompaniments to their own and men's consumer rites. Whether draping their entire bodies over automobiles or enveloping products with their breasts or thighs, women as sexual beings market products. The historical reality, however, is that a woman, an employee of the J. Walter Thompson Company, invented the use of sex appeal in advertising. Tired of the limited and limiting definitions advertising offered, Helen Lansdowne Resor hoped to create a more realistic woman, a sensual woman, and she did so proudly. She and the women who worked with her at J. Walter Thompson provide a vivid example of the potential, if not actual, liberatory elements of women's engagement with consumer culture.

The second essay, "In Spite of Women: *Esquire* Magazine and the Construction of the Male Consumer," by Kenon Brezeale, provides an example of the ways in which a men's magazine developed and maintained a definition of men as consumers. Founded in 1933, *Esquire* set out for itself a difficult task: providing a space for men to see themselves as consumers without acquiring the traits most commonly associated with consumption. In other words, *Esquire* had to create a male (not female) and heterosexual (not homosexual) consumer. It did so, as Brezeale illustrates, through a "simultaneous exploitation of and denial of the feminine."[6] In providing what Brezeale calls the first "thoroughgoing, conscious attempt to organize a consuming male audience," the powers that be at *Esquire* had their work cut out for them.[7] Men had been trained to abhor the female elements of their culture, and as Scanlon's article also illustrates, the consumer was seen, culturally, as female. To convince advertisers that men would consume the products advertised in *Esquire*, the magazine had to carefully cultivate a male culture of consumption.

The way in which *Esquire* did this, and did so successfully, is the subject of Brezeale's piece. Rewriting the scripts that intimated, if not outright stated, that only women and gay men had an interest in or talent for the art of consuming, *Esquire* wove together "misogynistic cultural threads" to create a new formula: men consumed whatever they wished, including, of course, women.[8] The visuals and editorial matter worked together in the magazine to balance "titillation and reassurance," to synthesize "fine arts and cheesecake," to make consumption as natural for men as it seemingly was for women.[9] Brezeale's exploration reveals the ways in which one group of men "understood" their peers and sought to create of them consumers of both their magazine and the goods they carefully marketed in order to underwrite, validate, and sustain this publication.

The third essay, "From Town Center to Shopping Center: The Reconfiguration of Community Marketplaces in Postwar America," by Lizabeth Cohen, explores the gendered nature of the restructured consumer marketplace that accompanied the growth of the suburbs after World War II. As Cohen points out, the majority of suburban developments were built without any attention given to the commercial needs of residents. As a result, regional shopping centers sprung up "aimed at satisfying suburbanites' consumption *and* community needs."[10] Interestingly, although several decades had passed since the founding and the success of *Esquire* magazine, the suburban shopping centers largely ignored the male consumer and most deliberately targeted women. In essence, they had reverted to nineteenth- and early-twentieth-century notions of women, men, and families. As "central sites of consumption," these shopping centers provided amenities unavailable in the city: parking, safety, cleanliness, and comfort—all aimed at female shoppers.[11] At the same time, they defined community for those same women in limited ways. As

Cohen puts it, the new shopping centers "filtered out not only the inefficiencies and inconveniences of the city but also the undesirable people who lived there."[12] The purveyors of consumer culture, in this case, offered white women the goods as well as what some might call "the goods": a limited definition of womanhood and a sanitized, white, and middle-class version of life.

Cohen also explores the relationship of women workers to the culture of consumption, as these new shopping centers invited housewives in as employees. The work fit the needs of these women in certain regards: it was part time and could be integrated into their family schedules; it was close to where they lived; and it provided them with some disposable income of their own. Cohen makes clear, however, that the benefits were limited: "Work became a way for women to maintain their status as consumers, but it did not significantly empower them as producers who could contribute substantially to—or be independent of—male earnings."[13] The purveyors of consumer culture—in this case, designers, owners, and managers of shopping centers—seemed quite comfortable with strictly gendered definitions of female and male citizenship.

The next essay in Part Three, "Narcissism as Liberation," by Susan J. Douglas, essentially takes on the purveyors of women's beauty products. "Forget the political already, and get back to the personal" is today's advertisers' smug, unspoken message, as they advise women that feminism is dead, that beauty is where it's at, and that the only way to maintain self-respect is to consume, consume, consume.[14] Douglas's exploration of advertising's stated and intended messages to the now-aging baby-boomer generation reveals the degree to which audience manipulation is key to advertisers' success. "You're worth it," for example, means you are not worth it, but if you purchase a particular product and use it religiously you might become worth it. Advertising of the 1980s and 1990s, as Douglas sees it, reveals the vulnerability of women to the impossible cultural standards of womanhood continually thrust at them.

Douglas explores the ways in which the advertising industry has interacted directly with the feminist movement in the United States. "The appropriation of feminist desires and feminist rhetoric by Revlon, Lancome, and other major corporations was nothing short of spectacular," she writes.[15] Cognizant of the inroads that feminism had made in women's consciousness, advertisers rightly felt they could profit by congratulating women on their movement forward and then urging those same women to reward themselves for their achievements. This fascinating approach worked. Rather than urge women back into the home or into outdated roles, cosmetics advertisers told women to continue to break free of the bonds, particularly the bond to put others first. "Narcissism was more in for women than ever," writes Douglas, who explores the ways in which the message makers look for and exploit real needs, real concerns, and real desires and turn those into profit-making advertisements.

The final essay in this part, " 'Young T'ing Is the Name of the Game': Sexual Dynamics in a Caribbean Romantic Fiction Series," by Jane Bryce, takes a somewhat different look at the purveyors of consumer culture. In her examination of

Caribbean Caresses, a romance fiction series aimed at women consumers in the Caribbean, Bryce explores how the purveyors of consumer culture can rework some of the exploitative, dominant messages as they rewrite the cultural context of a product. In this case, the romance fiction developed for the Caribbean features dark- rather than light-skinned women, but it also injects some interesting gendered differences into the romance formula. "Romance fiction is the most conservative and stereotypical of literature forms," writes Bryce, "and at same time one of the most potentially subversive."[16] Her aim is to explore the subversive elements in this contemporary romance fiction series.

In their attempt to "indigenize a Western formulaic genre," Bryce argues, romance writers in the Caribbean have problematized the romance. In most romance fiction, the Caribbean is the site where North American or British travelers frolic and where people of color form an "exotic" backdrop. The romance novels under consideration here, however, accept the Caribbean as a normal rather than an exotic setting; provide a cultural context that demands "insistence on gender equality, rather than swooning submission"; and provide a balance between exploring the real and the ideal of romantic relationships.[17] Like recent explorations of romance fiction in the United States, Bryce's portrait makes complex the relationship between the purveyors of this one element of consumer culture and their eager reading public.[18] Although she does not claim any "liberatory potential" for this romance fiction series, Bryce does make clear that the purveyors of consumer culture can adapt the formulas they follow to respect their readers and the realities of those readers' lives.

The archival material provided at the end of this section includes two cartoons published first in the early and mid–twentieth century. The first cartoon, from a 1934 edition of the *New Yorker*, refers specifically to the J. Walter Thompson Company discussed in Scanlon's "Advertising Women." In this case, the humor is aimed at the gendered nature of households and the "his" and "hers" marriages many women and men experienced. The advertising agent wants to know not if the woman is happily married but instead just what her complaints are. He can then offer to alleviate those complaints through her engagement with the consumer culture—redemption through consumption. In the second cartoon, from a 1956 volume of *Fortune*, the naive consumer, female, of course, and purse in hand, is the object of the gaze of a host of puzzled male observers, each of whom is trying to determine what makes her consume, what makes her female. In what ways do these comical depictions match observations made by scholars in the essays in Part Three? Like Scanlon's advertising women, Brezeale's magazine editors and publishers, Cohen's shopping-center designers and managers, and Bryce's romance writers, these comic characters make assumptions about the gendered nature of their audience. To what degree are they correct? What are they missing? What might be different if the purveyors of consumer culture operated with a larger picture of their audience? It is also valuable to ask what makes these cartoons humorous and to think about whether or not they would be considered humorous today. How far have the purveyors of consumer culture moved in the intervening years?

NOTES

1. R. W. Pollay, (Jung S. Lee, and David Carter-Whitney), "Separate, but Not Equal: Racial Segmentation in Cigarette Advertising," *Journal of Advertising* 21 (March 1992), 47.

2. Gloria Steinem explores the ways in which advertisers exercise control over women's magazines by demanding that they supply "complementary copy," copy that literally complements the products advertised. Steinem's history of the relationship between *Ms.* magazine and the advertising industry provides examples of advertisers refusing to feature people of color in their ads and refusing to include any ad copy in issues that explored controversial subjects. DeBeers, the famous diamond makers, prohibits magazines from placing DeBeers ads "with adjacencies to hard news or anti-love/romance themed editorials." Gloria Steinem, "Sex, Lies & Advertising," *Ms.*, July–August 1990, 18–28.

3. Henry Ward Beecher, quoted in Daniel Horowitz, *The Morality of Spending: Attitudes toward the Consumer Society in America, 1875–1940* (Baltimore: Johns Hopkins University Press, 1985), 11.

4. On the relationship between children and consumer culture, see Alison Alexander and Margaret A. Morrison, "Electric Toyland and the Structures of Power: An Analysis of Critical Studies on Children as Consumers," *Critical Studies in Mass Communication* 12 (September 1995), 344–353; Ellen Seiter, *Sold Separately: Children and Parents in Consumer Culture* (New Brunswick, NJ: Rutgers University Press, 1993).

5. Jennifer Scanlon, "Advertising Women: The J. Walter Thompson Company Women's Editorial Department," originally published as chap. 6 of her *Inarticulate Longings: The Ladies' Home Journal, Gender, and the Promises of Consumer Culture* (New York: Routledge, 1995), 181.

6. Kenon Brezeale, "In Spite of Women: *Esquire* Magazine and the Construction of the Male Consumer," originally published in *Signs* 20 (Autumn 1994), 5.

7. Ibid., 1.

8. Ibid., 7.

9. Ibid., 16.

10. Lizabeth A. Cohen, "From Town Center to Shopping Center: The Reconfiguration of Community Marketplaces in Postwar America," originally published in *American Historical Review* 101 (October 1996), 1050–1081, esp. 1052.

11. Ibid., 1057.

12. Ibid., 1060.

13. Ibid., 1077.

14. Susan Douglas, "Narcissism as Liberation," originally published as chap. 11 of her *Where the Girls Are: Growing Up Female with the Mass Media* (New York: Times Books, 1994), 245–268, esp. 247.

15. Ibid., 246.

16. Jane Bryce, " 'Young T'ing Is the Name of the Game': Sexual Dynamics in a Caribbean Romantic Fiction Series," originally published in Christine Barrow, ed., *Caribbean Portraits: Essays on Gender Ideologies and Identities* (Kingston: Ian Randle, 1998), 320.

17. Ibid., 325.

18. See Janice Radway, *Reading the Romance: Women, Patriarchy, and Popular Literature* (Chapel Hill: University of North Carolina Press, 1984).

Chapter Twelve

Advertising Women
The J. Walter Thompson Company Women's Editorial Department

Jennifer Scanlon

For the most part, historians have defined women's role in the cultural environment of consumer activity as that of the passive recipient, the consumer. Women who worked in the advertising business have been overlooked by historians of women, historians of advertising, and historians of consumer culture. Yet women played an active role in the development of the industry. In some fairly paradoxical ways, women helped create what has become a particularly female and, by most accounts, particularly disempowering twentieth-century consumer culture.[1] While they did, they also helped create new tiers of professional employment for educated women, and helped form a growing body of consumers whose needs would ultimately not be met by the *Ladies' Home Journal* or other strictly homemaking magazines.

While few today would deny the exploitation of women in advertisement copy or as consumers by the advertising industry, the early roots of this conflict are complicated rather than simplified by attention to issues of gender. Women did not unwittingly buy products or accept a consumer culture as their own; they sought an improved standard of living and a positive social identity, both of which advertising promised and sometimes delivered. In the same vein, women did not accept jobs in advertising with the intention of exploiting other women and subsequently getting ahead themselves, although on first glance early advertising women might seem to have done just that. Writing copy to persuade other women to consume, advertising women undoubtedly achieved a measure of autonomy, both personal and economic, that many of their readers lacked. However, these women often approached their work with a missionary spirit about the consumer culture, a spirit many of them carried over from the progressive politics of their college educations, suffrage activities, or social work experiences. They saw their work not as exploitation but as a positive good. The paradox of "advertising women" challenges commonly held assumptions about the hegemonic development of the advertising industry in the early twentieth century.

Women were recognized as consumers long before the twentieth century, but advertising agencies were quick to recognize and then exploit this consumer base during this century, especially through the medium of the women's magazine. "The proper study of mankind is man . . . but the proper study of market is women," wrote an ad executive in the 1920s.[2] Women were the purchasing agents in the nation's homes. In the 1920s, researchers estimated, women purchased at least 80 percent of the total goods accumulated in families.[3] They bought food, clothing, electrical appliances, linoleum, and home furnishings. They also purchased items one might expect men to have bought, such as automobiles and automotive accessories. Mary Louise Alexander, a researcher at the Batten, Barton, Durstine and Osborne advertising agency in New York City in the 1920s, believed that women's role in purchasing was an almost omnipotent one: "You might think the family car is under the man's thumb," she argued, "but no, our researchers show that women are a large factor in the buying of gasoline and oil so that it appears as though men determine for themselves little more than their hair cuts."[4] Although Alexander implies that advertising researchers were simply recording what they saw, the notion of women's omnipotence in purchasing goods was as much a social construction of these marketing experts as it was an observable social phenomenon.

Women's magazines were the most important medium for reaching these female consumers, and by 1917, advertising agencies handled 95 percent of the national advertising being promoted in the magazines.[5] The *Ladies' Home Journal* and others kept their subscription rates low and readership high by soliciting the most artistic and compelling advertisements for products from Crisco to Pond's Cold Cream, from Goodyear Tires to Yuban Coffee. While 56 percent of the magazine's revenues came from sales and subscriptions in 1879, the situation had changed dramatically by 1919, when nearly two-thirds of all magazine revenues came from advertising.[6]

Among the many prominent advertising agencies the *Ladies' Home Journal* dealt with, the J. Walter Thompson Company stands out. For one, it was the most successful agency in the United States, pulling ahead of its competition early in the 1920s and retaining that top spot well into the 1970s.[7] In 1925, the Thompson agency broke a world record by placing $230,000 worth of advertising in a single publication, the April volume of the *Ladies' Home Journal*. In October of that same year, the agency broke its own record by placing an additional $25,000 worth of advertising, again in the *Ladies' Home Journal*.[8] In an era in which people's incomes rose and manufactured products grew increasingly more affordable, the middle-class consumer could afford to make purchasing decisions based on considerations other than price.[9] J. Walter Thompson, with its reputation for expert quality and artistic originality, produced advertisements that spoke to existing consumer desires and, increasingly, defined new ones. The second reason the Thompson agency stands out is that it prided itself on providing professional opportunities for women. In an era in which male professions were increasingly defined by the degree to which they were not populated by females, the Thompson position is remarkable.

Women made up 35 percent of the professional workforce in 1900 and 45 percent of the professional workforce in 1930, but while their numbers grew quickly, their range of occupations did not. The majority of women educated at liberal arts institutions found work in teaching, social work, or home economics.

As Sharon Hartman Strom has demonstrated, it was opportunity rather than appropriate education they lacked, as the majority of men entering law or medicine had also been trained in the liberal arts.[10] Women looking for professional work generally found it only in what Joan Jacobs Brumberg and Nancy Tomes call "the dirtiest" of professional fields, those requiring the most human contact. Women's greatest opportunities, they argue, resulted from "the massive social dislocation caused by immigration, poverty, economic uncertainty, and labor exploitation—social problems that necessitated the creation of a vast army of social workers, public health nurses, and public school teachers."[11]

At a time when professional opportunities for women outside the helping professions were scarce, the J. Walter Thompson Company established a reputation for taking a more progressive position on the employment of women. In a 1924 publication intended for external use, the Thompson agency outlined the number of women employed in various departments, and then claimed, as one of the thirteen most important attributes of the agency, "The J. Walter Thompson Company employs more women in creative, responsible positions than does any other agency."[12] A female employee similarly argued that although women in other agencies got the "lesser and run of the mill jobs," women at Thompson had ample and unusual opportunities for success in the field.[13]

Further research will indicate the degree to which women also developed successful careers in other agencies. A 1926 study of fifteen agencies found women working in a variety of jobs including research, space buying, and writing copy.[14] The Thompson agency was not unique in hiring women, then, but its success in providing many women with "responsible" positions may have been due to its progressive attitude and to the fact that among other agencies, it alone organized its female copywriters into a separate department, the Women's Editorial Department. This department, run by women and, no less directly, primarily for women consumers, provided advertisements for products aimed at women: household and cleaning items, food and beauty products, clothing and accessories. The women copywriters' separate existence makes it difficult to measure their success relative to that of male copywriters; however, it may to a large degree account both for their professional success and their seemingly easy acceptance by male coworkers or male executives. Physical distance, in this case, may have both eased male insecurity and bolstered female opportunities for success. The few other exceptions to women's employment limitations during the period also occurred in "women-only" areas, namely women-supervised "women's departments" in banks, insurance companies, and investment agencies.[15] The women's separate existence does make it easy to measure their enormous economic contribution to the agency: in 1918, the billings for the copy written in the Women's Editorial Department totalled $2,264,759 out of the total of $3,902,601 for the company.[16] The Thompson agency clearly depended upon the work of these advertising women.

In the J. Walter Thompson Women's Editorial Department, a group comprised largely of white, native-born, middle- or upper-middle class, college-educated women was able to carve out for themselves an unmistakably successful professional workplace. Their employment applications and biographical files, as well as

Thompson Company newsletters and staff meeting minutes, provide a picture that adds significantly to our knowledge about women's entrance into the professions, female professionals' receptivity to the ethos of consumption, and the ways in which class and race in addition to gender informed cultural definitions of womanhood in the early twentieth century.

The J. Walter Thompson Company is remembered best not for the legacies of its namesake, James Walter Thompson, but for the legacies of Stanley Resor and Helen Lansdowne Resor, who took over the agency in 1916 and subsequently pushed it past all competition. From 1916 to 1918 they were part of a team of three which administered, in Helen's words, "all policies of the J. Walter Thompson agency, the payroll, and practically [sic] all personnel."[17] Stanley became the first president of the J. Walter Thompson agency, and although Helen never became vice president and did not even officially become a director for another eight years, she was clearly influential in the firm's policy making and instrumental in its success from the start. Helen Lansdowne started the Women's Editorial Department, and for this she was praised in an article Harriet Abbott wrote for the *Ladies' Home Journal* in 1920: "She not only put manufacturers' products and her own agency on the map; she made a place in advertising geography for women, a place no advertiser or agency ever before had granted them. She pioneered the way for women in advertising, marking a trail for which successful women today are grateful to her."[18]

In the Women's Editorial Department, Helen Lansdowne Resor assembled, as Stephen Fox has claimed, a "wing of women copywriters whom she hired, trained, and mothered."[19] Under her direction, women in copywriting worked as group heads, writers, and assistant writers. She set high standards for herself and for the women she employed, but she never doubted that either she or they were in any way less than able to produce the necessary results. When Helen Lansdowne Resor started working for J. Walter Thompson, the firm employed fewer than 100 people. When she died in 1964, the Thompson agency had 6,913 employees. She was largely responsible for this growth, because as she correctly saw it, the growth of modern advertising relied on the modern female consumer and hence on the work of the Women's Editorial Department. "The success of the J. Walter Thompson Company has been in large measure due to the fact that we have concentrated and specialized upon products sold to women," Resor argued in one of her few remaining written statements.[20]

Helen Lansdowne Resor, unlike most of her employees, was not college educated. After graduation as valedictorian of her high school class in Kentucky, Lansdowne secured her first job in advertising. She quickly became, as she herself acknowledged, "the first woman to be successful in writing and planning national, as opposed to retail, advertising."[21] Lansdowne first made her mark in the advertising world in 1910, when she worked for her future husband in the Cincinnati office of J. Walter Thompson. She was given responsibility for a new Thompson client, Woodbury's facial soap, manufactured by the Jergen's company. Lansdowne essentially invented the use of sex appeal in advertising with her advertisement, which she titled "A Skin You Love to Touch." Using muted sexuality and what may now appear to be tame physical contact between a man and a woman, Lansdowne created a sensation, and sales of Woodbury's facial soap increased 1000 percent in eight years.[22] Resor and the women she employed succeeded in addressing female consumers not only as women with money to spend but also as sensuous and sensitive women. What has turned into one of the major controversies in advertising—women as sex objects—was developed by a woman who most likely saw the recognition of women's sexuality as a step forward in an advertising world that had primarily portrayed women as asexual wives and mothers.

In January of 1911, Helen Lansdowne moved to Thompson's New York head-quarters. In 1916, at age 31, she married Stanley Resor, but her work did not stop at marriage. She continued to direct the Women's Editorial Department, where she left her legacies: decades of encouragement and an example of professional accomplishment for other women to follow. The *Ladies' Home Journal* article mentioned above described Helen Resor's techniques on the job. When she interviewed women for jobs she looked the woman, or "girl," in the eye, hoping to find a flicker of genius. If she caught that, she hired her. After that, she "coaches her and stands back of her and develops her into part of the company's corporate genius." A serious employer, this woman cautioned prospective candidates that the advertising world was not one of glamour and cleverness but of persistent hard work, based on research and statistics and the in-depth study of manufacturing and markets. Many of the women had college degrees, according to the article, but this employer did not believe that a college education alone dictated ability. She sought to determine the value of that education for the individual woman:

> The agency searches back into her interests in college. Was she attracted by economics, psychology, sociology, history? Was she a real student; did she really dig out the causes of things, think for herself, enjoy thinking for herself? Or did she learn texts and lectures by rote, pass "exams" with amazing A-pluses, bury her nose constantly in the alcoves of the college library or keep an eye forever over a 'scope? What was her mother like? Was she a constructively minded woman, seeing a big future dawning for women over the horizon, even though she herself stayed at the grindstone to put her daughter through college? Did she breathe this faith of hers into her daughter, filling her young mind with the vision of a new day for women when they should stand squarely beside men on the platform of achievement?[23]

Helen Lansdowne Resor was protective of her private life, and outside of a stockholder's affidavit and some biographical material on file in the Thompson Archives, few details of her private or work life were recorded. In her stockholder's affidavit she mentioned that various magazines and four large newspaper syndicates had requested that she write or provide interviews about herself. "As publicity of this kind does not appeal to me," she declared flatly in 1924, "I have refused these requests."[24] It is unlikely, then, that she agreed to an interview for the *Ladies' Home Journal* article. Nevertheless, unpublished biographical information about Resor and the personnel files of these 41 other women indicate that Harriet Abbott's remarks were not far off the mark.

Almost every one of these women's personnel files contains an employment application form. The applications changed slightly over time but follow the same

Fig. 12.1. Although the physical contact in this advertising series may seem tame now, it initially caused a great stir, and it is now widely accepted as the first "sex appeal" series in American advertising. This 1918 example features a World War I soldier. *Ladies' Home Journal*, March 1918, p. 116.

basic format, a company format used for both male and female employees. They first solicit personal information, including age, marital status, birthplace, occupation of parents, education, religion, and memberships. A series of questions follows which require slightly more descriptive answers. These questions, not unlike those suggested in Harriet Abbott's article, asked prospective employees to describe their interests, level of energy, judgment, self-confidence, optimism, and imagination. How serious were they in their work? How did they spend their unoccupied time? What ambitions did they have? Following this, the applicants provided information about previous employment, including what they were most proud of, why they left, and why they were now applying at J. Walter Thompson. The last part of the application form asked the women to choose three "effective" advertisements from a recent volume of the *Ladies' Home Journal* or *Saturday Evening Post* and discuss them. A few of the applications still have, attached to them, several-page long autobiographies. Although this is a fairly straightforward and perhaps typical application form, the collection of applications reveals a great deal about these women's personalities and interests, and provides us with a fascinating profile of the professional J. Walter Thompson woman in the 1910s and 1920s.

One must question the accuracy of self-description when a job is at stake, but the candid manner in which the women both praise and deride themselves suggests a sincerity, perhaps surprising to the late twentieth-century reader, that underscores the value of these documents. Florence Dorflinger, for example, when asked what she lacked, answered, "Patience, tolerance, experience, genius, money, beauty, and a position."[25] Alice Luiggi, when asked if she had poise, answered, "Have my balance in relation to my world pretty well now, particularly since a fairly complete mental analysis made by a psychoanalyst."[26] Frances Maule, replying to a question about previous employment experience, admitted that she had been fired, "Twice—for refusing to do certain things required by newspapers."[27] At other times the women were as forthcoming with self praise. Elizabeth Devree, for example, responded to the question about initiative in the following way: "Yes; my own decisions have governed my life."[28] Mary Tucker offered proof in response to the same question: "Yes. I changed my profession after four rather successful years of it."[29] Finally, Dorothy Lampe, when asked about self confidence, stated, "Goodness yes. But so far it has always been justified."[30]

An interesting set of responses reveals that many of the women took pride in their accomplishments at work. "Have done writing, editing and manuscript reading since my babies came in spite of my domestic preoccupations," Rebecca Hourwich wrote.[31] Janet Wing stated that "though I have been married more than ten years, though I have a small daughter, I have always worked."[32] Another, Eleanor Taylor, argued that her concentration was demonstrated by the fact that she had written "in the midst of large offices and even in the thick of a suffrage campaign in which women were being arrested all around me."[33] Finally, Eleanor McDonnell, who also mentioned suffrage, wrote of it in relation to her newspaper work and as though she felt responsibility for it: "I saw the suffrage bill safely through the House of Representatives in Washington."[34] If these women wrote to please their audience, they had specific and unusual expectations of what would please employers in the

J. Walter Thompson Women's Editorial Department. Certainly these statements did not reflect the images of womanhood the women saw in the *Journal* and *Saturday Evening Post* advertisements they evaluated.

These job applications reveal a fairly homogeneous group of women seeking employment in the Women's Editorial Department between 1915 and 1930. They ranged in age from 22 to 41 and were well spread out through these years. A slight majority of the women, 17, were in their twenties, 16 were in their thirties, 2 were in their forties, and the ages of 6 are unknown. Thirty of the 41 women hired by Helen Lansdowne Resor were single, 5 were married, 3 were separated from their husbands, and 3 were divorced. They came from many geographic regions, including the South, West, Midwest, and Northeast regions of the United States as well as Colombia and Cuba. Many of their fathers were professionals and numbered among them a judge, three lawyers, two clergymen, four farmers, several business men, a plantation owner, and a retail grocer. Only one woman mentioned her mother, who was an author.

A highly educated group, 40 of the applicants had attended some college; 29 had four-year degrees and 11 of those had master's or doctoral degrees. They were alumnae of the most prestigious women's colleges and numbered among them graduates of six of the Seven Sisters colleges: Vassar, Smith, Wellesley, Barnard, Mt. Holyoke, and Bryn Mawr. They also attended the fastest growing coeducational institutions, including the University of Michigan, University of Wisconsin, University of California, Cornell, and the University of Chicago. In addition, two of the women were graduates of the Carnegie Institute of Technology. Those who had done graduate work had attended Columbia University, the University of Pennsylvania, and the New York School for Social Research, among others.[35]

These women's educational achievements, for the most part, mirrored those occurring in the culture at large during this time period. By 1910 nearly 40 percent of all college students were women, and by 1920 nearly 47 percent of all students in four-year colleges were women.[36] The J. Walter Thompson Women's Editorial group was, however, overrepresented by graduates of women's colleges. The higher percentage of women's college graduates among the J. Walter Thompson women may be explained in several ways: women's college graduates may have exercised greater job mobility throughout their careers; there may have been a greater concentration of women's college graduates in New York City; or perhaps these women received the assistance of the women's colleges' vocational bureaus, which were set up specifically to help women find jobs in fields "other than teaching."[37] Several of the women's college graduates listed professors or deans of the women's colleges among their references, which suggests that they maintained close ties to their alma maters.

The women's group memberships, which included many feminist and suffragist causes, reveal a great deal about their interests and ambitions. They belonged to the YWCA, Suffrage League, Consumers League, National Woman's Party, and League of Women Voters. They also belonged to various college alumni groups, honorary societies, and sororities. Their associations were not unlike those of Helen Resor, who served as committee chairwoman for the babies' ward at New York Postgrad-

JUNIOR PROM NIGHT AT COLLEGE

We interviewed nearly two thousand girls at Smith, Bryn Mawr, Wellesley, and Barnard on the kind of soap they use for the care of the skin. Their answers brought out the fact that Woodbury's enjoys more than double the popularity of any other soap among these young college girls.

Four Hundred & Fifteen Girls
at WELLESLEY and BARNARD
tell why they are using this soap for their skin

This Treatment will keep a sensitive skin smooth and soft:—

She is one of the most charming things America has produced—the American college girl.

No other country has a type that at all compares with her. Eager, fearless, inquisitive—naïve, and at the same time self-possessed—joyously alive in mind, nerve, body—she has the flavor of America itself, a fresher, keener flavor than one finds in older countries.

HOW does the American college girl take care of that smooth, clear skin of hers? What soap does she use? Why does she choose it? What qualities about it especially appeal to her?

To get their own individual answers to these questions, we conducted an investigation among nearly two thousand college girls at Wellesley, Barnard, Smith, and Bryn Mawr.

Nearly two thousand college girls answer our questions

Of 804 girls at Wellesley and Barnard, more than half were Woodbury users. The rest showed a wide scattering of selection over 51 different brands of soap.

At Smith and Bryn Mawr, out of 927 girls, 520 said they were using Woodbury's Facial Soap. Four hundred and seven girls used other brands of soap, their choice ranging over 56 different kinds.

Why is it that among these nearly two thou-

sand college girls at Smith, Bryn Mawr, Wellesley, and Barnard Woodbury's enjoys more than double the popularity of any other soap?

Their answers, in their own words

The girls themselves answer the question—

"The only soap that doesn't irritate my skin."
"Seems to agree with my skin better than other soaps do."
"Keeps my skin in better condition than any other soap I have used."
"After trying other soaps, Woodbury's seemed to be the only one that helped me. Other soaps irritated my skin."

These were characteristic comments, repeated in varying language, over and over again.

Six hundred and forty-four girls spoke of the purity of Woodbury's Facial Soap, or its soothing non-irritating effect on their skin.

Many girls told at length how Woodbury's had helped them to overcome undesirable skin conditions and to gain a clear, flawless complexion.

Thirteen girls said they were using Woodbury's at the recommendation of their physician.

Dip a soft washcloth in warm water and hold it to the face. Do this several times. Then make a light warm-water lather of Woodbury's Facial Soap and dip your cloth in it until the cloth is "fluffy" with the soft white lather. Rub this lathered cloth gently over your skin until the pores are thoroughly cleansed. Rinse the face lightly with clear cool water and dry carefully.

Why Woodbury's is unique in its effect on the skin

A skin specialist worked out the formula by which Woodbury's is made. This formula not only calls for absolutely pure ingredients. It also demands greater refinement in the manufacturing process than is commercially possible with ordinary toilet soap. In merely handling a cake of Woodbury's one notices this extreme fineness.

Around each cake of Woodbury's Facial Soap is wrapped a booklet containing special cleansing treatments for overcoming common skin defects. Get a cake of Woodbury's today, and begin tonight, the treatment your skin needs!

A 25c cake of Woodbury's lasts a month or six weeks.

FREE—A guest size set, containing the new, large-size trial cake of Woodbury's Facial Soap, and samples of Woodbury's Facial Cream and Facial Powder.

Woodbury's Facial Soap

Fig. 12.2. College girls became a new target market as well as an important symbol for advertisers in the 1920s. *Ladies' Home Journal*, September 1925, p. 35.

uate Hospital, board member of the Museum of Modern Art, president of the Traveler's Aid Society, and supporter of woman suffrage and Planned Parenthood.[38] The women's varied interests included gardening, music, hiking, writing, driving a car, and rhythmic dancing. Several included feminism among their interests: "social betterment and improvement of the position of women," wrote one, and "the war and women and the modern trend of the evolution," wrote another.[39]

Is there a J. Walter Thompson Women's Editorial Department type, then? Clearly she was a well-educated, politically and/or socially active woman looking for job advancement. The majority of these women were not fresh out of school and looking for entry-level jobs. Thirty-nine leave records of their employment histories, but only one of those had applied to J. Walter Thompson for her first position. Twelve women applied after having held one or two previous jobs and 26 applied after having held three or more previous positions. The vast majority of these applicants were unmarried women who had been self-sufficient for at least a few years before they looked to Helen Lansdowne Resor for a job. They were working women who saw the possibility of improved work lives at the Thompson agency, and they were willing to make and often accustomed to making job or even career changes.

Since the world offered women of this generation few occupational choices, they had to create what Carroll Smith-Rosenberg calls "alternative institutions and careers."[40] Helen Resor created that for herself and for this group of women in the J. Walter Thompson Women's Editorial Department. Educated in women's colleges or as underrepresented students in coeducational institutions, and trained professionally, the Thompson women may have sought out such a female-centered workplace. And in an era in which college-educated women in business found themselves working, for the most part, in clerical work, opportunities to write advertising copy provided a good match for those women interested in exploring their creativity, maintaining their autonomy, and achieving job or career advancements.[41]

The job applications suggest the importance of work in these women's lives. "It is the most important thing I do and think about," wrote one. "I have to work to support myself, but I know I would work just the same if I did not have to," wrote Ruth Waldo.[42] "I get so absorbed in my work," another revealed, "that I do not lead a full enough life." This woman, Lucy Dunham, also described herself, however, as a "pioneer' in personnel management with an ambition to stand "head and shoulders above the crowd."[43]

Due to their class and educational backgrounds, these women had the opportunity to view work as something more than simply a means of support. In this light, their desire to work in advertising in general and in the J. Walter Thompson agency in particular is especially interesting. The application forms did not ask why the women wanted to work in advertising, but they did ask why the applicants chose this particular agency. Several wrote that J. Walter Thompson had an excellent reputation in the field: "The JWT agency is the only one to which I would like to belong," wrote Mary Tucker. Eight of the women, however, specifically wrote about the agency's reputation for providing opportunities to women. Perle Dienst chose Thompson "largely because of the opportunities it offers to women employees," while Rebecca Hourwich stated that "your company justly evaluates the service of women." Faith Kelley called the Thompson agency "broadminded" in its attitude toward women employees, and Frances Maule stated that she had heard that it "recognizes the special utility that women have in appealing to women as the chief purchasers of goods." Perhaps these women knew that a compliment to an agency might further their chances of employment, but it is noteworthy that so many applicants specifically referred to the agency's reputation concerning female employees.[44] They were conscious of themselves as workers and as women workers, and perhaps they expected the same of their employers.

The job applications outline each woman's employment history. Only 14, or 34 percent, of the women had worked in the advertising business before they applied at J. Walter Thompson. Of these, most had worked for department stores or advertising agencies; one had worked in banking. Mary Loomis Cook, for example, had been writing advertising copy for the John Wanamaker department store when she applied at J. Walter Thompson. "I have painted joyous pictures of drab merchandise for four years and a half," she stated in her application.[45] Apparently she believed her work would be more varied and more interesting at the Thompson agency. Most of these experienced women, who applied while they still worked at other jobs, saw the Women's Editorial Department as a step up professionally. Seven of the women had previously worked as teachers. Two mentioned that they left the field because of low pay; three others left because they did not like teaching. Elizabeth Gates complained of teaching stenography to "flighty young girls," while Mary Cook put it simply: "I hated teaching." These women had entered the business world hoping for better pay, more personal satisfaction, and more opportunities for professional advancement than they found in teaching, for as Sharon Strom puts it, "the teaching profession was full of women who could find little else to do with their education."[46]

A much larger group, 16 women, came from employment fields commonly identified as more feminist: paid suffrage work and social work. These women present what appears to be the most glaring paradox of advertising women. Not only did they remain independent by encouraging other women to be dependent consumers, but they also challenge what has been deemed an incompatibility between the worlds of progressive activity and business. Although they present a picture, on first glance, of women who, in their professional lives, changed from doing "for" women to doing "to" them, on closer examination, the example of the J. Walter Thompson women suggests the compatibility of social work and/or suffrage work and advertising work: social progressives could and did view advertising as a form of social service. Historians of the period must look more closely at the movement between the fields of social service and business and between the frames of reference that accompany those fields.

The J. Walter Thompson women's contemporaries found employment primarily in nursing, teaching, and social work; by 1930, women made up four out of every five people in or preparing for careers in teaching or social work.[47] They faced tremendous antagonism in the business world. As Dr. Alice Hamilton put it, "The American man gives over to the woman all the things he is profoundly disinterested in, and keeps business and politics to himself."[48] As the early decades of the century wore on, women in social work wanted to earn salaries that would enable them to be consumers as well as workers, but as Daniel Walkowitz has demonstrated, opportunities for advancement were extremely limited.[49] For reasons of salary and advancement alone, it is not surprising that female social workers would begin to look for opportunities outside their field. The seeming contradiction, though, is that they would choose the world of business, in particular the world of advertising. Like many other women and men of the day with progressive, social justice agendas, however, women in social work may have seen the world of business as highly compatible with their goals. Susan Curtis's research on the social gospel progressives, for example, reveals that in the teens and twenties this group did not abandon social justice; instead they saw business strength and the ethos of consumption as delivering "abundance, justice, and meaning to Americans."[50] Like Curtis's social gospel reformers, the Thompson women may have been satisfied with "an ideology of self-realization, a diminution of private anxieties, and an improved standard of living for many Americans," all of which both advertising and advertising work promised.[51]

The J. Walter Thompson Women's Editorial Department employees, although not the religious progressives described by Curtis, might have agreed that the home and family could be improved through institutions and "specialized agencies," advertising among them.[52] The image of the mother had served an earlier generation of reformers with inspiration, but this generation's motivation and inspiration came from the image of the woman worker, the professional. "Paid labor, not social mothering," argues Ellen Carol DuBois about the final generation of woman suffragists, "represented their route to women's emancipation, as well as the organizational basis for their reform efforts."[53] The J. Walter Thompson applicants may have viewed that agency as uniquely appealing, as meeting their own needs for personal autonomy and progressive social activity. New products could help women have an easier time of things at home, and helping other women indirectly through advertising could have been viewed personally as a better use of these women's talents: it provided less burn out and offered more creativity, higher salaries, increased professional responsibility, and greater prestige than social work. In addition, as the image of the social worker began, in the 1920s, to be equated with a meddling and hypocritical investigator, the image of a business professional grew increasingly more positive and more identified with progress.[54]

Employers in the advertising industry at large and in the J. Walter Thompson Women's Editorial Department in particular encouraged employees to contemplate the social and educational importance of their work. Advertisements educated consumers, namely women, in their new relationships with name-brand products and national manufacturers. According to the Thompson *Blue Book*, a compilation of company policies and achievements, selling a product was easily the equivalent of any social work project: "These advertisements educate the people to a knowledge of the comforts, conveniences, and luxuries of life and create the desire to share in their enjoyment. . . . Their minds are led to a national view of life and living and they reflect their broadened education in influence on the community as well as in the advertised articles which are consumed in the home."[55] Invited speakers reinforced the social service goals of advertising. Gertrude Battles Lane, for example, spoke to the Women's Editorial Department on the value of women's magazines in "speeding up and eliminating the usual daily drudgery." Lane argued further that the magazines for which the women at the Thompson agency provided copy lent stimulus to "better housing, dressing, furnishing, better care of children and raising the standard of living generally."[56] The *Ladies' Home Journal*, the most popular women's magazine of the day, provided a direct link between professional women with a social work spirit and, again, that illusory but ever more fully defined average woman, the woman who spent a great deal of money and needed professional guidance to spend it well.

Many in this group of women did, in fact, approach their work with the missionary spirit suggested by Lane. In her employment application, Eleanor Taylor wrote of the personal growth that accompanied her through college and into paid suffrage work and social work. "College meant to me a new world of ideas," she wrote. "What an interesting, exciting world it, after all, was! Dare I become a suffragist, socialist, atheist? I dared, and became them all." For Taylor, the progression from social work to advertising came naturally. "With a gradual decline of interest in great movements has come a much more satisfying interest in people," she wrote. "To understand the needs and the desires and the experiences of men and women, the things which give pleasure, which hurt, or which stir, has a fascination which far exceeds—poking at the roots to make them grow better." [57] Taylor entered the Women's Editorial Department with an impressive employment history including working as a social worker in the United States Children's Bureau in Washington, in publicity for the National Woman's Party, and as editor of *The Suffragist*.

Others of the women were not as specific about their progression from social work or suffrage work to advertising. Gertrude Coit was a graduate of Smith, Columbia, and the New York School for Social Research. Her previous jobs were at the Co-operative League of America, the People's Institute, and Madison House, a settlement. Her work experience included directing a community center and health center and supervising dances, camping trips, and other activities. Coit had no experience in the advertising or business worlds. She reported simply that she felt a "dissatisfaction with social work" that prompted her to seek work at the Thompson agency.[58] Charline Davenport stated that she had been doing social work at the Association for the Improvement of the Poor when her friends and her doctor advised her to look for "younger work,"[59] perhaps indicating a new push for female college graduates to enter the business world. And Ruth Waldo, who also joined the company with previous experience in social work but not in business, was a J. Walter Thompson success story. A graduate of Adelphi College and Columbia University, Waldo provided an extensive social work employment record. She had worked for the Bureau of Social Research, the Harlem and Jefferson County offices of the New York Charity Organization Society, and the Russell Sage Foundation. Waldo stated on her application that she wanted always to be moving ahead: "that is why I wish to leave social work, as I feel in a rut, and why I wish to go into advertising, as I believe that *moves*."[60]

Ruth Waldo was head of the copy department at the London office by 1922, the chief woman copywriter for the entire agency by 1930, and the first woman vice president of the firm by 1944. In addition to her work at Thompson, Waldo ran a working farm in Connecticut, received an honorary doctorate from Adelphi College, and served as president of the New York Friends Center and as a trustee of and the namesake of a dormitory at Adelphi College. Waldo retired from the agency in 1960 and died in 1975. She was remembered by former colleagues as "way ahead of her time" and "an inspiration to other women." That she learned to drive a car at age seventy was offered as further proof of her remarkable accomplishments.[61] Rebecca Hourwich, a Barnard graduate, had worked at the Henry Street Settlement, organized for suffrage in Massachusetts and New York, and held several paid positions in the National Woman's Party over a seven-year period. Hourwich, separated from her husband, had traveled to nineteen states giving speeches, lobbying, and raising funds for the party. She had organized the first civic club among women clothing workers in Chicago and met with them regularly at Hull House. Hourwich argued in her application that she would be good at copywriting because of these previous experiences: "I have had many contacts among average men and women," she wrote.[62]

Several of the women had combined careers in writing and suffrage work before they looked to the advertising industry for employment. Therese Olzendam, for example, worked as a typesetter and power press operator as well as a suffrage office worker. Her first career was with the Elm Tree Press in Woodstock, Vermont, where, she claimed, "I was the first woman to run a power press in that vicinity and also the fastest woman typesetter." She left Vermont to go to Washington, D.C., where she worked as a circulation manager for the *Suffragist*, and then left Washington to move to New York and work as a secretary at the National Woman's Party headquarters. At the time of her application, the Woman's Party office had closed, and Olzendam was looking for a new career as well as a new job. Therese Olzendam established herself solidly at J. Walter Thompson, where she wrote copy until 1951. She carved a niche for herself in the organization by becoming the resident expert on medical research. The company newsletter described her in the following way: "There must be few other men or women who are so knowledgeable in the medical-scientific field and at the same time so thoroughly grounded and experienced in practical advertising." Olzendam once brought a cage of rats to a creative staff meeting. "They are harmless unless they get out of the cage," she stated dryly. The Thompson agency provided this woman, who did not have a college degree, with real opportunities for responsibility and job advancement.[63]

Frances Maule, who also had experience in paid suffrage work but not in advertising, left perhaps the most intriguing job application of all. She had attended the University of Nebraska for two years, but received no degree. Her previous experience included working in publicity for the Henry Holt company, as a reporter for six different newspapers, and most importantly, at least for Maule herself and apparently for Helen Resor as well, as an organizer and speaker for the New York State Suffrage Party and the National Woman Suffrage Association. It was Maule who wrote that her biggest goal was to improve the position of women. When asked whether or not she was optimistic, Maule replied, "Yes—Believed we could put our woman suffrage in New York State (by federal amendment) throughout U.S." Maule was quite candid in her analysis of her newspaper career; she was the one who reported that she had been fired twice. When asked what part of her newspaper work she remembered with the most pride, her answer resonated: "That I got out of it early in life." Maule's application reveals a determined woman who, during the year when woman suffrage was passed, sought out a new career. Asked why she chose the Thompson agency, Maule's initial reply was succinct: "Had an introduction to Mrs. Resor." She went further, however: "Because I have heard that it recognizes the special utility that women must have in appealing to women as the chief purchasers of goods."[64]

A note written by Helen Resor in Frances Maule's personnel file recommended hiring Maule by highlighting her suffrage activities. She noted that Frances Maule's husband, from whom she was separated, was the Swedish scholar and translator Edwin Bjorkman. "I think she has not been living with him for some time, though there is, I believe, no scandal—simply temperamental incompatibility," wrote Resor.[65] Maule's application and Helen Resor's letter indicate the type of woman both welcome at and successful in the Women's Editorial Department: independent, resourceful, confident, and often, feminist. Helen Resor most likely not only understood these women but also fit in well with them. Her secretary later remembered the day that Helen Resor organized women at the office to take part in a large suffrage parade in New York City: "Mrs. Resor got us all big campaign hats to wear of various colors—green, purple, white. Mine was white." She also remembered that Augusta Nicoll, one of the women included in this profile, rode a white horse.[66]

When Frances Maule wrote that her goal was to improve the position of women, she had a clear idea of what she meant by that. Both Maule and her sister, novelist and suffrage lecturer Florence Maule Updegraff, were members of Heterodoxy, a "band of willful women" in New York City that met biweekly to discuss questions of personal life and social relationships. The women of Heterodoxy were among the first to use "feminism" in a self conscious and deliberate way.[67] The group also included women more well known than the Maule sisters: feminist lecturer and writer Charlotte Perkins Gilman, lawyer and social activist Crystal Eastman, and black leader and NAACP member Grace Neil Johnson. Part of the already established Greenwich Village community of artists and intellectuals, the Heterodoxy women pushed the boundaries of middle-class womanhood in the early twentieth century. As contemporary historian and Vassar College professor Caroline Ware noted in 1935, Greenwich Village attracted women and men who lived outside middle-class social conventions.[68]

One of the ways in which many of the Heterodoxy women and, apparently, several of the J. Walter Thompson women also lived outside middle-class conventions was through creating women-centered lives. Like several of the other J. Walter Thompson women, Frances Maule lived in Greenwich Village and shared her apartment with women friends. Several other of the applicants listed women as their housemates as well. Edith Lewis, another member of this group of applicants, lived for forty years with Willa Cather; fellow employees described her as being one of the best women writers and as being "devoted" to Cather.[69] A recent biography of Cather argues that the actions of both Lewis and Cather "make this lifelong companionship as hard to examine as they both would have wished," but also calls Lewis a "devoted, wifely companion" as well as a grieving widow who was buried at Cather's feet.[70] As Lillian Faderman argues, after the turn of the century and for the first time in American history, large numbers of women could make their lives with other women. College educations, careers, and the resulting economic independence fostered both the spirit and the money to make it happen.[71]

It is difficult, of course, to determine the ways in which the many single women of the day defined their relationships with other women. As Leila Rupp has argued, there was a broad category of women at this time period who were women-committed women. Judith Schwartz, who wrote about the "radical feminists of Heterodoxy," called Frances Maule a "probable lesbian" who lived an urban, women-centered life.[72] I would argue that Lewis was a lesbian, regardless of Cather's biographers' hesitations in placing the label and in spite of the fact that she herself may not have used that label. I have not yet determined if any others among this group identified themselves as lesbians, but several at least had primary commitments to other women.[73] Whether lesbian or not, many remained single, part of the group that could not marry, not only because they did not want to sacrifice career for family but also, as Lillian Faderman puts it, because "there were few husbands who could be expected to sacrifice their historically entrenched male prerogatives to revolutionary female notions."[74] If some of the other advertising women in this group were also lesbians or women-committed women, they shared with Maule and Lewis a further degree to which they were removed from their real clients: middle-class, married, heterosexual women.

All of these women lived lives far removed from the composite "woman" increasingly targeted by advertising. The advertising writers wrote appeals for the "average" woman, but they themselves, in many ways, were far from average. They were white, they were middle-class, but they were not the woman happily mopping her floor in the Wizard mop advertisement; they could not be defined by the "average woman" they promoted. At a staff meeting in 1936, Wallace Boren described the differences between Thompson writers and the people they wrote for. Only one of five writers went to church, except on rare occasions; half never went to Coney Island or similar resorts, the other half once in one or two years; over half had never lived at or below the average national income, and half couldn't name any relatives or friends who lived that way. While only 5 percent of all homes employed domestics, Boren continued, 66 percent of J. Walter Thompson writers employed domestics. Finally, only one in eight of the writers did her or his own shopping. The men writers, in fact, unanimously felt that shopping was "something to avoid entirely."[75] In 1930, according to former Thompson Company archivist Cynthia Swank, the median salary of women college graduates was $1900 while the average salary of all women at Thompson, including those without college degrees, was $2200.[76] It is unlikely that these women writers of the teens and twenties were less removed in salary and lifestyle from their readers.

The Thompson Company archives reveal some information about what the women writers thought of their consuming constituents, of this, "average" woman. They often praised the "woman at home," but they also grew frustrated with her, or at least with her limited and limiting image. These advertising women wrote effective advertisements for that consumer, but they attempted also to broaden the definition of woman consumer and citizen to include themselves. Helen Resor's few written statements suggest that she recognized that female consumers had been looked down upon—and that she saw it as the work of the Women's Editorial Department to change that. She attributed her own success not to having overcome her female nature but rather to having acknowledged it. Most of the clients produced items that women, as opposed to men, would purchase or not purchase. In advertising these products, Resor, as she later put it, "supplied the feminine point of view." She continued, "I watched the advertising to see that the idea, the wording, and the illustrating were effective for women." Resor argued further that effective advertising had to be "made with knowledge of the habits of women, their methods of reasoning, and their prejudices."[77] She assumed, then, that regardless of class or other differences, women writers and women readers shared a common knowledge of and appreciation for women.

However, because they were removed from the life experiences of the largest group of consumers, housewives, the advertising women occasionally revealed a degree of condescension in their views, although they never went as far as did Charles Austin Bates, one of the first men to write advertising copy full time. "Advertisers should never forget they are addressing stupid people," Bates wrote. "It is really astonishing how little a man may know and yet keep out of the way of the trolley cars."[78] The women in the Thompson agency generally felt more of an affinity with their readers than did Bates, even though recognition of class and other differences occasionally were exhibited in their descriptions of their work. Mildred Holmes, a graduate of Wellesley College and a writer and then temporary group head in the Women's Editorial Department, wrote an article entitled "Housewives Write the Copy" for the external news bulletin. She described the housewife who answered the investigator's ring as a woman far removed from the pictures in the advertisements. "Her skirt, grown too small in the waist-band, is anchored half way down the placket with a safety pin," she wrote. "Apron and shirt waist are somewhat soiled and on awry. Last year's high heels run over to the outside. She has discouraged wisps of hair about her ears and she eyes the investigators with disillusionment, faintly inquiring."[79] Holmes further describes the housewife as "inarticulate"; the investigator must listen carefully to discern her "motivating preferences." Holmes's article argues somewhat unconvincingly that these housewives, rather than Holmes and her colleagues, write the copy. Holmes sees little in the way of sisterhood between herself and these inarticulate, overweight, overworked women, and one wonders who Holmes really believed should write the copy, she or they. In addition, one wonders whom, considering the young, thin, and beautiful women whose images accompanied her advertisements, Holmes wrote the copy for.[80]

In an article "The Woman Appeal," Frances Maule urged advertisers to eliminate their practice of talking down to women. They would do well, she argued, to remember the suffrage slogan, "Women are People." There was no composite female; those who looked for one would end up only with an "angel-idiot" in their minds and in their advertisements. Maule argued that women could not easily be categorized, but then she placed all women in four neat categories: housewife, society woman, club woman, and business woman. Her group, business women, was "an ever-increasing class with an entirely different set of needs from the woman in the house." In trying to broaden the category of "woman" to include herself and her peers, Maule had to create another "average," who, although distinct from the housewife, formed little more than a composite herself.[81]

Interestingly enough, some women at the Thompson agency appear to have been openly critical of the narrow definition of womanhood set by the most popular women's magazines. They felt not that the stay-at-home women were inferior, but that magazines sold even these women short. In the late teens several letters and discussions at Thompson meetings centered on a potential conflict with the *Ladies' Home Journal*, the Women's Editorial Department's largest source for advertising placement. One letter stated that some women had written to the Thompson agency complaining that the *Journal* was somewhat "old maidish."[82] One meeting participant argued that "we have heard so many statements of this kind from so many different women that it seems to us worth asking ourselves whether the *Journal* is keeping abreast of the modern woman's needs." The *Ladies' Home Journal* was criticized as appealing to the "stand pat" woman who was likely to shy away from any broader vision for women. Another complaint centered around the magazine's policy on fiction. The *Journal* opposed what one Thompson employee called a movement toward "stronger" fiction in the women's magazines, and, further, did not allow its heroines to smoke.[83] Apparently the Women's Editorial Department women would have liked to dictate how the women's magazines defined womanhood, and their definitions would have expanded to include independent, strong-minded women.

One Women's Editorial Department campaign secured endorsements by famous women for Pond's Cold Cream. The first they secured featured Alva Belmont, the wealthy suffragist and feminist who provided her endorsement in exchange for a $1000 donation to a feminist cause. When Edith Lewis of the Thompson Company secured the endorsement and appeared in the office to share the good news, the other women hugged her and cheered the occasion. Evidently none of the other endorsements received the same response. On another occasion, the Women's Editorial Department received the contract to produce advertisements for *Pictorial Review*, a magazine with a more progressive reputation than that of the *Ladies' Home Journal*. One employee described the scene in the Women's Editorial Department once the word was out: for the first time women literally fought over the chance to write copy for that particular magazine. A newsletter article related their enthusiasm: "Fortunately, the account was big enough and the campaign was 'rush' enough to permit any one to drop anything she might be doing and to pitch in right away on our youngest 'greatest in the field.' " These advertising women looked forward to the chance to write advertisements for a magazine they described as "the most progressive and truly representative of women of wider interests." When they

Fig. 12.3. Women copywriters at the J. Walter Thompson Company celebrated when they secured the endorsement of feminist and suffragist Alva Belmont for their Pond's campaign. *Ladies' Home Journal*, February 1924, p. 65.

planned their campaign, one Women's Editorial Department member suggested they retell the story of Mabel Potter Daggett, a feminist who had written already in *Pictorial Review* about women and the war, "diluted" for male consumption, and then say, "This is the type of woman that PR reaches." The newsletter article ended by saluting the Women's Editorial Department and by suggesting that they urge *Pictorial Review* to play a greater role in the leadership of women.[84]

Some of the Women's Editorial Department women also appear to have been critical of their own limitations at work. The women's group heads apparently complained about the fact that they were not included in the representatives' meetings. Mr. William Day chastised those who felt discriminated against at a creative organization staff meeting, at which many of the copywriters would have been present. "I am no believer, being myself one of the mature members, in the young man's world; nor am I a believer in an old man's world; nor am I a believer in a man's world, nor in a woman's world," he stated. "Those things are hooey and you know them to be hooey, even those of you who advance them."[85] Day gave this speech but solicited no responses. The company rarely saved the minutes of the creative staff minutes, apparently believing they were less important than the representative meeting minutes. Some of the Women's Editorial Department staff recognized that distinction and protested their second-class status.

These advertising women, in writing ads that provided a narrow definition of women's lives—a definition confining women to home and market—secured their own independence, financial and otherwise. However condescending their views about women who did not work for pay, choose to vote, or broaden their sphere to include the public world, though, these women hoped to expand what they saw as a narrow definition of womanhood. They wanted to see themselves in the pages of the magazines. But simply entering the advertising profession would not guarantee that kind of freedom. Instead, as Susan Curtis argues about women's entrance into other professions during this period, "it meant a new kind of confinement, one in which women and men were bound by the rules of bureaucratic structure, professional standards, and the imperatives of consumer cultures."[86] And the link between consumer culture and a prescriptive, consumer role for women defined the advertising and magazine fields and ruled the day.

As history has it, *Pictorial Review,* with its more progressive attitude toward women, went out of business, and the *Ladies' Home Journal*, with its stand-pat attitude, remains strong today. The ultimate paradox for these advertising women is that the success of their work furthered the likelihood that they and women like them would not be featured on the pages of the most popular women's magazines for decades to come. Successful advertising like the majority of ads these women wrote was successful not only in reaching consumers but also in restricting the culture's definition of womanhood to include only white, middle-class, stay-at-home women. Like the African-American or immigrant women these advertising women ignored, they themselves remained nothing more than a "segment" of the population—and an insignificant one at that—as far as advertisers were concerned. As the emphasis for women moved, as Dorothy Brown argues, from "making a living to buying a living," the women who made a living in advertising remained behind the scenes in the development of their own industry.[87] Ironically, it was in part because they did such good work that these women, and the many others like them, remained invisible to the world of women's magazines and advertising for decades to come. Behind the scenes of in the 1910s and 1920s, and lost to history until now, the J. Walter Thompson women represent the complexities of women's history, the complex legacies of the consumer culture.

NOTES

1. Although the ratio of men to women working in advertising in these years was approximately ten to one, Roland Marchand argues that women played a more influential role in advertising than in any other industry except publishing, movies, and department store retailing. Roland Marchand, *Advertising the American Dream: Making Way for Modernity, 1920–1940* (Berkeley: University of California Press, 1985), 33. Because their numbers are so small, women have been mentioned but not discussed in much detail in any of the significant histories of advertising. Even Marchand makes clear in the first sentence of his book that he will use the term "advertising man" throughout, 1.

2. *Printer's Ink*, 7 (Nov. 1929), 133, quoted in Marchand, 66.

3. *News Bulletin, 191* (Dec. 1, 1927), 497, in J. Walter Thompson Company Archives, Duke University Library, Durham, North Carolina.

4. Marjorie Schuler, "Women's Role in Advertising Eased by Buyer's Point of View," *Christian Science Monitor*, 25 Nov. 1931.

5. Daniel Pope, *The Making of Modern Advertising* (New York, 1983), 144.

6. Pope, 137.

7. Stephen Fox, *The Mirror Makers: A History of American Advertising and Its Creators* (New York: William Morrow and Company 1984), 79.

8. "J. W. T. Establishes Another World's Record," J. Walter Thompson Company *News Bulletin*, 100 (Oct. 1, 1925), J. Walter Thompson Company Archives, Duke University Library, Durham, North Carolina.

9. For a discussion of changing patterns of manufacturing, packaging, and distribution of goods, see Susan Strasser, *Satisfaction Guaranteed: The Making of the American Mass Market* (New York: Pantheon Books, 1989).

10. Sharon Hartman Strom, *Beyond the Typewriter: Gender, Class, and the Origins of Modern American Office Work, 1900–1930* (Urbana: University of Illinois Press, 1992), 65.

11. Joan Jacobs Brumberg and Nancy Tomes, "Women in the Professions: A Research Agenda for American Historians," *Reviews in American History*, Vol. 10 (June 1982), 287–88.

12. "The J. Walter Thompson Company Portfolio Comprising of Facts and Figures," 1924, 9, 37, J. Walter Thompson Company Archives, Duke University Library, Durham, North Carolina.

13. Ruth Waldo, quoted in Marchand, 35.

14. Marchand, 33.

15. Strom, 93. On women's separatist political strategies in public life, see Estelle Freedman, "Separatism as Strategy: Female Institution Building and American Feminism, 1870–1930," *Feminist Studies*, No. 3 (Fall 1979), 512–29.

16. Helen Resor, Stockholder's Affidavit, March 1924, 70, J. Walter Thompson Company Archives, Duke University Library, Durham, North Carolina.

17. Helen Resor, Stockholder's Affidavit, 69, J. Walter Thompson Company Archives, Duke University Library, Durham, North Carolina.

18. Harriet Abbott, "Doctor? Lawyer? Merchant? Chief? Which Shall She Be? Women's New Leadership in Business," *Ladies' Home Journal*, (July 1920), 45, 164. Although Helen Resor is not mentioned by name in the article, an article published after Resor's death argues that "the reader familiar with the J. Walter Thompson Company and its history will have little trouble in linking up Harriet Abbott's words with Helen Lansdowne Resor" ("Mrs. Resor Lauded in 1920 Magazine Article," J. Walter Thompson Company *News*, January 10, 1964, 10, J. Walter Thompson Company Archives, Duke University Library, Durham, North Carolina).

19. Fox, 91.

20. Helen Lansdowne Resor, Stockholder's Affidavit, 69, J. Walter Thompson Company Archives, Duke University Library, Durham, North Carolina.

21. Helen Lansdowne Resor, Stockholder's Affidavit, 69, J. Walter Thompson Company Archives, Duke University Library, Durham, North Carolina.

22. Fox, 81. In 1948, the son and daughter of two followers of the famed efficiency expert Frederick Taylor wrote the story of their family life, *Cheaper By the Dozen*. The tale related the adventures of the Gilbreth family, twelve children and their two efficiency expert parents. The book was quite popular and followed later by a movie version. In one instance in the book the father described their car, "Foolish Carriage," with a take off on Helen Lansdowne Resor's advertisement: "Four Wheels, No Brakes. The Tin You Love to Touch." Frank Gilbreth and Ernestine Gilbreth Carey, *Cheaper By the Dozen* (New York, 1948), 222.

23. Abbott, 45.

24. Helen Resor, Stockholder's Affidavit, 70, J. Walter Thompson Company Archives, Duke University Library, Durham, North Carolina.

25. Florence I. Dorflinger, Personnel File, J. Walter Thompson Archives, Duke University Library, Durham, North Carolina.

26. Alice Luiggi, Personnel File, J. Walter Thompson Company Archives, Duke University Library, Durham, North Carolina.

27. Frances Maule, Personnel File, J. Walter Thompson Company Archives, Duke University Library, Durham, North Carolina.

28. Elizabeth Devree, Personnel File, J. Walter Thompson Company Archives, Duke University Library, Durham, North Carolina.

29. Mary Tucker, Personnel File, J. Walter Thompson Company Archives, Duke University Library, Durham, North Carolina.

30. Dorothy L. Lampe, Personnel File, J. Walter Thompson Company Archives, Duke University Library, Durham, North Carolina.

31. Rebecca Hourwich, Personnel File, J. Walter Thompson Company Archives, Duke University Library, Durham, North Carolina.

32. Janet Wing, Personnel File, J. Walter Thompson Company Archives, Duke University Library, Durham, North Carolina.

33. Eleanor Taylor, Personnel File, J. Walter Thompson Company Archives, Duke University Library, Durham, North Carolina.

34. Eleanor K. McDonnell, Personnel File, J. Walter Thompson Company Archives, Duke University Library, Durham, North Carolina.

35. Although the applicants mention the New York School for Social Research, they may have been referring to the New School for Social Research, which was founded in 1919.

None of the J. Walter Thompson women are listed in the Alumni Records of the New School, but they claimed to have taken graduate courses there, not to have earned degrees.

36. Strom, 73.

37. Strom found that between 1910 and 1923 women's college administrators and alumnae established 15 college placement bureaus. The most effective of these, the Intercollegiate Bureau of Occupations (IBO), founded in 1911 by alumnae of nine leading eastern women's colleges, registered nearly 4200 applicants by 1917 and placed more than half of those in jobs. The more prestigious of the women's colleges made arrangements for their graduates to study on the graduate level at "genteel" institutions like the Katherine Gibbs school (328–29). On the first women faculty at coeducational institutions, see Geraldine Joncich Clifford, *Lone Voyagers: Academic Women in Coeducational Universities, 1870–1937* (New York: Feminist Press, 1989).

38. Gar Schmidt, obituary of Helen Lansdowne Resor, Resor biography file, 3, J. Walter Thompson Company Archives, Duke University Library, Durham, North Carolina.

39. Frances Maule and Eleanor K. McDonnell, Personnel Files, J. Walter Thompson Company Archives, Duke University Library, Durham, North Carolina.

40. Carroll Smith-Rosenberg, "The New Woman as Androgyne: Social Disorder and Gender Crisis, 1870–1936," in her *Disorderly Conduct: Visions of Gender in Victorian America* (New York: Alfred A. Knopf, 1985), 245–96, quote from 257.

41. College vocational bureaus often promised that clerical work could lead to managerial or executive positions; this rarely happened. See Strom, 331. On college women in office work, see Strom, 336.

42. Ruth Waldo, Job Application Form, J. Walter Thompson Company Archives, Duke University Library, Durham, North Carolina.

43. Lucy H. Dunham, Personnel File, J. Walter Thompson Archives, Duke University Library, Durham, North Carolina.

44. Mary Tucker, Perle Dienst, Rebecca Hourwich, Faith Kelley, Frances Maule, Personnel Files, J. Walter Thompson Company Archives, Duke University Library, Durham, North Carolina.

45. Mary Cook, Personnel File, J. Walter Thompson Company Archives, Duke University Library, Durham, North Carolina.

46. Elizabeth Gates, Mary Cook, Personnel Files, J. Walter Thompson Company Archives, Duke University Library, Durham, North Carolina; Strom, 327.

47. Daniel Walkowitz, "The Making of a Feminine Professional Identity: Social Workers in the 1920s," *American Historical Review*, Vol. 95, No. 4 (October 1990), 1055. See also Brumberg and Tomes.

48. Dr. Alice Hamilton quoted in Rosalind Rosenberg, *Divided Lives: American Women in the Twentieth Century* (New York: Hill and Wang, 1992), 29.

49. Walkowitz, 1062; 1060.

50. Susan Curtis, *A Consuming Faith: The Social Gospel and Modern American Culture* (Baltimore: Johns Hopkins Univ. Press, 1991), xiii.

51. Curtis, 14.

52. Curtis, 33.

53. Ellen Carol DuBois, "Harriot Stanton Blatch and the Transformation of Class Relations Among Woman Suffragists," in Noralee Frankel and Nancy S. Dye, eds., *Gender, Class, Race, and Reform in the Progressive Era* (Lexington: The University Press of Kentucky, 1991), 162–79, quote from 163.

54. Walkowitz, 1062.

55. *J. Walter Thompson Company Blue Book*, 1910, 23, J. Walter Thompson Company Archives, Duke University Library, Durham, North Carolina.

56. *News Bulletin*, March 25, 1922, 14–15, J. Walter Thompson Company Archives, Duke University Library, Durham, North Carolina.

57. Eleanor Taylor, Personnel File, J. Walter Thompson Company Archives, Duke University Library, Durham, North Carolina.

58. Gertrude Coit, Personnel File, J. Walter Thompson Company Archives, Duke University Library, Durham, North Carolina.

59. Charline Davenport, Personnel File, J. Walter Thompson Company Archives, Duke University Library, Durham, North Carolina.

60. Ruth Waldo, Personnel File, J. Walter Thompson Company Archives, Duke University Library, Durham, North Carolina.

61. "Ruth Waldo Dies: Early Advertising Woman," *New York Times* (Sept. 5, 1975), J. Walter Thompson Company Archives, Duke University Library, Durham, North Carolina.

62. Rebecca Hourwich, Personnel File, J. Walter Thompson Archives, Duke University Library, Durham, North Carolina.

63. Therese Olzendam, Personnel File, J. Walter Thompson Company Archives; "Therese Olzendam—Thumbnail Sketch," Sept. 20, 1948, J. Walter Thompson Company Archives, Duke University Library, Durham, North Carolina.

64. Frances Maule, Personnel File, J. Walter Thompson Company Archives, Duke University Library, Durham, North Carolina.

65. Helen Resor, letter in Frances Maule's personnel file, J. Walter Thompson Company Archives, Duke University Library, Durham, North Carolina.

66. Helen Lansdowne Resor, Biographical File, J. Walter Thompson Company Archives, Duke University Library, Durham, North Carolina.

67. Judith Schwarz, Kathy Peiss, and Christina Simmons, " 'We Were a Band of Willful Women,' " in *Passion and Power*, ed. Kathy Peiss and Christina Simmons (Philadelphia: Temple University Press, 1989), 118.

68. Caroline F. Ware, *Greenwich Village, 1920–1930: A Comment on American Civilization in the Post-War Years* (Berkeley: University of California Press, 1994; 1935).

69. "Early Important Women," Bernstein Client Files: Chesebrough-Ponds, J. Walter Thompson Company Archives, Duke University Library, Durham, North Carolina.

70. Hermione Lee, *Willa Cather: Double Lives* (New York: Pantheon Books, 1989), 70, 71. Lillian Faderman, in *Odd Girls and Twilight Lovers: A History of Lesbian Life in Twentieth-Century America* (New York: Penguin, 1991), describes Willa Cather's practice of calling herself Dr. William and dressing in male drag while a student at the University of Nebraska. According to Faderman, Cather became more quiet about her relationships with women after the turn of the century "because she was aware of the fall from grace that love between women was beginning to suffer," 53.

71. Faderman, 12.

72. Judith Schwarz, *Radical Feminists of Heterodoxy* (Norwich, VT: New Victoria Publishers, 1986), 36.

73. Leila Rupp, " 'Imagine My Surprise': Women's Relationships in Historical Perspective," *Frontiers*, Vol. 5, No. 3 (1981), 61–70.

74. Faderman, 16.

75. Wallace Boren, Staff Meeting Minutes, January 7, 1936, J. Walter Thompson Company Archives, Duke University Library, Durham, North Carolina.

76. Cynthia Swank, "Not Just Another Pretty Face: Advertising Women in the 1920s," Slide Lecture to the Philadelphia Club of Advertising Women, March 9, 1982, 5–6.

77. Helen Lansdowne Resor, Stockholder's Affidavit, 69, J. Walter Thompson Company Archives, Duke University Library, Durham, North Carolina.

78. Charles Austin Bates quoted in Fox, 37.

79. Mildred Holmes, "Housewives Write the Copy," *News Bulletin*, No. 97, April, 1923, 7, J. Walter Thompson Company Archives, Duke University Library, Durham, North Carolina.

80. Walkowitz, 1062, provides an interesting parallel to the advertising woman's description of her clients in a contemporary drawing showing a young, thin, professionally dressed social worker talking with an older, heavier, toothless client.

81. Frances Maule, "The Woman Appeal," *News Bulletin*, No. 105, January 1925, 2, 5, J. Walter Thompson Company Archives, Duke University Library, Durham, North Carolina.

82. *News Bulletin*, July 11, 1916, 1, J. Walter Thompson Company Archives, Duke University Library, Durham, North Carolina.

83. *News Bulletin*, July 11, 1916, 2.

84. *News Bulletin*, No. 61, August 12, 1918, 1–5, J. Walter Thompson Company Archives, Duke University Library, Durham, North Carolina. *Pictorial Review* offered a $5000 annual award to the American woman who made, in the last ten years, the greatest contribution to national life in letters, arts, science, philanthropy, or social welfare. See "Win Pictorial Review Award," *The Independent Woman*, Vol. 7, No. 12 (December 1928), 561.

85. Minutes, Creative Organization Staff Meeting, March 5, 1932, 8, J. Walter Thompson Company Archives, Duke University Library, Durham, North Carolina.

86. Curtis, 71.

87. Dorothy Brown, *Setting a Course: American Women in the 1920s* (Boston: Twayne Pubs., 1987), 106.

Chapter Thirteen

In Spite of Women
Esquire *Magazine and the Construction of the Male Consumer*

Kenon Breazeale

> The proper study of mankind is man . . . but the proper
> study of markets is woman.
> —Ad in Printers Ink 1929

Much of what the modern world deems appropriate sex roles is embedded in a nutshell dichotomy—men produce and women shop. For years, this stereotype has been attracting feminist scholarly attention. From Betty Friedan's *The Feminine Mystique* (1963) to the upsurge of publication on the subject during the last decade, feminist scholars have asserted that the encoding of modern female identity has everything to do with attempts to construct women as consumers.[1] In this article I want to expand the discussion by offering a refocused premise—that precisely because consumption has been viewed as an attribute of middle-class femininity, some of our era's most aggressively one-dimensional representations of women have resulted from attempts to court men as consumers. Specifically, I want to examine *Esquire* magazine, which I would argue was the first thoroughgoing, conscious attempt to organize a consuming male audience. From the magazine's origin in 1933 until the 1946 departure of its influential founding editor, Arnold Gingrich, *Esquire*'s editorial staff sought to constitute consumption as a new arena for masculine privilege by launching in text and image what amounted to an oppositional meta-commentary on female identity. In other words, this "magazine for men" was to a great extent a magazine about women. Analyzing the magazine within the context of the twenties and thirties, I will explore why *Esquire*'s editors felt compelled so thoroughly to "take account" of the feminine and discuss the consequences for media culture of its need to represent women in certain ways.

Conventional scholarly wisdom holds that contemporary male socio-sexual identity was brought into focus during the 1950s when *Playboy*, inspired by the Kinsey Reports and enabled by postwar prosperity, proposed desire instead of responsibility as the key trope of bourgeois masculinity. The theory has been most influentially offered in Barbara Ehrenreich's *Hearts of Men* (1983). Ehrenreich asserts that the origins of modern sexual politics lie in a fifties revolt by American men against work and patriarchal authority as denominators of identity.[2] But I would contend that the new model of self-indulgent masculinity that she tracks across a spectrum of popular culture sources was by then an evolved formula, one that had originated under quite different historical circumstances.

It was not boom times and sexology but rather the crisis of the Depression that prompted the ideological work necessary to reshape attitudes about masculinity, desire, and consumption. Two recent social histories of image making and design, *All Consuming Images* (Ewen 1988) and *Making the Modern* (Smith 1993), persuasively argue that modern American commercial culture came into being during the 1930s. Driven by the felt necessity of reviving market demand, corporate and governmental attention shifted from production to the consumer, encouraging the marketing industry to new levels of influence and new subtleties of theory. Economists and industrial engineers collaborated with admen to originate a new pseudoscience: "consumption engineering." They evolved the logic (still in place today) that real profits lie in constantly organizing taste in new ways (Meikle 1979, 68–70). Only by sophisticated methods of manipulating and reconceptualizing consumer audiences, they posited, could corporate America revive and prosper.[3] *Esquire*, I will show, was one of the first and clearest sites of this consciousness at work.

Depression-bred anxiety about the impact of devastating economic change on traditional bourgeois sex roles provided the specific inspiration for *Esquire*'s creation. Lois Scharf and others have documented that twenties-formed habits of consumption collided during the early thirties with massive unemployment to push a cohort of middle-class married women into the workforce (Scharf 1980, chap. 7). Surely not by coincidence, social commentators rapidly developed a discourse that highlighted diminished male self-esteem as an outgrowth of the Depression. Pundits of Eleanor Roosevelt's stature argued that losing one's job, whether real or feared, and the possibility of seeing one's wife forced to become a breadwinner was resulting in a dislocating loss of masculine self-respect (Roosevelt 1933, 20). The opportunity seized by *Esquire* was recognizing that this multivalent "loss" could be refigured into the site of a marketable new male identity. Key to such sleight of hand was the notion of "leisure," a buzzword among Roosevelt braintrusters who hoped that commodifying the free time attendant on a reduced work week would lead to more consumer spending.[4] In deluxe promotional booklets meant to alert ad agency directors to his magazine's first issue, Gingrich appropriated the term, suggesting: "Men have had leisure thrust upon them. Now they've got it, they must spend it somehow. . . . What more opportune occasion for the appearance of a new magazine—a new kind of magazine—one that will answer the question of What to do? What to eat, what to drink, what to wear, how to play, what to read—in short a magazine dedicated to the improvement of the new leisure" (Gingrich 1971, 102). In other words, *Esquire* proposed to become the first magazine presenting an appeal to the desiring male subject (i.e., consumer) as a systematically developed editorial formula.

Not only New Deal rhetoric but the dynamic of attitudes about gender specific to the magazine industry circa 1930 created an opportune moment for *Esquire*'s founding. Understanding that occasion means understanding how rigidly sex-linked the ideology of consumption had become as the intertwined advertising/publishing industry grew to maturity during the 1920s. In a narrow sense that industry functioned on the interplay between two presumptions: the socially appropriate aim of women is to cultivate themselves as consumers; and shopping is what is wrong with women and women shoppers are what is wrong with the world.

First, the link forged between women's social role and consumption. As the ad industry of the twenties sought to professionalize itself, it generated a body of theory and research on marketing. No aspect of this lore made more of an impact than the "finding" that selling meant selling to women (Ewen 1976, 167). Articles touting women as the crucial market ran regularly in the advertising tradepaper *Printer's Ink*; and two influential books, Christine Frederick's *Selling Mrs. Consumer* (1929) and Carl Naether's *Advertising to Women* (1928), piled on statistics that demonstrated women's "buying power." The first line of Naether's introduction claimed, "Women are indeed the shoppers of the world." And it did not stop there. Such writers evolved a minisociology, couched in the language of the social sciences, that sought to conflate femininity and consumption as denominators of progressive modern life: "Having the purchasing power to practice it, they [American housewives] are increasingly applying the language of obsolesence to move ever upward to higher planes and standards of living. . . . A civilization like ours centers its genius upon improving the conditions of life. Inevitably in such a civilization women's influence grows increasingly larger, for woman is the logical center of peaceful living" (Frederick 1929, 29).

Widespread acceptance of not only the avalanche of statistics but also the mythology that accompanied it profoundly affected the publishing business. Women's magazines willing to organize editorial content around the presumption of "educated shopping" as a sign of responsible femininity benefited from an advertising bonanza (Matthews 1987, chap. 7). Both such values in and of themselves and the girlishly condescending style in which they were purveyed provided a ripe target for satire. Not surprisingly, some in the journalism fraternity began identifying the feminine with gullible vulnerability to consumerism's trashy faddishness. Throughout the 1920s a humorous discourse evolved that equated women's winning the vote with their gaining unbridled power as consumers. Male pundits (the best known being H. L. Mencken and Harold Nicholson) expressed a wide-ranging hostility toward women's (inferior) tastes and tendencies coming to dominate the cultural marketplace.[5]

Enter *Esquire*'s founders, David Smart and William Weintraub, partners whose backgrounds significantly lay in marketing rather than literature or journalism.[6] Both were in menswear, Smart as a producer of trade catalogs and Weintraub as an ad linage salesman. Their decision to found a magazine was inspired by *Fortune*, the surprise success story of early thirties publishing. Henry Luce had taken the trade paper formula (i.e., business-to-business advertising) and repackaged it as an immensely stylish vehicle for the new corporate culture. What *Fortune* "proved" to

Smart and Weintraub was that, with the right demographic, a male-identified magazine could arouse widespread interest among national advertisers. The partnership had expert knowledge of just such an audience. Customers of men's clothing stores were among the few reliably prosperous cohorts in U.S. society during the early thirties, and the partnership decided to launch a magazine that could serve as a vehicle for men's apparel ads.[7] Interestingly enough, the question of editorial content seems to have been a virtual afterthought. It was a young copywriter (soon to be editor) in their employ, Arnold Gingrich, who conceived the new magazine's core concept. Shrewdly surveying the popular media landscape, he perceived real promise in the collision point between the success of formula women's magazines and masculine journalism's contempt for this phenomenon. In language that would have done Mencken proud, Gingrich simultaneously identified a readership and a cause, the "neglected" male: "It is our belief, in offering *Esquire* to the American male, that we are only getting around at last to a job that should have been done a long time ago—that of giving the masculine reader a break. The general magazines, in the mad scramble to increase the woman readership that seems to be so highly prized by national advertisers, have bent over backwards in catering to the special interests and tastes of the feminine audience. This has reached the point where the male reader is made to feel like an intruder on gynaecic mysteries" (*Esquire* 1933, 4).

Gingrich's rhetoric reveals in a nutshell what would become the crucial dynamic of his new magazine—simultaneous exploitation and denial of the feminine. Not that the young editor would have admitted it. He pointedly claimed as inspiration the *New Yorker* and *Vanity Fair* and hoped his magazine's reputation would derive from publishing fiction by the likes of Hemingway and Fitzgerald. But in truth *Esquire* appropriated the mix of contents that has characterized women's magazines from the 1920s on: a centerpiece of seductive "lifestyle" features whose job is to service advertisers by transforming reader into consumer, leavened with visuals and fiction. Like the *Ladies' Home Journal, Vogue,* and *Harper's Bazaar, Esquire*'s nonfiction core sought to create a comprehensive set of expectations about what constitutes a desirable upper-middle-class identity. But that very parallel offered up an enormous difficulty for the magazine. Most of the activities being touted—cooking, interior decoration, and so on—were by definition fatally associated with housewifery. Somehow *Esquire* had to displace all the woman-identified associations so firmly lodged at the center of America's commodified domestic environment. The solution was a magazine replete with entire categories of nonfiction whose agenda, no matter what their surface content, was a thoroughgoing attempt to detach the imputation of femininity from that arena of domestic consumption *Esquire* planned to open for its male readers. From the beginning, a majority of its lifestyle articles were written to a formula, the tone arch but the point apocalyptic: American standards and taste are in decay, undermined by the pin-headed women who have come to dominate home and control pocketbook. In virtually every article on food, drink, home decor, gardening, etiquette, and the like published between 1933 and 1946, *Esquire* gave advice to counter the looming rhetorical prop of a woman who is doing things all wrong.

Articles and columns on food—what and how to eat in home and restaurant, recipes and cooking instructions—were a frequent locale for critiques of the appalling sway women's magazines and their "food disposition editors" supposedly maintained over the American housewife. In a 1936 article entitled "Dinner Bites Man," the author complained that "our table, once decorated by steaks, roasts and fowl . . . had been turned into a shambles of rosebud radishes and carrot teensie-weensies . . . our so-called dining room had taken on the aspect of a valentine store after an explosion" (Hough 1936, 46). Iles Brody, whose column "Man the Kitchenette" ran for years, not only held that women were inept cooks but also that they were so lacking in taste that when offered good food they refused to eat it. In evidence he recounted how a date invited for dinner, upon seeing the gourmet spread he had cooked, phoned a drugstore and ordered out "chop suey and a maple nut sundae" (Brody 1940, 105). "Will anyone explain why women can't cook?" another author pleaded. "My private summing up is that women can't cook as well as men because pro primo, they are less generous, pro secondo, they have less imagination, and protertio, they just do not enjoy good food" (Pine 1939, 51).

In home decor women were also accused of overvaluing appearance, this time at the expense of comfort. In putting forth a notion of masculine taste, the author of a regular decorating column noted with approval "the passing of the vogue for cluttering up the home with antiques of the most unlivable type, so long an ardent passion with most women and always a posterior pain to most men" (Jackson 1935, 109). But certainly the most consistently cranky vision of feminine incompetence was evoked in matters of strong drink. A 1936 article instructing how to give a cocktail party cautioned, "Remember, we are well into Repeal, and people . . . expect good liquor—especially because you are a man. That's another reason women say they like men's parties better—you get better drinks" (Powell 1936, 118). Less generously, another author claimed that women can't tell good from bad and advised the thrifty bachelor to pass off "cheap native fizzy water" as imported champagne (Nathan 1945, 106). If left to their own devices, it is darkly hinted, women prefer "fluffy, multi-colored abominations," or worse, do not like to drink at all.

In such monthly columns, *Esquire*'s staff knit misogynistic cultural threads familiar for decades into a wide-ranging set of assertions about the gendered meaning of good and bad taste. Apologists for modernism since the late nineteenth century had linked their favored style with masculinity—clean, functional, machine-based design, indeed innovation itself, was virile. By contrast, ornamentation meant the mire of reflexive tradition meant the feminine, an opposition rooted in late eighteenth-century reasoning that associated the corrupt excesses of the ancien régime with rococo as style and that, in turn, with illicit political influence à la Pompadour (Cheney and Cheney 1936, 48). A paradoxically reverse logic was contained in claims about women's attitudes toward food and drink. Here *Esquire* promoted a favorite canard: that women are deeply antisensual and, having no appreciation for the delights of the flesh, are given to irrational suspicion of all indulgence. Hence the female desire to interject irrelevant moral questions into areas of harmless pleasure and to call for controls where none are needed.

In concocting this take on femininity, *Esquire*'s writers drew on and powerfully reinforced a mythology basic to the twentieth century's "retelling" of nineteenth-century women's history. The temperance and social purity impulses were collapsed into the women's rights movement to create a one-dimensional historical cipher—a man-hating, prudish, censorious creature whose anti-alcohol obsession was a key to reimposing the worst aspects of Calvinist repression on the American psyche (Evans 1989, 175). Not coincidentally, such a caricature underwrote an agenda very important for the magazine. Repeal occurred in the year of *Esquire*'s founding, and reintroduction into the marketplace of a product strongly identified with masculinity was largely responsible for the magazine's initial success. Many periodicals disdained any connection with alcoholic beverages, so *Esquire*'s willingness to tout beer, wine, and liquor as adjuncts to the good life made those industries important early advertisers in its pages.[8] The magazine's equation of prohibitionist sentiments with powerful negative feminine stereotypes contributed a gender-loaded tilt to thirties arguments about public good and private enterprise. It identified support of economic opportunity with expressive individuality and linked both to tolerant, sophisticated masculinity.

In *Esquire*'s how-to's of consuming desire, women really had no place; they were merely a foil against which a superior male taste could be posited. This construction of femininity as lack was even more evident in a type of condescending tutelage that moved beyond consumption to provide a blueprint for class-appropriate behavior in the world at large. Presented as humorous commentaries on manners and mores, such pieces constituted a thorough, nuanced attempt to set standards and values for the professional-managerial bourgeoisie that was *Esquire*'s targeted readership. In every second or third issue there appeared a feature whose all-purpose subtitle could be "Women are Lousy at [fill in name of activity]." Among other things, it was variously claimed that women are irritating traveling companions (Bingham 1947, 89), demonic drivers (Marks and Stilwill 1941, 48), and uninformed hysterical sports fans (Graffis 1945, 66); cheat at cards (MacDougall and Kobler 1939, 61); have no sense of humor and talk too much and in the wrong tone of voice (Peet 1940, 42); and are less well-dressed (Brown 1935, 79), are worse letter writers (Horton 1939, 54), and make more dangerous criminals than men (Radin 1947, 72). In these articles femininity became the benchmark not only of bad taste but of boorish behavior and suspect intentions.

Esquire's assertions about gender, taste, consumption, and social identity radically subverted not only assumptions about the meaning of femininity and masculinity implicit in women's magazines but also the very structure of the periodicals industry. From its beginnings the industry had cultivated a mode of address ("Dear Reader . . .") that endowed readers with a specifically gendered identity and by the mid–nineteenth century had evolved editorial genres tied to sex-categorized interests and activities (Shevelow 1989, 3). In fact an argument could be made that the widespread acceptance of separate social roles for bourgeois men and women was to some extent a product of magazine culture.) Women's magazines of the twenties and thirties retained a strong echo of this worldview. They held that evident differences in masculine and feminine taste ultimately devolved from legitimately contrasting and mutually complementary biological and social roles. In embracing the women's magazine formula while trashing women, *Esquire* by definition confronted the popular periodical industry and its attendant arena of marketing culture with a very different premise—that women as women have no legitimate social role to play.

Taken as a whole, *Esquire*'s nonfiction of the thirties and forties added up to an ideological system, the project of which was remapping the territory on which difference was plotted. To recuperate successfully a female-identified role for men meant arguing against traditional sex-linked social roles. Yet claiming difference on some level was absolutely necessary to maintain male sex privilege. The magazine's lifestyle components—all of its advice and commentary modes—finessed this contradiction via a "postfeminist" argument. *Esquire*'s new domestic scenario was touted as "progress" for women as well as men, the enemy of both conceived of as some outmoded model of hyperdomestic femininity. Yet simultaneously the transformation of women's postsuffrage identity was read negatively. Modern womanhood, exploiting men's willingness to relinquish traditional modes of patriarchal dominance, was seen as out of control, a "problem" waiting to be "solved."[9] The solution was in essence proposed by the other body of contents in *Esquire* that sought to extensively represent women—its illustrations. As I will demonstrate below, *Esquire*'s pictorial contents offered its male audience what amounted to a system of compensatory control devised around the sexual gaze and specifically attuned to "modern" bourgeois sensibilities.

Before moving on to a discussion of *Esquire*'s visuals, a word about method. Most scholarly analysis of illustration follows art history's deeply embedded tendency to examine images in the context of like images and to construe significant meaning as flowing only from the mind of the artist. What research has been done on illustration in *Esquire* has met with this approach (histories of pinups as a generic category, e.g., or individual studies of illustrators who worked for the magazine). I want to argue for another kind of analysis. This study postulates that magazines are calculated packages of meaning whose aim is to transform the reader into an imaginary subject—as Louis Althusser put it, to "appellate" each reader.[10] Magazines are both devised and experienced as a whole and can be most meaningfully studied as a system entire. When seen that way, *Esquire*'s pictorial conter's can be understood as fulfilling a vital ideological function complementary to the text. Given that the text worked to deny the legitimacy of social roles proceeding from sexual difference, illustrations provided the site to which difference could be repositioned.

As with its female-focused nonfiction, *Esquire*'s visual images of women originated in a kind of hysteria. Basic to my argument about *Esquire* is a contention that the magazine was compelled to represent women in order to negotiate its relationship to the feminine. Only with the question of femininity "settled" could a credible space be opened up wherein to construct the consuming male. Hence the project of the text was to displace that archetype of consuming femininity, the housewife. And hence the function of the visuals was to deny an even more dangerous association with femininity, homosexuality. From the moment of its inception,

Esquire's founders were fearful that their magazine's interest in apparel, food, decor, and so on might make it appear to be targeted at homosexuals (as Gingrich wrote, that "a whiff of lavender" might seem to perfume its pages [1971, 81]). It had to be made unequivocally clear that women were the natural objects of its readership's desire.[11] Thus it was taken as given that the magazine would prominently feature erotically coded representations of women. Much of the magazine's tone and character was determined by the means devised both to include such illustrations and to reassure its readership about consuming them. Implicit in all this was, I would suggest, one of modern popular culture's most influential attempts to embody represented femininity as a signifier for specifically heterosexual masculinity.

Featuring erotic spectacle in a mainstream publication was possible only because *Esquire* was founded at a moment when the function of illustration was being transformed. During the thirties, the visual contents of periodicals became detached from illustrational function, a move facilitated by improved color reproduction techniques and encouraged by the fragmenting fact of increased full-page advertising. (Two new magazines of the thirties, *Life* and *Look*, made the focus on visuals their founding premise.) For the first time, images were presented to be consumed on their own, creating a potential distance in production of meaning between textual and visual contents. Nowhere was this possibility more shrewdly exploited than in *Esquire*. There it became the means to negotiate around taboos that had heretofore limited the profitability of "male-oriented" periodicals.

Throughout the late nineteenth century and the early decades of the twentieth, a whole "for-men-only" publishing category of sexual provocation had existed (magazines with photographs of nude models intended for "artists," e.g.). But it remained only a modestly profitable endeavor segregated from the high-circulation market, where major advertisers catered to a "family" audience thought to be regulated by female sensibilities (Gabor 1972, 5). Once the decision had been made by *Esquire*'s founders to feature cheesecake, the challenge was to contrive a balance, or better put, a tension, between a sub rosa assertion that the magazine was enjoyably salacious and a more overt claim that it was absolutely respectable, belonging on the coffee table, not hidden upstairs in the sock drawer. Playing off the contrast between verbal and visual, an editorial structure was evolved wherein sexy visuals could be both exploited and rendered in a sense "invisible." Through editorial cues the magazine presented its identity as a set of overlapped contrasts— text versus visuals, male subject versus female object, writing virtually always by men versus running features with titles like "Legs and the Woman"—that coalesced into an overarching contrast of serious, verbal masculinity versus frivolous, mute femininity. The pictorial material was constituted as a kind of bimbo zone, unworthy of serious consideration and (hopefully) of serious complaint.[12]

Within this overall modus operandi, the magazine deployed a recognizable semiotic—systematic categories of illustration that ran predictably from issue to issue.[13] Lynda Nead, in her recently published *The Female Nude* (1992, 85), observes the vital distinctions Western culture has structured into the oppositional categories of fine arts versus pornography/obscenity. Her point is that nude images tend to be firmly contexualized into one or the other category. *Esquire*'s crucial innovation was to embrace both, creating a dyad that appeared in virtually every number, "framing" the magazine's representation of women.

"Fine arts" was signified in portfolio presentations of works by prominent artists such as Rockwell Kent, Salvador Dali, and Yasuo Kuniyoshi where generic art modes like landscape and still life legitimated the inclusion of nudes. At the other end of the register was the type of image that specifically signified prurient appeal—the pinup. Society takes the significant boundary between acceptable and pornographic images to be whether the audience is moved to contemplation or sexual activity. While a majority of *Esquire*'s images of women were meant to be provocative, it was the pinup that was explicitly coded as a masturbatory aide.

No doubt in an attempt to evoke associations with the Gibson Girl, *Esquire*'s pinups were called Petty Girls in tribute to their originator.[14] George Petty's drawings are exemplars of the fetishizing possibilities inherent in airbrush: bodies encased in a flawlessly taut sheath of skin that resembles inflated rubber. It is instructive to follow the illustrator's codification of his formula throughout the thirties. First the Petty Girl was an air-headed cartoon character paired with a lecherous buffoon. By the late thirties, Petty had evolved both a simpler format—the telephone conversation—and a more intensely stylish presentation—the woman's highly volumetric body surrounded by and contrasted with an abbreviated, two-dimensional description of space. And by 1940 the illustration's presentation in each issue had gone from single page to gatefold to centerfold, clearly indicating an expectation that the reader would prop up or tear out this apotheosis of fetishism.[15] The Petty Girl was both source and example of the generic anatomical formula used to depict women in a vast majority of *Esquire*'s illustrations. Prototypically blonde with large breasts, tiny waist, small buttocks, and long, slender legs, she is a specifically Caucasian archetype of erotic appeal. And reinforcing her "whiteness" is the emphasis airbrush perforce gives to depicted surface; the Petty Girl's most noticeable attribute is her flawlessly smooth, pale peach-colored skin.

With fine arts and pinups, *Esquire* associated itself with recognized ways of seeing: aesthetic contemplation and consuming desire. The former bore just the highbrow associations desirable for (if not necessarily desired by) a middle-classy readership. But the pinup was highly problematic, fraught with downscale (i.e., working-class) suggestions of deprivation and sweaty need. *Esquire* had to somehow reframe the conditions under which images deemed sexually provocative were consumed so as to create an aura of sophisticated recreation. Two other regular pictorial features—the covers and cartoons—worked to do just that, socializing readers into a humorously presented vocabulary and point of view for sexual looking.

The magazine's agenda was effectively announced by a cover treatment that appeared in embryo form on the second issue and was fully developed by the mid-thirties. A word about magazine covers is in order. By the 1920s, major magazines had refined cover art into a site wherein the demographically targeted reader was endowed with an identity and appealed to on that basis. After Norman Rockwell's covers for the *Saturday Evening Post, Esquire*'s covers were the most effectively recognizable in the industry. Under the magazine's logo appeared a photographed tableau of puppet figures starring Esky, the magazine's trademark. Esky (a cartoonish send-up of the *New Yorker's* Edwardian dandy?) sported an upscale wardrobe, blonde walrus mustaches, and his most distinctive attribute, huge pop eyes with protruding button-like pupils that leered toward the complementary upthrust breasts of female companions who accompanied him in some seasonally themed scene. Repeated with minor variations for years, this cover design drove home *Esquire's* basic proposition that heterosexual social life consists of a mutually agreeable dialogue between male consciousness and female anatomy.

Cartoons were the other locale in which *Esquire* promoted the normalcy of what Freud clinically termed *scopophilia,* that is, the voyeuristic gaze. "Adult" cartoons already had a track record as a popular illustrational form. During and after World War I racy cartoon books that capitalized on themes of sexual looking found a sizable audience. *Esquire* adopted the genre with two innovations: transforming the traditional format of cursory line drawings into full-page color "artworks" and reorienting what had been a fairly gender-neutral humor (about themes like nudism, e.g.) around a specifically masculine position. In an average of about five cartoons per issue, the magazine rang variations on stock situations in which men could conceivably encounter a naked woman. All emphasized a kind of looking in which the man is an initiate and the woman a more or less unsuspecting object. Women are surprised in the bathtub by window washers, burglars, and firefighters. Or there is the accidental loss of clothes, particularly bathing suit tops, to vagaries of wind, weather, outboard motors, sharks, etc. Doctor-patient jokes present a particularly unnerving riff on vulnerable nudity. (To an undressed woman surrounded by slobbering male medicos, "But surely Miss Lonsdale, you've heard of consultations?") But by far the single favorite theme was artist and model, where the joke is the lustful look concealed behind the artistic regard ("Why Mr. DeMunson, you're not painting me at all!"). Male gallery-goers, whose reaction to painted and sculpted nudes pointedly collapses the distance between art and life, form a variation on the theme ("$2,500 is rather high; I can get a live one for less than that!").[16]

Reinforcing *Esquire's* commitment to dichotomized sexualities was the concentrated attention cartoons gave to two comic female types—the gold digger and the black domestic. The gold digger constituted the perfect ideological foil for the male gaze, a Menckenesque persona all too willing to trade sex for money.[17] *Esquire* presented her in a variety of guises, from naive young working-class girl to the calculating sophisticate who is an expert at coaxing ever larger "gifts" out of befuddled elderly plutocrats. In what appeared to be studied contrast are the numerous cartoons that featured black maids and housekeepers. While the gold digger's anatomy was derived from the pinup and signifies sexual attractiveness, black women were imaged as fat or as simian and stringy. And while the gold digger's desires were taken to be purely acquisatory, black women were seen as quite sexual, that is, as promiscuous baby machines. (White employer meets black housekeeper with baby carriage on the street, "Why Maisie, I thought you were an old maid!" "Yassum, but I ain't a fussy old maid.")[18] *Esquire* endorsed a significant double-think about race and gender. With ostentatious liberal rhetoric the magazine featured the work of black author Langston Hughes and illustrator Simms Campbell.[19] Yet in text as well as image *Esquire* constantly ridiculed black women. In addition to the cartoon features, the magazine published during the thirties a lengthy comic serial featuring one Mrs. Geranium Finn, a Harlem resident and the embodiment of every racist stereotype from nymphomania to illiteracy to comic social pretensions.

These monthly pictorial categories mapped the boundaries—art, sex, and ironic humor—within which women were to be represented and tutored the reader as to the position appropriate for him to assume when looking at women. But to my mind the most revealing *Esquire* visuals are the occasional features that deliberately put these elements into solution. With these features one can see clearly the ideological work—the veiling of contradiction—accomplished by *Esquire* during the thirties and forties that in turn made possible a postwar men's magazine industry predicated upon balancing titillation and reassurance.

Virtually all of *Esquire's* images of women attempted reference to the aesthetic, most obviously via use of a variety of art media and recognizably current art styles. Regularly included were oil, airbrush, and watercolor painting, pastels, sculpture, ceramics, collage, several printmaking media, and photography; stylistic codes ranged from cubism and fauvism to surrealism. (In sum, the virtual taxonomy of an art school curriculum.) Such arty manipulation was meant to transform not so much the woman in the image as the man looking at it—from voyeur to connoisseur. Certain pictorials pushed the signifier "fine arts" aggressively, hence fudging boundaries between high and low most obviously. A nicely literal example was a series created by Erwin Blumenthal in 1942. Semi-nude models were made-up, posed, accessorized, and sometimes trick-photographed "in the style of" famous artists such as Dürer, Renoir, and Picasso. In a more complex vein, the artistic eye as controlling presence was subtly figured in a series of glamour portraits of stars and starlets commissioned from Hollywood studio photographer George Hurrell during the late thirties. All are high-style black-and-white images wherein dramatic lighting seems literally to sculpt and paint the subject's face, transforming it into a fetishized mask. In one notable instance two photos of Simone Simon (entitled respectively "Sugar" and "Spice") were run back to back; "artistic" transformations in lighting, hairstyle, and expression make her appear to be two different people. A caption accompanying a self-portrait by Hurrell in another issue takes care to make the distinction between his art and mere photography: "The difference lies in the painter's eye, the painter's feel for form and composition, that brings black and white magic out of Hurrell's darkroom."[20]

Perhaps the single most revealing pictorial of these years was one entitled "Types of American Beauty" that ran for eight issues in 1940.[21] Here one sees the magazine ambitiously negotiating between regimes of meaning that had been the pretext for presenting provocative images of women in nineteenth- and early twentieth-century illustration and the stripped-down fetishism that was to become the norm in *Esquire* during the forties and *Playboy* in the fifties. This feature was based on the notion of women as "types" apotheosizing some aspect of American culture, a staple of magazine illustration for decades.[22] The premise of the *Esquire* project is that each woman represents a physiological category and that not only her character and personality but really her whole past and future are determined by and readable through her appearance. The apologia states: "These analyses are based upon a skilled reading of the model's physical attributes, permitting assignment of the individual to reasonably specific classification or category . . . and further permitting a projection of a possible behavior pattern. . . . Thus the figure reveals to the eye many a significant truth about its possessor's mental, spiritual and emotional pattern."[23] The images themselves reveal the ingenuity with which *Esquire* synthesized fine arts and cheesecake. Each month a specially commissioned sculpture of a nude woman was presented via gatefold photographs that combined an aura of artiness with the conventions of soft-core pornography—focus on breasts and buttocks. Typically the identities of the male "artists" involved, sculptor Frank Nagy and photographer Andre de Dienes, were foregrounded, together with the author of analytical captions, pen name Nostradamus, "a prominent New York medical specialist." Here are samples of the descriptive text. Number One was Perdita, "Hips full but not fleshy, denoting the broad feminine pelvis. . . . This constitutional type is common among those of Scandinavian ancestry. . . . She is a young woman who matured rather early and is in the first bloom of her active femininity. . . . Born on the wrong side of the tracks, crude sex is her ruin from the 6th Grade up. . . . If rescued into the haven of middle class domesticity, she promises to become the prize of the iceman." Number Two is Virginia, whose "breasts are on a broad base, their transversal diameter is greater than the vertical one. . . . The right date for a young man, good sport and no prude, but countenances petting only within strictly conventional limits. Will make a good wife and mother." In features such as these, the pleasures of sexual looking were annealed not only to aesthetic contemplation but also to the social scientific modes that employ inquiry via the visual. And if the highmindedness of the situation was not already sufficiently clear, *Esquire* typically took care to throw freedom of expression into the pot by publishing in the same issue a lengthy article on the history of censorship attempts against nudity in art.[24]

The captions accompanying "Types of American Beauty" are characteristic of *Esquire's* liminal content. It is from these informal enframing devices for occasional features that readers are most clearly appellated as subjects. Repeated, detailed guidance is given as to the attitudes "you," the *Esquire* Man, should bring to the illustrations and in turn take away from the magazine into your everyday reality.[25] Here is an excerpt from a whole paragraph hyping pinup calendars that suggests onanistic pleasures in a buzz of cute verbiage: "She restores your flagging sense of proportion, she is a tonic to your soul, a gladdener of the eye, a soft, sweet roustalont restorer of the old raison d'etre." Or this, from a pictorial featuring sketched models casually posed in studio settings that displaces the spectator's voyeuristic intent onto the woman herself: "While he was mixing his colors in preparation for the day's work, Mr. Smith the artist stole an amused glance at his model, noting the feline deliberation with which she preened herself for her portrait. . . . This cool creature remains like most models, as self-contained as a kitten—and as patently full of guile. . . . Her expressive eyes look thoughtful and faraway— well, at least as far as the mirror which hangs on the opposite wall."[26] And in case there was any doubt that sexual looking constituted a civilized recreational activity, in 1937 the magazine published a lengthy article that offered a history, philosophy, and guide to girl watching entitled "Essay on Jiggling":

> The jiggle . . . that champagne of movement which can only be accomplished by the human female . . . inspires more of the bubbly electric feeling of well-being for men than all the more publicized harbingers of spring. . . . It says in the language of the emotions . . . that it is not good for man to use all his energies in the grubby business of acquiring goods or to give all his thought to the injustices of society. . . . Everybody sees the girls walking along, and everybody is pleased. . . . And the remarkable part of it is that the girls have little to do with the cheer and good feeling they disseminate. . . . Young ladies are essentially serious creatures. They . . . worry enormously over the most trivial eventualities. It is only their bodies which are lively and irresponsible and keep them smiling and gay. (McNamara 1937, 43)

Here the frame of reference conceived for consuming images is effortlessly transferred into the world of lived experience.

Esquire's pictorial representations of women completed the logic premised by the text. If, as the text suggested, the relationship between the sexes is problematized by female waywardness, then here was the solution—"raw" femininity "cooked," so to speak, by the worldly wise *Esquire* Man's well-tutored gaze. And as with so much of *Esquire's* rhetoric, the pictorial content incorporated a smug liberality. Projected into a new zone beyond institutionalized oppression, masculine privilege was presented as something inherently benign. Men do not need the power to dominate women politically, the magazine implied (and, as evolved "modern" sorts, would not want it anyway), when they can exercise the pure control of fetishized pleasure over any woman who swims into their line of sight.

In 1946 Arnold Gingrich left *Esquire,* retiring to Switzerland on the competence that stock options had bought him.[27] As is typical of the publishing industry, within a year new editors had announced the fact of decision-maker change by reshaping the magazine. By 1948 content had shifted to a Western true-life adventure format. There were still illustrations of large-breasted women, but as lifestyle content rapidly diminished, so did the focus on femininity. Yet if *Esquire* seemed passé by the late forties—too "thirties" in its arch brittleness—this does not mean that its way of representing women had not been internalized by the periodicals industry itself. The magazine's combination of stylishness and cynical sophistication (not to mention high circulation figures) had long attracted admiration from industry professionals, and echos of its rhetoric on issues of gender are widely discernible within that milieu (Douglas 1991, 175).

I would like to suggest that one of those locales was Betty Friedan's *The Feminine Mystique* (1963). Often cited as a precipitator of second-wave feminism, the book analyzed what Friedan took to be a profound social malaise: the square peg of college-educated women fitted into the round hole of "homemaking." Much of the study focused on a critical analysis of women's magazines. Both the myopia and the wisdom of *The Feminine Mystique* were a function of Friedan's critiquing the values of a world she belonged to; she had written for mainstream women's and shelter magazines throughout the 1950s. What interests me in regard to all this are the assumptions she made about housewifery. Friedan proceeded from an acute conviction that homemaking as done by women is a pathetic and absurd excuse for a social role. In language that, minus the irony, sounds remarkably like *Esquire's,* she asserted that housewives are neurotic pill-poppers and that "homemaking" is a bogus, artificially expanded activity, proof being that men can do twice the amount of housework/childcare in half the time (1963, 247–49). Like *Esquire's* writers, Friedan seemed to be suggesting that the more women can identify themselves with (white, middle-class) male activities and value systems, the better off they will be. Many important feminist voices of the late sixties and early seventies had a background in the periodicals industry. Could they have transmitted to the movement solutions for "the dilemma of difference" that disdained traditional domesticity and privileged an identification with the styles of masculine sophistication?

At the other end of the periodical spectrum, a far more obvious recipient of *Esquire's* legacy was *Playboy.* It is not an exaggeration to say that the *Esquire* Man's model of urbane sophistication and cultivated sensuality constituted an enticing version of the American dream for a particular cohort of postwar masculinity. Certainly part of Hugh Hefner's self-evolved mythology was his early reverence for *Esquire* (he briefly worked in the magazine's circulation department during the late 1940s [Miller 1984, 27]). More to the point, when Hefner founded *Playboy* in 1953, it was very clearly a knock-off of the Gingrich version of *Esquire*—lifestyle articles and girlie visuals wrapped in a package of "serious" fiction and nonfiction. *Playboy* has been credited with first organizing and exploiting consuming masculine desire largely because its editors took for a starting premise the product of *Esquire's* ideological work. *Playboy* could present as unspoken givens certain assumptions about the legitimacy of catering to male desire that *Esquire* had labored to justify and put in place. Overall this meant that the new magazine was far less compelled to engage in rationalizing strategies regarding the feminine. Most notably, it indulged in relatively little of the housewife bashing that had structured and focused *Esquire's* lifestyle articles. The parent magazine had made the urban domestic scene safe for heterosexual men; a playboy could plunge right into "mixing up cocktails and an hors d'oeuvre or two" without having to denigrate woman as cook and drink—maker to justify his expertise.[28]

Not that *Playboy's* editors have not felt compelled to "settle" knotty problems regarding women, specifically the magazine's relationship to the women within its pages. Throughout the eighties and into the nineties, the magazine has combatted the accusation that its manner of representing women is exploitative and objectifying. I raise this issue because it relates to one final point I want to make about *Esquire's* place in modern media history. *Esquire's* contribution to the ideology of consumerism was to propose both the territory of market relations and the landscape of desire as gender-identified, zero-sum battlegrounds. In effect the magazine argued that, by catering to female desire, commercial culture of the twenties had robbed men of their rightful privileges. Hence its effort to fabricate the male consumer had to involve "putting women in their place." In other words, whether by route of perception or invention, *Esquire's* editorial staff convinced itself that what men are truly "in the market" for is status achieved at the expense of women. It is not difficult to perceive this nugget of received wisdom at work in *Playboy*, or in any other male-oriented magazine for that matter, where women are usually represented as servicing men, not just on the sexual level but via markers of class as well. (The playboy is an upscale professional, whereas bunnies, playmates, and so on often are working class.)

Misogyny existed in popular culture long before *Esquire*; what *Esquire* demonstrated was that woman-trashing as such could be packaged and sold to a large, prosperous bourgeois audience. When Barbara Ehrenreich (1983) traces the history of sexist social attitudes from the forties through the sixties, what she is in part examining is cultural product fabricated for a male-identified market. And although she does not put it this way, what Susan Faludi documents in *Backlash* (1991) is how sexist biases were rationalized in marketplace terms during the eighties—the appearance of antifeminist opinion in books, magazines, TV commentary, and the like supposedly indicating a market for antifeminism that in turn justified the production of ever more antifeminist opinion. Now in the mid-nineties, sexism is proposed routinely as a disinterested demand of the market. Market research's most recent "discovery" is a male demographic "neglected" because of the liberal media's supposed rush to service a politically correct feminist line. This time around the medium is radio—testosterone-saturated personas like Howard Stern cater to the eighteen- to thirty-four-year-old male market. But the mode of catering to that demographic—women, nothing but women, fantasized sexually and trashed socially—sounds all too familiar to anyone acquainted with *Esquire*'s attempt to seduce and construct the male consumer.

NOTES

Thanks are due to several friends and colleagues: most particularly Loralee MacPike, as well as John Broesamle, Cathryn Cheal, Susan Kaiser, Mary McArthur, Frances Pohl, Delia Rudiger, and Dianne Smith. I also would like to thank the editorial staff and reviewers for *Signs*, who patiently nursed this article through several versions.

1. Books published during the last decade that deal with female identity as inflected by consumerism include Bowlby 1985; Williamson 1985; Armstrong 1987; Winship 1987; Willis 1991; Spigel and Mann 1992; Radner 1994.

2. See also Bazin 1971 and Cranshaw 1983. Both theorize shifts in male sexual identity during the late 1940s regarding pinups and masturbation. Cranshaw credits the Kinsey Reports and Bazin looks to World War II barracks life.

3. Different conclusions appear to have been reached by Strasser 1989, 125. She argues that, by 1900, producers of new products like safety razors and soft drinks had begun to consciously focus on the market from a consumer-based viewpoint. She does not demonstrate, however, that this perspective had created the elaborately manipulative consciousness that characterized the marketing industry after 1929.

4. The lead article in *Esquire*'s first issue was an interview with Nicolas Murray Butler, then president of Columbia University, entitled "The New Leisure: What It Means in Terms of the Opportunity to Learn the Art of Living" (Butler 1933). Butler was a noted public figure during the early thirties who among other things argued for the economic benefits of

Repeal. As we shall see, much of *Esquire*'s earliest advertising revenue came from liquor and beer ads.

5. Mencken's definitively misogynistic social satire, *In Defense of Women* (1922), set a tone for ironic criticism of postsuffrage womanhood. Among others who capitalized on its arguments was Harold Nicholson, who functioned as a kind of in-house commentator on sex roles, marriage, and family for *Vanity Fair* from 1930 to 1933. In 1933 he authored a *Vanity Fair* article entitled "In Defense of the American Man," which asserted that the American husband was forced to "cut himself away from all that makes life worth living in order to minister to the competitive instincts of his . . . wife [so that] she may have the opportunity to do the same silly and expensive things as other women" (12). Women's supposed receptivity to the manipulative tactics of merchandising was such a truism of the early thirties that Aldous Huxley employed it as an important trope in *Brave New World* (Bowlby 1993, 2).

6. Wilson, in his article on the advent of mass market magazine publishing during the 1880s and 1890s, points out the shift in standard background from literature to journalism (Wilson 1983, 47). During the twenties, experience in advertising became more common as a route to work in magazines. Even so, Smart and Weintraub were unusual in their lack of literature- or journalism-related experience.

7. Smart eventually became the magazine's sole publisher. He went on to parlay *Esquire* into a small publishing empire that included the slick art folio *Minotaur, Coronet* magazine and educational films, and a short-lived magazine of liberal commentary, *Ken.*

8. Early on, *Esquire* made a thorough commitment to glamorizing the consumption of alcohol. To illustrate an article entitled "Cocktail Hour around the World" (*Esquire* 1934), the magazine's editors commissioned from Margaret Bourke-White a full-page color photograph of artistically arranged wine and liquor bottles. The photographer was celebrated for her work in *Fortune* heroically visualizing the new "process" imagery of corporate capitalism. *Esquire* was obviously hoping she could provide a visual rhetoric as convincing for consumption as she had for production.

9. Dick Pine in "Women Can't Cook" (1939, 51) linked women's gaining suffrage with loss of domestic skills and blamed both on "male supineness."

10. My use of the term derives from Williamson (1978, 50), who adapts Althusser's theoretical writing on ideology as a basis for analyzing how advertising constructs an imaginary "dialogue" with its audience.

11. *Esquire* put forward a negative commentary on homosexuality both overtly and covertly. In 1938 it published "Fashion Is a Fairy," an article on the supposedly "unhealthy" influence of homosexuals and lesbians in the design industries. And throughout the fashion features, good taste was defined in opposition to "effeteness."

12. While the strategy proved acceptable to readers and advertisers, contemporary media commentators complained about the hypocrisy of juxtaposing literature and cheesecake. One in *Scribner's* likened reading *Esquire* to listening to Mann, Dos Passos, or Hemingway "read aloud from his works in a burlesque house" (Pringle 1938, 33).

13. This format ultimately was owed to *Time*'s "fixed method of arrangement" of the news. Henry Luce's immensely important innovation pushed periodicals in the direction of becoming a reliable commodity, each issue predictably the same (Smith 1993, 164).

14. According to Gingrich's memoirs he discovered George Petty in the summer of 1933 while looking for visuals to fill out the magazine's first issue (Gingrich 1971, 100). Coming across posters that featured a girl "reminiscent of that line in T. S. Eliot about 'visions of pneumatic bliss,' " Gingrich was told they were by "an airbrush retoucher—you know does over photographs for catalogues . . . so they look like a bastard blend of photo and drawing—

all smoothed out." Petty executed all of the pinups published during the thirties. Most from the forties are the work of Alberto Vargas.

15. The pinup interpreted as archetypal fetish, "the phallus with breasts . . . a trophy of the symbolic and perverse defloration of the mother," is perceptively discussed by Cranshaw (1983, 28).

16. These three cartoons appeared respectively in the issues of June 1938, 79; July 1940, 56; and November 1941, 83.

17. The term *gold digger* came into popular usage during the 1920s to refer to chorus girls who "mined" admirers for gifts and money. Movie musicals of the early thirties appropriated the term as a euphemism for party girls.

18. The cartoon appeared in the May 1934 issue, 142.

19. In its sixth issue *Esquire* published a story by Hughes that involved the theme of miscegenation (1934), having earlier exploited potential controversy by inviting its readership to comment on whether the magazine should carry such material by a Negro author. Simms Campbell was, as Gingrich puts it in his memoirs, "a fantastically talented colored kid" unable to get much work. Gingrich happily recounts how, due to his own racial tolerance, he was thus able to acquire an excellent illustrator for very little money (Gingrich 1971, 95).

20. The photos of Simone Simon appeared in the May 1937 issue, 33–34; the Hurrell self-portrait in the November 1936 issue, 111.

21. The feature ran from April through December 1940. Number 1 (Perdita) appeared on 129–31 of the April issue; Number 2 (Virginia) was on 117–19 of the May issue.

22. Depicting women as "types" was an important mode of representation that evolved in art and literature throughout the nineteenth century. The immediate predecessor of *Esquire's* "Types of American Beauty" would have been the work of so-called girl illustrators like Gibson, Howard Chandler Christy, James M. Flagg, and Cole Phillips, who published variously in *Harper's, Scribner's, American Magazine,* and *Cosmopolitan* during the first three decades of the century (Banta 1987, chap. 9).

23. The caption ran in the April 1940 issue, 129.

24. See Laing 1940. This lengthy article conflates allowable depiction of nudity with freedom of expression and works hard to demonstrate that the censor is invariably rendered history's fool. It was not the first article *Esquire* had published on the subject. In September 1936 the magazine's editors commissioned a piece from Havelock Ellis entitled "What Is Obscenity?" (Ellis's ready answer: "Obscenity is an idea born of ignorance and superstition" [48]). *Esquire* constantly engaged in an obfuscating discourse, usually carried on in editorial asides, about the provocative intentions of its content. The January 1937 "Salute to New Subscribers" says, "The publishers personally guarantee that its cartoons are as clean as the paper on which they are printed. They only refuse to be responsible for the state of your mind" (1937, 3). In 1942 the magazine went to court (and won) over the U.S. postmaster general's attempt to revoke its second-class mail permit because of the provocative cartoons.

25. *Esquire's* chummy mode of address was a quite conscious strategy. In *The Sixth New Year,* the most lavish of its promotional booklets produced for ad agencies, Gingrich trumpeted "the relationship between the magazine and its readers that makes *Esquire* by all odds the most intimate of magazines" (*Esquire* 1939, 3).

26. The calendar ad appeared in the November 1941 issue, 33; Smith's illustration (one of a regular feature called "Esquidorables") ran in December 1945, 84.

27. Gingrich returned to edit *Esquire* during the 1950s and 1960s, but by then the formula niche he had originally carved out was occupied by *Playboy. Esquire* was sold during the seventies and began to be published in its current version in 1978.

28. This tag comes from Hefner's introduction to his first issue, wherein he distinguishes

Playboy from those magazines for men that "spend all their time out of doors—thrashing through thorny thickets or splashing about in fast flowing streams." In contrast, "we plan spending most of our time inside. We like our apartment. We enjoy mixing up cocktails and an hors d'oeuvre or two, putting a little mood music on the phonograph and inviting in a female for a quiet discussion of Picasso, Nietzsche, jazz and sex" (*Playboy* 1953, 3).

REFERENCES

Armstrong, Nancy. 1987. *Desire and Domestic Fiction: A Political History of the Novel.* New York: Oxford University Press.

Banta, Martha. 1987. *Imaging American Women: Idea and Ideals in Cultural History.* New York: Columbia University Press.

Bazin, Andre. 1971. "Entomology of the Pinup Girl." In *What Is Cinema,* ed. Andre Bazin, 15–23. Berkeley: University of California Press.

Bingham, Geary. 1947. "And Points West." *Esquire,* April.

Bowlby, Rachel. 1985. *Just Looking.* New York: Methuen.

———. 1993. *Shopping with Freud.* London: Routledge.

Brody, Iles. 1940. "Man the Kitchenette." *Esquire,* April, 105.

Brown, Carlton. 1935. "Nothing to Lose but Our Pants." *Esquire,* May, 79.

Butler, Nicolas Murray. 1933. "The New Leisure: What It Means in Terms of the Opportunity to Learn the Art of Living." *Esquire,* Autumn.

Cheney, Sheldon, and Martha Chandler Cheney. 1936. *Art and the Machine: An Account of Industrial Design in 20th Century America.* New York: Little, Brown.

Cranshaw, Robert. 1983. "The Object of the Centerfold." *Block* 9:26–33.

Douglas, George H. 1991. *The Smart Magazines.* Hamden: Archon.

Ehrenreich, Barbara. 1983. *The Hearts of Men: American Dreams and the Flight from Reality.* New York: Anchor.

Ellis, Havelock. 1936. "What Is Obscenity?" *Esquire,* September.

Esquire. 1933. "A Magazine for Men Only." *Esquire,* Autumn, 4.

———. 1934. "Cocktail Hour around the World." *Esquire,* January, 25–26.

———. 1937. "Salute to New Subscribers." *Esquire,* January, 5.

———. 1938. "Fashion Is a Fairy." *Esquire,* April, 35–36.

———. 1939. *The Sixth New Year.* Chicago: Esquire, Inc.

Evans, Sara M. 1989. *Born for Liberty: The History of Women in America* New York: Free Press.

Ewen, Stuart. 1976. *Captains of Consciousness: Advertising and the Social Roots of Consumer Culture.* New York: McGraw Hill.

———. 1988. *All Consuming Images: The Politics of Style in Contemporary Culture.* New York: Basic.

Faludi, Susan. 1991. *Backlash: The Undeclared War against American Women.* New York: Crown.

Frederick, Christine. 1929. *Selling Mrs. Consumer.* New York: Business Bourse.

Friedan, Betty. 1963. *The Feminine Mystique.* New York: Norton.

Gabor, Mark. 1972. *The Pinup: A Modest History.* New York: Bell.

Gingrich, Arnold. 1971. *Nothing but People.* New York: Crown.

Graffis, Herb. 1945. "Clamorous Janes." *Esquire,* October, 66.

Horton, Thomas. 1939. "What Men Don't Like about Women." *Esquire,* July.

Hough, Donald. 1936. "Dinner Bites Man." *Esquire,* October.

Hughes, Langston. 1934. "A Good Job Gone." *Esquire,* April.

Jackson, E. McKay. 1935. "The Bachelor at Home." *Esquire,* November.

Laing, Alexander. 1940. "The Struggle over Starko Barko." *Esquire,* April.

MacDougall, Michael, and John Kobler. 1939. "Ladies in Luck." *Esquire,* December.

McNamara, George. 1937. "Essay on Jiggling." *Esquire,* May.

Marks, Robert, and Hart Stilwill. 1941. "Ladies Are Lousy Drivers." *Esquire,* January, 48–49.

Matthews, Glenna. 1987. *Just a Housewife: The Rise and Fall of Domesticity in America.* New York: Oxford University Press.

Meikle, Jeffrey. 1979. *Twentieth Century Limited: Industrial Design in America, 1925–1939.* Philadelphia: Temple University Press.

Mencken, H. L. 1922. *In Defense of Women.* New York: Knopf.

Miller, Russell. 1984. *Bunny: The Real Story of Playboy.* New York: Holt, Rinehart & Winston.

Naether, Carl. 1928. *Advertising to Women.* New York: Prentice Hall.

Nathan, George G. 1945. "First Nights and Passing Judgments." *Esquire,* April, 106–7.

Nead, Linda. 1992. *The Female Nude: Art, Obscenity and Sexuality.* London: Routledge.

Nicholson, Harold. 1933. "In Defense of the American Male." *Vanity Fair,* July, 12–14.

Peet, Creighton. 1940. "Women Talk Too Much." *Esquire,* September, 42–43.

Pine, Dick. 1939. "Women Can't Cook." *Esquire,* September, 51.

Playboy. 1953. "From the Desk of the Publisher." *Playboy,* January, 5.

Powell, William B. 1936. "Cocktail Party, Masculine." *Esquire,* September.

Pringle, Henry. 1938. "Sex, Esq." *Scribner's,* March, 33–45.

Printer's Ink. 1929. Ad for market research firm of Emerson B. Knight. *Printer's Ink,* November 7, 133.

Radin, Edward. 1947. "Ladies in Stripes." *Esquire,* May.

Radner, Hillary. 1994. *Shopping Around.* London: Routledge.

Roosevelt, Eleanor. 1933. *It's Up to the Women.* New York: Frederick A. Stokes.

Scharf, Lois. 1980. *To Work and to Wed: Female Employment, Feminism and the Great Depression.* Westport, Conn.: Greenwood.

Shevelow, Kathryn. 1989. *Women and Print Culture: The Construction of Femininity in the Early Periodical.* London: Routledge.

Smith, Terry. 1993. *Making the Modern: Industry, Art and Design in America.* Chicago: University of Chicago Press.

Spigel, Lynn, and Denise Mann. 1992. *Private Screenings: Television and the Female Consumer.* Minneapolis: University of Minnesota Press.

Strasser, Susan. 1989. *Satisfaction Guaranteed: The Making of the American Mass Market.* New York: Pantheon.

Williamson, Judith. 1978. *Decoding Advertisements: Ideology and Meaning in Advertising.* London: Boyars.

———. 1985. *Consuming Passions.* London: Boyars.

Willis, Susan. 1991. *A Primer for Daily Life.* London: Routledge.

Wilson, Christopher. 1983. "The Rhetoric of Consumption: Mass-Market Magazines and the Demise of the Gentle Reader." In *The Culture of Consumption: Critical Essays in American History, 1880–1980,* ed. Richard Wightman Fox and T. J. Jackson Lears, 40–64. New York: Pantheon.

Winship, Janet. 1987. *Inside Women's Magazines.* New York: Pandora.

Chapter Fourteen

From Town Center to Shopping Center
The Reconfiguration of Community Marketplaces in Postwar America

Lizabeth Cohen

When the editors of *Time* magazine set out to tell readers in an early January 1965 cover story why the American economy had flourished during the previous year, they explained it in terms that had become the conventional wisdom of postwar America. The most prosperous twelve months ever, capping the country's fourth straight year of economic expansion, were attributable to the American consumer, "who continued spending as if there were no tomorrow." According to *Time*'s economics lesson, consumers, business, and government "created a nonvicious circle: spending created more production, production created wealth, wealth created more spending." In this simplified Keynesian model of economic growth, "the consumer is the key to our economy." As R. H. Macy's board chair Jack Straus explained to *Time*'s readers, "When the country has a recession, it suffers not so much from problems of production as from problems of consumption." And in prosperous times like today, "Our economy keeps growing because our ability to consume is endless. The consumer goes on spending regardless of how many possessions he has. The luxuries of today are the necessities of tomorrow." A demand economy built on mass consumption had brought the United States out of the doldrums of the Great Depression and World War II, and its strength in the postwar period continued to impress those like retail magnate Straus whose own financial future depended on it.[1]

Although Straus and his peers invested great energy and resources in developing new strategies for doing business in this mass-consumption economy, historians have paid far less attention to the restructuring of American commercial life in the postwar period than to the transformation of residential experience. An impressive literature documents the way the expansion of a mass consumer society encouraged a larger and broader spectrum of Americans to move into suburban communities after the war.[2] Between 1947 and 1953 alone, the suburban population increased by 43 percent, in contrast to a general population increase of only 11 percent.[3] At an astonishing pace, the futuristic highways and mass-built, appliance-equipped, single-family homes that had been previewed at the New York World's Fair in

1939–1940 seemed to become a reality. Thanks to a shortage in urban housing, government subsidies in highway building and home construction or purchase, and pent-up consumer demand and savings, a new residential landscape began to take shape in metropolitan areas, with large numbers of people commuting into cities for work and then back to homes in the suburbs. (Increasingly as the postwar era progressed, suburbanites worked, not just lived, outside cities.)

Less explored by historians and slower to develop historically was the restructuring of the consumer marketplace that accompanied the suburbanization of residential life. New suburbanites who had themselves grown up in urban neighborhoods walking to corner stores and taking public transportation to shop downtown were now contending with changed conditions. Only in the most ambitious suburban tracts built after the war did developers incorporate retail stores into their plans. In those cases, developers tended to place the shopping district at the core of the residential community, much as it had been in the pre-war planned community of Radburn, New Jersey, and in the earliest shopping centers, such as Kansas City's Country Club Plaza of the 1920s. These precedents, and their descendents in early postwar developments in Park Forest, Illinois, Levittown, New York, and Bergenfield, New Jersey, replicated the structure of the old-style urban community, where shopping was part of the public space at the settlement's core and residences spread outward from there.[4] But most new suburban home developers made no effort to provide for residents' commercial needs. Rather, suburbanites were expected to fend for themselves by driving to the existing "market towns," which often offered the only commerce for miles, or by returning to the city to shop. Faced with slim retail offerings nearby, many new suburbanites of the 1940s and 1950s continued to depend on the city for major purchases, making do with the small, locally owned commercial outlets in neighboring towns only for minor needs.

It would not be until the mid-1950s that a new market structure appropriate to this suburbanized, mass-consumption society prevailed. Important precedents existed in the branch department stores and prototypical shopping centers constructed between the 1920s and 1940s in outlying city neighborhoods and in older suburban communities, which began the process of decentralizing retail dollars away from downtown. But now the scale was much larger. Even more significant, the absence or inadequacy of town centers at a time of enormous suburban population growth offered commercial developers a unique opportunity to reimagine community life with their private projects at its heart.[5]

By the early 1950s, large merchandisers were aggressively reaching out to the new suburbanites, whose buying power was even greater than their numbers.[6] The 30 million people that *Fortune* magazine counted as suburban residents in 1953 represented 19 percent of the U.S. population but 29 percent of its income. They had higher median incomes and homeownership rates, as well as more children fourteen and under than the rest of the metropolitan population, all indicators of high consumption.

Merchandisers also realized that postwar suburbanites were finally living the motorized existence that had been predicted for American society since the 1920s. As consumers became dependent on, virtually inseparable from, their cars, traffic congestion and parking problems discouraged commercial expansion in central business districts of cities and smaller market towns, already hindered by a short supply of developable space.[7] Reaching out to suburbanites where they lived, merchandisers at first built stores along the new highways, in commercial "strips" that consumers could easily reach by car. By the mid-1950s, however, commercial developers—many of whom owned department stores—were constructing a new kind of marketplace, the regional shopping center aimed at satisfying suburbanites' consumption *and* community needs. Strategically located at highway intersections or along the busiest thoroughfares, the regional shopping center attracted patrons living within half an hour's drive, who could come by car, park in the abundant lots provided, and then proceed on foot (although there was usually some bus service as well). Here was the "new city" of the postwar era, a vision of how community space should be constructed in an economy and society built on mass consumption. Well-designed regional shopping centers would provide the ideal core for a settlement that grew by adding residential nodes off of major roadways rather than concentric rings from downtown, as in cities and earlier suburban communities. After spending several months in the late 1950s visiting these "modern-day downtowns," *Women's Wear Daily* columnist Samuel Feinberg was moved to invoke Lincoln Steffens's proclamation on his return from the Soviet Union in the 1920s: "I have seen the future and it works."[8]

This essay will analyze the larger social and political implications of the shift in community marketplace from town center to shopping center. Although I draw on national evidence, I pay special attention to the case of Paramus, New Jersey, a postwar suburb seven miles from the George Washington Bridge that sprouted virtually overnight in the vegetable fields of Bergen County and became the home of the largest shopping complex in the country by the end of 1957.[9] Within six months, R. H. Macy's Garden State Plaza and Allied Stores Corporation's Bergen Mall opened three quarters of a mile from each other at the intersection of Routes 4, 17, and the soon-to-be-completed Garden State Parkway. Both department store managements had independently recognized the enormous commercial potential of Bergen and Passaic counties; although the George Washington Bridge connected the area to Manhattan in 1931, the Depression and the war postponed major housing construction until the late 1940s. By 1960, each shopping center had two to three department stores as anchors (distinguishing it from many pre-war projects built around a single anchor), surrounded by fifty to seventy smaller stores. Attracting half a million patrons a week, these shopping centers dominated retail trade in the region.[10]

The Paramus malls have special significance because of their location adjacent to the wealthiest and busiest central business district in the nation. If these malls could prosper in the shadow of Manhattan, the success of their counterparts elsewhere should come as no surprise. Moreover, the Paramus case illuminates three major effects of shifting marketplaces on postwar American community life: in commercializing public space, they brought to community life the market segmentation that increasingly shaped commerce; in privatizing public space, they privileged the rights of private property owners over citizens' traditional rights of free speech in community forums; and in feminizing public space, they enhanced women's claim on the suburban landscape but also empowered them more as consumers than producers.

When planners and shopping-center developers envisioned this new kind of consumption-oriented community center in the 1950s, they set out to perfect the concept of downtown, not to obliterate it, even though their projects directly challenged the viability of existing commercial centers such as Hackensack, the political and commercial seat of Bergen County. It is easy to overlook this visionary dimension and focus only on the obvious commercial motives developers and investors shared. Of course, developers, department stores, and big investors such as insurance companies (who leapt at the promise of a huge return on the vast amounts of capital they controlled) were pursuing the enormous potential for profit in shopping-center development.[11] But they also believed that they were participating in a rationalization of consumption and community no less significant than the way highways were improving transportation or tract developments were delivering mass housing.

The ideal was still the creation of centrally located public space that brought together commercial and civic activity. Victor Gruen, one of the most prominent and articulate shopping-center developers, spoke for many others when he argued that shopping centers offered to dispersed suburban populations "crystallization points for suburbia's community life." "By affording opportunities for social life and recreation in a protected pedestrian environment, by incorporating civic and educational facilities, shopping centers can fill an existing void."[12] Not only did Gruen and others promote the construction of community centers in the atomized landscape of suburbia, but in appearance their earliest shopping centers idealized— almost romanticized—the physical plan of the traditional downtown shopping street, with stores lining both sides of an open-air pedestrian walkway that was landscaped and equipped with benches.[13] (See fig. 14.1)

While bringing many of the best qualities of urban life to the suburbs, these new "shopping towns," as Gruen called them, also sought to overcome the "anarchy and ugliness" characteristic of many American cities. A centrally owned and managed Garden State Plaza or Bergen Mall, it was argued, offered an alternative model to the inefficiencies, visual chaos, and provinciality of traditional downtown districts. A centralized administration made possible the perfect mix and "scientific" placement of stores, meeting customers' diverse needs and maximizing store owners' profits. Management kept control visually by standardizing all architectural and graphic design and politically by requiring all tenants to participate in the tenants' association. Common complaints of downtown shoppers were directly addressed: parking was plentiful, safety was ensured by hired security guards, delivery tunnels and loading courts kept truck traffic away from shoppers, canopied walks and air-conditioned stores made shopping comfortable year 'round, piped-in background music replaced the cacophony of the street. The preponderance of chains and franchises over local stores, required by big investors such as insurance companies, brought shoppers the latest national trends in products and merchandising tech-

Fig. 14.1. Garden State Plaza in the early 1960s featured open-air and landscaped walkways, suggesting a pedestrian Main Street. Courtesy of Garden State Plaza Historical Collection.

niques. B. Earl Puckett, Allied Stores' board chair, boasted that Paramus's model shopping centers were making it "one of the first preplanned major cities in America."[14] What made this new market structure so unique and appealing to businessmen like Puckett was that it encouraged social innovation while maximizing profit.

Garden State Plaza and Bergen Mall provide good models for how shopping centers of the 1950s followed Gruen's prescription and became more than miscellaneous collections of stores. As central sites of consumption, they offered the full range of businesses and services that one would previously have sought downtown. They not only sold the usual clothing and shoes in their specialty and department stores—Sterns and J. J. Newberry at Bergen Mall, Bamberger's (Macy's New Jersey division), J. C. Penney's, and Gimbels at Garden State Plaza—but also featured stores specifically devoted to furniture, hardware, appliances, groceries, gifts, drugs, books, toys, records, bakery goods, candy, jewelry, garden supplies, hearing aids, tires, even religious objects. Services grew to include restaurants, a post office, laundromat, cleaners, key store, shoe repair, bank, loan company, stock brokerage houses, barber shop, travel agency, real estate office, "slenderizing salon," and Catholic chapel. Recreational facilities ranged from a 550-seat movie theater, bowling alley, and ice-skating rink to a children's gymnasium and playground.

Both shopping centers made meeting rooms and auditoriums available to community organizations and scheduled a full range of cultural and educational activities to legitimize these sites as civic centers, which also attracted customers. (See fig. 14.2.) Well-attended programs and exhibitions taught shoppers about such "hot" topics of the 1950s and 1960s as space exploration, color television, modern art, and civics. Evening concerts and plays, ethnic entertainment, dances and classes for teenagers, campaign appearances by electoral candidates, community outreach for local charities: these were some of the ways that the Bergen Mall and Garden State Plaza made themselves indispensable to life in Bergen County. In sum, it was hard to think of consumer items or community events that could not be found at one or the other of these two shopping centers. (In the 1970s, a cynical reporter cracked that "the only institution that had not yet invaded" the modern shopping mall was the funeral home.) Furthermore, stores and services were more accessible than those downtown, as the centers were open to patrons from 10 a.m. to 9:30 p.m., at first four nights a week and by the 1960s, six nights a week. To a regional planner such as Ernest Erber, these postwar shopping centers helped construct a new kind of urbanism appropriate to the automobile age: the "City of Bergen," he named the area in 1960. The *New York Times* agreed, remarking of the Paramus commercial complex, "It lives a night as well as a day existence, glittering like a city when the sun goes down."[15]

When developers and store owners set out to make the shopping center a more perfect downtown, they aimed to exclude from this public space unwanted urban groups such as vagrants, prostitutes, racial minorities, and poor people. Market segmentation became the guiding principle of this mix of commercial and civic activity, as the shopping center sought perhaps contradictorily to legitimize itself as a true community center and to define that community in exclusionary socioeconomic and racial terms. The simple demographics of postwar America helped: when

Fig. 14.2. The in-house publication *Penney News* (November–December 1958) published this photo as part of a feature story on the recent opening of J. C. Penney's Garden State Plaza store. The caption read, "This community club room which can also serve as selling area will be made available free of charge to women's clubs and civic groups." Penney's created this community club room, its first ever, as part of the campaign to make the shopping center the heart of suburban life. P-N.J., Paramus-11. Courtesy of JCPenney Archives and Historical Museum, Dallas, Texas.

nine of the ten largest cities in the United States lost population between 1950 and 1960 while all metropolitan areas grew, three whites were moving out for every two non-whites who moved in, laying the groundwork for the racially polarized metropolitan populations of today.[16] In this way, suburbanization must be seen as a new form of racial segregation in the face of a huge wave of African-American migration from the South to the North during the 1950s.

Shopping centers did not exclude inadvertently by virtue of their suburban location. Rather, developers deliberately defined their communities through a combination of marketing and policing. Macy's reminded its stockholders in 1955 as it was building its first shopping center, the Garden State Plaza, "We are a type of organization that caters primarily to middle-income groups, and our stores reflect this in the merchandise they carry and in their physical surroundings."[17] It was this concern for "physical surroundings" that made the setting of the suburban shopping center appealing to retailers—and ultimately to customers. As Baltimore's Planning Council explained more explicitly than merchants ever would, "Greater numbers of low-income, Negro shoppers in Central Business District stores, coming at the same time as middle and upper income white shoppers are given alternatives in . . . segregated suburban centers, has had unfortunate implications [for downtown shopping]."[18]

Store selection, merchandise, prices, and carefully controlled access to suburban shopping centers supported the class and color line. A survey of consumer expenditures in northern New Jersey in 1960–1961 revealed that while 79 percent of all families owned cars, fewer than one-third of those with incomes below $3,000 did, and the low-income population included a higher percentage of non-white families than the average for the whole sample.[19] Although bus service was available for shoppers without cars, only a tiny proportion arrived that way (in 1966, a daily average of only 600 people came to the Garden State Plaza by bus compared to a mid-week daily average of 18,000 cars and a holiday peak of 31,000 cars, many carrying more than one passenger), and bus routes were carefully planned to serve non-driving customers—particularly women—from neighboring suburbs, not low-income consumers from cities such as Passaic, Paterson, and Newark.[20] Whereas individual department stores had long targeted particular markets defined by class and race, selling, for example, to "the carriage trade" at the upper end, shopping centers applied market segmentation on the scale of a downtown. In promoting an idealized downtown, shopping centers like Garden State Plaza and Bergen Mall tried to filter out not only the inefficiencies and inconveniences of the city but also the undesirable people who lived there.

If developers and retailers envisioned the regional shopping center as the new American city of postwar suburbia, what actually happened? How successful were shopping centers in attracting patrons and displacing existing urban centers? By investigating the behavior of consumers, on the one hand, and retail businessmen on the other, we can assess the impact of Bergen Mall and Garden State Plaza on the commercial and community life of Bergen County.

Consumer surveys of the late 1950s and early 1960s, carried out by sociologists and market researchers interested in evaluating the changes wrought by the new regional shopping centers, provide a remarkably good picture of consumer behavior in the era. Before the Bergen Mall and Garden State Plaza opened in 1957, Bergen County shoppers satisfied their immediate needs on the main streets of Hackensack and of smaller surrounding towns such as Ridgewood, Fair Lawn, Bergenfield, and Englewood. For more extensive shopping, people went to branches of Sears and Arnold Constable in Hackensack, Meyer Brothers and Quackenbush's department stores in Paterson, Bamberger's, Hahne's, and Kresge's in Newark, and quite often to the big stores in Manhattan. Even before the regional shopping centers opened, the huge influx of new suburban dwellers had raised retail sales in Bergen County from $400 million in 1948 to $700 million in 1954, an increase of 79 percent; by 1958, sales had increased another 23 percent to $866 million. Nonetheless, Bergen County residents in 1954 were still spending $650 million outside the county, almost as much as inside.[21]

Samuel and Lois Pratt, professors at Fairleigh Dickinson University, surveyed Bergen County consumers living within a ten-minute drive of the two new shopping centers in 1957, 1958, and 1959 to follow changes in their shopping habits over time. Prior to the opening of the shopping centers, seven in ten suburban families surveyed shopped in New York City to some extent. One year after the centers opened, the numbers shopping in New York dropped to six in ten, and two years after, fewer than five in ten families shopped there at all. In other words, one-fourth of the entire sample formerly had shopped in New York City but had now entirely stopped. The loss was even more substantial than that; the 15 percent of suburban families who formerly did most of their shopping in New York City—people the Pratts labeled "major shoppers"—showed the sharpest decline, 50 percent by 1958, 80 percent by 1959. Moreover, those who continued to shop in New York City were spending much less money there; the average annual expenditure in New York by suburban families dropped from $93 to $68 after the regional shopping centers opened. Furthermore, consumers were much less likely to shop in the New York stores that had opened suburban branches; by the end of the first year, the number of Bergen County families who had traded in the New York Macy's or Stern's dropped by half. A similar study of 1,100 shoppers by the New York University School of Retailing confirmed the Pratts' findings: shoppers for women's wear were half as likely to go to New York and a third as likely to go to Hackensack just one year after the shopping centers had opened. By the early 1960s, a survey of New York area shoppers by a Harvard Business School professor concluded that more than 80 percent of residents of the New Jersey suburbs were most likely to shop close to home for clothing and household items, while only 20 percent went most often to Manhattan and 38 percent to New Jersey cities. (Some multiple answers brought the total over 100 percent.) Nationwide, the trend was the same: retail sales in central business districts declined dramatically between 1958 and 1963, while overall metropolitan sales mushroomed from 10 to 20 percent.[22]

The reasons consumers routinely gave for shifting from downtown stores to shopping centers varied, but the overwhelming motivation they articulated was convenience—the ability to drive and park easily, more night hours, improved store layouts, increased self-selection, and simplified credit like the charge plate. The Pratts concluded that shoppers were not so much dissatisfied with New York and Hackensack stores as attracted to the ease and "progressiveness" of shopping-center shopping. People seemed to share the developers' sense that shopping centers were the modern way to consume.[23]

While it is hard to evaluate the extent to which people viewed the shopping centers as more than places to shop—as community centers—anecdotal evidence suggests that they did. Many reporters writing stories in the late 1950s and 1960s on the way malls were becoming central to the nation's culture made this point, and they routinely introduced their readers to people like Ernest J. Weinhold, a retired designer, who said that he and his wife came to the Cherry Hill Mall in southern New Jersey four days a week. "I love it here—there are things going on that you don't find anywhere else. I don't shop every day but what I do buy I get here."[24] The general manager of Willowbrook Mall, a shopping center not far from Paramus, explained that the Ernest Weinholds of the suburban world made it easy to program activities about forty-five weeks a year. "Whether it's charity fairs, 4-H exhibits, meetings of the Weight-Watchers or the concert by the local barbershop quartet, we find that people respond—and that's what counts."[25] In the new public place of the shopping center, consuming and leisure were becoming inseparably intertwined, constructing community experiences around the cultural tastes of white middle-class suburbanites.

The shift from downtown to shopping center entailed a feminization of public space. For at least the last two centuries, American women have been the major shoppers in their families. That pattern continued in the postwar period, with marketers estimating that women not only took on anywhere from 80 to 92 percent of the shopping but also spent a great deal of their time at it.[26] In a noteworthy departure from earlier times, however, the era of the shopping center saw significant public space—in private hands—being tailored to women's needs and desires as consumers. While the department store born of the nineteenth century created similarly feminized space, the urban commercial district of which it was a part catered as much to male consumption, leisure, and associational life—through bars, clubs, pool halls, and smoke shops, to say nothing of the male-dominated street resulting from the mix of commercial and corporate culture downtown. The shopping center, in contrast, created the equivalent of a downtown district dedicated primarily to female-orchestrated consumption.[27]

Shopping centers were planned with the female consumer in mind. As women patrons increasingly drove their own cars, they found parking spaces at the shopping center designed wider than usual for the express purpose of making it easier for them—many of whom were new drivers—to park.[28] Women then entered a well-controlled "public" space that made them feel comfortable and safe, with activities planned to appeal especially to women and children. From the color schemes, stroller ramps, baby-sitting services, and special lockers for "ladies' wraps," to the reassuring security guards and special events such as fashion shows, shopping centers were created as female worlds. "I wouldn't know how to design a center for a man," admitted Jack Follet of John Graham, Inc., a firm responsible for many shopping centers. And if New Jersey resident Mrs. Bonnie Porrazzo was any indication, designers like Follet knew what they were doing. Four or five times a week, she visited a shopping center three minutes from her suburban home because, "It's great for women. What else is there to do?"[29]

Not only did the shopping center pitch itself to women, it sought to empower them as orchestrators of their families' leisure. Marketing surveys revealed that almost half of all women shopped for four or more people, usually members of their families. With the advent of the suburban malls, they were increasingly bringing those family members along. Female shoppers in Bergen County surveyed by the Pratts in the first few years after the centers opened revealed that four in ten families were spending more time shopping, three in ten were making more shopping trips, two in ten were taking the children more often, and two in ten were including their husbands more frequently than before the malls were built. A study comparing family shopping in downtown Cincinnati with its suburban shopping centers concurred, finding that while 85 percent of downtown patrons shopped alone, only 43 percent of shopping-center patrons were alone; most of them were accompanied by family members. Accordingly, evenings and weekends were by far the busiest time in malls, creating peaks and valleys in shopping that had not affected downtown stores nearly as much. In many suburban centers, more than half the volume of business was done at night. At the Bergen Mall, the peak traffic count was at 8 p.m., and shopping was very heavy on Saturdays as well. A May Company executive described one of the largest problems in branch-store operation: "the biggest day in the suburban day in the suburban store will be ten times the poorest day, instead of five as it usually is downtown."[30]

Shopping centers responded with stores and programming specifically designed to appeal to families, to encourage them further to spend leisure time at the mall. William M. Batten, board chair of J. C. Penney, for example, recalled "the broadening of our lines of merchandise and our services to encompass a fuller spectrum of family activity" as the company began building stores in shopping centers rather than on Main Street in the late 1950s and 1960s; only then did Penney's start selling appliances, hardware, and sporting goods and offering portrait studios, restaurants, auto service, and Singer sewing instruction. As families strolled and shopped together at the mall, they engaged in what increasingly was becoming a form of leisure that was female directed and hence bore witness to a wife's or mother's control.[31] (See fig. 14.3.)

Female authority was also enhanced by shopping centers as they became associated with a huge expansion of consumer credit in the postwar era. In 1950, the ratio of credit to disposable income was 10.4 percent, with $21.5 billion worth of debt outstanding. By 1960, the ratio had grown to 16.1 percent, the debt to $56.1 billion; a decade later, they had reached 18.5 percent and $127 billion, respectively. The trend was apparent in Bergen County. Bamberger's promoted its Garden State Plaza store as offering "a credit plan to suit every need," a choice between Regular Charge Accounts, Budget Charge Accounts, and Deferred Payment Accounts. Once customers came into the store, an innovative teletype hook-up with the Bergen County Credit Bureau enabled charge accounts to be established quickly. Another Garden State Plaza anchor store, J. C. Penny, which had long built its identity around low price, cash-and-carry purchasing, finally recognized in 1957 that credit was expected, even demanded, by consumers, and became the last of the large nationwide retailers to introduce a company credit card. By 1962, national credit facilities and systems were operating with the latest electronic data-processing technology, and charging had become the standard way to buy. As credit cards increasingly became the legal tender of shopping-center purchasing, they expanded women's control over family finances from spending the domestic allowance assigned from the weekly or monthly paycheck to committing the family's present and future savings. It should also be noted, however, that credit cards at the same time reinforced women's economic dependence on men, since qualifying generally depended on husbands' or fathers' income, even when women earned money of their own.[32]

As the example of credit cards illustrates, even as women gained power in the family and in the public realm with the emergence of shopping centers, so, too, were their horizons limited by them. Women's public roles were expected to remain

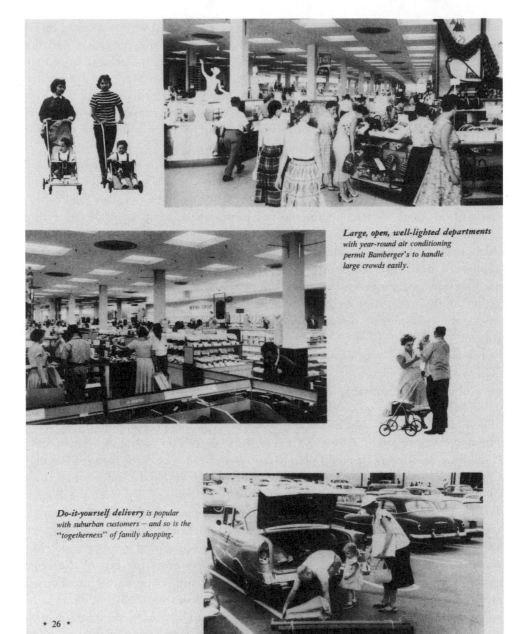

Large, open, well-lighted departments
with year-round air conditioning
permit Bamberger's to handle
large crowds easily.

Do-it-yourself delivery is popular
with suburban customers — and so is the
"togetherness" of family shopping.

Fig. 14.3. This page from Macy's annual report to shareholders the year its Garden State Plaza opened conveys the importance of the female-dominated family market to shopping-center merchandising. Note particularly the invocation of "the 'togetherness' of family shopping" in the bottom caption. Reproduced from R. H. Macy & Co., Inc., *1957 Annual Report*, courtesy of Robert F. Wagner Labor Archives, New York University, from its Department Store Workers—Local 1-S Collection, Box 2, Folder 61.

defined as consumers, and transcending that role was difficult. The most telling case involved the fate of women as workers in shopping centers like Bergen Mall and Garden State Plaza. As the department stores established branches, they increasingly turned to suburban housewives as retail clerks. The fit seemed perfect. Many women were interested in part-time work, and the stores were looking for part-time labor to service the notorious peaks and valleys in suburban shopping. As a Stanford Business School professor advised branch managers in the year the Bergen County shopping centers opened, "Fortunately, most of these suburban stores have in their immediate neighborhood a large number of housewives and other nonemployed women who have been willing to work during these evening and Saturday peak periods. . . . Many of these women apparently work as much because of interest as because of economic necessity, and, as a rule, they have proved to be excellent salespeople." The Paramus malls took heed: by the mid-1960s, the part-time employment of women had swelled the malls' combined employee ranks to almost 6,000 people, two-thirds of them part-time and many of them local residents.[33]

But according to New York–area labor unions such as Local 1-S, RWDSU (Retail, Wholesale and Department Store Union), which represented employees at Macy's and Bamberger's, and District 65, RWDSU, which represented them at Gimbels, Sterns, and Bloomingdale's, the department stores had another motive for hiring so many part-timers in their new suburban branches: they were trying to cut labor costs and break the hold of the unions, which had organized their New York stores successfully enough to make retail clerking a decent job. Certainly, retailers gave a lot of attention to keeping labor costs down, judging them to be the greatest obstacle to higher profits. Suburban branch managers sought to limit the number of salespeople needed by depending more on customer self-service and "pipe-racking," putting goods on floor racks rather than behind counters. Some stores, such as Sears Roebuck, Montgomery Ward, and J. C. Penney, expanded their catalog operations.[34] But the basic strategy of the suburban department store was to control wages through hiring more part-timers at minimum wages and benefits.

Organizing the new suburban branches became a life-and-death struggle for the unions beginning in the 1950s. They recognized that not only was the fate of new branch jobs at stake but, as retail dollars left the city for the suburbs, jobs in the downtown stores were threatened as well. The branch store was becoming, in effect, a kind of runaway shop that undermined the job security, wages, benefits, and working conditions of unionized downtown workers. Local 1-S and District 65 tried all kinds of strategies, such as demanding contract coverage of the new branches when renegotiating their existing contracts with downtown stores; getting permission from the National Labor Relations Board to split the bargaining units within particular branch stores (such as into selling, non-selling, and restaurant) to facilitate organization; assigning downtown store workers to picket suburban branches during strikes and organizing campaigns; and gaining the right for city-store employees to transfer to branches without losing accumulated seniority and benefits.

But still, successful labor organization of the suburban branches proved extremely difficult. Branch-store management at Sterns, Bamberger's, and a Bloomingdale's that opened nearby took an aggressive stand against unionism, harassing and firing employees who showed the least inclination to organize, particularly women. Bill Michelson, executive vice-president of District 65, pointed to the mentality of part-time employees as another obstacle to successful organizing: "The part-timer, usually a housewife in a suburban town, is interested in picking up extra money and does not have deep roots in her job." The large turnover among part-time workers—through lay-offs as well as voluntary resignation—made organizing them all the harder.[35]

Despite the determined efforts of Local 1-S and District 65 to organize all department store workers in the Paramus shopping centers, Gimbels was the only store to sign a union contract that covered its Paramus store, and this in exchange for a lesser wage increase and the cancellation of a threatened strike. At all the rest, an overwhelmingly female work force worked part-time at minimum wage, with few benefits, no union representation, and limited opportunities for career advancement. (See fig. 14.4.) Work became a way for women to maintain their status as consumers, but it did not significantly empower them as producers who could contribute substantially to—or be independent of—male earnings. At Bamberger's, in fact, the handbook for new employees urged them to use their staff discount to purchase store merchandise (20 percent off for apparel worn on the job, 10 percent on other items) so they could serve as model consumers for customers. The shopping center, then, contributed to a segmentation not only of consumers but of workers as well in a postwar labor market that offered new jobs to women but marked these jobs as less remunerative and more dead-end.[36] Furthermore, as a workplace, much like a public space, the shopping center constricted the rights available to the people who frequented it. That women came to dominate the ranks of workers and consumers there meant that their political freedom was particularly circumscribed. The shopping center thus posed a contradiction for women in the 1950s and 1960s: it empowered them in their families through creating a new community setting catering to female needs and desires, yet it contained them in the larger society as consumers and part-time workers. In this era before feminist revolt and affirmative action opened other opportunities, women's choices were limited not simply through peer pressure and personal priorities, as is often claimed, but also through the larger economic restructuring taking place in the metropolitan marketplace.

Mass consumption in postwar America created a new landscape, where public space was more commercialized, more privatized, and more feminized within the regional shopping center than it had been in the traditional downtown center. This is not to romanticize the city and its central business district. Certainly, urban commercial property owners pursued their own economic interests, political activity in public spaces was sometimes limited, and the priorities of women and men did not always peacefully coexist. Nonetheless, the legal distinction between public and private space remained significant; urban loitering and vagrancy laws directed against undesirables in public places have repeatedly been struck down by the courts, while privately owned shopping centers have been able to enforce trespassing laws.[37]

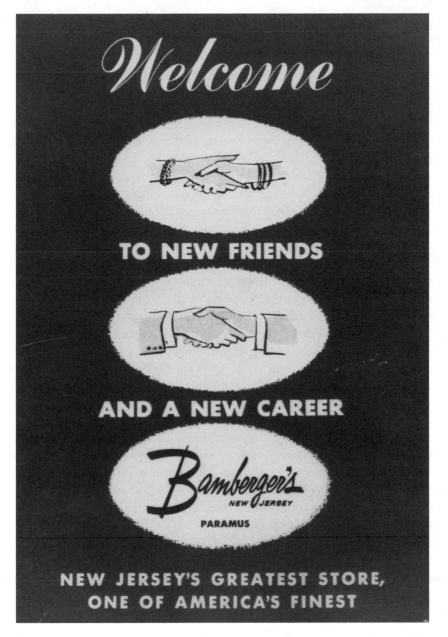

Fig. 14.4. Bamberger's Department Store prepared an employee handbook, of which this is the cover, for the opening of its Garden State Plaza store in 1957. Hoping to recruit part-time female employees among housewives in neighboring suburban towns, the store offered them "new friends," while male applicants were promised "a new career." Courtesy of the Robert F. Wagner Labor Archives, New York University, from its Department Store Workers— Local 1-S Collection, Box 7, Folder 16.

Overall, an important shift from one kind of social order to another took place between 1950 and 1980, with major consequences for Americans. A free commercial market attached to a relatively free public sphere (for whites) underwent a transformation to a more regulated commercial marketplace (where mall management controlled access, favoring chains over local independents, for example) and a more circumscribed public sphere of limited rights. Economic and social liberalism went hand in hand and declined together.

Not by accident, public space was restructured and segmented by class and race in New Jersey, as in the nation, just as African Americans gained new protections for their right of equal access to public accommodations. Although civil rights laws had been on the books in New Jersey since the late nineteenth century, comprehensive legislation with mechanisms for enforcement did not pass until the 1940s. With the "Freeman Bill" of 1949, African Americans were finally guaranteed equal access to schools, restaurants, taverns, retail stores, hotels, public transportation, and facilities of commercial leisure such as movie theaters, skating rinks, amusement parks, swimming pools, and beaches, with violators subject to fines and jail terms. Throughout the 1940s and 1950s, African-American citizens of New Jersey—and other northern states—vigilantly challenged discrimination by private property owners. Yet larger structural changes in community marketplaces were under way, financed by private commercial interests committed to socioeconomic and racial segmentation. While African Americans and their supporters were prodding courts and legislatures to eliminate legal segregation in public places, real-estate developers, retailers, and consumers were collaborating to shift economic resources to new kinds of segregated spaces.[38]

The landscape of mass consumption created a metropolitan society in which people were no longer brought together in central marketplaces and the parks, streets, and public buildings that surrounded them but, rather, were separated by class, gender, and race in differentiated commercial sub-centers. Moreover, all commercial sub-centers were not created equal. Over time, shopping centers became increasingly class stratified, with some like the Bergen Mall marketing themselves to the lower middle class, while others like the Garden State Plaza went upscale to attract upper middle-class consumers. If tied to international capital, some central business districts—such as New York and San Francisco—have prospered, although they have not been left unscarred from recent retail mergers and leveraged buy-outs. Other downtowns, such as Hackensack and Elizabeth, New Jersey, have become "Cheap John Bargain Centers" serving customers too poor and deprived of transportation to shop at malls. Even in larger American cities, poor urban populations shop downtown on weekends while the white-collar workers who commute in to offices during the week patronize the suburban malls closer to where they live. Some commercial districts have been taken over by enterprising, often newly arrived, ethnic groups, who have breathed new life into what would otherwise have been in decay, but they nonetheless serve a segmented market. Worst off are cities like Newark, once the largest shopping district in the state, which saw every one of its major department stores close between 1964 and 1992 and much of its retail space remain abandoned, leaving residents such as Raymond Mungin to wonder,

"I don't have a car to drive out to the malls. What can I do?" Mass consumption was supposed to bring standardization in merchandise and consumption patterns. Instead, diverse social groups are no longer integrated into central consumer marketplaces but rather are consigned to differentiated retail institutions, segmented markets, and new hierarchies.[39]

NOTES

I would like to acknowledge the skill and imagination of two research assistants, Deb Steinbach and Susan Spaet. My research was supported by grants from the National Endowment for the Humanities (1993), the American Council of Learned Societies (1994), and New York University (1993–1994). I am also grateful to several audiences who shared helpful reactions to versions of this article: the international conference "Gender and Modernity in the Era of Rationalization," Columbia University, September 1994; the conference "Significant Locales: Business, Labor, and Industry in the Mid-Atlantic Region," sponsored by the Center for the History of Business, Technology, and Society, Hagley Museum and Library, October 1994; the history department at George Washington University, February 1995; Tricia Rose's American Studies Colloquium, New York University, February 1995; the Historians of Greater Cleveland, May 1995; and my audience at Vassar College, November 1995. Individuals whose readings have especially helped me include Herrick Chapman, Michael Ebner, Ken Jackson, Richard Longstreth, Tricia Rose, Phil Scranton, David Schuyler, Sylvie Schweitzer, and two anonymous readers for the *American Historical Review*.

1. "The Economy: The Great Shopping Spree," *Time* (January 8, 1965): 58–62 (and cover).

2. See Kenneth T. Jackson, *Crabgrass Frontier: The Suburbanization of the United States* (New York, 1985); Robert Fishman, *Bourgeois Utopias: The Rise and Fall of Suburbia* (New York, 1987); Joel Garreau, *Edge City: Life on the New Frontier* (Garden City, N.Y., 1991); William Sharpe and Leonard Wallock, "Bold New City or Built-Up 'Burb? Redefining Contemporary Suburbia," with comments by Robert Bruegmann, Robert Fishman, Margaret Marsh, and June Manning Thomas, *American Quarterly* 46 (March 1994): 1–61; Carol O'Connor, "Sorting Out Suburbia," *American Quarterly* 37 (Summer 1985): 382–94.

3. The Editors of *Fortune, The Changing American Market* (Garden City, N.Y., 1995), 76.

4. Ann Durkin Keating and Ruth Eckdish Knack, "Shopping in the Planned Community: Evolution of the Park Forest Town Center," unpublished paper in possession of author; Howard Gillette, Jr., "The Evolution of the Planned Shopping Center in Suburb and City," *American Planning Association Journal* 51 (Autumn 1985): 449–60; Daniel Prosser, "The New Downtowns: Commercial Architecture in Suburban New Jersey, 1920–1970," in Joel Schwartz and Daniel Prosser, *Cities of the Garden State: Essays in the Urban and Suburban History of New Jersey* (Dubuque, Iowa, 1977), 113–15; "Park Forest Moves into '52," *House and Home: The Magazine of Building* 1 (March 1952): 115–16; William S. Worley, *J. C. Nichols and the Shaping of Kansas City: Innovation in Planned Residential Communities* (Columbia, Mo., 1990); Richard Longstreth, "J. C. Nichols, the Country Club Plaza, and Notions of Modernity," *The Harvard Architecture Review, Vol. 5: Precedent and Invention* (New York, 1968), 121–32; William H. Whyte, Jr., "The Outgoing Life," *Fortune* 47 (July 1953): 85; Michael Birkner, *A Country Place No More: The Transformation of Bergen-*

field, New Jersey, 1894–1994 (Rutherford, N.J., 1994), 174–77; *Bergen Evening Record*, Special Foster Village Edition, August 10, 1949.

5. Jackson, *Crabgrass Frontier*, 255–61. On precedents in the pre–World War II period, see Richard Longstreth, "Silver Spring: Georgia Avenue, Colesville Road, and the Creation of an Alternative 'Downtown' for Metropolitan Washington," in *Streets: Critical Perspectives on Public Space*, Zeynep Celik, Diane Favro, and Richard Ingersoll, eds. (Berkeley, Calif., 1994), 247–57; Longstreth, "The Neighborhood Shopping Center in Washington, D.C., 1930–1941," *Journal of the Society of Architectural Historians* 51 (March 1992): 5–33; Longstreth, "The Perils of a Parkless Town," in *The Car and the City: The Automobile, the Built Environment, and Daily Urban Life*, Martin Wachs and Margaret Crawford, eds. (Ann Arbor, Mich., 1992), 141–53.

6. Editors of *Fortune, Changing American Market*, 78–80, 90. Also see "New Need Cited on Store Centers," *New York Times* (February 13, 1955): 7.

7. Richard Longstreth, "The Mixed Blessings of Success: The Hecht Company and Department Store Branch Development after World War II," Occasional Paper No. 14, January 1995, Center for Washington Area Studies, George Washington University.

8. Samuel Feinberg, "Story of Shopping Centers," *What Makes Shopping Centers Tick*, reprinted from *Women's Wear Daily* (New York, 1960), 1. For useful background on the development of regional shopping centers, see William Severini Kowinski, *The Malling of America: An Inside Look at the Great Consumer Paradise* (New York, 1985); Neil Harris, *Cultural Excursions: Marketing Appetites and Cultural Tastes in Modern America* (Chicago, 1990), 7, 76–77, 278–88; Margaret Crawford, "The World in a Shopping Mall," in Michael Sorkin, ed., *Variations on a Theme Park: The New American City and the End of Public Space* (New York, 1992), 3–30; Gillette, "Evolution of the Planned Shopping Center."

9. On the postwar growth of Paramus and Bergen County, see Raymond M. Ralph, *Farmland to Suburbia, 1920–1960*, Vol. 6, Bergen County, New Jersey History and Heritage Series (Hackensack, N.J., 1983), 62–71, 76–90; Catherine M. Fogarty, John E. O'Connor, and Charles F. Cummings, *Bergen County: A Pictorial History* (Norfolk, Va., 1985), 182–93; *Beautiful Bergen: The Story of Bergen County, New Jersey*, 1962; Patricia M. Ryle, *An Economic Profile of Bergen County, New Jersey* (Office of Economic Research, Division of Planning and Research, New Jersey Department of Labor and Industry, March 1980); League of Women Voters of Bergen County, *Where Can I live in Bergen County: Factors Affecting Housing Supply* (Closter, N.J., 1972).

10. Feinberg, *What Makes Shopping Centers Tick*, 2, 94–102; Ralph, *Farmland to Suburbia*, 70–71, 84–85; Mark A. Stuart, *Our Era, 1960–Present*, Vol. 7, Bergen County, New Jersey History and Heritage Series (Hackensack, N.J., 1983), 19–22; Prosser, "New Downtowns," 119–20; Edward T. Thompson, "The Suburb That Macy's Built," *Fortune* 61 (February 1960): 195–200; "Garden State Plaza Merchant's Manual," May 1, 1957, and certain pages revised in 1959, 1960, 1962, 1963, 1965, 1969, Garden State Plaza Historical Collection.

11. On the financing of shopping centers and the great profits involved, see Jerry Jacobs, *The Mall: An Attempted Escape from Everyday Life* (Prospect Heights, Ill., 1984), 52.

12. Victor Gruen, "Introverted Architecture," *Progressive Architecture* 38, no. 5 (1957): 204–8; Victor Gruen and Larry Smith, *Shopping Towns USA: The Planning of Shopping Centers* (New York, 1960), 22–24; both quoted in Gillette, "Evolution of the Planned Shopping Center." For more on Gruen, see Kowinski, *Malling of America*, 118–20, 210–14; "Exhibit of Shopping Centers," *New York Times* (October 19, 1954): 42. Paul Goldberger recently profiled shopping-center builder Martin Bucksbaum in "Settling the Suburban Frontier," *New York Times Magazine* (December 31, 1995): 34–35.

13. Robert Bruegmann made the same point about the way the earliest design of suburban shopping centers resembled downtown shopping streets in a talk to the Urban History Seminar of the Chicago Historical Society, February 17, 1994.

14. Quoted in Feinberg, *What Makes Shopping Centers Tick*, 101. In addition to sources already cited on the control possible in a shopping center versus a downtown, see "Shopping Centers Get 'Personality,' " *New York Times* (June 29, 1958): 1.

15. Ernest Erber, "Notes on the 'City of Bergen,' " September 14, 1960, Box B, Ernest Erber Papers (hereafter, Erber), Newark Public Library (hereafter, NPL), Newark; "Paramus Booms as a Store Center," *New York Times* (February 5, 1962): 33–34; "The Mall the Merrier, or Is It?" *New York Times* (November 21, 1976): 62. For details on particular stores and activities at Bergen Mall and Garden State Plaza, see Feinberg, *What Makes Shopping Centers Tick*, 97–100; Fogarty et al., *Bergen County*, 189; Prosser, "New Downtowns," 119. Almost every issue of the *Bergen Evening Record* from 1957 and thereafter yields valuable material (in articles and advertisements) on mall stores, services, and activities. The discussion here is based particularly on issues from November 8, 13, and 19, 1957, January 8, 1958, June 10, 1959, and March 2, 1960. Also see "Shoppers! Mass Today on Level 1," *New York Times*, June 14, 1994; press release on Garden State Plaza's opening in the Historical Collection of Garden State Plaza, folder "GSP history"; "It Won't Be Long Now . . . Bamberger's, New Jersey's Greatest Store, Comes to Paramus Soon," promotional leaflet, stamped August 22, 1956, file "Bergen County Shopping Centers," Johnson Free Public Library, Hackensack, N.J.; "The Shopping Center," *New York Times* (February 1, 1976): 6–7.

For data on the allocation of shopping-center space in ten regional shopping centers in 1957, see William Applebaum and S. O. Kaylin, *Case Studies in Shopping Center Development and Operation* (New York, 1974), 101. For evidence of the community orientation of shopping centers nationwide, see Arthur Herzog, "Shops, Culture, Centers—and More," *New York Times Magazine* (November 18, 1962): 34–35, 109–10, 112–14; in the *New York Times*: "A Shopping Mall in Suffolk Offering More Than Goods," June 22, 1970: 39; "Supermarkets Hub of Suburbs," February 7, 1971: 58; "Busy Day in a Busy Mall," April 12, 1972: 55. On the community-relations efforts of branch stores, see Clinton L. Oaks, *Managing Suburban Branches of Department Stores* (Stanford, Calif., 1957), 81–83.

16. George Sternlieb, *The Future of the Downtown Department Store* (Cambridge, Mass., 1962), 10.

17. R. H. Macy & Company, *Annual Report* (New York, 1955). The *Times-Advocate*, March 14, 1976, argues that Bamberger's, Macy's store at the Garden State Plaza, was at the forefront of the chain's appeal to the middle- to upper-income shopper. On market segmentation of shopping centers, also see William H. Whyte, Jr., *The Organization Man* (New York, 1956), 316–17; Jacobs, *The Mall*, 5, 12; and Albert Bills and Lois Pratt, "Personality Differences among Shopping Centers," *Fairleigh Dickinson University Business Review* 1 (Winter 1961), which distinguishes between the customers of the Bergen Mall and Garden State Plaza in socioeconomic terms. Crawford's "World in a Shopping Mall," in Sorkin, *Variations on a Theme Park*, discusses the sophisticated strategies that market researchers use to analyze trade areas and pitch stores to different kinds of customers, 8–9.

18. George Sternlieb, "The Future of Retailing in the Downtown Core," *AIP Journal* 24 (May 1963), as reprinted in Howard A. Schretter, *Downtown Revitalization* (Athens, Ga., 1967), 96, and quoted in Jon C. Teaford, *The Rough Road to Renaissance: Urban Revitalization in America, 1940–1985* (Baltimore, Md., 1990), 129.

19. United States Department of Labor, Bureau of Labor Statistics, "Consumer Expenditures and Income, Northern New Jersey, 1960–61," BLS Report No. 237–63, December

1963, Schomburg Center, New York Public Library, Clipping File "Consumer Expenses & Income-NJ."

20. "The Wonder on Routes 4 and 17: Garden State Plaza," brochure, file "Bergen County Shopping Centers," Johnson Free Public Library, Hackensack, New Jersey; "Notes on Discussion Dealing with Regional (Intermunicipal) Planning Program for Passaic Valley Area (Lower Portion of Passaic Co. and South Bergen," n.d., Box A, Folder 3, Erber, NPL; "Memorandum to DAJ and WBS from EE," November 22, 1966, Box B, Erber, NPL; National Center for Telephone Research (A Division of Louis Harris and Associates), "A Study of Shoppers' Attitudes toward the Proposed Shopping Mall in the Hudson County Meadowlands Area," conducted for Hartz Mountain Industries, February 1979, Special Collections, Rutgers University, New Brunswick, New Jersey.

21. Stuart, *Our Era*, 20; Lois Pratt, "The Impact of Regional Shopping Centers in Bergen County," unpublished conference paper delivered April 23, 1960, in possession of the author.

22. Samuel Pratt and Lois Pratt, "The Impact of Some Regional Shopping Centers," *Journal of Marketing* 25 (October 1960): 44–50; Samuel Pratt, "The Challenge to Retailing," an address to the 1957 Annual Meeting of the Passaic Valley Citizens Planning Association, April 24, 1957, in possession of the author; L. Pratt, "Impact of Regional Shopping Centers in Bergen County"; Samuel Pratt and James Moran, "How the Regional Shopping Centers May Affect Shopping Habits in Rochelle Park (Preliminary)," *Business Research Bulletin* 1, Bureau of Business Research, Fairleigh Dickinson University (1956); New York University study cited in Thompson, "Suburb That Macy's Built," 196, 200; Regional Plan Association, Committee on the Second Regional Plan, "Work Book for Workshops," Princeton, N.J., May 25–26, 1966, Box D, pp. V-7–9, Erber, NPL; Stuart U. Rich, *Shopping Behavior of Department Store Customers: A Study of Store Policies and Customer Demand, with Particular Reference to Delivery Service and Telephone Ordering* (Boston, 1963), esp. 133–56, 228; Plan One Research Corporation, New York City, for the Bergen Evening Record Corporation, *The Mighty Market* (Hackensack, N.J., 1971). For national statistics on the decline of retail sales in central business districts while they mushroomed in metropolitan areas between 1958 and 1963, see Teaford, *Rough Road to Renaissance*, 129–31.

23. Pratt and Moran, "How the Regional Shopping Centers May Affect Shopping Habits in Rochelle Park"; Pratt, "Challenge to Retailing," 13–15. For surveys of consumers outside of the New York area, see C. T. Jonassen, *Downtown versus Suburban Shopping*, Ohio Marketing Studies, The Ohio State University Special Bulletin Number X-58 (Columbus, Ohio, 1953); Sternlieb, *Future of the Downtown Department Store*, 33, 131–33; Rich, *Shopping Behavior of Department Store Customers*; and several important studies described in Pratt, "Challenge to Retailing," 15–19.

24. Herzog, "Shops, Culture, Centers—And More," 110, quote on 114.

25. "The Shopping Centers," *New York Times* (February 1, 1976): 7.

26. Jonassen, *Downtown versus Suburban Shopping*, 15; Alan Voorhees, *Shopping Habits and Travel Patterns* (Washington, D.C., 1955), 6; Rich, *Shopping Behavior of Department Store Customers*, 61–64; on the long history of women as shoppers, see Steven Lubar, "Men and Women, Production and Consumption," keynote address to the "His and Hers: Gender and the Consumer" conference, Hagley Museum and Library, April 1994. The increasingly sophisticated field of market research addressed itself to motivating the female consumer. An excellent example is Janet L. Wolff, *What Makes Women Buy: A Guide to Understanding and Influencing the New Woman of Today* (New York, 1958).

27. My thanks to William Becker and Richard Longstreth, both of George Washington University, for their suggestions on comparing the gendered character of the downtown street

to the shopping center. Also see Gunther Barth, *City People: The Rise of Modern City Culture in Nineteenth-Century America* (New York, 1980); Elaine Abelson, *When Ladies Go A-Thieving: Middle-Class Shoplifters in the Victorian Department Store* (New York, 1989); William Leach, "Transformations in a Culture of Consumption: Women and Department Stores, 1890–1925," *Journal of American History* 71 (September 1984): 319–42.

28. On women driving, and specifically using a car for shopping, see Rich, *Shopping Behavior of Department Store Customers*, 84–85, 137–38; L. Pratt, "Impact of Regional Shopping Centers in Bergen County"; Voorhees, *Shopping Habits and Travel Patterns*, 17.

29. Herzog, "Shops, Culture, Centers—and More," 35; "Busy Day in Busy Willowbrook Mall," *New York Times* (April 2, 1972): 55, 65; Harris, *Cultural Excursions*, 281.

30. Rich, *Shopping Behavior of Department Store Customers*, 64, 71–74; L. Pratt, "Impact of Regional Shopping Centers in Bergen County"; Sternlieb, *Future of the Downtown Department Store*, 27–28, 184; Feinberg, *What Makes Shopping Centers Tick*, 97; Oaks, *Managing Suburban Branches of Department Stores*, 72.

31. JCPenney, "An American Legacy, A 90th Anniversary History" (1992), brochure, 22, 25, JCPenney Archives, Dallas, Texas; Mary Elizabeth Curry, *Creating an American Institution: The Merchandising Genius of J. C. Penney* (New York, 1993), 311–13; William M. Batten, *The Penney Idea: Foundation for the Continuing Growth of the J. C. Penney Company* (New York, 1967), 17. The opening of the J. C. Penney store in Garden State Plaza in 1958 is featured in a film, *The Past Is a Prologue* (1961), which is one of several fascinating movies made by the company that have been collected on a video. *Penney Premieres*, available through the JCPenney Archives. Also see *Penny News* 24 (November–December 1958): 1, 7, on the new Paramus store, JCPenney Archives; R. H. Macy & Company, *Annual Report for 1957* (New York, 1957), 26.

32. Barry Bluestone, Patricia Hanna, Sarah Kuhn, and Laura Moore, *The Retail Revolution: Market Transformation, Investment, and Labor in the Modern Department Store* (Boston, 1981), 46–47; Rich, *Shopping Behavior of Department Store Customers*, 100–01; " 'It Won't Be Long Now . . . ': Bamberger's New Jersey's Greatest Store, Comes to Paramus Soon," stamped August 22, 1956, file "Bergen County Shopping Centers," Johnson Free Public Library, Hackensack; press release, "The Garden State Plaza Opens Wednesday, May 1st at the Junction of Routes 4 and 17, Paramus," Garden State Plaza Historical Collection; JCPenney, "An American Legacy," 21–22; Curry, *Creating an American Institution*, 305–7.

On the expansion of credit in the postwar period, see Marie de Vroet Kobrak, "Consumer Installment Credit and Factors Associated with It" (M.A. thesis, University of Chicago, 1958); Lewis Mandell, *The Credit Card Industry: A History* (Boston, 1990); Hillel Black, *Buy Now Pay Later* (New York, 1961). For a 1971 study documenting the possession of bank cards and store charge cards in the counties of Bergen, Passaic (New Jersey), and Rockland (New York) and when they were last used, see Plan One Research Corporation, *Mighty Market*, 382–85. In 1958, the *Paterson Evening News* cited a recent newspaper poll on family finances showing that the wife has full control of the family purse in 90 percent of all families; "Even as You and I," *Bergen Evening Record* (January 10, 1958): 58; also "Handling Your Money," January 25, 1958, *Bergen Evening Record*, Weekend Magazine, 4.

33. Oaks, *Managing Suburban Branches of Department Stores*, 73; "Paramus Booms as a Store Center," *New York Times* (February 5, 1962): 34; "Sales Personnel Ready to Work," *Bergen Evening Record*, November 13, 1957.

34. Rich, *Shopping Behavior of Department Store Customers*, 20; Sternlieb, *Future of the Downtown Department Store*, 27; R. H. Macy & Company, *Annual Report for 1955*, 29; JCPenney, "An American Legacy," 25; Stuart, *Our Era*, 20.

35. My understanding of labor conditions and organizing in the New York area, and in the Paramus malls specifically, comes from two manuscript collections at the Robert F. Wagner Labor Archives, New York University: the papers of Local 1-S, Department Store Workers' Union (RWDSU), and District 65, now of the UAW, then of the RWDSU. I have based my analysis on the clippings, meeting minutes, and legal files in those collections, which I have not cited individually unless I quoted from them. Michelson quote from "NLRB Ruling Spurs New York Area Union: Target—50 Stores," Box 4, Folder 36, District 65; similar statement with two-thirds figure from "Report to General Council Meeting, Department Store Section, by William Michelson," January 12, 1965, Box 5, Folder 4, District 65. On department store efforts with part-timers, see "Part-Timer: New Big Timer," *Women's Wear Daily*, January 8, 1964, Box 4, Folder 35, Local 1-S; also see the records of a fascinating case that Local 1-S brought before the NLRB concerning the firing of a young woman employee who had shown interest in the union: Box 9, Folder 21, Local 1-S.

On industrial relations in department stores nationally, with a case study of the Boston metropolitan area, see Bluestone et al., *Retail Revolution*, 70, 80–119, 148–49, which provides an excellent analysis of the restructuring of the labor market in the retail trade. Also see Jacobs, *The Mall*, 49.

36. Bamberger's Paramus, "Welcome to New Friends and a New Career," Employee Handbook, 1957, Box 7, Folder 16, pp. 4, 9–12, Local 1-S.

37. "Amtrak Is Ordered Not to Eject the Homeless from Penn Station," *New York Times* (February 22, 1995): A1.

38. Article on passage of New Jersey Civil Rights Bill, *New York Times*, March 24, 1949; Marion Thompson Wright, "Extending Civil Rights in New Jersey through the Division Against Discrimination," *Journal of Negro History* 38 (1953): 96–107; State of New Jersey, Governor's Committee on Civil Liberties, "Memorandum on Behalf of Joint Council for Civil Rights in Support of a Proposed Comprehensive Civil Rights Act for New Jersey," 1948, 11, B 8, Folder "Civil Rights, New Jersey, 1941–48," NAACP Papers, Library of Congress, Washington, D.C.; "Report of Legislative Committee, NJ State Conference of NAACP Branches," March 26, 1949, 11, B 8, Folder "Civil Rights, New Jersey, 1941–48," NAACP Papers. Other NAACP files on discrimination document the actual experiences of African Americans in New Jersey during the 1940s and 1950s.

39. "Closing of 'Last' Department Store Stirs Debate on Downtown Trenton," *Star-Ledger*, June 5, 1983; "Urban Areas Crave Return of Big Markets," *Star-Ledger*, July 17, 1984; "Elizabeth Clothier Mourns Demise of Century-Old Customized Service," *Sunday Star-Ledger*, January 10, 1988; "President's Report to the Annual Meeting, Passaic Valley Citizens Planning Association," Box A, Folder 3, Erber, NPL. On Newark, see for Raymond Mungin quotation, "Two Guys Will Be Missed," *Star-Ledger*, November 23, 1981. Also see "Last-Minute Bargain Hunters Abound as Chase Closes Up," *Newark News*, February 12, 1967; "Ohrbach's Will Close Store in Newark, Cites Drop in Sales and Lack of Lease," *New York Times*, December 7, 1973; and, in the *Star-Ledger*, "S. Klein to Shut Last State Stores Sometime in June," May 9, 1975; "Sears to Shut Newark Store," June 13, 1978; "Hahne's Bids a Farewell to Newark," June 18, 1986; "Macy's to Shut Stores in Newark, Plainfield," May 21, 1992; "Newark & Lewis Is Closing 11 Stores," October 15, 1993; Greater Newark Chamber of Commerce, "Survey of Jobs and Unemployment," May 1973, NPL "Q" File; Greater Newark Chamber of Commerce, "Metro New Jersey Market Report" [1991], NPL "Q" File.

Chapter Fifteen

Narcissism as Liberation

Susan J. Douglas

"I'm worth it," insists Cybill Shepherd in her brattiest, na-na-na-poo-poo voice as she swirls her blond hair in my face. Since I have to be restrained, physically, from hatcheting my television set to death whenever this ad appears (and every woman I know has the same reaction), it is amazing to think it actually sells hair dye. But it must, since this campaign has been harassing us for nearly a decade. "I'm worth it" became the motto for the 1980s woman we saw in television and magazines ads. Endless images of women lounging on tiled verandas, or snuggling with their white angora cats while wearing white silk pajamas, exhorted us to be self-indulgent, self-centered, private, hedonistic. In stark contrast to the selfless wife and mom of *The Feminine Mystique*, not to mention those hideous, loudmouthed feminists who thought sisterhood and political activism mattered, women of the 1980s were urged to take care of themselves, and to do so *for* themselves. An ad for Charles of the Ritz, featuring a gorgeous model dripping with pearls and staring off into space, summed up women's recent history. "I'm not the girl I used to be. Now I want to surround myself with beautiful things. And I want to look beautiful too. I've discovered that it's easier to face the world when I like what I see in the mirror."

By the 1980s, advertising agencies had figured out how to make feminism—and antifeminism—work for them. There had been a few clumsy starts in the 1970s, like the Virginia Slims "You've Come a Long Way, Baby" campaign, which equated liberation with the freedom to give yourself lung cancer. And feminine hygiene sprays like Massengill's pictured the product with a political button reading "Freedom Now" and touted the crotch rot in the can as "The Freedom Spray." But the approaches got more subtle and certainly more invidious as America's multibazillion-dollar cosmetics industry realized that all those kids who once bought Clearasil and Stri-Dex were now getting something even worse than acne—wrinkles. Here was an enormous market—the women who grew up with, who in fact made possible, a youth culture—now getting old. You could almost hear the skin cream moguls in their boardrooms yelling yippie-kiyo-kiyay.

The appropriation of feminist desires and feminist rhetoric by Revlon, Lancôme, and other major corporations was nothing short of spectacular. Women's liberation metamorphosed into female narcissism unchained as political concepts and goals like liberation and equality were collapsed into distinctly personal, private desires.

Women's liberation became equated with women's ability to do whatever they wanted for themselves, whenever they wanted, no matter what the expense. These ads were geared to the woman who had made it in a man's world, or who hoped she would, and the message was Reward yourself, you deserve it. There was enormous emphasis on luxury, and on separating oneself from the less enlightened, less privileged herd. The ability to spend time and money on one's appearance was a sign of personal success and of breaking away from the old roles and rules that had held women down in the past. Break free from those old conventions, the ads urged, and get *truly* liberated: put yourself first.

Narcissism was more in for women than ever, and the ability to indulge oneself, pamper oneself, and focus at length on oneself without having to listen to the needy voices of others was the mark of upscale female achievement. These were the years when we were supposed to put the naive, idealistic, antimaterialistic 1960s behind us and, instead, go to polo matches and wash our hair with bottled water from the Alps. Ralph Lauren, in his ads for sheets and oxford cloth shirts, used manor houses, antique furniture, riding boots, and safari gear to make us long for the days when the sun never set on the British Empire, when natives (and women) knew their place, and robber barons ran America. Huge museum exhibits celebrated England's "Treasure Houses" and the gowns favored by Marie Antoinette and her pals, each of which represented the work of 213 starving peasant seamstresses.[1] *The Big Chill* suggested that even radical baby boomers had sold out to Wall Street, a move portrayed as inevitable and perfectly understandable.

For women in the age of Reagan, elitism and narcissism merged in a perfect appeal to forget the political already, and get back to the personal, which you might be able to do something about. But let's not forget the most ubiquitous and oppressive anatomical symbol of the new woman's achievement that came into its own in the 1980s: the perfectly sculpted, dimple-free upper thigh and buttock. A tour through the land of smooth faces and even smoother buttocks and thighs makes one appreciate why the women of the 1980s who had reason to feel pride in their accomplishments still felt like worthless losers when they looked in the mirror or, horror of horrors, put on a bathing suit. Of course, these feelings were hardly confined to baby boomers. Nor are they confined to the past. Though I write about what emerged in the 1980s in the past tense, I feel awkward about doing so, because the ad strategies established then are still in high gear, and we watch their effects with sorrow, anger, and empathy. When I go to any number of college or university swimming pools, I see women twenty years younger than I, at their physical peak, healthy and trim, walk out to the pool with towels wrapped around their waists so their thighs will be exposed to the world only for the few nanoseconds it takes to drop the towel and dive into the pool. I have *never* seen a young man do this. Then they go back to the locker room and slather their sweet, twenty-year-old faces with Oil of Olay so they can fight getting old "every step of the way."

Advertisers in the 1980s, especially those targeting women, apparently had a new bible: Christopher Lasch's 1979 best-seller, *The Culture of Narcissism.* Lasch identified what he saw as a new trend, the emergence of people who seemed self-centered and self-satisfied but were really deeply anxious about what others thought of them. Americans were becoming increasingly self-absorbed, he wrote, but not because they were conceited. On the contrary, Americans were desperately insecure, consumed by self-doubt and self-loathing, and totally obsessed with competing with other people for approval and acclaim. The "narcissistic personality," according to Lasch, was compulsively "other-directed" and consumed by self-doubt, even self-hatred. As a result, the narcissist craved approval and fantasized about adulation. Any sense of self-esteem was fleeting, hinging on things like whether someone looked at you funny or laughed at one of your jokes. This obsessive need for admiration prompted the narcissist to become skilled at managing impressions, at assuming different roles, and at developing a magnetic personality. Narcissists were always measuring themselves against others; being envied, for example, had become infinitely more important than being admired or respected. Narcissists had a strong belief in their right to be gratified and were constantly searching for heightened emotional experiences, for instant gratification, to stave off the fear that life is unreal, artificial, and meaningless. Narcissists were especially terrified of aging and death. Lasch particularly emphasized how the messages and ploys of American advertising had cultivated such narcissistic personalities.

When I read this book, I was struck by two things. First, Lasch kept using the pronoun *he* to talk about the narcissist, and this helped make the trend he was describing seem new. But for women, this wasn't so new, this was the story of our lives, of how we had been socialized since childhood. Second, it was in ads geared specifically to women, especially ads for cosmetics and other personal care items. that we saw advertisers applying, with a vengeance, the various insights of Lasch's book. Under the guise of addressing our purported new confidence and self-love, these ads really reinforced how we failed to measure up to others. Hanes, for example, in a classic campaign, skillfully resolved the tensions surrounding new womanhood in its series of ads titled "Reflections On . . ." A woman was pictured sitting across the arms of a leather chair, or in a wicker patio lounger, with her legs prominently displayed. She was usually dressed up in a glittery cocktail dress, exchanging smiles with a man in a tux. She was always white. In one ad, the admiring male voice said, "She messes up the punch line of every joke; can tell a Burgundy from a Bordeaux; and her legs . . . Oh yes, Joanna's legs." In another version, the copy read: "She does this flawless imitation of Groucho Marx; recites the most astonishing passages from Hemingway; ahh, and her legs . . . Emily's legs."

Joanna's and Emily's nonanatomical achievements were impressive—they knew things only elite men used to know, like how to select a wine, and their favorite writer wasn't Edith Wharton or Alice Walker, it was Mr. Macho himself. They didn't imitate Mae West (too threatening), they imitated a constantly lecherous man. They had cracked the male code, but, because of Hanes, they were still ladies. These women were huge successes at managing the impressions they gave to others, coming across as distinctive, nonconformist women who nonetheless conform perfectly to dominant standards of beauty. They were self-satisfied and self-assured, yet their value came from male admiration and approval. The ads suggested that without inner confidence, and a core self that is assured and discriminating (made possible, one can infer, by feminism), these women would not be the charmers they are today. But without male approval and admiration, they would not have the acclaim on which narcissistic self-esteem rests. It was in campaigns such as this that the appearance of female self-love and achievement was used to reinforce female dependence on male approval. If you wore Hanes, in other words, you would feel the contradictions between feminism and prefeminism thread together smoothly as you pulled them up over your legs and hips and then strode confidently out into the world.

The cult of narcissism Lasch saw in the 1970s exploded in the 1980s, nurtured by Reagan's me-first-and-to-hell-with-everyone-else political and moral philosophies. Under the guise of telling women, "You're worth it," advertisers suggested we weren't worth it at all but could feel we were, for a moment, if we bought the right product. Here we were again, same as it ever was, bombarded by the message that approval from others, especially men, means everything, and without it you are nothing, an outcast, unworthy and unloved. We were right back to Tinker Bell and Cinderella, urged to be narcissistic yet ridiculed if it was discovered that we were.

The narcissism as liberation campaign found its happiest home in certain television ads, such as those that sponsored shows like *Dynasty*, and in women's magazines like *Vogue, Harper's Bazaar, Mademoiselle, Glamour, Cosmopolitan*, and the aptly named *Self*. These magazines, with their emphasis on clothes, makeup, and dieting, were much more hospitable than *Ladies' Home Journal* or *McCall's*, which acknowledged that women couldn't be completely self-indulgent since they still were the ones responsible for pureeing bananas for the baby and getting dinner on the table at night. *Vogue* et al. didn't contaminate their pages with such gritty reminders of reality, thank God. Instead, they created a narcissistic paradise, a luxurious daydream, in which women focused on themselves and their appearance, and in which any change was possible, as long as it was personal.

Now, before I get on my high horse about cures for what the fashion magazines call "orange peel skin" and subdermal rehydrating systems, let me be perfectly honest about my own vulnerability to these really preposterous ploys. Like a lot of women, I look at ads for things like Elizabeth Arden's Ceramide Time Complex Capsules, little gelatinous spheres that look like a cross between a diaphragm and a UFO, which claim to—get this—"boost [the] skin's hydration level over 450% after one hour" because they are "supercharged with HCA, a unique alpha-hydroxy complex," and I think—or sometimes yell—would you puleeze get real here. I know that in 1987 the FDA had cracked down on cosmetics ads then in print because they were, to put it euphemistically, inflated in their claims. I know that putting collagen on your skin does nothing. Nevertheless, there's this perfectly airbrushed model, young, beautiful, and carefree, her eyebrows the only lines on her face, and I sigh a longing sigh. Even when we are fully able to deconstruct these pseudoscientific sales pitches, which would make any self-respecting snake oil salesman blush, there we are, a part of us still wanting to believe that we can look younger and that it's desirable to do so. I don't "read" *Vogue* or *Glamour*; if you'll pardon the masculine metaphor, I enter them. I escape into them, into a world where I have nothing more stressful to do than smooth on some skin cream, polish my toenails, and lie on the beach. But despite these soft spots, I'm here to say that deconstruction can make us strong, so let's be on with it.

In ads for personal care products in the 1980s, especially skin creams, makeup, and perfume, we confronted our ideal selves, eternally young, flawless, confident, assured of the envy of others, yet insulated from the needs of others. The Lutèce Bath, for example, created "your private world of luxury." In these ads, the contradictions that we'd lived with all our lives, the tensions between the need to be passive and the need to be active, were subtly and brilliantly resolved. Usually the women pictured were enjoying leisure moments, or what *Glamour* called "private time." They were sitting alone on their enormous porches, or reclining in beds of satin sheets, or soaking in bubble baths, sometimes with their eyes closed, in a state of relaxation and escape. In one of my favorites, an ad for something called Terme di Montecatini, we saw the profile of a woman at a spa, covered from forehead to rib cage with a kind of mud we assumed would make her even more beautiful while she just rested. Women like this are passive, inactive, supine. Yet make no mistake about it, these women are in complete control: they are dependent on no one, their time is their own, they are beyond the cares of the world, they long for nothing they don't already have. Those symbols of wealth—a huge veranda, the Riviera, art objects, unusual breeds of dogs, the omnipresent glass of white wine—convey comfort, luxury, insulation from the masses, and control.

It wasn't enough to put some Lubriderm on your face—my God, that was like consigning your skin to the soup kitchens of moisturizers. No, you had to spend money, and plenty of it, to be a discriminating, knowledgeable, accomplished woman. An ad for a product called Oligo-Major lectured, "No woman can afford to be without it." The cosmetics industry employed three main strategies to get women to buy the high-priced spreads for their faces instead of using the cheap shit, Pond's or Nivea—the building construction approach, the haute cuisine approach, and the high-tech approach, all intended to flatter the "new woman." They were designed to convey one basic message: you get what you pay for, and if you scrimp on skin-care products, you get what you deserve—crow's-feet, eye bags, turkey neck, the worst. Fail to spend $42.50 on one-thirty-second of an ounce of skin cream and the next time you look in the mirror, you'll see Lyndon Johnson in drag.

The building construction approach was best represented by a fabulous new product, Line Fill, a kind of Silly Putty for the face. Line Fill was also called skin Spackle—now we were supposed to think of ourselves as a slab of drywall—and was best used to "fill those character lines we can all do without." In the same age when "character," particularly for male politicians, became an obsession, women didn't dare look like they had any character at all. Chanel's Lift Sérum Anti-Wrinkle Complex relied on Plastoderm, which, despite its name, operated as a kind of hydraulic jack for sagging skin. "Wrinkles," informed the ad, "are 'lifted' by gentle upward pressure." The haute cuisine approach reached its apotheosis with "skin caviar," an "intensive concentration of vitamins, humectants, emollients and plant naturals." The assumption here was that aging skin was merely malnourished; so in a gesture reminiscent of our new heroine, Marie Antoinette, the truly discriminating woman should say, "Let it eat caviar."

But without doubt the most prevalent approach was the high-tech approach, the one that introduced us to "delivery systems," "collagen," and lots of words starting with *micro-* and *lipo-*. What women's liberation really meant was that now the labs of America would turn to our real concerns: our crow's-feet. Science and technology, those onetime villains that had brought us napalm, the bomb, Three Mile Island, Love Canal, and the Dalkon Shield, were themselves given a face-lift for women. They were rehabilitated as our allies and our minions. Science and technology were the most effective agents of luxurious narcissism, and the various forms of white goop that we slopped on our faces had amazing names that cloaked the products in mystery while keeping supposedly technophobic and techno-dumbo females engaged and credulous.

Here we see another clever twist on feminism. The women's health movement of the 1970s, as embodied in *Our Bodies, Ourselves*, insisted that doctors not treat women like morons but that they talk to us as adults, provide us with information and choices, and give us more control over our bodies. Advertisers said OK, you want technical, medical information, we'll give it to you. They got to have it both ways—they flattered the "new woman" with all this pseudoscientific jargon, suggesting that this was the kind of information she wanted, needed, and could easily understand, and they got to make the goop they were selling sound as if it had been developed at Cal Tech.

In the 1980s, in nearly every cosmetic ad we saw, science and technology were women's servants, and servants not just to expedite domestic chores (as in the bad, selfless old days) but through which women could remake themselves, conquer time, and conquer nature by overcoming their genetic heritage. Here women's desires for more control over and more autonomy in their lives were shrewdly co-opted. Naomi Wolf argues that the high-tech approach sought to speak to women whose work was increasingly dominated by computers and the microchip.[2] The words *performance, precision,* and *control* were used repeatedly, and products such as Swiss Performing Extract or Niosôme Système Anti-Age performed on you (you are passive) while performing for you (you are in command). One product's slogan was, simply, "The Victory of Science over Time." This product, like so many, contained "patented liposomes," which, in case you needed an explanation, were "micro-capsules of select ingredients of natural origin which fuse with the membrane restoring fluidity, promoting reactivation of cells in your skin." Niosôme produced "an exclusive action, 'Biomimitism.'" This was not supposed to make you think of conjugating spirogyra; it was supposed to make you feel privy to the world of the scientist. It was very important to feature microscopes, women in white lab jackets, and lots of footnotes about patents pending to suggest the weight of a scientific abstract.

As we read other ads for competing products (and there was no shortage of them), a pattern started to emerge. Nearly all the cosmetics companies referred to their products as "systems." These systems "penetrate" the "intercellular structure" of the skin, increasing "microcirculation." Using only the most advanced "delivery systems," presumably inspired by NASA, the Pentagon, and Star Wars, these creams and lotions deployed "advanced microcarriers" or "active anti-age agents," presumably trained by the CIA to terminate wrinkles with extreme prejudice. So cosmetics actually became weapons, and the word *defense* began to proliferate in ads at the same time, interestingly, that the Pentagon's budget was going through the roof.

In copy sounding as if it had been written by Alexander Haig, our skin was put in a bunker or, better yet, behind Reagan's version of Star Wars, as "protective barriers" and "invisible shields" deflected "external aggressors." These muscular products relied on the same high-tech weaponry we saw in *The Empire Strikes Back* and had straightforward names like Defense Cream and Skin Defender. You could almost see Luke Skywalker, backed up by the Green Berets, zapping those wrinkles back to kingdom come. Turning on its head the feminist argument that the emphasis on beauty undermines women's ability to be taken seriously and to gain control over their lives, advertisers now assured women that control *comes* from cosmetics. Cosmetics were sold as newly engineered tools, precision instruments you could use on yourself to gain more control than ever over the various masks and identities you as a woman must present to the world.

But lest all this high-tech talk alienate women, cosmetics firms also made sure to give their products European-, and especially French-sounding names. System was usually spelled *système*; concentrated became *concentré*. Accent signs became essential, as did the pronoun *Le*. Several product names simply went for broke, as in this little gem, Crème Multi Modelanté bio-suractiveé, or Lift Extrême Nutri-Collagène Concentré. What were brilliantly brought together were the seemingly opposite worlds of advanced, ever-changing, American engineering technology and laboratory science (traditionally the province of men) and the preindustrialist, timeless, beauty-oriented cultural authority of Europe (which caters to women). For new beauty products to sell, it seems, the ads had to refer to and unite recent scientific breakthroughs and the language of engineering with references to France, Switzerland, or Italy. The words *extract, serum*, and *molecular* suggested both the lab *and* elements found in nature. Thus Niosôme, from Lancôme, is an antiaging "system" with a French-sounding name that "recreates the structure of a young skin." Cosmetics ads straddled the Atlantic, linking American technology with European culture, and the traditions of the old world with the futurism of the new.

With the union of science and aesthetics, women now could draw from the achievements of men in a world in which science and technology did what we always wished they would do—slow the passage of time, provide us with cost-free luxury and convenience, and allow us to remake ourselves. It was through the female form, and the idealized female face in particular, that science and technology were made to seem altruistic, progressive, relevant to everyday needs, and responsive to women's desires. They were made humane and romantic, and allied with the realms of art, nature, and tradition.

At the same time, the pseudoscientific language not only legitimated cosmetic companies' claims but also assured women that these products were for discriminating, upscale consumers. The new woman was now sophisticated enough and privileged enough to benefit from a scientific enterprise designed specifically for elite white women. The linking of American science and technology with European cultural authority served to unite narcissism with elitism, to make elitism seem natural, legitimate, and inevitable, and to suggest that if you truly loved yourself, you had to aspire to the privileged, idle, self-indulgent world of the rich, who were the rightful beneficiaries of technology, and the true arbiters of high art. Here we had a new kind of magic. How could products that relied on herbal treatments, molecular biology, and chemistry fail to transform us into newer, better selves?

Of course, if you'd been derelict in your moisturizing duties, there were more heroic methods to combat the signs of aging. Article after article touted plastic surgery, so that no woman would ever have to go out in public again looking like Eleanor Roosevelt, Simone de Beauvoir, or Margaret Mead did in their later years. Experts from skin-care labs, their names trailed by twenty-eight initials signifying their degrees and affiliations, happily agreed to interviews for *Harper's Bazaar* and elsewhere, promoting the knife. They always said these really informative and logical things, like that the first part of the body people usually look at is the face, which is why you shouldn't have any lines on yours. So what if, after a few tucks, you were laid up for six weeks and looked like you'd gone eighteen rounds with George Foreman? It was true, some women did experience a little facial paralysis after a lift, and you might not look as Occidental as you used to or have enough skin to smile in quite the same way, but these concerns were all picky, picky, picky. Did you want to look like Cher, or not?

The other intermediate step was promoted in full-page ads by the Collagen Corporation. Here we met Sunny Griffin, "mother, building contractor, and former TV correspondent and model." Already I felt pretty inferior, but it quickly got worse. Sunny was ten years older than I and easily looked ten years younger. Sunny, it turned out, "didn't like those 'little commas' at the corners of her mouth, her crow's feet, or the lines on her forehead. So she did something about them." But, unlike me, she was a woman of action. She went to a doctor who stuck needles in her face, filling in those hideous lines with "injectable Zyderm© and Zyplast© Collagen." Now those wrinkles were "mere memories." Here were prefeminism and feminism beautifully reconciled in Sunny Griffin, Collagen poster girl. As a feminist, this superwoman had tackled male jobs and female jobs and combined them successfully with motherhood. This gave her permission to indulge her prefeminist side, the one still obsessed with little commas and crow's-feet, especially if she took decisive medical action to take control of her face and herself.

In the collagen ad, it was the beautiful, rich, and successful Sunny Griffin versus the rest of us. And that was the other important thrust of the narcissism as liberation campaign, the continuation of the catfight, the war between women. In all these ads, sisterhood was out, competitive individualism was in. It got worse if you actually fell for these ads (hey, I was in my thirties, what did I know?) and went out to buy some skin defender. If you've ever bought anything at a Clinique, Lancôme, or other such counter, you know what I mean. The saleswoman's face is made up like a Kabuki mask to put you off balance right away. And, clearly, all these women were trained wherever that awful secret place is that they train used car salesmen. Using a combination of intimidation, pressure, and highly uncharitable assessments of your existing skin-care regimen, these women sought to shame you into buying everything they had, which could come to the equivalent of a monthly car payment. The worst, and I mean the worst, thing you could say to one of these women was that you mixed products—you know, used a cleanser from one company and moisturizer from another. Then they'd nearly croak from exasperation at your stupidity and your self-destructive tendencies. Didn't you know, these cosmetic lines were *integrated* systems; each component worked with the other components as a unit. Mixing products was akin to putting a Chevy carburetor inside a Porsche engine and expecting the car to run. You'd wreck your face by mixing products; you had to buy into the entire system or risk waking up one morning to discover your face turning into melting wax.

The notion of sisterhood being powerful seemed a real joke under this onslaught. Fisticuffs seemed more appropriate. It took work to remember that the salesclerks needed these jobs, that many of them were supporting kids with their salaries, and that while we squared off against each other across the glass-cased counter, the big boys upstairs who didn't need face cream were getting ready for their three-martini lunches and their affairs with women twenty years younger than they.

Tensions between technology and nature, between feminism and antifeminism, and between self-love and self-doubt were played out not only on the terrain of the flawless female face. Everywhere we looked, in the incessant "get-back-in-shape" TV ads and magazine articles, on billboards, in the catalogs that jammed our mailboxes, and in the endless diet soda and cereal ads on the airwaves, the perfectly smooth, toned buttocks and thighs of models and actresses accosted the women of America. They jutted out at us from the new, high-cut, split-'em-in-two bathing suits and exercise outfits, challenging us and humbling us, reminding all women that nothing in the world is more repulsive and shameful than "orange peel skin," a.k.a. "cellulite." They provided women, whether black or white, rich or poor, with a universal standard of achievement and success. They insisted that the rest of us should feel only one thing when we put on a bathing suit: profound mortification.

It's true that we also started seeing more female biceps, and every few months *The New York Times* asserted that breasts were back "in." But, still, it was the slim, dimple-free buttock and thigh that became, in the 1980s and the 1990s, the ultimate signifier of female fitness, beauty, and character. To make sure you couldn't hide them, the fashion industry gave us bathing suits with legs cut up to just below the armpit. Trim, smug models were positioned with their knees bent or their bodies curled so that their superhuman hindquarters were front and center. And not just in *Vogue* or *Cosmo*, either: even in *The Village Voice*, between the exposés on racism and government malfeasance, ads appeared for products like the videotape *Buns of Steel*, which promised, "Now you can have the buns you've always wanted." Saddlebag-busting products like Biotherm appeared, which actually suggested that if you just rubbed some cream on your buttocks, the dimples would go into remission.

Why this part of the body? Why were we suddenly but constantly confronted by these perfectly sculpted rumps? During the mammary mania of the 1950s and '60s, bust creams, exercisers, and padded bras suggested that women could compensate for what nature forgot. Yet while less-endowed women might buy such products, and bemoan their lack of voluptuousness, there was also a basic understanding that, short of surgery, there was little a woman could do to actually change the size of her breasts. The thigh was different: this body part could be yoked to another pathology of the 1980s, the yuppie work ethic. Thin thighs and dimple-free buttocks became instant, automatic evidence of discipline, self-denial, and control. You, too, the message went, can achieve perfect thighs through dieting and exercise. As Jane Fonda put it, "Discipline Is Liberation."[3]

Emphasis on the thigh, which still harasses us, stems from the fitness craze of the past fifteen years, when increasing numbers of women discovered the physical and psychic benefits of exercise. I learned in graduate school, for example, that if I swam sixty-seven laps in the pool I was less likely to strangle the pompous white male professors making my life miserable, and I'd also sort out some problem with my own work as well. Plus, for inspiration to get off your butt, there were women like Billie Jean King, one of my heroes, a fabulous athlete and a feminist, and the first woman athlete to earn more than $100,000 a year. When she beat the living crap out of Bobby Riggs in the much touted "Battle of the Sexes" in 1973, as women like me screamed with delight in our living rooms, she not only vindicated female athletes and feminism but also inspired many of us to get in shape—not because it would make us beautiful but because it would make us strong and healthy.

What too many of us forget is that the fitness movement began as a radical reaction against the degradation of food by huge conglomerates, and against the work routines and convenience technologies that encouraged us to be passive and sedentary. The organic health food movement was, initially, at its core, anticapitalist. The women's fitness movement, too, was a site of resistance, as women sought to break into sports previously restricted to men and other women simply sought to get strong. But one of capitalism's great strengths—perhaps its greatest—is its ability to co-opt and domesticate opposition, to transubstantiate criticism into a host of new, marketable products. And so it was with fitness.

Corporations saw immediately that there was gold in them thar thighs. The key to huge profits was to emphasize beauty over health, sexuality over fitness, and to equate thin thighs with wealth and status. What had worked so well in the past was to set up standards of perfection that were cast as unattainable yet somehow within reach if only the right product were purchased. So we got a new, even narrower ideal of beauty that continues to bombard us from every media outlet and serves the needs of a host of corporations.

Yet there was much more going on here than just the media capitalizing on a trend or the standard let's-make-'em-feel-inferior-so-they'll-buy-our-product routine. The flawless rump became *the* most important female body part of the 1980s because its cultivation and display fit in so well with the great myth of Reaganism: that superficial appearances really can be equated with a person's deepest character strengths and weaknesses. The emphasis on streamlined rumps allowed for a dramatic reshaping of feminist urgings that women take control of their bodies and their health. All we had to do was listen to Cher in those health spa ads, she'd tell us: thin thighs and dimple-free buttocks meant you worked hard, took yourself seriously, and were ready to compete with anyone. They were indicators of a woman's potential for success. Any woman, so the message went, could achieve perfect thighs through concentrated effort, self-denial, and deferred gratification, the basic tenets of the work ethic. All she had to do was apply herself and, of course, be a discriminating, upscale consumer. "You don't get this far by accident," proclaimed one sneaker ad displaying a tight, toned rump; "you've worked hard." Another magazine ad, this one for a spa, also spotlighted a machine-tooled hind-quarter, intoning, "When you work at it, it shows." Meaning, if you've been slacking off, that will show too. Only "new women" had buns of steel; out-of-date women who had failed to have their consciousnesses raised didn't.

It didn't matter if you were healthy, exercised regularly, and weren't overweight. If wearing one of the new, ultrahigh-cut bathing suits would reveal too much roundness, a little fat (what the cosmetics industry christened "cellulite" in the 1970s), you would be dismissed as slothful and lacking moral fiber and self-respect, not to mention lazy, self-indulgent, insufficiently vigorous, lacking control, seden-tary, and old. (The only acceptable sedentary indulgence was to lie on a chaise longue, slathered from head to toe in sludge, à la Terme di Montecatini.) No matter that the female hip area is naturally more fatty than the male (a function of reproduction), or that most women's jobs require constant sitting, two factors that tend to work against developing buns of steel. Over and again we were told that a real woman, whatever her age, would get off her butt and, by overcoming her sloth, not just get in shape but conquer genetics and history. Her buns of steel would instantly identify her as someone who subscribed to the new yuppie ethic that insisted that even in leisure hours, the truly tough, the truly deserving, never stopped working. The sleek, smooth, tight butt was—and is—a badge, a medal asserting that anal compulsiveness is an unalloyed virtue.

Perfect thighs, in other words, were an achievement, a product, and one to be admired and envied. They demonstrated that the woman had made something of herself, that she had character and class, that she was the master of her body and, thus, of her fate. If she had conquered her own adipose tissue, she could conquer anything. She was a new woman, liberated and in control. She had made her buttocks less fatty, more muscular, more, well . . . like a man's. So here we have one of the media's most popular—and pernicious—distortions of feminism: that ambitious women want, or should want, to be just like men. The woman whose upper thigh best approximated a fat-free male hindquarter was the woman most entitled to enjoy the same privileges as men. Orange-peel skin should be a source of shame, not only because it's "ugly," but also because it's inherently female. It indicates that, as a woman, you aren't working hard enough, aren't really taking responsibility for your own life. You aren't really liberated because you haven't overcome being a woman. A desirable woman doesn't look like a real woman looks; thus, one of the basic physical markers of femaleness is cast as hideous.

Yet well-toned, machine-tooled thighs suggested that women could compete with men while increasing their own desirability. Thighs, rather than breasts, became the focus in the 1980s because presumably everyone, the flat-chested and the stacked, men as well as women, could work toward buns of steel. Women could develop the same anatomical zones that men did, giving their muscles new definition, a definition meant to serve simultaneously as a warning and as an enticement to men. Buns of steel marked a woman as a desirable piece of ass, and as someone who could kick ass when necessary.

What made these thighs desirable was that, while they were fat-free, like men's, they also resembled the thighs of adolescent girls. The ideal rump bore none of the marks of age, responsibility, work, or motherhood. And the crotch-splitting, cut-up-to-the-waistline, impossible-to-swim-in bathing suits featured in such publications as the loathsome *Sports Illustrated* swimsuit issue could never reveal that other marker of adulthood, pubic hair. So, under the guise of female fitness and empowerment, of control over her own body, was an idealized image that infantilized women, an image that kept women in their place.

The upper thigh thus became freighted with meaning. The work ethic, the ethos of production and achievement, self-denial and deferred gratification was united there with egoism, vanity, self-absorption, and other-directedness. With the work ethic moved from the workplace to the private sphere, the greatest female achievement became, ironically, her body, her self. The message was that women were capable of remaking themselves and that this remaking required not only intelligent consumption but also hard work. Thus could women be, simultaneously, self-indulgent consumers, buying high-priced exercise shoes and spa memberships, and self-denying producers who were working hard to remake something—their bodies. They could be active subjects in control of their own images and passive objects judged by those images. They could be profeminists and new women at the same time.

By the middle of the 1980s, these buttocks and thighs were making me and all the other women I knew really hostile and defensive. Their sleek, seemingly healthy surfaces really demanded that we all be pathological: compulsive, filled with self-hate, and schizophrenic, and we were already schizophrenic enough, thank you very much. Aside from the impossible standards of perfection they imposed, these buns of steel urged women to never stop and to be all things to all people: to be both competitive workaholics *and* sex objects, to be active workers in control of their bodies *and* passive ornaments for the pleasure of men, to be hard-as-nails super-women *and* vulnerable, unthreatening, teenage beach bunnies. Straddling such contradictions, even on toned, fat-free, muscular legs is, in real life, impossible. And buns of steel were meant to separate the truly classy, deserving women from the rest of the lumpy female proletariat. Buns of steel, like a Pierre Cardin label, were a mark of well-earned exclusivity. Lumpy thighs were Kmart thighs, not the thighs of Rodeo Drive.

The 1980s are over, but buns of steel are very much with us, in Diet Pepsi ads, Victoria's Secret catalogs, and women's magazines. A 1993 survey reported that while only 6 percent of women wished their breasts were either bigger or smaller, a whopping 72 percent wished they had "better thighs."[4] That same year, the cover of *Glamour* promised, in a two-inch headline, "A Better Butt, Fast!" The cover also promised to explain "Why 15 Million Women Own Guns."[5] I figure it's to shoot everyone involved in the campaign to make us think we need buns of steel. The article inside, titled euphoniously enough "The World-Class Butt," accompanied by exercise instructions and an enormous photo of a smooth, sixteen-year-old butt in white eyelet short shorts, lectured, "A toned, firm bottom has plenty to recommend it, as the photo on the right confirms." I also learned that the "flat bottom featured in those beach-blanket movies" was really out. "Now women want a defined, sculpted look with higher, rounder cheeks." Yep, this has been an overarching goal I've wanted to devote a lot of time to in the 1990s. But there's the same old hitch: "You have to work hard to firm them up. So get busy." No need to repeat which expletives I use when reading an exhortation such as this.

So where do these buttocks and thighs leave the rest of us, the real women of America who sit at desks or stand at sinks, who are over sixteen, and who don't have the time, money, personal trainer, or surgical team to help us forge our own buns of steel? Even nonoverweight women, and women who do and should know better, have been worked over so well that whenever we look at ourselves in the mirror or, worse, have to be seen in public in a bathing suit, all we can feel is disgust and shame. But it isn't just shame of our bodies. Buns of steel have taught us to be ashamed of the way we live our day-to-day lives; of the fact that whatever we're doing, we aren't working hard enough; that we don't have that badge of entitlement; that we don't really have enough self-respect and dignity; that we aren't enough like men; and worst of all, that we're adult females in a culture that still prefers, by and large, little girls. All it takes is the slightest roundness, the smallest dimple, to mark a woman as a lazy, and therefore worthless, unattractive person whose thighs obliterate whatever other admirable traits or impressive accomplishments she might possess.

I'm tired of being told never to stop, and that some physical exertion, like pumping a Nautilus machine, is more valuable than some other exertion, such as chasing a two-year-old. I'm tired of Cher's rump, Christie Brinkley's thighs, and countless starved, airbrushed, surgically enhanced hindquarters being shoved in my face. I'm tired of being told that if I just exercise a lot more and eat a lot less, I, too, can conquer biology, make my thighs less female, and thus not be eyed with derision. I'm *real* tired of the marquis de Sade "bathing suits" foisted on us by the fashion industry. Most of all, I'm tired of the endless self-flagellation we women subject ourselves to because of the way this latest, unattainable, physical ideal has been combined with the yuppie work ethic.

And I'm not alone. Backlash works two ways, and women, especially cranky women my age, are really getting the fed-up-skis with advertisers' obsession with machine-tooled faces and thighs. I think that catalogs like Lands' End must be making a fortune on this backlash against buns of steel. They sell bathing suits that fit and that you can actually swim in. If you make the mistake of waiting until late June to order one, they're out of stock because furious women all over the country now refuse to try on a glorified G-string under fluorescent lights that make you look like a very fat dead person.

At the same time that we can't exorcise such long-standing inferiority complexes about our bodies, we see women trying to reclaim the fitness movement from

Kellogg's, Diet Pepsi, Biotherm, and all the rest of the buttocks and thighs cartel. Women know, in their heads if not their hearts, that buns of steel are not about fitness: they are about pretending that some anorexic, unnatural, corporate-constructed ideal is really a norm. Buns of steel are designed to humiliate women, and to make us complicit in our own degradation, and most women know this too. Silly as they may seem, buns of steel are worth being angry about because of the eating disorders they promote among young women and the general sexism they reinforce in society. So the next time some curled-up rump is forced into your field of vision, view it not with envy but with contempt. For it doesn't reflect hard work or entitlement so much as mindless narcissism, unproductive self-absorption, and the media's ongoing distortion of feminism to further their own misogynistic, profit-maximizing ends. Buns of steel are just another media Trojan horse, pretending to advance feminism but harboring antifeminist weaponry.

Narcissism as liberation gutted many of the underlying principles of the women's movement. Instead of group action, we got escapist solitude. Instead of solidarity, we got female competition over men. And, most important, instead of seeing personal disappointments, frustrations, and failures as symptoms of an inequitable and patriarchal society, we saw these, just as in the 1950s, as personal failures, for which we should blame ourselves. Smooth, toned thighs and buttocks obstruct any vision of social change and tell us that, as women, personal change, physical change, is our last, best, and most realistic hope. Women are to take control of their bodies not for political or health reasons but to make them aesthetically pleasing. The "new woman" of the 1980s, then, perpetuated and legitimated the most crass, selfish aspects of consumer capitalism and thus served to distort and deny the most basic and revolutionary principles of feminism. Narcissism as liberation is liberation repackaged, deferred, and denied. Again women felt pinioned, trapped in a web of warring messages. We were supposed to work harder than ever; in fact, the mark of success was having no time for your friends, your family, or yourself. But we were also supposed to indulge ourselves, and to know when and how to kick back, and to do so with style.

Let's take, for example, the politics of the face-lift. Baby boomers with sufficient discretionary income are starting to confront this one, and with the explosion in celebrity journalism, stars' face-lifts and other nips and tucks have become headline news, serving as an enticement and a warning. Cosmetic surgery is being presented as a perfectly natural, affordable, routine procedure, and increasing numbers of women are heeding the call. Cosmetic surgery is growing at a faster rate than any other medical specialty and grosses approximately $300 million a year.[6] The decision to get a face-lift or not is, inescapably, a political decision. Getting one means you're acquiescing to our country's sick norms about beauty, youth, and being "worth it." Not getting one means you're gonna tough it out, be baggy-faced, and take the heat. Actresses and models have no choice. The rest of American women are pulled between these nodes.

But here's what doesn't come out in the war against wrinkles and cellulite: women are as conflicted about aging as they are about other aspects of their lives. For example, when I was twenty and had streaked blond hair, walking down pretty much any street was a nightmare. The incessant yells of "Hey, baby," and other more anatomically graphic remarks, the whistles and other simianlike sounds some men seem to spend an inordinate amount of time perfecting, all these infuriated me and kept me constantly on the defensive. Now that doesn't happen anymore—and I love it. I can walk—no comments; I can jog—no comments; I can walk along the beach—no leers. My eye bags and my "cellulite" are now my friends, my protectors, my armor, and I love them for that. At the same time, part of me will always want to sandpaper them off.

Then there's the love-hate relationship with the eye bags. No woman wants to look like George Shultz after a bad night, but a woman's facial lines are the story of her life. I got mine from pulling too many all-nighters in college, from smoking pot, from drinking tequila with my brother and champagne with my husband, from baking way too long in the sun, from putting in sixty-hour workweeks, from having a child unfamiliar with the concept of sleep, and, of course, from growing older. They've tracked my joys and sorrows, my failures and successes, and I'm supposed to want to chop them off so I can look like an empty vessel, a bimbette? Besides, my husband, who hates it when his favorite actresses get face-lifts and don't look like themselves anymore, likes them. They go with his; they're a team.

So here's the question, girls. And it's one you guys should consider too as Grecian Formula, Clinique, and Soloflex eye your sagging faces and bodies greedily. What if every woman in America woke up tomorrow and simply decided that she was happy with the way she looked? She might exercise to keep herself healthy, and get some Vaseline Intensive Care from CVS to soothe her dry skin, but, basically, that would be the extent of it. Think of the entire multibillion-dollar industries that would crumble. This is one of the reasons lesbians are so vilified—many of them have already made this choice, thereby costing the beauty industry millions. If women decided in the war between feminism and antifeminism being waged in skin-care and diet soda ads that antifeminism had way too big an advantage, women might decide to shift the odds a bit. For example, they might decide to take the $42.50 for skin caviar or skin Spackle and send it, instead, to the Fund for the Feminist Majority, the International Red Cross, the Children's Defense Fund, or some other organization that works for the benefit of women and children.

The reason this won't happen is that advertising, women's magazines, movies, and TV shows have been especially effective in alienating women from their faces and bodies. Women of all ages, who are perfectly capable of denouncing sexist news coverage, or making their own empowering and subversive meanings out of TV shows and films, find it extremely difficult to resist the basic tenet that a face with lines or a thigh with dimples means you are worthless. The media's relentlessly coercive deployment of perfect faces and bodies, and the psychologically, politically, and economically punitive measures taken against women who fail to be young, thin, and beautiful, have intersected seamlessly with age-old American ideals about the work ethic, being productive, and being deserving of rewards. The "I'm Worth It" campaign and all its allies and imitators co-opt the feminist effort to promote female self-esteem to reassure women that, deep down, they aren't worth it at all. The same women who have been able to find feminist empowerment in the most unlikely places—from Harry Reasoner's editorials to Krystle and Alexis's cat-fights—find nothing but self-hatred and disempowerment here. Of all the disfigure-ments of feminism, this, perhaps, has been the most effective.

NOTES

1. For a funny and very smart discussion of elite culture in the 1980s see Debora Silver-man, *Selling Culture: Bloomingdale's, Diana Vreeland and the New Aristocracy of Taste in Reagan's America* (New York: Pantheon. 1986).

2. Naomi Wolf, *The Beauty Myth* (New York: Doubleday, 1991). p. 109.

3. Ibid., p. 99.

4. Melissa Stanton, "Looking After Your Looks," *Glamour*, August 1993, p. 233.

5. "A Better Butt, Fast!" and "Why 15 Million Women Own Guns" in *Glamour*, May 1993. p. 270ff and p. 260ff.

6. Wolf, *The Beauty Myth*, p. 232.

Chapter Sixteen

"Young T'ing Is the Name of the Game"
Sexual Dynamics in a Caribbean Romantic Fiction Series

Jane Bryce

In 1993 a new romantic fiction series appeared in the Caribbean, modeled on the British series Mills and Boon but specifically aimed at readers in the region. The English publisher, Heinemann, had spotted the potential for a local version of mass market romance, and invited writers in the English-speaking Caribbean to try their hand. Caribbean Caresses were the result. Identical in format to Mills and Boon, the titles of the six-volume series apparently challenge nothing in their bland invocation of stereotype (*Fantasy of Love, Love in Hiding, Merchant of Dreams, Heartaches and Roses, Sun Valley Romance* and *Hand in Hand*). The crucial difference is the covers. Where regular romance readers are accustomed to seeing white heroines, all the couples depicted on the front of the Caribbean Caresses are dark-skinned: of the six, four are obviously African, one obviously East Indian, and one of the couples shows the influence of the different racial groups which have historically occupied Trinidad. This simple difference alone signals innovation. But it is when we proceed beyond the covers that really interesting deviations begin to emerge.

Romantic fiction is the most conservative and stereotypical of literature forms, and at the same time one of the most potentially subversive. It is bound by rules which derive from the medieval European chivalric code, with its highly conventional and idealized concept of the relationship between the sexes, known as Courtly Love. Central to the convention is the idea of the Lady, who represents an ideal version of femininity which, filtered through a repressive Victorian morality became in turn the Angel in the House—restricted to the domestic sphere, virginal or maternal, nurturing, forbearing, submissive and pure. This myth of desirable femininity still, against all the odds, exerts its influence today, even in unlikely contexts. The Jamaican writer Erna Brodber, documenting stereotypes in the Caribbean, describes the appearance of "Excellent Ellen" in the Jamaican *Daily Gleaner* of 1834, whose characteristics—of delicacy, paleness, tact, diffidence and submissive suffering—were even then far from the norm for Jamaican women, whether white or black (Brodber 1982: 22). The Barbados *Advocate* in 1950 reprinted a report entitled "A Husband's Dream," on the selection by a French club for the introduction of "bachelors to prospective brides," of their "Household Pearl of 1950" (p. 15). Brodber, having detailed the ways in which Barbadian women did not conform to this domestic ideal, goes on to show how, by the 1970s, "Upwardly mobile women have become willing to design their lives to fit the stereotypes which, with economic progress, [have] entered creole culture as an alternative course of behavior for women and which they have obviously internalized" (p. 21). This image, which—in its various guises of Lady, Excellent Ellen or Household Pearl— is fundamentally a European cultural icon, becomes, in the Caribbean setting, at best a travesty, at worst a repressive mechanism for the devaluing of other, more realistic, attributes of women. The Lady, above all, is white. In her guise of romantic heroine she may be found on Caribbean beaches, attracting the gaze of the white hero, while a black waiter offers them exotic cocktails. How is she transformed into the dark-skinned, Caribbean heroines of the Caribbean Caresses? Is it just a matter of internalizing the stereotype, a process which could perhaps be seen as the literary equivalent of hair-straightening or skin-lightening? Or do these novels attempt something more subversive?

Lorna Skeete, the heroine of *Merchant of Dreams*, is a hard-working advertising executive. Her search for a male model for an Atlas Stout commercial brings her face to face with a picture of Damien Bradshaw, "a gorgeous hunk" she briefly fantasizes over, before reminding herself severely that "great-looking guys like Mr Damien Bradshaw didn't usually have much time for girls who looked like Lorna Skeete. 'Young t'ing' was the name of the game" (p. 12). Lorna's description is uncompromising: "Her round, dark brown face looked back at her. She wore no make-up or jewelry except for a pair of plain pearl studs in her ears. Oh, dear, she really ought to lose some weight again, she thought and went out of the door" (p. 3).

Lorna, it turns out, is a contradictory character. Ambitious, talented and confident at work (though underpaid and exploited), she is prey to insecurity when it comes to men. Having successfully dodged the cultural expectations that dictate particular professions (nursing and teaching, for example) as being appropriately "feminine," Lorna retains a surprising level of vulnerability in her emotional life. This shows up in her now ended relationship with Colin, in which "she was so happy that this big, beautiful, sexy man was all hers, when he could have had any number of pretty young chicks just by looking at them" (p. 13), that she doesn't notice he's using her until it hits her in the face. Needless to say, this lack of self-esteem is the major factor in her failure to realize the Hero is serious about her. How could he be, when pretty "slim t'ing" Gillian is all over him in her tiny pink bikini? How is she to know that here is one man who likes women to have a brain, and appreciates a full bosom and muscular legs? Lorna's blind spot is, moreover, very convenient in terms of the romantic formula, which decrees that there must always be an Obstacle in the way of true love. *Merchant of Dreams* quite consciously (perhaps the title is less innocent than it appears) plays with the romantic formula, exposing the gap between Real and Ideal, turning stereotypes upside down and in the process, pointing toward the possibility of a different way of doing things.

The gap between the Real and the Ideal has been noted by researchers in other contexts than romantic fiction. Merle Hodge, introducing Brodber's study of stereotypes, extends her findings, drawn from the church and the press, to literature. The Caribbean novel, she suggests, is marked by "the tension between official and real culture," which she sees as "a permanent feature of Caribbean culture, and the discrepancy between Ideal Woman and Real Woman documented by Brodber is but one aspect of this phenomenon" (Brodber 1982: viii). In a similar vein, Olive Senior, another Jamaican writer and researcher, observes that

> the vacillation in women's behaviour might be seen as expressing the dichotomy of their cultural inheritance, where the stereotypes are European (protected/dominated female) but the role models and role performance are West African (woman as independent actor). Thus part of the vacillation arises from contradictions within the society itself. (Senior 1991: 180)

In this sense, then, the heroine of *Merchant of Dreams* is "realistic," since her behavior reproduces this vacillation between European stereotype (slim, dependent) and West African role model (pragmatic, independent). Yet there is a danger in seeking to demonstrate the Real in what is, after all, a fantasy form. If the gap between Real and Ideal exerts an alienating effect in the lives of actual ("real") women, the fictional heroines of *Caribbean Caresses* are inevitably at one further remove. The extent to which they can claim to be more "real" than Western romance heroines is therefore a function of reader response and identification, and of the genre itself. Possibly the most that can be said is that the series, by envisaging a *new* Ideal, is closer to the Real than most Western mass market romance, at least as far as Caribbean readers are concerned. Yet most "real" of all, as Brodber and Senior indicate, is, not the resolution, but the tension between the two. The difference between the female protagonists of "serious" contemporary West Indian fiction (by writers who include the researchers from whom I quote in this article), and *Caribbean Caresses* heroines, is that, while the former negotiate this tension in a variety of ways, including leaving the Caribbean, the latter do, ultimately, resolve it in marriage. This resolution, however, is by no means a wholesale capitulation to the romantic stereotype, but part of a larger utopian vision, of which gender equality is metonymic. This revisioning of social reality, with all its attendant tensions and contradictions, is a partial answer to Olive Senior when she posits: "A fundamental question is: what is the ideal of womanhood that is being projected and absorbed in the Caribbean today?"

To answer this question more fully, I intend to examine the representations of women and men in the *Caribbean Caresses* series—particularly the heroines and heroes—to see how far they are determined by prevailing stereotypes and to what extent they rework them and thus subvert the formula. This exercise would be quite pointless if I did not share the view, put forward by Karin Barber, that popular culture does more than merely reflect social norms; it also contributes to shaping them (Barber 1987). The fundamental characteristic of popular formulaic genres, whether horror movies, love lyrics or romantic fiction, is their predictability, and much of the pleasure of these forms of entertainment is derived precisely from the fact that their devotees know what to expect and get it, with the resulting sense of fulfillment and resolution. Caribbean Caresses would fail as romantic fiction if they did not overtly adhere to the formula, including obstacles in the way of love, and a happy ending. What is interesting about them, however, is the way their attempt to transplant the formula to the Caribbean context works against the straightforward reproduction of stereotypes, and results in significant deviations which, in turn, point to a changing social consciousness.

Real and Ideal: Exploring the Tension

The relocation of romantic fiction from a Western to a West Indian frame necessitates an ontological, as well as a geographical shift. The Caribbean, along with numerous other non-Western locations, from "the jungles of Borneo" to "the deserts of North Africa," features in conventional romantic fiction as a site of the exotic. However diverse these settings, they are all marked by the same characteristics of sensuousness and latent danger, which typify the "non-civilized world." The logic of the series of oppositions implicit in conventional romance—Western/other, familiar/exotic, civilized/wild, home/away—disintegrates the moment the focus of subjectivity shifts from white Western outsider to native of the exotic territory: suddenly "other" becomes self, exotic becomes familiar, and "away" becomes the site of "home" itself. And yet, since it is part of the formula and therefore a source of pleasure for the reader, some of the old logic must be retained—a sense of escape from the everyday, of lurking danger, of the otherness which is an essential part of the experience of being in love. How is this simultaneous conformity and deviation accomplished by Caribbean Caresses? What sort of world do the protagonists of these novels inhabit, and to what extent does it participate in the dichotomy of Real and Ideal?

Olive Senior, summing up aspects of "woman's 'true' situation" in the Caribbean, points to the progress of younger women in particular:

> There are in some of our larger cities and towns numbers of highly visible, well-dressed, apparently self-confident women, who in their lifestyles and manner appear to have gained equality with their male counterparts. The majority of these women are young, well educated and largely from the middle class or have adopted a middle class lifestyle. (Senior 1991: 187)

This is without doubt the group to which the Caribbean Caresses heroines belong—professional, independent, educated, and highly motivated to succeed. Their occupations include dress designer, advertising executive, adult education project worker, flower shop owner (businesswoman), linguistics researcher and personal assistant. None of them, however, comes from a particularly privileged background. Typically, they are from "ordinary" families, and fully aware of the interrelationship of class and poverty, as anyone in the Caribbean must be. Giselle of *Sun Valley Romance*, for instance, the dress designer, is forced to give up her university career when her family can no longer support her, and, though she falls back on her own artistic talent, dressmaking is also a traditional feminine skill inherited from her mother. Lorna of *Merchant of Dreams*, the advertising executive, far from finding her profession glamorous, is exploited by her boss, underpaid and subjected to large amounts of routine drudgery. John Gilmore, alias Lucille Colleton, her creator, is explicit about the extent to which he sought to invoke the Real over the Ideal in his representation of Lorna and her working life. He wanted, he says,

> to present a somewhat more realistic view of the Caribbean [as] a place where people are getting on with things in an ordinary manner. The heroine is the creative director in an advertising agency and there's a lot of routine work which has to be done to deadlines, a lot of pressure and very little glamour.[1]

Similarly, asked about the role reversal whereby the heroine of his novel hires the hero as a model, Gilmore/Colleton claims this is a deliberate reference to the fact that "in Caribbean society you get a lot of professional women who make their way in the world because they have to and I wanted to use this for my heroine." What Gilmore is pointing to here is both the fact that West Indian women have been traditionally self-supporting, and to the ongoing reality that reliance on a man is for most of them simply not an option, romantic fantasy notwithstanding. The implication of this for the relationships which drive the narratives is that, implicit in the heroine's choice of a man, marriage and romantic resolution, is an insistence on gender equality, rather than swooning submission. Valerie Belgrave, author of *Sun Valley Romance*, maintains that while "you can hardly have a romance in a setting of great poverty and suffering," there is still the potential for subversion of what she sees as an essentially middle-class form:

> One of the things is to subvert the conflict of dominance and subservience by the woman. I try to strengthen the harmonising of the sexes, to lessen the antagonism between the hero and the heroine, to make the heroine have a career, to have her family and the socio-political situation be of importance, and to do all this while maintaining the romantic canon [*sic*] to a large extent.

It would seem, then, that these authors' self-conscious use of the romance form is partly an effect of their positioning as West Indians, for whom representation is not only a matter of "reflecting reality" but also an act of reclamation. In their context, the formula cannot be employed innocently, for it invites interrogation every step of the way. An attempt to insert the Real into the artificial conventions of the romance form is part of that interrogation.

Apart from work and the construction of a specific notion of femininity, other aspects of the Real may be traced in such factors as the attention given in the series as a whole to family, community, local cultural manifestations such as Carnival, and the importance of all these in creating a sense of place, and ultimately a sense of identity. Nor is this is a question of isolated individualism, as is so often the case with formula romances in exotic settings, where the couple are divorced from their familiar environments, including family ties. A distinct sense of national pride emerges from the specificity of place, custom and language—the subdued but nonetheless assertive use of creole inflections within a largely standard English narrative. Beyond these manifestations of cultural specificity, how far does the Real inform the driving narrative force of Caribbean Caresses: love between a man and a woman?

"Rip, Torn, Stretch and Kick Apart"

Romantic fiction is quintessentially about love: love realized, love triumphant, mutual, monogamous, faithful, till death us do part. This construction of love is idealistic in any context, and the Caribbean is no exception. Love as an aspiration is, however, given a different inflection in a context where, according to social science studies of West Indian gender relations, the attitudes of the sexes to each other are predominantly negative. In her study "Male Images of Women in Barbados," Christine Barrow finds, "the Barbadian male image of today's women is almost totally negative" (Barrow 1986: 61). "Young women of today," in contrast to an "idealised view of how women were in the past," are seen as no longer subservient or submissive. Rather, they are "out fulfilling their own ambitions and desires," as a result of which they have become "aggressive, ugly and 'flashy', no longer deserving of the respect (men) allege was traditionally accorded to women" (p. 60). At the same time, the men participating in the survey "argued that Caribbean man perceives women as existing for his sexual pleasure"; they also claimed that women are avaricious, and see men primarily in terms of financial gain (p. 58). This means that to love a woman "is to be 'foolish' and vulnerable," since "if a woman say she love you, it is something you have that she want" (p. 59). In these circumstances, love will inevitably be "rip, torn, stretch and kick apart" (p. 60).[2]

On the other side, Olive Senior (1991), examining "general views of male-female behaviour" in her chapter "Women and Men," finds "women citing certain negative behaviors on the part of men which our informants almost seem to take for granted as part of the male repertoire: unreliability, infidelities, and a wide range of oppressions including physical violence, humiliation, mental cruelty, drunkenness, desertion, financial irresponsibility, etc" (p. 166). Senior also cites Merle Hodge's view that "the whole range of mental cruelty [from men] is part and parcel of women's experience in the Caribbean" (p. 167), and ponders that, in the light of these complaints, "the Caribbean woman seems to 'put up with a lot' from her man" (p. 170). Senior's examination of women in the whole range of available relationships—as "outside women" of married men, in sharing partnerships, often with parallel families, as well as, less commonly, as wives—reveals a contradictory tendency on the part of women to pursue an Ideal which is all too rarely realized. She concludes that women are in quest of "warmth, love and tenderness," and their "emotional vulnerability lies precisely in this desire for satisfactory 'relationships' and a susceptibility to male charms, despite everything" (p. 179).

What is striking is the extent to which the heroes and heroines of Caribbean Caresses, the very "young women of today" of whom the men in Barrow's study speak so disparagingly, and their love objects, fail to conform to these prevailing norms or stereotypes. In the "world of Caribbean romance" created by the novels, such features of Caribbean society as male violence, unfaithfulness and the "outside woman" phenomenon are absent, as are teenage pregnancies, conflict with parents, and, to a large extent, sex. Using these parameters, the novels could be deemed to be quite unrealistic. Reading them another way, however, it's possible that the very way the romantic formula translates into the Caribbean context, is informed and shaped by the kind of presuppositions about gender roles and behavior pointed to by Barrow, Senior, Brodber and Hodge. Citing Hermione McKenzie, Senior suggests that the dissatisfaction shown by both sexes toward the prevailing status quo is driven by a need for an elusive Something Other: "In a social structure which so often defeats fidelity and tenderness, the shift from partner to partner by both men and women may still be seen as a persistent quest for exactly these qualities in a relationship" (p. 179). Caribbean Caresses' lovers, then, are only removed from the Real in that they actually *attain* fidelity and tenderness. The obstacles in the way of their doing so may arise in part from the generalized distrust already noted, negative previous experiences, contradictions between appearances and reality, and the failure to credit behavior which deviates from the stereotype as real.

The obstacles which, according to formulaic convention, create difficulties for the lovers, often consist in a misunderstanding, such as the hero being seen with another woman he seems to be involved with, or his suppressed desire for the heroine coming out in brutish behavior. Caribbean Caresses follow this convention fairly closely, with a narrative pattern emerging as follows: the heroine's experience with another man has put her on her guard toward the hero, who is, nonetheless, quite recognizable to the reader. This other man is, therefore, not-the-hero. Because of this experience, when the hero is seen with another woman, she instantly constitutes the Obstacle. The heroine's refusal to be used or strung along by the hero is one of the ways Caribbean Caresses work against the social stereotype, which decrees that men are intrinsically unfaithful and women must take what they get. In this way, the novels not only conform to, but also manipulate the formula so as to speak to a specifically Caribbean context.

To take one example, Erica, the heroine of *Fantasy of Love*, is first seen in the company of Mark, her escort at a party where he is ignoring her. Erica longs to dance, but can only tug gently at his arm, "knowing if his friends noticed they'd laugh and tease him, saying that she was trying to control him" (p. 1). Mark, a "typical" Caribbean man in his need for control and his sensitivity to peer group opinion, is instantly signaled as not-the-hero. His subsequent behaviour bears this out—his annoyance when Erica shows him up by lying down at the party, his casual ordering of her to collect him a plate of food, his duplicity and two-timing of Erica, which finally makes her retort, "Men [are] something else again. All of them" (p. 69). Meanwhile, although she misrecognizes him, the tall, dark stranger who watches Erica at the party definitely is the hero. We know this by his sensitivity, the way he takes care of Erica when Mark is neglecting her, his teasing of her which she takes for arrogance ("all men were the same . . . unreliable . . . spoilt" [p. 5]), and above all his effect on the heroine. Apart from noticing his "beautiful warm brown eyes . . . a clear contrast to his ebony skin . . . the strength of his arms and shoulders . . ." (p. 12), "she didn't feel intimidated by him. He didn't make her feel small and insecure . . . she was spurred on, her mind racing ahead to match wits with him" (p. 14). In other words, he is *not* the typical West Indian man, and this is borne out at a further meeting, where Erica discovers he is in fact Dr. Julian Baird, her project consultant, and that he is black British.

A not uncommon feature of the Caribbean Caresses hero is that he has been in some way removed from the Caribbean, so that he is simultaneously a part of the heroine's society, and also different, marked by his experience abroad. Gary, hero of *Sun Valley Romance*, has been educated in England, with the result, he claims, that he is "more of a free thinker than a capitalist leader" (p. 69), a trained architect with "finesse and sensitivity and who loved art and beautiful things" (p. 86). In the house he designed himself, he appears "wiping his hands on a kitchen towel. The little domestic gesture pulled at her heart" (p. 67). Like Erica, Giselle, heroine of *Sun Valley Romance*, is taken by "the lack of mockery, the absence of the desire to master her that she had known in other men" (p. 74). Ironically, it is Gary's idealism and sheltered class position which conspire to blind him to the depredations being wrought on Giselle's village by one of the companies in his conglomerate. It is through his association with Giselle that he is awakened to the reality of class conflict, poverty and powerlessness, and their effects on people's lives. More down-to-earth, Damien of *Merchant of Dreams*, impresses Lorna, apart from being a "hunk," by the fact that he sells for a living, forcing her to acknowledge "this guy's got more than good looks—you've got to have drive and initiative for a job like that" (p. 63). Like Julian and Gary, his winning card is his lack of machismo and his ability to put the heroine at her ease: "It made such a change to find a man who talked about his failures as well as his successes" (p. 64).

The profile of the Ideal Man that begins to emerge is one which deviates sharply from the stereotypical West Indian man. He is sensitive, caring, domesticated, trustworthy, straightforward and easy to talk to, and accepts the heroine as she is. The heroine's inability to believe he is all these things, and her readiness to see him as a user and manipulator, is perhaps testimony to the power of the very stereotype to which he does not conform. This has a great deal to do with the socialization of Caribbean men, and a construction of masculinity which almost requires men to adopt a hard-bitten and exploitative attitude to women. Social science studies suggest that the relative absence of fathers as role models for boys growing up is a defining factor in male behavior. Senior posits: "The paradigm of absent father, omniscient mother, is central to the ordering and psyche of the Caribbean family," the mother's power resulting in an ambivalent relationship with women, both fearful and resentful (Senior 1991: 8). Julian of *Fantasy of Love* exemplifies this attitude when he comments drily: "Ah, the indomitable West Indian woman again, I have no doubt" (p. 42). This sore point is explained at the end of the novel by an elderly relation describing his parents' relationship: "Julian feels that she dominated his father too much, she controlled him. The marriage eventually broke up and Julian hasn't seen much of him over the years. He has always seen his mother as the typical strong, controlling West Indian woman" (p. 135). Again the stereotype interposes itself between hero and heroine, exerting a negative effect.

The "paradigmatic ordering" pointed to by Senior is reproduced in the typical Caribbean Caresses family. Two of the heroines have lost both parents, one being brought up by her grandmother; two have lost their fathers but live with their mothers, one with a stepfather; Erica's mother features but her father is asthmatic and plays no role, and Lorna regularly goes to her mother's for Sunday lunch, but her father is absent. In *Sun Valley Romance*, Gary's father is dead and his stepfather is "presently unwell" and does not appear. His mother, however, is formidable: "Gloria Henshaw was one of the wealthiest women on the island of Trinidad, as clever at keeping her glamorous image as she was in her business ventures," one of the first black beauty queens, a poor girl who married two rich husbands and now requires that her son, Gary, run her business empire (p. 11). Part of the drama of the novel lies in her attempt to dictate to Gary, and his eventual standing up to her. The heroine Giselle's stepfather is an example of a "bad" West Indian man, shiftless and bullying, always at loggerheads with her brother, Garnet, but who reforms through participation in the community's resistance to the mining conglomerate which threatens the village. Probably the most deliberately negative masculine characterization is that of Randy (not-the-hero) of *Heartaches and Roses*, who controls and exploits all three of the women in his life—Betty, his fiancée, his aging mother and his secretary, Susan, who is also his "outside woman." Having convinced Betty that, having had a hysterectomy, no one else will want to marry her, he then persuades his mother to move into Betty's house, ostensibly for her greater comfort and safety, but actually so that so he can use the rent from her own house to pay for his mistress. All this becomes apparent when Betty visits his office and overhears Randy and Susan in conversation about his mother. Susan wants her sent to a home, to which Randy replies: "My mother worked very hard for many years to support me, and I would like to be able to take care of her when she's old" (p. 98). He explains to Susan that since she (Susan) refuses to take care of mother, he is prepared to marry Betty, who "really loved and cared for her own mother, and that's one thing I've always admired about her" (p. 99). When Susan points out that what the old lady really wants is grandchildren, Randy responds: "I'm certainly planning to have a few. I can assure you, before mother gets much older, she'll see her first grandchild" (p. 99). Randy's breathtaking selfishness and casual sexual exploitativeness epitomize stereotypical West Indian male behavior, behavior which must also be partly attributable to his mother's over-indulgence of her precious son. All three women are represented as being in competition for his economic and/or sexual favors, and the mother, at least, endorses this power relationship when she comments: "I hope my son will be able to control his wife" (p. 100). How closely this approximates the Real may once more be assessed by comparison with the evidence from social science, as for example this statement from one of Graham Dann's respondents in *The Barbadian Male: Sexual Attitudes and Practices*: "I think a woman should always be under the man. A man should always be over she" (Dann 1987: 52), or the following comment from pastoral counselor Neilson Waithe's study, *Caribbean Sexuality*: "The belief that men must satisfy their sexual urges, and women want men to be in control of them, are motivating factors in the approach to sexuality of the Caribbean male" (Waithe 1993: 53).

It is highly significant of course that the masculine representation which approximates most closely to the Real is, not the hero but quite the reverse, the monitory image of an exploiter from whom the heroine is rescued by her alliance with the true hero. Yet even among the hero-figures, elements of the stereotype may be found, which quite naturally contribute to the heroine's confusion over whether he is, in fact, a hero. In *Love in Hiding*, the heroine, Rena, is an orphan brought up by her grandmother. Thierry is the boy next door, whom she idolized as a big brother until he was sent away to Canada to become an engineer, returning years later intent on marrying her. Unfortunately, as she is already involved with the gentlemanly Raj, he feels unable to reveal this to her, and concentrates instead on interfering in her life, telling her what to do and demonstrating his sexual power over her, in a way which borders on the sadistic. The fact that he is able to do so speaks to the vacillation between Real and Ideal noted by Brodber *et al.*, for it evidently reforms Rena's behavior and self-concept. Most notably, she is obsessively afraid of being thought a "tramp," and construes her sexual response to Thierry as coming dangerously close to this undesirable feminine stereotype. At his 21st birthday party, when she is 15, Thierry rescues Rena from a drunken older boy, but promptly turns the blame on her: "What the hell are you trying to do? Incite rape? My god! You're going to stop behaving like a tramp," whereupon he proceeds to "administer four hard slaps to her rear" (p. 8). This scene is described in language implicitly suggestive of rape, with Thierry "making her look at him by holding her chin while the fingers of his other hand tangled in her hair to keep her head just where he wanted it," while she listens to him with "streaming eyes, bitten lips, torn dress and misery she couldn't conceal" (p. 9). This relationship of dominance and submission continues at work, where she finds he is now her boss, insists on driving her to work, carries her into the house, undresses her, and generally acts the role of protective elder brother/jealous lover. Thierry is characterized by his "raw animal magnetism" (p. 32) and his "tiger's eyes" (repeatedly). Rena is alternately helpless victim and rebellious convent schoolgirl (her last resort is in fact to run away back to her convent in Barbados with the intention of joining the order, from which she is saved at the last minute by Thierry's arrival). In this novel, sex is both a woman's most precious gift to a man, and the source of her vulnerability, used as a weapon against Rena by Thierry, whose "response" opens her up to male power and the possibility of abuse:

> Then he kissed her angrily. She fought him silently. Her teeth ground together to prevent his entry. His teeth savaged her lips and she was forced to open her mouth. She would have bruises tomorrow. Then he was plundering the sweetness of her mouth. His kiss had changed. He no longer sought to punish and she felt the heat shooting through her. At her total response he went wild. Then he suddenly seized her wrists in a grasp that hurt and pushed her away. (p. 84)

Again, the language here is suggestive of rape, but when she starts to submit, he withdraws, leaving her disheveled and panting. The extent of his power over her may be seen when Rena announces her engagement to Raj. Thierry reacts furiously, ordering her to come and stand in front of him with a mixture of suppressed sexual arousal and latent violence, to which she responds with absolute submission: "She walked slowly towards him in the manner of a sacrificial maiden aware that he willed her to come to him. Those few steps were the hardest she had ever had to take, but she made it, and stood before him with bowed head" (p. 65). Given the reality of male violence, and in the context of the earlier scene where he actually beat her, this passage carries a very uneasy sub-textual message.

The construction of the hero in this novel is a long way from the gentle, sensitive, caring men of most of the others, or indeed from Raj, Rena's fiancé, who plays Edgar to Thierry's Heathcliff. Like Heathcliff, Thierry is, significantly, also a brother figure, as is Andel, hero of *Hand in Hand*, who has, like Thierry, known the heroine as a child, gone abroad and returned years later. Experience overseas marks the hero as older and more worldly than the heroine, and Andel too is in possession of a secret to which he alone holds the key. Unlike Thierry, however, he is a revisionary hero—gentle, protective, responsible, patient and faithful. What most obviously links the hero figures though, beyond coincidences of plot, is of course their single-minded attraction to the heroine, their ability to discriminate even when surrounded by beautiful women, and their steadfastness, which wins them the prize in the end. In a context, as already described by Hermione McKenzie, "which so often defeats fidelity and tenderness," and makes multiple relationships almost inevitable, this must be read as a quite deliberate reconstruction of the stereotypical philandering male. Who then are the women fortunate enough to attract these unrepresentative men?

As already mentioned, while all the heroines are West Indian women, four are African, one East Indian and one deliberately unspecified. It is expected of a romantic heroine that she will be beautiful, but the question of what actually constitutes beauty is not so easily answered. In a context where the Western stereotype—slim, delicate, blonde, white skinned—exerts its sway via the media, beauty contests, Barbie, even the dark-skinned Pocahontas, romance authors are faced once again with the necessity of deliberate reconstruction, although they have chosen different strategies to accomplish this. Betty of *Heartaches* and *Roses*, for example, answers most closely to a conventionally held notion of attractiveness, even while her blackness is emphasized: "long, dark lashes enhancing a pair of sleepy, slanting brown eyes . . . a small, round nose and lips as rosy as a ripe mango in a round, smooth face black hair braided into a bundle of small plaits . . . her body was slim and lithe" (p. 24). The physical characteristics of Khadija of *Hand in Hand*, are given to us in the context of her morning run along the beach, "her waist length black hair streaming behind her as she pounded down the edge of the surf, practising her Spanish grammar as she ran" (p. 1). Dressing for a date with the hero, she laughs at herself for going to so much trouble—the implication being that she usually has more important things on her mind: "Her outfit was a shalawar in royal blue silk which brought out her well-defined brows and deep sparkling brown eyes . . . (she) swept her silky black hair up and coiled it around in a neat roll. She secured it with a brass comb and two black lacquered chopsticks" (p. 21). Again, the details emphasize a specific cultural background, here East Indian, and while she is undoubtedly alluring, the author takes pains not to objectify or exoticize her, by giving her sister a comic reaction: "Ay, ay, girl! You going to kill the man!" (p. 21). This is a difficult line to tread, when romance fiction has traditionally characterized dark-skinned, dark-haired beauty as the exotic Other of fair, pale-skinned, golden-haired, etc. Giselle, of *Sun Valley Romance*, has to contend with a white-skinned rival referred to as Gary's "Carnival blonde": "an exceptional beauty . . . the exotic look of a perfectly tanned skin contrasted with the long blonde hair that framed her face and fell down her back like a golden waterfall" (p. 80). Giselle herself is constructed as a quintessentially Caribbean beauty, most notably at Carnival, jumping with a band called, emblematically, the Barbaric Warriors: "The choice of costume with its heavily 'ethnic' look suited her exotic beauty . . . made her appear regal and distant and added to the effect of sensuous, savage beauty" (p. 41). The problem of revisioning physical attractiveness in a specific cultural context is demonstrated here by the way the description, while consciously invoking a Carib past, teeters danger-ously on the brink of exotic stereotype.

Apart from the somewhat ambivalent question of physical appearance, the her-oine is characterized in all these novels as deviating conspicuously from the Sexual and Economic Exploiter stereotype. She is, typically, a self-supporting, professional woman who need not rely on a man financially, even though a number of the heroes are richer and can offer her social and material elevation. Her need for a man is therefore primarily emotional and, to a lesser extent, sexual, but the true heroine, though beautiful, never flaunts herself, and, though passionate, never loses control. In this she conforms fairly closely to the Ideal, or, to put it another way, to the Western-inspired Lady stereotype. Other women may use their bodies to try and attract the hero, but the true hero remains impervious, preferring the innocence, the unspoilt charm of the heroine.

We have already looked at the way Lorna of *Merchant of Dreams* makes few concessions to stereotypical femininity, while still being insecure about her power to attract. Along the continuum the heroines represent, Lorna is the most deliber-ately non-conformist, as we see in relation to her celebration of her blackness. Out on a shoot in the hot sun, Damien offers her lotion, which she refuses bluntly, all too conscious of Gillian, the model, with her "flawless golden brown skin": "Look, I'm not one of those people who are afraid of the sun making them too black, you know" (p. 23).[3] There is an obvious ironic inversion here, since what they are shooting is an ad for Atlas Stout, and the ubiquitous beer posters which adorn the walls of rum shops in the Caribbean invariably favor fair-skinned models, or dark-skinned women lit in such a way as to *appear* fair. Lorna moreover is shown tucking into her mother's lunch of "pork chops, fried plantain and sweet potato pie," classic West Indian cooking, even while she worries about its effect on her figure (p. 34). The novel incorporates and plays with the tension between Real and Ideal, both in its construction of the heroine's subjectivity, and in relation to her professional function as a "merchant of dreams" as analogous with the romance form itself. The author deliberately exposes the mechanisms underlying fantasy, whether that of advertising or of romantic fiction, by realistic descriptions of the techniques used to create the illusion. At work, for example, Lorna and others are shown to be at the mercy of unscrupulous employers, with no recourse to outside arbitration:

> Being an executive meant working all hours on evenings, plus weekends and bank holidays. She'd never actually worked on Christmas Day, but two years running she'd had to come into the office on Boxing Day. The junior artists got paid overtime, though it always seemed to be next to nothing, but executives didn't. (p. 49)

Lorna recalls the annual Christmas party, where everyone receives a bottle of rum which she suspects comes free from a client of the agency, and the time an account executive asked the boss for "some of the twelve-year-old Scotch whisky he was drinking," and promptly got the sack (p. 50).

What the heroines *do* is integral to their characterization, though, in accordance with the Real, their jobs are far from being glamorized. As Olive Senior testifies: "Many women in high executive and administrative positions have got the opportunity to be there because they are willing to accept far less in salaries and perquisites and operate under conditions that men of much lesser qualifications and capabilities would consider insulting" (Senior 1991: 191). Erica of *Fantasy of Love* works on an adult education project aimed at three groups of women: rural women, women in prison and higglers. Though these women barely appear, apart from as supporting extras in a scene where Erica takes Julian to a market, the fact that they are visible at all points to the relatively privileged position of the project workers, and to the social and economic hierarchy to which they too are subject. At a meeting with the board Erica observes: "They were all men, all grey-haired, all wearing glasses . . . men in charge on one side of the table, women implementing on the other" (p. 19). Compounding this imbalance is the fact that the consultant is a foreigner, so that, when challenged by him, Erica defends herself and her project with nationalistic fervor: "The nature of Jamaicans is such, Dr Baird, that they are always willing to surpass their wildest dreams" (p. 80). Betty of *Heartaches and Roses* is attracted to the hero, who runs a hotel in Tobago, partly because, like her, he is a businessperson. His proposal of marriage is entwined with a discussion of how much money Betty would lose if she didn't go back to her flower shop, and part of what brings them together finally is her skill as an accountant, which enables her to keep the hotel going when he is in hospital after an accident. Giselle of *Sun Valley Romance* also ends up with her own business, and learns very quickly how to defend herself against exploitation by the formidable Gloria Henshaw, whose guise of fairy godmother conceals pragmatic self-interest: "It was all so miraculous, like a fairy tale. How lucky she was! But, just as she was starting to express her appreciation and gratitude, Mrs. Henshaw, 'the patron', turned into Mrs. Henshaw 'the shrewd businesswoman' "(p. 76). These examples demonstrate one of the most significant features of the construction of femininity in the Caribbean Caresses series, and one which is closer to Real than Ideal. As always, though, Real and Ideal are in tension, and nowhere more so than in the heroines' relationship to sexuality.

The Heinemann authors' guidelines for the series are quite specific on this score, and bring into focus questions of marketing, target audience and preconceptions as to what is or is not appropriate for young, mainly feminine readers in the Caribbean: "As we would hope to sell to the upper level of the school market, please treat any sex scenes carefully—you can lead your couple into the bedroom, and even into bed but suggestion, rather than explicit detail, says the rest." At least three of the authors agreed with this circumspection. Asked to comment, Annette Charles (*Love in Hiding*) responded that most family groups in Trinidad "still prefer girls to be innocent until they get married." Dorothy Jolly (*Heartaches and Roses*) agreed: "The way I was brought up, you get married and then you have sex, especially in a small country like Dominica." Annette Charles (*Love in Hiding*), whose heroine Rena is engaged to Raj, an East Indian, pointed out that in the Trinidadian Indian community it is still common for "a fellow to go to a dance and see a girl, and the next thing, he goes to the father and they arrange a marriage."[4] Valerie Belgrave (*Sun Valley Romance*) declared: "I myself am a good convent girl. I think one of the things about this book is that it's a wholesome book, and the characters are both wholesome so sex didn't come into the story."[5] Of the six heroines, three—Erica, Lorna and Khadija—do have sex by the end of the novel. Rena and Thierry end up in bed, but apparently confine themselves to passionate caresses. Betty could be assumed to be sexually experienced since she has been in and out of an engagement, but to what extent is never specified. Nonetheless, this sexual reticence is possibly the least realistic aspect of the novels, and certainly the one most complained about by readers I have canvassed.[6] Myra Murby, commissioning editor for the series, asked whether it could not have been a little more daring, responded: "We had to be very careful because the Caribbean is quite a moral place and certain things are definitely frowned upon . . . things that happen in Europe are not considered the thing in the Caribbean."[7] Though this may be true at the level of the Ideal, the evidence of social science research, popular culture, from calypso to dancehall, and the popularity of imported television serials and upper school-age fiction like the American series Sweet Valley High, is that, once again, Real and Ideal diverge quite sharply on the issue.

It appears that the Caribbean Caresses series can best be characterized as an experiment in negotiating the tension between Real and Ideal which plays so conspicuous a part in Caribbean life and fiction. In attempting to indigenize a Western formulaic genre, these little novels confront fundamental issues of identity, gender and sexuality, as well as the way these intersect with economic and social factors—access to education, types of work, status and independence. Implicit in their revisioning of gender relationships is a critique of both Real and Ideal, and the negative effects of these on the lives of women and men in the Caribbean. The fact that they answer to a felt need of many people is testified to here in a quotation from one of Olive Senior's respondents, described as "an Antiguan in her forties": "I don't think a woman can live without love . . . women need to be loved. I mean, when you're loved you feel wanted, you feel appreciated . . . you have somebody that you can talk to, you can exchange ideas with, you need a companion you know" (Senior 1991: 166).

NOTES

1. These remarks and those of Valerie Belgrave which follow, are taken from an interview with John Gilmore for the BBC Radio 3 program "Books Abroad," broadcast June 15, 1996.

2. In the Content and Methodology section of this paper, Barrow explains that it deals with "the images that two groups of Barbadian men have of women" and, "while it is likely that these images have crystallised into more widely held stereotypes . . . we were unable to investigate this in much detail. Neither were we able to examine the effect they have on women's self-image and performance, though we cannot deny that this occurs. These limitations result largely from the Focus Group Research Methodology which was considered the most appropriate within the severe time and resource constraints of the Women in the Caribbean Project" (Barrow 1986: 54). In other words, it is a very partial survey, but may be taken as part of a collective testimony, which would also include the group discussions drawn on by Earl Warner for his dramatization "Mantalk," shown in Barbados and Trinidad in 1995 and 1996 respectively, and reviewed by Jane Bryce in *Caribbean Week*, December 1995.

3. For this insight and others, I am grateful to my student Armel Drayton, whose paper, "Representations of Women in Selected Caribbean Romance," was submitted as part of her degree in English at the University of the West Indies, Cave Hill, in 1995.

4. The remarks quoted here by Dorothy Jolly and Annette Charles are taken from a joint interview with Jane Bryce, in the home of Dorothy Jolly in Valsayn, Port of Spain, Trinidad, August 6, 1996.

5. BBC Radio 3 interview.

6. Without claiming to have done a systematic reader survey, I have had reactions from students on the MA course at Cave Hill, Women Writing and Feminist Theory (co-taught by Evelyn O'Callaghan and Jane Bryce), who read the whole series for the module on romance; also from students on the Creative Writing course (taught by Jane Bryce), some of whom participated in the BBC Radio 3 program "Books Abroad."

7. Interviewed on the BBC Radio 3 program "Books Abroad."

REFERENCES

Barber, Karin. 1987. "Popular Arts in Africa." African Studies Review, Volume 30, Number 3, September, 1–78.

Barrow, Christine. 1986. "Male Images of Women in Barbados." Social and Economic Studies, Volume 35, Number 3, September, 51–64.

Brodber, Erna. 1982. *Perceptions of Caribbean Women: Towards a Documentation of Stereotypes*. Introduction by Merle Hodge. Women in the Caribbean Project, Volume 4. ISER, University of the West Indies, Cave Hill, Barbados.

Bryce, Jane. 1996 "A World of Caribbean Romance: Reformulating the Language of Love, or Can A Caress Be Culturally Specific." In *Framing the Word: Gender and Genre in Caribbean Women's Writing*, ed Joan Anim-Addo. (London: Whiting and Birch) 108–127.

Caribbean Caress series. 1993. Oxford: Heinemann.

Ali, Lyn-Anne. *Hand in Hand.*

Belgrave, Valerie. *Sun Valley Romance.*

Charles, Annette. *Love in Hiding.*

Colleton, Lucille. *Merchant of Dreams*.

D'Allan, Deidre. *Fantasy of Love*.

Jolly, Dorothy. *Heartaches and Roses*.

Dann, Graham. 1987. *The Barbadian Male: Sexual Attitudes and Practices*. London: Macmillan.

Drayton, Armel. 1995. "Representations of Women in Selected Caribbean Romance." Unpublished paper toward the Literatures in English degree, University of the West Indies, Cave Hill, Barbados.

Senior, Olive. 1991. *Working Miracles: Women's Lives in the English-Speaking Caribbean*. London: James Currey: Bloomington and Indianapolis: Indiana University Press.

Waithe, Nelson. 1993. *Caribbean Sexuality*. Bethlehem, PA: Department of Publications, Moravian Church.

Chapter Seventeen

Archival Material
New Yorker and *Fortune* Cartoons

"*Good morning, Madam, the J. Walter Thompson Company would like to know if you are happily married.*"

Fig. 17.1. *New Yorker* cartoon. Advertisers sought out women's complaints not to alleviate them but rather to find ways to promise convincingly to do so with the assistance of consumer goods. Drawing by P. Barlow; © 1934 (renewed). Originally in the *New Yorker* June 9, 1934, p. 19. All rights reserved.

Fig. 17.2. *Fortune* drawing. The woods of the 1950s were filled with marketing men trying to understand what made women buy. The article that followed this drawing argued that the world of business "is launching a great new assault with enlarged forces and all the latest in psychological ammunition." *Fortune* 54 (August 1956), 93.

Part Four

Purchasing Possibilities
Sexuality, Pleasure, and Resistance in Consumer Culture

It will be clear to readers who have ventured this far that consumer culture is not a one-way street, regardless of the best attempts of the best marketing people. Perhaps the most fascinating thing about consumer culture is the interplay between the purveyors and the purchasers. One advertiser calls the process "partipulation," with the consuming audience participating in its own manipulation.[1] Nicholas Abercrombie puts it this way: "Producers try to commodify meaning, that is try to make images and symbols into things which can be bought or sold. Consumers, on the other hand, try to give their own, new meanings to the commodities and services that they buy."[2] The tension between the two is most apparent in this part of the book, which explores the various forms of resistance engaged in by everyday people as they try to define consumer culture and their role in it in ways that fit their needs and their sense of self. Sometimes they resist the proffered images; other times they reshape them; other times they embrace them literally rather than as intended. This dance, as it were, provides rich material for study and enormous promise for those who hope to see consumers even more deliberately engaged as active agents in the culture of consumption.

What forms might resistance to consumer culture take? The authors in Part Four explore women's shoplifting as one response to both the lures and the pressures of consumer culture; women's outright use of their sexuality as they interact with the consumer culture; Chicano and black men's resistance to dominant themes of manhood and citizenship through fashion; the contested nature of beauty pageants as mediated through race, gender, and nation; and the entrance of lesbians into consumer culture on their own, advertisers', and contested terrains. In each case, the notion of the possibilities as well as the limitations of consumer culture predominates. The demand side of consumer culture, rich in motivation and varied in approach, takes its rightful place in scholarly discourse. That is not to say, however, that these scholars make light of the message makers. They do not. As Yiannis Gabriel puts it, and as these scholars also recognize, "Consumer capitalism has an extraordinary capacity to look at what directly threatens it and, after a deep intake of breath, convert it into a marketing opportunity."[3] The essays in this part reveal the complexities of those relationships.

The scholars here are not alone in exploring sites of resistance in consumer culture. Hazel Carby's and Angela Davis's examinations of African American women and the blues tradition reveal the ways in which black women, through the blues, an aspect of consumer culture, constructed themselves as sexual subjects rather than sexual objects.[4] Dana Frank, Robert Weems, and Dwight Brooks explore in different contexts the uses of the boycott as a consumer tool to effect change.[5] The "Don't Buy Where You Can't Work Campaign" staged by black consumers during the Great Depression, for example, included pickets and boycotts of white-owned businesses that refused to hire African Americans. Not all resistance comes through rejection of consumer culture, however; consumers also use the process of shopping, the products they purchase, and the sites of consumption in unintended and often oppositional ways. Rosemary Hennessy has examined groups such as the Queer Shopping Network of New York and SHOP (Suburban Homosexual Outreach Program) of San Francisco, which stages mall actions both to establish an open presence and to educate heterosexual shoppers about the lives of gay men and lesbians.[6] Feminist critics recently have explored the ways in which women use anorexia or other eating disorders as forms of resistance to the messages of consumer culture.[7] The marketplace is not simply a site of consumption; it is also a site where consumers engage in cultural appropriation, identity construction, imitation, and innovation.

The first essay in this part, "Shoplifting Ladies," by Elaine S. Abelson,[8] explores the relationship between two seemingly incongruous groups: shoplifters and "ladies." In turn-of-the-twentieth-century New York City, middle-class female kleptomaniacs "lifted" items from the department stores that invited them in and provided, for store owners then and historians now, the "reverse image" of the ideal woman shopper.[9] In the case of this particular group of women, resistance to consumer culture comes in the form of theft. Women who felt overwhelmed by the dazzling array of goods, under pressure to stretch their dollars, or conflicted by the images of consumption and the obvious contrasts between that world and their domestic lives, stole, compulsively or deliberately, occasionally or repeatedly.

Abelson's essay makes clear that the middle-class woman, the darling of advertisers and merchants alike, had a vexed relationship to the consumer culture she in many ways both represented and furthered. When she acted as a criminal by stealing from the department stores, she so disturbed middle-class and consumer culture definitions of the female, however, that no one seemed to know how to respond to her. Stores proved particularly unwilling to prosecute shoplifters of the middle class; the public saw such women largely as victims unable to resist the "lust of possession;" and the women themselves threw out any number of excuses for their own behavior.[10] The privilege of being defined in a particular way by the consumer culture clearly worked to these women's advantage, as stores would more readily pursue and prosecute poor or working-class than middle-class women. Abelson examines these women's economic dependency on their husbands, sense of their class and gender privilege, and response to "the pathology of consumption" to explain their clearly unexpected and problematic behaviors.

The second essay, " 'Charity Girls' and City Pleasures: Historical Notes on Working-Class Sexuality, 1880–1920," by Kathy Peiss,[11] moves the focus from the middle class to the working class and explores the gendered nature of the relationship between consumer culture and sexual expression. Peiss examines the lives of a group of women, the children of immigrants, also at the turn of the twentieth century. These young women, as Peiss puts it, "dressed in the latest finery, negotiated city life with ease, and sought intrigue and adventure with male companions."[12] They differed from their parents and from their middle-class contemporaries in that they defined themselves as sexual actors and not simply the objects of male sexual interest. For example, in words that sound familiar to young people today, the dances these women engaged in were described as "so suggestive that they are absolutely indecent."[13] In their other leisure-time pursuits, including social clubs and amusement resorts, young women experimented with a "free and easy" sexuality.[14]

What is perhaps most interesting about this sexuality is the way in which it was tied to consumer culture and gendered cultural relationships. Women and men interacted with each through the custom of "treating," whereby men would purchase entrance tickets to events, drinks and refreshments, and other incidentals for women. Peiss argues that since women's work was undervalued and underpaid, "women relied on these treats to see them through the night."[15] The act of treating, however, was not a one-way proposition; women essentially paid with sexual favors while men paid with money. Such relationships extended to the workplace as well, where some young working-class women made up for their poor salaries through these exchange relationships with men. As Peiss puts it, perhaps few women were "charity girls" or occasional prostitutes, but few women would have been exempt from the clearly economic relationship between women's participation in consumer culture and their participation in the world of dating. Like Abelson's "thieving ladies," Peiss's working-class women engaged in consumer culture in unanticipated and culturally revealing ways.

The third essay in Part Four "The Zoot-Suit and Style Warfare," by Stuart Cosgrove,[16] moves the discussion forward to the 1940s and to the engagement primarily of men rather than women with consumer culture. In this case, young Mexican American youths, "pachucos," part of what Cosgrove calls a "disinherited generation within a disadvantaged sector of North American society," signified their difference by flaunting it to whites through dress. The resulting fashion, the zoot suit, a long suit jacket with exaggerated shoulders and trousers with tapered ankles, provided for both Chicano and black men a means of rebelling against white norms as well as an excuse, on the part of their white peers, for ethnic and racial oppression.

The zoot suit emerged in the late 1930s but became a belligerent means of engagement with consumer culture during World War II, when rationing extended to fabrics and "streamlined suits" became both the norm and a visible symbol of patriotism. Disenchanted youths, aware of the discrepancies between the nationalist rhetoric and the realities of their own lives, chose to voice their alienation by purchasing and wearing bootlegged zoot suits. The resulting zoot-suit riots provide evidence of the contentious relationships between white servicemen and Chicano and black youths and between the seemingly irreversible economic hardships of certain groups of Americans and the consumer culture that offered them images that reflected as well as distorted their realities. In this case, resistance to racism came through active and oppositional engagement with consumer culture. As Cosgrove makes clear, although the zoot-suit riots were not overtly political in the strictest sense, they provide an example of the political uses consumers can make of the products they purchase and the ways in which they use them.

The fourth article in this part, "Face of the Nation: Race, Nationalisms, and Identities in Jamaican Beauty Pageants," by Natasha B. Barnes,[17] explores the contested nature of consumer culture as it defines and projects ideals of female beauty. The beauty pageant, a popular event worldwide, represents in many ways the epitome of the gendered nature of consumer culture: women are both sold a model of womanhood and "sold" as beauties on stage. However, as Barnes illustrates, not all consumers of beauty pageants are eager and supportive. In this case, Barnes explores the significance of the selection of a white Miss Jamaica in a country where, thirty years into independence and with a 90 percent black population, whiteness still evokes privilege. The beauty pageant remains, as she puts it, one of several "spectacular public events that dramatized in visceral ways the disenfranchisement of people of color"[18] and a reminder that beauty remains, in the end, "not natural but ideological."[19]

The resistance in Barnes's essay comes in the form of outright protest. Audience members at the pageant threw oranges at the winner, who, interestingly, is defined as "white" in Jamaica but well may have been defined as a person of color in the United States. The protest continued after the pageant in the newspapers, and similar protests to the commodification and cultural reward of beauty emerged in Trinidadian calypsos, where active male cultural "work," the calypso, was contrasted with passive female "leisure," the beauty pageant. "She does nothing for Carnival," the Mighty Sparrow said of the Carnival Queen. "She only pretty and that is all."[20] In both Trinidad and Jamaica, the response to commodified female beauty, black or white, points to the ways in which gender and race interact, in a postcolonial context, with consumer culture and everyday life. In this clearly global element of consumer culture, the female body is a site of representation and contestation, a place of multiple tensions.

The final essay, "Commodity Lesbianism," by Danae Clark,[21] is itself a form of protest against the consumer culture, as it reads into that culture a group of people largely overlooked, if not deliberately ignored, by those who supply us with invitations to consume. As Clark states bluntly and demonstrates aptly, "Lesbians too are consumers."[22] Lesbians form an interesting group in relation to consumer culture; because they have not deliberately been targeted for the most part, they have historically had to place themselves into the consumer culture by providing their own readings of that culture. Recently, however, advertisers have seen fit, recognizing the purchasing power of gay men and lesbians, to target those audiences. In targeting lesbians, advertisers have to recognize what Clark calls the "uneasy" relationship these women have historically had with advertising, which largely offers heterosexual women messages about consumer culture and making oneself pleasing to men. Lesbians' resistance to those messages has provided a means of both rejecting heterosexual cultural messages and identifying with the lesbian community. The integration of lesbians into consumer culture, then, provides a fascinating picture of changes in both advertising and the lesbian community.

As they tread the thin line between explicitly targeting gay and lesbian audiences and maintaining the heterosexist illusions of their heterosexual audiences, Clark argues, advertisers merge consumer identities in potentially liberating and oppressive ways. "The seamless connections that have traditionally been made between heterosexuality and consumerism are broken apart to allow straight and lesbian women alternative choices," writes Clark.[23] The "insider status" that lesbians achieve through interaction with consumer culture may simply draw them in in apolitical ways, but it may also politicize heterosexual women with more autonomous images of womanhood. The hitch, however, is that lesbians, in becoming the latest target of what Judith Williamson calls "capitalism's constant search for new areas to colonize," may be reduced, culturally, to a product choice themselves.[24]

The archival materials in this part explore in different ways the contested nature of people's relationships with consumer culture. The lyrics "Nobody Makes a Pass at Me" were first sung in a musical, *Pins and Needles*, produced in the main auditorium at the International Ladies' Garment Workers Union on November 27, 1937, in New York City. This working-class production ran for three years and featured on stage a cast of forty-four cutters, pressers, operators, and finishers in the needle trades. The satire of the production is evident in the words of "Nobody Makes a Pass at Me," which reveal the promises as well as the disappointments of an active engagement with consumer culture, particularly as it pertains to sexuality.

The second piece of archival material is a poem, "Among the Things That Use to Be," by Willie Coleman. This poem, originally published in 1979, was reprinted in Barbara Smith's *Home Girls: A Black Feminist Anthology* in 1983. It reveals the tensions involved in disengaging from certain elements of the consumer culture. In this case, as black women in the period rejected consumer culture's invitations to straighten their hair, they engaged with a powerful image of female blackness equated with beauty. At the same time, they lost something: spending time in a female cultural space, the beauty parlor, where Coleman locates the potential for not just social conformity but also radical social change. Like the women portrayed in "Nobody Makes a Pass at Me," the women in Coleman's poem engage with the consumer culture on several levels and in ways of their own choosing.

NOTES

1. Tony Schwartz, quoted in Sut Jhally, "Image-Based Culture: Advertising and Popular Culture," in Gail Dines and Jean M. Humez, eds., *Gender, Race and Class in Media* (Thousand Oaks, CA: Sage, 1995), 77–87, esp. 80.

2. Nicholas Ambercrombie, quoted in Celia Lury, *Consumer Culture* (New Brunswick, NJ: Rutgers University Press, 1996), 53.

3. Yiannis Gabriel and Tim Lang, *The Unmanageable Consumer: Contemporary Consumption and Its Fragmentation* (Thousand Oaks, CA: Sage, 1995), 145.

4. Hazel Carby, "It Jus Be's Dat Way Sometimes: The Sexual Politics of Women's Blues," *Radical America* 20 (1986), 922; Angela Davis, *Blues Legacies and Black Feminism: Gertrude "Ma" Rainey, Bessie Smith, and Billie Holiday* (NY: Pantheon Books, 1998).

5. On boycotts, see Dwight Ernest Brooks, *Consumer Markets and Consumer Magazines:*

Black America and the Culture of Consumption, 1920–1960, (Ph.D. diss. Ann Arbor: University Microfilms, 1991); Dana Frank, "Housewives, Socialists, and the Politics of Food: The 1917 New York Cost-of-Living Protests," *Feminist Studies,* 11 (Summer 1985), 255–285; Dana Frank, *Purchasing Power: Consumer Organizing, Gender and the Seattle Labor Movement, 1919–1929* (Cambridge: Cambridge University Press, 1994); Robert Weems, *Desegregating the Dollar: African American Consumerism in the Twentieth Century* (New York: New York University Press, 1998).

6. Rosemary Hennessy, "Queer Visibility in Consumer Culture," *Cultural Critique* 29 (Winter 1994–95), 31–76. See also Lisa Penaloza, "We're Here, We're Queer, and We're Going Shopping! A Critical Perspective on the Accommodation of Gays and Lesbians in the U.S. Marketplace," *Journal of Homosexuality* 31 (1996), 9–41.

7. On women's bodies and consumer culture, see Susan Bordo, *Unbearable Weight: Feminism, Western Culture, and the Body* (Berkeley: University of California Press); Rosalyn Coward, *Female Desires: How They Are Sought, Bought and Packaged* (New York: Grove, 1985); L. Pemmenis, "The Ritual of Anorexia Nervosa in Cultural Context," *Journal of American Culture* 14 (Winter 1991), 49–59; Judith Williamson, "Woman Is an Island: Femininity and Colonization," in Tania Modleski, ed., *Studies in Entertainment* (Bloomington: Indiana University Press, 1986), 99–118.; Naomi Wolf, *The Beauty Myth: How Images of Beauty Are Used against Women* (New York: Doubleday, 1991).

8. Elaine S. Abelson, "Shoplifting Ladies," originally published as chap. 6 of her *When Ladies Go a-Thieving: Middle-Class Shoplifters in the Victorian Department Store* (New York: Oxford University Press).

9. Ibid., 149.

10. Ibid., 151.

11. Kathy Peiss, " 'Charity Girls' and City Pleasures: Historical Notes on Working-Class Sexuality, 1880–1920," originally published in Ann Snitow, Christine Stansell, and Sharon Thompson, eds., *Powers of Desire: The Politics of Sexuality* (New York: Monthly Review Press, 1983).

12. Ibid., 76.

13. Ibid.,

14. Ibid., 77.

15. Ibid., 78.

16. Stuart Cosgrove, "The Zoot-Suit and Style Warfare," originally published in *History Workshop* 18 (Autumn 1984), 77–91.

17. Natasha Barnes, "Face of the Nation: Race, Nationalisms, and Identities in Jamaican Beauty Pageants," originally published in *Massachusetts Review* and then republished in Consuelo Lopez Springfield, ed., *Daughters of Caliban: Caribbean Women in the Twentieth Century* (Bloomington: Indiana University Press, 1997), 285–306. Page numbers cited here are from *Daughters of Caliban.*

18. Ibid., 287.

19. Ibid., 293.

20. Ibid., 291.

21. Danae Clark, "Commodity Lesbianism," originally published in *Camera Obscura* 25 (1991), 180–201.

22. Ibid., 181.

23. Ibid., 194.

24. Ibid., Williamson quoted on 197.

Chapter Eighteen

Shoplifting Ladies

Elaine S. Abelson

The Kleptomaniac, Edwin S. Porter's 1905 silent movie, gave powerful definition to the late nineteenth-century female shoplifter. Dealing directly with the pattern of relations that had developed within class, gender, and consumerism in America, Porter told the parallel but very different stories of the thefts committed by two women. The story is simple. A wealthy woman is arrested for shoplifting in Macy's. In court the elegantly attired defendant is accompanied by her husband and a frock-coated lawyer. She is treated with sympathy and given a chair. The two men are treated with deference; they are obviously important. The Macy detectives who argue the case have no chance; the woman goes free over their strenuous objections. In the same courtroom, a poor woman who has stolen a loaf of bread for her starving children goes to jail. Justice, Porter says in this biting social commentary, is not blind, but blinded by money and power.[1]

What made the movie work so well, what made such a blunt point seem more subtle and compelling, was the popular acceptance of a stereotype. American audiences recognized the kleptomaniac instantly. The nineteenth-century women who went "a-thieving" in the department stores had quickly become a type of cultural artifact, remarkable for the very fact that they were "Ladies." Far removed from the subculture of crime—the professional women shoplifters, pickpockets, and sneak thieves who, traditionally, had plagued merchants—these late nineteenth-century thieving women were from an entirely different class and background.[2] The new breed of shoplifter seemed to fly in the face of all previously understood relations of crime, class, and gender.

In April 1908, after years of reporting on shoplifting by the "fair fine ladies," the *New York Times* still wondered at the phenomenon.

> It seems impossible that these beautifully gowned, gracefully moving creatures, all polish and delicacy and poise, should harbor among them all one single thief. The word seems absurd, an affront to their well-bred faces and their well-filled purses hanging on jeweled chains. And yet it is indeed from this class that the army of shoplifters is largely made up.[3]

A highly visible paradox to merchants and the public alike from the time of the Elizabeth Phelps–Rowland Macy furore in 1870, the middle-class woman shoplifter became the reverse image of the ideal woman shopper. Key elements of the nine-teenth century's definition of "female" were worked into an image of female weak-ness that made sense of the shoplifting phenomenon. But this cultural construct, however serviceable to consumer society and middle-class respectability, profoundly undermined the self-respect of women as individuals and as a group, even while freeing them of the onus of criminality.

The problem of shoplifting exposed the contradictions at the heart of department store consumerism. Middle-class women were the backbone of the stores' clientele, and the shoplifters among them, who seemed to appear so suddenly and in such great numbers in the dry-goods bazaars after 1870, were indistinguishable from other shoppers. But they represented a new category of crime as well as a new social danger. The controversy was not simply over arresting shoplifting suspects. Defini-tive action would have meant action against the very group merchants were loath to accuse, and in many instances dared not accuse. The interrelation between the store and the middle-class customers was such that there was a widespread reluc-tance to make demands on the customers even when they were acting against the interests of the institution. Management preferred not to "catch" many of these women, and given this reluctance, the problem ultimately proved insoluble.

Obviously, a few middle-class women were arrested and some names were pub-lished in the daily newspapers. Personal embarrassment and family shame must have been high in these instances. However, because of the special characteristics of the crime and of the group committing the crime, there was no immediate moral isolation of the arrested women and little in the way of harsh or judgmental pronouncements by the stores. Merchants were well aware of the fact that exposure of shoplifters fascinated the public, and too often publicity meant sympathy for the thieves.[4] After the well-publicized arrests of four respectable women in Lynn, Mas-sachusetts, the *Boston Globe* commented on the "many . . . expressions of sorrow and sympathy heard for the women who had been tempted and fell."[5] Newspaper articles about the four women dramatized just how ensnared late nineteenth-century men and women were by the phenomenon. At the bail hearing, the reporter for the *New York Times* described a scene bordering on hysteria. A mob of women filled the court room, the corridors, and the streets in the vicinity of the court.

> Some of the best known and most highly respected women in this city came in carriages or walked and stood with their sisters outside the doors waiting anxiously for the signal to enter. . . . When finally some of the accused women were allowed to depart, the waiting crowd surged around them, endeavoring to get a glimpse of their faces which were concealed by thick veils and even tried to look into the carriages in waiting to drive them away.[6]

The reporter concluded that "such a scene was never before witnessed here."

The Lynn shoplifters wondered what their friends would say, and, according to the *Globe*, one of the women "broke down," but there is little evidence that there was any social ostracism of such women; quite the contrary. Newspapers, maga-zines, and fiction in various guises all suggest an intense curiosity about and a sentimental attachment to such "unfortunate women." The object of gentle and generally silly satire in a variety of literary forms, the lady shoplifter was a nonthreatening figure, often seen as irresponsible, more childlike than adult, unable to resist momentary temptation and ready to succumb to the "lust of possession." The popular image of the middle-class shoplifter, sometimes called a kleptomaniac, was that of victim.[7]

Beyond periodic determined pronouncements about the scourge by retail trade groups by the 1890s, only in the occasional newspaper editorial was there ever any serious condemnation of the woman herself.[8] The *Boston Globe* took note of the public's fascination with the massive shoplifting caper uncovered in Lynn and warned that "education and social position" should not make these women exempt from the fullest penalties of the law. The excuse of "pride and vanity" must not mark their escape from such punishment as would be meted out to the humblest working girl in Boston guilty of a similar offense.[9]

Despite their obvious reluctance to act, in the face of substantial losses department stores were forced to confront the problem of the middle-class shoplifter. The Retail Dry-Goods Association of New York offered one solution—prosecution— but the member stores never consistently supported such a hard line.

The situation in New York during 1904 and 1905 demonstrates the ambivalence of the stores toward the middle-class shoplifter. A spokesman for the association announced in the *New York Times* that shoplifting losses for 1905 had increased significantly and were expected to reach an astonishing $500,000. This was followed by the claim that the stores were fully prepared to deal with the depredations during the Christmas season already under way. Headlined "Harvest Time of The Shoplifter," the article was in fact a report on the state of the art in New York City. In what was to become a perennial threat/promise, the Dry-Goods Association declared, "No mercy is to be shown to shoplifters, all are to be punished to the limit of the law, no matter what 'influence' there may be behind them."[10] Obviously the prospect of such huge dollar losses demanded a tough stance, but in fact such pronouncements remained little more than that. There would be a spurt of selective shoplifting arrests accompanied by an occasional jail sentence, but it was a hit or miss situation at best, and publicity, which might have deterred some of the thefts, was kept to a minimum.[11]

A perfect example of this contradictory attitude toward shoplifters was revealed in the account of the arrest of a socially prominent woman in November 1904. "Lawyer's Wife Accused" ran the headline in the *New York Times*. Mrs. Caroline Hobart, a name everyone agreed was fictitious, was arrested after being observed taking several pins from a jewelry counter in a well-known 23rd Street store. Coming at the height of one of the sporadic efforts by the New York Retail Dry-Goods Association "to restrict as much as possible this form of theft," the arrest of the woman became a real problem for the judge, store detectives, and managers alike. Special Sessions Magistrate Martin Whitman made his feeling very clear in the overblown prose typical of the period. "This is one of the saddest cases that has ever come to my attention. Here is a woman who is the wife of one of the most respected members of the bar of New Jersey and a mother of some very promising children." But prodded by the determination of the Dry-Goods Association to pursue these cases, Whitman felt compelled to hold Mrs. Hobart for trial, "much as I would any other person."[12]

The store manager appeared in Whitman's court the next day and attempted to withdraw the charge. "We have made an investigation and have learned that this woman is a member of one of the best families in the city and, moreover, that she has been suffering from severe illness for three years. We believe that in this instance she committed the theft under stress of some sudden mental defection."[13] Here was the essential contradiction: A socially prominent, wealthy woman had given patronage to a store, and even when the woman was caught stealing, management did not want to jeopardize that relationship. Here, too, was the basic confrontation between the courts and the medical profession. Was this theft or disease? Was the woman who called herself Caroline Hobart suffering from a physical or mental disorder, or was she simply a shoplifter who relied on the court to treat her as it had countless other middle-class women? Was this form of shoplifting to be exonerated as a disease or prosecuted as a crime?[14] In this case the ambiguities and unanswered questions remain. Apologizing that he had a duty to perform as a public official, Judge Whitman remanded Mrs. Hobart for trial in spite of the manager's attempt to withdraw from the case. There is no further mention of Mrs. Hobart in any of the newspapers.

Occasionally judges were determined to prosecute. When John Wanamaker attempted to drop charges against a customer arrested for shoplifting in December 1882, the judge was adamant. Wanamaker asked his lawyers to intervene and stop the procedure.

> I wrote a note to the Magistrate on the 25th of December saying that I did not desire to prosecute the case; but I am informed that he refused to be governed by my note. . . . I do not wish to prosecute the case and wish you could withdraw the Bill before it is called by the Grand Jury.[15]

Faced with a typical action in 1893—wherein a genteel young woman "from one of the best known families in the city" was before him on the charge of stealing a piece of silk and two pairs of gloves at Stern Brothers—a Judge Voorhis displayed his skepticism. "I suppose," he said, "this is *another* of those respectable family cases."[16] The judge interpreted the situation perfectly. When Stern's discovered the woman's identity, they withdrew the charge and the case was dismissed.

When Siegel-Cooper detective George Bernard arrested two middle-class women for shoplifting, one who, it was charged, stole a bottle of perfume, and the other an umbrella, which she unsuccessfully attempted to hide in the folds of her skirt, the store quickly withdrew both complaints the following day: the explanation was that "restitution had been made."[17] The judge in the case was clearly unhappy with the situation, but felt he had little room to maneuver. "I don't see what I can do in the matter," Judge Olmsted said regretfully. With no complaint there could be no case.

These cases of shoplifting by the middle-class and socially prominent were replete with contradictions. Judges routinely faced instances of stores backing off from prosecution, and without strong pressure from an interest group comparable to that which Whitman confronted, most judges felt they were left with no choice but to discharge the prisoner.

Many judges were openly resentful of a system that forced them to participate in such visibly class-based justice. Whitman responded like many magistrates in Special Sessions who heard the shoplifting cases: while he maintained an unconcealed class alliance with many of the suspects, as a judge he was frustrated by a system that resolutely discriminated in favor of the middle class. But with stores rarely willing to prosecute, and defendants able to marshall doctors and lawyers to plead extenuating circumstances and friends to attest to their unblemished respectability, cases of shoplifting by middle-class women were routinely dismissed. Throughout this period it was generally accepted that the poor had simple motives for these crimes, while the rich had complex explanations that required sympathy and understanding.

One further example will demonstrate how a number of these strands interacted and temporarily worked in the woman's favor. Louisa Schloss was arrested for shoplifting in the Siegel-Cooper store in New York in December 1908. Caught leaving the store with a variety of small trinkets in her possession, the woman challenged the arrest on the ground of its absurdity. She was, she said, the wife of a respectable merchant, and she had credit accounts in all the big department stores. Her lawyer, Daniel Blumenthal, produced an affadavit from her physician, which read: "This is to certify that Mrs. Schloss is a patient of mine; that she is a very nervous woman, and I feel that it would be very injurious to her health if she had to go to court tonight. She is very subject to nervous shocks." In spite of the strong objections of store detectives David (Daniel) Kash and Rose McCauley, who swore in court that the woman was a thief, and that they had witnessed her repeated shoplifting, the woman went free. Siegel-Cooper overrode their own detectives and decided that "a mistake had been made." Indeed it had; the mistake was the arrest of a well-connected woman.[18]

Lawyers were obviously aware of the dual system in effect in the Special Session courts. In 1905, counsel for a woman suspected of being a professional shoplifter challenged the magistrate on this very issue; he demanded the same show of "mercy" for his client that the court had shown when it released a wealthy woman convicted of shoplifting the preceding week.[19] The plea, of course, failed. While Judge Whitman could refuse to dismiss the case against Mrs. Hobart, maintaining that "there should be no discrimination, and there will be none in this court whether the accused be poor or rich, socially prominent or unknown," other judges, feeling there was no strong public support for such a position, shied away from prosecuting the middle-class shoplifter.[20]

The situation remained constant into the second decade of the twentieth century. Secrecy remained endemic. While acknowledging that stolen merchandise represented "sums sufficiently large to constitute a source of real anxiety . . . it is impossible to estimate accurately how much is lost in this way." The editors of the influential *Merchant's Record and Show Window* despaired of reducing the losses. Without publicity, the journal said, without the stores' determination to prosecute, the amateur shoplifter seemed to be in very little danger. In the few instances where the stores did act decisively, "pressure is generally brought to bear through friends of the culprit, nothing appears in the papers about any shoplifters being punished, and those who have a propensity for casual thievery [think] that none are ever detected."[21]

The group of women who were the cause of the escalating losses and the object of all the concern were neither as rich as the stereotype would have us believe, nor poor in any observable, material way.[22] While the exact dimensions of the problem are unclear, the vital statistics of the women accused of shoplifting in the New York City department stores between 1870 and 1910 lack any distinguishing features. Assembled from reports in daily newspapers, the profile of the women who were caught and whose names entered the public record appear to represent the middle-class shopper.[23]

Popular understanding underscored medical "fact" to connect many important characteristics of shoplifters with the female life cycle, particularly the onset of middle age and the beginning of menopause. Yet of the ninety-seven women whose ages are given, the average age is thirty-six and a half, an age without any particular significance in the reproductive cycle. Many of the ages are probably estimates; occasionally the reporter guesses "between forty-five and fifty" or simply settles on "middle-aged." Of the 190 women in the sample, over one hundred women were "married"; a few were widowed, some were listed as "Miss," but for others there is no indication of marital status. All were white; only two were foreign born, and they were both wealthy Cubans.

Whatever their exact ages and specific nationalities, the largest number of women were in the middle stages of life—set in their domestic, housewifely roles, responsible for home, children and husbands. Age was significant not in its connection to the reproductive cycle but in what the women were doing: shopping. The overwhelmingly female presence in the department stores represents both the strength of conventional gender boundaries and the "social changes which had occurred in the day to day functioning of the urban middle-class home." Shopping denoted freedom from one sort of labor and signified, as well, the intricate texture of women's lives in which domestic work and leisure were often confused.[24]

A great many women were out-of-town visitors: Chicago; Dayton; Philadelphia; New Orleans; San Francisco; Canton, Ohio; Charlestown, Massachusetts; and Corning, New York, were a few of the more distant permanent addresses. Many of the women were from various parts of New Jersey, southern Connecticut, Westchester and Rockland Counties, and Brooklyn, and appeared to be in the city on legitimate shopping expeditions that culminated in their arrest for shoplifting. For women from the more remote suburbs and smaller cities—such as Sophie Hall, the visitor from Wilmington, Delaware—the atmosphere in the large department stores must have been particularly intoxicating. The unusual crowds of women, the profusion of merchandise and choices, and the routine overselling contributed to what all observers agree was often an over-stimulating environment. We tend to forget that both the size and the special atmosphere in the stores were unique to large urban centers at the end of the nineteenth century.

The occupations of only three alleged shoplifters were specified: one woman worked as a milliner, another was an insurance agent, and the third, the wife of a suburban minister, was the superintendent of the primary department in the Sunday School of the Church of the Puritans in New York City.[25] Presumably, some of the other women, particularly the unmarried women, were employed; but statistically, most of these middle-class women, married or single, would not have held paying jobs. They would have been engaged primarily in the domestic sphere, and shopping was one of their major domestic roles. "The task may be a pleasant one or it may be a trial," the *New York Tribune* explained to readers in 1901, "but it is one of the duties connected with housekeeping."[26] Women had become the purchasing agents for the family; men were the primary wage earners, but women were the unchallenged wage spenders. Even the masculine trade often came through the women in the family. They were "the natural and regular customers in the department stores."[27]

The occupation of the husband or father, the public badge of female identity, was mentioned often enough to give us a good sense of the economic circumstances of the family. While there was wide variation in employment patterns, in no case was the male a common laborer or a factory worker, or unemployed. In only one instance was the husband described in a way that might suggest working-class status: Mr. Lynch, the *New York Times* reported, was "a respectable, hard working mechanic."[28] Of the other men, three were Protestant ministers, two were described as engineers, four were in insurance, one was an artist, and one a town official in Newton, New Jersey. One man was a conductor on the New Jersey Railroad and another was a superintendent on the Jersey City Railroad. The largest number of the husbands (and the father of one woman) were in a range of businesses: produce merchant, liquor dealer, shoe dealer, contractor's supplies, hardware merchant, grocer, and representative of a large machinery house. There were three lawyers, a judge from Sandusky, Ohio, a retired physician, and a Republican politician from Brooklyn. A number of these men were simply described as "an influential man," "well connected," or "wealthy retired businessman." The most important-sounding title was that of Mr. Russell Raymond, who was secretary and manager of the American Safe Deposit Company and a trustee of the American Savings Bank.[29] These men were, with few exceptions, solidly middle class, more often than not from the professional, managerial, and business ranks.

What conclusions can be drawn from this sample? The women do not appear to typify the "new woman," the college-educated social worker or the woman prominent in local community or national affairs who has been studied in this period.[30] While there were, undoubtedly, some club women and active feminists among them, the women arrested for shoplifting epitomize the traditional nineteenth-century domestic model, that vast majority of women who were enmeshed in what what some observers demeaned as the "idle busyness" of housekeeping.[31] Certainly the middle-class status and respectability of the women is evident. They belong to that broad, amorphous, middling group of women whose role lacked a degree of definition and whose contribution, in a culture that valued hard work and money, was ill-defined.

The scenario of arrests had certain common features. The drama began when the suspect was stopped and told the manager wished to see her.[32] Detectives generally waited until the women were leaving the store—in fact they often stopped suspects on the sidewalk—both to minimize possible disturbance in the store and to ensure that the intention to steal was unmistakable. In most instances the woman apparently made little objection to this part of the routine and quietly followed the detective to the manager's office or special room used to question suspected shoplifters. Creating a case was the next step. Away from crowds and curious eyes the suspect was asked about the unpaid merchandise thought to be on her person. At this point she was usually charged with shoplifting by the manager or the detective, often in the presence of the salesperson.

Virtually all the women became indignant, loudly denying they had stolen merchandise in their possession, and frequently insisting a mistake had been made for which the store was going to be very sorry! If she consented, a search of the woman usually followed; invariably it yielded hidden articles. This discovery often produced hysterical weeping, occasionally even fainting, followed by impassioned pleading, desperate promises, and a variety of excuses for "what must have happened." The drama was enacted at a high emotional pitch; it was a scene that obviously had to be played out just as it was played up.

There is always the question of how to analyze such scenes. Were the excuses true, or were they created on the spot in self-defense? It is entirely possible that a woman picked up for shoplifting could not have described what provoked her particular response to the store environment, but true or false, more or less fanciful, the explanations would seem to be part of the play.

Store managers readily acknowledged that every effort was made to "hush up the cases." Shoplifters were routinely allowed to give back the goods, sign a release admitting the theft, and promise never to enter the store again; refusal could mean arrest and exposure.[33] If there were a prosecution, the store had sufficient leverage that its name was "usually withheld," even when that of the suspect became public knowledge.[34] Hesitancy to arrest the amateur shoplifter may have fallen within the concept of store service. Managers were protecting themselves and the image of the store, but they were also concerned with the broad circle of potential customers. "To ruin the reputation not only of a possible unwilling offender but also her family, throwing a stain upon the fair reputation of all connected with the accused, is too serious a subject for the average merchant, or man for that matter, to carelessly handle."[35]

Not only was there a distinction drawn between "the shoplifter who deliberately and willfully 'lifts' things for a living" and the "unfortunate beings who just happened to take it because inclination and impulse got together"; lenient treatment was a service to the reputation and social status of husbands and families, society, and especially the stores themselves.[36] With people generally unaware of individual instances of shoplifting, the trouble-free, dream-world image of the store remained intact. Detective Daniel Kash felt many shoplifters were so skillful that "the next neighbors of the shoplifter who is caught in the act never know anything about it."[37] Henry Blades, the chief detective at Wanamaker's, readily admitted that "no good end can be served by such exposure. Moreover it would be a *bad advertisement* for the house, for such cases would receive extended newspaper comment, to the the detriment of the firm exposing the culprits."[38]

Repeat customers who were suspected of shoplifting by store detectives were, not uncommonly, left alone just because they were recognized as good customers. Daniel Kash, a former New York City policeman and a well-known detective at Siegel-Cooper at the turn of the century, recalled "accidentally" finding an expensive handkerchief in a wealthy charge customer's muff. Although the woman had been suspected of shoplifting for some time, Kash took no action, merely commenting, "Why Mrs. B. you must have picked this up by mistake with your bundle." We let her go, he told the reporter, and "she continued to trade at the store, as there was no apparent reason for stopping her charge account."[39] The repeat shopper was a mainstay, and one that the stores assiduously cultivated. Management interpreted store loyalty as a signal that the store was providing the material and psychological satisfaction customers were thought to require. But this very constancy often made shoplifting arrests difficult. When such shoppers were stopped or finally arrested, the store often declined to prosecute. "Caution and discrimination" were essential in making arrests of this kind, warned detective Henry Blades.[40]

The *New York Times* reported an offshoot of the problem of the repeat customer as shoplifter. In this instance a "well-dressed woman" shoplifter was caught but not arrested because another customer intervened. The woman who interceded on the shoplifter's behalf did so purely for personal reasons, but the superintendent felt, pragmatically, that he could not deny her refusal to become further involved: "Being one of our best customers, we could not afford to offend her by pushing the matter."[41]

Many of the detained women gave false names and addresses; the police knew it and so did the courts, and neither group seemed unduly alarmed by the practice. A case with a fictitious name was the stuff of cheap novels and daily newspapers alike; such a case might appear in the *Times* or the *Tribune* two or three times under such tantalizing headlines as "Who is the Mysterious Shoplifter?" "Mystery About a Shoplifter," "Keeps Her Secrets Well," or "She Gave the Wrong Name."[42]

There was a special kind of anonymity in the central city. In an age where personal documentation was not a necessity, women could give any name they wished, and without a good deal of investigation their real identity need never be known. Lawyers even stood up in court and swore they did not know their client's true name.[43] Mrs. Caroline Hobart was patently a "nom de guerre," as were the names of at least thirty to thirty-five other women in this sample. The excuses were of a kind and seemed, in part, to be a response to the reporting of the arrests in the daily press. Some of the women were frankly afraid of their husbands' reaction.[44] In 1880, for example, Mrs. Catherine King refused to reveal her legal identity when arrested for shoplifting in both B. Altman and Arnold Constable, claiming, "she did not want to disgrace her family; her husband is a well known businessman of Newark." In court nine days later, she still maintained her silence, refusing to give any clue to her identity "on account of her family and connections."[45]

The rationalization changed little over the years. Annie Smith was the name given in Special Sessions Court by a "handsome, matronly woman dressed in black silk . . . and wearing expensive diamond earrings."[46] The justification for the pseudonym (for there was no pretense that the name was bona fide) lay in the fact that the putative Annie Smith was a respectable, well-connected lady. "Why should I disgrace my family?" asked a woman who called herself Maria Miller.[47] One woman said she was Jane Doe, and another, who called herself Mary Brown, was paroled to her husband, John Doe.[48]

Mary Smith was a commonly used fictitious name, but other, far less ordinary, names were used: May Hues, Josephine Durand, Emma Webster, Adelaid Martin, Louise Bryson, Leone Greenberg, Gertrude Price, and Nellie O'Brien are just a few. The list goes on, the names becoming more or less fanciful, but the attempt to protect the family, and obviously themselves, does not change. These women had something tangible to lose—their reputation and, with it, their self-esteem.

There is evidence of moral confusion in these attempts to hide behind fictitious names. Attempting to cope in the Gilded Age environment of rampant commercialism and speculation, some women found traditional virtues and inhibitions ineffective tools. Momentarily submerging the distinction between right and wrong, the women had taken what they thought they wanted from department store counter tops. When caught, they found that what they really wanted was the facade of middle-class respectability. They coveted "things" and seized and opportunity to take them, but when arrested they held tenaciously to the security of class.[49] On another level, however, these explanations shed light on certain cultural understandings of the period. In refusing to be named, women seized control of their own stereotype; they remained non-actors, non-participants, who hoped thereby to escape the consequences of their behavior.

Often, of course, the real woman emerged despite the fictions, and notwithstanding any attempt to dissociate the actions from the person one really was. Maria Miller turned out to be Mrs. W. D. Burnett of West 124th Street, New York City, whose husband was "entirely at a loss to understand his wife's actions."[50] Similarly, one Jane Doe was in fact a Mrs. Cornelius I. Wigham, the wife of a retired and quite "astonished" liquor dealer in Brooklyn.[51] It is a mark of this woman's presumed social position that the court papers continued to carry the pseudonym Jane Doe.

Whatever the repercussions and personal shame, it was not felt by the women alone. Shame attached to these men as well. The untoward notoriety threatened their status, community standing, and possibly their jobs. The newspaper statements of the men who were dragged into the situation were strikingly similar in tone, expressing concern with the implicit threat to their own position.

> Dr. Swift (The Rev. Dr.) said he was "dumbfounded" when the telegram arrived; he was sure there must be some mistake. . . . Mr. Swift further declared in court that "it stands to reason that my wife would not stoop to take an umbrella and disgrace her own and my good name."[52]

> He was at a loss to understand his wife's actions. She was very absent minded but. . . .[53]

Mr. Guinzberg stated that there was *no* reason for his wife to steal. They have a fine residence and Mr. Guinzberg is well-to-do.[54]

Her husband took the stand to testify "his wife was given plenty of money and did not *need* to steal."[55]

These denials of motivation or of need denied, as well, the possibility that social and material ambitions spurred the behavior.[56] But given the uneasy economic position of many middle-class families in the decades following the Civil War, one can assume that wives felt the twin pressures of money and status as keenly as their husbands did. The department store gave concrete expression to these pressures, tying the aspirations of class to material objects. The very existence of the grand bazaars suggested that commodities had redemptive power, and that their possession signified individual worth.[57] Thorstein Veblen understood this. In his language, reputation and status rested on the strength of the outward manifestations of success. Symbols replaced reality. Conspicuous consumption, or at least emulative spending, even at the risk of economic strain, was a necessary concomitant of social standing.

The quartet of middle-class women from Lynn, Massachusetts, who amassed "Trunkfuls of Booty" before they were caught in 1897 had no hesitation in giving their reasons for shoplifting: "They saw things they wanted, could not buy them, so took them from the counters when they were not watched."[58] Because we are aware that there is no necessary correlation between income and class in the late twentieth century, we should not be too quick to dismiss the possibility of economic motives in some of these cases. In a mobile society, in which appearances meant so much, the appearance of not being able to afford "things" was a threat of serious proportions.[59]

Obviously, no husband would ever say of his wife's shoplifting, "I suspected it all along." Husbands insisted that because their wives had an established social position, based of course on *their* wealth or position, and had what they considered to be a suitable allowance, the possibility the wives might shoplift did not exist. There seemed to be a growing distance between what men and women thought necessary to maintain the appearance of class. It was the woman who spent, "largely to bring about fulfillment of some idea or other of what [the] conditions for a pleasant environment should be for herself and for others."[60]

Most middle-class men had little firsthand knowledge of the realities of day-to-day consumption. Their understanding of what things cost was probably vague, and they were unlikely to take into account what having enough money meant in the social context of the department store. This was the first generation for whom material abundance was an everyday possibility. "The question today," Bertha June Richardson wrote in her 1904 study of women's economic function, "is not what shall be produced to supply my needs, but *how shall I spend to satisfy my needs*." (Italics mine.)[61] There was an infinite variety of things to buy, a push by the stores and their advertisers to buy them, and, increasingly, a society in which one's social position was tied to material possessions.

For the middle-class woman, financially dependent, without income or economic position of her own, having sufficient money did not necessarily mean freedom or control over spending. Even as they turned over part of their salary to their wives, husbands still regarded it as their own. It was *their* money. In an early feminist tract, *Fettered for Life, or Lord and Master* (1874), Lilly Devereux Blake observed that women had to justify and account for everything they spent, including ordinary expenses.[62] Echoing Blake, the author of an 1889 treatise on domestic economy demanded, "Let women have money to spend as *they* see fit [and] avoid annoying explanations as to *why* they need to buy another spool of thread today when they just bought one yesterday!"[63] Years later a woman reminisced, "In my girlhood we spoke with awe of my contemporary, Louise de Koven, who had a bank account and could sign checks!"[64] Empowered in the domestic arena as mothers and home-makers, women dominated the consumption process—there was little division of labor here—yet they had virtually no control over money. A woman's allowance or pocket money was generally a gift bestowed, not something to which she was entitled. Dismissed as "pin money," a woman's allowance reflected the explicit power relationships within the family.[65]

Feminists were aware of the problems surrounding money. "The Poor Little Rich Girls" was how the *Business Woman's Journal* described unmarried girls of comfortable families who were expected to "keep up" but either were never given money of their own to spend (Daddy paid the bills), or were given a wholly inadequate allowance. From their sheltered economic position many of these young women resorted to various strategems to get what they felt they needed—and wanted; a "demoralizing" state of affairs that, columnist Ella Wheeler Wilcox charged, "leads the weak and irresolute to shoplifting and petty larceny. . . ."[66]

An article in the *Boston Herald* in September 1890 tackled the problem of women and money head-on. The author, a Mrs. Ives, declared the failure of men to see that their unwillingness to allow their wives a discretionary income left them often "unable to meet the demands laid upon them by the social conditions surrounding them." Unnamed "social tragedies" were the result: "Women lie and steal and resort to all sorts of questionable expedients in order to obtain the spending money which they require for their own private purposes."[67] There was a reality to Mrs. Ives' argument. Many of the women had legitimate purchases in their possession and money in their purses when they were caught. Their shoplifting was that extra something that they felt they could not afford or possibly could not justify buying.

Women generally took things for their personal use, citing needs, or perceived needs, that often exceeded their ability to pay. Purchasing some things—most things—and stealing others, many women seemed to use shoplifting as a kind of budget-stretching device.[68] To many shoppers, the stores seemed so rich, so large, and so impersonal that it was a simple thing to maintain the illusion that what they did was not really theft; theft was something someone else committed. Women who would never steal from an individual took merchandise from the department stores and denied the implications of the act. For these women, shoplifting was a form of consumer behavior. Contrary to all logic and to the evidence, more than one woman rejected any conscious motive and adamantly defended herself with the assertion, "I am an honest and respectable woman."[69]

This level of denial was pervasive. If suspect Maria Miller had thought herself to be a shoplifter or had let others brand her "shoplifter," she would have had to question why she knowingly violated her own ethical precepts; and, even more troubling, she would have had to face the moral implications of her lapse. She would have been guilty of something more than irresponsibility. Aware of the normative distinctions between stealing and not stealing, these women were seemingly incapable of sensing emotionally that their shoplifting was wrong. They told themselves they were innocent, and, however fragile their defenses, they did not think of themselves as thieves. [70]

How, then, did these women see their own actions? Some women were quite frank about their reasons: like the quartet in Lynn, Massachusetts, whose "motive for stealing was the desire for fine apparel which they could not afford to buy." Others cited the example of women they had observed or had heard about—these women were imitators; they did what they knew other women were doing.[71] The more difficult responses to interpret were those of the women who readily acknowledged they could pay for what they wanted, but stole the merchandise just the same. The Brooklyn woman who decided to shoplift instead of spending the twelve dollars she had been given to buy Christmas presents suggests the taking of a calculated risk, a conscious level of action quite different from that of the woman who was at a loss to explain what had happened.[72]

Many of the women described the overwhelming temptation, the "physical inability to resist" the magnetism and lure of the displays. This was a common defense, and one that store personnel and magistrates came to expect. Although this routine explanation quickly became a cliché, it fulfilled social expectations. Women were expected to succumb to temptation. The claim that she had "no recollection of taking the articles found on her person," was a variation of this common defense.[73]

These stories, with their close relationship between truth and plausibility, become evidence for the mentality of the group.[74] It is not unlikely that some women were genuinely confused by their own actions. Their shoplifting was a spur-of-the-moment act, and their shame emerged as total denial. Even when a suspect pleaded guilty, as Mrs. Abbie Long did in 1898, it was not unusual for her to implore the judge to understand that "I did not mean to take the articles, indeed I did not. I had money and I could buy them. . . . I did not do it. I *could not* have done it."[75] For Mrs. Long, the wife of a clergyman, the expanding material economy posed choices even more difficult than those faced by other women. Hers was a public role and her conduct was minutely scrutinized. Expected to embody traditional values, the minister's wife was supposed to eschew the more blatant manifestations of the material culture.[76] That she often did not is evident. Mrs. Long's refusal to believe what she had done was the shocked reaction of a woman for whom the stakes were high.

The available cultural stereotypes focusing on woman's weak state of mind and frequent episodes of irresponsible behavior played into these explanations. In one highly publicized case in 1893, Dr. W. Gill Wylie, a prominent New York gynecologist and Professor of Medicine at Bellevue and Polyclinic Hospitals, appeared on the scene and posted bond for a suspected shoplifter. The doctor, who had a private sanitarium at 215 West 43rd Street, explained that he had been treating the woman for "seven or eight years for a reflex nervous trouble which rendered her at times unaccountable for her actions."[77] "Reflex nervous trouble" was a pervasive, if ill-defined, female symptom, and Dr. Wylie was probably saying little more than that his patient was hysterical. In providing this excuse for shoplifting, the doctor thus reinforced the common assumption that the female was often unstable, ruled by her nervous system and her emotions.[78]

Many times the woman's unconscious became the culprit. "I had no intention to steal anything," the putative Mary Smith told the judge, "[I] took the things unconsciously."[79] Mrs. Eladia Rubria protested that she did not know what she was doing when she took the candies, needles, kid gloves, silk scarves, and a comb, which were all jumbled together in a Gladstone bag she carried on her arm.[80] Laura Little's defense was classic. Not only was she described as "one of those apparently inexplicable cases of a young woman [she was thirty-one years old and unmarried] of respectable parentage being detected in shoplifting," but she, too, confessed that "she did not realise what she was doing when she took the fichu and other articles." She said she felt "possessed of an impulse to seize things and walk off." A variation on this theme was replayed with dismaying regularity.[81] The women used it to explain themselves, their lawyers used it to justify their clients' actions, and doctors used it to legitimize their diagnoses.

What they were describing, of course, was the pathology of consumption. Modern merchandising was geared to self-gratification, to the impulsive purchase, the irrational desire. Merchants wanted to make shoppers feel the propriety of such responses. Whetting the consumer's appetite with their emphasis on spending and material possessions, merchants, paradoxically, helped to promote the legitimacy of wants over needs, and "wants," sociologist Daniel Bell writes, "by their nature are unlimited and insatiable."[82]

In most cases the likelihood of being detected seemed never to have occurred to the women, for the general absence of caution was a hallmark of their behavior. On the other hand, some suspects probably did mean to get caught. For these women shoplifting was possibly a rational act of defiance to punish others—husbands and families—by punishing themselves. It is also possible that some women were reacting against their own dependence and economic powerlessness. As women began to move from the limited framework of domesticity and into a different self-definition, they might have been reacting to a crisis internal to the middle-class family. In shoplifting they were exercising both power and control, even if it was also what one psychiatrist has labeled a form of "moral suicide."[83] The four women from Lynn certainly were rational and aware of what they were doing and why they were doing it. Respectable women, who were ostensibly dedicated to the maintenance of middle-class values—which included the prohibition, "Thou Shalt Not Steal"—the Lynn shoplifters seemed not unduly burdened by such standard moral values until they were caught.

Although the source of the behavior was located in the individual and the

changes taking place in the middle-class family, the relationship between consciousness and activity can never be fully charted. Valid reasons may not be operative
reasons.[84] But whether the opportunity was there, or whether the women created it,
the ease of shoplifting in the modern department store made it seem like an invitation. The culture of the big store, the diverse stimuli within the shopping milieu,
created the environment that affected the behavior of so many women. Given the
free entry, the immense and almost seductive display of all kinds of objects, the
"freedom to pass unnoticed in the middle of a crowd" that constantly pressed on
all sides, and the possibility of touching whatever she found pleasing—given all
these factors and the virtual assurance that her class position protected her—it is
entirely probable that the middle-class woman shoplifted without thinking seriously
of the consequences.

There is no dearth of evidence that the impact of these middle-class shoplifters
was substantial. A relatively specific form of activity that became as much a female
symptom as a crime, shoplifting was decisively important because of the meaning
placed on it by physicians, the legal profession, the stores, the individuals involved,
and the larger society.

NOTES

1. Edwin S. Porter, *The Kleptomaniac,* Edison, 1905. Film.

2. Loren E. Edwards, *Shoplifting and Shrinkage Protection for Stores* (Springfield, Illinois: Charles C. Thomas, 1958), chap. II, 4–15.

3. *New York Times* (April 26, 1908), III, 8.

4. *Dry Goods Economist* (Oct. 27, 1900), 57; *Merchants Record and Show Window*
(Jan. 1910), 40.

5. *Boston Globe* (Dec. 6, 1897), 1:1.

6. *New York Times* (Dec. 11, 1897), 1:2; also see *Boston Globe* (Dec. 10, 1897), 1:5.

7. *Dry Goods Economist* (Oct. 27, 1900), 57. The DGE wrote that the situation was
different in London and Paris. Merchants in those cities were "vengeful," less interested in
the good will of friends and relatives. American stores and the general public viewed the
middle-class shoplifter very differently from the pickpocket or professional shoplifter; see
also Barbara Hobson, *Sex in the Marketplace* (Ph.D. diss., Boston University, 1982)

8. *New York Herald* (Feb. 7, 1886), 21:3–4; *Dry Goods Economist* (Feb. 1, 1902), 75
and (March 15, 1902), 75.

9. *Boston Globe* (Dec. 6, 1897), 6:2, editorial.

10. *New York Times* (Dec. 11, 1904), III, 1; *New York Daily Tribune* (Dec. 17, 1905),
V, 3:1.

11. These trends are evident in the 1880s in the correspondence of John Wanamaker.
Wanamaker wrote to one G. Harry Davis that he had reviewed "Mrs. Miller's case, and
considering the long period of time that she was stealing from us and the large quantity of
goods that you would readily admit, I think the sentence was an extremely light one. . . . I
cannot see my way clear to interfere with the sentence of the judge." On the following day
he wrote to the judge in the case. "I understand efforts are being made to get you to shorten
the sentence of Mrs. Miller who was convicted of stealing at the Grand Depot. But little of
her long continued offenses came before you and her sentence was light. I would suggest it

stand as it is." See John Wanamaker to G. Harry Davis, May 2, 1883, and John Wanamaker to Judge Allison, May 3, 1883, *Letterbook*, 33–34, Wanamaker Archives, Philadelphia, Pa. Bill Leach was kind enough to share this correspondence with me.

12. *New York Times* (Nov. 30, 1904), 1:2.

13. Ibid.

14. Joan Jacobs Brumberg, *Fasting Girls, The Emergence of Anorexia Nervosa as a Modern Disease* (Cambridge, MA: Harvard University Press, 1988), introduction.

15. John Wanamaker to Messrs. Rothermel Brown, *Letterbook,* 493, J. W. Personal from 1881–1883, Wanamaker Archives. Thanks are due, once again, to Bill Leach for uncovering this correspondence and sharing it with me.

16. *New York Times* (Feb. 18, 1893), 12:4.

17. Ibid. (Dec. 11, 1898), 3:5; see also *Brooklyn Eagle* (Dec. 22, 1896), 4:5, and (Oct. 27, 1896), 16:2.

18. *New York Times* (Dec. 9, 1908), 2:2, and (Dec. 12, 1908), 3:1.

19. *New York Times* (April 27, 1905), 18:5. In her autobiography, the notorious shoplifter Sophie Lyons related how, in the 1880s, she successfully convinced a store detective that she was a kleptomaniac: "Did you pay for that hat?" "No, Sir, I didn't pay a cent for it. You see, I am a Kleptomaniac, and I just cannot help taking any pretty thing I see in the stores. My husband has done everything to stop me, but the habit seems to be incurable." *Autobiography of Sophie Lyons* (Chicago: Star Publishing Co., 1913) typescript, from the files of the Pinkerton National Detective Agency.

20. *New York Times* (Dec. 2, 1904), 7:3. The unequal application of criminal law was a problem at all levels of the legal system. See Gerard C. Brandon, "The Unequal Application of the Criminal Law," *Journal of the American Institute of Criminal Law and Criminology* I, no. 6 (March 1911), 893–95; see also Barbara Hobson's dissertation, "Sex in the Marketplace." The discussion of the varying responses of the courts and the implicit class bias underlying the discretionary practices in the policing and treatment of prostitutes is applicable to the treatment of shoplifters; see personal correspondence of merchant John Wanamaker to attorneys, Messrs. Rothermel Brown, Jan. 8, 1883, *Letterbook*, 493, J. W. Personal from 1881–1883, Wanamaker Archives. Bill Leach passed this correspondence on to me.

21. *Merchant's Record and Show Window* (June 1916), 9, and (Jan. 1910), 40.

22. T. C. N. Gibbens and Joyce Prince, *Shoplifting* (London: The Institute for the Study and Treatment of Delinquency, 1962); T. C. N. Gibbens, Clare Palmer, Joyce Prince, "Mental Health Aspects of Shoplifting," *British Medical Journal* (Sept. 11, 1971), 612–15. English psychiatrist T. C. N. Gibbens was the author of a major study of shoplifting in London stores between July 1959 and August 1960. Interested in shoplifting behavior, Gibbens and his associate, Joyce Prince, investigated 532 cases of female shoplifting. While not applicable in all respects, the methodology and analytical categories used and the questions asked in this and in the ten-year follow-up study allowed me to look at my sample of about 190 shoplifters with a keener eye.

23. I have checked every women mentioned in a shoplifting case in the *New York Times* index for the years covered by this study, along with those so mentioned in the *Brooklyn Eagle* (1891–1903) and the *New York World* (sporadic index for a few years). I attempted to verify the addresses and occupations of the husbands in one of three New York City directories: *Phillips Elite Directory, Trows* New York City Directory (some New Jersey towns included), and the *Brooklyn City Directory*. Only 35 addresses were fully documented. Additional names that appeared in the pages of the store journals or other New York City newspapers were similarly checked.

The 190 names represent only a tiny fraction of the total number of shoplifting arrests. Other than middle-class female shoplifters, one was the son of the King of Spain, some were shopgirls, another was a Canadian minister, and another was a former church sexton. See *New York Times* (July 2, 1911), 3:7, (Dec. 20, 1907), 1:5, (Dec. 3, 1897), 5:3, and (July 20, 1898), 12:2.

24. Margaret Gibbons Wilson, *The American Woman in Transition: The Urban Influence, 1870–1920* (Westport, CT: Greenwood Press, 1979), 86; Katherine Kish Sklar, *Catharine Beecher: A Study in American Domesticity* (New York: W. W. Norton, 1973).

25. *New York Times* (Dec. 9, 1898), 1:3. Mrs. Abbie Long was the Sunday School Superintendent at The Church of the Puritans, located on 130th Street near Fifth Avenue. About one suspect arrested in 1893 we know nothing more than her name, Mary Arthur, and the intriguing fact that "she spent time in a cell reading a French novel." *New York Times* (Feb. 21, 1893), 3:4.

26. *New York Daily Tribune* (July 21, 1901), supplement, 1:4; Emma Churchman, *Queen of Home* (Philadelphia: Miller-Megee Co., 1889), 401–43, 458. Hewitt wrote of new avenues of employment opening for women, e.g., bookkeeping, shorthand, and typewriting, but these were careers for single women. She felt married women "should have one profession . . . from choice, let no mother relegate her duties to another, while she preaches science and knowledge away from home."

27. *Dry Goods Economist* (Dec. 4, 1897), 13, editorial, and (March 23, 1901), 153. See also Nathan C. Fowler, Jr. "Reaching the Men Through the Women," *Printers' Ink* 5 (July 22, 1891), 51–53, "The woman buys, or she directs the buying of everything from shoes to shingles."

28. *New York Times* (Nov. 29, 1904), 16:3.

29. Ibid. (Dec. 11, 1898), 3:5.

30. Sheila Rothman, *Woman's Proper Place: A History of Changing Ideals and Practices, 1870 to the Present* (New York: Basic Books, 1978); Karen J. Blair, *The Clubwoman as Feminist: True Womanhood Redefined, 1868–1914* (New York: Holmes & Meier, 1980); see also, Barbara J. Balliet, "What Shall We Do With Our Daughters? Middle-Class Women's Ideas About Work, 1840–1920" (Ph.D. diss., New York University, 1988).

31. Daniel T. Rodgers, *The Work Ethic in Industrial America, 1850–1920* (Chicago: University of Chicago Press, 1979), 183. Among the many articles on the "new woman," see Kate Gannett Wells, "The Transitional American Woman," *Atlantic Monthly* 46 (Dec. 1880), 817–23, and Caroline Ticknor, "The Steel-Engraved Lady and the Gibson Girl," *Atlantic Monthly* 88 (July 1901), 105–8.

32. This scenario appears in a variety of sources. See *New York Times* (April 26, 1908), 8; (Dec. 12, 1904), 6:4; (Jan. 2, 1906), 15:1; *New York Evening Post* (June 3, 1903), 5:1; *New York Tribune* (Dec. 17, 1905), V, 3:1.

33. Many sources deal with the sequence of these events. See *New York Times* (Dec. 11, 1904), III, 1; *New York Evening Post* (Feb. 18, 1899), 16:1. Some stores had women sign a release exonerating the store from any damage claims or suits for false arrest. See *New York Times* (Dec. 12, 1904), 6:4, and (Jan. 2, 1906), 15:1.

34. *Merchant's Record and Show Window* (Jan. 1910), 40; *New York Evening Post* (Feb. 18, 1899), 16:1; *New York World* (March 3, 1872).

35. *Dry Goods Economist* (Oct. 27, 1900), 57; *Merchant's Record and Show Window* (Jan. 1910), 40–41.

36. *Dry Goods Economist* (Aug. 31, 1901), 75.

37. *New York Times* (Dec. 11, 1904), III, 1.

38. *Dry Goods Economist* (Nov. 23, 1901), 21.

39. *New York Times* (Dec. 11, 1904), III, 1.

40. *Dry Goods Economist* (Nov. 23, 1901), 21.

41. *New York Times* (Dec. 20, 1900), 1:3.

42. There are numerous citations in the daily press for this practice of giving false names. See for example *New York Times* (Feb. 18, 1893), 12:4; (March 1, 1895), 13:6; (Dec. 19, 1895), 14:2; (Dec. 11, 1904), III:1; *San Francisco Chronicle* (Dec. 1, 1896), 5:2; *Boston Globe* (Dec. 25, 1897), 1:7.

43. *New York Daily Tribune* (Feb. 20, 1893), 12:2, and (Dec. 17, 1905), V, 3:1. One well-dressed woman was reported as crying, "Oh, what will my husband say . . . I shall be disgraced for life."

44. *Boston Globe* (Dec. 21, 1897), 3:7.

45. *New York Times* (Dec. 19, 1880), 8:1 and (Dec. 28, 1880), 8:5.

46. Ibid. (Nov. 8, 1883), 8:1 and (Dec. 28, 1880), 8:5.

47. Ibid. (Dec. 19, 1895), 14:2. The lawyer for many of these cases was Mark Alter. Claiming to have defended over 500 shoplifting cases, Alter gave a dramatic interview to a *Times* reporter. "If I could give the real names of the 500 women whom I have defended on the charge of shoplifting, it would make a sensation that would startle New York. One was the wife of a Supreme Court judge, another a near relative of an ambassador; one, a well-known society woman, had several hundred dollars in her pocketbook when she was arrested for stealing a trinket worth a few dollars. Out of 4000 arrests every year, only about 700 ever get into the courts and of this number not more than 50 are convicted." *New York Times* (Jan. 2, 1906), 15:1.

48. Ibid. (Feb. 2, 1898), 3:4.

49. Mark Twain, *The Gilded Age*, (Hartford, CT: American Publishing Co., 1874), 355; Stowe Persons, *The Decline of American Gentility* (New York: Columbia University Press, 1963), 101; John G. Cawelti, *Apostles of the Self-Made Man* (Chicago: The University of Chicago Press, 1965), 36, 178–80.

50. *New York Times* (Dec. 20, 1895), 9:6. The *Times* ran a full-page article with illustrations, "Harvest-Time of the Shoplifter," in a Sunday edition in 1904 that discussed the battle of wits between store detectives and women shoppers. "More important than the explanation of the theft . . . is to ascertain the real name and address of the shoplifter." (Dec. 11, 1904), III, 1:1.

51. *Brooklyn Eagle* (Aug. 28, 1899), 2:4; (Aug. 29), 2:4; (Aug. 31), 1:7. It was not an accident that the final court appearance of the richly attired Mrs. Whigham ran on page one.

52. *New York Times* (Jan. 11, 1898), 3:5.

53. Ibid. (Dec. 20, 1895), 9:6.

54. Ibid. (May 16, 1897), 11:2.

55. Ibid. (March 28, 1898), 8:7. Testimony in the Castle shoplifting incident pointed out that "Mr. Castle was very generous with his wife." See *San Francisco Chronicle* (Oct. 14, 1896), 1:1.

56. Psychologists had advanced this very possibility in 1862. Writing in the *Journal of Mental Science* and excerpted in the *American Journal of Insanity*, the prominent English authority on insanity, Dr. John C. Bucknill, analyzed early evidence of "the thieving madness." It is, he wrote, "part of the struggle for existence in the middle and even upper-classes of our complex social system." Such madness "combined with the prevailing fashion of an emulative and showy expenditure, [to] make the *sense* of want keenly felt . . . where no traces of vulgar poverty are discernible. . . . Women . . . spend no inconsiderable portion of her [*sic*] time in the discharge of that new and peculiar duty of life called 'shopping,' can we be

surprised that when the means fail to satisfy the desires thus stimulated . . . that in some few instances the desire of the eye should prove too strong for the moral sense. . . . It would be more true than gallant to consider these fair thieves as an elder kind of children." *AJI* XIX (Oct. 1862), 150–51. See full article "Kleptomania," *Journal of Mental Science* VIII, 42 (London 1863), 262–75.

57. Paul Michael Rogin, *Subversive Genealogy*: The Politics and Art of Human Melville (New York: Knopf, 1983), 126; for a sardonic view of consumerism, see James Fenimore Cooper, *Autobiography of a Pocket Handkerchief* (Evanston, Illinois: R. R. Donnelley, 1897).

58. *Boston Globe* (Dec. 5, 1897), 2:2.

59. Thorstein Veblen, *Theory of the Leisure Class* (New York: Viking, 1931); Abba Goold Woolson, *Women in American Society*, (Boston: Roberts Brothers, 1873), 108–9; Patricia Branca, *Silent Sisterhood*, (Pittsburgh: Carnegie-Mellon University Press, 1975), 52–53; Neil McKendrick, John Brewer, and J. H. Plumb, *The Birth of a Consumer Society* (Bloomington: Indiana University Press, 1982), chap. II, "The Commercialization of Fashion," 34–99. Although he is dealing with Georgian England, McKendrick sees emulative and taste-induced spending among increasingly wide sectors of English society a century before similar developments in the United States. For a new examination of American spending habits and ideology, see Daniel Horowitz, *The Morality of Spending* (Baltimore: John Hopkins University Press, 1985).

For two personal views see Josephine Pitcairn Knowles, *The Upholstered Cage* (New York: Hodder & Stoughton, 1913), 26, and Mrs. Ives, "Pin Money for Married Women," The *Boston Herald* (Sept. 13, 1890), 9:3. For the quintessential statement about the importance of "things" as the expression of the person, see Henry James, *The Portrait of a Lady* (New York: New American Library, 1979); also Theodore Dreiser, *Sister Carrie* (Indianapolis: Bobbs-Merrill, 1970).

60. Bertha June Richardson, *The Woman Who Spends* (Boston: Whitcomb & Barrows, 1904), 40.

61. Ibid., 38.

62. Lilly Devereux Blake, *Fettered for Life*; (New York: Sheldon Co., 1874); Abraham Meyerson, M.D., *The Nervous Housewife* (Boston: Little, Brown, 1920), 146; see also Nathan C. Fowler, "Reaching the Men through the Women *Printer's Ink* 5 (July 22, 1891)," 51. For an interpretation of female dependence in a market world in 19th-century France, see Bonnie Smith, *Ladies of the Leisure Class* (New Jersey: Princeton University Press, 1981), 64–65.

63. Hewitt, *Queen of Home*, 38.

64. Adeline Hibbard Gregory, *A Great Grandmother Remembers* (Chicago: A. Kroch, 1940), 114.

65. William Dean Howells, *A Woman's Reason* (Boston: Osgood & Co., 1883), 185. Describing the fierce concentration of women shopping, Howells asked, "Where does the money all come from? It is a fearful problem, and the imagination must shrink from following these multitudinous shoppers to their homes, in city and suburb, when they arrive frayed and limp and sore, with overspent allowances, and the hard task before them of making the worst appear the better reason." Some historians see women in control of the household budget. See Branca, *Silent Sisterhood*, 22.

66. *Business Woman's Journal* (Feb. 1892), 55–56, and (Nov. 1892), 59, "Progress." Lucy M. Salamon, "The Economics of Spending," *Outlook* 91 (April 17, 1909), 889; Veblen, *Theory of the Leisure Class*, 193; Blake, *Fettered for Life*, 160.

67. *Boston Herald* (Sept. 13, 1890), 9:3, excerpted from *Forum* magazine, Sept. 1890.

For the crippling effects of economic dependence on women, see Charlotte Perkins Gilman, *Women and Economics: A Study of the Economic Relation between Men and Women as a Factor in Social Evolution* (1898) (New York: Harper and Row, 1966).

68. David John Thomas, "The Demographics of Shoplifting" (Ph.D. diss., University of Nebraska–Lincoln, 1979), 222. In 1902 a spokesman for Ehrich Bros. commented, ". . . there is that innate love of shopping which many a woman feels obliged to gratify even with an impoverished purse." *Dry Goods Economist* (Feb. 22, 1902), 37.

69. *New York Times* (Dec. 19, 1895), 14:2.

70. David Brion Davis, *Homicide in American Fiction, 1798–1860: A Study in Social Values* (Ithaca: Cornell Univ. Press, 1957), 21. For a discussion about the repression of guilt as an expression of anxiety, see Melvin Zax and George Strickler, *The Study of Abnormal Behavior* (New York: Macmillan Publ. Co., 1974), 28. In an article entitled "City Shoplifters," the *Boston Herald* noted, "conscience stifled by cupidity is dormant, and the lust of possession is all that possesses her." *Boston Herald* (Feb. 7, 1886), 21:3–4. For another statement to this effect, see *Merchant's Record and Show Window* (Jan. 1910), 40; see also Sigmund Freud, *Totem and Taboo* (New York: W. W. Norton, 1950), 29–34, 70–71, 85–87.

71. *Boston Globe* (Dec. 5, 1897), 1:6; *New York Times* (Dec. 8, 1907), 5:3. The former head of protection at Marshall Field suggests that nonprofessional shoplifters maintain conventional attitudes toward theft. Loren E. Edwards, *Shoplifting and Shrinkage Protection for Stores* (Springfield, Ill.: Charles C. Thomas, 1958). It is interesting to note that Lizzie Borden was also a shoplifter. See Edward Rowe Snow, *Piracy, Mutiny and Murder* (New York: Dodd, Mead, 1959), 275–77.

72. *Boston Globe* (Dec. 21, 1897), 3:7; *Brooklyn Eagle* (Nov. 9, 1901), 2:6.

73. *New York Times* (Feb. 4, 1886), 2:6; for a similar, French interpretation, see Maurice Bontemps, *Du vol dans les grands magasins et du vol à l'étalage* (Paris: Étude medico-legale, 1894), 10. American detectives were not unaware of this possibility; see *New York Daily Tribune* (Dec. 17, 1905), V, 3:1.

74. Natalie Zemon Davis, *Fiction in the Archives: Pardon Tales and Their Tellers in Sixteenth-Century France* (Stanford, Calif.: Stanford Univ. Press, 1987), chap. 3, 77–109.

75. *New York Times* (Dec. 10, 1898), 3:2; T. C. N. Gibbens, "Shoplifting," *British Journal of Psychiatry* 138 (April 1981), 347.

76. Leonard I. Sweet, *The Minister's Wife: Her Role in Nineteenth-Century American Evangelism* (Philadelphia: Temple University Press, 1983), 221.

77. *New York Times* (Feb, 19, 1893), 9:4. The "medical history" of Mrs. Louisa Schloss, mentioned earlier, was quite similar to this episode, although the two incidents took place fifteen years apart; see Dr. Walker Gill Wylie's obituary in the *New York Times* (March 14, 1923), 19:5.

78. *New York Herald* (Feb. 7, 1886), 21:3–4. Some women "are simply not strong in resisting the temptations to which their sex are most subject." The article continues, "Some really absent-minded have carried some article away from the counter utterly unconscious of it." There are so many comments of this nature that it is difficult to choose only one.

79. *New York Times* (Feb. 18, 1893), 8:6.

80. Ibid. (Dec. 26, 1892), 5:7.

81. Ibid. (May 24, 1893), 9:2. It is interesting that Miss Little was a repeat customer in Stern's. See also *New York Times* (Jan. 18, 1882), 8:6; (Aug. 14, 1887), 1:4; (March 27, 1889), 2:5.

82. Daniel Bell, *The Cultural Contradictions of Capitalism* (New York: Basic Books, 1976), 224; Rosalind H. Williams, *Dream Worlds*, (Berkeley: University of California Press, 1982).

83. Gibbens and Prince, *Shoplifting*, 86.

84. Nina Auerbach, *Woman and the Demon* (Cambridge: Harvard University Press, 1982), 189. Gibbens and Prince: "A simple confession does not imply a simple motive." *Shoplifting*, 81. Cushing Strout, "The Uses and Abuses of Psychology in American History," *American Quarterly* 28 (1976) 332–39.

Chapter Nineteen

"Charity Girls" and City Pleasures
Historical Notes on Working-Class Sexuality, 1880–1920

Kathy Peiss

Uncovering the history of working-class sexuality has been a particularly intractable task for recent scholars. Diaries, letters, and memoirs, while a rich source for studies of bourgeois sexuality, offer few glimpses into working-class intimate life. We have had to turn to middle-class commentary and observations of working people, but these accounts often seem hopelessly moralistic and biased. The difficulty with such sources is not simply a question of tone or selectivity, but involves the very categories of analysis they employ. Reformers, social workers, and journalists viewed working-class women's sexuality through middle-class lenses, invoking sexual standards that set "respectability" against "promiscuity." When applied to unmarried women, these categories were constructed foremost around the biological fact of premarital virginity, and secondarily by such cultural indicators as manners, language, dress, and public interaction. Chastity was the measure of young women's respectability, and those who engaged in premarital intercourse, or, more importantly, dressed and acted as though they had, were classed as promiscuous women or prostitutes. Thus labor investigations of the late nineteenth century not only surveyed women's wages and working conditions, but delved into the issue of their sexual virtue, hoping to resolve scientifically the question of working women's respectability.[1]

Nevertheless, some middle-class observers in city missions and settlements recognized that their standards did not always reflect those of working-class youth. As one University Settlement worker argued, "Many of the liberties which are taken by tenement boys and girls with one another, and which seem quite improper to the 'up-towner,' are, in fact, practically harmless."[2] Working women's public behavior often seemed to fall between the traditional middle-class poles: they were not truly promiscuous in their actions, but neither were they models of decorum. A boarding-house matron, for example, puzzled over the behavior of Mary, a "good girl": "The other night she flirted with a man across the street," she explained. "It is true she dropped him when he offered to take her into a saloon. But she does go to picture shows and dance halls with 'pick up' men and boys."[3] Similarly, a city missionary noted that tenement dwellers followed different rules of etiquette, with the observation: "Young women sometimes allow young men to address them and caress them in a manner which would offend well-bred people, and yet those girls would indignantly resent any liberties which they consider dishonoring."[4] These examples suggest that we must reach beyond the dichotomized analysis of many middle-class observers and draw out the cultural categories created and acted on by working women themselves. How was sexuality "handled" culturally? What manners, etiquette, and sexual style met with general approval? What constituted sexual respectability? Does the polarized framework of the middle class reflect the realities of working-class culture?

Embedded within the reports and surveys lie small pieces of information that illuminate the social and cultural construction of sexuality among a number of working-class women. My discussion focuses on one set of young, white working women in New York City in the years 1880 to 1920. Most of these women were single wage earners who toiled in the city's factories, shops, and department stores, while devoting their evenings to the lively entertainment of the streets, public dance halls; and other popular amusements. Born or educated in the United States, many adopted a cultural style meant to distance themselves from their immigrant roots and familial traditions. Such women dressed in the latest finery, negotiated city life with ease, and sought intrigue and adventure with male companions. For this group of working women, sexuality became a central dimension of their emergent culture, a dimension that is revealed in their daily life of work and leisure.[5]

These New York working women frequented amusements in which familiarity and intermingling among strangers, not decorum, defined normal public behavior between the sexes. At movies and cheap theaters, crowds mingled during intermissions, shared picnic lunches, and commented volubly on performances. Strangers at Coney Island's amusement parks often involved each other in practical jokes and humorous escapades, while dance halls permitted close interaction between unfamiliar men and women. At one respectable Turnverein ball, for example, a vice investigator described closely the chaotic activity in the barroom between dances:

> Most of the younger couples were hugging and kissing, there was a general mingling of men and women at the different tables, almost everyone seemed to know one another and spoke to each other across the tables and joined couples at different tables, they were all singing and carrying on, they kept running around the room and acted like a mob of lunatics let lo[o]se.[6]

As this observer suggests, an important aspect of social familiarity was the ease of sexual expression in language and behavior. Dances were advertised, for example, through the distribution of "pluggers," small printed cards announcing the particulars of the ball, along with snatches of popular songs or verse; the lyrics and pictures, noted one offended reformer, were often "so suggestive that they are absolutely indecent."[7]

The heightened sexual awareness permeating many popular amusements may also be seen in working-class dancing styles. While waltzes and two-steps were common, working women's repertoire included "pivoting" and "tough dances."

While pivoting was a wild, spinning dance that promoted a charged atmosphere of physical excitement, tough dances ranged from a slow shimmy, or shaking of the hips and shoulders, to boisterous animal imitations. Such tough dances as the grizzly bear, Charlie Chaplin wiggle, and the dip emphasized bodily contact and the suggestion of sexual intercourse. As one dance investigator commented, "What particularly distinguishes this dance is the motion of the pelvic portions of the body."[8] In contrast, middle-class pleasure-goers accepted the animal dances only after the blatant sexuality had been tamed into refined movement. While cabaret owners enforced strict rules to discourage contact between strangers, managers of working-class dance halls usually winked at spieling, tough dancing, and unrestrained behavior.[9]

Other forms of recreation frequented by working-class youth incorporated a free and easy sexuality into their attractions. Many social clubs and amusement societies permitted flirting, touching, and kissing games at their meetings. One East Side youth reported that "they have kissing all through pleasure time, and use slang language, while in some they don't behave nice between [sic] young ladies."[10] Music halls and cheap vaudeville regularly worked sexual themes and suggestive humor into comedy routines and songs. At a Yiddish music hall popular with both men and women, one reformer found that "the songs are suggestive of everything but what is proper, the choruses are full of double meanings, and the jokes have broad and unmistakable hints of things indecent."[11] Similarly, Coney Island's Steeplechase amusement park, favored by working-class excursionists, carefully marketed sexual titillation and romance in attractions that threw patrons into each other, sent skirts flying, and evoked instant intimacy among strangers.[12]

In attending dance halls, social club entertainments, and amusement resorts, young women took part in a cultural milieu that expressed and affirmed heterosocial interactions. As reformer Belle Israels observed, "No amusement is complete in which 'he' is not a factor."[13] A common custom involved "picking up" unknown men or women in amusement resorts or on the streets, an accepted means of gaining companionship for an evening's entertainment. Indeed, some amusement societies existed for this very purpose. One vice investigator, in his search for "loose" women, was advised by a waiter to "go first on a Sunday night to 'Hans'l & Gret'l Amusement Society' at the Lyceum 86th Str & III Ave, there the girls come and men pick them up."[14] The waiter carefully stressed that these were respectable working women, not prostitutes. Nor was the pickup purely a male prerogative. "With the men they 'pick up,'" writer Hutchins Hapgood observed of East Side shop girls, "they will go to the theater, to late suppers, will be as jolly as they like."[15]

The heterosocial orientation of these amusements made popularity a goal to be pursued through dancing ability, willingness to drink, and eye-catching finery. Women who would not drink at balls and social entertainments were often ostracized by men, while cocktails and ingenious mixtures replaced the five-cent beer and helped to make drinking an acceptable female activity. Many women used clothing as a means of drawing attention to themselves, wearing high-heeled shoes, fancy dresses, costume jewelry, elaborate pompadours, and cosmetics. As one working woman sharply explained, "If you want to get any notion took of you, you gotta have some style about you."[16] The clothing that such women wore no longer served as an emblem of respectability. "The way women dress today they all look like prostitutes," reported one rueful waiter to a dance hall investigator, "and the waiter can some times get in bad by going over and trying to put some one next to them, they may be respectable women and would jump on the waiter."[17]

Underlying the relaxed sexual style and heterosocial interaction was the custom of "treating." Men often treated their female companions to drinks and refreshments, theater tickets, and other incidentals. Women might pay a dance hall's entrance fee or carfare out to an amusement park, but they relied on men's treats to see them through the evening's entertainment. Such treats were highly prized by young working women; as Belle Israels remarked, the announcement that "he treated" was "the acme of achievement in retailing experiences with the other sex."[18]

Treating was not a one-way proposition, however, but entailed an exchange relationship. Financially unable to reciprocate in kind, women offered sexual favors of varying degrees, ranging from flirtatious companionship to sexual intercourse, in exchange for men's treats. "Pleasures don't cost girls so much as they do young men," asserted one saleswoman. "If they are agreeable they are invited out a good deal, and they are not allowed to pay anything." Reformer Lillian Betts concurred, observing that the working woman held herself responsible for failing to wangle men's invitations and believed that "it is not only her misfortune, but her fault; she should be more attractive."[19] Gaining men's treats placed a high premium on allure and personality, and sometimes involved aggressive and frank "overtures to men whom they desire to attract," often with implicit sexual proposals. One investigator, commenting on women's dependency on men in their leisure time, aptly observed that "those who are unattractive, and those who have puritanic notions, fare but ill in the matter of enjoyments. On the other hand those who do become popular have to compromise with the best conventional usage."[20]

Many of the sexual patterns acceptable in the world of leisure activity were mirrored in the workplace. Sexual harassment by employers, foremen, and fellow workers was a widespread practice in this period, and its form often paralleled the relationship of treating, particularly in service and sales jobs. Department store managers, for example, advised employees to round out their meager salaries by finding a "gentleman friend" to purchase clothing and pleasures. An angry saleswoman testified, for example, that "one of the employers has told me, on a $6.50 wage, he don't care where I get my clothes from as long as I have them, to be dressed to suit him."[21] Waitresses knew that accepting the advances of male customers often brought good tips, and some used their opportunities to enter an active social life with men. "Most of the girls quite frankly admit making 'dates' with strange men," one investigator found. "These 'dates' are made with no thought on the part of the girl beyond getting the good time which she cannot afford herself."[22]

In factories where men and women worked together, the sexual style that we have seen on the dance floor was often reproduced on the shop floor. Many factories lacked privacy in dressing facilities, and workers tolerated a degree of familiarity and roughhousing between men and women. One cigar maker observed that his workplace socialized the young into sexual behavior unrestrained by parental and community control. Another decried the tendency of young boys "of thirteen or fourteen casting an eye upon a 'mash.' " Even worse, he testified, were the

> many men who are respected—when I say respected and respectable, I mean who walk the streets and are respected as working men, and who would not under any circumstances offer the slightest insult or disrespectful remark or glance to a female in the streets, but who, in the shops, will whoop and give expressions to "cat calls" and a peculiar noise made with their lips, which is supposed to be an endearing salutation.[23]

In sexually segregated workplaces, sexual knowledge was probably transmitted among working women. A YWCA report in 1913 luridly asserted that "no girl is more 'knowing' than the wage-earner, for the 'older hands' initiate her early through the unwholesome story or innuendo."[24] Evidence from factories, department stores, laundries, and restaurants substantiates the sexual consciousness of female workers. Women brought to the workplace tales of their evening adventures and gossip about dates and eligible men, recounting to their co-workers the triumphs of the latest ball or outing. Women's socialization into a new shop might involve a ritualist exchange about "gentlemen friends." In one laundry, for example, an investigator repeatedly heard this conversation:

> "Say, you got a feller?"
> "Sure. Ain't you got one?"
> "Sure."[25]

Through the use of slang and "vulgar" language, heterosexual romance was expressed in a sexually explicit context. Among waitresses, for example, frank discussion of lovers and husbands during breaks was an integral part of the work day. One investigator found that "there was never any open violation of the proprieties but always the suggestive talk and behavior." Laundries, too, witnessed "a great deal of swearing among the women." A 1914 study of department store clerks found a similar style and content in everyday conversation:

> While it is true that the general attitude toward men and sex relations was normal, all the investigators admitted a freedom of speech frequently verging upon the vulgar, but since there was very little evidence of any actual immorality, this can probably be likened to the same spirit which prompts the telling of risqué stories in other circles.[26]

In their workplaces and leisure activities, many working women discovered a milieu that tolerated, and at times encouraged, physical and verbal familiarity between men and women, and stressed the exchange of sexual favors for social and economic advantages. Such women probably received conflicting messages about the virtues of virginity, and necessarily mediated the parental, religious, and educational injunctions concerning chastity, and the "lessons" of urban life and labor.

The choice made by some women to engage in a relaxed sexual style needs to be understood in terms of the larger relations of class and gender that structured their sexual culture.

Most single working-class women were wage-earners for a few years before marriage, contributing to the household income or supporting themselves. Sexual segmentation of the labor market placed women in semi-skilled, seasonal employment with high rates of turnover. Few women earned a "living wage," estimated to be $9.00 or $10.00 a week in 1910, and the wage differential between men and women was vast. Those who lived alone in furnished rooms or boarding houses consumed their earnings in rent, meals, and clothing. Many self-supporting women were forced to sacrifice an essential item in their weekly budgets, particularly food, in order to pay for amusements. Under such circumstances, treating became a viable option. "If my boy friend didn't take me out," asked one working woman, "how could I ever go out?"[27] While many women accepted treats from "steadies," others had no qualms about receiving them from acquaintances or men they picked up at amusement places. As one investigator concluded, "The acceptance on the part of the girl of almost any invitation needs little explanation when one realizes that she often goes pleasureless unless she does accept free treats.' "[28] Financial resources were little better for the vast majority of women living with families and relatives. Most of them contributed all of their earnings to the family, receiving only small amounts of spending money, usually 25¢ to 50¢ a week, in return. This sum covered the costs of simple entertainments, but could not purchase higher priced amusements.[29]

Moreover, the social and physical space of the tenement home and boarding house contributed to freer social and sexual practices. Working women living alone ran the gauntlet between landladies' suspicious stares and the knowing glances of male boarders. One furnished-room dweller attested to the pressure placed on young, single women: "Time and again when a male lodger meets a girl on the landing, his salutation usually ends with something like this: 'Won't you step into my place and have a glass of beer with me?' "[30]

The tenement home, too, presented a problem to parents who wished to maintain control over their daughters' sexuality. Typical tenement apartments offered limited opportunities for family activities or chaperoned socializing. Courtship proved difficult in homes where families and boarders crowded into a few small rooms, and the "parlor" served as kitchen, dining room, and bedroom. Instead, many working-class daughters socialized on streetcorners, rendezvoused in cafes, and courted on trolley cars. As one settlement worker observed, "Boys and girls and young men and women of respectable families are almost obliged to carry on many of their friendships, and perhaps their love-making, on tenement stoops or on street corners."[31] Another reformer found that girls whose parents forebade men's visits to the home managed to escape into the streets and dance halls to meet them. Such young women demanded greater independence in the realm of "personal life" in exchange for their financial contribution to the family. For some, this new freedom spilled over into their sexual practices.[32]

The extent of the sexual culture described here is particularly difficult to establish, since the evidence is too meager to permit conclusions about specific groups of working women, their beliefs about sexuality, and their behavior. Scattered evidence does suggest a range of possible responses, the parameters within which most women would choose to act and define their behavior as socially acceptable. Within this range, there existed a subculture of working women who fully bought into the system of treating and sexual exchange, by trading sexual favors of varying degrees for gifts, treats, and a good time. These women were known in underworld slang as "charity girls," a term that differentiated them from prostitutes because they did not accept money in their sexual encounters with men. As vice reformer George Kneeland found, they "offer themselves to strangers, not for money, but for presents, attention, and pleasure, and most important, a yielding to sex desire."[33] Only a thin line divided these women and "occasional prostitutes," women who slipped in and out of prostitution when unemployed or in need of extra income. Such behavior did not result in the stigma of the "fallen woman." Many working women apparently acted like Dottie: "When she needed a pair of shoes she had found it easy to 'earn' them in the way that other girls did." Dottie, the investigator reported, was now known as a respectable married woman.[34]

Such women were frequent patrons of the city's dance halls. Vice investigators note a preponderant number of women at dances who clearly were not prostitutes, but were "game" and "lively"; these charity girls often comprised half or more of the dancers in a hall. One dance hall investigator distinguished them with the observation, "Some of the women . . . are out for the coin, but there is a lot that come in here that are charity."[35] One waiter at La Kuenstler Klause, a restaurant with music and dancing, noted that "girls could be gotten here, but they don't go with men for money, only for good time." The investigator continued in his report, "Most of the girls are working girls, not prostitutes, they smoke cigarettes, drink liquers and dance dis.[orderly] dances, stay out late and stay with any man, that pick them up first."[36] Meeting two women at a bar, another investigator remarked, "They are both supposed to be working girls but go out for a good time and go the limit."[37]

Some women obviously relished the game of extracting treats from men. One vice investigator offered to take a Kitty Graham, who apparently worked both as a department store clerk and occasional prostitute, to the Central Opera House at 3 A.M.; he noted that "she was willing to go if I'd take a taxi; I finally coaxed her to come with me in a street car."[38] Similarly, Frances Donovan observed waitresses "talking about their engagements which they had for the evening or for the night and quite frankly saying what they expected to get from this or that fellow in the line of money, amusement, or clothes."[39] Working women's manipulation of treating is also suggested by this unguarded conversation overheard by a journalist at Coney Island:

"What sort of a time did you have?"
"Great. He blew in $5 on the blow-out."
"You beat me again. My chump only spent $2.50."[40]

These women had clearly accepted the full implications of the system of treating and the sexual culture surrounding it.

While this evidence points to the existence of charity girls—working women defined as respectable, but who engaged in sexual activity—it tells us little about their numbers, social background, working lives, or relationships to family and community. The vice reports indicate that they were generally young women, many of whom lived at home with their families. One man in a dance hall remarked, for example, that "he sometimes takes them to the hotels, but sometimes the girls won't go to [a] hotel to stay for the night, they are afraid of their mothers, so he gets away with it in the hallway."[41] While community sanctions may have prevented such activity within the neighborhood, the growth of large public dance halls, cabarets, and metropolitan amusement resorts provided an anonymous space in which the subculture of treating could flourish.

The charity girl's activities form only one response in a wide spectrum of social and sexual behavior. Many young women defined themselves sharply against the freer sexuality of their pleasure-seeking sisters, associating "respectability" firmly with premarital chastity and circumspect behavior. One working woman carefully explained her adherence to propriety: "I never go out in the evenings except to my relatives because if I did, I should lose my reputation and that is all I have left." Similarly, shop girls guarded against sexual advances from co-workers and male customers by spurning the temptations of popular amusements. "I keep myself to myself," said one saleswoman. "I don't make friends in the stores very easily because you can't be sure what any one is like."[42] Settlement workers also noted that women who freely attended "dubious resorts" or bore illegitimate children were often stigmatized by neighbors and workmates. Lillian Betts, for example, cites the case of working women who refused to labor until their employer dismissed a co-worker who had born a baby out of wedlock. To Betts, however, their adherence to the standard of virginity seemed instrumental, and not a reflection of moral absolutism: "The hardness with which even the suggestion of looseness is treated in any group of working girls is simply an expression of self-preservation."[43]

Other observers noted an ambivalence in the attitudes of young working women toward sexual relations. Social workers reported that the critical stance toward premarital pregnancy was "not always unmixed with a certain degree of admiration for the success with the other sex which the difficulty implies." According to this study, many women increasingly found premarital intercourse acceptable in particular situations: " 'A girl can have many friends,' explained one of them, 'but when she gets a "steady," there's only one way to have him and to keep him; I mean to keep him long.' "[44] Such women shared with charity girls the assumption that respectability was not predicated solely on chastity.

Perhaps few women were charity girls or occasional prostitutes, but many more must have been conscious of the need to negotiate sexual encounters in the workplace or in their leisure time. Women would have had to weigh their desire for social participation against traditional sanctions regarding sexual behavior, and charity girls offered to some a model for resolving this conflict. This process is exemplified in Clara Laughlin's report of an attractive but "proper" working woman who could not understand why men friends dropped her after a few dates. Finally she receives the worldly advice of a co-worker that social participation involves an exchange relationship: "Don't yeh know there ain't no feller goin' t'spend coin on yeh fer nothin'? Yeh gotta be a good Indian, Kid—we all gotta!"[45]

For others, charity girls represented a yardstick against which they might measure their own ideas of respectability. The nuances of that measurement were expressed, for example, in a dialogue between a vice investigator and the hat girl at Semprini's dance hall. Answering his proposal for a date, the investigator noted, she "said she'd be glad to go out with me but told me there was nothing doing [i.e., sexually]. Said she didn't like to see a man spend money on her and then get disappointed." Commenting on the charity girls that frequented the dance hall, she remarked that "these women get her sick, she can't see why a woman should lay down for a man the first time they take her out. She said it wouldn't be so bad if they went out with the men 3 or 4 times and then went to bed with them but not the first time."[46]

For this hat girl and other young working women, respectability was not defined by the strict measurement of chastity employed by many middle-class observers and reformers. Instead, they adopted a more instrumental and flexible approach to sexual behavior. Premarital sex *could* be labeled respectable in particular social contexts. Thus charity girls distinguished their sexual activity from prostitution, a less acceptable practice, because they did not receive money from men. Other women, who might view charity girls as promiscuous, were untroubled by premarital intimacy with a steady boyfriend.

This fluid definition of sexual respectability was embedded within the social relation of class and gender, as experienced by women in their daily round of work, leisure, and family life. Women's wage labor and the demands of the working-class household offered daughters few resources for entertainment. At the same time, new commercial amusements offered a tempting world of pleasure and companionship beyond parental control. Within this context, some young women sought to exchange sexual goods for access to that world and its seeming independence, choosing not to defer sexual relations until marriage. Their notions of legitimate premarital behavior contrast markedly with the dominant middle-class view, which placed female sexuality within a dichotomous and rigid framework. Whether a hazard at work, fun and adventure at night, or an opportunity to be exploited, sexual expression and intimacy comprised an integral part of these working women's lives.

NOTES

1. See, for example, Carroll D. Wright, *The Working Girls of Boston* (1889; New York: Arno Press, 1969).

2. "Influences in Street Life," University Settlement Society *Report* (1900), p. 30.

3. Marie S. Orenstein, "How the Working Girl of New York Lives," New York State, Factory Investigating Commission, *Fourth Report Transmitted to Legislature*, February 15, 1915, Senate Doc. 43, vol. 4, app. 2 (Albany: J. B. Lyon Co., 1915), p. 1697.

4. William T. Elsing, "Life in New York Tenement-Houses as Seen by a City Missionary," *Scribner's* 11 (June 1892): 716.

5. For a more detailed discussion of these women, and further documentation of their social relations and leisure activities, see my dissertation, "Cheap Amusements: Gender Relations and the Use of Leisure Time in New York City, 1880 to 1920," Ph.D. diss., Brown University, 1982.

6. Investigator's Report, Remey's, 917 Eighth Ave., February 11, 1917, Committee of Fourteen Papers, New York Public Library Manuscript Division, New York.

7. George Kneeland, *Commercialized Prostitution in New York City* (New York: The Century Co., 1913), p. 68; Louise de Koven Bowen, "Dance Halls," *Survey* 26 (3 July 1911): 384.

8. Committee on Amusements and Vacation Resources of Working Girls, two-page circular, in Box 28, "Parks and Playgrounds Correspondence," Lillian Wald Collection, Rare Book and Manuscripts Library, Columbia University, New York.

9. See, for example, Investigator's Report, Princess Cafe, 1206 Broadway, January 1, 1917; and Excelsior Cafe, 306 Eighth Ave., December 21, 1916, Committee of Fourteen Papers. For an excellent discussion of middle-and upper-class leisure activities, see Lewis A. Erenberg, *Steppin' Out: New York Nightlife and the Transformation of American Culture, 1890–1930* (Westport, Conn.: Greenwood Press, 1981).

10. "Social Life in the Streets," University Settlement Society Report (1899), p. 32.

11. Paul Klapper, "The Yiddish Music Hall," *University Settlement Studies* 2, no. 4 (1905): 22.

12. For a description of Coney Island amusements, see Edo McCullough, *Good Old Coney Island; A Sentimental Journey into the Past* (New York: Charles Scribner's Sons, 1957), pp. 309–13; and Oliver Pilot and Jo Ransom, *Sodom by the Sea: An Affectionate History of Coney Island* (Garden City, N.J.: Doubleday, 1941).

13. Belle Lindner Israels, "The Way of the Girl," *Survey* 22 (3 July 1909): 486.

14. Investigator's Report, La Kuenstler Klause, 1490 Third Ave., January 19, 1917, Committee of Fourteen Papers.

15. Hutchins Hapgood, *Types from City Streets* (New York: Funk and Wagnalls, 1910), p. 131.

16. Clara Laughlin, *The Work-A-Day Girl: A Study of Some Present Conditions* (1913; New York: Arno Press, 1974), pp. 47, 145. On working women's clothing, see Helen Campbell, *Prisoners of Poverty: Women Wage-Earners, Their Trades and Their Lives* (1887; Westport, Conn.: Greenwood Press, 1970), p. 175; "What It Means to Be a Department Store Girl as Told by the Girl Herself," *Ladies Home Journal* 30 (June 1913): 8; "A Salesgirl's Story," *Independent* 54 (July 1902): 1821. Drinking is discussed in Kneeland, *Commercialized Prostitution*, p. 70; and Belle Israels, "Diverting a Pastime," *Leslie's Weekly* 113 (27 July 1911): 100.

17. Investigator's Report, Weimann's, 1422 St. Nicholas Ave., February 11, 1917, Committee of Fourteen Papers.

18. Israels, "Way of the Girl," p. 489; Ruth True, *The Neglected Girl* (New York: Russell Sage Foundation, 1914), p. 59.

19. "A Salesgirl's Story," p. 1821; Lillian Betts, *Leaven in a Great City* (New York: Dodd, Mead, 1902), pp. 251–52.

20. New York State, Factory Investigating Commission, *Fourth Report*, vol. 4, pp. 1585–86; Robert Woods and Albert Kennedy, *Young Working-Girls: A Summary of Evidence from Two Thousand Social Workers* (Boston: Houghton Mifflin, 1913), p. 105.

21. New York State, Factory Investigating Commission, *Fourth Report*, vol. 5, p. 2809; see also Sue Ainslie Clark and Edith Wyatt, *Making Both Ends Meet: The Income and Outlay of New York Working Girls* (New York: Macmillan, 1911), p. 28. For an excellent analysis of sexual harassment, see Mary Bularzik, *Sexual Harassment at the Workplace: Historical Notes* (Somerville, Mass.: New England Free Press, 1978).

22. Consumers' League of New York, *Behind the Scenes in a Restaurant: A Study of 1017 Women Restaurant Employees* (n.p., 1916), p. 24; Frances Donovan, *The Woman Who Waits* (1920; New York: Arno Press, 1974), p. 42.

23. New York Bureau of Labor Statistics, *Second Annual Report* (1884), pp. 153, 158; *Third Annual Report* (1885), pp. 150–51.

24. Report of Commission on Social Morality from the Christian Standpoint, Made to the 4th Biennial Convention of the Young Women's Christian Associations of the U.S.A., 1913, Records File Collection, Archives of the National Board of the YWCA of the United States of America, New York, N.Y.

25. Clark and Wyatt, *Making Both Ends Meet*, pp. 187–88; see also Dorothy Richardson, *The Long Day, in Women at Work*, ed. William L. O'Neill (New York: Quadrangle, 1972); Amy E. Tanner, "Glimpses at the Mind of a Waitress," *American Journal of Sociology* 13 (July 1907): 52.

26. Committee of Fourteen in New York City, *Annual Report for 1914*, p. 40; Clark and Wyatt, *Making Both Ends Meet*, p. 188; Donovan, *The Woman Who Waits*, pp. 26, 80–81.

27. Esther Packard, "Living on Six Dollars a Week," New York State, Factory Investigating Commission, *Fourth Report*, vol. 4, pp. 1677–78. For a discussion of women's wages in New York, see ibid., vol. 1, p. 35; and vol. 4, pp. 1081, 1509. For an overview of working conditions, see Barbara Wertheimer, *We Were There: The Story of Working Women in America* (New York: Pantheon Books, 1977), pp. 209–48.

28. Packard, "Living on Six Dollars a Week," p. 1685.

29. New York State, Factory Investigating Commission, *Fourth Report*, vol. 4, pp. 1512–13, 1581–83; True, *Neglected Girl*, p. 59.

30. Marie Orenstein, "How the Working Girl of New York Lives," p. 1702. See also Esther Packard, *A Study of Living Conditions of Self-Supporting Women in New York City* (New York: Metropolitan Board of the YWCA, 1915).

31. "Influences in Street Life," p. 30; see also Samuel Chotzinoff, *A Lost Paradise* (New York: Knopf, 1955), p. 81.

32. On the rejection of parental controls by young women, see Leslie Woodcock Tentler, *Wage-Earning Women: Industrial Work and Family Life in the United States, 1900–1930* (New York: Oxford University Press, 1979), pp. 110–13. For contemporary accounts, see True, *Neglected Girl*, pp. 54–55, 62–63, 162–63; Lillian Betts, "Tenement House Life and Recreation," *Outlook* (11 February 1899): 365.

33. "Memoranda on Vice Problem: IV. Statement of George J. Kneeland," New York State, Factory Investigating Commission, *Fourth Report*, vol. 1, p. 403. See also Committee of Fourteen, *Annual Report* (1917), p. 15, and *Annual Report* (1918), p. 32; Woods and Kennedy, *Young Working-Girls*, p. 85.

34. Donovan, *The Woman Who Waits*, p. 71; on occasional prostitution, see U.S. Senate, *Report on the Condition of Women and Child Wage-Earners in the United States*, U.S. Sen. Doc. 645, 61st Cong., 2nd Sess. (Washington, D.C.: GPO), vol. 15, p. 83; Laughlin, *The Work-A-Day Girl*, pp. 51–52.

35. Investigator's Report, 2150 Eighth Ave., January 12, 1917, Committee of Fourteen Papers.

36. Investigator's Report, La Kuenstler Klause, 1490 Third Ave., January 19, 1917, Committee of Fourteen Papers.

37. Investigator's Report, Bobby More's, 252 W. 31 Street, February 3, 1917, Committee of Fourteen Papers.

38. Investigator's Report, Remey's, 917 Eighth Ave., December 23, 1916, Committee of Fourteen Papers.

39. Donovan, *The Woman Who Waits*, p. 55.

40. Edwin Slosson, "The Amusement Business," *Independent* 57 (21 July 1904): 139.

41. Investigator's Report, Clare Hotel and Palm Gardens/McNamara's, 2150 Eighth Ave., January 12, 1917, Committee of Fourteen Papers.

42. Marie Orenstein, "How the Working Girl of New York Lives," p. 1703; Clark and Wyatt, *Making Both Ends Meet*, pp. 28–29.

43. Bctts, *Leaven in a Great City*, pp. 81, 219.

44. Woods and Kennedy, *Young Working-Girls*, pp. 87, 85.

45. Laughlin, *The Work-A-Day Girl*, p. 50.

46. Investigator's Report, Semprini's, 145 W. 50 Street, October 5, 1918, Committee of Fourteen Papers.

Chapter Twenty

The Zoot-Suit and Style Warfare

Stuart Cosgrove

Introduction: The Silent Noise of Sinister Clowns

> What about those fellows waiting still and silent there
> on the platform, so still and silent they clash with the
> crowd in their very immobility, standing noisy in their
> very silence; harsh as a cry of terror in their quietness?
> What about these three boys, coming now along the
> platform, tall and slender, walking with swinging shoul-
> ders in their well-pressed, too-hot-for-summer suits,
> their collars high and tight about their necks, their iden-
> tical hats of black cheap felt set upon the crowns of
> their heads with a severe formality above their conked
> hair? It was as though I'd never seen their like before:
> walking slowly, their shoulders swaying, their legs
> swinging from their hips in trousers that ballooned up-
> ward from cuffs fitting snug about their ankles; their
> coats long and hip-tight with shoulders far too broad
> to be those of natural western men. These fellows
> whose bodies seemed—what had one of my teachers
> said of me?—"You're like one of those African sculp-
> tures, distorted in the interest of design." Well, what
> design and whose?[1]

The zoot-suit is more than an exaggerated costume, more than a sartorial statement,
it is the bearer of a complex and contradictory history. When the nameless narrator
of Ellison's *Invisible Man* confronted the subversive sight of three young and ex-
travagantly dressed blacks, his reaction was one of fascination not of fear. These
youths were not simply grotesque dandies parading the city's secret underworld,
they were "the stewards of something uncomfortable,"[2] a spectacular reminder that
the social order had failed to contain their energy and difference. The zoot-suit was
more than the drape-shape of 1940s fashion, more than a colorful stage-prop
hanging from the shoulders of Cab Calloway, it was, in the most direct and obvious
ways, an emblem of ethnicity and a way of negotiating an identity. The zoot-suit

was a refusal: a subcultural gesture that refused to concede to the manners of subservience. By the late 1930s the term "zoot" was in common circulation within urban jazz culture. Zoot meant something worn or performed in an extravagant style, and since many young blacks wore suits with outrageously padded shoulders and trousers that were fiercely tapered at the ankles, the term zoot-suit passed into everyday usage. In the sub-cultural world of Harlem's nightlife, the language of rhyming slang succinctly described the zoot-suit's unmistakable style: "a killer-diller coat with a drapeshape, reat-pleats and shoulders padded like a lunatic's cell." The study of the relationships between fashion and social action is notoriously under-developed, but there is every indication that the zoot-suit riots that erupted in the United States in the summer of 1943 had a profound effect on a whole generation of socially disadvantaged youths. It was during his period as a young zoot-suiter that the Chicano union activist Cesar Chavez first came into contact with community politics, and it was through the experiences of participating in zoot-suit riots in Harlem that the young pimp "Detroit Red" began a political education that transformed him into the Black radical leader Malcolm X. Although the zoot-suit occupies an almost mythical place within the history of jazz music, its social and political importance has been virtually ignored. There can be no certainty about when, where or why the zoot-suit came into existence, but what is certain is that during the summer months of 1943 "the killer-diller coat" was the uniform of young rioters and the symbol of a moral panic about juvenile delinquency that was to intensify in the post-war period.

At the height of the Los Angeles riots of June 1943, the *New York Times* carried a front page article which claimed without reservation that the first zoot-suit had been purchased by a black bus worker, Clyde Duncan, from a tailor's shop in Gainesville, Georgia.[3] Allegedly, Duncan had been inspired by the film "Gone with the Wind" and had set out to look like Rhett Butler. This explanation clearly found favor throughout the USA. The national press forwarded countless others. Some reports claimed that the zoot-suit was an invention of Harlem night life, others suggested it grew out of jazz culture and the exhibitionist stage-costumes of the band leaders, and some argued that the zoot-suit was derived from military uniforms and imported from Britain. The alternative and independent press, particularly *Crisis* and *Negro Quarterly*, more convincingly argued that the zoot-suit was the product of particular social context.[4] They emphasized the importance of Mexican-American youths, or *pachucos*, in the emergence of zoot-suit style and, in tentative ways, tried to relate their appearance on the streets to the concept of *pachuquismo*.

In his pioneering book, *The Labyrinth of Solitude*, the Mexican poet and social commentator Octavio Paz throws imaginative light on *pachuco* style and indirectly establishes a framework within which the zoot-suit can be understood. Paz's study of the Mexican national consciousness examines the changes brought about by the movement of labor, particularly the generations of Mexicans who migrated northwards to the USA. This movement, and the new economic and social patterns it implies, has, according to Paz, forced young Mexican-Americans into an ambivalent experience between two cultures.

> What distinguishes them, I think, is their furtive, restless air: they act like persons who are wearing disguises, who are afraid of a stranger's look because it could strip them and leave them stark naked. . . . This spiritual condition, or lack of a spirit, has given birth to a type known as the pachuco. The pachucos are youths, for the most part of Mexican origin, who form gangs in southern cities; they can be identified by their language and behaviour as well as by the clothing they affect. They are instinctive rebels, and North American racism has vented its wrath on them more than once. But the pachucos do not attempt to vindicate their race or the nationality of their forebears. Their attitude reveals an obstinate, almost fanatical will-to-be, but this will affirms nothing specific except their determination . . . not to be like those around them.[5]

Pachuco youth embodied all the characteristics of second generation working-class immigrants. In the most obvious ways they had been stripped of their customs, beliefs and language. The *pachucos* were a disinherited generation within a disadvantaged sector of North American society; and predictably their experiences in education, welfare and employment alienated them from the aspirations of their parents and the dominant assumptions of the society in which they lived. The *pachuco* subculture was defined not only by ostentatious fashion, but by petty crime, delinquency and drug-taking. Rather than disguise their alienation or efface their hostility to the dominant society, the *pachucos* adopted an arrogant posture. They flaunted their difference, and the zoot-suit became the means by which that difference was announced. Those "impassive and sinister clowns" whose purpose was "to cause terror instead of laughter,"[6] invited the kind of attention that led to both prestige and persecution. For Octavio Paz the *pachucos*'s appropriation of the zoot-suit was an admission of the ambivalent place he occupied. "It is the only way he can establish a more vital relationship with the society he is antagonising. As a victim he can occupy a place in the world that previously ignored him; as a delinquent, he can become one of its wicked heroes."[7] The zoot-suit riots of 1943 encapsulated this paradox. They emerged out of the dialectics of delinquency and persecution, during a period in which American society was undergoing profound structural change.

The major social change brought about by the United States' involvement in the war was the recruitment to the armed forces of over four million civilians and the entrance of over five million women into the war-time labor force. The rapid increase in military recruitment and the radical shift in the composition of the labor force led in turn to changes in family life, particularly the erosion of parental control and authority. The large scale and prolonged separation of millions of families precipitated an unprecedented increase in the rate of juvenile crime and delinquency. By the summer of 1943 it was commonplace for teenagers to be left to their own initiatives while their parents were either on active military service or involved in war work. The increase in night work compounded the problem. With their parents or guardians working unsocial hours, it became possible for many more young people to gather late into the night at major urban centers or simply on the street corners.

The rate of social mobility intensified during the period of the zoot-suit riots.

With over 15 million civilians and 12 million military personnel on the move throughout the country, there was a corresponding increase in vagrancy. Petty crimes became more difficult to detect and control; itinerants became increasingly common, and social transience put unforeseen pressure on housing and welfare. The new patterns of social mobility also led to congestion in military and industrial areas. Significantly, it was the overcrowded military towns along the Pacific coast and the industrial conurbations of Detroit, Pittsburgh and Los Angeles that witnessed the most violent outbreaks of zoot-suit rioting.[8]

"Delinquency" emerged from the dictionary of new sociology to become an everyday term, as wartime statistics revealed these new patterns of adolescent behavior. The *pachucos* of the Los Angeles area were particularly vulnerable to the effects of war. Being neither Mexican nor American, the *pachucos*, like the black youths with whom they shared the zoot-suit style, simply did not fit. In their own terms they were "24-hour orphans," having rejected the ideologies of their migrant parents. As the war furthered the dislocation of family relationships, the *pachucos* gravitated away from the home to the only place where their status was visible, the streets and bars of the towns and cities. But if the *pachucos* laid themselves open to a life of delinquency and detention, they also asserted their distinct identity, with their own style of dress, their own way of life and a shared set of experiences.

The Zoot-Suit Riots: Liberty, Disorder, and the Forbidden

The zoot-suit riots sharply revealed a polarization between two youth groups within wartime society: the gangs of predominantly black and Mexican youths who were at the forefront of the zoot-suit subculture, and the predominantly white American servicemen stationed along the Pacific coast. The riots invariably had racial and social resonances but the primary issue seems to have been patriotism and attitudes to the war. With the entry of the United States into the war in December 1941, the nation had to come to terms with the restrictions of rationing and the prospects of conscription. In March 1942, the War Production Board's first rationing act had a direct effect on the manufacture of suits and all clothing containing wool. In an attempt to institute a 26% cut-back in the use of the fabrics, the War Production Board drew up regulations for the wartime manufacture of what *Esquire* magazine called "streamlined suits by Uncle Sam."[9] The regulations effectively forbade the manufacture of zoot-suits and most legitimate tailoring companies ceased to manufacture or advertise any suits that fell outside the War Production Board's guidelines. However, the demand for zoot-suits did not decline and a network of bootleg tailors based in Los Angeles and New York continued to manufacture the garments. Thus the polarization between servicemen and *pachucos* was immediately visible: the chino shirt and battledress were evidently uniforms of patriotism, whereas wearing a zoot-suit was a deliberate and public way of flouting the regulations of rationing. The zoot-suit was a moral and social scandal in the eyes of the authorities, not simply because it was associated with petty crime and violence, but because it openly snubbed the laws of rationing. In the fragile harmony of wartime society, the zoot-suiters were, according to Octavio Paz, "a symbol of love and joy of horror and loathing, an embodiment of liberty, of disorder, of the forbidden."[10]

The zoot-suit riots, which were initially confined to Los Angeles, began in the first few days of June 1943. During the first weekend of the month, over 60 zoot-suiters were arrested and charged at Los Angeles County jail, after violent and well publicized fights between servicemen on shore leave and gangs of Mexican-American youths. In order to prevent further outbreaks of fighting, the police patrolled the eastern sections of the city, as rumors spread from the military bases that servicemen were intending to form vigilante groups. The *Washington Post*'s report of the incidents, on the morning of Wednesday 9 June 1943, clearly saw the events from the point of view of the servicemen.

> Disgusted with being robbed and beaten with tire irons, weighted ropes, belts and fists employed by overwhelming numbers of the youthful hoodlums, the uniformed men passed the word quietly among themselves and opened their campaign in force on Friday night.
>
> At central jail, where spectators jammed the sidewalks and police made no efforts to halt auto loads of servicemen openly cruising in search of zoot-suiters, the youths streamed gladly into the sanctity of the cells after being snatched from bar rooms, pool halls and theaters and stripped of their attire.[11]

During the ensuing weeks of rioting, the ritualistic stripping of zoot-suiters became the major means by which the servicemen re-established their status over the *pachucos*. It became commonplace for gangs of marines to ambush zoot-suiters, strip them down to their underwear and leave them helpless in the streets. In one particularly vicious incident, a gang of drunken sailors rampaged through a cinema after discovering two zoot-suiters. They dragged the *pachucos* on to the stage as the film was being screened, stripped them in front of the audience and as a final insult, urinated on the suits.

The press coverage of these incidents ranged from the careful and cautionary liberalism of the *Los Angeles Times* to the more hysterical hate-mongering of William Randolph Hearst's west coast papers. Although the practice of stripping and publicly humiliating the zoot-suiters was not prompted by the press, several reports did little to discourage the attacks:

> . . . zoot-suits smouldered in the ashes of street bonfires where they had been tossed by grimly methodical tank forces of service men. . . . The zooters, who earlier in the day had spread boasts that they were organized to "kill every cop" they could find, showed no inclination to try to make good their boasts. . . . Searching parties of soldiers, sailors and Marines hunted them out and drove them out into the open like bird dogs flushing quail. Procedure was standard: grab a zooter. Take off his pants and frock coat and tear them up or burn them. Trim the "Argentine Ducktail" haircut that goes with the screwy costume.[12]

The second week of June witnessed the worst incidents of rioting and public disorder. A sailor was slashed and disfigured by a *pachuco* gang; a policeman was run down when he tried to question a car load of zoot-suiters; a young Mexican was stabbed at a party by drunken marines; a trainload of sailors were stoned by *pachucos* as their train approached Long Beach; streetfights broke out daily in San Bernardino; over 400 vigilantes toured the streets of San Diego looking for zoot-suiters, and many individuals from both factions were arrested.[13] On 9 June, *The Los Angeles Times* published the first in a series of editorials designed to reduce the level of violence, but which also tried to allay the growing concern about the racial character of the riots.

> To preserve the peace and good name of the Los Angeles area, the strongest measures must be taken jointly by the police, the Sheriff's office and Army and Navy authorities, to prevent any further outbreaks of "zoot suit" rioting. While members of the armed forces received considerable provocation at the hands of the unidentified miscreants, such a situation cannot be cured by indiscriminate assault on every youth wearing a particular type of costume.
>
> It would not do, for a large number of reasons, to let the impression circulate in South America that persons of Spanish-American ancestry were being singled out for mistreatment in Southern California. And the incidents here were capable of being exaggerated to give that impression.[14]

The Chief, the Black Widows, and the Tomahawk Kid

The pleas for tolerance from civic authorities and representatives of the church and state had no immediate effect, and the riots became more frequent and more violent. A zoot-suited youth was shot by a special police officer in Azusa; a gang of *pachucos* were arrested for rioting and carrying weapons in the Lincoln Heights area; 25 black zoot-suiters were arrested for wrecking an electric railway train in Watts; and 1000 additional police were drafted into East Los Angeles. The press coverage increasingly focused on the most "spectacular" incidents and began to identify leaders of zoot-suit style. On the morning of Thursday 10 June 1943, most newspapers carried photographs and reports on three "notorious" zoot-suit gang leaders. Of the thousands of *pachucos* that allegedly belonged to the hundreds of zoot-suit gangs in Los Angeles, the press singled out the arrests of Lewis D. English, a 23-year-old-black, charged with felony and carrying a "16-inch razor sharp butcher knife"; Frank H. Tellez, a 22-year-old Mexican held on vagrancy charges; and another Mexican, Luis "The Chief" Verdusco (27 years of age), allegedly the leader of the Los Angeles *pachucos*.[15]

The arrests of English, Tellez and Verdusco seemed to confirm popular perceptions of the zoot-suiters widely expressed for weeks prior to the riots. Firstly, that the zoot-suit gangs were predominantly, but not exclusively, comprised of black and Mexican youths. Secondly, that many of the zoot-suiters were old enough to be in the armed forces but were either avoiding conscription or had been exempted on medical grounds. Finally, in the case of Frank Tellez, who was photographed wearing a pancake hat with a rear feather, that zoot-suit style was an expensive fashion often funded by theft and petty extortion. Tellez allegedly wore a colorful long drape coat that was "part of a $75 suit" and a pair of pegged trousers "very full at the knees and narrow at the cuffs" which were allegedly part of another suit. The caption of the Associated Press photograph indignantly added that "Tellez holds a medical discharge from the Army."[16] What newspaper reports tended to suppress was information on the marines who were arrested for inciting riots, the existence of gangs of white American zoot-suiters, and the opinions of Mexican-American servicemen stationed in California, who were part of the war-effort but who refused to take part in vigilante raids on *pachuco* hangouts.

As the zoot-suit riots spread throughout California, to cities in Texas and Arizona, a new dimension began to influence press coverage of the riots in Los Angeles. On a day when 125 zoot-suited youths clashed with marines in Watts and armed police had to quell riots in Boyle Heights, the Los Angeles press concentrated on a razor attack on a local mother, Betty Morgan. What distinguished this incident from hundreds of comparable attacks was that the assailants were girls. The press related the incident to the arrest of Amelia Venegas, a woman zoot-suiter who was charged with carrying, and threatening to use, a brass knuckleduster. The revelation that girls were active within *pachuco* subculture led to consistent press coverage of the activities of two female gangs: the Slick Chicks and the Black Widows.[17] The latter gang took its name from the members' distinctive dress, black zoot-suit jackets, short black skirts and black fish-net stockings. In retrospect the Black Widows, and their active part in the subcultural violence of the zoot-suit riots, disturb conventional understandings of the concept of *pachuquismo*.

As Joan W. Moore implies in *Homeboys*, her definitive study of Los Angeles youth gangs, the concept of *pachuquismo* is too readily and unproblematically equated with the better known concept of *machismo*.[18] Undoubtedly, they share certain ideological traits, not least a swaggering and at times aggressive sense of power and bravado, but the two concepts derive from different sets of social definitions. Whereas *machismo* can be defined in terms of male power and sexuality, *pachuquismo* predominantly derives from ethnic, generational and class-based aspirations, and is less evidently a question of gender. What the zoot-suit riots brought to the surface was the complexity of *pachuco* style. The Black Widows and their aggressive image confounded the *pachuco* stereotype of the lazy male delinquent who avoided conscription for a life of dandyism and petty crime, and reinforced radical readings of *pachuco* subculture. The Black Widows were a reminder that ethnic and generational alienation was a pressing social problem and an indication of the tensions that existed in minority, low-income communities.

Although detailed information on the role of girls within zoot-suit sub-culture is limited to very brief press reports, the appearance of female *pachucos* coincided with a dramatic rise in the delinquency rates among girls aged between 12 and 20 years old. The disintegration of traditional family relationships and the entry of young women into the labor force undoubtedly had an effect on the social roles and responsibilities of female adolescents, but it is difficult to be precise about the relationships between changed patterns of social experience and the rise in delinquency. However, war-time society brought about an increase in unprepared and irregular sexual intercourse, which in turn led to significant increases in the rates of abortion, illegitimate births and venereal diseases. Although statistics are difficult to trace, there are many indications that the war years saw a remarkable increase in the numbers of young women who were taken into social care or referred to penal institutions, as a result of the specific social problems they had to encounter.

Later studies provide evidence that young women and girls were also heavily involved in the traffic and transaction of soft drugs. The *pachuco* sub-culture within the Los Angeles metropolitan area was directly associated with a widespread growth in the use of marijuana. It had been suggested that female zoot-suiters concealed quantities of drugs on their bodies, since they were less likely to be closely searched by male members of the law enforcement agencies. Unfortunately, the absence of consistent or reliable information on the female gangs makes it particularly difficult to be certain about their status within the riots, or their place within traditions of feminine resistance. The Black Widows and Slick Chicks were spectacular in a sub-cultural sense, but their black drape jackets, tight skirts, fish-net stockings and heavily emphasized make-up, were ridiculed in the press. The Black Widows clearly existed outside the orthodoxies of war-time society: playing no part in the industrial war effort, and openly challenging conventional notions of feminine beauty and sexuality.

Toward the end of the second week of June, the riots in Los Angeles were dying out. Sporadic incidents broke out in other cities, particularly Detroit, New York and Philadelphia, where two members of Gene Krupa's dance band were beaten up in a station for wearing the band's zoot-suit costumes; but these, like the residual events in Los Angeles, were not taken seriously. The authorities failed to read the inarticulate warning signs proffered in two separate incidents in California: in one a zoot-suiter was arrested for throwing gasoline flares at a theater; and in the second another was arrested for carrying a silver tomahawk. The zoot-suit riots had become a public and spectacular enactment of social disaffection. The authorities in Detroit chose to dismiss a zoot-suit riot at the city's Cooley High School as an adolescent imitation of the Los Angeles disturbances.[19] Within three weeks Detroit was in the midst of the worst race riot in its history.[20] The United States was still involved in the war abroad when violent events on the home front signaled the beginning of a new era in racial politics.

Official Fears of Fifth Column Fashion

Official reaction to the zoot-suit riots varied enormously. The most urgent problem that concerned California's State Senators was the adverse effect that the events might have on the relationship between the United States and Mexico. This concern stemmed partly from the wish to preserve good international relations, but rather more from the significance of relations with Mexico for the economy of Southern California, as an item in the *Los Angeles Times* made clear. "In San Francisco Senator Downey declared that the riots may have 'extremely grave consequences' in impairing relations between the United States and Mexico, and may endanger the program of importing Mexican labor to aid in harvesting California crops."[21] These fears were compounded when the Mexican Embassy formally drew the zoot-suit riots to the attention of the State Department. It was the fear of an "international incident"[22] that could only have an adverse effect on California's economy, rather than any real concern for the social conditions of the Mexican-American community, that motivated Governor Warren of California to order a public investigation into the causes of the riots. In an ambiguous press statement, the Governor hinted that the riots may have been instigated by outside or even foreign agitators:

> As we love our country and the boys we are sending overseas to defend it, we are all duty bound to suppress every discordant activity which is designed to stir up international strife or adversely affect our relationships with our allies in the United Nations.[23]

The zoot-suit riots provoked two related investigations; a fact finding investigative committee headed by Attorney General Robert Kenny and an un-American activities investigation presided over by State Senator Jack B. Tenney. The un-American activities investigation was ordered "to determine whether the present zoot-suit riots were sponsored by Nazi agencies attempting to spread disunity between the United States and Latin-American countries."[24] Senator Tenney, a member of the un-American Activities Committee for Los Angeles County, claimed he had evidence that the zoot-suit riots were "axis-sponsored" but the evidence was never presented.[25] However, the notion that the riots might have been initiated by outside agitators persisted throughout the month of June, and was fueled by Japanese propaganda broadcasts accusing the North American government of ignoring the brutality of US marines. The arguments of the un-American activities investigation were given a certain amount of credibility by a Mexican pastor based in Watts, who according to the press had been "a pretty rough customer himself, serving as a captain in Pancho Villa's revolutionary army."[26] Reverend Francisco Quintanilla, the pastor of the Mexican Methodist church, was convinced the riots were the result of fifth columnists. "When boys start attacking servicemen it means the enemy is right at home. It means they are being fed vicious propaganda by enemy agents who wish to stir up all the racial and class hatreds they can put their evil fingers on."[27]

The attention given to the dubious claims of nazi-instigation tended to obfuscate other more credible opinions. Examination of the social conditions of *pachuco* youths tended to be marginalized in favor of other more "newsworthy" angles. At no stage in the press coverage were the opinions of community workers or youth leaders sought, and so, ironically, the most progressive opinion to appear in the major newspapers was offered by the Deputy Chief of Police, E. W. Lester. In press releases and on radio he provided a short history of gang subcultures in the Los Angeles area and then tried, albeit briefly, to place the riots in a social context.

> The Deputy Chief said most of the youths came from overcrowded colorless homes that offered no opportunities for leisure-time activities. He said it is wrong to blame law enforcement agencies for the present situation, but that society as a whole must be charged with mishandling the problems.[28]

On the morning of Friday, 11 June 1943, the *Los Angeles Times* broke with its regular practices and printed an editorial appeal, "Time For Sanity" on its front page. The main purpose of the editorial was to dispel suggestions that the riots were racially motivated, and to challenge the growing opinion that white servicemen from the Southern States had actively colluded with the police in their vigilante campaign against the zoot-suiters.

> There seems to be no simple or complete explanation for the growth of the grotesque gangs. Many reasons have been offered, some apparently valid, some farfetched. But it does appear to be definitely established that any attempts at curbing the movement have had nothing whatever to do with race persecution, although some elements have loudly raised the cry of this very thing.[29]

A month later, the editorial of July's issue of *Crisis* presented a diametrically opposed point of view:

> These riots would not occur—no matter what the instant provocation—if the vast majority of the population, including more often than not the law enforcement officers and machinery, did not share in varying degrees the belief that Negroes are and must be kept second-class citizens.[30]

But this view got short shrift, particularly from the authorities, whose initial response to the riots was largely retributive. Emphasis was placed on arrest and punishment. The Los Angeles City Council considered a proposal from Councillor Norris Nelson, that "it be made a jail offense to wear zoot-suits with reat pleats within the city limits of LA,"[31] and a discussion ensued for over an hour before it was resolved that the laws pertaining to rioting and disorderly conduct were sufficient to contain the zoot-suit threat. However, the council did encourage the War Production Board (WPB) to reiterate its regulations on the manufacture of suits. The regional office of the WPB based in San Francisco investigated tailors manufacturing in the area of men's fashion and took steps "to curb illegal production of men's clothing in violation of WPB limitation orders."[32] Only when Governor Warren's fact-finding commission made its public recommendations did the political analysis of the riots go beyond the first principles of punishment and proscription. The recommendations called for a more responsible co-operation from the press; a program of special training for police officers working in multi-racial communities; additional detention centers; a juvenile forestry camp for youth under the age of 16; an increase in military and shore police; an increase in the youth facilities provided by the church; an increase in neighborhood recreation facilities and an end to discrimination in the use of public facilities. In addition to these measures, the commission urged that arrests should be made without undue emphasis on members of minority groups and encouraged lawyers to protect the rights of youths arrested for participation in gang activity. The findings were a delicate balance of punishment and palliative; it made no significant mention of the social conditions of Mexican laborers and no recommendations about the kind of public spending that would be needed to alter the social experiences of *pachuco* youth. The outcome of the zoot-suit riots was an inadequate, highly localized and relatively ineffective body of short term public policies that provided no guidelines for the more serious riots in Detroit and Harlem later in the same summer.

The Mystery of the Signifying Monkey

> The pachuco is the prey of society, but instead of hiding he adorns himself to attract the hunter's attention. Persecution redeems him and breaks his solitude: his salvation depends on him becoming part of the very society he appears to deny.[33]

The zoot-suit was associated with a multiplicity of different traits and conditions. It was simultaneously the garb of the victim and the attacker, the persecutor and the persecuted, the "sinister clown" and the grotesque dandy. But the central opposition was between the style of the delinquent and that of the disinherited. To wear a zoot-suit was to risk the repressive intolerance of wartime society and to invite the attention of the police, the parent generation and the uniformed members of the armed forces. For many *pachucos* the zoot-suit riots were simply hightimes in Los Angeles when momentarily they had control of the streets; for others it was a realization that they were outcasts in a society that was not of their making. For the black radical writer Chester Himes, the riots in his neighborhood were unambiguous: "Zoot Riots are Race Riots."[34] For other contemporary commentators the wearing of the zoot-suit could be anything from unconscious dandyism to a conscious "political" engagement. The zoot-suit riots were *not* "political" riots in the strictest sense, but for many participants they were an entry into the language of politics, an inarticulate rejection of the "straight world" and its organization.

It is remarkable how many post-war activists were inspired by the zoot-suit disturbances. Luis Valdez of the radical theater company El Teatro Campesino allegedly learned the "chicano" from his cousin the zoot-suit Billy Miranda.[35] The novelists Ralph Ellison and Richard Wright both conveyed a literary and political fascination with the power and potential of the zoot-suit. One of Ellison's editorials for the journal *Negro Quarterly* expressed his own sense of frustration at the enigmatic attraction of zoot-suit style.

> A third major problem, and one that is indispensable to the centralization and direction of power is that of learning the meaning of myths and symbols which abound among the Negro masses. For without this knowledge, leadership, no matter how correct its program, will fail. Much in Negro life remains a mystery; perhaps the zoot-suit conceals profound political meaning; perhaps the symmetrical frenzy of the Lindy-hop conceals clues to great potential powers, if only leaders could solve this riddle.[36]

Although Ellison's remarks are undoubtedly compromised by their own mysterious idealism, he touches on the zoot-suit's major source of interest. It is in everyday rituals that resistance can find natural and unconscious expression. In retrospect, the zoot-suit's history can be seen as a point of intersection, between the related potential of ethnicity and politics on the one hand, and the pleasures of identity and difference on the other. It is the zoot-suit's political and ethnic associations that have made it such a rich reference point for subsequent generations. From the music of Thelonious Monk and Kid Creole to the jazz-poetry of Larry Neal, the zoot-suit has inherited new meanings and new mysteries. In his book *Hoodoo Hollerin' Bebop Ghosts*, Neal uses the image of the zoot-suit as the symbol of Black America's cultural resistance. For Neal, the zoot-suit ceased to be a costume and became a tapestry of meaning, where music, politics and social action merged. The zoot-suit became a symbol for the enigmas of Black culture and the mystery of life, the signifying monkey:

> But there is rhythm here
> Its own special substance:
> I hear Billie sing, no Good Man, and dig Prez, wearing the Zoot suit of life, the Porkie hat tilted at the correct angle; through the Harlem smoke of beer and whiskey, I understand the mystery of the Signifying Monkey.[37]

NOTES

1. Ralph Ellison *Invisible Man* New York 1947 p. 380.

2. *Invisible Man* p 381.

3. "Zoot Suit Originated in Georgia" *New York Times* 11 June 1943 p. 21.

4. For the most extensive sociological study of the zoot-suit riots of 1943 see Ralph H. Turner and Samuel J Surace "Zoot Suiters and Mexicans: Symbols in Crowd Behavior" *American Journal of Sociology* 62 1956 pp 14–20.

5. Octavio Paz *The Labyrinth of Solitude* London 1967 pp 5–6.

6. *Labyrinth of Solitude* p 8.

7. As note 6.

8. See K. L. Nelson (ed) *The Impact of War on American Life* New York 1971.

9. O. E. Schoeffler and W. Gale, *Esquire's Encyclopedia of Twentieth-Century Men's Fashion* (New York 1973) p 24.

10. As note 6.

11. "Zoot-Suiters Again on the Prowl as Navy Holds Back Sailors" *Washington Post* June 1943 p 1.

12. Quoted in S. Menefee *Assignment USA* New York 1943 p 189.

13. Details of the riots are taken from newspaper reports and press releases for the weeks in question, particularly from the *Los Angeles Times, New York Times, Washington Post, Washington Star* and *Time Magazine*.

14. "Strong Measures Must be Taken Against Rioting" *Los Angeles Times* 9 June 1943 p 4

15. "Zoot-Suit Fighting Spreads On the Coast" *New York Times* 10 June 1943 p 23.

16. As note 15.

17. "Zoot-Girls Use Knife in Attack" *Los Angeles Times* 11 June 1943 p 1.

18. Joan W. Moore, *Homeboys: Gangs, Drugs and Prison in the Barrios of Los Angeles* Philadelphia 1978.

19. "Zoot Suit Warfare Spreads to Pupils of Detroit Area" *Washington Star* 11 June 1943 p 1.

20. Although the Detroit Race Riots of 1943 were not zoot-suit riots, nor evidently about "youth" or "delinquency" the social context in which they took place was obviously comparable. For a lengthy study of the Detroit riots see R Shogun and T Craig *The Detroit Race Riot: A Study in Violence* Philadelphia and New York 1964.

21. "Zoot Suit War Inquiry Ordered by Governor" *Los Angeles Times* 9 June 1943.

22. "Warren Orders Zoot Suit Quiz; Quiet Reigns After Rioting" *Los Angeles Times* 10 June 1943 p 1.

23. As note 22.

24. "Tenney Feels Riots Caused by Nazi Move for Disunity" *Los Angeles Times* 9 June 1943 p A.

25. As note 24.

26. "Watts Pastor Blames Riots on Fifth Column" *Los Angeles Times* 11 June 1943 p A.

27. As note 26.

28. "California Governor Appeals for Quelling of Zoot Suit Riots" *Washington Star* 10 June 1943 p A3.

29. "Time for Sanity" *Los Angeles Times* 11 June 1943 p 1.

30. "The Riots" *The Crisis* July 1943 p 199.

31. "Ban on Freak Suits Studied by Councilmen" *Los Angeles Times* 9 June 1943 p A3.

33. *Labyrinth of Solitude* p 9.

34. Chester Himes "Zoot Riots are Race Riots" *The Crisis* July 1943; reprinted in Himes *Black on Black: Baby Sister and Selected Writings* London 1975.

35. El Teatro Campesino presented the first Chicano play to achieve full commercial Broadway production. The play, written by Luis Valdez and entitled "Zoot Suit" was a drama documentary on the Sleepy Lagoon murder and the events leading to the Los Angeles riots. (The Sleepy Lagoon murder of August 1942 resulted in 24 *pachucos* being indicated for conspiracy to murder.)

36. Quoted in Larry Neal "Ellison's Zoot Suit" in J. Hersey (ed) Ralph Ellison: A Collection of *Critical Essays* New Jersey 1974 p 67.

37. From Larry Neal's poem "Malcolm X: An Autobiography" in L. Neal *Hoodoo Hollerin' Bebop Ghosts* Washington DC 1974 p 9.

Chapter Twenty-One

Face of the Nation
Race, Nationalisms, and Identities in Jamaican Beauty Pageants

Natasha B. Barnes

In September 1986, the Jamaican *Daily Gleaner*, the island's leading newspaper, gave a front-page report of the proceedings of a Miss Jamaica beauty pageant headlined "Missiles Barrage at Beauty Contest."

> Deafening shouts of protest rang through the National Arena. Patrons sprang to their feet screaming and gesticulating their disagreement on Saturday night when twenty-two-year-old Lisa Mahfood . . . was announced winner of Miss Jamaica (World) 1986.
>
> Many in the jampacked arena, estimated to hold about 9,000, booed and shouted, "No . . . no . . . no!" Some banged the metal chairs to the chant "We want Majorie," referring to Majorie Tolloch . . . who placed fourth.
>
> Some patrons in the angry crowd threw crushed paper cups and oranges at the new queen, who was struck in the face with an orange. Others threw bottles, one of which struck a photographer on the side of the head.
>
> Pandemonium reigned. Confusion broke out among those on the platform. The new queen found it impossible to make the usual victory walk. At this stage, the new Miss Jamaica 1986 had to be escorted from the stage by promotor Mickey Haughton-James to prevent further harm to her by flying objects.[1]

How is it that a beauty pageant could arouse such passions? While the Miss Jamaica contest has been both popular and controversial, Jamaican beauty pageants, unlike Reggae Sunsplash concerts and working-class dance halls, are meant to be dignified public affairs; the showcasing of feminine charm and grace is expected to produce an atmosphere of congeniality and good will among contestants and onlookers alike. A fanfare evening patronized by the governor general, choreographed and staged by the prestigious Jamaican Institute of Dance, and featuring a parade of twenty lithe and lovely women in lace bathing suits and lavish evening gowns is hardly the kind of event to conclude with hurled bottles and oranges. A few days later, an interview with Lisa Mahfood clarified the reasons why her unexpected coronation drew such a violent response. Mahfood was white. The daughter of a Lebanese Jamaican entrepreneurial family, she was "European" by the standards of Jamaican racial identity and hence had no business representing what was to many of the Miss Jamaica onlookers a black country. The reporter from the *Gleaner* found her in her family's large suburban home recovering from "shock and surprise" at the outburst of the Jamaican people. "Their behavior . . . ," she stuttered, "and to talk about our [national] motto—Out of many one people . . . and I said to myself how can these people be like this. Jamaica is made up of more than one race. How come they are not living by it?"[2]

Like all good beauty queens, Mahfood wore her crown and represented her country with dignity and grace. Even when she was forced to abandon her coronation walk on the pageant night, she waved and blew kisses at a crowd that was taunting her with racial epithets and assaulting her with oranges. But the fans of the Miss Jamaica pageant felt that they were victims of a larger, more historically rooted insult. A few months earlier, twenty-year-old Lilliana Antonette Cisneros, a woman who declared herself Venezuelan (she was born of a Jamaican father and a Colombian mother), walked away with the Miss Jamaica Universe crown. During the same year, a former contestant, Ruth Cammock, filed a suit in the Supreme Court alleging that as a black woman she was a victim of color discrimination.[3] But the court cases and hurled oranges are only recent manifestations of a crisis brewing within the Miss Jamaica pageant that was hardly new to most Jamaicans. Although images of Rastafarians, reggae music, and tourist brochures have made many of us associate blackness as the very picture of Jamaica, the struggles within the beauty contest reflect the fact that as far as representation on the island goes, Jamaica has yet to assert its identity as a black country. In spite of demographic figures identifying some 90 percent of the inhabitants as black and thirty years of a postcolonial legacy that attempted to shift economic and hegemonic power away from European creole elites to a disenfranchised black mass, many dark-skinned Jamaicans still see their color as a handicap in their efforts to secure good jobs, access to education, decent housing, even polite service from store clerks, bank tellers, etc. For these Jamaicans, the coronation of a white Miss Jamaica is not a trivial matter; nor is it removed from the everyday manifestation of power and privilege on the island. Rather it strikes a violent blow at the very heart of their sense of personhood, viscerally reenacting the failure of the postcolonial promise to give black people their symbolic and material due after centuries of colonial domination. With Jamaica suffering from an unemployment rate at 30 percent, a political party system that has abandoned the social-uplift commitments made during independence, poor inner-city dwellings stunted by neglect and crime, it is the arena of culture—the site of cricket, music, and beauty pageants—that has become the place black people, resigned to the fact that there will be no piece of the economic pie for them, have come to claim and sometimes violently defend as their own.

To understand how white women and the ideological specter of beauty have come to constitute such a viciously contested terrain of representative power one only needs to look at who beauty queens were in the forties and fifties. In the long and troubled history of beauty pageants throughout the Anglophone Caribbean, it was only the daughters of the white-identified business and plantocratic elite who were encouraged to enter and eventually win the many lavishly financed contests that sprang up. In the colonial Caribbean, where local assemblies hardly provided money for schools let alone cultural events, the extravagant private and govern-mental sponsorship made affairs like the Miss Jamaica pageant[4] or the "Carnival Queen" contest in Trinidad spectacular public events that dramatized in visceral ways the disenfranchisement of people of color. While the coronation of light-skinned black women today generates the same charges of exclusion and discrima-tion that surround white winners, in the forties few women whose black or Asian ancestry was obvious, let alone prominent, would have access to these hallowed sororities. When calls for decolonization and black assertiveness became increas-ingly strident and linked, it became politically expedient to include mulatto, Indian, and Chinese women, but these contestants of color had no illusions about their potential to win. Contemporary commentators rightly argued that the philosophy and practice of such contests made the commodification of beauty a public but decidedly closed affair. Wrapped in a mantle of respectability and civility that was denied to black people in general and black women in particular, beauty contests became the place for the making of feminine subjectivity in a racial landscape where femininity was the jealously guarded domain of white womanhood.

The very infrastructure of the pageants upheld and reflected the fact, often crudely so, that people of color—not just *women* of color—were unfit subjects for national representation, that in spite of their efforts to prove to the contrary, nothing noble and enlightened could be reflected in their image. Beauty contests gave prizes to contestants judged as possessing the "best eyes," prizes that would never be awarded to anyone with brown or black eyes. Prize trips for winning queens habitually included destinations like Miami, Florida, a city that was vehe-mently Jim Crow at the time. Judges were often members of the island's political and business elites and were closely associated with the sponsors of the competition as well as with the contestants themselves. One reporter for the *Spotlight*, a weekly Jamaican newsmagazine, smitten that the "soft-voiced, olive-colored Peggy Dick-ard" lost to the white "lux complexioned" winner of the 1948 Buy Jamaican queen contest, noted that although the queen was a "lovely, accomplished and exception-ally pretty miss," she was nonetheless related to one of the "heavily white panel of judges [who] seemed to regard her Nordic beauty as typically Jamaicanesque or West Indian."[5] Likewise Una Marson, one of Jamaica's early twentieth-century black feminists, had ample reason to take the organizers of the pageant to task for their routine choice of blond-haired, blue-eyed women as Miss Jamaicas. As early as 1931 Marson sardonically called attention to the pageant as a segregated arena for the reification of plantocratic dominance and in so doing uncovered the "invisi-bility" of the its hegemonic work: "[S]ome amount of expense and disappointment could be saved numbers of dusky ladies who year after year enter the beauty competition if the promoters of the contest would announce in the daily press that very dark or black 'beauties' would not be considered."[6]

The tensions expressed here between the contemporary ideals of beauty—which in no way included black women—and the emphasis on the queen as a national representative in a country that was increasingly attempting to identify itself as "black" would reach its crescendo in the Miss Jamaica pageant of the 1950s. It was in this contest that the contrast between a white queen and her public role as a

Jamaican representative would become as dramatic as it was fiercely controversial. Unlike previous island beauty pageants where queens would have undefined or limited roles as crowned winners, the Jamaica Tourist Board (with its sponsorship of the Miss Jamaica pageant in 1954) conceived of the queen as a professional of sorts, a cultural broker who would now be charged with a year-long job of "selling" the island to prospective European and white North American tourists. The construction of the queen as a worker, as someone with clearly-defined "professional" and public responsibilities infused the contest with a sense of purpose that changed white women's symbolic function as invisible, leisured wives and daughters whose absence from the rigors of wage-labor work reinscribed the patriarchal privilege of white men. By contrast, the prevailing discourse surrounding black women's public identities as laborers was seen as evidence of black men's inability to assert patriarchal control over the sphere of "home" and "family" and the inevitable consequence of the black family's tendency toward "breakdown" and "pathology." Indeed the concept of the white queen's "work," in its ideological refractions, operated on a number of levels to further antagonize the already hostile relationship between the white owner/managerial caste and an increasingly politicized black labor force—both camps using the rhetoric of masculinity to define and orchestrate their struggle. The white beauty queen's public and well-financed cultural "work" as Jamaica's hostess to the world built and depended upon an eroticized and "exotic" black female presence but outrightly excluded women of color as suitable representatives of this ideal. Miss Jamaica winners not only went on to represent their island at regional and international pageants, but were frequently sent on publicity campaigns to the United States and Canada garbed in the picturesque costume of the creole black women folk—embroidered white blouse, madras plaid head-kerchief and matching skirt, heavy earrings and bead necklaces—to show off the "native" charm of Jamaica's fairer sex. Publicity photographs often showed them superimposed over the map of Jamaica itself inviting their onlookers to read the island as a space of civility and heterosexual pleasure through their white bodies. By the coronation of the second such Miss Jamaica in 1955, the editorial page of the *Daily Gleaner* used the occasion of seventeen-year-old Marlene Fenton's victory to warn the pageant organizers of the growing racial divisiveness that the Miss Jamaica contest was increasingly coming to signify at home through her public image abroad. It rightly identified the Tourist Board's concept of the beauty queen's role as "island ambassadress" as a source of a continuing discrepancy between the insurgent trade union attempts to inscribe Jamaica's postcolonial identity as "proud," "manly," and "black" with the Tourist Board's marking and marketing of the island as "comely," "womanly," and "white." The editorial warned that "constructive care" should be taken "not to let Americans or Canadians or Europeans imagine that this is a Caucasian country. . . . We in countries like Jamaica should not lead the world overseas to think that all the lovely people in the island are of one [racial] sort and the woman on the donkey is of another."[7]

The white beauty queen's high visibility as a symbol of plantocratic hierarchy and racism pitted her against an emergent multifaceted male-identified black labor force that increasingly portrayed her privilege as an insult directed less toward black women than to black men. Nationalist efforts to regain control over the Carnival festivities in Trinidad in the middle of this century show how the segregated beauty institution formed the axis upon which a competitive struggle between the white colonial managerial elite and an emergent black political force was waged. Between 1946 to 1954, a group of colonial business and political interests organized into the Carnival Improvement Committee attempted to transform the black working class celebrations—celebrations that were remembered as an arena for black women's riotous and disorderly public behavior—into a "decent" and well ordered tourist attraction by initiating the Dimarche Gras Carnival Queen competition, an event which quickly became the most prestigious and well-financed show of the season's festivities. Indeed it is possible to argue that the strategic deployment of white female bodies as Carnival Queens was constitutive of the history of crisis and concession that regulated the evolution of Carnival as an embattled sphere of social culture. If the Canbolay Riots of the late nineteenth century showed that black people would violently resist colonial efforts to ban or threaten the autonomy linked their symbolic "ownership" of Carnival festivities, the colonial elite through a redirected campaign of "refinement" and "Europeanization" successfully, if unevenly, challenged black control of Carnival on precisely this notion of proprietorship. The evolution of the Carnival Queen competition into a beauty pageant (the contest saw its beginnings in the 1920s as a costume competition open to married women and women of color) secured its transformation as a public but "boundaried" social arena, operating within black people's public space but off-limits to them.

By the mid 1950s, the Carnival Queen pageant, like the Miss Jamaica contest, was a lucrative debutante ball for the daughters of Trinidad's white elite, with the winner getting prizes valued at some $7,500—a figure which Gordon Rohlehr estimates was $2,500 more than the prize money given to all the winning masquerade bands put together.[8] In 1957, after unsuccessful attempts to persuade the Carnival Development Committee to substantially raise the value of the Calypso Monarch prizes, the Mighty Sparrow, a young calypsonian enjoying ample career opportunities abroad as a nightclub entertainer in British and American cities, organized a famous boycott of the calypso competition specifically targeting the CDC's unfair privileging of the Carnival Queen show. As his "Carnival Boycott" calypso goes, the promotion of the queen came at the expense of the "real" artistes of the season—steelband players, calypsonians and masqueraders—figures that are identified as black and male. Sparrow's song reflected what a letter writer to the Trinidadian *Guardian* complained of as the unfairness of the " 'Carnival Queen' get[ting] so many prizes [yet] a man who buys a costume for about $200 gets a prize and a silver cup costing perhaps $5. What a reward for showing the skill and art of the natives of our country!"[9] Perhaps more than in any other episode in the history of Trinidadian spectatorial culture are the lines sharply drawn between the struggle of undeserving white privilege—dramatized here in the body of the debutante queen—and that of an unappreciated and exploited black labor mass—identified in discourse of the controversy as male cultural workers. In spite of the efforts to give the Carnival Queen a public but short-lived "career" as an "ambassadress,"[10] the calypsonian's discourse, using the politicized rhetoric of the emergent labor activism, claims that she is rewarded by the authorities for doing "nothing" while the "real" legitimate cultural workers go unrecognized. As the Mighty Sparrow sang in "Carnival Boycott":

> What really cause the upset
> Is the motor-car the queen does get
> She does nothing for Carnival
> She only pretty and that is all
> But men like me an' you
> Saving money to play "history" and Ju Ju[11]
> All we getting is two case of beer
> And talk up as Band of the Year.

Chorus:
> I intend to keep all my costume on the shelf
> Let them keep the prizes in the Savannah for they own self
> Let the Queen run the show
> Without Steelband and Calypso
> Who want to go can go up dey
> But me ain't going no way
>
> Calypsonians with the talent
> Hardly getting a cent
> I think its overbearing
> So now give me a hearing;
> Calypso is the root of Carnival
> Steelband is the foot of Carnival
> Without Calypso, no road march could beat
> Without Steelband, I'll bet you don't move your feet.

Sparrow's "Carnival Boycott" identifies the cultural work of the steelbandmen and calypsonians as the motor and machinery that drives Carnival's activity. Indeed Sparrow's eruption into the Trinidad calypso scene in the 1950s and the leadership he brought to the organized boycott inaugurated a period in Trinidadian popular music that was marked by a growing awareness of local music as a source of profit and professionalism. The calypsonians' awareness of themselves as professionals formed a critical dimension of their shifting status in the 1950s and upon which their targeting of the white debutante beauty queen earns its legitimacy. Sparrow's career launched the beginning of the calypsonian's self-definition as professionals, as valued cultural workers whose labor, unlike that of their earlier status as "roving minstrels," could be exchanged and marketed for profit and social veneration. What is established here and in the discourse of Lord Superior's calypso "Brass Crown" is the dangerous symbolic opposition between white female leisure and deserving but unpaid black *male* work. We can see from "Brass Crown" how the dichotomy between the paid Queen who is not, by the calypsonian's estimation, a "real" cultural worker inscribes a dangerous notion of postcolonial culture as being the province of black men—a notion that has serious implications for *all* women's cultural activity:

> They doesn't send the King Calypso
> As far as Tobago
> But the Queen and her family
> Goes to New York City
> When she comes back, before she steps out the plane
> You hear she gone again
> This time, they send she to Stalingrad
> And she can't whistle to represent Trinidad.

From this short history it is not hard to imagine why these beauty contests would become central targets in the efforts of trade unionists, burgeoning anticolonial politicians and black upliftment societies to dismantle the material and psychological effects of colonialism and Eurocentrism. The fact that Jamaica's earliest black feminists rallied against the exclusion of women of color from the contest—rather than the patriarchal structure of the pageant itself—reminds us that the struggle for black women everywhere to be recognized as women, as feminine subjects, is not, as Nancy Caraway puts it, simply "derived from vanity . . . but is a crucial component of a larger collective effort at self definition."[12] The public nature of the Miss Jamaica pageant, the fact that the reigning queen needs validation from the nation's subjects because of her representational status—she goes on to represent Jamaica at an international beauty pageant and hence is to be the embodiment of all that *is* Jamaican—means that a white winner, like the idea of beauty itself, is the site of dangerous contradictions. Like beauty which, as commonly held platitudes on the subject attest, has no race or class referents—you're either pretty or you're not—the repeated coronation of a white Miss Jamaica lays bare the ugly truth that beauty is not "natural" but ideological: it has a certain kind of face, certain features, hair texture, eye color, shape of nose and lips. Indeed, the public scope of the pageant served to underscore this very fact. Contestants were routinely paraded in Kingston's public places followed by a train of reporters and photographers who eulogized and fetishized the women in newspaper tabloid spreads. In these flashy pictorials, white women, historically sheltered and made off-limits to black men and men of color in general, are now flagrantly displayed and eroticized. Full-page photographs and accompanying copy detail the trappings of power and privilege that they embody: expensively styled "light auburn hair," fashionably made-up "grayish-green" and "twinkling sea-blue eyes"—details that in a highly charged racial atmosphere were read for what they were: transparent fetishes of the phenotypes associated with whiteness.

Beauty contests in the Caribbean are a continual reminder of both the transparency of race as a historical construction and the concreteness of its social reality. The first Miss Jamaica, Evelyn Andrade, a woman recognized as white on the island, was sent as the regional representative to the 1954 Miss Universe contest held in Long Beach, California. Here Andrade, now Miss West Indies, was noticed by *Ebony* magazine, which produced a lavish four-page spread of the photogenic

Fig. 21.1. A spectrum of Jamaican beauty displayed before a cannon of Fort Charles, Port Royal. "Ten types; one people" was the heading of this contest, run in 1955 as part of the "Jamaica 300" celebrations.

beauty retranslating her as "black": "Jamaican girl is the first Negro to enter top beauty contest."[13] For *Ebony* blackness becomes identified, as it usually is in the United States, simply through the presence of a black progenitor, and hence the proof of Andrade's "Negro" identity is located in her family: her father, *Ebony* reports, is a "Syrian Jew, well-known in business circles . . . married to a colored woman in Kingston." But in Jamaica, the wealth of the Syrian and Lebanese elites had already canceled their prior immigrant and religious identities and the progressive whitening of the island's elite mulatto castes made individuals of Andrade's background—irrespective of black ancestry—white to most Jamaicans.

By the late forties the controversies surrounding the Miss Jamaica pageant and the many other beauty contests organized prior to it led to a well-publicized and spectacular effort to satisfy the public's growing taste for beauty contests while infusing them with a more egalitarian and representative quality. In 1955 the *Star*, the evening tabloid of the *Gleaner*, announced its sponsorship of a "Ten Types, One People" contest organized as part of the island's tercentennial anniversary of British rule. "Ten Types, One People," echoing what would become Jamaica's national motto—"Out of many one people"—was to celebrate the island's racial diversity as well as manage, through the showcasing of race and color "types," concerns about the bias and discrimination that were by now regular complaints about the beauty business. This pageant was in fact made up of a coterie of pageants based on what the *Star* identified as the ten distinct racial types on the island. As the *Gleaner* reported, this was a beauty pageant "break[ing] new ground . . . [by] trying to bring out all the shades and types in one great contest—European, African, Indian, Chinese and those that come from the Near East."[14] Hence there was a Miss Ebony for black-complexioned women, Miss Mahogany for women of "cocoa-brown complexion," Miss Satinwood for "girls of coffee and milk complexion," Miss Golden Apple for "peaches and cream" Jamaican women, Miss Apple-blossom for "a Jamaican girl of white European parentage," Miss Pomegranate for "white Mediterranean girls," Miss Sandalwood for women of "pure Indian parentage," Miss Lotus who was to be "pure Chinese," Miss Jasmine for a Jamaican of "part-Chinese parentage," and Miss Allspice for "part-Indian" women.[15] Each winner was to be chosen by a group of twenty judges, ten of whom were to be of the complexion category of the judged—clearly a logistical nightmare for the organizers, who not only had to recruit and categorize the contestants but also match each competition with suitably complexioned judges in an island of only one and a half million people. While the idea of the "Ten Types, One People" contest was as sensational and indeed laughable in 1955 as it sounds to us today, for many of the region's journalists, politicians, and public opinion makers, the fact that this pageant was organized not only to include diverse representation of all Jamaica's ethnicities but also to ensure that a winner would emerge from each group made it a showpiece of racial tolerance to the region and the world. Although the sensationalism of the pageant attracted attention from journalists around the world—both *Life* and *Ebony* magazines sent photographers to cover the event—for Caribbean opinion makers the "Ten Types" contest was a humane and egalitarian way to build racial pride among those communities never represented at beauty pageants. One journalist heralded the pageant for its "revolutionary" potential and declared that it reflected the "culture and civilization" of a peaceful and plural emergent nation. The report in the *Havana Post*, for example, waxed poetic and political:

> I do not know who made up that list of ten names, but it is a masterpiece of poetry, dignity and good taste. The various qualifications are beautifully prepared, and I find myself admiring particularly the little Jamaican girl who does not protest that it is undemocratic to have a class for "MISS APPLE BLOSSOM," but who readily admits that she is a "Jamaican girl of black complexion" and proudly enters her name in the competition for the title of "MISS EBONY." Such dignity is worthy of the highest praise because it is an acceptance of reality, of the immutable truth.[16]

The focus on the Miss Ebony contest here is no accidental emphasis. Since Caribbean beauty contests had traditionally denied a place to dark-skinned women, this pageant was envisioned as a social experiment in which black contestants, and by extension black people in general, would have their dignity and sense of self-worth validated through their access to the institutions that regulated cultural norms of physical attractiveness. The very idea that beauty was a quality that could embrace African-descended people and that "black" was a racial description that could be declared proudly and without embarrassment was, in 1955, well before the "black is beautiful" stridency of the 1970s, quite a startling concept. The fourteen finalists for the Miss Ebony title, lithe, well-proportioned, and, as a *Spotlight* report remarked, "coal black," drew stares of amazement from white tourist onlookers and smiles of pride and joy from black islanders. Lady Allen, widow of a prominent black Jamaican government minister and member of the Jamaica Federation of Women, brought in to help organize the "Ten Types" contest, told a reporter that the Miss Ebony show was of particular social significance: "[It] brings out some of our really good-looking Jamaican girls—if I use the term natives they might not like, it, but that is what I mean—it brings out the girls who would otherwise not get a chance."[17] In this spirit contest organizers made a point of recruiting young black women outside of the urban areas to have them photographed for consideration. The *Star* gave its islandwide correspondents hundreds of leaflets advertising both the contest and the date and time that newspaper photographers would be in the area to take pictures. Clifton Neita, a *Gleaner* editorial executive, was appointed to search out such women and even employ some rather unusual tactics to coax possible contestants into allowing themselves to be photographed. As he told a *Spotlight* reporter, "Some of the objections those girls made for not coming forward! A favorite was: 'But my hair don't look nice.' I soon learned to squash that by providing comb, brush, mirror, even advice on hair style."[18] The enterprise had its desired effect. Villagers took pride in the fact that the *Star* featured pictures of local women in its pages whether they made it to the finals or not. Young women themselves, emboldened by the fact that their dark skin and "bad" hair did not disqualify them from cultural norms of attractiveness, felt a new sense of confidence and self-worth. As the *Spotlight* editorialized, "Forever after, the shy servant girls of Little River (St. James) and Bluefields (Westmoreland) could say to their friends: 'I *am* pretty. Didn't you see my picture in the Star?' "[19]

The idea of a racialized beauty contest proudly announcing itself as such took on a decidedly more strident and eventually controversial tone with the introduction of a Miss Chinese Jamaica competition the year after the first Tourist Board–sponsored Miss Jamaica was crowned. Like earlier pageants, the Miss Chinese Jamaica contest had its beginnings as a fund raiser for the Chinese Benevolent Society, the central social welfare institution for people of Chinese descent on the island. Its organizer, Cecil Chuck, then a charismatic member of the younger Chinese Jamaican social set, envisioned the competition as an attraction to the society's already popular annual Garden Party—an outdoor bazaar sponsored by the Chinese Athletic Club and well patronized by a wide cross-section of the Afro-Jamaican public.[20] Like the annual Garden Party, where the Chinese community threw open its doors to the larger public, the Miss Chinese Jamaica pageant soon became a showpiece of ethnic revitalization and pride, a "coming out" of the entire Chinese community enthusiastically received by most Jamaicans. The organizers had no trouble recruiting politicians, ambassadors, and governors' wives as patrons and sponsors, as well as former beauty queens who acted as coaches to the young contestants, instructing them in the finer points of poise, make-up application, and public speaking. Like the "Ten Types" contest, Miss Chinese Jamaica was prominently covered in local and regional magazines and newspapers, a publicity spectacle which proved Cecil Chuck's assertion that "everyone liked Chinese girls."[21]

While Jamaicans may have liked Chinese girls, they may not necessarily have liked the Chinese. Some fifty years earlier the Chinese bore the brunt of the region's most dramatic protest against Asian immigration. During the 1918 Anti-Chinese

Riots, a complex social disturbance fueled by a depressed colonial economy that hit working-class black Jamaicans particularly hard, many Chinese shopkeepers were killed or maimed and their properties destroyed by black residents who saw them as unwelcome competitors in strained economic times.[22] While the Chinese have always been seen as a recalcitrant and unassimilated ethnic group, Chinese women entered and were popular contestants throughout the entire troubled history of Caribbean beauty pageants. Dorothy Wong, for example, an entrant in the 1958 Miss Jamaica competition, was the crowd favorite, although she lost to Joan Duperly, a white Jamaican who, a *Gleaner* report enthused, had "the same type of face as Marilyn Monroe."[23] (That same year Wong entered the Miss Chinese Jamaica pageant and won easily.) Indeed, the first time the Miss Jamaica color bar was broken, it was by the Chinese-identified Sheila Chong, whose "Polynesian demeanor" made her the first woman of color to be crowned Miss Jamaica, in 1959. But the presence of Chinese women in these national beauty contests was not without the tensions that have historically surrounded the question of Chinese identity in the Caribbean. In 1958 the Trinidadian representative to the Miss British Caribbean competition, Angela Tong, found herself having to tell reporters that although her father was born in Hong Kong, she spoke no Chinese—a situation that was not repeated for the other regional contestants, who were also members of recently arrived immigrant communities but felt no pressure to explain their legitimacy as Caribbean representatives.[24] Indeed, the crowning of Sheila Chong in 1959 drew a petition signed by several black Jamaican shopkeepers complaining of the fact that since in their knowledge a Jamaican girl was never crowned Miss China, a Chinese woman had no right to be Miss Jamaica.

Clearly it was the color and ethnicity tensions surrounding who was a "typical" Jamaican that led to the inauguration of a Miss Chinese Jamaica pageant in the first place. While such debates about the color and caste identity of the emergent nation were hardly new in the 1950s and certainly not confined to beauty pageants, the spectacle of such competitions had for a long time made such debates ritualized and feminized. Indeed, beauty pageants were precisely the place where public battles over representation and identity would commodify women for a variety of constituent *and* overwhelmingly male interests. By the early sixties the editorials and writers of letters to the editor made the color and caste controversies surrounding the pageants ostensibly about women, but between men. For the island's white elites, caught in a rapidly decolonizing landscape where it was clear that political leadership would soon have a black face, control over the beauty contests was its last effort to preserve Eurocentric social and cultural values. For precisely the same reasons, women of color—black, mulatto, and Chinese—were recruited in these political battles to challenge colonial and European dominance from the podium of the beauty contest.

Something of this effort can be seen in the organization and recruitment practices of the Miss Chinese Jamaica competition. In spite of its popularity among spectators, the organizers of the pageant were quickly faced with the herculean task of finding slim, attractive, and unmarried young women who were willing to enter the contest among a fairly small population grouping.[25] Although many of the older generation were opposed to the idea of parading the community's young women in bathing suits and strapless ball gowns, the Miss Chinese Jamaica contest was actively supported by the economic and print institutions serving the Chinese community. The *Pagoda*, the fortnightly Chinese Jamaican newsmagazine, soon found itself conducting an active campaign to solicit women to enter the contest—one year the pageant almost had to be canceled because of the lack of entrants—and reward those who did enter with lavish prizes that would normally be awarded only to a crowned winner. In 1955, a particularly sparse year for contestants, a *Pagoda* editorial launched an appeal for entrants that could best be described as desperate, particularly given the fact that in the same year the *Star*'s Miss Ebony contest drew some 1,200 applicants from hopeful dark-skinned women all over the island:

> What have other girls got that the Jamaican-born Chinese girls haven't got? Why do they shy away from beauty contests? These are the questions that must be giving the organizers of the "Miss Chinese Jamaica 1955" contest a big headache. Yet there is no reason why Jamaican-born Chinese girls shouldn't make ideal beauty queens.
>
> I understand this year's winner of the coveted "Miss Chinese Jamaica" title will get a two-week expense-paid trip to Miami. Now every girl dreams of travelling and of being a Beauty Queen, and when the two are offered in one package, there should be a new crop of entrants every year to show up the beauty of Jamaican-born Chinese girls.
>
> And speaking of beauty, the girls have it. I see them every day, in offices, in stores, in their homes, and they have the figure that wins the contests. So girls, why not step out and enter the year's "Miss Chinese Jamaica" contest?[26]

The exhortation drew this letter to the editor from a male reader:

> Although I have never sponsored a beauty contest, I know the difficulties the organizers run into, and I wonder if it's worth all the organizers' time to urge the girls to join in for their own sake. After all, if they are too shy to convince us that there are indeed lovely girls in our community, why should we waste time to get them to do so? We do have lovely girls, yes, but if they want to keep it a secret, let them play hide and seek.[27]

From the rhetoric of this letter the reader mistakenly identifies the pageant as an unmediated parade of beautiful women, separate from the heady political and racial atmosphere which made all such contests on the island embodiments of the decolonization struggle. As this exchange makes clear, the Miss Chinese Jamaica competition was not just about the "winning figures" of "our girls," it was about recruiting and investing women with the symbolic worth of the community itself. Soon the pageant became the major public event of Chinese Jamaica and its popularity drew accolades as well as hostility from some of the island's black cultural nationalists concerned about what the resurgence of Chinese nationalism would mean in a future decolonized landscape. Evon Blake, a popular black journalist and editor of the *Spotlight* newsmagazine, charged the pageant organizers as well as the *Pagoda* itself with making unpatriotic and "un-Jamaican" displays of ethnic pride, even though his magazine featured the Miss Ebony winner on its cover and endorsed her as "our girl," a not-so-veiled reference to the Afro-Jamaican nationalism that he and his magazine promoted. With Jamaican independence on its heels and the ruling party with its strong links to the black trade union movement facing the impossible task of having to fulfill its mandate to a dispossessed black mass while mouthing platitudes about the island's multiracial destiny, Chinese Jamaicans soon realized that the integrity of their cultural institutions would be at risk. To avert charges of divisiveness, not only did the Chinese Benevolent Society and its umbrella institutions—the Sanitorium, the Chinese Public School, and the Athletic Club—have to publicly dismantle themselves, but the Miss Chinese Jamaica pageant had to reinvent itself to survive. But even before independence, the organizers found it expedient to rename the contest from the Miss Chinese Jamaica pageant—a title both calling attention to the national aspirations of Jamaicans of Chinese descent and signaling their distinct identity—to the less politically charged Miss Chinese Athletic Club. By 1962, the year of independence and the public assertion of Jamaica as a "black" nation, the final Chinese identified beauty pageant was held on the island, an event that marked not just the close of an openly racialized beauty contest, but signaled the beginning of the end of ethnically organized cultural activity among the Chinese in Jamaica.[28]

The postindependence period, an era in which black Jamaicans hoped that they could assert economic and cultural dominance, proved to be a difficult and frustrating time in this regard. Colin Palmer, in his essay on black power in independent Jamaica, rightly sees the creation of a distinct racial identity as "one of the most agonizing and protracted struggles" waged by Jamaican people in the last half of this century.[29] Although many racial minorities abandoned their symbolic hold over privilege and power during this period—white-only clubs were desegregated and cultural events like Miss Jamaica were relinquished to government authority—they still maintained a firm, if less visible, hand in the economic affairs of the island. But even as Jamaica was being publicly declared as a "black" or multicultural country, the residual effects of Eurocentric definitions of personhood continued to haunt the nation's psyche well into the present. While such concerns reveal a rather problematic essentialist linkage between race and nation, the vigor in which Afro-Caribbean scholars, artists, novelists, and poets campaigned for the legitimacy and justness of the region's identity as "black" attests to the importance that such racial assertiveness, however one-dimensional, still holds as a political ideal. The real test of the anticolonial struggle was thought to be measured not only in concrete material gains, but in the success that the centuries-old stigma attached to black skin could be eradicated. And it is in this regard that the beauty contest, more so than any other arena of cultural production, was seen as the ideal place where the readiness to accept these values could be tested.

Ideally the postindependence beauty pageant would inscribe Jamaica's new political identity as proud, dignified, and black. In the midsixties sponsorship of the Miss Jamaica pageant was taken over by the government and it was conducted under the umbrella of independence day celebrations. During this period attempts were made to select queens who epitomized the racial ideals of the emergent nation. Jeanette Bartley's study of beauty pageants in this period noted that the preferred contestants were described in newspaper advertisements as "Mahogany Types"—defined as "Jamaican cocoa-brown, neither full black, nor very light-skinned."[30]

Although light-skinned and racially mixed women formed the majority of the contestants, virtually no white or Chinese women dared to enter the pageant for fear of the controversy that their presence would inevitably bring. The fact that Chinese and white Jamaicans had to take a back seat in the beauty business—Indian Jamaican women who epitomized the "Mahogany" ideal continued to enter and receive no hostility on account of their race—is indicative of the manner in which these two racial minorities became increasingly linked in the popular Jamaican imagination. The economic success of the Chinese Jamaican community elevated the group into whiteness and in the barter for monetary security the Chinese community had to render itself culturally invisible. Walter Rodney, the most influential Afro-Caribbean intellectual embracing the grassroots politics of Black Power at the time, pointedly excluded the Chinese in his discussions of Afro-Asian regional solidarity. For him, Indian Caribbean people who shared a similar history of oppression had to be embraced within the fold of Black Power; by contrast, the Chinese were an exploiting class who would "have either to relinquish or be deprived of that function before they can be reintegrated into a West Indian society where the black man walks with dignity."[31] Since beauty contests were always a reflection or contestation of prevailing political values, the Miss Jamaica pageants of the late sixties and seventies, although touched by occasional quarrels over class and color, were not events of outright hostility. In this climate the pageants were functioning as they were supposed to: creating consensus about the kind of image Jamaica wanted to project of itself.

But the reign of brown-skinned beauty queens of this era was broken in 1973 by a young Chinese Jamaican model Patsy Yuen. Although reluctant to enter the competition because of her race, Yuen proved to be a successful, if controversial, Caribbean representative because of her willingness to perform Jamaica's ideal of itself. Since her Asian ancestry disrupted the official picture of the country's identity, Yuen's vehement defense of herself as Jamaican gave her an edge in styling herself as a symbol of national pride. But because the nation was already publicly pronounced as "black," Yuen's efforts to prove her Jamaicanness inevitably forced her into a problematic and overzealous denial of her Chinese ancestry. Her efforts in this regard dramatized the fact that the multiraciality of the Caribbean experience was still a problem in the official discourse of national identity. Both at home and abroad Yuen had to remind reporters everywhere that although she may look Chinese, her heart and soul were Jamaican: "I'm Jamaican and I'm proud to be a Jamaican. When I travel and I am asked where I am from, I don't say I'm Chinese. I say I am a Jamaican. Look. I don't even like Chinese food . . . give me my ackee and saltfish any day!"[32] As Jamaica's entry in the Miss World competition in London, Yuen placed third, a feat, in a country intoxicated by the drama of beauty pageants, that elevated her to the status of national hero.

This victory was significant, as it reveals both the paradox of the representation of women within the body politic and the eventual disillusionment with Jamaica's self-styled "black" face. The last time such an event took place was when Carol Crawford, Miss Jamaica 1963, brought home the Miss World crown. Crawford, like all Caribbean women who win international pageants, was given a momentous celebration upon her return to the island, festivities which subdued local arguments about her near-white complexion and her green eyes. In a postindependence climate where women never get representation status as national heroes, the idolatry that surrounds winning Caribbean beauty queens is dramatic and unique: Crawford's image was issued on a series of Jamaican postage stamps and she was given the keys to the city of Kingston, the second woman up to that date—Queen Elizabeth II was the first—who was honored in such a manner. But the troubled political and economic times of the 1980s made the Miss Jamaica enterprise much too expensive for an increasingly impoverished public sector to endure. When the contest was turned over once again to private sponsorship, the focus on choosing queens who were "typically Jamaican" gave way to a new concern over the type of entrant who would have the best chance of winning an international pageant and garnering increased financial rewards for the local sponsors. The fracas over the 1986 coronation of "white" Lisa Mahfood is indicative of the peculiarly postcolonial dilemma facing Third World cultural production in an era of late capitalism. It makes Jamaica's conversation with itself over questions of identity and autonomy as bitter as it is ongoing.

NOTES

1. "Missiles Barrage at Beauty Contest," *Daily Gleaner*, 8 September 1986.

2. Christine King, "Says Lisa Mahfood, Miss Jamaica (World), 'I Did Not Expect to Win' . . . Neither Did the Crowd," *Sunday Gleaner Magazine*, 14 September 1986.

3. "Girl from Venezuela Wins 'Miss Jamaica Universe' amidst Sea of Controversy," *Daily Gleaner*, 12 May 1986.

4. Although there was a series of Miss Jamaicas held before the pageant came under the sponsorship of the Jamaican Tourist Board in 1954, the infusion of cash and sense of purpose that the organization gave to the pageant makes it important to start my discussion from this date. But there were several beauty contests that emerged in the island and ran side-by-side with the Miss Jamaica contest. Many of the earlier events were tied to commercial publicity campaigns with the winner usually sent to regional or international contests, such as the Miss British Caribbean pageant, as a national representative. In 1948, for example, the island witnessed a Buy Jamaican campaign sponsored by the Jamaica Manufacturers Association which featured an island-wide beauty contest and the coronation of a Buy Jamaican campaign queen.

5. "Carload of Queens," *Spotlight* 9, no. 5 (May 1948), pp. 35–36.

6. "Miss Jamaica," editorial, *Daily Gleaner*, 5 December 1955.

7. See Gordon Rohlehr's excellent account of the tensions that surrounded the Carnival Queen competition in the chapter "Calypso: From the Mucurapo Stadium to the Savannah Boycott" in Rohlehr's *Calypso and Society in Pre-Independence Trinidad* (Port of Spain: Gordon Rohlehr, 1990), pp. 401–456.

8. Ibid.

9. Quoted in ibid., pp. 445–446.

10. "Ambassadress" was the title of choice for the organizers and sponsors of Caribbean beauty queens to justify their choice of winning girls and the large sum of money that was spent on the pageants. As the winner of the 1957 Carnival Queen competition, Diana Timpsy

was described in the *Trinidad Guardian*: "She speaks five languages and will be a perfect Ambassadress for Trinidad overseas." Ibid., p. 447.

11. These are two popular forms of working-class masquerades.

12. Nancy Caraway makes the point that the black female struggle for "cultural acceptance as attractive, 'respectable' beings" has been misinterpreted by white feminists who see this emphasis on "negative imagery" as trivial and politically misguided. Although Caraway's argument is made within the specific contexts of U.S. feminisms, her point here has particular relevance to this discussion. See Caraway's *Segregated Sisterhood: Racism and the Politics of American Feminism* (Knoxville: University of Tennessee Press, 1991), p. 78.

13. "Miss West Indies in Miss Universe," *Ebony*, November 1954, pp. 79–83.

14. Edward Scott, "Beauty Contest of a "Revolutionary Quality," *Daily Gleaner*, 10 August 1955. Although the "Ten Types" pageant was supposed to be held consecutively over a ten-year period, only five of them actually took place: Miss Ebony, 1959, Miss Mahogany, 1960, Miss Satinwood, 1961, Miss Golden Apple, 1962, Miss Appleblossom, 1963.

15. Ibid.

16. Quoted in ibid.

17. Quoted in "Black Beauty," *Spotlight* 20, no, 12 (December 1959), p. 32.

18. Ibid.

19. Ibid.

20. The Miss Chinese Jamaica pageant was only open to members of the Chinese Athletic Club who were members of the Benevolent Society. Although this group comprised both foreign and local-born Chinese people and mixed-race populations of Chinese ancestry, I am not aware of any formal rules concerning the size of the society's mixed-race membership, nor any strict formula about how Chinese ancestry is determined. In a small community like Jamaica's where Chinese-descended people knew each other intimately, Chinese ancestry was frequently determined through kinship lines and it was commonly accepted that an individual needed to be at least one fourth Chinese to be considered eligible for membership in Chinese Jamaican social institutions. However, a 1945 article of the memorandum of the Chinese Association of Trinidad stipulated that "at no time must the membership of persons of half or less than Chinese exceed more than 20 percent of total membership." See Trevor M. Millett, *The Chinese in Trinidad* (Port of Spain, Trinidad: Inprint Caribbean Ltd., 1993), p. 78.

21. Cecil Chuck, personal interview, 10 November 1993.

22. The reasons for the 1918 Anti-Chinese Riots are symptomatic of the complex relationship between race, class, and sexuality in colonial Jamaica. According to Howard Johnson, the disturbances began with a squabble between Fung Sue, an immigrant Chinese shopkeeper, and a black policeman over the attentions of Fung Sue's live-in companion, Caroline Lindo. The feud between the two men quickly led to rumors that the policeman had been murdered by the shopkeeper and some of his Chinese friends. Within a few days the incident drew mobs of local residents who attacked Chinese shopkeepers throughout the district and looted their stores. See Johnson, "The Anti-Chinese Riots of 1918," paper delivered at the 1979 Postgraduate Seminar, Department of History, University of the West Indies, Mona, Jamaica. Also see Jacqueline Levy, "The Economic Role of the Chinese in Jamaica: The Grocery Retail Trade," paper delivered at the 1967 Postgraduate Seminar, Department of History, University of the West Indies, Mona, Jamaica.

23. "Girl to Stop the Traffic," *Daily Gleaner*, 14 July 1959.

24. "Carib Beauties Reach the U.S.," *Trinidad Guardian*, 17 July 1958.

25. Estimates of the percentages of Chinese-identified Jamaicans at that time range between 6 and 7 percent.

26. "Miss Chinese Jamaica," *Pagoda*, 29 October 1955, p. 3.

27. "Letter to the Editor," *Pagoda*, 6 October 1956, p. 3.

28. The Chinese Benevolent Society still exists, but it has abandoned its social and cultural emphasis and exists mainly as a business organization. However, it is being refurbished and there are plans to revitalize its cultural scope.

29. Colin A. Palmer, "Identity, Race and Black Power in Independent Jamaica," in Franklin W. Knight and Colin A. Palmer, eds., *The Modern Caribbean* (Chapel Hill: University of North Carolina Press, 1989), p. 111.

30. Jeanette M. Bartley, "The Search for a Jamaican Identity," M.A. thesis, University of the West Indies, Mona, Jamaica, 1987, p. 54.

31. The Chinese in the Caribbean were to be distinguished from the Chinese of the People's Republic of China who, for Rodney, a Marxist intellectual, had a long and noble history of antiimperialist and pro-Communist activism. "*Our* Chinese," he writes, "have nothing to do with that movement. They are to be identified with Chiang Kai-shek and not Chairman Mao Tse-tung. They are to be put in the same bracket as the lackeys of capitalism and imperialism who are to be found in Hong Kong and Taiwan." See Walter Rodney, *The Groundings with My Brother* (London and Chicago: Bogle L'Ouverture Publications, Research Associates School Publications, 1990), p. 29.

32. Joan Fairweather, "Patsy Lets It All Hang Out," *Daily News*, 12 August 1973.

Chapter Twenty-Two

Commodity Lesbianism

Danae Clark

A commodity appears, at first sight, a very trivial thing, and easily understood. Its analysis shows that it is, in reality, *a very queer thing* ...

Karl Marx, Capital[1]

In an effort to articulate the historical and social formation of female subjectivity under capitalism, feminist investigations of consumer culture have addressed a variety of complex and interrelated issues, including the construction of femininity and desire, the role of consumption in media texts, and the paradox of the woman/commodity relationship. Implicit in these investigations, however, has been an underlying concern for the heterosexual woman as consuming subject.[2] Perhaps because, as Jane Gaines notes, "consumer culture thrives on heterosexuality and its institutions by taking its cues from heterosexual 'norms,' "[3] theories *about* consumerism fall prey to the same normalizing tendencies. In any event, analyses of female consumerism join a substantial body of other feminist work that "assumes, but leaves unwritten, a heterosexual context for the subject" and thus contributes to the continued invisibility of lesbians.[4]

But lesbians too are consumers. Like heterosexual women they are major purchasers of clothing, household goods and media products. Lesbians have not, however, been targeted as a separate consumer group within the dominant configuration of capitalism, either directly through the mechanism of advertising or indirectly through fictional media representations; their relation to consumerism is thus necessarily different. This "difference" requires a careful look at the relation between lesbians and consumer culture, representations of lesbianism and consumption in media texts, and the role of the lesbian spectator as consuming subject. Such an investigation is especially timely since current trends in both advertising and commercial television show that lesbian viewers (or at least some segments of the lesbian population) are enjoying a certain pleasure as consumers that was not available to them in the past. An analysis of these pleasures should therefore shed light not only on the place that lesbians occupy within consumer culture, but on the identificatory processes involved in lesbian reading formations.

Dividing the Consumer Pie

Lesbians have not been targeted as consumers by the advertising industry for several historical reasons. First, lesbians as a social group have not been economically powerful; thus, like other social groups who lack substantial purchasing power (for example, the elderly), they have not been attractive to advertisers. Second, lesbians have not been easily identifiable as a social group anyway. According to the market strategies commonly used by advertisers to develop target consumer groups, four criteria must be met. A group must be: (1) identifiable, (2) accessible, (3) measurable, and (4) profitable.[5] In other words, a particular group must be "knowable" to advertisers in concrete ways. Lesbians present a problem here because they exist across race, income and age (three determinants used by advertisers to segment and distinguish target groups within the female population). To the extent that lesbians are not identifiable or accessible, they are not measurable and, therefore, not profitable. The fact that many lesbians prefer not to be identified because they fear discrimination poses an additional obstacle to targeting them. Finally, most advertisers have had no desire to identify a viable lesbian consumer group. Advertisers fear that by openly appealing to a homosexual market their products will be negatively associated with homosexuality and will be avoided by heterosexual consumers.[6] Thus, although homosexuals (lesbians and gay men) reputedly comprise 10% of the overall U.S. market population—and up to 20–22% in major urban centers such as New York and San Francisco—advertisers have traditionally stayed in the closet when it comes to peddling their wares.[7]

Recently, however, this trend has undergone a visible shift—especially for gay men. According to a 1982 review in *The New York Times Magazine* called "Tapping the Homosexual Market," several of today's top advertisers are interested in "wooing . . . the white, single, well-educated, well-paid man who happens to be homosexual."[8] This interest, prompted by surveys conducted by *The Advocate* between 1977 and 1980 that indicated that 70% of their readers aged 20–40 earned incomes well above the national median, has led companies such as Paramount, Seagram, Perrier, and Harper & Row to advertise in gay male publications like *Christopher Street* and *The Advocate*.[9] Their ads are tailored specifically for the gay male audience. Seagram, for example, ran a "famous men of history" campaign for Boodles Gin that pictured men "purported to be gay."[10]

A more common and more discreet means of reaching the gay male consumer, however, is achieved through the mainstream (predominantly print) media. As one marketing director has pointed out, advertisers "really want to reach a bigger market than just gays, but [they] don't want to alienate them" either.[11] Thus, advertisers are increasingly striving to create a dual marketing approach that will "speak to the homosexual consumer in a way that the straight consumer will not notice."[12] As one observer explains:

> It used to be that gay people could communicate to one another, in a public place, if they didn't know one another, only by glances and a sort of *code behavior* . . . to indicate to the other person, but not to anybody else, that you, too, were gay. Advertisers, if they're smart, can do that too. (Emphasis added)[13]

One early example of this approach was the Calvin Klein jeans series that featured "a young, shirtless blond man lying on his stomach" and, in another ad, "a young, shirtless blond man lying on his side, holding a blue-jeans jacket." According to Peter Frisch, a gay marketing consultant, one would "have to be comatose not to realize that it appeals to gay men" (I presume he is referring to the photographs' iconographic resemblance to gay pornography).[14] Calvin Klein marketing directors, however, denied any explicit gay element:

> We did not try *not* to appeal to gays. We try to appeal, period. With healthy, beautiful people. If there's an awareness in that community of health and grooming, they'll respond to the ads.[15]

This dual marketing strategy has been referred to as "gay window advertising."[16] Generally, gay window ads avoid explicit references to heterosexuality by depicting only one individual or same-sexed individuals within the representational frame. In addition, these models bear the signifiers of sexual ambiguity or androgynous style. But "gayness" remains in the eye of the beholder: gays and lesbians can read into an ad certain subtextual elements that correspond to experiences with or representations of gay/lesbian subculture. If heterosexual consumers do not notice these subtexts or subcultural codes, then advertisers are able to reach the homosexual market along with the heterosexual market without ever revealing their aim.

The metaphor of the window used by the advertising industry to describe gay marketing techniques is strikingly similar to feminist descriptions of women's relation to consumer culture and film representation. Mary Ann Doane, for example, remarks that "the film frame is a kind of display window and spectatorship consequently a form of window shopping."[17] Jane Gaines likewise suggests that cinema-going is "analogous to the browsing-without-obligation-to-buy pioneered by the turn-of-the-century department store, where one could, with no offense to the merchant, enter to peruse the goods, exercising a kind of *visual connoisseurship*, and leave without purchase" (emphasis added).[18] Gaines further argues that the show window itself is "a medium of circulation" and that "commodification seems to facilitate circulation by multiplying the number of possible contexts."[19] The metaphor of the window, in other words, posits an active reader as well as a multiple, shifting context of display.

The notion of duality that characterizes gay window advertising's marketing strategy is also embodied in various theoretical descriptions and approaches to consumer culture in general. Within the Frankfort School, for example, Adorno speaks of the dual character or dialectic of luxury that "opens up consumer culture to be read as its opposite," and Benjamin suggests that consumer culture is a dual system of meaning whereby "the economic life of the commodity imping[es] upon its life as an object of cultural significance."[20] More recently, a duality has been located in feminist responses to consumer culture and fashion culture in particular. As Gaines notes, the beginning of the Second Wave of feminist politics and scholarship was marked by a hostility toward fashion, perceiving it as a patriarchal codification and commodification of femininity that enslaved women and placed their bodies on display. But this "anti-fashion" position is now joined by a feminist perspective that sees fashion culture as a site of female resistance, masquerade and self-representation.[21] At the heart of this "fabrication," says Gaines, is a gender confusion and ambiguity that disrupts and confounds patriarchal culture.[22]

Lesbians have an uneasy relationship to this dual perspective on fashion. First of all, lesbians have a long tradition of resisting dominant cultural definitions of female beauty and fashion as a way of separating themselves from heterosexual culture politically and as a way of signaling their lesbianism to other women in their subcultural group. This resistance to or reformulation of fashion codes thus distinguished lesbians from straight women at the same time that it challenged patriarchal structures. As Arlene Stein explains in a recent article on style in the lesbian community:

> Lesbian-feminist anti-style was an emblem of refusal, an attempt to strike a blow against the twin evils of capitalism and patriarchy, the fashion industry and the female objectification that fueled it. The flannel-and-denim look was not so much a style as it was anti-style—an attempt to replace the artifice of fashion with a supposed naturalness, free of gender roles and commercialized pretense.[23]

Today, however, many lesbians, particularly younger, urban lesbians, are challenging this look, exposing the constructedness of "natural" fashion, and finding a great deal of pleasure in playing with the possibilities of fashion and beauty.

This shift, which is not total and certainly not without controversy, can be attributed to a number of factors. First of all, many lesbians are rebelling against a lesbian-feminist credo of political correctness that they perceive as stifling. As a *Village Voice* writer observes:

> A lesbian can wag her fingers as righteously as any patriarchal puritan, defining what's acceptable according to what must be ingested, worn, and especially desired. . . . In a climate where a senator who doesn't like a couple of photographs tries to do away with the National Endowment for the Arts, censorious attacks within the lesbian community begin to sound a lot like fundamentalism. . . . They amount to a policing of the lesbian libido.[24]

Stein thus notes that while the old-style, politically correct(ing) strain of lesbian feminism is on the wane, "life style" lesbianism is on the rise. Lifestyle lesbianism is a recognition of the "diverse subcultural pockets and cliques—corporate dykes, arty dykes, dykes of color, clean and sober dykes—of which political lesbians are but one among many."[25] But it may also be a response to the marketing strategies of consumer culture.

The predominant research trend in U.S. advertising for the past two decades has been VALS (values and life styles) research. By combining information on demographics (sex, income, educational level), buying habits, self-image, and aspirations, VALS research targets and, in the case of yuppies, effectively *creates* consumer lifestyles that are profitable to advertisers.[26] Given lesbian-feminism's countercultural, anticapitalist roots, it is not surprising that lesbians who "wear" their life-styles or flaunt themselves as "material girls" are often criticized for trading in their politics for a self-absorbed materialism. But there is more to "lipstick lesbians" or "style nomads" than a freewheeling attitude toward their status as consumers or a boredom with the relatively static nature of the "natural look" (fashion, after all, implies change). Fashion-conscious dykes are rebelling against the idea that there is a clear one-to-one correspondence between fashion and identity. As Stein explains:

> You can dress as a femme one day and a butch the next. You can wear a crew-cut along with a skirt. Wearing high heels during the day does not mean you're a femme at night, passive in bed, or closeted on the job.[27]

Seen in this light, fashion becomes an assertion of personal freedom as well as political choice.

The new attitudes of openness toward fashion, sexuality and lifestyle would not have been possible, of course, without the lesbian-feminist movement of recent decades. Its emergence may also have an economic explanation. According to a recent survey in OUT/LOOK, a national gay and lesbian quarterly, the average annual income for individual lesbians (who read OUT/LOOK) is $30,181; the average lesbian household income is approximately $58,000.[28] Since lesbians as a group are beginning to raise their incomes and class standing, they are now in a position to afford more of the clothing and "body maintenance" that was once beyond their financial capabilities. Finally, some credit for the changing perspectives on fashion might also be given to the recent emphasis on masquerade and fabrication in feminist criticism and to the more prominent role of camp in lesbian criticism. At least within academic circles these factors seem to affect, or to be the effect of, lesbian theorists' fashion sensibilities.

But regardless of what has *caused* this shift, or where one stands on the issue of fashion, advertisers in the fashion industry have begun to capitalize upon it. Given the increasing affluence and visibility of one segment of the lesbian population—the predominantly white, predominantly childless, middle-class, educated lesbian with disposable income—it appears that advertisers are now interested in promoting "lesbian window advertising." (Even while recognizing the highly problematic political implications of such a choice, I will continue to use the term "gay" instead of "lesbian" when referring to this marketing strategy since "gay window advertising" is the discursive phrase currently employed by the advertising industry.) In fashion magazines such as *Elle* and *Mirabella*, and in mail-order catalogs such as *Tweeds, J. Crew* and *Victoria's Secret*, advertisers (whether knowingly or not) are capitalizing upon a dual market strategy that packages gender ambiguity and speaks, at least indirectly, to the lesbian consumer market. The representational strategies of gay window advertising thus offer what John Fiske calls "points of purchase" or points of identification that allow readers to make sense of cultural forms in ways that are meaningful or pleasurable to them.[29] The important question here is how these consumer points of purchase become involved in lesbian notions of identity, community, politics, and fashion.

When Dykes Go Shopping...

In a recent issue of *Elle*, a fashion layout entitled "Male Order" shows us a model who, in the words of the accompanying ad copy, represents "the zenith of masculine allure." In one photograph the handsome, short-haired model leans against the handlebars of a motorcycle, an icon associated with bike dyke culture. Her man-styled jacket, tie, and jewelry suggest a butch lesbian style that offers additional points of purchase for the lesbian spectator. In another photograph from the series, the model is placed in a more neutral setting, a cafe, that is devoid of lesbian iconography. But because she is still dressed in masculine attire and, more importantly, exhibits the "swaggering" style recommended by the advertisers, the model incorporates aspects of lesbian style. Here, the traditional "come on" look of advertising can be read as the look or pose of a cruising dyke. Thus, part of the pleasure that lesbians find in these ads might be what Elizabeth Ellsworth calls "lesbian verisimilitude," or the representation of body language, facial expression, and general appearance that can be claimed and coded as "lesbian" according to current standards of style within lesbian communities.[30]

A fashion layout from *Mirabella*, entitled "Spectator," offers additional possibilities for lesbian readings. In this series of photographs by Deborah Turbeville, two women (not always the same two in each photograph) strike poses in a fashionable, sparsely decorated apartment. The woman who is most prominently featured has very short, slicked-back hair and, in three of the photographs, she is wearing a tank top (styled like a man's undershirt) and baggy trousers. With her confident poses, her broad shoulders and strong arms (she obviously pumps iron), this fashion model can easily be read as "high-style butch." The other women in the series are consistently more "femme" in appearance, though they occasionally wear masculine-style apparel as well. The lesbian subtext in this fashion layout, however, is not limited to the models' appearances. The adoption of butch and femme *roles* suggests the possibility of interaction or a "playing out" of a lesbian narrative. Thus, while the women are physically separated and do not interact in the photographs,[31] their stylistic role-playing invites the lesbian spectator to construct a variety of (butch-femme) scenarios in which the two women come together. The eroticism of these imaginary scenes is enhanced by compositional details such as soft lighting and a rumpled bedsheet draped over the apartment window to suggest a romantic encounter. The variation of poses and the different combination of models also invite endless possibilities for narrative construction. Have these two women just met? Are they already lovers? Is there a love triangle going on here? and so on.

Much of what gets negotiated, then, is not so much the contradictions between so-called "dominant" and "oppositional" readings, but the details of the subcultural reading itself. Even so, because lesbians (as members of a heterosexist culture) have been taught to read the heterosexual possibilities of representations, the "straight" reading is never entirely erased or replaced. Lesbian readers, in other words, know that they are not the primary audience for mainstream advertising, that androgyny is a fashionable and profitable commodity, and that the fashion models in these ads are quite probably heterosexual. In this sense, the dual approach of gay window advertising can refer not only to the two sets of readings formulated by homosexuals and heterosexuals, but to the dual or multiple interpretations that exist *within* lesbian reading formations. The straight readings, however, do not simply exist alongside alternative readings, nor do they necessarily diminish the pleasure found in the alternate readings. As "visual connoisseurs" lesbians privilege certain readings (styles) over others, or, in the case of camp readings, the straight reading itself forms the basis of (as it becomes twisted into) a pleasurable interpretation.

Here, as Sue-Ellen Case might argue, is the locus of a true masquerade of readership.[32] Lesbians are accustomed to playing out multiple styles and sexual roles as a tactic of survival and thus have learned the artifice of invention in defeating heterosexual codes of naturalism:

> The closet has given us the lie; and the lie has given us camp—the style, the discourse, the *mise-en-scène* of butch-femme roles. The survival tactic of hiding and lying [has] produced a camp discourse . . . in which gender referents are suppressed, or slip into one another, fictional lovers are constructed, [and] metaphors substitute for literal descriptions.[33]

I would not argue, as Case does, that "the butch-femme couple inhabit the [lesbian] subject position together"[34] since the butch-femme aesthetic is a historically specific (and even community and lifestyle specific) construct that ranges from the rigid butch-femme roles of the 1950s to the campy renaissance of today's butch-femme role-playing, and thus cannot represent a consistent subject position. But a lesbian subject's recognition of the butch-femme binarism, as it has been historically styled by lesbian communities, is an essential component of a reading practice that distances, subverts and plays with both heterosexist representations and images of sexual indeterminacy. Another aspect of reading that must be considered is the pleasure derived from seeing the dominant media "attempt, but fail, to colonize 'real' lesbian space."[35] Even in representations that capitalize upon sexual ambiguity there are certain aspects of lesbian subculture that remain (as yet) inaccessible or unappropriated. By claiming this unarticulated space as something distinct and separable from heterosexual (or heterosexist) culture, lesbian readers are no longer outsiders, but insiders privy to the inside jokes that create an experience of pleasure and solidarity with other lesbians "in the know." Thus, as Ellsworth notes, lesbians "have responded to the marginalization, silencing and debasement" found in dominant discourse "by moving the field of social pleasures . . . to the center of their interpretive activities" and reinforcing their sense of identity and community.[36]

This idea assumed concrete dimensions for me during the course of researching and presenting various versions of this paper. Lesbians across the country were eager to talk about or send copies of advertisements that had "dyke appeal" (and there was a good deal of consensus over how that term was interpreted). A number of lesbians admitted to having an interest in *J. Crew* catalogs because of a certain model they looked forward to seeing each month. Another woman told me of several lesbians who work for a major fashion publication as if to reassure me that gay window fashion photography is not an academic hallucination or a mere coincidence. Gossip, hearsay and confessions are activities that reside at the center of lesbian interpretive communities and add an important discursive dimension to lesbians' pleasure in looking.

This conception of readership is a far cry from earlier (heterosexist) feminist analyses of advertising that argued that "advertisements help to endorse the powerful male attitude that women are passive bodies to be endlessly looked at, waiting to have their sexual attractiveness matched with *active* male sexual desire," or that women's relation to advertisements can only be explained in terms of anxiety or "narcissistic damage."[37] These conclusions were based on a conspiracy theory that placed ultimate power in the hands of corporate patriarchy and relegated no power or sense of agency to the female spectator. Attempts to modify this position, however, have created yet another set of obstacles around which we must maneuver with caution. For in our desire and haste to attribute agency to the spectator and a means of empowerment to marginal or oppressed social groups, we risk losing sight of the interrelation between reading practices and the political economy of media institutions.

In the case of gay window advertising, for example, appropriation cuts both ways. While lesbians find pleasure (and even validation) in that which is both accessible and unarticulated, the advertising industry is playing upon a material and ideological tension that simultaneously appropriates aspects of lesbian subculture and positions lesbian reading practices in relation to consumerism. As John D'Emilio explains: "This dialectic—the constant interplay between exploitation and some measure of autonomy—informs all of the history of those who have lived under capitalism."[38] According to D'Emilio's argument that capitalism and the institution of wage labor have created the material conditions for homosexual desire and identity, gay window advertising is a logical outgrowth of capitalist development, one which presumably will lead to more direct forms of marketing in the future. But the reasons behind this development can hardly be attributed to a growing acceptance of homosexuality as a legitimate lifestyle. Capitalist enterprise creates a tension: materially it "weakens the bonds that once kept families together," but ideologically it "drives people into heterosexual families." Thus, "while capitalism has knocked the material foundations away from family life, lesbians, gay men, and heterosexual feminists have become the scapegoats for the social instability of the system."[39] The result of this tension is that capitalists welcome homosexuals as consuming subjects but not as social subjects. Or, as David Ehrenstein remarks, "the market is there for the picking, and questions of 'morality' yield ever so briefly to the quest for capital."[40]

The sexual indeterminacy of gay window advertising's dual market approach thus allows a space for lesbian identification, but must necessarily deny the representation of lesbian identity politics. This is a point that has so far been overlooked in the ongoing feminist and lesbian/gay debates over the issue of identity politics.[41] At the core of these debates is the post-structuralist challenge to essentialist definitions of identity. While theorists and activists alike agree that some shared sense of identity is necessary to build a cohesive and visible political community, some theorists argue that any unified conception of gay/lesbian identity is reductive and ahistorical. They thus opt for a historically constructed notion of *identities* that is contradictory, socially contingent, and rooted in progressive sexual politics. But while the controversies are raging over whether gay/lesbian identity is essential or constructed, media industries are producing texts that deny the very politics feminists and lesbians are busy theorizing.

Mainstream media texts employ representational strategies that generally refer to gays and lesbians in *anti-essentialist* terms. That is, homosexuals are not depicted as inherently different from heterosexuals; neither does there exist a unified or authentic "gay sensibility." As Mark Finch observes, "[t]he most recuperable part of the gay movement's message is that gay people are individuals."[42] The result is a liberal gay discourse that embraces humanism while rejecting any notion of a separate and authentic lesbian/gay subject. The homosexual, says John Leo, is thus "put together from disarticulating bits and pieces of the historical discourse on homosexual desire, which become a narrative pastiche for middle-class 'entertainment.' "[43] As a mode of representation that lacks any clear positioning toward what it shows, pastiche embodies "the popular" in the sense that people are free to make their own meanings out of the cultural bits and ideological pieces that are presented to them.

But this postmodern, anti-essentialist (indeed, democratic) discourse could also be interpreted as a homophobic response. As Jeffrey Weeks ironically points out, "The essentialist view lends itself most effectively to the defence of minority status."[44] (For example, if homosexuality were to be classified by the courts as biologically innate, discrimination would be more difficult to justify. By contrast, when a sense of lesbian or gay identity is lost, the straight world finds it easier to ignore social and political issues that directly affect gays and lesbians as a group.) The constructionist strategies of the media are thus not as progressive as anti-essentialist theorists (or media executives) might have us believe. The issue is not a matter of choosing between constructionism or essentialism, but a matter of examining the political motivations involved in each of these approaches—whether they appear in theory or media texts.

If we take politics as our starting point, then media and advertising texts can be analyzed in terms of their (un)willingness or (in)ability to represent the identity politics of current lesbian communities. Gay window advertising, as suggested earlier, consciously disavows any explicit connection to lesbianism for fear of offending or losing potential customers. At the same time, an appropriation of lesbian styles or appeal to lesbian desires can also assure a lesbian market. This dual approach is effective because it is based on two key ingredients of marketing success: style and choice. As Dick Hebdige has noted, "it is the subculture's stylistic innovations which first attract the media's attention."[45] Because style is a cultural construction, it is easily appropriated, reconstructed and divested of its original political or subcultural signification. Style as resistance becomes commodifiable as chic when it leaves the political realm and enters the fashion world. This simultaneously diffuses the political edge of style. Resistant trends (such as wearing men's oversized jackets or oxford shoes—which, as a form of masquerade, is done in part for fun, but also in protest against the fashion world's insistence upon dressing women in tightly-fitted garments and dangerously unstable footwear) become restyled as high-priced fashions.

In an era of "outing" (the practice of forcing gay and lesbian public figures to come out of the closet as a way to confront heterosexuals with our ubiquity as well as our competence, creativity or civicmindedness), gay window advertising can be described as a practice of "ining." In other words, this type of advertising invites us to look *into* the ad to identify with elements of style, invites us *in* as consumers, invites us to be part of a fashionable "*in* crowd," but negates an identity politics based on the act of "coming out." Indeed, within the world of gay window advertising, there is no lesbian community to come out to, no lesbian community to identify with, no indication that lesbians or "lesbian style" is a political issue. This stylization furthermore promotes a liberal discourse of choice that separates sexuality from politics and connects them both with consumerism. Historically, this advertising technique dates back to the 1920s, as Roland Marchand explains:

> The compulsion of advertising men to regulate women's modernity to the realm of consumption and dependence found expression not only in pictorial styles but also in tableaux that sought to link products with the social and political freedoms of the new woman. Expansive rhetoric that heralded women's march toward freedom and equality often concluded by proclaiming their victory only in the narrower realm of consumer products.[46]

Just as early twentieth-century advertisers were more concerned about women's votes in the marketplace than their decisions in the voting booth, contemporary advertisers are more interested in lesbian consumers than lesbian politics. Once stripped of its political underpinnings, lesbianism can be represented as a style of consumption linked to sexual preference. Lesbianism, in other words, is treated as merely a sexual style that can be chosen—or not chosen—just as one chooses a particular mode of fashion for self-expression.

But within the context of consumerism and the historical weight of heterosexist advertising techniques, "choice" is regulated in determinate ways. For example, gay window advertising appropriates lesbian subcultural style, incorporates its features into commodified representations, and offers it back to lesbian consumers in a packaged form cleansed of identity politics. In this way, it offers lesbians the opportunity to solve the "problem" of lesbianism: by choosing to clothe oneself in fashionable ambiguity, one can pass as "straight" (in certain milieux) while still choosing lesbianism as a sexual preference; by wearing the privilege of straight culture, one can avoid political oppression. Ironically, these ads also offer heterosexual women an alternative as well. As Judith Williamson notes, "[t]he bourgeois always wants to be in disguise, and the customs and habits of the oppressed seem so much more fascinating than his [sic] own."[47] Thus, according to Michael Bronski, "when gay sensibility is used as a sales pitch, the strategy is that gay images imply distinction and non-conformity, granting straight consumers a longed-for place outside the humdrum mainstream."[48] The seamless connections that have traditionally been made between heterosexuality and consumerism are broken apart to allow straight and lesbian women alternative choices. But these choices, which result in a rearticulated homogenized style, deny the differences among women as well as the potential antagonisms that exist between straight and lesbian women over issues of style, politics, and sexuality. As Williamson might explain, "femininity needs the 'other' in order to function . . . even as politically [it] seek[s] to eliminate it."[49]

Similar contradictions and attempts at containment occur within the discourses surrounding women's bodybuilding. As Laurie Schulze notes, "The deliberately muscular woman disturbs dominant notions of sex, gender, and sexuality, and any discursive field that includes her risks opening up a site of contest and conflict, anxiety and ambiguity."[50] Thus, within women's fashion magazines, bodybuilding has been recuperated as a normative ideal of female beauty that promotes self-improvement and ensures attractiveness to men. This discourse

> also assures women who are thinking about working out with weights that they need not fear a loss of privilege or social power; despite any differences that may result from lifting weights, they will still be able to "pass."[51]

The assurances in this case are directed toward heterosexual women who fear that bodybuilding will bring the taint of lesbianism. The connection between bodybuilding and lesbianism is not surprising, says Schulze, for "the ways in which female bodybuilders and lesbians disturb patriarchy and heterosexism . . . draw very similar responses from dominant culture."[52] Both the muscular female and the butch lesbian are accused of looking like men or wanting to be men. As Annette Kuhn puts it, "Muscles are rather like drag."[53] Lesbian style, too, tends toward drag, masquerade and the confusion of gender. Thus, both are subjected to various forms of control that either refuse to accept their physical or sexual "excesses" or otherwise attempt to domesticate their threat and fit them into the dominant constructions of feminine appearances and roles.

Both bodybuilders and lesbians, in other words, are given opportunities to "pass" in straight feminine culture. For body builders, this means not flexing one's muscles while walking down the street or, in the case of competitive bodybuilders, exhibiting the signs of conventional feminine style (for example, makeup, coiffed hair and string bikinis) while flexing on stage.[54] For lesbians, as discussed earlier, this means adopting more traditionally feminine apparel or the trendy accoutrements of gender ambiguity. But within these passing strategies are embodied the very seeds of resistance. As Schulze argues, muscle culture is a "terrain of resistance/ refusal" as well as a "terrain of control."[55] It's simply a matter of how much muscle a woman chooses to flex. Within bodybuilding subculture, flexing is encouraged and admired; physical strength is valorized as a new form of femininity. Lesbians engage in their own form of "flexing" within lesbian subcultures (literally so for those lesbians who also pump iron) by refusing to pass as straight.

This physical and political flexing calls the contradictions of women's fashion culture into question and forces them out of the closet. It thus joins a long history of women's subversive and resistant responses to consumer culture in general. Although consumer culture has historically positioned women in ways that benefit heterosexist, capitalist patriarchy, women have always found ways to exert their agency and create their own pleasures and spaces. Fiske, for example, discusses the way that shopping has become a "terrain of guerrilla warfare" where women change price tags, shoplift or try on expensive clothing without the intent of purchase.[56] The cultural phenomenon of shopping has also provided a homosocial space for women (for example, mothers and daughters, married and single adult women, teenage girls) to interact and bond. Lesbians have been able to extend this pleasure by shopping with their female lovers or partners, sharing the physical and erotic space of the dressing room, and, afterwards, wearing/exchanging the fashion commodities they purchase. Within this realm, the static images of advertising have even less control over their potential consumers. Gay window advertising, for example, may commodify lesbian masquerade as legitimate high-style fashion, but lesbians are free to politicize these products or reappropriate them in combination with other products/fashions to act as new signifiers for lesbian identification or ironic commentaries on heterosexual culture.

This is not to suggest that there exists an authentic "lesbian sensibility" or that all lesbians construct the same, inherently progressive, meanings in the realm of consumption. One must be wary of the "affirmative character" of a cultural studies that leans toward essentialist notions of identity at the same time as it tends to overestimate the freedom of audience reception.[57] Since lesbians are never simply lesbians but also members of racial groups, classes, and so on, their consumption patterns and reading practices always overlap and intersect those of other groups. In addition, there is no agreement within lesbian communities on the "proper" response or relationship to consumer culture. This is precisely why the lesbian "style wars" have become a topic of such heated debate. Arlene Stein pinpoints the questions and fears that underlie this debate:

> Are today's lesbian style wars skin-deep, or do they reflect a changed conception of what it means to be a dyke? If a new lesbian has in fact emerged, is she all flash and no substance, or is she at work busily carving out new lesbian politics that strike at the heart of dominant notions of gender and sexuality?[58]

The answers are not simple, not a matter of binary logic. Some lesbians choose to mainstream. Others experience the discourse of fashion as an ambivalence—toward power, social investment, and representation itself.[59] Still others engage a camp discourse or masquerade that plays upon the lesbian's ambivalent position within straight culture. These responses, reading practices, interpretive activities—whatever one might call them—are as varied as the notions of lesbian identity and lesbian community.

Given the conflicts that lesbians frequently experience within their communities over issues of race, class and life style, lesbians are only too aware that a single, authentic identity does not exist. But, in the face of these contradictions, lesbians are attempting to forge what Stuart Hall calls an *articulation*, "a connection, a linkage that can establish a unity among different elements within a culture, under certain conditions."[60] For lesbians, the conditions are *political*. Lesbian identity politics must therefore be concerned with constructing political agendas and articulating collective identities that take into account our various needs and differences as well as our common experiences and oppressions *as a social group*. So too a theory of lesbian reading practices rooted in identity politics must stretch beyond analyses of textual contradictions to address the history of struggle, invisibility and ambivalence that positions the lesbian subject in relation to cultural practices.

Ironically, now that our visibility is growing, lesbians have become the target of "capitalism's constant search for new areas to colonize."[61] This consideration must remain central to the style debates. For lesbians are not simply forming a new relationship with the fashion industry, *it* is attempting to forge a relationship with us. This imposition challenges us and is forcing us to renegotiate certain aspects of identity politics. (I can't help but think, for example, that the fashion controversy may not be about "fashion" at all but has more to do with the fact that it is the femmes who are finally asserting themselves.) In the midst of this challenge, the butch-femme aesthetic will undoubtedly undergo realignment. We may also be forced to reconsider the ways in which camp can function as a form of resistance. For once "camp" is commodified by the culture industry, how do we continue to camp it up?

The only assurance we have in the shadow of colonization is that lesbians *as lesbians* have developed strategies of selection, (re)appropriation, resistance, and subversion in order to realign consumer culture according to the desires and needs of lesbian sexuality, subcultural identification, and political action. Lesbian reading/ social practices, in other words, are informed by an identity politics, however that politics may be formulated historically by individuals or by larger communities. This does not mean that the readings lesbians construct are always "political" in the strictest sense of the term (for example, one could argue that erotic identification is not political, and there is also the possibility that lesbians will identify with mainstreaming). Nonetheless, the discourses of identity politics—which arise out of the lesbian's marginal and ambivalent social position—have *made it possible* for lesbians to consider certain contradictions in style, sexual object choice and cultural representation that inform their reading practices, challenge the reading practices of straight culture, and potentially create more empowered, or at least pleasurable, subject positions as lesbians. Because identities are always provisional, lesbians must also constantly assert themselves. They must replace liberal discourse with camp discourse, make themselves visible, foreground their political agendas and their politicized subjectivities.

This may explain why feminists have avoided the issue of lesbian consumerism. Lesbians may present too great a challenge to the heterosexual economy in which they are invested, or lesbians may be colonizing the theoretical and social spaces they wish to inhabit. As long as straight women focus on the relation between consumer culture and women in general, lesbians remain invisible, or are forced to pass as straight, while heterosexual women can claim for themselves the oppression of patriarchal culture or the pleasure of masquerade that offers them "a longed for place outside the humdrum mainstream." On the other hand, straight feminists may simply fear that lesbians are better shoppers. When dykes go shopping in order to "go camping," they not only subvert the mix 'n' match aesthetic promoted by dominant fashion culture, they do it with very little credit.

NOTES

1. Karl Marx, *Capital*, Vol. I (London: Lawrence and Wishart, 1970) 71.

2. For a recent overview of the literature see Lynn Spigel and Denise Mann, "Women and Consumer Culture: A Selective Bibliography," *Quarterly Review of Film and Video* 11.1 (1989): 85–105. Spigel and Mann's compilation does not so much reproduce as *reflect* the heterosexual bias of scholarship in this field.

3. Jane Gaines, "The Queen Christina Tie-Ups: Convergence of Show Window and Screen," *Quarterly review of Film and Video* 11.1 (1989): 50. Gaines is one of the few feminist critics who acknowledges gays and lesbians as consuming subjects.

4. Sue-Ellen Case, "Towards a Butch-Femme Aesthetic," *Discourse* 11.1 (1988–89): 56.

5. Roberta Astroff, "Commodifying Cultures: Latino Ad Specialists as Cultural Brokers," Paper presented at the 7th International Conference on Culture and Communication, Philadelphia, PA, 1989.

6. Karen Stabiner, "Tapping the Homosexual Market," *The New York Times Magazine*, May 2, 1982: 80.

7. Stabiner 79.

8. Stabiner 34.

9. Stabiner 34.

10. Stabiner 75.

11. Stabiner 81.

12. Stabiner 80.

13. Stabiner 80.

14. Stabiner 81.

15. Stabiner 81.

16. Stabiner 80.

17. Mary Ann Doane, "The Economy of Desire: The Commodity Form in/of the Cinema," *Quarterly Review of Film and Video* 11.1 (1989): 27.

18. Gaines, "The Queen Christina Tie-Ups," 35.

19. Gaines, "The Queen Christina Tie-Ups," 56.

20. Jane Gaines, "Introduction: Fabricating the Female Body," *Fabrications: Costume and the Female Body*, ed. Jane Gaines and Charlotte Herzog (New York: Routledge, 1990) 12–13.

21. Gaines, "Fabricating the Female Body," 3–9. Also see Kaja Silverman, "Fragments of a Fashionable Discourse," *Studies in Entertainment: Critical Approaches to Mass Culture*, ed. Tania Modleski (Bloomington: Indiana University Press, 1986) 139–152.

22. Gaines, "Fabricating the Female Body," 27.

23. Arlene Stein, "All Dressed Up, But No Place to Go? Style Wars and the New Lesbianism," *OUT/LOOK* 1.4 (1989): 37.

24. Alisa Solomon, "Dykotomies: Scents and Sensibility in the Lesbian Community," *Village Voice*, June 26, 1990: 40.

25. Stein 39.

26. Stan LeRoy Wilson, *Mass Media/Mass Culture* (New York: Random House, 1989) 279.

27. Stein 38.

28. "*OUT/LOOK* Survey Tabulations," *Queery* #10, Fall 1990.

29. John Fiske, "Critical Response: Meaningful Moments," *Critical Studies in Mass Communications* 5 (1988): 247.

30. Elizabeth Ellsworth, "Illicit Pleasures: Feminist Spectators and *Personal Best*," Wide Angle 8.2 (1986): 54.

31. Cathy Griggers, "A Certain Tension in the Visual/Cultural Field: Helmut Newton, Deborah Turbeville and the VOGUE Fashion Layout," *differences* 2.2 (1990): 87–90. Griggers notes that Turbeville's trademark is photographing women (often in pairs or groups) who "stand or sit like pieces of sculpture in interiors from the past in [a] grainy, nostalgic soft-focused finish."

32. Case 64.

33. Case 60.

34. Case 58.

35. Ellsworth 54.

36. Ellsworth 54.

37. Jane Root, *Pictures of Women* (London: Pandora, 1984) 68; Rosalind Coward, *Female Desires* (New York: Grove Press, 1985) 80.

38. John D'Emilio, "Capitalism and Gay Identity," *Powers of Desire: The Politics of Sexuality*, ed. Ann Snitow, Christine Stansell and Sharon Thompson (New York: Monthly Review Press, 1983) 102.

39. D'Emilio 109.

40. David Ehrenstein, "Within the Pleasure Principle or Irresponsible Homosexual Propaganda," *Wide Angle* 4.1 (1980): 62.

41. See, for example, Teresa de Lauretis, "The Essence of the Triangle or, Taking the Risk of Essentialism Seriously: Feminist Theory in Italy, the U.S., and Britain," *differences* 1.2 (1989): 3–37; Diana Fuss, *Essentially Speaking* (New York: Routledge, 1989); Diana Fuss, "Reading Like a Feminist," *differences* 1.2 (1989): 72–92; Carol Vance, "Social Construction Theory: Problems in the History of Sexuality," *Which Homosexuality?* (London: GMP, 1989) 13–34; Jeffrey Weeks, "Against Nature," *Which Homosexuality?* 99–213; Jeffrey Weeks, *Sexuality and Its Discontents* (London: Routledge, 1985).

42. Mark Finch, "Sex and Address in 'Dynasty,'" *Screen* 27.6 (1986): 36.

43. John R. Leo, "The Familialism of 'Man' in American Television Melodrama," *South Atlantic Quarterly* 88.1 (1989): 42.

44. Weeks, *Sexuality*, 200.

45. Dick Hebdige, *Subculture: The Meaning of Style* (London: Methuen, 1979) 93.

46. Roland Marchand, *Advertising the American Dream* (Berkeley: University of California Press, 1985) 186.

47. Judith Williamson, "Woman Is an Island: Femininity and Colonization," *Studies in Entertainment: Critical Approaches to Mass Culture* (Bloomington: Indiana University Press, 1986) 116.

48. Michael Bronski, *Culture Clash: The Making of Gay Sensibility* (Boston: South End Press, 1984) 187.

49. Williamson 109, 112.

50. Laurie Schulze, "On the Muscle," *Fabrications*:59.

51. Schulze 63.

52. Schulze 73.

53. Annette Kuhn, "The Body and Cinema: Some Problems for Feminism," *Wide Angle* 11.4 (1989): 56.

54. Schulze 68.

55. Schulze 67.

56. John Fiske, *Reading the Popular* (Boston: Unwin Hyman, 1989): 14–17. Fiske cites the research of M. Pressdee, "Agony or Ecstasy: Broken Transitions and the New Social State

of Working-Class Youth in Australia," Occasional Papers, S. Australian Centre for Youth Studies, S. A. College of A. E., Magill, S. Australia, 1986.

57. Mike Budd, Robert M. Entman and Clay Steinman, "The Affirmative Character of U.S. Cultural Studies," *Critical Studies in Mass Communication* 7.2 (1990): 169–184.

58. Stein 37.

59. Griggers 101.

60. Jacqueline Bobo, "*The Color Purple*: Black Women as Cultural Readers," Female Spectators, ed. E. Deidre Pribram (London: Verso, 1988) 104–5. See also Stuart Hall, "Race, Articulation and Societies Structured in Dominance," *Sociological Theories: Race and Colonialism* (UNESCO, 1980) 305–45.

61. Williamson 116.

Chapter Twenty-Three

Archival Material
Nobody Makes a Pass at Me

Harold Rome

I want men that I can squeeze,
that I can please, that I can tease
Two or three or four or more!
What are those fools waiting for?
I want love and I want kissing,
I want more of what I'm missing—
Nobody comes knocking at my front
door.
What do they think my knocker's for?
If they don't come soon there won't be
any more!
What can the matter be?

I wash my clothes with Lux,
my etiquette's the best,
I spend my hard-earned bucks on just
what the ads suggest,
Oh, dear, what can the matter be?
Nobody makes a pass at me!
I'm full of Kellogg's bran,
eat Grape-Nuts on the sly,
A date is on the can of coffee that I buy
Oh, dear, what can the matter be?
Nobody makes a pass at me!

Oh Beatrice Fairfax,
give me the bare facts,
How do you make them fall?
If you don't save me,
the things the Lord gave me,
never will be any use to me at all.
I sprinkle on a dash of Fragrance de
Amour,

The ads say "Makes Men Rash"
but I guess their smell is poor
Oh, dear, what can the matter be?
Nobody makes a pass at me.

I use Ovaltine and Listerine,
Barbasol and Musterole,
Life Buoy soap and Flit,
So why ain't I got it?
I use Coca Cola and Marmola,
Crisco, Lesco and Mazola,
Exlax and Vapex,
So why ain't I got sex?
I use Albolene and Maybelline,
Alka Seltzer and Bromo Seltzer,
Odorono and Sensation
So why ain't I got fascination?

My girdles come from the best,
the Times ads say they're chic,
And up above I'm dressed in the
brassiere of the week,
Oh, dear, what can the matter be?
Nobody makes a pass at me!
I use Pond's on my skin,
with Rye-crisp I have thinned,
I get my culture in,
I began "Gone With the Wind,"
Oh, dear, what can the matter be?
Nobody makes a pass at me!

Oh Dorothy Dix, show me some tricks,
please, I want some men to hold.
I want attention and things I won't
mention,
And I want them all before I get too old.
I use Mum every day and Angelus Lip-
lure,
But still men stay away
Just like Ivory soap I'm pure
Oh, dear, what can the matter be?
Nobody makes a pass at me.

The lyrics above were first sung in *Pines and Needles,* a musical produced in the main auditorium at the International Ladies Garment Workers Union on November 27, 1937, in New York City.

Among the Things That Use to Be

Willie M. Coleman (ca. 1979)

Use to be

Ya could learn
a whole lot of stuff
sitting in them
beauty shop chairs

Use to be

Ya could meet
a whole lot of other women
sittin there
along with hair frying
            spit flying
                    and babies crying

Use to be

you could learn
a whole lot about
how to catch up
        with yourself
and some other folks
        in your household
Lots more got taken care of
                than hair
Cause in our mutual obvious dislike
            for nappiness
we came together
        under the hot comb
to share
        and share
                and share

But now we walk
            heads high
naps full of pride
with not a backward glance

at some of the beauty in
                 that which
use to be

Cause with a natural
there is no natural place
for us to congregate
to mull over
our mutual discontent

Beauty shops
could have been
a hell-of-a-place
                 to ferment
                              a   revolution.

Permissions

Every effort has been made to trace or contact copyright holders. The publishers will be pleased to make good in future editions or reprints any omissions or corrections brought to their attention.

Andrew Heinze, "Jewish Women and the Making of an American Home," from *Adapting to Abundance, Jewish Immigrants, Mass Consumption, and the Search for American Identity*. Andrew Heinze © 1990 Columbia University Press. Reprinted by permission of the publisher.

Erika D. Rappaport, "A New Era of Shopping': The Promotion of Women's Pleasure in London's West End, 1909–1914," from *Cinema and the Invention of Modern Life*, edited by Leo Charney and Vanessa R. Schwartz © 1995 The Regents of the University of California. Reprinted by permission.

George Chauncey, "Lots of Friends at the YMCA: Rooming Houses, Cafeterias, and Other Gay Social Centers," from his book *Gay New York: Gender, Urban Culture, and the Making of the Gay Male World, 1890–1940*. Copyright © 1994 by George Chauncey. Reprinted by permission of Basic Books, a member of Perseus Books, L.L.C.

Steven M. Gelber, "Do-It-Yourself: Constructing, Repairing and Maintaining Domestic Masculinity," *American Quarterly* 49, 1 (March 1997) © 1997 The American Studies Association. Reprinted by permission of the Johns Hopkins University Press.

"Playboy's Penthouse Apartment." Reproduced by Special Permission of *Playboy* magazine. Copyright © 1956 by Playboy.

Jeffrey Steele, "Reduced to Images: American Indians in Nineteenth-Century Advertising," from *Dressing in Feathers: The Construction of the Indian in American Popular Culture*, by S. Elizabeth Bird. Copyright © 1996 by Westview Press, Inc. Reprinted by permission of Westview Press, a member of Perseus Books, L.L.C.

Anne McClintock, "Soft-Soaping Empire: Commodity Racism and Imperial Advertising." Copyright © 1995. From *Imperial Leather: Race, Gender, and Sexuality in the Colonial Contest*, by Anne McClintock. Reproduced by permission of Routledge, Inc.

Lillian Faderman, "Lesbian Chic: Experimentation and Repression in the 1920s," from *Odd Girls and Twilight Lovers: A History of Lesbian Life in Twentieth Century America*.© 1991 Columbia University Press. Reprinted by permission of the publisher.

Malcolm Gladwell, "Listening to Khakis," originally appeared in the *New Yorker* magazine, July 26, 1997. Reprinted by permission.

Jennifer Scanlon, "Advertising Women: The J. Walter Thompson Company Women's Editorial Department." Copyright © 1995. From *Inarticulate Longings: The Ladies' Home*

Contributors

Elaine S. Abelson is associate professor of history and director of the Urban Studies Program at Eugene Lang College, the undergraduate division of the New School for Social Research in New York City. She is currently working on a book-length manuscript titled *The Dimensions of Inequality: Gender and Homelessness in the Great Depression*.

Natasha B. Barnes is assistant professor of English and African American Studies at Emory University. She is working on a manuscript on gender and cultural theory in the Caribbean.

Kenon Breazeale is a professor of art history at California State University at Northridge. She has done work on magazine illustration, public sculpture, and African American folk art. She produced an exhibit, *The Courthouse Steps*, on the material culture produced during the O. J. Simpson trial. Her current research deals with body image and tabloid photography.

Jane Bryce teaches African literature and film, as well as creative writing, at the University of the West Indies, Cave Hill, Barbados. She was born and raised in Tanzania and studied and worked for five years in Nigeria. Her current research interests include feminist theory and women's writing, contemporary African fiction, film theory and African/black cinema, and popular culture, and she has published in all of these areas.

George Chauncey is a professor of history at the University of Chicago and the author of *Gay New York: Gender, Urban Culture, and the Making of the Gay Male World, 1890–1940* (Basic Books, 1994), which won the Turner and Curtis Awards from the Organization of American Historians, as well as the Los Angeles Times Book Prize and the Lambda Literary Award. He is also the co-editor of *Hidden from History: Reclaiming the Gay and Lesbian Past* (NAL Books, 1989) and is currently working on *The Strange Career of the Closet: Gay Culture, Consciousness, and Politics from the Second World War to the Gay Liberation Era*.

Danae Clark is associate professor of Media Studies in the Department of Communications at the University of Pittsburgh. She is the author of *Negotiating Hollywood: The Cultural Politics of Actors' Labor* (University of Minnesota Press, 1995) and is currently working on the topic of consumption and collectibles.

Lizabeth Cohen is Howard Mumford Jones Professor of American Studies in the History Department at Harvard University. She is currently writing a book titled *A Consumers' Republic: The Politics of Mass Consumption in Postwar America*, to be published by Alfred A. Knopf, from which the essay in this collection is drawn. Her previous work includes *Making a New Deal: Industrial Workers in Chicago, 1919–1939* (Cambridge University Press, 1990).

Stuart Cosgrove, from Perth, Scotland, has written for *Theater Quarterly, New York Live*, and *History of Rock and Screen*. He has also written for a variety of music magazines and newspapers, including *Collusion* and *Black Echoes*. His research on the social history of the zoot suit was supported by a British Academy postdoctoral research grant.

Susan J. Douglas is the Catherine Neafie Kellogg Professor of Communication Studies at the University of Michigan. She is the author of *Listening In: Radio and the American Imagination* (Times Books, 1999), *Where the Girls Are: Growing up Female with the Mass Media* (Times Books, 1994), and *Inventing American Broadcasting, 1899–1922* (John Hopkins University Press, 1987). She has written for *The Nation, Ms.,* and other publications and was media critic for *The Progressive* from 1992 to 1998. She is currently working on an examination of how motherhood has been portrayed in the mass media from the late 1960s to the present.

Lillian Faderman is the author/editor of nine books, including *Surpassing the Love of Men* (Morrow, 1981), *Odd Girls and Twilight Lovers* (Columbia University Press, 1991), and *Chloe Plus Olivia* (Viking, 1994). Her most recent book is *To Believe in Women: What Lesbians Have Done for America — A History* (Houghton Mifflin, 1999).

Steven M. Gelber is professor of history and chair of the department at Santa Clara University. His publications on American social and cultural history include "Working at Playing: The Construction of the Workplace and the Rise of Baseball," *Saving the Earth: The History of a Middle-Class Millenarian Movement* (University of California Press, 1990), and *Hobbies: Leisure and the Culture of Work in America* (Columbia University Press, 1999).

Malcolm Gladwell is a 1984 graduate from the University of Toronto. From 1987 to 1996, he was a reporter with the *Washington Post*, and at present he is a staff writer for the *New Yorker*. He is the author of *The Tipping Point* (Little, Brown, 2000).

Andrew Heinze is associate professor of history and director of the Swig Judaic Studies Program at the University of San Francisco. He is the author of *Adapting to Abundance: Jewish Immigrants, Mass Consumption and the Search for American Identity*, and much of his scholarship focuses on the intersections of Jewish and American culture. He is now writing a book on the ways in which Jewish men and women reshaped twentieth-century American thought through the mass market of inspirational and self-help literature.

Anne McClintock is the Simone de Beauvoir Professor of English and Women's Studies at the University of Wisconsin at Madison. She is the author of *Imperial Leather: Race Gender and Sexuality in the Colonial Contest* (Routledge, 1994), as well as monographs on Olive Schreiner and Simone de Beauvoir. She co-edited with Ella Shohut and Aamir Mufti *Dangerous Liaisons: Gender, Nation and Postcolonial Perspectives* (University of Minnesota Press, 1997). She also edited a special issue of *Social Text* called *Sexworkers* and *Sexwork* and co-edited a special issue of *Social Text* called *Queer Transexions of Race, Nation and Gender*. She is the recipient of two SSRS-MacArthur Awards, is currently completing a creative nonfiction book called *Skin Hunger: A Chronicle of the Sex Trade*, and is editing a collection of writings by sex workers called *Screwing the System*.

Kathy Peiss teaches American history at the University of Massachusetts. Her research interests have focused on women's history, sexuality, and consumer culture. She is the author of *Cheap Amusements: Working Women and Leisure in Turn-of-the-Century New York* (Temple University Press, 1986), and *Hope in a Jar: The Making of America's Beauty Culture* (Metropolitan, 1998).

Erika D. Rappaport is associate professor of history at the University of California, Santa Barbara. She works on the interconnections between gender, consumerism, and Victorian culture and most recently published *Shopping for Pleasure: Gender in the Making of London's West End* (Princeton University Press, 1999).

Jennifer Scanlon is associate professor and director of Women's Studies at Plattsburgh State University of New York. She is the author of *Inarticulate Longings: The Ladies' Home Journal, Gender, and the Promises of Consumer Culture* (Routledge, 1995), coauthor of *American Women Historians, 1700s–1990s: A Biographical Dictionary* (Greenwood, 1996), and editor of *Significant Contemporary American Feminists* (Greenwood, 1999). She has also published widely in the area of feminist pedagogy.

Jeffrey Steele is professor of English at the University of Wisconsin at Madison. He is the author of *The Representation of the Self in the American Renaissance* (University of North Carolina Press, 1997), *The Essential Margaret Fuller* (Rutgers University Press, 1992), a forthcoming study of Margaret Fuller, and articles on the American Renaissance, African American literature, and popular culture. He is currently working on two projects: one involving the politics of mourning in American culture; the other, the connection between the racial and gender stereotypes of nineteenth-century American advertising.

Robert E. Weems, Jr., is professor of history at the University of Missouri, Columbia. His publications include *Desegregating the Dollar: African American Consumerism in the Twentieth Century* (New York University Press, 1998) and *Black Business in the Black Metropolis: The Chicago Metropolitan Insurance Company, 1925–1985* (Indiana University Press, 1996).